Eye-Witness
The 20th Century

Eye-witness Accounts of the
Moments that Shaped Our Century

Edited by
JON E. LEWIS

ROBINSON

London

For Penny and Tristram Lewis-Stempel

Robinson Publishing Ltd
7, Kensington Church Court
London W8 4SP

First published in the UK by Robinson Publishing Ltd 1994

A copy of the British Library Cataloguing in Publication Data for this title is available from the British Library.

ISBN 1-85487-278-8

Typeset in 11/12pt Baskerville by Hewer Text, Edinburgh
Printed by HarperCollins Manufacturing, Glasgow

10 9 8 7 6 5 4 3 2

CONTENTS

INTRODUCTION

A man walks on the moon. To the crowds which gathered in London and New York to see the new century on the winter's evening of 31 December 1899, such an event was the stuff of the wildest fantasy. The aeroplane itself was still on the drawing board of an obscure duo of North Carolina brothers, Orville and Wilbur Wright. Yet humankind's ability to escape from the confining gravity of Earth is neatly symbolic of how far the frontiers of technology and knowledge have been conquered in the twentieth century. The fact that many millions could watch the 1969 moon landing live at home through the medium of television only proves the point that this has been, without doubt, the most revolutionary century in history.

It has also been the most turbulent. On the eve of 1900 about a quarter of the world's population looked to Britain as their ruling nation. The Empire on which the 'sun never sets' stretched from Cardiff to Calcutta. Yet, even as the new century dawned, Britain's imperial grip was starting to slacken. The most prescient of the revellers in Trafalgar Square may have realized the future belonged to others; a portent of this was the surprising trouble the British were having in winning the then recent, remote war against uppity Dutch settlers in South Africa.

Paradoxically, the two great events which finished Britain as the world's premier power were the two she 'won': the World Wars of 1914–18 and 1939–45. The slaughter of the trenches in the First World War caused everywhere – including Britannia's own empire – the rise of nationalism. It also, *inter alia*, ushered in the 1917 communist revolution in Russia and led, almost inexorably, to the growth of Nazism in defeated Germany, the holocaust and the Second World War – midnight in the century, its defining event. (It is one of the contradictions of war, that its violence often stimulates potentially beneficial inventions; the Apollo rocket is a direct descendant of the V-1 'doodlebugs' which harass London civilian Vere Hodgson.) The nation which has emerged pre-eminent from these conflagrations is the USA; if the nineteenth century was British, the twentieth has been the American Century.

In these pages you can follow the events of the twentieth century through the eyes and words of those who were there, from the assassination of John F. Kennedy to the sinking of the *Titanic*, from the My Lai massacre in Vietnam to the première of Charlie Chaplin's *Modern Times*. Many of the eye-witnesses are professionals – journalists and writers – while others are soldiers, explorers, and artists. Not a few are those lucky, or more unusually unlucky, enough to be by-standers at history, like McMillan Adams, a passenger on the ill-fated *Lusitania*. The great advantage of eye-witness history is that it has the ring of truth, and is more alive than formal history. If the strength of the latter is its studied analysis, the product of long hours amid dusty shelves, the unsurpassed pleasure and quality of the eye-witness account is that it offers the reader the thrill of experiencing the event. I have consciously played to this quality by selecting 'good' reportage, that which communicates itself by the sort of images and language which imprint themselves on the mind's eye, or is told with an emotion which can still strike the reader, despite distances across time, and even culture. The importance of the eye-witness report, as opposed to its pleasure, is that it is a record. At a time when resurgent Nazism would deny the genocide of the Jews by Hitler, the importance of record becomes vital.

It would be an exaggeration to say that every event reported here is truly historic; occasionally I have included descriptions of happenings because they epitomize a mood, a moment or a decade (like Tom Wolfe's account of the Beatles arriving in America). There are also accounts of meetings with the people who have shaped the century, like psychoanalyst Sigmund Freud, Hitler and gangster Al Capone. After all, people make history, and some people make history more than others.

This book tells the story of the century by its witnesses, in chronological order. Part of its appeal is in the juxtaposition of events: robberies, football matches, executions, AIDS, rock concerts, funerals, battles, political protest and social unrest. For some the eye-witnesses' accounts will evoke memories; for everyone they will recapture a world and its events that we are already beginning to leave behind.

As ever, my thanks are due to the many who have helped in the compilation of this book, especially Jan Chamier, Alex Stitt, Eryl Humphrey Jones, Dinah Glasier and Nick Robinson at Robinson Publishing, Elfreda Powell, Julian Alexander of Jacintha Alexander Associates, the staffs of the Imperial War Museum and British Library, and Penny Stempel. A long overdue thanks goes to John Tomlinson, the sort of bookseller writers need.

Jon E. Lewis
12 August 1994

Part I

The New Age
1900–14

THE BOER WAR: SKIRMISH AT KARI SIDING, 29 March 1900

Rudyard Kipling

The new century began as the old ended for the British, fighting the Boer War (1899–1902) in South Africa. The war had initially been prompted by the discovery of vast quantities of diamonds and gold in a territory of South Africa that was outside Britain's jurisdiction. Although the British army outnumbered the Boers by more than five to one, the country in which they were fighting was difficult and hostile. The British campaign against the Afrikaner nationalists had been initially an exercise in humiliation, but the arrival of Generals Robert and Kitchener in January 1900 began to see the tide of war turn in imperial favour, with victories such as that at Kari Siding. At the time of the skirmish, the novelist Rudyard Kipling was working as a correspondent for the *Friend*, a newspaper for British soldiers.

So there had to be a battle, which was called the Battle of Kari Siding. All the staff of the Bloemfontein *Friend* attended.

I was put in a Cape cart, with native driver, containing most of the drinks, and with me was a well-known war correspondent. The enormous pale landscape swallowed up 7,000 troops without a sign, along a front of seven miles. On our way we passed a collection of neat, deep and empty trenches well undercut for shelter on the shrapnel side. A young Guards officer, recently promoted to *Brevet-Major* – and rather sore with the paper that we had printed it *Branch* – studied them interestedly. They were the first dim lines of the dug-out, but his and our eyes were held. The Hun had designed them *secundum artem*, but the Boer had preferred the open within reach of his pony. At last we came to a lone farmhouse in a vale adorned with no less than five white flags. Beyond the ridge was a sputter of musketry and now and then the whoop of a field-piece. 'Here,' said my guide and guardian, 'we get out and walk. Our driver will wait for us at the farmhouse.' But the driver loudly objected. 'No, sar. They shoot. They shoot me.' 'But they are white-flagged all over,' we said. 'Yess, sar. That *why*,' was his answer, and he preferred to take his mules down into a decently remote donga and wait our return.

The farmhouse (you will see in a little why I am so detailed) held two men and, I think, two women, who received us disinterestedly. We went on into a vacant world of sunshine and distances, where now and again a single bullet sang to himself. What I most objected to was the sensation of being under aimed fire – being, as it were, required as a head. 'What are they doing this for?' I asked my friend. 'Because they think we are the Something Light Horse. They ought to be just under this slope.' I prayed that the particularly Something Light Horse would go elsewhere, which they presently did, for the aimed fire slackened and a wandering Colonial, bored to extinction, turned up with news from a far flank. 'No; nothing doing and no one to see.' Then more cracklings and a most cautious move forward to the lip of a large hollow where sheep were grazing. Some of them began to drop and kick. 'That's both sides trying sighting-shots,' said my companion. 'What range do you make it?' I asked. 'Eight hundred, at the nearest. That's close quarters nowadays. You'll never see anything closer than this. Modern rifles make it impossible. We're hung up till something cracks somewhere.' There was a decent lull for meals on both sides, interrupted now and again by sputters. Then one indubitable shell – ridiculously like a pipsqueak in that vastness but throwing up much dirt. 'Krupp! Four or six pounder at extreme range,' said the expert. 'They still think we're the — Light Horse. They'll come to be fairly regular from now on.' Sure enough, every twenty minutes or so, one judgmatic shell pitched on our slope. We waited, seeing nothing in the emptiness, and hearing only a faint murmur as of wind along gas-jets, running in and out of the unconcerned hills.

Then pom-poms opened. These were nasty little one-pounders, ten in a belt (which usually jammed about the sixth round). On soft ground they merely thudded. On rock-face the shell breaks up and yowls like a cat. My friend for the first time seemed interested. 'If these are *their* pom-poms, it's Pretoria for us,' was his diagnosis. I looked behind me – the whole length of South Africa down to Cape Town – and it seemed very far. I felt that I could have covered it in five minutes under fair conditions – but *not* with those aimed shots up my back. The pom-poms opened again at a bare rock-reef that gave the shells full value. For about two minutes a file of racing ponies, their tails and their riders' heads well down, showed and vanished northward. 'Our pom-poms,' said the correspondent. 'Le Gallais, I expect. *Now* we shan't be long.' All this time the absurd Krupp was faithfully feeling for us, *vice* – Light Horse, and, given a few more hours, might perhaps hit one of us. Then to the left, almost under us, a small piece of hanging woodland filled and fumed with our shrapnel much as a man's moustache fills with cigarette-smoke. It was most impressive and lasted for quite twenty minutes. Then silence; then a movement of men and horses from our side up the slope, and the hangar our guns had been hammering spat steady fire at them. More Boer ponies on more skylines; a flurry of pom-poms on the right and a little frieze of far-off meek-tailed ponies, already out of rifle range.

'*Maffeesh*,' said the correspondent, and fell to writing on his knee. 'We've shifted 'em.'

Leaving our infantry to follow men on ponyback towards the Equator, we returned to the farmhouse. In the donga where he was waiting someone squibbed off a rifle just after we took our seats, and our driver flogged out over the rocks to the danger of our sacred bottles.

Then Bloemfontein, and Gwynne storming in late with his accounts complete – 125 casualties, and the general opinion that 'French was a bit of a butcher' and a tale of the General commanding the cavalry who absolutely refused to break up his horses by galloping them across raw rock – 'not for any dam' Boer'.

Months later, I got a cutting from an American paper, on information from Geneva – then a pest-house of propaganda – describing how I and some officers – names, date, and place correct – had entered a farmhouse where we found two men and three women. We had dragged the women from under the bed where they had taken refuge (I assure you that no Tantie Sannie of that day could bestow herself beneath any known bed) and, giving them a hundred yards' start, had shot them down as they ran.

Even then, the beastliness struck me as more comic than significant. But by that time I ought to have known that it was the Hun's reflection of his own face as he spied at our back-windows. He had thrown in the 'hundred yards' start' touch as a tribute to our national sense of fair play.

From the business point of view the war was ridiculous. We charged ourselves step by step with the care and maintenance of all Boerdom – women and children included. Whence horrible tales of our atrocities in the concentration camps.

One of the most widely exploited charges was our deliberate cruelty in making prisoners' tents and quarters open to the north. A Miss Hobhouse among others was loud in this matter, but she was to be excused.

We were showing off our newly built little 'Woolsack' to a great lady on her way up-country, where a residence was being built for her. At the larder the wife pointed out that it faced south – that quarter being the coldest when one is south of the Equator. The great lady considered the heresy for a moment. Then, with the British sniff which abolishes the absurd, 'Humm! I shan't allow *that* to make any difference to *me*.'

Some Army and Navy Stores Lists were introduced into the prisoners' camps, and the women returned to civil life with a knowledge of corsets, stockings, toilet-cases, and other accessories frowned upon by their clergymen and their husbands. *Qua* women they were not very lovely, but they made their men fight, and they knew well how to fight on their own lines.

In the give-and-take of our work our troops got to gauge the merits of the commando leaders they were facing. As I remember the scale, De Wet, with 250 men, was to be taken seriously. With twice that number he was likely to fall over his own feet. Smuts (of Cambridge), warring, men assured me, in a black suit, trousers rucked to the knees, and a top-hat, could handle 500 but, beyond that, got muddled. And so with the others. I had the felicity of meeting Smuts as a British General, at the Ritz during the Great War. Meditating on things seen and suffered, he said that being hunted about the veldt on a pony made a man think quickly, and that perhaps Mr Balfour (as he was then) would have been better for the same experience.

Each commando had its own reputation in the field, and

the grizzlier their beards the greater our respect. There was
an elderly contingent from Wakkerstroom which demanded
most cautious handling. They shot, as you might say, for the
pot. The young men were not so good. And there were
foreign contingents who insisted on fighting after the manner
of Europe. These the Boers wisely put in the forefront of the
battle and kept away from. In one affair the Zarps – the
Transvaal Police – fought brilliantly and were nearly all
killed. But they were Swedes for the most part, and we were
sorry.

Occasionally foreign prisoners were gathered in. Among
them I remember a Frenchman who had joined for pure
logical hatred of England, but, being a professional, could
not resist telling us how we ought to wage the war. He was
quite sound but rather cantankerous.

The 'war' became an unpleasing compost of 'political
considerations', social reform, and housing; maternity work
and variegated absurdities. It is possible, though I doubt it,
that first and last we may have killed 4,000 Boers. Our own
casualties, mainly from preventible disease, must have been
six times as many.

The junior officers agreed that the experience ought to be
a 'first-class dress-parade for Armageddon', but their practical conclusions were misleading. Long-range, aimed rifle-
fire would do the work of the future: troops would never get
near each other than half a mile, and Mounted Infantry
would be vital. This was because, having found men on foot
cannot overtake men on ponies, we created 80,000 of as good
Mounted Infantry as the world had seen. For these Western
Europe had no use. Artillery preparation of wire-works, such
as were not at Magersfontein, was rather overlooked in the
reformers' schemes, on account of the difficulty of bringing
up ammunition by horse-power. The pom-poms, and Lord
Dundonald's galloping light gun-carriages, ate up their own
weight in shell in three or four minutes.

In the ramshackle hotel at Bloemfontein, where the

correspondents lived and the officers dropped in, one heard free and fierce debate as points came up, but – since no one dreamt of the internal-combustion engine that was to stand the world on its thick head, and since our wireless apparatus did not work in those landscapes – we were all beating the air.

Eventually the 'war' petered out on political lines. Brother Boer – and all ranks called him that – would do everything except die. Our men did not see why they should perish chasing stray commandos, or festering in block-houses, and there followed a sort of demoralizing 'handy-pandy' of alternate surrenders complicated by exchange of Army tobacco for Boer brandy which was bad for both sides.

THE BOER WAR: THE SIEGE OF MAFEKING, April–May 1900

J. E. Neilly

Besieged by the Boers from October 1899, the British garrison and the civilian population at Mafeking was by spring 1900 reduced to starvation levels.

Words could not portray the scene of misery. The best thing I can do is ask you to fancy 500–600 human frameworks of both sexes and all ages, from the tender infant upwards, dressed in the remains of tattered rags, standing in lines, each holding an old blackened can or beef tin, awaiting turn to crawl painfully up to the kitchen where the food was distributed. Having obtained the horse soup, fancy them tottering off a few yards and sitting down to wolf up the life-fastening mess, and lick the tins when they had finished. It was one of the most heart-rending sights I ever witnessed, and I have seen many . . .

When a flight of locusts came it was regarded as a godsend – this visitation that is looked upon by farmer as hardly less of a curse than the rinderpest or drought. The starving ones gathered the insects up in thousands, stripped them of their heads, legs, and wings, and ate the bodies. They picked up meat-tins and licked them; they fed like outcast curs. They went further than the mongrel. When a dog gets a bone he polishes it white and leaves it there. Day afer day I heard outside my door continuous thumping sounds. They were caused by the living skeletons who, having eaten all that was outside the bones, smashed them up with stones and devoured what marrow they could find. They looked for bones on the dust-heaps, on the roads everywhere, and I pledge my word that I saw one poor fellow weakly follow a dog with a stone and with unerring aim strike him on the ribs, which caused the lean and hungry brute to drop a bone, which the Kaffir carried off in triumph to the kerb, where he smashed it and got what comfort he could from it.

THE BOER WAR: THE RELIEF OF MAFEKING, 18 May 1900

Filson Young

A British column led by Colonel Mahon reached Mafeking on 18 May 1900, finally breaking the Boer siege.

They were twenty-four very exciting hours. Many miles were travelled, a great enterprise was brought to a successful issue, a tough battle was fought, men received wounds and died, Mafeking was relieved – enough incident and adventure to fill months of ordinary life. The bare events I may describe, but the emotional history of those twenty-four hours will probably never be written, simply because there is no one here able to set it forth. But read the narrative, put yourself in the place of those to whom it was not a story but a piece of life, and then perhaps you will realize something of what it meant to them.

The country consisted of a succession of ridges lying at right angles to our line of march, and as each one rose before us the staff galloped forward to the summit, only to see another lying beyond. But at last, while some of us were buying eggs at a Kaffir kraal, a more adventurous person climbed upon a rubbish heap and shouted 'There's Mafeking.' There was a rush for the coign of vantage, and a great levelling of glasses. There it lay, sure enough, the little town that we had come so far to see – a tiny cluster of white near the eastward horizon, glistening amid the yellowish-brown of the flats. We looked at it for a few moments in silence, and then Colonel Mahon said, 'Well let's be getting on'; and no one said anything more about Mafeking, but everyone thought a great deal.

There was one more brisk engagement to be fought.

The commando that had been holding on for days on our right had effected a junction with a force sent out from Mafeking to oppose us, and had just arrived in position near Israel's Farm when we came up against them. From the large outline of their attack there must have been at least 2,000 of them, and from the cleverness with which they were disposed we at first estimated them at twice that number. We held them on our right while we sent a strong force working round on our left, which ultimately got out far enough to turn their right. Of course we were too few to do more than dislodge them; surrounding was out of the question; so when we had fairly turned them we 'let go' on the right and they fled in that direction. The house at Israel's Farm they held until the very end, shelling our rear-guard briskly. The engagement lasted close on five hours, during which our

casualties amounted to less than forty. It seems strange that
there are five hours of fighting to be accounted for. Five
hours! Was it for so long that one listened to the voices of
guns and rifles?

The fight was over, but as the convoy began to work its
way cautiously through the bush in the dusk we began to talk
about it, and to fit it together from the pieces of our
individual experience. What had they been trying to do?
The Boers had once more given us a lesson in tactics, and we
had given them one in dealing with a nasty situation. They
had bluffed us by extending their attack round a large
perimeter, leading us to suppose their strength to be far
greater than it really was, and but for the really excellent
fighting on our side might have held us where we were until
the want of supplies forced us to retire or surrender. As we
had so few casualties, it is probable that they had not many;
but it is possible to have very warm fighting with few
casualties. Our cover was excellent; so was theirs; and
Colonel Peakman, who with the rearguard bore the heaviest
burden of the fight, lost hardly a man, although he lost
heavily in horses. Everyone is agreed that the honours of the
day fall chiefly to this gallant business man, who in his spare
time has made himself so good a soldier.

Major Karri-Davies had ridden on into Mafeking, and,
with the luck which rewards daring people, had found the
road clear and sent back a messenger with that information
to Colonel Mahon. I think people were never so willingly
awakened from sleep; not even the wounded grumbled, who
had also to be roused from their beds on the grass and
repacked into the stuffy ambulance. At about twelve-thirty
we were ready to start, but during the first mile there were
long halts and delays while the guides argued and boggled
about the roads. At last the strain became too great, and
Major Gifford, Captain Smith, and I resolved to ride on and
trust to finding the right road. We knew the direction by the
stars, and started across the veldt a little south of east. It was

bitterly cold, and we were all both sleepy and hungry, but there was an excitement in the air that kept us easily going. After about half an hour we heard voices ahead, and descried the shapes of horses and men. Our hearts sank for a moment, only to rise again when we recognized Colonel Peakman, who, having been in command of the rearguard on the previous day up till nine o'clock at night, was now taking his turn at advance guard at one o'clock the next morning. As a Kimberley man, it had long been his ambition to lead the relieving force into Mafeking, and I think no one grudged him the honour. Amongst all, indeed, there was a certain amount of competition, and the four correspondents who survived to the end of the expedition became strangely silent about their intentions for the evening. I pinned my faith to Peakman, as I knew he was as anxious as anyone to be in first. For an hour we jogged on at a fast walk, until we had clearly 'run the distance,' as they say at sea. Still no sign of the trenches or forts which should mark the outward boundary of the defended area. We pulled up, and the guide was questioned. 'Two miles more,' he said. We rode on for another quarter of an hour, but still found nothing before us but the rolling veldt; not a light, not a sound except the beating of the horses' feet. Again we halted, and this time Colonel Peakman himself questioned the guide, and the man had to admit that he had mistaken his way, and that we were on the lower road, longer by a good three miles than that originally intended. We had no connecting files with the main column, and, as it had a guide of its own, it was certain that it would take the shorter road, and probably be in before its own advance guard.

So we went on again, this time at a trot; the excitement seemed to extend to the horses, so that even they could not be restrained. In ten minutes we saw men sitting by the road-side, and found a hundred very weary Fusiliers, who had been sent to Israel's Farm at the end of the fight and told to go on afterwards. 'Had anyone passed along the road before us?' 'No'; and with a gasp of relief we hurried on. In a few moments the group in advance pulled up, shouting, "Ware barbed wire!' We all stopped, and there were frantic calls for wire-cutters. With four reports like the snapping of big fiddle-strings the last barrier before Mafeking was removed, and we passed on again, this time at a hard canter. In a few minutes we heard the sound of a galloping horse on the road, and a mounted man challenged us. 'Halt! Who goes there?' 'Friend.' 'Who are you?' (The excitement was too high for the preservation of the proper formula.) 'Colonel Peakman, in command of the advance guard of the relief column.' 'By Jove, ain't I glad to see you, sir!' It was an officer sent out by Colonel Baden-Powell to meet us and bring us in. We left the squadron, and the five of us went on, this time at a gallop, over trenches, past breastworks and redoubts and little forts, until we pulled up at the door of the headquarters mess. Ah, the narrative is helpless here. No art could describe the hand-shaking and the welcome and the smiles on the faces of these tired-looking men; how they looked with rapt faces at us commonplace people from the outer world as though we were angels, how we all tried to speak at once, and only succeeded in gazing at each other. One man tried to speak; then he swore; then he buried his face in his arms and sobbed. We all gulped at nothing, until someone brought in cocoa and we gulped that instead; and then the Colonel came in, and one could only gaze at him, and search in vain on his jolly face for the traces of seven months' anxiety and strain.

After an hour we went out and found the column safely encamped just outside the town. Everyone was dog-tired, and although it was half-past five in the morning and the moon was sinking, we lay down and were immediately asleep – in Mafeking.

THE BOER WAR: A BRITISH CONCENTRATION CAMP, SOUTH AFRICA, January 1901

Emily Hobhouse

After the tide of war began to turn, the British retaliated: they rounded up the Boers and their families and set fire to their farms. The Boers were herded into camps. The plight of the women and children in the filthy, insanitary, overcrowded camps became an international scandal – more than 20,000 were to die there.

Diary: January 31
Some people in town still assert that the camp is a haven of bliss. Well, there are eyes and no eyes. I was at the camp today, and just in one little corner this is the sort of thing I found. A girl of twenty-one lay dying on a stretcher – the father, a big, gentle Boer, kneeling beside her; while, next tent, his wife was watching a child of six, also dying, and one of about five drooping. Already this couple had lost three children in the hospital, and so would not let these go, though I begged hard to take them out of the hot tent. 'We must watch these ourselves,' he said. I sent — to fetch brandy, and got some down the girl's throat, but for the most part you must stand and look on, helpless to do anything because there is nothing to do anything with. Then a man came up and said, 'Sister, come and see my child, sick for three months.' It was a dear little chap of four, and nothing left of him but his great brown eyes and white teeth from which the lips were drawn back, too thin to close. His body was emaciated. The little fellow had craved for fresh milk, but of course there had been none until these last two days, and now the fifty cows only give four buckets. I can't describe what it is to see these children lying about in a state of collapse. It's just exactly like faded flowers thrown away. And one has to stand and look on at such misery and be able to do almost nothing.

QUEEN VICTORIA'S FUNERAL CORTÈGE, 1 February 1901

Countess of Denbigh

The death of Victoria, Queen of Great Britain and Ireland, Empress of India, on 22 January 1901 at Osborne on the Isle of Wight, truly marked the end of the old century. Her reign of almost sixty-four years had been the longest in British history, and she had spent the last forty years of it in mourning for her late husband, Prince Albert. She had imprinted her personality upon a whole era.

I think you will like to hear of my going down to Southampton to see the passing of our dear Queen from Osborne to Portsmouth.

I went on the *Scot*, where both Houses were embarked. We steamed out, and took up our position between the last British ship and the first foreign ships of war, on the south side of the double line down which the procession was to pass. The day was one of glorious sunshine, with the smoothest and bluest of seas. After a while a black torpedo destroyer came dashing down the line signalling that the *Alberta* was leaving Osborne and from every ship, both British and foreign, boomed out the minute guns for close on an hour before the procession reached us. The sun was now (three p.m.) beginning to sink, and a wonderful golden pink appeared in the sky and as the smoke slowly rose from the guns it settled in one long festoon behind them, over Haslar, a purple festoon like the purple hangings ordered by the King.

Then slowly down the long line of battleships came eight torpedo destroyers, dark gliding forms, and after them the white *Alberta* looking very small and frail next the towering battleships. We could see the motionless figures standing round the white pall which, with the crown and orb and sceptre, lay upon the coffin. Solemnly and slowly, it glided over the calm blue water, followed by the other three vessels, giving one a strange choke, and a catch in one's heart as memory flew back to her triumphal passage down her fleet in the last Jubilee review. As slowly and as silently as it came the cortège passed away into the haze: with the solemn booming of the guns continuing every minute till Portsmouth was reached. A wonderful scene and marvellously impressive, leaving behind it a memory of peace and beauty and sadness which it is impossible to forget.

THE FIRST RADIO SIGNAL ACROSS THE ATLANTIC, 12 December 1901

Guglielmo Marconi

Marconi awaited the signal transmitted from Poldhu in Cornwall in a hut on the cliffs of Newfoundland. Until this time few scientists had believed that radio signals could follow the curvature of the earth for more than a hundred miles or so. Marconi's achievement created a sensation worldwide, and paved the way for the vast development in radio communications and broadcasting.

Shortly before midday I placed the single earphone to my ear and I started listening. The receiver on the table before me was very crude – a few coils and condensers and a coherer – no valves, no amplifiers, not even a crystal. But I was at last on the point of putting the correctness of all my beliefs to test. The answer came at twelve-thirty when I heard, faintly but distinctly, *pip-pip-pip*. I handed the phone to Kemp: 'Can you hear anything?' I asked. 'Yes,' he said, 'the letter S' – he could hear it. I knew then that all my anticipations had been justified. The electric waves sent out into space from Poldhu had traversed the Atlantic – the distance, enormous as it

seemed then, of 1,700 miles – unimpeded by the curvature of
the earth. The result meant much more to me than the mere
successful realization of an experiment. As Sir Oliver Lodge
has stated, it was an epoch in history. I now felt for the first
time absolutely certain that the day would come when
mankind would be able to send messages without wires
not only across the Atlantic but between the farthermost
ends of the earth.

THE FIRST POWERED FLIGHT, 17 December 1903

Orville Wright

The feat of powered flight was finally achieved on a blustery
winter's day at Kitty Hawk, North Carolina, by the brothers
Orville and Wilbur Wright. In a telegram to their father Orville
wrote: SUCCESS FOUR FLIGHTS THURSDAY MORNING ALL AGAINST
TWENTY-ONE MILE WIND STARTED FROM LEVEL WITH ENGINE POWER
ALONE AVERAGE SPEED THROUGH AIR THIRTY-ONE MILES LONGEST 59
SECONDS INFORM PRESS HOME CHRISTMAS.
     The longest flight was the last of the day, with Wilbur flying the
600-pound biplane. Orville later recorded in his diary:

At just twelve o'clock Will started on the fourth and last trip.
The machine started with its ups and downs as it had before,
but by the time he had gone 300 or 400 feet he had it under
much better control, and was travelling on a fairly even
course. It proceeded in this manner till it reached a small
hummock out about 800 feet from the starting ways, when it
began pitching again and suddenly darted to the ground.
The front rudder frame was badly broken up, but the main
frame suffered none at all. The distance over the ground was
852 feet in 59 seconds. The engine turns was 1,071, but this
included several seconds while on the starting ways and

probably about half a second after landing. The jar of the landing had set the watch on the machine back, so we have no exact record for the 1,071 turns.

BLOODY SUNDAY, ST PETERSBURG, 9 January 1905*

Georgy Gapon

Discontent at the autocratic Russian social and political system had been mounting. A Russian Orthodox priest, Georgy Gapon, led a peaceful demonstration which hoped to present a group of workers' request for reforms directly to Tsar Nicholas II. He had forewarned the authorities of his plan. Workers carried icons, pictures of the Tsar and petitions citing their grievances. The Chief of Security, Grand Duke Vladimir stopped the march and ordered the police to open fire as it approached the Winter Palace.

'Shall we go straight towards the gate, or by a roundabout route to avoid the soldiers?' I was asked. I shouted huskily, 'No; straight through them. Courage! Death or Freedom!' and the crowd shouted in return, 'Hurrah!' We then started forward, singing in one mighty, solemn voice the Tsar's hymn, 'God Save thy People'. But when we came to the line, 'Save Nicholas Alexandrovitch', some of the men who belonged to the Socialist Party were wicked enough to substitute the words 'Save George Appolonovich' [Gapon], while others simply repeated the words, 'Death or Freedom!' The procession moved in a compact mass. In front of me were my two bodyguards and a young fellow with dark eyes from whose face his hard labouring life had not yet

---

* 22 January 1905. Russia at this time was still using the Julian Calendar: by the calendar in operation in the West at this time the Revolution happened 13 days later.

wiped away the light of youthful gaiety. On the flanks of the
crowd ran the children. Some of the women insisted on
walking in the first rows, in order, as they said, to protect me
with their bodies, and force had to be used to remove them. I
may mention also as a significant fact that at the start the
police not only did not interfere with the procession, but
moved with us with bared heads in recognition of the
religious emblems. Two local police officers marched bareheaded in front of us, preventing any hindrance to our
advance and forcing a few carriages that we met to turn
aside in our favour. In this way we approached the Narva
Gate, the crowd becoming denser as we progressed, the
singing more impressive, and the whole scene more dramatic.

At last we reached within 200 paces of where the troops
stood. Files of infantry barred the road, and in front of them
a company of cavalry was drawn up, with their swords
shining in the sun. Would they dare to touch us? For a
moment we trembled, and then started forward again.

Suddenly the company of Cossacks galloped rapidly
towards us with drawn swords. So, then, it was to be a
massacre after all! There was no time for consideration, for
making plans, or giving orders. A cry of alarm arose as the
Cossacks came down upon us. Our front ranks broke before
them, opening to right and left, and down this lane the
soldiers drove their horses, striking on both sides. I saw the
swords lifted and falling, the men, women and children
dropping to the earth like logs of wood, while moans, curses
and shouts filled the air. It was impossible to reason in the
fever of this crisis. At my order the front rows formed again in
the wake of the Cossacks, who penetrated further and
further, and at last emerged from the end of the procession.

Again we started forward, with solemn resolution and
rising rage in our hearts. The Cossacks turned their horses
and began to cut their way through the crowd from the rear.
They passed through the whole column and galloped back

towards the Narva Gate, where – the infantry having
opened their ranks and let them through – they again
formed a line. We were still advancing, though the bayonets raised in threatening rows seemed to point symboli-
cally to our fate. A spasm of pity filled my heart, but I felt no
fear. Before we started, my dear friend, a workman called
K—, had said to me, 'We are going to give your life as a
sacrifice.' So be it!

We were not more than thirty yards from the soldiers,
being separated from them only by the bridge over the
Tarakanovskii Canal, which here marks the border of the
city, when suddenly, without any warning and without a
moment's delay, was heard the dry crack of many rifle-shots.
I was informed later on that a bugle was blown, but we could
not hear it above the singing, and even if we had heard it we
should not have known what it meant.

Vasiliev, with whom I was walking hand in hand,
suddenly let go of my arm and sank upon the snow. One
of the workmen who carried the banners fell also. Immediately one of the two police officers to whom I had referred
shouted out, 'What are you doing? How dare you fire upon
the portrait of the Tsar?' This, of course, had no effect, and
both he and the other officer were shot down – as I learned
afterwards, one was killed and the other dangerously
wounded.

I turned rapidly to the crowd and shouted to them to lie
down, and I also stretched myself out upon the ground. As
we lay thus another volley was fired, and another, and yet
another, till it seemed as though the shooting was continuous. The crowd first kneeled and then lay flat down, hiding
their heads from the rain of bullets, while the rear rows of the
procession began to run away. The smoke of the fire lay
before us like a thin cloud, and I felt it stiflingly in my throat.
An old man named Lavrentiev, who was carrying the Tsar's
portrait, had been one of the first victims. Another old man
caught the portrait as it fell from his hands and carried it till

he too was killed by the next volley. With his last gasp the old man said, 'I may die, but I will see the Tsar.' One of the banner-carriers had his arm broken by a bullet. A little boy of ten years, who was carrying a church lantern, fell pierced by a bullet, but still held the lantern tightly and tried to rise again, when another shot struck him down. Both the smiths who had guarded me were killed, as well as all those who were carrying the icons and banners; and all these emblems now lay scattered on the snow. The soldiers were actually shooting into the courtyards of the adjoining houses, where the crowd tried to find refuge and, as I learned afterwards, bullets even struck persons inside, through the windows.

At last the firing ceased. I stood up with a few others who remained uninjured and looked down at the bodies that lay prostrate around me. I cried to them, 'Stand up!' But they lay still. I could not at first understand. Why did they lie there? I looked again, and saw that their arms were stretched out lifelessly, and I saw the scarlet stain of blood upon the snow. Then I understood. It was horrible. And my Vasiliev lay dead at my feet.

Horror crept into my heart. The thought flashed through my mind, 'And this is the work of our Little Father, the Tsar.' Perhaps this anger saved me, for now I knew in very truth that a new chapter was opened in the book of the history of our people. I stood up, and a little group of workmen gathered round me again. Looking backward, I saw that our line, though still stretching away into the distance, was broken and that many of the people were fleeing. It was in vain that I called to them, and in a moment I stood there, the centre of a few scores of men, trembling with indignation amid the broken ruins of our movement.

More than 100 demonstrators were killed. The massacre sparked off uprisings and mutinies that came to be known as the Russian Revolution of 1905. It brought the regime to the verge of collapse, and the authoritarian Tsar was compelled to introduce some measures of parliamentary democracy.

A BALL AT THE PARIS *OPÉRA*, 17 February 1906

Arnold Bennett

Diary: Opéra masked ball on Saturday night. The Atkinses supped with me at the Place Blanche. We got to the restaurant too soon, and found all the waiters asleep in odd corners, and the room darkened. It was like going into an enchanted palace. We woke it up, and lighted it up, in an instant. By the time we left, 12.30, there was a noisy band playing, and a crowd of guests.

We got to the ball at 12.45. Already an enormous crowd. Great cohorts of men in silk hats. I should say the men outnumbered the women by 5 to 1. The people who looked really well were the chorus girls etc. from the Opéra who were thoroughly used to fancy dress and knew how to walk and how to dine. Outside these, and a few professional men, there was almost no fancy dress; but plenty of dominoes. The *coup d'œil* in the *salle* was superb, and the orchestras (3) fine and deafening, as they ought to be.

There was, relatively, very little dancing. Not a single well-bred Frenchwoman there, so far as I could see, and very few *toilettes* worth a damn. But the general effect was dazzlingly immense. And the cohorts of men, all on the look-out for something nice, seemed to lurch from time to time in one direction or another, as crowds do, bodily, and sometimes even to stampede. There was something undignified in these masses of masculinity. The waiters and *ouvreuses* seemed politer and gayer than usual. We left at 3.15. Many people had preceded us.

I was a wreck on Sunday, and the noises of people overhead got on my nerves. However I wrote a brief

account of the ball for the *Standard*, rather sardonic, and took
it down to the office.

THE SAN FRANCISCO EARTHQUAKE, 17 April 1906

Jack London

Fires raged for four days after the earthquake. Some 28,000
buildings were destroyed; 700 people were killed; some quarter
of a million made homeless.

San Francisco is gone! Nothing remains of it but memories
and a fringe of dwelling houses on the outskirts. Its industrial
section is wiped out. Its social and residential section is wiped
out. The factories and warehouses, the great stores and
newspaper buildings, the hotels and the palaces of the
nabobs, are all gone. Remains only the fringe of dwelling
houses on the outskirts of what was once San Francisco.

Within an hour after the earthquake shock the smoke of
San Francisco's burning was a lurid tower visible a hundred
miles away. And for three days and nights this lurid tower
swayed in the sky, reddening the sun, darkening the sky, and
filling the land with smoke.

On Wednesday morning at a quarter past five came the
earthquake. A minute later the flames were leaping
upward. In a dozen different quarters south of Market
Street, in the working-class ghetto, and in the factories,
fires started. There was no opposing the flames. There was
no organization, no communication. All the cunning
adjustments of a twentieth-century city had been smashed
by the earthquake. The streets were humped into ridges
and depressions and piled with debris of fallen walls. The
steel rails were twisted into perpendicular and horizontal
angles. The telephone and telegraph systems were dis-

rupted. And the great water mains had burst. All the shrewd contrivances and safeguards of man had been thrown out of gear by thirty seconds' twitching of the earth crust.

By Wednesday afternoon, inside of twelve hours, half the heart of the city was gone. At that time I watched the vast conflagration from out on the bay. It was dead calm. Not a flicker of wind stirred. Yet from every side wind was pouring in upon the city. East, west, north, and south, strong winds were blowing upon the doomed city. The heated air rising made an enormous suck. Thus did the fire of itself build its own colossal chimney through the atmosphere. Day and night this dead calm continued, and yet, near to the flames, the wind was often half a gale, so mighty was the suck.

The edict which prevented chaos was the following proclamation by Mayor E. E. Schmitz:

'The Federal Troops, the members of the Regular Police Force, and all Special Police Officers have been authorized to KILL any and all persons found engaged in looting or in the commission of any other crime.

'I have directed all the Gas and Electric Lighting Companies not to turn on gas or electricity until I order them to do so; you may therefore expect the city to remain in darkness for an indefinite time.

'I request all citizens to remain at home from darkness until daylight of every night until order is restored.

'I warn all citizens of the danger of fire from damaged or destroyed chimneys, broken or leaking gas pipes or fixtures, or any like cause.'

Wednesday night saw the destruction of the very heart of the city. Dynamite was lavishly used, and many of San Francisco's proudest structures were crumbled by man himself into ruins, but there was no withstanding the onrush of the flames. Time and again successful stands were made by the fire fighters, and every time the flames flanked around on either side, or came up from the rear, and turned to defeat the hard-won victory . . .

A PORTRAIT OF PABLO PICASSO AND THE INVENTION OF CUBISM, 1906

Max Jacob

Pablo Picasso (1881–1973), one of the greatest, most innovative artists of this century, had gone to live in Paris in 1901, where he became part of a group of Bohemians, among them Henri Matisse and Max Jacob.

The art dealers who today are so proud of having discovered Picasso thought he was mad. 'Your friend has gone mad!' M. V — said to me. One day, when Picasso was sick and I had tried to sell this same M. V. a landscape, he said to me disdainfully, 'The bell tower is crooked!' and turned his back on me.

Picasso sold some drawings for ten *sous* to a junk shop on the rue des Martyrs, and those ten *sous* were welcome.

In the evenings we acted out plays by the light of an oil lamp, as we were not able to see other people's performances. We took all the parts in turn, including that of the producer, the stage manager, the electricians and the stage hands, and brought them all into the play. (Pirandello did not invent anything.)

We used to go to a restaurant which gave us credit and we always paid in the end. Later we took all our friends there, and the place was full, if not rich. Père Vernin deserves a chapter in a book . . .

One morning, when I arrived as usual from my lodgings on the boulevard Barbès, Picasso, whom I had not seen the previous evening, told me he had spent the evening in a bar on the rue d'Amsterdam with an extraordinary man, Guillaume Apollinaire, and that he would introduce me to him that same evening. I then met Guillaume Apollinaire, who was impressive. He was seated on a leather bench, surrounded by a thousand little books which he brought out from everywhere, and by a group of rather common people. He gave me his hand, and from that moment a triple friendship started, which lasted until Apollinaire's death. This all happened in 1905. Picasso and Apollinaire understood one another marvellously. Picasso painted harlequins and saltimbanques; Apollinaire put them in his poems. The figure of Apollinaire was often repeated in his paintings; mine too. We were never apart: we used to wait for Apollinaire at the entrance to the bank where he was employed on the rue Lepelletier. We had lunch and dinner together. Our literary opinions were summed up in the words that were so important at the time: 'Down with Laforgue! Long live Rimbaud!' The 'Long live Rimbaud' was prophetic, as we all know.

One winter morning, when I arrived in the corridor which led to the studio, a tall thin young man asked me where Picasso lived. I said to him 'Are you André Salmon?' And he replied 'Are you Max Jacob?' A minute later we were seated on the garnet-red mattress with no feet which served as the studio divan. Salmon became Picasso's friend.

At the time he also knew Derain, Vlaminck and Matisse. For a while, we used to go on Thursday evenings to Matisse's for dinner, Picasso, Salmon, Apollinaire and myself. I think it was at Matisse's that Picasso saw Negro sculpture, or at least that he was struck by it, for the first time. Picasso has never confided in me at all about the invention of Cubism, so that I have to rely on guesswork, and I will venture to say this: Cubism was born from Negro sculpture. Picasso began some large figures (in 1906 or 1907) with their noses attached to their eyes. He absorbed himself in deep meditation, simplifying animals and objects and arriving at a single stroke at drawings of a kind that recall those in prehistoric caves. I doubt that any still exist.

ARRIVAL AT THE NORTH POLE, 6 April 1909

Commander Robert Edwin Peary

In the early years of the twentieth century, parts of the globe remained unexplored. Commander Peary had already made two previous attempts to reach the North Pole and failed. Some now question whether he indeed reached the North Pole on this attempt, but rather ended up at a point some thirty to sixty miles south of it.

This was the time for which I had reserved all my energies, the time for which I had worked for twenty-two years, for which I had lived the simple life and trained myself as for a race. In spite of my years, I felt fit for the demands of the coming days and was eager to be on the trail. As for my party, my equipment, and my supplies, they were perfect, beyond my most sanguine dreams of earlier years. My party might be regarded as an ideal which had now come to realization – as loyal and responsive to my will as the fingers of my right hand.

My four Eskimos carried the technique of dogs, sledges, ice, and cold as their racial heritage. Henson and Ootah had been my companions at the furthest point on the expedition three years before. Egingwah and Seegloo had been in Clark's division, which had such a narrow escape at that time, having been obliged for several days to subsist upon their sealskin boots, all their other food being gone.

And the fifth was young Ooqueah, who had never before served in any expedition; but who was, if possible, even more willing and eager than the others to go with me wherever I should elect. For he was always thinking of the great treasures which I had promised each of the men who should go to the furthest point with me – whale-boat, rifle, shotgun, ammunition, knives, etc. – wealth beyond the wildest dreams of Eskimos, which should win for him the daughter of old Ikwah of Cape York, on whom he had set his heart.

All these men had a blind confidence that I would somehow get them back to land. But I recognized fully that all the impetus of the party centred in me. Whatever pace I set, the others would make good; but if I played out, they would stop like a car with a punctured tyre. I had no fault to find with the conditions, and I faced them with confidence . . .

With every passing day even the Eskimos were becoming more eager and interested, notwithstanding the fatigue of the long marches. As we stopped to make camp, they would climb to some pinnacle of ice and strain their eyes to the north, wondering if the Pole was in sight, for they were now certain that we should get there this time . . .

The bitter wind burned our faces so that they cracked, and long after we got into camp each day they pained us so that we could hardly go to sleep. The Eskimos complained much, and at every camp fixed their fur clothing about their faces, waists, knees, and wrists. They also complained of their noses, which I had never known them to do before. The air was as keen and bitter as frozen steel . . .

The last march northwards ended at ten o'clock of the forenoon of 6 April. I had now made the five marches planned from the point at which Bartlett turned back, and my reckoning showed that we were in the immediate neighbourhood of the goal of all our striving. After the usual arrangements for going into camp, at approximate local noon, on the Columbia meridian, I made the first observation at our polar camp. It indicated our position as 89° 57'.

We were now at the end of the last long march of the upward journey. Yet with the Pole actually in sight I was too weary to take the last few steps. The accumulated weariness of all those days and nights of forced marches and insufficient sleep, constant peril and anxiety, seemed to roll across me all at once. I was actually too exhausted to realize at the moment that my life's purpose had been achieved. As soon as our igloos had been completed, and we had eaten our dinner and double-rationed the dogs, I turned in for a few hours of absolutely necessary sleep, Henson and the Eskimos having unloaded the sledges and got them in readiness for such repairs as were necessary. But, weary though I was, I could not sleep long. It was, therefore, only a few hours later when I woke. The first thing I did after awaking was to write these words in my diary: 'The Pole at last. The prize of three centuries. My dream and goal for twenty years. Mine at last! I cannot bring myself to realize it. It seems all so simple and commonplace . . .'

After I had planted the American flag in the ice, I told Henson to time the Eskimos for three rousing cheers, which they gave with the greatest enthusiasm. Thereupon, I shook hands with each member of the party – surely a sufficiently unceremonious affair to meet with the approval of the most democratic. The Eskimos were childishly delighted with our success. While, of course, they did not realize its importance fully, or its worldwide significance, they did understand that it meant the final achievement of a task upon which they had seen me engaged for many years . . .

We had now left the ice of the polar sea and were practically on *terra firma*. When the last sledge came to the almost vertical edge of the glacier's fringe, I thought my Eskimos had gone crazy. They yelled and called and danced until they fell from utter exhaustion. As Ootah sank down on his sledge he remarked in Eskimo: 'The devil is asleep or having trouble with his wife, or we should never have come back so easily . . .'

It was almost exactly six o'clock on the morning of April 23 when we reached the igloo of 'Crane City' at Cape Columbia and the work was done. That day I wrote these words in my diary: 'My life work is accomplished. The thing which it was intended from the beginning that I should do, the thing which I believed could be done, and that I could do, I have done. I have got the North Pole out of my system after twenty-three years of effort, hard work, disappointments, hardships, privations, more or less suffering, and some risks. I have won the last great geographical prize, the North Pole, for the credit of the United States. This work is the finish, the cap and climax of nearly 400 years of effort, loss of life, and expenditure of fortunes by the civilized nations of the world, and it has been accomplished in a way that is thoroughly American. I am content.'

BLÉRIOT FLIES THE CHANNEL, 25 July 1909

Louis Blériot

In 1909, the London *Daily Mail* offered a prize of £1,000 to the first aviator to fly the English Channel. The prize was won by Frenchman Louis Blériot who achieved the crossing in a 28 hp monoplane. It took a little over forty minutes.

At four-thirty we could see all around: daylight had come. M. Le Blanc endeavoured to see the coast of England, but could not. A light breeze from the south-west was blowing. The air was clear.

Everything was prepared. I was dressed as I am at this moment, a khaki jacket lined with wool for warmth over my tweed clothes and beneath an engineer's suit of blue cotton overalls. My close-fitting cap was fastened over my head and ears. I had neither eaten nor drunk anything since I rose. My thoughts were only upon the flight, and my determination to accomplish it this morning.

Four-thirty five! *Tout est prêt!* Le Blanc gives the signal and in an instant I am in the air, my engine making 1,200 revolutions – almost its highest speed – in order that I may get quickly over the telegraph wires along the edge of the cliff. As soon as I am over the cliff I reduce my speed. There is now no need to force my engine.

I begin my flight, steady and sure, towards the coast of England. I have no apprehensions, no sensations, *pas du tout*.

The *Escopette* has seen me. She is driving ahead at full speed. She makes perhaps 42 kilometres [about 26 miles per hour]. What matters? I am making at least 68 kilometres [42 miles per hour].

Rapidly I overtake her, travelling at a height of 80 metres [about 260 feet].

The moment is supreme, yet I surprise myself by feeling no exultation. Below me is the sea, the surface disturbed by the wind, which is now freshening. The motion of the waves beneath me is not pleasant. I drive on.

Ten minutes have gone. I have passed the destroyer, and I turn my head to see whether I am proceeding in the right direction. I am amazed. There is nothing to be seen, neither the torpedo-destroyer, nor France, nor England. I am alone. I can see nothing at all – *rien du tout*!

For ten minutes I am lost. It is a strange position, to be alone, unguided, without compass, in the air over the middle of the Channel.

I touch nothing. My hands and feet rest lightly on the levers. I let the aeroplane take its own course. I care not whither it goes.

For ten minutes I continue, neither rising nor falling, nor turning. And then, twenty minutes after I have left the French coast, I see the green cliffs of Dover, the castle, and away to the west the spot where I intended to land.

What can I do? It is evident that the wind has taken me out of my course. I am almost at St Margaret's Bay and going in the direction of the Goodwin Sands.

Now it is time to attend to the steering. I press the lever with my foot and turn easily towards the west, reversing the direction in which I am travelling. Now, indeed, I am in difficulties, for the wind here by the cliffs is much stronger, and my speed is reduced as I fight against it. Yet my beautiful aeroplane responds. Still I fly westwards, hoping to cross the harbour and reach the Shakespear Cliff. Again the wind blows. I see an opening in the cliff.

Although I am confident that I can continue for an hour and a half, that I might indeed return to Calais, I cannot resist the opportunity to make a landing upon this green spot.

Once more I turn my aeroplane, and, describing a half-circle, I enter the opening and find myself again over dry land. Avoiding the red buildings on my right, I attempt a landing; but the wind catches me and whirls me round two or three times.

At once I stop my motor, and instantly my machine falls straight upon the land from a height of twenty metres [65 ft]. In two or three seconds I am safe.

Soldiers in khaki run up, and a policeman. Two of my compatriots are on the spot. They kiss my cheeks. The conclusion of my flight overwhelms me. I have nothing to say, but accept the congratulations of the representatives of the *Daily Mail* and accompany them to the Lord Warden Hotel.

Thus ended my flight across the Channel. The flight could be easily done again. Shall I do it? I think not. I have promised my wife that after a race for which I have entered I will fly no more.

A SUFFRAGETTE IN HOLLOWAY PRISON, LONDON, 1909

Lucy Burns

Ever since 1792, with the publication of Mary Wollstonecraft's plea, women had been demanding the right to vote. By the end of the nineteenth century their campaign had become a major political issue. Only New Zealand, Australia and Finland had granted women the right to vote by 1909, and in Britain they would not fully achieve it until 1928.

We remained quite still when ordered to undress, and when they told us to proceed to our cells we linked arms and stood with our backs to the wall. The Governor blew his whistle and a great crowd of wardresses reappeared, falling upon us, forcing us apart and dragging us towards the cells. I think I had twelve wardresses for my share, and among them they managed to trip me so that I fell helplessly to the floor. One of the wardresses grasped me by my hair, wound the long braid around her waist and literally dragged me along the ground. In the cell they fairly ripped the clothing from my back, forcing on me one coarse cotton garment and throwing others on the bed for me to put on myself. Left alone exhausted by the dreadful experience I lay for a time gasping and shivering on the floor. By and by a wardress came to the door and threw me a blanket. This I wrapped around me, for I was chilled to the bone by this time. The single cotton garment and the rough blanket were all the clothes I wore during my stay in prison. Most of the prisoners refused everything but the blanket. According to agreement we all broke our windows and were immediately dragged off to the punishment cells. There we hunger struck, and after enduring great misery for nearly a week, we were one by one released.

THE ARREST OF DR H. H. CRIPPEN, 31 July 1910

Captain H. G. Kendall

After murdering his wife – with the exotic poison, hyoscine – Crippen tried to flee to Canada with his paramour, Ethel LeNeve, but became the first criminal to be caught by wireless. Captain Kendall was the master of the steamship *Montrose*.

The *Montrose* was in port at Antwerp when I read in the *Continental Daily Mail* that a warrant had been issued for Crippen and LeNeve. They were reported to have been traced to a hotel in Brussels but had then vanished again.

Soon after we sailed for Quebec I happened to glance through the porthole of my cabin and behind a lifeboat I saw two men. One was squeezing the other's hand. I walked along the boat deck and got into conversation with the elder man. I noticed that there was a mark on the bridge of his nose through wearing spectacles, that he had recently shaved off a moustache, and that he was growing a beard. The young fellow was very reserved, and I remarked about his cough.

'Yes,' said the elder man, 'my boy has a weak chest, and I'm taking him to California for his health.'

I returned to my cabin and had another look at the *Daily Mail*. I studied the description and photographs issued by Scotland Yard. Crippen was fifty years of age, 5 ft 4 ins high, wearing spectacles and a moustache; Miss LeNeve was twenty-seven, 5 ft 5 ins, slim, with pale complexion. I then examined the passenger list and ascertained that the two passengers were travelling as 'Mr Robinson and son'. I arranged for them to take meals at my table.

When the bell went for lunch I tarried until the coast was clear, then slipped into the Robinsons' cabin unobserved, where I noticed two things: that the boy's felt hat was packed round the rim to make it fit, and that he had been using a piece of a woman's bodice as a face flannel. That satisfied me. I went down to the dining saloon and kept my eyes open. The boy's manners at table were ladylike. Later, when they were promenading the saloon deck, I went out and walked behind them, and called out, 'Mr Robinson!' I had to shout the name several times before the man turned and said to me, 'I'm sorry, Captain, I didn't hear you – this cold wind is making me deaf.'

In the next two days we developed our acquaintance. Mr Robinson was the acme of politeness, quiet-mannered, a non-smoker; at night he went on deck and roamed about on his own. Once the wind blew up his coat tails and in his hip pocket I saw a revolver. After that I also carried a revolver, and we often had pleasant little tea parties together in my cabin, discussing the book he was reading, which was *The Four Just Men*, a murder mystery by Edgar Wallace – and when that little fact was wirelessed to London and published it made Edgar Wallace's name ring, so agog was everybody in England over the Crippen case.

That brings me to the wireless. On the third day out I gave my wireless operator a message for Liverpool: *One hundred and thirty miles west of Lizard . . . have strong suspicions that Crippen London cellar murderer and accomplice are among saloon passengers . . . Accomplice dressed as boy; voice, manner, and build undoubtedly a girl.*

I remember Mr Robinson sitting in a deckchair, looking at the wireless aerials and listening to the crackling of our crude spark-transmitter, and remarking to me what a wonderful invention it was.

I sent several more reports, but our weak transmitting apparatus was soon out of communication with land. We could hear other ships at a great distance, however, and you may imagine my excitement when my operator brought me a message he had intercepted from a London newspaper to its representative aboard the White Star liner *Laurentic* which was also heading westward across the Atlantic: *What is Inspector Dew doing? Is he sending and receiving wireless messages? Is he playing games with passengers? Are passengers excited over chase? Rush reply.*

This was the first I knew that my message to Liverpool had caused Inspector Dew to catch the first boat out – the *Laurentic*. With her superior speed I knew she would reach the Newfoundland coast before me. I hoped that if she had any news for me the *Laurentic* would leave it at the Belle Island station to be transmitted to me as soon as I passed that point on my approach to Canada.

She had news indeed: *Will board you at Father Point . . .*

strictly confidential . . . from Inspector Dew, Scotland Yard, on board Laurentic.

I replied: *Shall arrive Father Point about 6 a.m. tomorrow . . . should advise you to come off in small boat with pilot, disguised as pilot . . .*

This was confirmed. The last night was dreary and anxious, the sound of our fog-horn every few minutes adding to the monotony. The hours dragged on as I paced the bridge; now and then I could see Mr Robinson strolling about the deck. I had invited him to get up early to see the 'pilots' come aboard at Father Point in the River St Lawrence. When they did so they came straight to my cabin. I sent for Mr Robinson. When he entered I stood with the detective facing the door, holding my revolver inside my coat pocket. As he came in, I said, 'Let me introduce you.'

Mr Robinson put out his hand, the detective grabbed it, at the same time removing his pilot's cap, and said, 'Good morning, Dr Crippen. Do you know me? I'm Inspector Dew, from Scotland Yard.'

Crippen quivered. Surprise struck him dumb. Then he said, 'Thank God it's over. The suspense has been too great. I couldn't stand it any longer.'

Ethel LeNeve was acquitted of aiding Crippen in the murder of his wife. The doctor, however, was found guilty and sentenced to be hanged at Pentonville Prison.

CRIPPEN'S LAST LETTER

Dr H. H. Crippen

This is my farewell letter to the world. After many days of anxious expectation that my innocence might be proved, after enduring the agony of a long trial and the suspense of an appeal, and after the final endeavour of my friends to obtain a reprieve, I see that at last my doom is sealed and that in this life I have no more hope.

With all the courage I have I face another world and another Judge – from Whom I am sure of justice greater than that of this world and of mercy greater than that of men.

I have no dread of death, no fear of the hereafter, only the dread and agony that one whom I love best may suffer when I have gone . . .

About my unhappy relations with Belle Elmore I will say nothing. We drifted apart in sympathy; she had her own friends and pleasures, and I was a rather lonely man and rather miserable. Then I obtained the affection and sympathy of Miss Ethel LeNeve.

I confess that according to the moral laws of Church and State we were guilty, and I do not defend our position in that respect. But what I do say is that this love was not of a debased and degraded character.

It was, if I may say so to people who will not, perhaps, understand or believe, a good love. She comforted me in my melancholy condition. Her mind was beautiful to me. Her loyalty and courage and self-sacrifice were of a high character. Whatever sin there was – and we broke the law – it was my sin, not hers.

In this farewell letter to the world, written as I face eternity, I say that Ethel LeNeve has loved me as few women love men, and that her innocence of any crime, save that of yielding to the dictates of the heart, is absolute.

To her I pay this last tribute. It is of her that my last thoughts have been. My last prayer will be that God may protect her and keep her safe from harm and allow her to join me in eternity . . .

I make this defence and this acknowledgment – that the love of Ethel LeNeve has been the best thing in my life – my only happiness – and that in return for that great gift I have been inspired with a greater kindness towards my fellow-beings, and with a greater desire to do good.

We were as man and wife together, with an absolute communion of spirit. Perhaps God will pardon us because we were like two children in the great unkind world, who clung to one another and gave each other courage . . .

I myself have endeavoured to be equally courageous, yet there have been times during her visits to me when an agony of intense longing has taken possession of me, when my very soul has cried out to clasp her hand and speak those things which are sacred between a man and a woman who have loved.

Alas! We have been divided by the iron discipline of prison rules, and warders have been the witnesses of our grief.

Why do I tell these things to the world? Not to gain anything for myself – not even compassion. But because I desire the world to have pity on a woman who, however weak she may have seemed in their eyes, has been loyal in the midst of misery, and to the very end of the tragedy, and whose love has been self-sacrificing and strong.

These are my last words.

I belong no more to the world.

In the silence of my cell I pray that God may pity all weak hearts, all the poor children of life, and His poor servant.

THE FIRST POST-IMPRESSIONIST EXHIBITION, LONDON, 1910

Wilfrid Blunt

The first ever showing in Britain of an exhibition of paintings of Van Gogh, Gauguin, Cézanne, Matisse, Seurat and Picasso was organized at the Grafton Gallery in London by the artist and critic Roger Fry. He knew that it would cause outrage, and it did: it came to be known as 'The Artquake'. The art critic Wilfrid Blunt was at the opening and recorded in his diary:

The exhibition is either an extremely bad joke or a swindle. I am inclined to think the latter for there is no trace of humour in it. Still less is there a trace of sense or skill or taste, good or bad, or art or cleverness . . . Apart from the frames, the whole collection should not be worth £5, and then only for the pleasure of making a bonfire of them . . . These are not works of art at all; unless throwing a handful of mud against a wall may be called one. They are the work of idleness and impotent stupidity. A pornographic show.

THE TONYPANDY RIOT, SOUTH WALES, November 1910

J. V. Radcliffe

Churchill has often been blamed for the escalating violence of the Tonypandy riots when coal miners on strike clashed with the police and military. In fact, he had ordered that the troops who had been sent in 'should not come into direct contact with rioters unless and until action had been taken by the police'. However, as this eye-witness account reveals, his message arrived too late for strike leaders to calm the situation.

The centre stretch of the Rhondda Valley, where it lies deep between mountain slopes all autumn brown and ashen grey, was in wild turmoil late last night and early this morning. Strikers and policemen were in furious conflict, stones were thrown in showers, truncheons were drawn and vigorously used, colliery property was smashed, and more than a hundred strikers and six or seven policemen were injured, some of them badly. What set the bad spirit abroad cannot be known. It seemed to fall with the gathering darkness. High above the Llwynypia pit is a frowning head of rock, which the clouds wrapped round last night in sullen gloom,

and if they had distilled riot and fury down its threatening
front the effect in the valley could scarcely have been more
sombre and wild. The first mutterings of trouble were heard
about nine o'clock. Four thousand men marched to the pit
and halted at its gate. This was a repetition so far of the
morning and midday marches, but the temper of the men
underwent a sudden change. Some youths showed the first
symptoms of what was stirring. They made a rush towards
the gates, where the police kept guard. It was not a
formidable movement, and the police withstood the shock
without a tremor, but the repulse set more evil designs on
foot. A sober-minded collier very bravely ventured to set
himself against the current of feeling. Climbing a bank, he
began a speech of counsel to his fellow workmen to act
humanely and justly. The counsel was too quiet for distem-
pered minds, and if it had any effect at all it was only to
divert attention from the colliery gates and their police guard
to the long line of palisading that shuts off the pit yard from
the road.

One common motive actuated the thousands of men
massed together. It was to get to the electric power-house,
to drive out the men in charge and stop the machinery. The
power-house since Sunday has been manned by under-
managers and other officials of the Glamorgan Colliery
Company, with Mr Llewellyn, the general manager, at
their head. The regular enginemen and stokers have been
frightened away. The power station is the citadel of the
situation so far as the Glamorgan Company is concerned. It
supplies the power for pumping and ventilating five pits. The
pits, at any rate, will be in danger of flooding, the ventilation
has already ceased, and as a consequence the fate of
hundreds of horses is only a matter of hours. To stop every
bit of work at the collieries, to stop the pumping as well as the
ventilating, was what one man called the trump card that
the strikers were now to play. They rushed at the palisading
to tear it down. They dare not push it before them lest they

should fall with it on the railway below. It had to come down on the road. Thick stumps were snapped and props and stays torn up by the pulling of thousands of hands, and the men began to swarm into the pit yard. The brightly lighted power-station was in front of them, and to hinder their advance only the railway, a line of trucks, and a score or two of policemen advancing in scouting order. Not one of the strikers got behind the line of trucks. Big, active men more than their match physically drove them violently back, and they did not try that way any more. Worse things were in store. Stone-throwing began. The road that skirts the colliery is cut low down on the hillside. Another road descends the hill to join it fast by the colliery, and for 150 yards it overlooks the colliery entrance. A band of strikers had taken up places here as well as on the slope between the two highways. Stones were plentiful, and big and small, just as they came to hand, they were hurled at the policemen at the gates.

The policemen were unfortunately conspicuous. The light from the power station, without which the men there could not work, shone on the silver facings of their helmets and made them an easy mark. Man after man was hit, and when the line was weakened and another attempt was made to carry the pit by storm the policemen gave way, and the strikers were already within the gates when reinforcements came from another part of the yard. These men had their truncheons drawn, and laying freely about them they drove the crowd beyond the gates and some distance along the lower road. The men on the higher road were at the moment beyond reach, but when the stone-throwing commenced Captain Lionel Lindsay, Chief Constable of the county, called his men together and led them in a charge up the hill. The attacking force consisted of 118 men, every one of them 6 ft tall or thereabouts. With their truncheons in their hands they advanced with long swinging strides. The colliers did not wait. They preferred throwing stones from a distance to a personal encounter, in which, indeed, they would have been completely overmatched. They scuttled off as fast as their legs would carry them, but not fast enough for all to escape the horrid thud of truncheons on their heads and shoulders. It was a wild, headlong flight for safety, only limited by the necessity for the policemen to remain in touch with their base. Even after this there was no quietness. The strikers re-formed once and again, and other though minor charges were made. The night passed into morning, and still the road was in turmoil. About four o'clock there was a second but this time half-hearted attempt to storm the power-house. It was easily defeated.

Daylight revealed in a striking manner the part of the conflict that darkness had hidden. Most fearful-looking of the wreckage was the litter of stones, half-bricks, and bits of rock that lay all about the colliery gate. It was appalling to think of enduring that merciless, invisible hail. In less profusion, the missiles lay a considerable distance along the road, and a walk up to the hill showed where the supply had come from and the commanding position the throwers held. The best-placed would be thirty or forty feet above the heads of the police and scarcely more than a street's width from them. Standing in a body, as they were obliged to do, and picked out by the colliery lights, the police were completely exposed, a mark for any coward who chose to aim from a distance.

The power-house itself, though it stands well back from the road, had not escaped scot-free. A number of its windows were perforated by stones, but no one inside was hurt. Those of its garrison who were struck were hit while passing to and from the boilers. Twenty men who are really prisoners in this building are waging a hard, unresting struggle against a flood of water in the mine. Amateurs at stoking as they are, they find it almost beyond their power to keep a sufficient head of steam to run the pumping machinery. None of them has slept since Sunday night, and weariness compels them t lie down sometimes on the hard concrete floor, but the rest is brief. They are doing all that men can do to save the pits, and are just keeping the water down. If it overflows the dam it will invade the steam coal pit, and incalculable damage may be done and some 300 horses drowned. As it is three fates threaten the horses – by starvation, asphyxiation, or drowning – and one can scarcely tell which is coming fastest.

I was permitted this morning to enter the power-house. I found its occupants as eager to gain news from outside as I was to know what had happened within. We therefore exchanged information. Their great physical needs, I ascertained, were first sleep and second cigarettes. The strain of the past thirty hours' vigil and the constant exertion were marked in weary lines on their faces. Some of them were on duty and alert, and the remainder were getting some relief in the easiest attitudes they could assume on the floor. There was not a chair or a form in the place.

There was hope for a time during the afternoon that troops would not be necessary to enforce order in the Valley. The morning had passed quietly, and the afternoon was occupied chiefly, so far as the strikers were concerned, with a mass meeting at which 10,000 were present, and a huge parade round the district. The long delay in the arrival of troops known to have started for the coalfield caused wonder and surprise, and the explanation came later in the afternoon. The strike leaders received a telegram from Mr Winston Churchill inviting them to meet him in London tomorrow. The Home Secretary's telegram added (according to a statement made by the strike leaders) that he was reluctant to have troops quartered in the Valley, and that if quietness were maintained the troops on the way would not be sent to their destination. It was extremely unfortunate that this telegram had not arrived in time to be read at the mass meeting. The strike leaders met immediately afterwards to consider what reply they should send, and decided to accept Mr Churchill's offer and to advise the men to keep the peace.

There were, however, no effective means of promulgating their decision, and tonight Tonypandy has been the scene for hours of a terrible uproar. Rioting broke out again as soon as twilight fell. It began down at the Llwynypia (Glamorgan Colliery) pit. The police in strong force were again on duty at the gates and in the yard concentrating their force so as to defend the power-house. A great crowd drew up in the road. All at once stones began to hurtle through the air. Another attack was made on the palisading, and the wreckage of last night was piled up in the road to prevent the mounted police from charging. The fusilade on the police was unendurable. The Chief Constable took advantage of a temporary cessation of the onslaught to make a last appeal for order. The reply was another volley of stones.

The Chief Constable himself was hit and knocked to the ground. There was a menacing rush to the gates, and the police replied by drawing their staves and charging. They drove the men before them until they had cleared a good space, and just the same as last night it was necessary to clear the higher road with truncheons. This space the police resolved to defend. Their line was weakened by being extended, but they were in a less vulnerable position. On each side of them was a desperate crowd, but for a time they won a breathing space. The tale of the injured has yet to be told, however. Nobody knows how many are injured, but news comes from the pit that nine constables are lying there in a serious condition. The riot is spreading throughout the town, and it is unsafe to venture into the street. A fellow-journalist has just come in bleeding from a wound in the head, inflicted by a stone. He was a stranger, and that alone seems to account for the attack. A reckless crowd is marching through the streets. There seem to be no police about. The rioters swarm down the main street.

A number of men started a short time ago on a mission of wanton destruction bringing half bricks with them. They hurled them right and left into the shop windows. I followed safely in their tracks and saw the damage they had done. Some shops have not a particle of glass left in their fronts, and it is impossible to say how many windows are smashed. There has also been unrestricted looting. In the central square of the town a dozen shops have had their fronts completely broken out, and the goods that filled the windows three hours ago are now lying in the street. Companies of strikers have climbed to the upper floors and are rifling the stores, throwing them out of the windows to the people below, who are bearing them away in armfuls. The square is littered with clothing, millinery, groceries, confectionery, and chemists' wares. It is an amazing sight and quite indescribable.

The scene in the centre of the town is one of utter confusion. People stand about in small groups, either silent or discussing under their breath the events of the past few hours. The looting of shops is still going on. I have just seen a man standing behind the broken glass of a clothier's window emptying a broken bale of goods. He called out, 'Who wants a waistcoat?' and handed one to the man who first spoke; then a pair of trousers, then a coat; in this way the goods were distributed until the bale was empty. To assist the distribution the gas in the shop window had been lighted. Everything was done openly. There are no police about. Carpenters are already at work boarding up the broken windows.

Tonypandy, Wednesday 9 November. The town was awake all night. Excitement and fear kept many out of bed, and only the dawn scattered the prevailing alarm. All night long men were boarding up the shattered shop fronts and carts were going round for the sweepings of plate glass that littered the main street for three quarters of a mile. Now and again there was the heavy tramp of large bodies of police going or returning from the Glamorgan pit at Llwynypia, but nothing occurred to remove or increase the anxious suspense. Today is also full of fear. The few shops that escaped damage yesterday are being barricaded today, and the night is awaited with dread. Soldiers have arrived. A squadron of the 18th Hussars reached Pontypridd early this morning, and after a rest a troop came here by road, a distance of seven miles, while the other troop went to Aberdare. Their places at Pontypridd were taken by another squadron brought from Cardiff, where they had been overnight. The troop here rode through the town about one o'clock to their quarters at the New Colliery offices. The Metropolitan Mounted Constabulary have also arrived. Superficially there is nothing but curiosity in the minds of the slow-moving crowds that are in the streets, but the same could have been said yesterday, and those who know the temper of the Rhondda miners predict more trouble. Let us hope the prophets of evil are wrong.

Ten o'clock. Tonypandy tonight and Tonypandy last night are not like the same town. Even within the past two hours there has been a great change. There is not even a crowd about except in the square, where the number of people is perhaps large enough to be called a crowd. At first the disappearance of the strikers caused misgiving. It seemed as if they had acted on a common understanding, and the fear was that they might be congregating elsewhere. A good effect was produced by a proclamation in the square inviting all well-disposed persons to avoid associating themselves with riotous assemblies. I have walked to Llwynypia and as far as the grounds of Mr Llewellyn's house. There are only curious sightseers about. The colliery is brightly lighted, and the loud hum of the machinery in the power-house shows that it is running at full speed. The police, chilled by the cold night air, are stamping up and down to keep themselves warm. Mr Llewellyn's house looks as secure as Buckingham Palace. No doubt there are many police guarding it, but they are all hidden by the darkness, and it has not been thought necessary to secure the gates.

WINNING THE RACE FOR THE SOUTH POLE, December 1911

Roald Amundsen

The Norwegian explorer Roald Amundsen set out with four companions and fifty-two dogs on 19 October to reach the South Pole, arriving thirty-five days before his British rival, Robert Falcon Scott.

It was like the eve of some great festival that night in the tent. One could feel that a great event was at hand. Our flag was taken out again and lashed to the same two ski-sticks as before. Then it was rolled up and laid aside, to be ready when the time came. I was awake several times during the night, and had the same feeling that I can remember as a little boy on the night before Christmas Eve – an intense expectation of what was going to happen. Otherwise I think we slept just as well that night as any other.

On the morning of 14 December the weather was of the finest, just as if it had been made for arriving at the Pole. I am not quite sure, but I believe we dispatched our breakfast rather more quickly than usual and were out of the tent sooner, though I must admit that we always accomplished this with all reasonable haste. We went in the usual order – the forerunner, Hanssen, Wisting, Bjaaland, and the reserve forerunner. By noon we had reached 89° 53' by dead reckoning, and made ready to take the rest in one stage . . . We advanced that day in the same mechanical way as before; not much was said, but eyes were used all the more. Hanssen's neck grew twice as long as before in his endeavour to see a few inches further. I had asked him before we started to spy out ahead for all he was worth, and he did so with a vengeance. But, however keenly he stared, he could not descry anything but the endless flat plain ahead of us. The dogs had dropped their scenting, and appeared to have lost their interest in the regions about the earth's axis.

At three in the afternoon a simultaneous 'Halt!' rang out from the drivers. They had carefully examined their sledge-meters, and they all showed the full distance – our Pole by reckoning. The goal was reached, the journey ended. I cannot say – though I know it would sound much more effective – that the object of my life was attained. That would be romancing rather too bare-facedly. I had better be honest and admit straight out that I have never known any man to be placed in such a diametrically opposite position to the goal of his desires as I was at that moment. The regions around the North Pole – well, yes, the North Pole itself – had attracted me from childhood, and here I was at the South Pole. Can anything more topsy-turvy be imagined?

We reckoned now that we were at the Pole. Of course, every one of us knew that we were not standing on the absolute spot; it would be an impossibility with the time and the instruments at our disposal to ascertain that exact spot. But we were so near it that the few miles which possibly separated us from it could not be of the slightest importance. It was our intention to make a circle round this camp, with a radius of twelve and a half miles, and to be satisfied with that. After we had halted we collected and congratulated each other. We had good grounds for mutual respect in what had been achieved, and I think that was just the feeling that was expressed in the firm and powerful grasps of the fist that were exchanged. After this we proceeded to the greatest and most solemn act of the whole journey – the planting of our flag. Pride and affection shone in the five pairs of eyes that gazed upon the flag, as it unfurled itself with a sharp crack, and waved over the Pole. I had determined that the act of planting it – the historic event – should be equally divided among us all. It was not for one man to do this; it was for *all* who had staked their lives in the struggle, and held together through thick and thin. This was the only way in which I

could show my gratitude to my comrades in this desolate
spot. I could see that they understood and accepted it in the
spirit in which it was offered. Five weather-beaten, frost-
bitten fists they were that grasped the pole, raised the waving
flag in the air, and planted it as the first at the geographical
South Pole. 'Thus we plant thee, beloved flag, at the South
Pole, and give to the plain on which it lies the name of King
Haakon VII's Plateau.' That moment will certainly be
remembered by all of us who stood there.

One gets out of the way of protracted ceremonies in those
regions – the shorter they are the better. Everyday life began
again at once. When we had got the tent up, Hanssen set
about slaughtering Helge, and it was hard for him to have to
part from his best friend. Helge had been an uncommonly
useful and good-natured dog; without making any fuss he
had pulled from morning to night, and had been a shining
example to the team. But during the last week he had quite
fallen away, and on our arrival at the Pole there was only a
shadow of the old Helge left. He was only a drag on the
others, and did absolutely no work. One blow on the skull,
and Helge had ceased to live. 'What is death to one is food to
another' is a saying that can scarcely find a better application than these dog meals. Helge was portioned out on the
spot, and within a couple of hours there was nothing left of
him but his teeth and the tuft at the end of his tail. This was
the second of our eighteen dogs that we had lost. The Major,
one of Wisting's fine dogs, left us in 88° 25′ S, and never
returned. He was fearfully worn out, and must have gone
away to die. We now had sixteen dogs left, and these we
intended to divide into two equal teams, leaving Bjaaland's
sledge behind.

Of course, there was a festivity in the tent that evening –
not that champagne corks were popping and wine flowing –
no, we contented ourselves with a little piece of seal meat
each, and it tasted well and did us good. There was no other
sign of festival indoors. Outside we heard the flag flapping in

the breeze. Conversation was lively in the tent that evening, and we talked of many things. Perhaps, too, our thoughts sent messages home of what we had done.

ANTARCTIC EXPEDITION: THE FINAL DIARIES AND LETTERS OF CAPTAIN R.F. SCOTT, January 1912

Captain Scott

Scott had set out with eleven others on 24 October, only to find that the Norwegians had arrived first. On their return journey, in 1912, Scott and his companions all perished. Their bodies were found by searchers later that year on 12 November. This diary entry leaves some confusion as to the date of his actual death, but it is now generally assumed that he mistakenly wrote 'March' for 'January'.

It is wonderful to think that two long marches would land us at the Pole. We left our depot today with nine days' provisions, so that it ought to be a certain thing now, and the only appalling possibility the sight of the Norwegian flag forestalling ours. Little Bowers continues his indefatigable efforts to get good sights, and it is wonderful how he works them up in his sleeping-bag in our congested tent. (Minimum for night −27.5°.) Only 27 miles from the Pole. We *ought* to do it now.

Tuesday, 16 January . . . The worst has happened, or nearly the worst. . . . About the second hour of the march Bowers' sharp eyes detected what he thought was a cairn; he was uneasy about it, but argued that it must be a sastrugus. Half an hour later he detected a black speck ahead. Soon we knew that this could not be a natural snow feature. We marched on, found that it was a black flag tied to a sledge bearer; near by the remains of a camp; sledge tracks and ski tracks going and coming and the clear trace of dogs' paws – many dogs. This told us the whole story. The Norwegians have forestalled us and are first at the Pole. It is a terrible disappointment, and I am very sorry for my loyal companions. Many thoughts come and much discussion have we had. Tomorrow we must march on to the Pole and then hasten home with all the speed we can compass. All the daydreams must go; it will be a wearisome return. We are descending in altitude – certainly also the Norwegians found an easy way up.

Wednesday, 17 January . . . The Pole. Yes, but under very different circumstances from those expected. We have had a horrible day – add to our disappointment a head wind 4 to 5, with a temperature −22°, and companions labouring on with cold feet and hands.

We started at 7.30, none of us having slept much after the shock of our discovery. We followed the Norwegian sledge tracks for some way; as far as we make out there are only two men. In about three miles we passed two small cairns. Then the weather overcast, and the tracks being increasingly drifted up and obviously going too far to the west, we decided to make straight for the Pole according to our calculations . . . Great God! this is an awful place and terrible enough for us to have laboured to it without the reward of priority. Well, it is something to have got here, and the wind may be our friend tomorrow. We have had a fat Polar hoosh in spite of our chagrin, and feel comfortable inside – added a small stick of chocolate and the queer taste of a cigarette brought by Wilson. Now for the run home and a desperate struggle. I wonder if we can do it.

Thursday morning, 18 January . . . We have just arrived at this tent, 2 miles from our camp, therefore about 1½ miles from the Pole. In the tent we find a record of five Norwegians having been here, as follows: 'Roald Amundsen, Olav Olavson Bjaaland, Hilmer Hanssen, Sverre H. Hassel, Oscar Wisting; 16 Dec. 1911'. The tent is fine – a small, compact affair supported by a single bamboo. A note from Amundsen, which I keep, asks me to forward a letter to King Haakon!

The following articles have been left in the tent: three half-bags of reindeer containing a miscellaneous assortment of mitts and sleeping socks, very various in description, a sextant, a Norwegian artificial horizon and a hypsometer without boiling-point thermometers, a sextant and hyps-ometer of English make. Left a note to say I had visited the tent with companions . . .

This morning started with southerly breeze, set sail and passed another cairn at good speed; half-way, however, the wind shifted to W by S or WSW, blew through our wind clothes and into our mitts. Poor Wilson horribly cold, could not get off ski for some time. Bowers and I practically made camp, and when we got into the tent at last we were all deadly cold. Then temp. now midday down −43° and the wind strong. We *must* go on, but now the making of every camp must be more difficult and dangerous. It must be near the end, but a pretty merciful end. Poor Oates got it again in the foot. I shudder to think what it will be like tomorrow. It is only with greatest pains rest of us keep off frostbites. No idea there could be temperatures like this at this time of year with such winds. Truly awful outside the tent. Must fight it out to the last biscuit, but can't reduce rations.

Friday, 16 March or Saturday 17. Lost track of dates, but think the last correct. Tragedy all along the line. At lunch, the day before yesterday, poor Titus Oates said he couldn't go on; he proposed we should leave him in his sleeping-bag. That we could not do, and induced him to come on, on the afternoon march. In spite of its awful nature for him he struggled on and we made a few miles. At night he was worse and we knew the end had come.

Should this be found I want these facts recorded. Oates' last thoughts were of his mother, but immediately before he took pride in thinking that his regiment would be pleased with the bold way in which he met his death. We can testify to his bravery. He has borne intense suffering for weeks without complaint, and to the very last was able and willing to discuss outside subjects. He did not – would not – give up hope to the very end. He was a brave soul. This was the end. He slept through the night before last, hoping not to wake; but he woke in the morning – yesterday. It was blowing a blizzard. He said, 'I am just going outside and may be some time.' He went out into the blizzard and we have not seen him since.

I take this opportunity of saying that we have stuck to our sick companions to the last. In case of Edgar Evans, when absolutely out of food and he lay insensible, the safety of the remainder seemed to demand his abandonment, but Providence mercifully removed him at this critical moment. He died a natural death, and we did not leave him till two hours after his death. We knew that poor Oates was walking to his death, but though we tried to dissuade him, we knew it was the act of a brave man and an English gentleman. We all hope to meet the end with a similar spirit, and assuredly the end is not far.

I can only write at lunch and then only occasionally. The cold is intense, –40° at midday. My companions are unendingly cheerful, but we are all on the verge of serious frostbites, and though we constantly talk of fetching through I don't think any one of us believes it in his heart.

We are cold on the march now, and at all times except meals. Yesterday we had to lay up for a blizzard and today we move dreadfully slowly. We are at No. 14 pony camp, only two pony marches from One Ton Depot. We leave here our theodolite, a camera, and Oates' sleeping-bags. Diaries, etc., and geological specimens carried at Wilson's special request, will be found with us or on our sledge.

Sunday, 18 March. Today, lunch, we are 21 miles from the depot. Ill fortune presses, but better may come. We have had more wind and drift from ahead yesterday; had to stop marching; wind NW, force 4, temp. –35°. No human being could face it, and we are worn out *nearly*.

My right foot has gone, nearly all the toes – two days ago I was proud possessor of best feet. These are the steps of my downfall. Like an ass I mixed a small spoonful of curry powder with my melted pemmican – it gave me violent indigestion. I lay awake and in pain all night; woke and felt done on the march; foot went and I didn't know it. A very small measure of neglect and have a foot which is not pleasant to contemplate. Bowers takes first place in condition, but there is not much to choose after all. The others are still confident of getting through – or pretend to be – I don't know! We have the last *half* fill of oil in our primus and a very small quantity of spirit – this alone between us and thirst. The wind is fair for the moment, and that is perhaps a fact to help. The mileage would have seemed ridiculously small on our outward journey.

Monday, 19 March. Lunch. We camped with difficulty last night and were dreadfully cold till after our supper of cold pemmican and biscuit and a half a pannikin of cocoa cooked over the spirit. Then, contrary to expectation, we got warm and all slept well. Today we started in the usual dragging manner. Sledge dreadfully heavy. We are 15½ miles from the depot and ought to get there in three days. What progress! We have two days' food but barely a day's fuel. All our feet are getting bad – Wilson's best, my right foot worst, left all right. There is no chance to nurse one's feet till we can get hot food into us. Amputation is the least I can hope for now, but will the trouble spread? That is the serious question. The weather doesn't give us a chance – the wind from N to NW and −40° temp. today.

Wednesday, 21 March. Got within 11 miles of depot Monday night; had to lay up all yesterday in severe blizzard. Today forlorn hope, Wilson and Bowers going to depot for fuel.

Thursday, 22 and 23 March. Blizzard bad as ever – Wilson and Bowers unable to start – tomorrow last chance – no fuel and only one or two of food left – must be near the end. Have decided it shall be natural – we shall march for the depot with or without our effects and die in our tracks.

Thursday, 29 March. Since the 21st we have had a continuous gale from WSW and SW. We had fuel to make two cups of tea apiece and bare food for two days on the 20th. Every day we have been ready to start for our depot *11 miles* away, but outside the door of the tent it remains a scene of whirling drift. I do not think we can hope for any better things now. We shall stick it out to the end, but we are getting weaker, of course, and the end cannot be far.

It seems a pity, but I do not think I can write more.

R. SCOTT

For God's sake look after our people.

LETTER TO J. M. BARRIE

My dear Barrie,

We are pegging out in a very comfortless spot. Hoping this letter may be found and sent to you, I write a word of farewell . . . More practically I want you to help my widow and my boy – your godson. We are showing that Englishmen can still die with a bold spirit, fighting it out to the end. It will be known that we have accomplished our object in reaching the Pole, and that we have done everything possible, even to sacrificing ourselves in order to save sick companions. I think this makes an example for Englishmen of the future, and that the country ought to help those who are left behind to mourn us. I leave my poor girl and your godson, Wilson leaves a widow, and Edgar Evans also a widow in humble circumstances. Do what you can to get their claims recognized. Goodbye. I am not at all afraid of the end, but sad to miss many a humble pleasure which I had planned for the future on our long marches. I may not have proved a great explorer, but we have done the greatest march ever made and come very near to great success. Goodbye, my dear friend.

Yours ever,

R. Scott

Later . . . As a dying man, my dear friend, be good to my wife and child. Give the boy a chance in life if the State won't do it. He ought to have good stuff in him . . . I never met a man in my life whom I admired and loved more than you, but I never could show you how much your friendship meant to me, for you had much to give and I nothing.

LETTER TO HIS WIFE, KATHLEEN SCOTT

Make the boy [his son Peter] interested in natural history if you can; it is better than games; they encourage it at some schools. I know you will keep him in the open air.

Above all, he must guard and you must guard him against indolence. Make him a strenuous man. I had to force myself into being strenuous as you know – had always an inclination to be idle.

Kathleen Scott succeeded in her husband's dying wish; Peter Scott became a leading ornithologist and wildlife painter.

THE *TITANIC* SINKS, 15 April 1912

Harold Bride

Hailed by its makers and owners as 'unsinkable', the liner *Titanic* had a total complement of 2,224 passengers and crew but, it was to transpire, room for only 1,178 passengers in its lifeboats when it struck an iceberg in the Atlantic on its maiden voyage. A total of 1,513 lives were lost. Harold Bride was a *Titanic* wireless operator.

From aft came the tunes of the band. It was a ragtime tune. I don't know what. Then there was 'Autumn' . . . I went to the place I had seen the collapsible boat on the boat deck, and to my surprise I saw the boat, and the men still trying to push it off. I guess there wasn't a sailor in the crowd. They couldn't do it. I went up to them and was just lending a hand when a large wave came awash of the deck. The big wave carried the boat off. I had hold of an oarlock and I went with it. The next I knew I was in the boat. But that was not all. I was in the boat, and the boat was upside-down, and I was under it. And I remember realizing I was wet through and that whatever happened I must not breathe, for I was under water. I knew I had to fight for it, and I did. How I got out from under the boat I do not know but I felt a breath of air at last. There were men all around me – hundreds of them. The sea was dotted with them, all depending on their lifebelts. I felt I simply had to get away from the ship. She was a beautiful sight then. Smoke and sparks were rushing out of her funnel. There must have been an explosion, but we heard none. We only saw the big stream of sparks. The ship was turning gradually on her nose – just like a duck that goes for a dive. I had only one thing on my mind – to get away from the suction. The band was still playing. I guess all of them went down. They were playing 'Autumn' then. I swam with all my might. I suppose I was 150 feet away when the *Titanic*, on her nose, with her after-quarter sticking straight up in the air, began to settle – slowly.

When at last the waves washed over her rudder there wasn't the least bit of suction I could feel. She must have kept going just so slowly as she had been . . . I felt after a little while like sinking. I was very cold. I saw a boat of some kind near me, and put all my strength into an effort to swim to it.

It was hard work. I was all done when a hand reached out from the boat and pulled me aboard. It was our same collapsible. The same crowd was on it. There was just room for me to roll on the edge. I lay there not caring what happened. Somebody sat on my legs. They were wedged in between slats and were being wrenched. I had not the heart left to ask the man to move. It was a terrible sight all around – men swimming and sinking.

I lay where I was, letting the man wrench my feet out of shape. Others came near. Nobody gave them a hand. The bottom-up boat already had more men than it would hold, and it was sinking. At first the larger waves splashed over my clothing. Then they began to splash over my head, and I had to breathe when I could. As we floated around on our capsized boat and I kept straining my eyes for a ship's lights, somebody said, 'Don't the rest of you think we ought to pray?' The man who made the suggestion asked what the religion of the others was. Each man called out his religion. One was a Catholic, one a Methodist, one a Presbyterian. It was decided the most appropriate prayer for all was the Lord's Prayer. We spoke it over in chorus with the man who first suggested that we pray as the leader. Some splendid people saved us. They had a right-side-up boat and it was full to capacity. Yet they came to us and loaded us all into it. I saw some lights off in the distance and knew a steamship was coming to our aid.

A PERFORMANCE OF MUSIC BY SCHOENBERG, STETTIN, 16 October 1912

Anton Webern

The twelve-tone or serial technique invented by Austrian composer Arnold Schoenberg caused a Modernistic revolution in classical music.

The reception of the recitations was enthusiastic. Naturally there were a few people who hissed after the first part and one person who blew on a key. But that meant nothing. There was enthusiasm after the second part, and in the third there was one place where unrest was caused by an idiot who was laughing, so that Schoenberg stopped the performance and waited until calm was restored again. But at the end there was no trace of opposition. Schoenberg and the performers had to appear again and again on the platform, especially Schoenberg, naturally; people shouted for him in the hall over and over again. It was an unqualified success.

A SUFFRAGETTE COMMITS SUICIDE AT THE DERBY, 1913

Anon.

They had just got round the Corner, and all had passed but the King's horse, when a woman squeezed through the railings and ran out into the course. She made straight for Anmer, and made a sort of leap for the reins. I think she got hold of them, but it was impossible to say. Anyway the horse knocked her over, and then they all came down in a bunch. They were all rolling together on the ground. The jockey fell with the horse, and struck the ground with one foot in the stirrup, but he rolled free. Those fellows know how to tumble. The horse fell on the woman and kicked out furiously, and it was sickening to see his hoofs strike her repeatedly. It all happened in a flash. Before we had time to realize it was over. The horse struggled to its feet – I don't think it was hurt – but the jockey and the woman lay on the ground.

The ambulance men came running up, put them on stretchers, and carried them away. Most of the other jockeys saw nothing of it. They were far ahead. It was a terrible thing.

The woman who died was Emily Wilding, a well-known activist in the cause of women's suffrage.

THE PREMIÈRE OF STRAVINSKY'S *RITE OF SPRING*, 29 May 1913

Jean Cocteau

Stravinsky's ballet of pagan ritual has also been hailed as the beginning of Modernism in music. The opening night practically started a riot.

It was the first *scandale* ever witnessed. *The Rite of Spring* was performed . . . in a brash, brand-new theatre, too comfortable and too lacking in atmosphere for a Paris audience accustomed to experiencing its theatrical emotions while packed like sardines amidst the warmth of much red plush and gold. I have no thought that the *Rite* would have been more properly received in less pretentious surroundings; but this deluxe theatre symbolized very strikingly the mistake of pitting a strong, youthful work against a decadent public. An enervated public that spent its life lolling amid Louis XVI garlands and in Venetian gondolas, and on soft divans – and on pillows of an orientalism for which one can only say the Russian Ballet itself was responsible. Such an existence is like digesting one's lunch in a hammock; lying in a doze, you brush away anything really new as if it were a fly. It's troublesome.

I myself heard this historic work amid such a tumult that the dancers could no longer hear the orchestra and had to follow the rhythm as Nijinsky, stamping and shouting, beat it out for them from the wings.

Now come with me through the little metal door leading to the auditorium. Every seat is taken. The experienced eye perceives that every possible ingredient of a *scandale* is here: a society audience, décolleté, festooned with pearls, aigrettes, ostrich plumes; and, along with the tail-coats and the tulle, daytime jackets and women's hair that never saw a hairdresser – the ostentatiously drab trappings of that race of aesthetes who invariably acclaim the new out of mere hatred for the people in the boxes. (The ignorant applause of such aesthetes is more intolerable than the sincere boos of the society folk.) Then there were the feverish musicians, like so many Panurge's sheep, torn between the opinion expressed by the smart set and the respect due the Ballets Russes. No more of this: were I to continue, I would have to describe a thousand shades of snobbism, supersnobbism, countersnobbism, which would fill a chapter by themselves.

The house played its appointed role: it rebelled, instantly. It laughed, booed, whistled, imitated the cries of animals: perhaps it would have tired more quickly if the crowd of aesthetes and some of the musicians, carried away by excessive enthusiasm, hadn't taken to insulting and even physically threatening the people in the boxes. What had begun as an uproar turned into a veritable battle.

Standing in her box, red in the face, her coronet askew, the old Comtesse de Pourtalès brandished her fan and shouted: 'This is the first time in sixty years that anyone has dared make fun of me.' The good lady was sincere: she thought the whole thing was a practical joke.

Practical requirements had obliged Diaghilev to present in the form of a gala a première that should have been for artists alone.

Quel bombe! Quel chef d'oeuvre!

GERSHWIN COMPOSES *RHAPSODY IN BLUE*, 7 January 1914

George Gershwin

At this stage of the piece I was summoned to Boston for the première of *Sweet Little Devil*. I had already done some work on the rhapsody. It was on the train, with its steely rhythms, its rattle-ty bang that is often so stimulating to a composer . . . I frequently hear music in the very heart of noise. And there I suddenly heard – and even saw on paper – the complete construction of the rhapsody, from beginning to end. No new themes came to me, but I worked on the thematic material already in mind and tried to conceive the composition as a whole. I heard it as a sort of musical kaleidoscope of America – of our vast melting pot, of our unduplicated national pep, of our blues, our metropolitan madness. By the time I reached Boston I had a definite *plot* of the piece, as distinguished from its actual substance.

Part II

Armageddon
The First World War
1914–18

THE ASSASSINATION OF THE ARCHDUKE FRANZ FERDINAND, SARAJEVO, 28 June 1914

Borijove Jevtic

The murder of the heir to the Habsburg throne by Serb nationalist Gavrilo Princip was the incident which ignited the First World War. Austria made the assassination the pretext to declare war on Serbia, and within weeks the major powers had begun to mobilize. Jevtic was one of Princip's co-conspirators.

A tiny clipping from a newspaper mailed without comment from a secret band of terrorists in Zagreb, a capital of Croatia, to their comrades in Belgrade, was the torch which set the world afire with war in 1914. That bit of paper wrecked old proud empires. It gave birth to new, free nations.

I was one of the members of the terrorist band in Belgrade which received it and, in those days, I and my companions were regarded as desperate criminals. A price was on our heads. Today my little band is seen in a different light, as pioneer patriots. It is recognized that our secret plans hatched in an obscure café in the capital of old Serbia, have led to the independence of the new Yugoslavia, the united nation set free from Austrian domination.

The little clipping was from the *Srobobran*, a Croatian journal of limited circulation, and consisted of a short telegram from Vienna. This telegram declared that the Austrian Archduke Franz Ferdinand would visit Sarajevo, the capital of Bosnia, 28 June, to direct army manoeuvres in the neighbouring mountains.

It reached our meeting place, the café called Zeatna Moruana, one night the latter part of April, 1914 . . . At a small table in a very humble café, beneath a flickering gas jet we sat and read it. There was no advice nor admonition sent with it. Only four letters and two numerals were sufficient to make us unanimous, without discussion, as to what we should do about it. They were contained in the fateful date, 28 June.

How dared Franz Ferdinand, not only the representative of the oppressor but in his own person an arrogant tyrant, enter Sarajevo on that day? Such an entry was a studied insult.

28 June is a date engraved deeply in the heart of every Serb, so that the day has a name of its own. It is called the vidovnan. It is the day on which the old Serbian kingdom was conquered by the Turks at the battle of Amselfelde in 1389. It is also the day on which in the second Balkan War the Serbian arms took glorious revenge on the Turk for his old victory and for the years of enslavement.

That was no day for Franz Ferdinand, the new oppressor, to venture to the very doors of Serbia for a display of the force of arms which kept us beneath his heel.

Our decision was taken almost immediately. Death to the tyrant!

Then came the matter of arranging it. To make his death certain twenty-two members of the organization were selected to carry out the sentence. At first we thought we would choose the men by lot. But here Gavrilo Princip intervened. Princip is destined to go down in Serbian history as one of her greatest heroes. From the moment Ferdinand's death was decided upon he took an active leadership in its planning. Upon his advice we left the deed to members of our band who were in and around Sarajevo under his direction and that of Gabrinovic, a linotype operator on a Serbian newspaper. Both were regarded as capable of anything in the cause.

The fateful morning dawned. Two hours before Franz Ferdinand arrived in Sarajevo all the twenty-two conspirators were in their allotted positions, armed and ready. They were distributed 500 yards apart over the whole route along which the Archduke must travel from the railroad station to the town hall.

When Franz Ferdinand and his retinue drove from the station they were allowed to pass the first two conspirators. The motor cars were driving too fast to make an attempt feasible and in the crowd were Serbians: throwing a grenade would have killed many innocent people.

When the car passed Gabrinovic, the compositor, he threw his grenade. It hit the side of the car, but Franz Ferdinand with presence of mind threw himself back and was uninjured. Several officers riding in his attendance were injured.

The cars sped to the Town Hall and the rest of the conspirators did not interfere with them. After the reception in the Town Hall General Potiorek, the Austrian Commander, pleaded with Franz Ferdinand to leave the city, as it was seething with rebellion. The Archduke was persuaded to drive the shortest way out of the city and to go quickly.

The road to the manoeuvres was shaped like the letter V, making a sharp turn at the bridge over the River Nilgacka. Franz Ferdinand's car could go fast enough until it reached this spot but here it was forced to slow down for the turn. Here Princip had taken his stand.

As the car came abreast he stepped forward from the curb,

drew his automatic pistol from his coat and fired two shots. The first struck the wife of the Archduke, the Archduchess Sofia, in the abdomen. She was an expectant mother. She died instantly.

The second bullet struck the Archduke close to the heart.

He uttered only one word; 'Sofia' – a call to his stricken wife. Then his head fell back and he collapsed. He died almost instantly.

The officers seized Princip. They beat him over the head with the flat of their swords. They knocked him down, they kicked him, scraped the skin from his neck with the edges of their swords, tortured him, all but killed him.

Then he was taken to the Sarajevo gaol. The next day he was transferred to the military prison and the round-up of his fellow conspirators proceeded, although he denied that he had worked with anyone.

He was confronted with Gabrinovic, who had thrown the bomb. Princip denied he knew him. Others were brought in, but Princip denied the most obvious things.

The next day they put chains on Princip's feet, which he wore till his death.

His only sign of regret was the statement that he was sorry he had killed the wife of the Archduke. He had aimed only at her husband and would have preferred that any other bullet should have struck General Potiorek.

The Austrians arrested every known revolutionary in Sarajevo and among them, naturally, I was one. But they had no proof of my connection with the crime. I was placed in the cell next to Princip's, and when Princip was taken out to walk in the prison yard I was taken along as his companion.

A GERMAN DIARY, 28 June–25 July 1914

Herbert Sulzbach

Frankfurt-am-Main, 28 June 1914 Archduke Francis Ferdinand has been murdered, with his wife [the Duchess of Hohenberg], by two Serbs at Sarajevo. What follows from this is not clear. You feel that a stone has begun to roll downhill and that dreadful things may be in store for Europe.

I am proposing on 1 October to start my military service instead of going to Hamburg as a commercial trainee. I'm twenty, you see, a fine age for soldiering, I don't know a better.

July 14 I travel to Würzburg, report to the 2nd Bavarian Field Artillery Regiment and get accepted.

Böhm, the German airman, has scored a world record with 24½ hours of continuous flight.

July 23 Ultimatum delivered to Serbia by Austria-Hungary. No strong action by Austria appeared to have been taken since the assassination of 28 June until suddenly this note was presented, containing ten demands which among other things were supposed to allow Austria herself to take action on Serbian soil against activities hostile to Austria. Serbia has to accept the ultimatum within 48 hours, otherwise Austria reserves the right to take military action. A world war is hanging by a thread.

July 25 Unbelievably large crowds are waiting outside the newspaper offices. News arrives in the evening that Serbia is rejecting the ultimatum. General excitement and enthusiasm, and all eyes turn towards Russia – is she going to support Serbia?

The days pass from 25 to 31 July. Incredibly exciting; the whole world is agog to see whether Germany is now going to mobilize. I've hardly got enough peace of mind left to go to the bank and do my trainee job. I play truant as though it were school and stand about all day outside the newspaper offices, feeling that war is inevitable.

JEAN JAURÈS IS MURDERED, PARIS, 31 July 1914
Robert Dell

Jean Jaurès was the leader of the French Socialist Party and founder of the socialist newspaper, *L'Humanité*. He had stood up for the working classes against Clemenceau and opposed long-term military service. Many considered him anti-patriotic. However, his assassin, Raoul Villain, would be found to be mentally unstable and at his trial would be acquitted.

Grave as is the international situation even the probable imminence of war has been overshadowed for the moment in Paris by the appalling crime this evening of which I was an eye-witness. It is impossible to one who knew M. Jaurès, whom one could not help loving, to write about it calmly with the grief fresh upon one. I was dining with a member of my family and a friend at the Café du Croissant, the well-known resort of journalists in the rue Montmartre close to many newspaper offices including that of *L'Humanité*. M. Jaurès was also dining there with some Socialist deputies and members of the staff of *L'Humanité*. He came in later than we did. I spoke to him just as he entered and had a short conversation with him about the prospects of war and peace. Like everyone else, he feared that war was probable, but he still had some faith that Sir Edward Grey might succeed in inducing Germany to be conciliatory. If some sort of conference could be arranged, he thought, peace might even yet be secured; and if the French Government would bring pressure to bear on Russia and the German Government on Austria an arrangement might be possible. He added, however, that he feared the French Government might not do that. What a crime war will be and what a monstrous folly. The last words that he said to me was an inquiry about M. Anatole France, who, he said, must be deeply distressed by the situation.

At about half-past nine, when we were just finishing dinner, two pistol shots suddenly resounded in the restaurant. At first we did not understand what had happened, and for a moment thought that there was shooting in the street outside. Then we saw that M. Jaurès had fallen sideways on the bench on which he was sitting, and the screams of the women who were present told us of the murder. It should be explained that M. Jaurès and his friends were sitting on a bench with their backs to the open window of the restaurant, and the shots were fired from the street through the window. M. Jaurès was shot in the head, and the murderer must have held the pistol close to his victim. A surgeon was hastily summoned, but he could do nothing, and M. Jaurès died quietly without regaining consciousness a few minutes after the crime. Meanwhile the murderer had been seized and handed over to the police, who had to protect him from the crowd which had quickly collected in the street. At that hour in the evening the rue Montmartre is filled with newsvendors waiting for the late editions of the evening papers.

It is said that the murderer is a member of the Royalist society Action Française, but I have not yet been able to discover whether this report is true or not. A more cold-blooded and cowardly murder was never committed. The scene in and about the restaurant was heartrending; both men and women were in tears and their grief was terrible to see. It is as yet too early to say what the effect of the murder will be, but it may be considerable. M. Jaurès has died a victim to the cause of peace and humanity.

A GERMAN DIARY, 31 July–1 August 1914

Herbert Sulzbach

Friday, 31 July State of war declared and total mobilization announced in Austria-Hungary.

Saturday, 1 August 6.30 p.m. The Kaiser orders mobilization of the Army and Navy. That word 'mobilize', it's weird, you can't grasp what it means. First mobilization day is 2 August.

Try as I may I simply can't convey the splendid spirit and wild enthusiasm that has come over us all. We feel we've been attacked, and the idea that we have to defend ourselves gives us unbelievable strength.

Russia's dirty intrigues are dragging us into this war; the Kaiser sent the Russians an ultimatum as late as 31 July. You still can't imagine what it's going to be like. Is it all real, or just a dream?

BRITAIN DECLARES WAR, 4 August 1914

King George V

Great Britain entered the First World War on 4 August 1914 after Germany refused to respect Belgian neutrality.

I held a council at 10.45 to declare war with Germany. It is a terrible catastrophe but it is not our fault. An enormous crowd collected outside the Palace; we went on the balcony both before and after dinner. When they heard that war had been declared, the excitement increased and May and I with David went on to the balcony; the cheering was terrific. Please to God it may soon be over and that He will protect dear Bertie's life.

King George V

JOINING UP, Autumn 1914

Oskar Kokoschka

Austrian by birth, Kokoschka went on to become one of Europe's most eminent painters.

In 1914 I was twenty-eight years old, and thus liable for military service. It seemed to me better to volunteer before I was conscripted. I had no wife or child to await my happy return. I had nothing to lose or to defend. I felt melancholy at the sight of the young bank clerks, the little office workers, whom I saw hurrying with their suitcases to enlist, and yet I did not share the doom-laden mood that prevailed on the streets. The air was thick with rumours that part of the army had gone into the field wearing peacetime clothing.

Arthur Conan Doyle

The British author of the *Sherlock Holmes* stories writes a letter to the War Office.

I have been told that there may be some difficulty in finding officers for the New Army. I think I may say that my name is well-known to the younger men of this country and that if I were to take a commission at my age it might be of help. I can drill a company – I do so every evening. I have seen something of campaigning, having served as a surgeon in South Africa. I am fifty-five but I am very strong and hardy, and can make my voice audible at great distances which is useful at drill. Should you entertain my application, I should prefer a regiment which was drawn from the South of England – Sussex for choice.

Robert Graves

At the time of writing, Robert Graves was a student. He later joined the Royal Welch Fusiliers, and wrote one of the classic memoirs of the conflict, *Goodbye to All That*.

I had just finished with Charterhouse and gone up to Harlech, when England declared war on Germany. A day or two later I decided to enlist. In the first place, though the papers predicted only a very short war – over by Christmas at the outside – I hoped that it might last long enough to delay my going to Oxford in October, which I dreaded. Nor did I work out the possibilities of getting actively engaged in the fighting, expecting garrison service at home, while the regular forces were away. In the second place, I was outraged to read of the Germans' cynical violation of Belgian neutrality. Though I discounted perhaps twenty per cent of the atrocity details as wartime exaggeration, that was not, of course, sufficient.

FLEEING THE GERMAN ADVANCE THROUGH FRANCE, October 1914

Frederick Delius

At the time of the German invasion of France, the composer Delius was living at Grez-sur-Loing, some sixty miles south of Paris.

We have been having very exciting times here – During the German advance there was an ever growing panic here caused, no doubt, by the refugees from Belgium & the North of France streaming thro' Grez – The high road to

Nemours was a terrifying sight & we sat for hours watching this terrified stream of humanity pass by in every sort of vehicle possible – We had hundreds every night in Grez & they told terrible tales of German atrocities – On Sept 5th it got too much for us & we also could hear the booming of the canon [Battle of the Marne] so we decided to get out also, so we left for Orleans in a cattle truck with 50 or 60 others. We took 16½ hours to go 75 kilometres & arrived in Orleans at 3.30 in the morning & as there was not a room to be had in the whole town we spent the rest of the night on a bench on the boulevard near the railway station – We had the great luck to get a room at night so we decided to stay there & await further developements (*sic*) – We had a most interesting & exciting time in Orleans watching the soldiers going off to the front & the wounded coming back – trainload after trainload – this was awful – Some of the poor soldiers, carried on stretchers, with one or both legs shot off – As soon as we heard of the great Victory of the allies we quietly returned to Grez & found everything as quiet & peaceful as ever – Your uncle had gone off the same day as we did with his 2 servants en route for Guernsey – At Havre he got a steamer for Cherbourg & had a most fearful passage in a miserable little dirty boat. On arriving in some port or other they were fired on 3 times, it appears, as they had no flag up. I nearly died with laughter when Joe told me of his adventures – We are thinking of going to America until all this is over – I am entirely sick of it – We shall leave about Christmas probably from England – I may come to London a fortnight or 3 weeks before sailing & then I should just love to roam about London with you – I am glad you have not enlisted – I hate & loathe this German militarism & autocracy & hope it may be crushed for ever – but I can get up no enthusiasm whatever for the war. My sympathies are with the maimed & slaughtered on both sides. My North Country sketches are ready & also my 'Requiem'. I shall take them with me to America & perhaps conduct them myself – I shall have to

make some money over there in some way or other. Music
will be dead in Europe for a year or more & all countries will
be ruined – It makes one despair of humanity – Lloyd
Osbourne & his wife were here thro' the panic – They were
seized with it 24 hours before we were & left for Nantes but
they returned a fortnight ago here to Grez & are now on
their way to London. We had great fun burying our best
wine & silver – I would not have missed this experience for
anything. The world has gone mad.

THE SOUND OF BULLETS, FRANCE, 2 October 1914

André Fribourg

It is understood that bullets whistle, just as horses neigh . . .
But how poor the word is. How pale and niggardly in
expressing the extraordinary richness of the music! . . . the
differences of distance, of speed, of calibre, of direction, of the
grouping of the guns . . . of dampness, heat, cold wind; the
differences of the setting of the battle, whether in plain,
valley, forest, glade or on a hill; the differences of intensity of
fire are such that there is a veritable scale of sounds of an
infinite variety of combinations . . . Very soon you learn to
distinguish the sound of the Mannlicher from the sound of a
Lebel. The S bullet leaves the rifle dryly, with a sharp note.
The cry of the D is deeper, making many echoes . . .

NIGHT PATROL, YPRES, October 1914

Private Frank Richards, Royal Welch Fusiliers

That night we heard the enemy working on our front, but
we didn't know whether they were entrenching themselves
or not. The next morning a heavy mist hung over every-

where and it was impossible to see ten yards ahead. Buffalo Bill decided to send a patrol out, consisting of a corporal and two men; in my battalion throughout the whole of the War no privates were ever warned to go out on patrol – volunteers were always called for. Corporal Pardoe, Private Miles and I went out on that patrol; our orders were simply to proceed as far as we could up the willow ditch and to discover what we could. We had gone a considerable way past our listening-post when we halted. Pardoe said: 'How far do you think we have come?' 'Over 200 yards,' said Miles, and I agreed with him. The mist was still heavy and we were listening intently. Presently we heard voices not far off and the sounds of men working. We were wondering whether to work up closer or to go back and report, when all of a sudden the mist blew away, and there, a little over 100 yards in front of us, were new enemy trenches. The enemy were taking advantage of the mist and working on the parapet: some were a good thirty yards from their trench – they had been levelling some corn-stacks so as to have a clear line of fire. Pardoe got one side of the ditch, and Miles and I on the other, and opened out with rapid fire. We had our rifles resting on the bank. The three of us had been marksmen all through our soldiering: each of us could get off twenty-five aimed rounds a minute and it was impossible to miss at that distance. We had downed half a dozen men before they realized what was happening; then they commenced to jump back in the trench. Those that were out in front started to run, but we bowled them over like rabbits. It put me in mind of firing at the 'running man' on a peace-time course of musketry. Against we had expended our magazines which held ten rounds there wasn't a live enemy to be seen, and the whole affair had not lasted half a minute. We quickly reloaded our magazines, which took us a couple of seconds, turned around, and ran towards our trench, each of us in turn halting to fire five rounds covering fire at the enemy's trench.

The mist had now lifted everywhere: we could see our own trench quite plainly and bullets were zipping around us. Our men on the extreme left of the platoon had opened fire on the enemy's trench, but the men in line with the ditch were not allowed to fire for fear of hitting us (we learned this when we got back). We arrived at our listening-post, jumped the little bank and laid down, properly winded. We were not out of the soup yet: we still had forty yards to travel before we got back in our trench. We were safe from rifle-fire as long as we crawled on our bellies to the parapet but when we got to the end of the ditch we would have to jump out in the open before getting into the trench, and we knew full well that the enemy would be waiting for that move. We arrived at the end of the ditch and there we heard Buffalo Bill shouting over for us to remain where we were for a couple of minutes, and then to get back in the trench one by one. He passed word up the trench for the whole platoon to open out with rapid fire which would make the enemy keep their heads down and give us a decent chance to get home without being hit. We got back safely; I never knew how well I could jump until that morning. I was out of the ditch and into the trench in the twinkling of an eye: Duffy said that I cleared the parapet like a Grand National winner. The corporal made his report to Buffalo Bill who was delighted at our brush-up. Miles and I did not know what narrow squeaks we had had until someone noticed a bullet-hole through Miles's trousers and two more through the right sleeve of my tunic.

LIFE IN THE TRENCHES, WESTERN FRONT, Winter 1914

Alan Seeger

After the first battle of Ypres ('Wipers' as it became known to the British soldier), the opposing sides on the Western Front settled

down into a double line of entrenchments that stretched from
Switzerland to the English Channel.

This style of [trench] warfare is extremely modern and for
the artillerymen is doubtless very interesting, but for the poor
common soldier it is anything but romantic. His role is
simply to dig himself a hole in the ground and to keep
hidden in it as tightly as possible. Continually under the fire
of the opposing batteries, he is yet never allowed to get a
glimpse of the enemy. Exposed to all the dangers of war, but
none of its enthusiasms or splendid élan, he is condemned to
sit like an animal in its burrow and hear the shells whistle
over his head and take their little daily toll from his comrades
. . . His feet are numb, his canteen frozen, but he is not
allowed to make a fire . . . he is not even permitted to light a
candle, but must fold himself in his blanket and lie down
cramped in the dirty straw to sleep as best he may. How
different from the popular notion of the evening campfire,
the songs and good cheer.

Private Frank Richards

Our dead we used to put on the back of the parapet and we
carried them at night to a place just behind the line and
buried them there. All companies carried their dead to the
same place. If a dead man's clothes or boots were in good
condition we never hesitated to take them off him, especially
when they would fit a man. My own puttees were in ribbons,
so I took the Corporal's, which were in good condition. In a
belt that Corporal Pardoe wore next to his skin they found
about sixty English sovereigns, besides French money. None
of it went back to his next-of-kin. I could have had some but
I didn't want to touch it: I was satisfied with his puttees. We
began to sap out to our left and right platoons and dug a

trench from the officers' bay back to a dip in the ground about twenty yards from a farmhouse. We used to fill our water-bottles at the farm at night, and each man's water-bottle had to last him twenty-four hours.

There was no such thing as cooked food or hot tea at this stage of the War, and rations were very scarce: we were lucky if we got our four biscuits a man daily, a pound tin of bully between two, a tin of jam between six, and the rum ration which was about a tablespoonful and a half. Even at this early period the jam was rotten and one firm that supplied it must have made hundreds of thousands of pounds profit out of it – the stuff they put in instead of fruit and sugar! One man swore that if ever he got back to England he would make it his first duty to shoot up the managing director and all the other heads of that particular firm. Tobacco, cigarettes and matches were also very scarce. We had plenty of small-arm ammunition but no rifle-oil or rifle-rag to clean our rifles with. We used to cut pieces off our shirts for use as rifle-rags, and some of us who had bought small tins of vaseline (in villages we passed through during our Aisne advance) for use on sore heels or chafed legs, used to grease our rifles with that. A rifle soon got done up without oil in these conditions. Our sanitary arrangements were very bad: we used empty bully-beef tins for urinating in, throwing it over the back of the parapet. If a man was taken short during the day he had to use the trench he was in and then throw it over the back of the trench and throw earth after it.

One night there was an enemy attack which we beat off and the next morning some corpses were to be seen lying just out in front of us: they were wearing spiked helmets. We crawled out the next night and went through their packs, taking anything they had of value from them. The spiked helmets we intended to keep as souvenirs, but we soon came to the conclusion that it was no good keeping souvenirs of that sort when any moment we may be dancing a two-step in another world. So we used them as latrine buckets, throwing them over the parapet at the back when we had used them.

A PILOT ENCOUNTERS THE ENEMY, WESTERN FRONT, 1914

Sholto Douglas, Royal Flying Corps

The first time I ever encountered a German plane in the air both the pilot, Harvey-Kelley, and myself were completely unarmed . . . We were taking photographs . . . of the trench system to the north of Neuve Chapelle when I suddenly espied a German two-seater about 100 yards away and just below us. The German observer did not appear to be shooting at us. There was nothing to be done. We waved a hand to the enemy and proceeded with our task. The enemy did likewise. At the time this did not appear to me in any way ridiculous – there is a bond of sympathy between all who fly, even between enemies. But afterwards just for safety's sake I always carried a carbine with me in the air. In the ensuing two or three months I had an occasional shot at a German engine. But these encounters can hardly be dignified by the name of 'fights'. We scarcely expected to shoot the enemy down . . .

CHRISTMAS IN THE TRENCHES, WESTERN FRONT, 1914

Private Frank Richards

On Christmas morning we stuck up a board with 'A Merry Christmas' on it. The enemy had stuck up a similar one. Platoons would sometimes go out for twenty-four hours' rest – it was a day at least out of the trench and relieved the monotony a bit – and my platoon had gone out in this way the night before, but a few of us stayed behind to see what would happen. Two of our men then threw their equipment off and jumped on the parapet with their hands above their heads. Two of the Germans done the same and commenced to walk up the river bank, our two men going to meet them. They met and shook hands and then we all got out of the trench. Buffalo Bill rushed into the trench and endeavoured to prevent it, but he was too late: the whole of the Company were now out, and so were the Germans. He had to accept the situation, so soon he and the other company officers climbed out too. We and the Germans met in the middle of no-man's-land. Their officers was also now out. Our officers exchanged greetings with them. One of the German officers said that he wished he had a camera to take a snapshot, but they were not allowed to carry cameras. Neither were our officers.

We mucked in all day with one another. They were Saxons and some of them could speak English. By the look of them their trenches were in as bad a state as our own. One of their men, speaking in English, mentioned that he had worked in Brighton for some years and that he was fed up to the neck with this damned war and would be glad when it was all over. We told him that he wasn't the only one that was fed up with it. We did not allow them in our trench and they did not allow us in theirs. The German Company-Commander asked Buffalo Bill if he would accept a couple of barrels of beer and assured him that they would not make his men drunk. They had plenty of it in the brewery. He accepted the offer with thanks and a couple of their men rolled the barrels over and we took them into our trench. The German officer sent one of his men back to the trench, who appeared shortly after carrying a tray with bottles and glasses on it. Officers of both sides clinked glasses and drunk one another's health. Buffalo Bill had presented them with a plum pudding just before. The officers came to an understanding that the unofficial truce would end at midnight. At dusk we went back to our respective trenches.

We had a decent Christmas dinner. Each man had a tin of Maconochie's and a decent portion of plum pudding. A tin of Maconochie's consisted of meat, potatoes, beans and other vegetables and could be eaten cold, but we generally used to fry them up in the tin on a fire. I don't remember any man ever suffering from tin or lead poisoning through doing them in this way. The best firms that supplied them were Maconochie's and Moir Wilson's, and we could always depend on having a tasty dinner when we opened one of their tins. But another firm that supplied them at this time must have made enormous profits out of the British Government. Before ever we opened the first tins that were supplied by them we smelt a rat. The name of the firm made us suspicious. When we opened them our suspicions were well founded. There was nothing inside but a rotten piece of meat and some boiled rice. The head of that firm should have been put against the wall and shot for the way they sharked us troops. The two barrels of beer were drunk, and the German officer was right: if it was possible for a man to have drunk the two barrels himself he would have bursted before he had got drunk. French beer was rotten stuff.

Just before midnight we all made it up not to commence firing before they did. At night there was always plenty of firing by both sides if there were no working parties or patrols out. Mr Richardson, a young officer who had just joined the Battalion and was now a platoon officer in my company wrote a poem during the night about the Briton and the Bosche meeting in no-man's-land on Christmas Day, which he read out to us. A few days later it was published in *The Times* or *Morning Post*, I believe. During the whole of Boxing Day we never fired a shot, and they the same, each side seemed to be waiting for the other to set the ball a-rolling. One of their men shouted across in English and inquired how we had enjoyed the beer. We shouted back and told him it was very weak but that we were very grateful for it. We were conversing off and on during the whole of the day. We were relieved that evening at dusk by a battalion of another brigade. We were mighty surprised as we had heard no whisper of any relief during the day. We told the men who relieved us how we had spent the last couple of days with the enemy, and they told us that by what they had been told the whole of the British troops in the line, with one or two exceptions, had mucked in with the enemy. They had only been out of action themselves forty-eight hours after being twenty-eight days in the front-line trenches. They also told us that the French people had heard how we had spent Christmas Day and were saying all manner of nasty things about the British Army.

GALLIPOLI, 25 April 1915

The landing of Allied troops – predominantly British and Anzac (Australian and New Zealand Army Corps) – at the entrance to the Dardenelles, the straits between the Mediterranean and Sea of Marmara, giving access to Istanbul (Constantinople), was intended to open a front against the Turks, and so lessen the pressure on the Russian Army. At the outset, it was regarded as a highly dangerous and almost unachievable move, and it proved one of the greatest military disasters of the First World War, with the Allies slaughtered as they tried to struggle ashore. Even those that made it found themselves unable to break out of a narrow bridgehead on the rocky, sun-beaten Gallipoli peninsula.

Major Shaw

About 100 yards from the beach the enemy opened fire, and bullets came thick all around, splashing up the water. I didn't see anyone actually hit in the boats, though several were; e.g. my Quartermaster-Sergeant and Sergeant-Major sitting next to me; but we were so jammed together that you couldn't have moved, so that they must have been sitting there, dead. As soon as I felt the boat touch, I dashed over the side into three feet of water and rushed for the barbed wire entanglements on the beach; it must have been only three feet high or so, because I got over it amidst a perfect storm of lead and made for cover, sand dunes on the other side, and got good cover. I then found Maunsell and only two men had followed me. On the right of me on the cliff was a line of Turks in a trench taking pot shots at us, ditto on the left. I looked back. There was one soldier between me and the wire, and a whole line in a row on the edge of the sands. The sea behind was absolutely crimson, and you could hear the groans through the rattle of musketry. A few were firing. I signalled to them to advance. I shouted to the soldier behind me to signal, but he shouted back 'I am shot through the chest'. I then perceived they were all hit.

Chief Petty Officer Johnson, Royal Navy

For quite an hour the huge guns blazed away, whilst we in the trenches lay full length on the ground or stuffed ourselves into small holes cut in the trench side. It was good if two fellows could get together in one of these holes – it meant company. Your feet and legs stuck well out into the trench, but your back and head were safely protected by perhaps two feet of earth which any ordinary size of shell would cut a way through in the hundredth part of a second. You are both squeezed together, you don't dare think how easily a piece of shell would penetrate your shelter. You light a cigarette, look at each other, and wait . . . You press your back harder against the wall and your head harder into the roof. You know you are not safe, but you press harder and that seems to help a bit. You can only see in front of you the opposite side of the sandy trench, at which you gaze in a vacant stare. The shells scream louder and more often, the screeches, whistles and bangs are hopelessly intermingled, and the ground beneath and around you is rocking and trembling.

Thick fumes float into your hole and you cough and your pal coughs. Your knees and legs are covered with pieces of dirt and a layer of dust, and half of the ground that was above your head has gone by way of your neck to the seat of your trousers. You wonder if the bombardment will ever cease . . .

The crashes suddenly cease, the air becomes clearer at once, and you realize that for the time being at any rate the bombardment is over. You wait a few minutes to make quite sure, and then you struggle out of the hole into the trench . . . You look over the parapet, and see a stretch of country with no sign of life.

OVER THE TOP, WESTERN FRONT, 1915

H.S. Clapham

We started again at dusk and passed down the railway cutting, but, instead of turning off into the fields, we went on as far as the Menin Road, at what is known as 'Hell Fire Corner'. A few hundred yards down the road we turned into the fields on the left, and found a resting-place for the night in some shallow 'jumping-off' trenches, a few yards back from the front line. It was very dark, and the trench was small, and sitting in a huddle I got cramp and felt miserable.

The Huns started by putting over big crumps all around us. They seemed to aim for the relics of a building 100 yards in the rear, and there the bricks were flying, but otherwise they did no damage. Still, they kept us guessing, and, knowing what was in front of us, I found sleep impossible.

Then at 2.50 a.m. our own guns started and kept up a

heavy bombardment of the trenches in front until 4.15, by which time it was quite light. I don't know whether the Huns kept it up, too. In any case, one couldn't have heard them or their explosions: there was such a devil of a row going on.

At 4.15 a whistle blew. The men in the front line went over the top, and we scrambled out and took their places in the front trench. In front of us was a small field, with grass knee-high, split diagonally by an old footpath. On the other side of the field was a belt of trees, known as Y Wood, in which lay the first Hun trench.

In a few moments flags went up there, to show that it had been captured and that the troops were going on. Another whistle, and we ourselves scrambled over the parapet and sprinted across the field. Personally, I was so overweighted that I could only amble, and I remember being intensely amused at the sight of a little chap in front of me who seemed in even worse case than myself. Without thinking much about it, I took the diagonal path, as the line of least resistance, and most of my section did the same.

When I dropped into the Hun trench I found it a great place, only three feet wide, and at least eight deep, and beautifully made of white sandbags, back and front. At that spot there was no sign of any damage by our shells, but a number of dead Huns lay in the bottom. There was a sniper's post just where I fell in, a comfortable little square hole, fitted with seats and shelves, bottles of beer, tinned meats, and a fine helmet hanging on a hook.

THE *LUSITANIA* IS TORPEDOED, 7 May 1915

McMillan Adams

The sinking of the British cruise liner *Lusitania* off the coast of Ireland by a German U-boat caused the drowning of over 1,000 people, including 100 Americans. It provoked outrage in the USA, and paved the way for America to enter the First World War. McMillan Adams was an American passenger aboard the liner.

I was in the lounge on A Deck . . . when suddenly the ship shook from stem to stern, and immediately started to list to starboard . . . I rushed out into the companionway . . . While standing there, a second, and much greater explosion occurred. At first I thought the mast had fallen down. This was followed by the falling on the deck of the water spout that had been made by the impact of the torpedo with the ship . . . My father came up and took me by the arm . . . We went to the port side . . . and started to help in the launching of the lifeboats. Owing to the list of the ship, the lifeboats . . . had a tendency to swing inwards across the deck and before they could be launched, it was necessary to push them over the side of the ship. While working there, the staff Captain told us that the boat was not going to sink, and ordered the lifeboats not to be lowered. He also asked the gentlemen to help in clearing the passengers from the boat deck (A Deck) . . . it was impossible to lower the lifeboats safely at the speed at which the *Lusitania* was still going . . . I saw only two boats launched from this side. The first boat to be launched for the most part full of women fell sixty or seventy feet into the water, all the occupants being drowned. This was owing to the fact that the crew could not work the davits and falls properly, so let them slip out of their hands, and sent the lifeboats to destruction . . . I said to my father 'We shall have to swim for it. We had better go below and get our lifebelts.'

When we got down to Deck D, our cabin deck, we found it was impossible to leave the stairs, as the water was pouring in at all the port holes . . . Finally, we reached the boat deck again, this time on the starboard side, and after filling a lifeboat with women and children, we jumped into it. The lifeboat [No. 19] was successfully lowered until we were about twelve feet from the water, when the man at the bow davit lost his nerve, and let the rope go. Most of the occupants were thrown into the water, but we, being in the stern, managed to stay in. The lifeboat was full of water, but the sailors said it would float if only we could get it away from the *Lusitania* which was now not far from sinking. My Father threw off his overcoat, and worked like a slave trying to help loose the falls from the boat. This, however, was impossible. B. Deck was then level with the water, and I suggested to my Father we should climb up and get into another lifeboat. He, however, looked up, saw the *Lusitania* was very near its end, and was likely to come over on us, and pin us beneath. He shouted to me to jump, which I did. We were both swimming together in the water, a few yards from the ship, when something separated us. That was the last I saw of him. . . . After about an hour I was helped on to a collapsible boat which was upside down. It was at this time that we saw smoke coming towards us on the horizon out to sea, but as soon as the funnel was just in sight, it went away again from us. This must have been one of the boats that the German submarine stopped from coming to our rescue.

Later, another collapsible boat, full of water but right side up and with oars, came and picked us off our upturned boat. We rowed several miles in this sinking condition to [a] fishing boat.

ZEPPELIN RAID ON LONDON, Summer 1915

Freiharr Treusch von Buttlar Brandenfels

We were flying at a height of 15,000 feet. Suddenly the steersman called out to me: 'Searchlights on our starboard bow!' Then the whole car became alive, and with our binoculars to our eyes we leant out of the control car down to our waists.

What a magnificent sight! How wonderful to see the

beams of the searchlights exploring the heavens inch by inch, intersecting one another, then collecting into groups of three, four and five from different directions, and cutting each other again, and at last, at the point where they intersected, possibly finding a Zeppelin hanging like a huge incandescent cigar in the sky!

In a moment red lights were scattered through the blackness. They were the shrapnel-bursts.

Soon corresponding red lights appeared below on the ground. They were our own bombs.

There could not be the slightest doubt that our ship, too, was now quite close to the English coast.

Suddenly I staggered and was enveloped in blackness. In the heat of the fight I had lost my liquid-air pipe. It had dropped off the mouthpiece. It grew darker and darker. I felt I was going to be sick. I groped madly about the floor and seized hold of legs, cables, machine-gun belts. At last, just as I felt I should faint from the leaden weight on my head, I found the pipe!

It was marvellous. The moment I was able to breathe in the liquid air again I felt I could have knocked down whole barricades of brick walls, or lifted our tender with my little finger, or juggled with the machine-gun as though it were a billiard-cue, so elemental and powerful is the sudden fresh breath of life that is breathed into one!

'Climb to 18,000 feet!'

Minus twenty-one degrees, thirty degrees, thirty-five degrees Centigrade! Splendid! We met with no inversion. On the contrary, the temperature decreased appreciably the higher we rose.

A quarter of an hour later we had made the coast. We could see the lights of towns and villages, and of railways with their red and green signals, quite plainly. Suddenly everything below went black again. The district was certainly very skilful at putting out or concealing lights. It knew all about airship raids!

Ahead of us, I should say about ten miles away, one of our ships was attacking, and it immediately occurred to me that I ought to keep a more southerly course. So I changed my direction, intending, as soon as I had the attacking ship on my starboard beam, to course about and, flying north-east, to attack the same objective.

Everything depended on our reaching our objective unobserved. We were lucky. It was not long before we located the brightly illumined ship four points abaft the starboard beam, and I gave the order to steer north-east with rudder hard aport. The attack could begin.

The trap-doors for the bombs, which were in the catwalk, could be opened by the *Wachoffizier* by simply pressing a button. We were on the western edge of our objective. I gave the order for action!

Schiller pressed the first button and the first ten-pounder bomb whistled down to the depths. In spite of the buzz of the engines we could hear it whizzing through the air. The whole thing happened in a flash; the next bomb followed, then the third and fourth.

The bombs were plainly visible. A tiny blob of light appeared 18,000 feet below us, a few seconds later we heard the dull thud above the hum of the engines.

There could be no doubt that we were well over our objective, so the heavier fellows, the one-hundredweight and two-hundredweight bombs, were also dropped. They were released at regular intervals and crashed down below with a loud whine, followed quite rhythmically by a heavy thud as they reached the ground. The last three bombs were released simultaneously, and a heavy roll of thunder resounded below.

The crew knew what to do. Out with the ammunition!

It was so light that my eyes began to smart. Immediately after the first burst the searchlights had found us. One, two, three, four! We were flying through a cloud of glaring light. I could read the smallest print on the map before me.

How magnificent the huge, dazzlingly bright form of the ship must have looked 18,000 feet up in the sky, as she steered her way across the heavens!

The shrapnel salvoes drew nearer and nearer. At first they burst 3,000 feet below us. Oh, so the man in front of us had been flying at 15,000 feet!

But they corrected their range damnably quickly. Now they were getting very close indeed. We could hear the shells bursting all round and the whine of the splinters as they hurtled through space – high-explosive shells.

Should we climb higher, exhaust our last reserve strength, and, for the sake of 300 feet, risk being brought down by a hit, in which case all would be lost?

Suddenly on our port bow we saw a brilliant light, but no searchlight beam. It was deep and broad, a regular bank of light. The searchlight was penetrating a cloud.

'All engines full throttle.' We were saved! Up we climbed into the cloud. The next salvo would certainly have hit the ship if we had not been able to hide.

A SOLDIER'S LIFE, EASTERN FRONT, September 1915

Karl Liebknecht

The way we are being used is careless and criminal. Please inform Hugo Haase [socialist member of the Reichstag] if necessary. The whole battalion has only one doctor, and what kind of! . . . For our company of 500 men there are two medical orderlies – and what kind of! . . . The food leaves much to be desired, only potatoes are in the fields plentifully, and very good ones. No tobacco – that hurts especially, because it is the only stimulant. In the rear area there are all sorts of things, for instance two cigars and two cigarettes per day. Aside from this the greatest hardship is the lack of lighting. After half past six it is dark. No candles, nothing. You hang around, cannot read or write and crawl into your 'bed', that is your straw and wrap yourself in the unheated stable or barn into your coat or a thin blanket, often dripping wet, freezing all night . . .

SHOOTING DOWN A ZEPPELIN, POTTERS BAR, LONDON, October 1915

Lt W. J. Tempest, RFC

I decided to dive at her . . . firing a burst straight into her as I came. I let her have another burst as I passed under her and then banked my machine over, sat under her tail and flying along underneath her pumped lead into her for all I was worth . . . As I was firing, I noticed her to begin to go red inside like an enormous Chinese lantern. She shot up about 200 feet, paused, and came roaring down straight on to me before I had time to get out of the way. I nose-dived for all I was worth, with the Zeppelin tearing after me . . . I put my machine into a spin and just managed to corkscrew out of the way as she shot past me, roaring like a furnace . . . then proceeded to fire off dozens of green Very lights in the exuberance of my feelings.

RETREAT FROM GALLIPOLI, 21 December 1915

H. W. Nevinson

The stores began to go first, slowly. Various ruses and accidents served to deceive the enemy, who even thought that the increased number of ships off the bay signified a strongly renewed attack about Christmas. To maintain this apprehension, parties of our men were taken off at night and returned by day, like a stage army. On the final day, an ironic order commanded that the immemorial custom of our men showing themselves on the skyline should be carefully maintained, and we all did our best to serve our country by walking everywhere round Suvla in the enemy's sight. Orders were further received that mule-carts were to be driven slowly up and down. The mules were singular fine animals; happily all were saved at Suvla, and nearly all at Anzac. Native Indians managed them as though mules were well-trained dogs, and served with great patience and fortitude, even under the severe trial of tempest and frost.

After the strain of carefully organized preparations, the excitement of the final hours was extreme, but no signs of anxiety were shown. Would the sea remain calm? Would the moon remain veiled in a thin cloud? Would the brigades keep time and place? Our own guns continued firing duly till the moment for withdrawal came. Our rifles kept up an intermittent fire, and sometimes came sudden outbursts from the Turks. An aeroplane whirred overhead, but was invisible. We could not be sure it was our own until we saw a green star blaze for a few seconds just below Saturn. On the earth a few fires still blazed where camps or dug-outs were once inhabited, but gradually they went out. Only far off the hospital tents along the curving shore showed lights, and there were only two of these. The sea glimmered white through a moonlit haze, and over its surface thin black lines kept moving. Could an enemy see, or could he possibly miss the significance of those thin black lines?

Mules neighed, chains rattled, steamers hooted low, and sailor men shouted into megaphones language strong enough to carry a hundred miles. Still the enemy showed no sign of life or hearing, though he lay almost visible in the moonlight across the familiar scene of bay and plain and hills to which British soldiers have given such unaccustomed names. So the critical hours went by slowly, and yet giving so little time for all to be done. At last the final bands of silent defenders began to come in from the nearest lines. Sappers began to come in, cutting all telephone wires and signals on their way. Some sappers came after arranging slow fuses to kindle our few abandoned stores of biscuits, bully beef, and bacon left in the bends of the shore. Silently the staffs began to go. The officers of the beach party, who had accomplished such excellent and sleepless work, collected. With a smile they heard the distant blast of Turks still labouring at the trenches – a peculiar instance of labour lost. Just before three a pinnace took me off to one of the battleships. At half-past three the last-ditchers put off. From our familiar northern point of Suvla Bay itself, I am told, the General commanding the Ninth Army Corps was himself the last to leave, motioning his chief of staff to go first. So the Suvla expedition came to an end after more than five months of existence. I do not discuss policy, but the leaving of the existence well became it.

THE SOMME, July 1916

Sergeant Major Ernest Shephard

The Battle of the Somme, which began on 1 July 1916, claimed 60,000 British casualties on the first day alone. By the battle's end in mid-November 1916, 420,000 British and 200,000 French lives had been lost. For all this, the Allies had gained only five miles of ground.

Diary: Saturday, 1 July
A lovely day, intensely hot. Lot of casualties in my trench. The enemy are enfilading us with heavy shell, dropping straight on us. A complete trench mortar battery of men killed by one shell, scores of dead and badly wounded in trench, now one p.m. Every move we make brings intense fire, as trenches so badly battered the enemy can see all our

movements. Lot of wounded in front we got in, several were hit again and killed in trench. We put as many wounded as possible in best spots in trench and I sent a lot down, but I had so many of my own men killed and wounded that after a time I could not do this. Sent urgent messages to Brigade asking for RAMC bearers to be sent to evacuate wounded, but none came, although Brigade said they had been dispatched. Meanwhile the enemy deliberately shelled the wounded between the trenches with shrapnel, thus killing, or wounding, again most of them. Our own Regtl stretcher bearers worked like niggers to take cases away. Counted all Dorsets at one p.m. Total 53 all ranks. At three p.m. the Manchesters went through the Russian Sap and made an attack, captured a portion of the Leipzig Redoubt. Brigade sent message to say we would be relieved by 15th HLI as soon as possible. Meanwhile we were to hold tight.

We needed to; literally we were blown from place to place. Men very badly shaken. As far as possible we cleared trenches of debris and dead. These we piled in heaps, enemy shells pitching on them made matters worse.

Wounded suffering agonies. I got them water from bottles of dead, a few managed to crawl away to the Aid Post in wood. At dusk we got more wounded in from the front. Eight p.m. we got shelled intensely, and continued at intervals. I had miraculous escapes. The HLI arrived at midnight. I handed care of wounded to them, and took remnants of B and C Coys, only 10 NCOs and men, back via Mounteagle and Rock St, through Wood Post and over same track (Dumbarton) through Blighty Wood, down the valley to Crucifix Corner. Arrived there at one a.m. on

Sunday 2 July

Had a halt there, then on as ordered to the Authuille defences in Kintyre St. Got to top of hills, met messenger, orders to go to Blackhorse dug-outs for night, arrived there absolutely dead beat at two a.m. No dug-outs available, place crammed with troops of another division, camped out in the open. Very cold, had some sleep for an hour. Terrible bombardment going on all the time. The 17th HLI and 11th Borders say their Bns nearly wiped out, also the Ulster Div. who attacked Thiepval on left.

A number of our men came in at four a.m., some had been mixed up with other units, others had to lie in shell holes unable to budge owing to machine-gun fire, some from various jobs detailed for before the attack, and a number from the enemy trenches on relief by 15th HLI. This party had been commanded by Capt. Lancaster. He got wounded but held on and our men did very good work there. They bombed and captured a large portion of the enemy second line, and completed the capture of enemy 1st and 2nd line up to the Hindenburg Fort on right and Leipzig Redoubt on left. Very strong position held them up. We lost a lot of men there, but we have satisfaction over them as they killed a large number of the enemy. The enemy troops against us were the Prussian Guards, whom we have fought against at Ypres and previously at La Bassée. A prisoner said they only came there two days ago, and had lost heavily. Our men say they fought very bravely, and were of splendid physique, all over 6 feet in height. Also, they say enemy trenches very substantial and wanting nothing. Good dug-outs fitted luxuriously with electric lights, boarded and even wallpapered, plenty of good food, cigars, wines, in fact everything required. Plenty of German helmets as souvenirs. Enemy trenches choked with their own dead. Three Companies of 15th HLI are holding enemy trenches now, with two companies of Manchesters. At six-thirty a.m. came orders we were to be at Kintyre Trench by seven-thirty a.m. On arrival there we had a roll call of the Bn. After all were in I mustered ninety all ranks, out of 201 who went into action. I lost 111 all ranks. Total casualties in Battalion reckoned as 490 NCOs and men, and 20 officers. I lost all my Platoon Sgts and three Platoon Officers.

A fine day. I reorganized my remnants, made new Platoon Sgts, etc., sent in my list of casualties and had a little sleep. Major Thwaytes now arrived and took over command of Bn. Needless to say, we are all bitterly cut up at practically losing our fine Battalion in getting to our own fire trenches. Had we lost so many in actual grip with the enemy we should have felt more satisfaction. This is a repetition of Hill 60, where we lost nearly the Battalion with hardly a fighting chance. That happened on 1st of month as well.

Of course the 8th Division caused it through not being able to capture the ridge with machine guns on our right. Really our Division ought never to have attacked until that ridge had been gained, but either the 97th and 96th Brigade Commanders did not inform our Divisional Commander of the situation (possibly the orderly was killed or wires destroyed) or else, if our General did know and yet decided that we should carry on, he is not fit for his job.

At two-thirty p.m. an intense bombardment of our artillery started on Beaumont Hamel. At four-thirty p.m. smoke bombs were used, so I presume our troops attacked. We could see quite plainly, but no troops. The enemy retaliated on us, and we had a hot time from 'Jack Johnsons'. Great aerial activity going on. Rumour at six p.m. that the cavalry are in action on left. Got rations up later and just going to settle down for a decent sleep at eight-thirty p.m. when we were sent for and told to be ready to move in one hour for trenches to relieve 17th HLI. All day we have been expecting to go right back out of it for the Division to reorganize. I sent a Sgt to take over our portion of trench. Our Bn is to hold our own original front line from Chequerbent St to Tyndrum St as support to 2nd Manchesters in enemy trench in front between the Leipzig and Hindenburg Forts. The 15th HLI are relieving Manchesters at three a.m. and are to make an attack to capture the forts. We act as supports to them with 19th Lancs and Manchesters in reserve. Stood by for orders which came at one-thirty a.m. on

Monday 3rd

We moved up via Campbell Av. and got blocked there by a company of Cheshires with 'wind up'. Hell's own bombardment going on by our artillery preparatory to the attack, and enemy retaliating heavily all round us. Got clear of Cheshires and cut across the New MG Trench. Here we found ½ of our men had got cut off by Cheshires and lost touch. Waited ½ hour trying to connect up, nothing doing so I sent on what we had and went back to find the others. I found nine of them and they said the remainder were sure of the way on, so I decided to get the nine up. Got to Oban Av. and up to the front trench expecting to find the others there. Most terrible fire from enemy on the trench from howitzer shells dropping dead in trench, also the enemy were using gas shells, which almost stifled us. Evidently by the intense shelling from enemy, they have news of our attack and shelling this trench to prevent troops getting up. Shells dropping all round us, hairbreadth escapes. L/Cpl Lillington and Jenkins killed by one shell. The trench almost level with ground. Finally got to Chowbent St, still no sign of our men so came to conclusion they had all been killed and buried by debris in trench. I turned into Chowbent, worked way to junction of Bury Av.-Hough St, and through Hough St to Oban Av., met no one so I put the men in a shelter for a rest, while the HLI passed up to relieve Manchesters. Now almost break of dawn. At four a.m. the remainder of lost party came up, so I decided to hold Hough St (instead of the first trench), and I put two groups on duty there. Later I found my OC Coy at the Aid Post and found that he had, on arrival with first party, decided not to hold fire trench owing to intense fire, and he had put his party on duty in Chequerbent St on the right of Hough St. Time now six a.m., devilish row going on ahead.

The attack started at six-thirty a.m. I went along the fire trench and put out another post in the new communicating trench across the salient from Chowbent to Iona St. From there I had fine view of the attack. Apparently the HLI are getting on alright, as they have not asked for our help yet. We are getting a lot of heavy shell and machine gun fire. I returned to Coy HQ at eleven a.m. to find the OC in a great stew over my absence. They thought I had been killed and reported me as 'Missing' to Bn HQ. Had breakfast. Enemy brought one of our aeroplanes down at noon. I have only one officer in the Company, i.e. the OC, Lt Webb. In afternoon had little sleep. Heavy shelling continues all day. At seven p.m. message to say we are being relieved by 1st Wilts tonight, so sent guides down and made all preparations. They arrived at nine-thirty p.m. and we got out fairly easily as enemy eased down a little at that time. The Wilts have a lot of raw reinforcements of officers and men. We led out via Oban Av. through Authuille, over Blackhorse Bridge and Road to Pioneer Road, Northumberland Av., skirted Martinsart and arrived Bouzincourt at midnight. Here we collected the Company, a few enemy shells dropped close by. We pushed on and got in by singing, quite exhausted, at one a.m. on [billets in Senlis].

A WALK AMONG THE DEAD, THE SOMME, July 1916

Robert Graves

The next two days we spent in bivouacs outside Mametz Wood. We were in fighting kit and felt cold at night, so I went into the wood to find German overcoats to use as blankets. It was full of dead Prussian Guards Reserve, big men, and dead Royal Welch and South Wales Borderers of the New Army battalions, little men. Not a single tree in the wood remained unbroken. I collected my overcoats, and came away as quickly as I could, climbing through the wreckage of green branches. Going and coming, by the only possible route, I passed by the bloated and stinking corpse of a German with his back propped against a tree. He had a green face, spectacles, close-shaven hair; black blood was dripping from the nose and beard. I came across two other unforgettable corpses: a man of the South Wales Borderers and one of the Lehr Regiment had succeeded in bayoneting each other simultaneously.

WOUNDED IN ACTION, THE SOMME, July 1916

Robert Graves

One piece of shell went through my left thigh, high up, near the groin; I must have been at the full stretch of my stride to escape emasculation. The wound over the eye was made by a little chip of marble, possibly from one of the Bazentin cemetery headstones. (Later, I had it cut out, but a smaller piece has since risen to the surface under my right eyebrow, where I keep it for a souvenir.) This, and a finger-wound which split the bone, probably came from another shell bursting in front of me. But a piece of shell had also gone in two inches below the point of my right shoulder-blade and came out through my chest two inches above the right nipple.

My memory of what happened then is vague. Apparently Dr Dunn came up through the barrage with a stretcher-party, dressed my wound, and got me down to the old German dressing-station at the north end of Mametz Wood. I remember being put on the stretcher, and winking at the stretcher-bearer sergeant who had just said: 'Old Gravy's got it, all right!' They laid my stretcher in a corner of the dressing-station, where I remained unconscious for more than twenty-four hours.

Late that night, Colonel Crawshay came back from High Wood and visited the dressing-station; he saw me lying in the corner, and they told him I was done for. The next morning, 21 July, clearing away the dead, they found me still breathing and put me on an ambulance for Heilly, the nearest field hospital. The pain of being jolted down the Happy Valley, with a shell hole at every three or four yards of the road, woke me up. I remember screaming. But back on the better roads I became unconscious again. That morning, Crawshay wrote the usual formal letters of condolence to the next-of-kin of the six or seven officers who had been killed. This was his letter to my mother:

Dear Mrs Graves,   22.7.16
  I very much regret to have to write and tell you your son has died of wounds. He was very gallant, and was doing so well and is a great loss.
  He was hit by a shell and very badly wounded, and died on the way down to the base I believe. He was not in bad pain, and our doctor managed to get across and attend to him at once.
  We have had a very hard time, and our casualties have been large. Believe me you have all our sympathy in your loss, and we have lost a very gallant soldier.
                                             Yours sincerely,
                                             G. Crawshay, Lt-Col.

Then he made out the official casualty list – a long one, because only eighty men were left in the battalion – and reported me 'died of wounds'. Heilly lay on the railway; close to the station stood the hospital tents with the red cross prominently painted on the roofs, to discourage air-bombing. Fine July weather made the tents insufferably hot. I was semi-conscious now, and aware of my lung-wound through a shortness of breath. It amused me to watch the little bubbles of blood, like scarlet soap-bubbles, which my breath made in escaping through the opening of the wound. The doctor came over to my bed. I felt sorry for him; he looked as though he had not slept for days.

I asked him: 'Can I have a drink?'

'Would you like some tea?'

I whispered: 'Not with condensed milk.'

He said, most apologetically: 'I'm afraid there's no fresh milk.'

Tears of disappointment pricked my eyes; I expected better of a hospital behind the lines.

'Will you have some water?'

'Not if it's boiled.'

'It is boiled. And I'm afraid I can't give you anything alcoholic in your present condition.'

'Some fruit then?'

'I have seen no fruit for days.'

Yet a few minutes later he returned with two rather unripe greengages. In whispers I promised him a whole orchard when I recovered.

The nights of the 22nd and 23rd were horrible. Early on the morning of the 24th, when the doctor came round the ward, I said: 'You must send me away from here. This heat will kill me.' It was beating on my head through the canvas.

'Stick it out. Your best chance is to lie here and not to be moved. You'd not reach the Base alive.'

'Let me risk the move. I'll be all right, you'll see.'

Half an hour later he returned. 'Well, you're having it your way. I've just got orders to evacuate every case in the hospital. Apparently the Guards have been in it up at Delville Wood, and they'll all be coming down tonight.' I did not fear that I would die, now – it was enough to be honourably wounded and bound for home.

A CAVALRY CHARGE, THE SOMME, July 1916

Frederick Palmer

Gunners rubbed their eyes at the vision as they saw the horsemen pass and infantry stood amazed to see them crossing trenches, Briton and Indian on their way up to the Ridge. How they passed the crest without being decimated by a curtain of fire would be a mystery if there were any mysteries in this war, where everything seems to be worked out like geometry or chemical formulae . . . There had been some Germans in hiding in the grass who were taken unawares by this rush of gallopers with lances. Every participant agreed to the complete astonishment of the enemy.

A TANK CHARGE, THE SOMME, 15 September 1916

Bert Chaney

The menacing rumble of a tank was heard for the first time in warfare when thirty-six British Mark ls were used in an attack on the Somme on 15 September 1916. The Mark 1 weighed 30 tons and was developed from the agricultural tractor of American engineer Benjamin Holt. Its top speed was 5mph.

We heard strange throbbing noises, and lumbering slowly towards us came three huge mechanical monsters such as we had never seen before. My first impression was that they looked ready to topple on their noses, but their tails and the two little wheels at the back held them down and kept them level. Big metal things they were, with two sets of caterpillar wheels that went right round the body. There was a bulge on each side with a door in the bulging part, and machine-guns on swivels poked out from either side. The engine, a petrol engine of massive proportions, occupied practically all the inside space. Mounted behind each door was a motor-cycle type of saddle seat and there was just about enough room left for the belts of ammunition and the drivers . . .

Instead of going on to the German lines the three tanks assigned to us straddled our front line, stopped and then opened up a murderous machine-gun fire, enfilading us left and right. There they sat, squat monstrous things, noses stuck up in the air, crushing the sides of our trench out of shape with their machine-guns swivelling around and firing like mad.

Everyone dived for cover, except the colonel. He jumped on top of the parapet, shouting at the top of his voice, 'Runner, runner, go tell those tanks to stop firing at once. At once, I say.' By now the enemy fire had risen to a crescendo but, giving no thought to his own personal safety as he saw the tanks firing on his own men, he ran forward and furiously rained blows with his cane on the side of one of the tanks in an endeavour to attract their attention.

Although, what with the sounds of the engines and the firing in such an enclosed space, no one in the tank could hear him, they finally realized they were on the wrong trench and moved on, frightening the Jerries out of their wits and making them scuttle like frightened rabbits.

THE RED BARON CLAIMS HIS THIRTY-SECOND VICTORY, 2 April 1917

Rittmeister Manfred Freiharr von Richthofen ('The Red Baron')

The legendary Baron von Richthofen was Germany's leading fighter pilot in the First World War, credited with the destruction of eighty Allied planes before his death in action in 1918. The nickname 'The Red Baron' derived from his affectation in having his Fokker aircraft painted brilliant red.

The second of April, 1917, was another hot day for my squadron. From our field we could hear the sounds of the bombardment, and it was certainly very heavy that day.

I was still in bed when the orderly rushed in crying: '*Herr Leutnant*, the English are here!' Still somewhat sleepy, I looked out of the window and there circling over the field were my dear 'friends'. I got out of bed, quickly put my things on and got ready. My red bird was all set to begin the morning's work. My mechanics knew that I would not let this favourable moment go by without taking advantage of it. Everything was ready. I quickly donned my flying suit and was off.

Even so, I was the last to start. My comrades got much closer to the enemy. Then, suddenly, one of the impudent fellows fell on me, attempting to force me down. I calmly let him come on, and then we began a merry dance. At one point my opponent flew on his back, then he did this, then that. It was a two-seater. I was superior to him, and he soon realized that he could not escape me. During a pause in the fighting I looked around and saw that we were alone. Therefore, whoever shot better, whoever had the greatest calm and the best position in the moment of danger, would win.

It did not take long. I squeezed under him and fired, but without causing serious damage. We were at least two kilometres from the Front and I thought he would land, but I miscalculated my opponent. When only a few metres above the ground, he suddenly levelled off and flew straight ahead, seeking to escape me. That was too bad for him. I attacked him again and went so low that I feared I would touch the houses in the village beneath me. The Englishman kept fighting back. Almost at the end I felt a hit on my machine. I must not let up now, he must fall. He crashed at full speed into a block of houses, and there was not much left. It was again a case of splendid daring. He defended himself right up to the end.

Very pleased with the performance of my red 'bicycle' in the morning's work, I turned back. My comrades were still in the air and were very surprised when, as we later sat down to breakfast, I told them of my number thirty-two. A very young lieutenant had shot down his first, and we were all happy.

A FIRING SQUAD AT DAWN, WESTERN FRONT, 1917

Brig.-Gen. F. P. Crozier

During the 1914–18 war 307 British soldiers were executed for offences against the Army Act, mainly desertion.

Now, in peace-time, I and the rest of us would have been very upset indeed at having to shoot a colleague, comrade, call him what you will, at dawn on the morrow. We would not, in ordinary circumstances, have slept. Now the men don't like it, but they have to put up with it. They face their ordeal magnificently. I supervise the preliminary arrangements myself. We put the prisoner in a comfortable warm place. A few yards away we drive in a post, in a back garden, such as exists with any villa residence. I send for a certain junior officer and show him all. 'You will be in charge of the firing-party,' I say; 'the men will be cold, nervous and excited, they may miss their mark. You are to have your revolver ready loaded and cocked; if the medical officer tells you life is not extinct you are to walk up to the victim, place the muzzle of the revolver to his heart and press the trigger. Do you understand?' 'Yes, sir,' comes the quick reply. 'Right,' I add, 'dine with me at my mess tonight.' I want to keep this young fellow engaged under my own supervision until late at night, so as to minimize the chance of his flying to the bottle for support. As for Crocker, he leaves this earth, in so far as knowing anything of his surroundings is concerned, by midnight, for I arrange that enough spirituous liquor is left beside him to sink a ship. In the morning, at dawn, the snow being on the ground, the battalion forms up on the public road. Inside the little garden on the other side of the wall, not ten yards from the centre of the line, the victim is carried to the stake. He is far too drunk to walk. He is out of view save from myself, as I stand on a mound near the wall. As he is produced I see he is practically lifeless and quite unconscious. He has already been bound with ropes. There are hooks on the post; we always do things thoroughly in the Rifles. He is hooked on like dead meat in a butcher's shop. His eyes are bandaged – not that it really matters, for he is already blind. The men of the firing-party pick up their rifles, one of which is unloaded, on a given sign. On another sign they come to the 'Present' and, on the lowering of a handkerchief by the officer, they fire – a volley rings out – a nervous ragged volley it is true, yet a volley. Before the fatal shots are fired I had called the battalion to attention. There is a pause, I wait. I see the medical officer examining the victim. He makes a sign, the subaltern strides forward, a single shot rings out. Life is now extinct. We march back to breakfast while the men of a certain company pay the last tribute at the graveside of an unfortunate comrade. This is war.

BLOWING UP A TRAIN ON THE HEJAZ RAILWAY, PALESTINE 1917

Colonel T.E. Lawrence (Lawrence of Arabia)

The British leader of an irregular Arab army fighting the Turks in the First World War, T.E. Lawrence spent much of 1917 sabotaging the Hejaz Railway, the main Turkish supply line in the Palestinian desert.

Through my powerful glasses we saw a hundred Turkish soldiers issue from Mudowwara Station and make straight across the sandy plain towards our place. They were coming very slowly, and no doubt unwillingly, for sorrow at losing their beloved midday sleep: but at their very worst marching and temper they could hardly take more than two hours before they reached us.

We begun to pack up, preparatory to moving off, having decided to leave the mine and its leads in place on chance that the Turks might not find them, and we be able to return and take advantage of all the careful work. We sent a messenger to our covering party on the south, that they should meet us farther up, near those scarred rocks which served as screen for our pasturing camels.

Just as he had gone, the watchman cried out that smoke in clouds was rising from Hallat Ammar. Zaal and I rushed uphill and saw by its shape and volume that indeed there must be a train waiting in that station. As we were trying to see it over the hill, suddenly it moved out in our direction. We yelled to the Arabs to get into position as quick as possible, and there came a wild scramble over sand and rock. Stokes and Lewis, being booted, could not win the race; but they came well up, their pains and dysentery forgotten.

The men with rifles posted themselves in a long line behind the spur running from the guns past the exploder to the mouth of the valley. From it they would fire directly into the derailed carriages at less than 150 yards, whereas the ranges for the Stokes and Lewis guns were about 300 yards. An Arab stood up on high behind the guns and shouted to us what the train was doing – a necessary precaution, for if it carried troops and detrained them behind our ridge we should have to face about like a flash and retire fighting up the valley for our lives. Fortunately it held on at all the speed the two locomotives could make on wood fuel.

It drew near where we had been reported, and opened random fire into the desert. I could hear the racket coming, as I sat on my hillock by the bridge to give the signal to Salem, who danced round the exploder on his knees, crying with excitement, and calling urgently on God to make him fruitful. The Turkish fire sounded heavy, and I wondered with how many men we were going to have affair, and if the mine would be advantage enough for our eighty fellows to equal them. It would have been better if the first electrical experiment had been simpler.

However, at that moment the engines, looking very big, rocked with screaming whistles into view around the bend. Behind them followed ten box-waggons, crowded with rifle-muzzles at the windows and doors; and in little sand-bag nests on the roofs Turks precariously held on, to shoot at us. I had not thought of two engines, and on the moment decided to fire the charge under the second, so that however little the mine's effect, the uninjured engine should not be able to uncouple and drag the carriages away.

Accordingly, when the front 'driver' of the second engine was on the bridge, I raised my hand to Salem. There followed a terrific roar, and the line vanished from sight behind a spouting column of black dust and smoke 100 feet high and wide. Out of the darkness came shattering crashes and long, loud metallic clangings of ripped steel, with many lumps of iron and plate; while one entire wheel of a locomotive whirled up suddenly black out of the cloud against the sky, and sailed musically over our heads to fall slowly and heavily into the desert behind. Except for the flight of these, there succeeded a deathly silence, with no cry of men or rifle-shot, as the now grey mist of the explosion drifted from the line towards us, and over our ridge until it was lost in the hills.

In the lull, I ran southward to join the sergeants. Salem

picked up his rifle and charged out into the murk. Before I had climbed to the guns the hollow was alive with shots, and with the brown figures of the Beduin leaping forward to grips with the enemy. I looked round to see what was happening so quickly, and saw the train stationary and dismembered along the track, with its waggon sides jumping under the bullets which riddled them, while Turks were falling out from the far doors to gain the shelter of the railway embankment.

As I watched, our machine-guns chattered out over my head, and the long rows of Turks on the carriage roofs rolled over, and were swept off the top like bales of cotton before the furious shower of bullets which stormed along the roofs and splashed clouds of yellow chips from the planking. The dominant position of the guns had been an advantage to us so far.

When I reached Stokes and Lewis the engagement had taken another turn. The remaining Turks had got behind the bank, here about eleven feet high, and from cover of the wheels were firing point-blank at the Beduin twenty yards away across the sand-filled dip. The enemy in the crescent of the curving line were secure from the machine-guns; but Stokes slipped in his first shell, and after a few seconds there came a crash as it burst beyond the train in the desert.

He touched the elevating screw, and his second shot fell just by the trucks in the deep hollow below the bridge where the Turks were taking refuge. It made a shambles of the place. The survivors of the group broke out in a panic across the desert, throwing away their rifles and equipment as they ran. This was the opportunity of the Lewis gunners. The sergeant grimly traversed with drum after drum, till the open sand was littered with bodies. Mushagraf, the Sherari boy behind the second gun, saw the battle over, threw aside his weapon with a yell, and dashed down at speed with his rifle to join the others who were beginning, like wild beasts, to tear open the carriages and fall to plunder. It had taken nearly ten minutes.

I looked up-line through my glasses and saw the Mudow-wara patrol breaking back uncertainly towards the railway to meet the train-fugitives running their fastest northward. I looked south, to see our thirty men cantering their camels neck and neck in our direction to share the spoils. The Turks there, seeing them go, began to move after them with infinite precaution, firing volleys. Evidently we had a half-hour respite, and then a double threat against us.

I ran down to the ruins to see what the mine had done. The bridge was gone; and into its gap was fallen the front waggon, which had been filled with sick. The smash had killed all but three or four and had rolled dead and dying into a bleeding heap against the splintered end. One of those yet alive deliriously cried out the word typhus. So I wedged shut the door, and left them there, alone.

Succeeding waggons were derailed and smashed: some had frames irreparably buckled. The second engine was a blanched pile of smoking iron. Its driving wheels had been blown upward, taking away the side of the fire-box. Cab and tender were twisted into strips, among the piled stones of the bridge abutment. It would never run again. The front engine had got off better: though heavily derailed and lying half-over, with the cab burst, yet its steam was at pressure, and driving-gear intact.

Our greatest object was to destroy locomotives, and I had kept in my arms a box of gun-cotton with fuse and detonator ready fixed, to make sure such a case. I now put them in position on the outside cylinder. On the boiler would have been better, but the sizzling steam made me fear a general explosion which would sweep across my men (swarming like ants over the booty) with a blast of jagged fragments. Yet they would not finish their looting before the Turks came. So I lit the fuse, and in the half-minute of its burning drove the plunderers a little back, with difficulty. Then the charge burst, blowing the cylinder to smithers, and the axle too. At the moment I was distressed with uncertainty whether the damage were enough; but the Turks, later, found the engine beyond use and broke it up.

The valley was a weird sight. The Arabs, gone raving mad, were rushing about at top speed bareheaded and half-naked, screaming, shooting into the air, clawing one another nail and fist, while they burst open trucks and staggered back and forward with immense bales, which they ripped by the rail-side, and tossed through, smashing what they did not want. The train had been packed with refugees and sick men, volunteers for boat-service on the Euphrates, and families of Turkish officers returning to Damascus.

There were scores of carpets spread about; dozens of mattresses and flowered quilts, blankets in heaps, clothes for men and women in full variety; clocks, cooking-pots, food, ornaments and weapons. To one side stood thirty or forty hysterical women, unveiled, tearing their clothes and hair; shrieking themselves distracted. The Arabs without regard to them went on wrecking the household goods; looting their absolute fill. Camels had become common property. Each man frantically loaded the nearest with what it could carry and shooed it westward into the void, while he turned to his next fancy.

Seeing me tolerably unemployed, the women rushed, and caught at me with howls for mercy. I assured them that all was going well: but they would not get away till some husbands delivered me. These knocked their wives off and seized my feet in a very agony of terror of instant death. A Turk so broken down was a nasty spectacle: I kicked them off as well as I could with bare feet, and finally broke free.

Next a group of Austrians, officers and non-commissioned officers, appealed to me quietly in Turkish for quarter. I replied with my halting German whereupon one, in English, begged for a doctor for his wounds. We had none: not that it mattered, for he was mortally hurt and dying. I told them the Turks would return in an hour and care for them. But he was dead before that, as were most of the others (instructors in the new Skoda mountain howitzers supplied to Turkey for the Hejaz war), because some dispute broke out between them and my own bodyguard, and one of them fired a pistol shot at young Rahail. My infuriated men cut them down, all but two or three, before I could return to interfere.

THE RUSSIAN REVOLUTION, 24 October 1917*

Leon Trotsky

In February 1917 strikes and demonstrations had brought down Tsar Nicholas II's regime, which was replaced by a republican provisional government led by the moderate reformer, Alexander Kerensky. The new body proved unwilling to extract Russia from the war and was quickly overtaken by the revolutionary left. On the evening of 24 October the Marxist Bolshevik party of V. I. Lenin seized power in Petrograd. Leon Trotsky was Lenin's chief comrade-in-arms and the main overseer of the insurrection, which was organized via the Bolshevik-dominated Military Revolutionary Committee. The Committee's headquarters were the Smolny building, where Trotsky spent the fateful night.

On the night of the 24th the members of the Revolutionary Committee went out into the various districts, and I was left alone. Later on Kamenev came in. He was opposed to the uprising, but he had come to spend that deciding night with me, and together we stayed in the tiny corner room on the third floor, so like the captain's bridge on that deciding night of the revolution.

There is a telephone booth in the large empty room adjoining us, and the bell rings incessantly about important things and trifles. Each ring heightens the alertness of the

* 6 November in Western Calendar.

silence. One can readily picture the deserted streets of Petrograd, dimly lit, and whipped by the autumn winds from the sea; the bourgeois and officials cowering in their beds, trying to guess what is going on in those dangerous and mysterious streets; the workers' quarters quiet with the tense sleep of a war-camp. Commissions and conferences of the government parties are exhausting themselves in impotence in the Tsar's palaces, where the living ghosts of democracy rub shoulders with the still hovering ghosts of the monarchy. Now and again the silks and gildings of the halls are plunged into darkness – the supplies of coal have run short. In the various districts detachments of workers, soldiers, and sailors are keeping watch. The young proletarians have rifles and machine-gun belts across their shoulders. Street pickets are warming themselves at fires in the streets. The life of the capital, thrusting its head from one epoch into another on this autumn night, is concentrated about a group of telephones.

Reports from all the districts, suburbs, and approaches to the capital are focused in the room on the third floor. It seems that everything has been foreseen; the leaders are in their places; the contacts are assured; nothing seems to have been forgotten.

Once more, let us go over it in our minds. This night decides. Only this evening in my report to the delegates of the second congress of the Soviets, I said with conviction: 'If you stand firm, there will be no civil war, our enemies will capitulate at once, and you will take the place that belongs to you by right. There can be no doubt about victory; it is as assured as the victory of any uprising can be. And yet these hours are still tense and full of alarm, for the coming night decides. The government while mobilizing cadets yesterday, gave orders to the cruiser *Aurora* to steam out of the Neva. They were the same Bolshevik sailors whom Skobelev, coming hat in hand, in August begged to protect the Winter Palace from Kornilov. The sailors referred to the Military-

Revolutionary Committee for instructions, and consequently the *Aurora* is standing tonight where she was yesterday. A telephone call from Pavlovsk informs me that the government is bringing up from there a detachment of artillery, a battalion of shock troops from Tsarskoye Syelo, and student officers from the Peterhof military school. Into the Winter Palace Kerensky has drawn military students, officers, and the women shock troops. I order the commissaries to place dependable military defences along the approaches to Petrograd and to send agitators to meet the detachments called out by the government. All our instructions and reports are sent by telephone and the government agents are in a position to intercept them. Can they still control our communications?

'If you fail to stop them with words, use arms. You will answer for this with your life.'

I repeat this sentence time and time again. But I do not believe in the force of my order. The revolution is still too trusting, too generous, optimistic and light-hearted. It prefers to threaten with arms rather than really use them. It still hopes that all questions can be solved by words, and so far it has been successful in this – hostile elements evaporate before its breath. Earlier in the day (the 24th) an order was issued to use arms and to stop at nothing at the first sign of pogroms. Our enemies don't even dare think of the streets; they have gone into hiding. The streets are ours; our commissaries are watching all the approaches to Petrograd. The officers' school and the gunners have not responded to the call of the government. Only a section of the Oraniembaum military students have succeeded in making their way through our defences, but I have been watching their movements by telephone. They end by sending envoys to the Smolny. The government has been seeking support in vain. The ground is slipping from under its feet.

The outer guard of the Smolny has been reinforced by a

new machine-gun detachment. The contact with all sections of the garrison is uninterrupted. The companies on duty are on watch in all the regiments. The commissaries are in their places. Delegations from each garrison unit are in the Smolny, at the disposal of the Military-Revolutionary Committee, to be used in case the contact with that unit should be broken off. Armed detachments from the districts march along the streets, ring the bells at the gates or open the gates without ringing, and take possession of one institution after another. Nearly everywhere these detachments are met by friends who have been waiting impatiently for them. At the railway terminals, specially appointed commissaries are watching the incoming and outgoing trains, and in particular the movement of troops. No disturbing news comes from there. All the more important points in the city are given over into our hands almost without resistance, without fighting, without casualties. The telephone alone informs us: 'We are here!'

All is well. It could not have gone better. Now I may leave the telephone. I sit down on the couch. The nervous tension lessens. A dull sensation of fatigue comes over me.

'Give me a cigarette,' I say to Kamenev. (In those years I still smoked, but only spasmodically.) I take one or two puffs, but suddenly with the words, 'Only this was lacking!' I faint. (I inherited from my mother a certain susceptibility to fainting spells when suffering from physical pain or illness. That was why some American physician described me as an epileptic.) As I come to, I see Kamenev's frightened face bending over me. 'Shall I get some medicine?' he asks.

'It would be much better,' I answer after a moment's reflection, 'if you got something to eat.' I try to remember when I last had food, but I can't. At all events it was not yesterday.

THE RUSSIAN REVOLUTION: STORMING THE WINTER PALACE, PETROGRAD, 25 October 1917

John Reed

The Winter Palace was the seat of the moderate provisional government led by Kerensky. The so-called 'storming' of the Palace like most of the early acts of the Russian Revolution was a peculiarly bloodless affair. John Reed, an American socialist journalist, was later immortalized in the film *Reds*.

. . . It was absolutely dark, and nothing moved but pickets of soldiers and Red Guards, grimly intent. In front of the Kazan Cathedral a three-inch field-gun lay in the middle of the street, slewed sideways from the recoil of its last shot over the roofs. Soldiers were standing in every doorway talking in loud tones and peering down towards the Police Bridge. I heard one voice saying: 'It is possible that we have done wrong . . .' At the corners patrols stopped all passers-by – and the composition of these patrols was interesting, for in command of the regular troops was invariably a Red Guard . . . The shooting had ceased.

Just as we came to the Morskaya somebody was shouting: 'The *yunkers* have sent word that they want us to go and get them out!' Voices began to give commands, and in the thick gloom we made out a dark mass moving forward, silent but for the shuffle of feet and the clinking of arms. We fell in with the first ranks.

Like a black river, filling all the street, without song or cheer we poured through the Red Arch, where the man just ahead of me said in a low voice: 'Look out, comrades! Don't trust them. They will fire, surely!' In the open we began to run, stooping low and bunching together, and jammed up suddenly behind the pedestal of the Alexander Column.

'How many of you did they kill?' I asked.

'I don't know. About ten . . .'

After a few minutes huddling there, some hundreds of men, the Army seemed reassured and without any orders suddenly began again to flow forward. By this time, in the light that streamed out of all the Winter Palace windows, I could see that the first 200 or 300 men were Red Guards, with only a few scattered soldiers. Over the barricade of fire-wood we clambered, and leaping down inside gave a triumphant shout as we stumbled on a heap of rifles thrown down by the *yunkers* who had stood there. On both sides of the main gateway the doors stood wide open, light streamed out, and from the huge pile came not the slightest sound.

Carried along by the eager wave of men we were swept into the right-hand entrance, opening into a great bare vaulted room, the cellar of the East wing, from which issued a maze of corridors and staircases. A number of huge packing cases stood about, and upon these the Red Guards and soldiers fell furiously, battering them open with the butts of their rifles, and pulling out carpets, curtains, linen, porcelain, plates, glass-ware . . . One man went strutting around with a bronze clock perched on his shoulder; another found a plume of ostrich feathers, which he stuck in his hat. The looting was just beginning when somebody cried, 'Comrades! Don't take anything. This is the property of the People!' Immediately twenty voices were crying, 'Stop! Put everything back! Don't take anything! Property of the People!' Many hands dragged the spoilers down. Damask and tapestry were snatched from the arms of those who had them; two men took away the bronze clock. Roughly and hastily the things were crammed back in their cases, and self-appointed sentinels stood guard. It was all utterly spontaneous. Through corridors and up staircases the cry could be heard growing fainter and fainter in the distance, 'Revolutionary discipline! Property of the People . . .'

We crossed back over to the left entrance, in the West

wing. There order was also being established. 'Clear the Palace!' bawled a Red Guard, sticking his head through an inner door. 'Come, comrades, let's show that we're not thieves and bandits. Everybody out of the Palace except the Commissars, until we get sentries posted.'

Two Red Guards, a soldier and an officer, stood with revolvers in their hands. Another soldier sat at a table behind them, with pen and paper. Shouts of 'All out! All out!' were heard far and near within, and the Army began to pour through the door, jostling, expostulating, arguing. As each man appeared he was seized by the self-appointed committee, who went through his pockets and looked under his coat. Everything that was plainly not his property was taken away, the man at the table noted it on his paper, and it was carried into a little room. The most amazing assortment of objects were thus confiscated; statuettes, bottles of ink, bed-spreads worked with the Imperial monogram, candles, a small oil-painting, desk blotters, gold-handled swords, cakes of soap, clothes of every description, blankets. One Red Guard carried three rifles, two of which he had taken away from *yunkers*; another had four portfolios bulging with written documents. The culprits either sullenly surrendered or pleaded like children. All talking at once the committee explained that stealing was not worthy of the people's champions; often those who had been caught turned around and began to help go through the rest of the comrades.

Yunkers came out in bunches of three or four. The committee seized upon them with an excess of zeal, accompanying the search with remarks like, 'Ah, Provocators! Kornilovists! Counter-revolutionists! Murderers of the People!' But there was no violence done, although the *yunkers* were terrified. They too had their pockets full of small plunder. It was carefully noted down by the scribe, and piled in the little room . . . The *yunkers* were disarmed. 'Now, will you take up arms against the People any more?' demanded clamouring voices.

'No,' answered the *yunkers*, one by one. Whereupon they were allowed to go free.

We came out into the cold, nervous night, murmurous with obscure armies on the move, electric with patrols. From across the river, where loomed the darker mass of Peter-Paul came a hoarse shout . . . Underfoot the sidewalk was littered with broken stucco, from the cornice of the Palace where two shells from the battleship *Aurora* had struck; that was the only damage done by the bombardment.

It was now after three in the morning. On the Nevsky all the street-lights were again shining, the cannon gone, and the only signs of war were Red Guards and soldiers squatting around fires. The city was quiet – probably never so quiet in its history; on that night not a single hold-up occurred, not a single robbery.

TANKS AT CAMBRAI, WESTERN FRONT, November 1917

Major W. H. L. Watson

Although introduced at the Somme in 1916, the tank's first main success came at Cambrai.

Until the 17th, the enemy apparently suspected nothing at all; but on the night of the 17th-18th he raided and captured some prisoners, who fortunately knew little. He gathered from them that we were ourselves preparing a substantial raid, and he brought into the line additional companies of machine-gunners and a few extra field-guns.

The 19th came with its almost unbearable suspense. We did not know what the Germans had discovered from their prisoners. We could not believe that the attack could be really a surprise. Perhaps the enemy, unknown to us, had concentrated sufficient guns to blow us to pieces. We looked up for the German aeroplanes, which surely would fly low over the wood and discover its contents. Incredibly, nothing happened. The morning passed and the afternoon – a day was never so long – and at last it was dusk.

At eight forty-five p.m. my tanks began to move cautiously out of the wood and formed into a column. At nine-thirty p.m., with engines barely turning over, they glided imperceptibly and almost without noise towards the trenches. Standing in front of my own tanks, I could not hear them at 200 yards.

By midnight we had reached our rendezvous behind the reserve trenches and below the crest of the slope. There we waited for an hour. The Colonel arrived, and took me with him to pay a final visit to the headquarters of the battalions with which we were operating. The trenches were packed with Highlanders, and it was with difficulty that we made our way through them.

Cooper led the tanks for the last half of the journey. They stopped at the support trenches, for they were early, and the men were given hot breakfast. The enemy began some shelling on the left, but no damage was done.

At six-ten a.m. the tanks were in their allotted positions, clearly marked out by tapes which Jumbo had laid earlier in the night . . .

I was standing on the parados of a trench. The movement at my feet had ceased. The Highlanders were ready with fixed bayonets. Not a gun was firing, but there was a curious murmur in the air. To right of me and to left of me in the dim light were tanks – tanks lined up in front of the wire, tanks swinging into position, and one or two belated tanks climbing over the trenches.

I hurried back to the Colonel of the 6th Black Watch, and I was with him in his dug-out at six-twenty a.m. when the guns began. I climbed on to the parapet and looked.

In front of the wire, tanks in a ragged line were surging

forward inexorably over the short down grass. Above and around them hung the blue-grey smoke of their exhausts. Each tank was followed by a bunch of Highlanders, some running forward from cover to cover, but most of them tramping steadily behind their tanks. They disappeared into the valley. To the right the tanks were moving over the crest of the shoulder of the hill. To the left there were no tanks in sight. They were already in among the enemy.

Beyond the enemy trenches the slopes, from which the German gunners might have observed the advancing tanks, were already enveloped in thick, white smoke. The smoke shells burst with a sheet of vivid red flame, pouring out blinding, suffocating clouds. It was as if flaring bonfires were burning behind a bank of white fog. Over all, innumerable aeroplanes were flying steadily to and fro.

The enemy made little reply. A solitary field-gun was endeavouring pathetically to put down a barrage. A shell would burst every few minutes on the same bay of the same trench. There were no other enemy shells that we could see. A machine-gun or two were still trained on our trenches, and an occasional vicious burst would bring the venturesome spectator scrambling down into the trench.

Odd bunches of men were making their way across what had been No-Man's Land. A few, ridiculously few, wounded were coming back. Germans, in twos and threes, elderly men for the most part, were wandering confusedly towards us without escort, putting up their hands in tragic and amazed resignation, whenever they saw a Highlander.

The news was magnificent. Our confidence had been justified. Everywhere we had overrun the first system and were pressing on.

A column of tanks, equipped with a strange apparatus, passed across our front to clear a lane through the wire for the cavalry.

On our left another column of tanks had already disappeared into the valley on their way to Flesquieres. It was

Ward's company, but Ward was not with them. A chance bullet had killed him instantly at the head of his tanks. When we heard of his death later, the joy of victory died away . . .

THE RUSSIAN REVOLUTION: TSAR NICHOLAS II AND THE RUSSIAN ROYAL FAMILY ARE SHOT AT EKATERINBURG, 16 July 1918

Pavel Medvedev

In the evening of 16 July, between seven and eight p.m., when the time for my duty had just begun, Commandant Yurovsky [the head of the guard] ordered me to take all the Nagan revolvers from the guards and to bring them to him. I took twelve revolvers from the sentries as well as from some other of the guards, and brought them to the commandant's office. Yurovsky said to me, 'We must shoot *them all* tonight, so notify the guards not to be alarmed if they hear shots.' I understood, therefore, that Yurovsky had it in his mind to shoot the whole of the Tsar's family, as well as the doctor and the servants who lived with them, but I did not ask him where or by whom the decision had been made. I must tell you that in accordance with Yurovsky's order the boy who assisted the cook was transferred in the morning to the guardroom (in the Popov house). The lower floor of Ipatiev's house was occupied by the Letts from the Letts Commune, who had taken up their quarters there after Yurovsky was made commandant. They were ten in number. At about ten o'clock in the evening, in accordance with Yurovsky's order, I informed the guards not to be alarmed if they should hear firing. About midnight Yurovsky woke up the Tsar's family. I do not know if he told them the reason they had been awakened and where they were to be taken, but I positively affirm that it was Yurovsky who entered the rooms occupied by the Tsar's family. Yurovsky had not ordered me or Dobrynin to awaken the family. In about an hour the whole of the family, the doctor, the maid and the waiters got up, washed and dressed themselves. Just before Yurovsky went to awaken the family, two members of the Extraordinary Commission [of the Ekaterinburg Soviet] arrived at Ipatiev's house. Shortly after one o'clock a.m., the Tsar, the Tsaritsa, their four daughters, the maid, the doctor, the cook and the waiters left their rooms. The Tsar carried the heir in his arms. The Emperor and the heir were dressed in *gimnasterkas* [soldiers' shirts] and wore caps. The Empress and her daughters were dressed but their heads were uncovered. The Emperor, carrying the heir, preceded them. The Empress, her daughters and the others followed him. Yurovsky, his assistant and the two above-mentioned members of the Extraordinary Commission accompanied them. I was also present. During my presence none of the Tsar's family asked any questions. They did not weep or cry. Having descended the stairs to the first floor, we went out into the court, and from there by the second door (counting from the gate) we entered the ground floor of the house. When the room (which adjoins the store room with a sealed door) was reached, Yurovsky ordered chairs to be brought, and his assistant brought three chairs. One chair was given to the Emperor, one to the Empress, and the third to the heir. The Empress sat by the wall by the window, near the black pillar of the arch. Behind her stood three of her daughters (I knew their faces very well, because I had seen them every day when they walked in the garden, but I didn't know their names). The heir and the Emperor sat side by side almost in the middle of the room. Doctor Botkin stood behind the heir. The maid, a very tall woman, stood at the left of the door leading to the store room; by her side stood one of the Tsar's daughters (the fourth). Two servants stood against the wall on the left from the entrance of the room.

The maid carried a pillow. The Tsar's daughters also brought small pillows with them. One pillow was put on the

Empress's chair; another on the heir's chair. It seemed as if all of them guessed their fate, but not one of them uttered a single sound. At this moment eleven men entered the room: Yurovsky, his assistant, two members of the Extraordinary Commission, and seven Letts. Yurovsky ordered me to leave, saying, 'Go on to the street, see if there is anybody there, and wait to see whether the shots have been heard.' I went out to the court, which was enclosed by a fence, but before I got to the street I heard the firing. I returned to the house immediately (only two or three minutes having elapsed) and upon entering the room where the execution had taken place, I saw that all the members of the Tsar's family were lying on the floor with many wounds in their bodies. The blood was running in streams. The doctor, the maid and two waiters had also been shot. When I entered the heir was still alive and moaned a little. Yurovsky went up and fired two or three more times at him. Then the heir was still.

A BLACK DAY FOR THE GERMAN ARMY, 8 August 1918

General Ludendorff

August 8th was the black day of the German Army in the history of this War. This was the worst experience that I had to go through, except for the events that, from September 15th onwards, took place on the Bulgarian Front and sealed the fate of the Quadruple Alliance.

Early on 8 August, in a dense fog, rendered still thicker by artificial means, the English, mainly with Australian and Canadian divisions, and the French attacked between Albert and Moreuil with strong squadrons of tanks, but otherwise in no great superiority. Between the Somme and the Luce they penetrated deep into our positions. The divisions in line at that point allowed themselves to be completely overwhelmed. Divisional staffs were surprised in their head-quarters by enemy tanks. The breach very soon extended across the Luce stream; the troops that were still gallantly resisting at Moreuil were rolled up. To the northward the Somme imposed a halt. Our troops in action north of the river had successfully parried a similar assault. The exhausted divisions that had been relieved a few days earlier and were now resting in the region south-west of Peronne, were immediately warned and set in motion by the commander of the Second Army. At the same time he brought forward into the breach all other available troops. The Rupprecht Army Group dispatched reserves thither by train. The Eighteenth Army threw its own reserves directly into the battle from the south-east, and pushed other forces forward in the region north-west of Roye. On an order from me, the Ninth Army too, although itself in danger, had to contribute. Days, of course, elapsed before the troops from more distant areas could reach the spot. For their conveyance the most extensive use was made of motor lorries.

By the early hours of the forenoon of 8 August I had already gained a complete impression of the situation. It was a very gloomy one. I immediately dispatched a General Staff officer to the battlefield, in order to obtain an idea of the condition of the troops.

The losses of the Second Army had been very heavy. Heavy demands had also been made on its reserves to fill up the gaps. The infantry of some divisions had had to go into action straight off the lorries, whilst their artillery had been sent to some other part of the line. Units were badly mixed up. It could be foreseen that a number of additional divisions would become necessary in order to strengthen the Second Army, even if the enemy continued the offensive, and that was not certain. Besides, our losses in prisoners had been so heavy that GHQ was again faced with the necessity of breaking up more divisions to form reserves. Our reserves dwindled. The losses of the enemy, on the other hand, had been extraordinarily small. The balance of numbers had moved heavily against us; it was bound to become increasingly unfavourable as more American troops came in. There was no hope of materially improving our position by a counter-attack. Our only course, therefore, was to hold on.

We had to resign ourselves now to the prospect of a continuation of the enemy's offensive. Their success had been too easily gained. Their wireless was jubilant, and announced – and with truth – that the morale of the German Army was no longer what it had been. The enemy had also captured many documents of inestimable value to them. The Entente must have gained a clear idea of our difficulty in finding reserves, a further reason why they should pursue the offensive without respite.

The report of the Staff Officer I had sent to the battlefield as to the condition of those divisions which had met the first shock of the attack on the 8th, perturbed me deeply. I summoned divisional commanders and officers from the line to Avesnes to discuss events with them in detail. I was told of deeds of glorious valour, but also of behaviour which, I openly confess, I should not have thought possible in the German Army; whole bodies of our men had surrendered to single troopers, or isolated squadrons. Retiring troops, meeting a fresh division going bravely into action, had shouted out things like 'Blackleg,' and 'You're prolonging the War,' expressions that were to be heard again later. The officers in many places had lost their influence and allowed themselves to be swept along with the rest. At a meeting of Prince Max's War Cabinet in October, Secretary Scheidemann called my attention to a Divisional Report on the occurrences of August 8th, which contained similar unhappy stories. I was not acquainted with this report, but was able to verify it from my own knowledge. A battalion commander from the front, who came out with a draft from home shortly before August 8th, attributed this to the spirit of insubordination and the atmosphere which the men brought back with them from home. Everything I had feared, and of which I had so often given warning, had here, in one place, become a reality. Our war machine was no longer efficient. Our fighting power had suffered, even though the great majority of divisions still fought heroically.

The 8th of August put the decline of that fighting power beyond all doubt, and in such a situation as regards reserves, I had no hope of finding a strategic expedient whereby to turn the situation to our advantage. On the contrary, I became convinced that we were now without that safe foundation for the plans of GHQ, on which I had hitherto been able to build, at least so far as this is possible in war. Leadership now assumed, as I then stated, the character of an irresponsible game of chance, a thing I have always considered fatal. The fate of the German people was, for me, too high a stake.

Part III

Jazz, Slump and Fascism
1919–38

THE SIGNING OF THE TREATY OF VERSAILLES, 28 June 1919

Harold Nicolson

After the capitulation of Germany on 11 November 1918 she was required by the victorious Allies to sign a punitive peace treaty. The signing took place in the Hall of Mirrors at Versailles Palace – the Hall which had witnessed the humiliation of France and the proclamation of the German Empire in 1871.

La journée de Versailles. Lunch early and leave the Majestic in a car with Headlam Morley. He is a historian, yet he dislikes historical occasions. Apart from that he is a sensitive person and does not rejoice in seeing great nations humbled. I, having none of such acquirements or decencies, am just excited.

There is no crowd at all until we reach Ville d'Avray. But there are poilus at every crossroad waving red flags and stopping all other traffic. When we reach Versailles the crowd thickens. The avenue up to the Château is lined

with cavalry in steel-blue helmets. The pennants of their
lances flutter red and white in the sun. In the Cour
d'Honneur, from which the captured German cannon have
tactfully been removed, are further troops. There are Generals, Pétain, Gouraud, Mangin. There are St Cyriens. Very
military and orderly. Headlam Morley and I creep out of
our car hurriedly. Feeling civilian and grubby. And wholly
unimportant. We hurry through the door.

Magnificent upon the staircase stand the Gardes Républicains – two caryatides on every step – their sabres at the
salute. This is a great ordeal, but there are other people
climbing the stairs with us. Headlam and I have an eye-
meet. His thin cigaretted fingers make a gesture of dismissal.
He is not a militarist.

We enter the two anterooms, our feet softening on to the
thickest of savonnerie carpets. They have ransacked the
Garde Meubles for their finest pieces. Never, since the
Grand Siècle, has Versailles been more ostentatious or more
embossed . . .

We enter the Galerie des Glaces. It is divided into three
sections. At the far end are the Press already thickly installed.
In the middle there is a horseshoe table for the plenipotentiaries. In front of that, like a guillotine, is the table for the
signatures. It is supposed to be raised on a dais but, if so, the
dais can be but a few inches high. In the nearer distance are
rows and rows of tabourets for the distinguished guests, the
deputies, the senators and the members of the delegations.
There must be seats for over 1,000 persons. This robs the
ceremony of all privilege and therefore of all dignity. It is like
the Aeolian Hall.

Clemenceau is already seated under the heavy ceiling as
we arrive. 'Le roi', runs the scroll above him, 'gouverne par
lui-même.' He looks small and yellow. A crunched homun-
culus.

Conversation clatters out among the mixed groups around
us. It is, as always on such occasions, like water running into

a tin bath. I have never been able to get other people to
recognize that similarity. There was a tin bath in my house
at Wellington: one turned it on when one had finished and
ran upstairs shouting 'Baath ready' to one's successor: 'Right
ho!' he would answer: and then would come the sound of
water pouring into the tin bath below, while he hurried into
his dressing-gown. It is exactly the sound of people talking in
undertones in a closed room. But it is not an analogy which I
can get others to accept.

People step over the Aubusson benches and escabeaux to
talk to friends. Meanwhile the delegates arrive in little
bunches and push up the central aisle slowly. [Woodrow]
Wilson and Lloyd George are among the last. They take
their seats at the central table. The table is at last full.
Clemenceau glances to right and left. People sit down upon
their escabeaux but continue chattering. Clemenceau makes
a sign to the ushers. They say 'Ssh! Ssh! Ssh!' People cease
chattering and there is only the sound of occasional coughing
and the dry rustle of programmes. The officials of the
Protocol of the Foreign Office move up the aisle and say,
'Ssh! Ssh!' again. There is then an absolute hush, followed by
a sharp military order. The Gardes Républicains at the
doorway flash their swords into their scabbards with a loud
click. 'Faîtes entrer les Allemands,' says Clemenceau in the
ensuing silence. His voice is distant but harshly penetrating.
A hush follows.

Through the door at the end appear two huissiers with
silver chains. They march in single file. After them come four
officers of France, Great Britain, America and Italy. And
then, isolated and pitiable, come the two German delegates.
Dr Müller, Dr Bell. The silence is terrifying. Their feet upon
a strip of parquet between the savonnerie carpets echo
hollow and duplicate. They keep their eyes fixed away from
those 2,000 staring eyes, fixed upon the ceiling. They are
deathly pale. They do not appear as representatives of a
brutal militarism. The one is thin and pink-eyelidded: the

second fiddle in a Brunswick orchestra. The other is moon-faced and suffering: a privat-dozent. It is all most painful.

They are conducted to their chairs. Clemenceau at once breaks the silence. 'Messieurs,' he rasps, 'la séance est ouverte.' He adds a few ill-chosen words. 'We are here to sign a Treaty of Peace.' The Germans leap up anxiously when he has finished, since they know that they are the first to sign. William Martin, as if a theatre manager, motions them petulantly to sit down again. Mantoux translates Clemenceau's words into English. Then St Quentin advances towards the Germans and with the utmost dignity leads them to the little table on which the Treaty is expanded. There is general tension. They sign. There is a general relaxation. Conversation hums again in an under-tone. The delegates stand up one by one and pass onwards to the queue which waits by the signature table. Meanwhile people buzz round the main table getting autographs. The single file of plenipotentiaries waiting to approach the table gets thicker. It goes quickly. The officials of the Quai d'Orsay stand round, indicating places to sign, indicating procedure, blotting with neat little pads.

Suddenly from outside comes the crash of guns thundering a salute. It announces to Paris that the second Treaty of Versailles has been signed by Dr Müller and Dr Bell. Through the few open windows comes the sound of distant crowds cheering hoarsely. And still the signature goes on.

We had been warned it might last three hours. Yet almost at once it seemed that the queue was getting thin. Only three, then two, and then one delegate remained to sign. His name had hardly been blotted before the huissiers began again their 'Ssh! Ssh!' cutting suddenly short the wide murmur which had again begun. There was a final hush. 'La séance est levée,' rasped Clemenceau. Not a word more or less.

We kept our seats while the Germans were conducted like prisoners from the dock, their eyes still fixed upon some distant point of the horizon.

THE RUSSIAN REVOLUTION: I CAPTURE VLADIVOSTOK, 31 December 1919

Frazier Hunt

Frazier Hunt was a *Chicago Tribune* journalist who reported the civil war between the Bolsheviks and the rightist forces (the White Guard) in Russia following the Revolution of 1917.

It isn't every war correspondent who can capture a city. I don't mean to say that I got one all by myself, but at least I was the first man in. And, different from the immortal Kipling's tale of how 'Privit Mulvaney tuk the town av Lungtungpen,' I had my trousers on when I took mine.

I've never written the story before, and I doubt if I would do it now if Frank Martinek, one-time US Naval Intelligence Officer in Vladivostok, had not told what youthful critics, not quite dry behind the ears, like to call the *dénouement* of the yarn in introducing me to a Chicago audience.

I had landed in the colourful and war-weary Siberian port from a miserable little Japanese tub that had bobbed across the Sea of Japan like a champagne cork. It was the last day of 1919, and Vladivostok was being held by a bobtail White Guard army, supported by Japanese troops. Ten thousand homesick, disgusted American soldiers were scattered for 1,000 miles up and down the single line of steel that pointed towards Moscow. About this time Admiral Kolchak, dictator and White saviour, once head of the British- and Japanese-supported anti-Bolshevik hopes, had a rather frightful accident: his own troops mutinied, held a drumhead court-martial, quietly led him out to a convenient wall and filled him full of lead (although I believe it is actually steel bullets they use in such emergencies).

The whole White Guard movement in Siberia was crumbling rapidly, and old Tsarist officials, Japanese generals,

Cossack *atamans*, and thick-skinned British advisers did not know what to do about it. The American commander, the incorruptible, wise Major-General Graves, however, did know exactly what to do: simply keep his troops out of mixing in the internal affairs of Russia, and see to it that the 50,000 Japanese soldiers there did not move the hills and the rivers. It was a cinch they were going to try to move everything else.

I was primed for this situation like an Indiana pump in frosty weather. In the previous winter I had spent two months with the North Russian Expedition in the desolate country around Archangel. I had ridden almost 1,000 miles by sledge up frozen rivers and through forests of glistening Christmas-trees, visiting American outposts and snow-bound fronts.

When I left the unsavoury mess I was bitter and resentful. I could not stand the sight of American doughboys being commanded to do British officers' dirty work. A 5,000-word *exposé* cable that I had sneaked out and sent from the transmitting office in Narvik, Norway, had been read in the United States Senate, and, I think, had had a little to do with the promise of the White House to remove the American troops as soon as the ice thawed.

Following this pleasant adventure in the shadow of the Arctic Circle, I had worked my way through the Allied blockade into the heart of the Soviets. For two months I had enjoyed the exclusive privilege of working the greatest news goldmine in history. . . . And now I was at the other end of the world in a second intervention mess, and ready for trouble.

It took less than a day for me to see that this American Expeditionary Force was run in quite a different manner from the North Russia fiasco. A Lieutenant-General of the Japanese Army had unanimously elected himself Commander-in-Chief of the Allied Forces, and before General Graves had arrived had sent the two American regiments, rushed up from Manila, westward to pick up a fight with the anti-White peasant outfits called 'Partisans'. But the very day General Graves disembarked he called in his troops, and figuratively set the high-ranking little gentleman from Nippon squarely on his west end. So my anticipated story of how American soldiers were a second time doing filthy jobs for someone else evaporated into the cold dry air. And I needed a few good pieces to keep the *Chicago Tribune* contented.

Now, I have always operated on the general theory that the best place to get a story is directly from the people who are mixed up in it. So it was that after I had been a few days in Vladivostok I decided to get out with the fighting Red Siberian moujiks and see for myself how they were feeling about their revolution, their war with the Whites, and their near-war with the Japanese. For my interpreter I found a gentle, old-fashioned Social Democrat named Kolko, who years before had escaped from a Siberian prison, then denned up in New York until the first revolution had broken, and was now a sort of anti-White spy around Vladivostok.

We had a great time for ten days living with the Partisans. As I look back over a long series of 'great times' I'm inclined to say this tops my purple list. We rode, slept, drank vodka, and sang with these young peasant soldiers – and I made speeches to bearded old grandfathers on how friendly America really was, and how I wished them luck with their Japanese problem.

I used to do this volunteer lecturing in school-houses, or crowded peasant homes, or anywhere they asked me. At first most of them would be suspicious of me, but when they understood that I'd been in Moscow, and that I was really on their side, they were like eager children. They used to ask all sorts of questions about America, and how people lived and ran their affairs in a free country. Most of the time they would keep the soldiers from coming in, and there would be only Kolko, the interpreter, myself, and the grizzled old fellows in their sheepskin coats and felt boots.

I was surprised too at the depth of the feeling of the youthful Partisan soldiers. They knew what they were fighting for; they were against the return of the ways of the Tsar, and against the interference of the Japanese. They still felt that they wanted some form of assembly and democratic constitution, but the futile efforts of Kerensky, and the coming of Kolchak and the intervention, had shaken their faith in half-way measures.

They were thrilled by the magic of the word 'soviet'. They thought that possibly that was what they needed too. And somehow or other they knew that Lenin was their true leader. . . . When they heard that I had met Lenin and had talked with him for a few minutes they barraged me with a hundred questions. The revolution was vague and shadowy in their minds, but at least it meant land and freedom for them.

Probably it is a bit far-fetched, but time and again I could not help but think how similar this must have been to the mood and dreams of Putnam's men and the Green Mountain boys – when the name of George Washington thrilled the hearts of hungry, beaten soldiers with the same imagery and the same fervour that Lenin's name was doing now, 140 years later, and 10,000 miles to the westward. I'd like to have been a correspondent in those days, too.

Then one day, far back in the snow-covered hills, I joined up with a small Partisan detachment that had five Japanese soldier prisoners, who were eating them out of house and home. They had captured the lads from a *makaka* garrison some twenty miles away. Incidentally, to call a Japanese soldier a *makaka* was like calling him a so-and-so and not smiling when you did it. The Japs had been doing a little village-burning and bayonet practice among the peasant villages, and all the emotional tinder for a nice little war was laid out ready to be lit.

The young Red commander couldn't think of anything to do with his five prisoners except to shoot them humanely. I explained through my interpreter that it would be a fine lesson in hospitality if he'd turn these boys over to me and let me put them in Lieutenant-General Oi's lap, with the word that his troops didn't have to shoot every Partisan soldier they got their hands on. Finally we traded the lot for my watch.

It was all good, clean fun, and in due time I got back to Vladivostok with my Japanese quintuplets. The able little Japanese commander rubbed his bald pate while I gave him a lengthy discourse on the beauty of letting his soldiers have their target practice on something else besides captured Siberians.

Then I heard that down Nikolsk way real fighting was about to start between the Japanese-supported Whites and the Red Partisans. Kolko and I took the twice-a-week train the 100 *versts* or so towards this latest front.

We missed the show by four hours – but it wasn't much of a war to brag about at that. The Whites had quickly surrendered, and, while there was some question as to what to do with the old Tsarist officers, the White troopers themselves had gladly melted into the Partisan forces.

And now they were moving to attack and capture the key city of Vladivostok, still in the hands of the Whites. Two troop trains were being made up directly in front of the station. They would be pulling out very soon.

We hurried back to the Red commander. 'Tell him I must go in on that first train,' I instructed Kolko.

But the commander shook his head. 'There'll be some heavy fighting before we get there,' he answered. 'The Whites have plenty of artillery, and they'll try to stop us.'

But I insisted that I'd like to go along; that I had to go. Then it was that the commander got his brilliant idea. 'You might ride in the armoured truck we've just captured,' he suggested. 'It'll be ahead of the engine on the first train, but it ought to be safe enough in there.'

I pumped his hand. I patted his shoulder. It was too good
to be true: a war in an armoured truck. Send me there right
now!

He called a smiling kid soldier and rolled out a few yards of
orders; then we followed the boy down the track to a home-
made armoured truck, with steel plates bolted to the sides. In
the armour were cut half a dozen oblong slits. I noticed the
muzzles of machine-guns sticking out from two or three of
these loopholes.

Behind the armoured truck an ancient wood-burning
engine was champing at the bit – or whatever it is engines
do. Ahead of the armoured truck there was nothing but snow
and two steel rails gleaming in the late afternoon sunlight –
and down the track other boys were getting ready to blow
this pleasant little armoured truck to kingdom come. It
seemed a very silly idea, but it was a bit romantic at that.

Our guide ducked under the truck and disappeared
through a trapdoor in the floor. We followed, and pulled
ourselves into the car. Two tin lanterns, with candles stuck in
them, hung from the ceiling. In the flickering light I could
make out six or seven men. A young lad, certainly not over
nineteen years old, stepped up, and our guide reeled off his
instructions. The truck commander turned to me, welcomed
me with a hand-shake and a broad smile. Then one by one I
shook hands with the two machine-gun crews. Someone
pushed up an ammunition box, and I took off my old fur-
lined trench coat, folded it on top of the box, and sat down.
Next I took out a package of cigarettes and passed them
round, leaving the remainder of the package on a second
ammunition box. I could have had the car after that.

We settled back in the stifling heat. A pot-bellied stove in
the centre of the truck was roaring. It was 20 degrees below
zero outside, but we were baking here inside our steel oven.

The young commander said something, then slipped down
through the trapdoor. Silence settled over the truck. A giant
tow-headed boy, astride the seat of a Vickers-Maxim, started

humming a Slav song in the inevitable minor chords. Soon we were all dreaming of our worlds outside this hot armoured truck . . . Time drifted by. Then the young chief pushed his head up through the door, popped in, and closed the steel trap behind him. His voice was pitched high with excitement.

'We're starting, comrades!' he announced dramatically. 'Let every man do his duty! If anyone falters he knows what to expect!'

Almost immediately we heard the muffled tones of an engine bell and the echoes of men's voices. Then came a violent bump that all but sent us sprawling from our cartridge-box seats. At last we were actually rolling. One of the wheels was a bit flat, and it soured the song the other wheels were singing. I'm sure each of us was making up his own words. Mine were: 'This is life! . . . This is life! . . . This is life!'

The young commander pulled up an ammunition case close to mine. It was evident that he was of a little different breed from these square-faced Slav peasants, with their wide cheek-bones and their heavy bodies. Finally Kolko and I got him to talk about himself: he was from Petrograd, and his father had in the Tsar's days been captain of a Russian battleship. He was now a Red Admiral. This boy, Ivan Vasilievitch Trestiakoff, had been a naval cadet for a year; then, when the revolution broke, he had joined up with the Bolshies, and had been swept by one of the strange tides of war to this distant land of Far Eastern Siberia.

I asked him what he wanted to do. He answered straight off. 'When we've finished the Whites and driven out the Japs I would like to take my armoured truck to Petrograd and say, "Here I am, Papa, with my brave machine-gunners."'

He took a turn round the little truck. Then he came back and went on with his talk. 'These Whites thought we were all stupid fools. Well, we were foolish like a fox. You know how they always had trouble getting their engines to run. Our people in the railway shops saw to that. They're running all right now.'

As a matter of fact, this particular engine of ours that was pushing us into the night and its black uncertainty wasn't running any too well. Or maybe it was something else that kept us starting and stopping every few miles. We'd get a series of good healthy bumps from both operations. Sometimes we'd pull up, and for what seemed like hours we'd stand dead still. Then there would be that clanking engine bell and the shouting, and we'd get a couple of bumps; then off we'd go again. We were not troubled with any fancy air-brakes on this makeshift troop train.

In one of these long stops our young chief slipped down through the manhole in the bottom of the car. He wore a short curved sword that he'd taken from some dead Cossack, and it would catch on the sides of the narrow trapdoor when he climbed in or out. It was the only side-arm he had, and I thought seriously of giving him my own 45-calibre Colt automatic army pistol which I carried deep in the right-hand pocket of my breeches. But General Graves had presented it to me, and I couldn't get myself around to parting with it.

Our commander was gone for some minutes, and when he finally stuck his head up through the hole he had a broad grin on his face. In his right hand he held a stubby automatic. He announced that we had stopped opposite a station platform, and that he'd just lifted the pistol from an unsuspecting civilian. He dug up a heavy cord, looped it round his neck, tied the ends to the pistol butt, and stuck the gun in his belt. He was a real officer now; he had both a sword and a pistol.

Before long we got our usual bumping, and slowly pushed our way on towards our unknown fate. Kolko and I moved over next to the tow-headed machine-gunner. He'd been fighting with the Partisan troops for almost a year now. He'd had a bad break, and he was disconsolate. 'I'm thinking about my wife all the time,' he explained. 'We'd only been married a month when I had to join up with the Partisans. I can hardly think of anything else but how I'd like to have her right now.'

We offered him our condolences. Maybe he could go home before so very long. If he didn't get there pretty soon some other man might be keeping her warm on these cold nights . . . He only shook his head sadly when we suggested that possibility.

Leaning against the wall was a red-bearded boy who wore his sheepskin jacket despite the incredible heat of this steel baking oven. He was a new recruit; he'd joined up with the Partisans only that morning. 'I was afraid to desert from the Whites,' he explained to us. 'You see, I live in the country near Nikolsk, and they might have punished my family.'

A third peasant soldier cut in: 'Kolchak and the *makakas* made us all Partisans. While we were fighting for Kolchak the Japs were burning our villages and killing our people. When we finish off the Whites we'll give them something! America understands us. They are men like we are. If America would only help us we could whip the Japs. We never had anything against the Americans. They did a little something against us at the start when they first got here, but that didn't amount to much. They're our friends now.'

The blond giant, with the wide mouth and the shining teeth, and the big yearn for his wife, muscled into the conversation. 'Did you hear about that American who brought back five Jap prisoners we had and turned them over to the Jap General? He told him that was the way we treated our prisoners, and for him to quit killing ours.'

I didn't say anything. It was too hot and stuffy in that truck to be even your own hero. I drifted back to my old seat on the ammunition case.

The boy commander started talking about some mystical thing he called *svoboda* – freedom. He would have made quite a rabble-rouser if he'd put his mind to it.

We jogged along through the interminable hours. The two lanterns, swaying from their hooks, cast weird shadows. The little stove threw off enough heat to barbecue a mule.

We'd talk a few sentences, and then we'd turn to our own dreams. Once in a while the tow-headed homesick lover on the Vickers-Maxim saddle-seat would hum a song. Maybe the others would join in, and, again, maybe they wouldn't.

The young commander would make his rounds and examine the two heavy guns. Their barrels were blanketed, and their water-coolers warm and ready for action. He was a true machine-gunner. He'd pet the guns and call them 'Baby'. You could get action from the seat of a Vickers-Maxim – especially if you put your heart in your work.

He was a bit of a sentimentalist too. 'Wish you could take a picture so you'd remember us,' he suggested. Then he began looking around the car again. 'I'd like to give you a souvenir of some kind or other, but I can't find any,' he went on.

Then he got his inspiration. He hurried to the far end of the truck and pulled the lid off a box.

'Here's something to take home,' he said in eager earnestness. Then he rolled a pineapple hand-grenade on the floor straight towards my feet.

I didn't know much about hand-grenades, but I'd seen plenty of men who'd been mangled by them. At least I knew they weren't to play handball with. . . . I watched this little package of bad news as it bounced and rolled towards me. I started to count to ten: most grenades were supposed to burst on the fatal ten. Then a sort of sickly grin spread over my face. I was conscious that my comrades were watching me – me, the over-sized American who was supposed to know all the answers.

I casually reached down and picked up the grenade. If it was going to explode it might as well do the job right, and not just mess around. I knew a few Russian words, and, with the steel pineapple cupped in my two hands, I nodded to the young commander and said, 'Thanks, comrade!'

I looked it over with feigned professional interest. I saw that the pin was in its proper place and securely bent over. I knew now that we were safe: it couldn't go off as long as that pin was in its place. Then, with just a trace of bravado, I shoved the gift in my trousers-pocket, opposite the one that held my Colt.

I imagine it was an hour later, when we'd got up near Razdolne, that we bumped to another stop. Again there was a long wait. Through the gun slits we could make out, far down the track, what looked to be a bonfire. After a while our commander lifted the trapdoor and slipped down through it.

Within three or four minutes he came back. He was excited, and his dark eyes were snapping. 'The White cadets are entrenched 300 yards down the track with three-inch guns!' he shouted. 'We'll have a fight now!'

He pushed the tow-headed gunner off the saddle-seat of the gun in the front of the truck, pulled the blankets off the barrel, and squared himself for action. There was tense silence in the car. Any second now we might be pushing forward towards that dull red glow and into those three-inch guns.

I reached behind me and felt the steel sides of the truck. I remembered that the armour-plate was not more than three-eighths of an inch thick. That would be pie for a three-inch high explosive. I'd seen the twisted, pathetic wrecks of dozens of armour-plated tanks that had tried to stop German 77s up in the Soissons area in France. One direct hit on this car of ours and they wouldn't be able to tell which had been me and which the blond gunner with the yearn for his bride.

My throat was parched, and I smacked my dry lips. The heat, the cigarette smoke, and the foul air, smelling of unwashed bodies and sheepskin jackets, were even making my eyes smart. I wanted to get out of here. I didn't want to be blown to bits by some nervous White cadet, pulling a lanyard that would send an unlucky shell, with my number on it, to its unnecessary mission.

The voice of the commander broke the long, hot silence. Kolko whispered that he had said he would slip out and find what was happening. The blond giant took his old seat on the machine-gun, and the boy hurried to the trapdoor and disappeared.

He was gone for what seemed a very long time. Then his Cossack cap popped up from the manhole, and his white teeth showed in the candlelight. He shouted something in Russian.

'What's that? What d'he say?' I demanded of Kolko.

My interpreter did not answer me. He had jumped to his feet and was shouting to the commander. The gunners were talking loudly and excitedly.

'What's doing?' I questioned. But no one paid the slightest attention to me.

'What in hell did he say?' I demanded again, grabbing Kolko's sleeve. But he had no time to answer me.

'God damn it! What d'he say?' I yelled, striking at him.

Kolko came out of his trance. 'He said the cadets had surrendered!' he answered, gulping. 'The road to Vladivostok is open!'

I joined in the cheering. Two or three of the men were hugging each other. The tow-headed gunner gleefully shouted that maybe he'd get to see his bride again before very long.

Slowly we settled back to our waiting game. Then we got the go-ahead bump and crept on towards what the doughboys called 'Bloodyvostok.'

I awoke from sleep with a jerk. We were coming to a stop. The boy commander peered out through a loophole. Kolko translated what he said: 'It's getting light . . . Looks as if we're almost in Vladivostok.'

I stretched my cramped legs. I drew a deep breath of the foul, dead air and immediately regretted it. I couldn't stand this truck any longer. I'd rather freeze than toast, and I'd rather be shot in the open than smothered to death in a heated vacuum.

Again the commander disappeared through the manhole. I slipped on my fur-lined coat and cap, pulled on my great gloves, and told Kolko I was going to get out of here. He presented arguments and recited pledges. I answered that I didn't give a damn about anything except to leave this steel pigsty. He picked up his coat and started to follow me. But I wouldn't let him come. I explained that I'd only get some fresh air, look round, and report back.

I crawled out between the wheels. We were in a gap in the snow-blanketed hills that surrounded the magnificent 'Golden Horn'. We couldn't be more than three or four miles from the railway station.

Dawn was just breaking, but here in the Far North it would be a late dawn. It was almost eight o'clock. Several groups of men were evidently conferring by the side of the train, a carriage or two below the engine. I snooped around to see what I could see. A narrow steel ladder on the rear of our armoured truck, that led to the roof, caught my eye. I climbed up and made a quick survey. The truck had a flat wooden roof. I scrambled down, ducked between the wheels, and stuck my head up through the trapdoor. The hot blast and the stench were almost like a smash in the face. I told Kolko not to worry about me, that I was going to stay outside in the clear air. He said he'd join me, but I begged him not to: his clothes were not as warm as mine. Then I slipped out, returned to the ladder, and mounted it to the top of the truck. Carefully I tucked the skirts of my long coat under me, and, with my legs dangling over the front end, sat squarely on the roof. Vladivostok was straight ahead of me.

The engine bell rang, men shouted and scurried to their carriages, and off we started. Suddenly I realized that I was doing a very silly thing. If there was fighting at the station I'd be the first man to be picked off. But the air was champagne to me, and I was intoxicated with this blessed oxygen, the lovely morning, and the whole thrilling business of living gaily and dangerously.

We were getting into town now. A little group of workmen along the track cheered and waved as we went by. Then there was more shouting and waving.

I was taking the salute. I was the man on the white horse at the head of the procession. I chuckled to myself. From my high seat at the front of the No. 1 truck I sang out '*Tovarish!*' ('Comrade!') to everyone we passed.

Now we were pushing into the station. There was a wild crowd of cheering men here. They had no uniforms, but they were waving rifles and yelling.

I looked down from my box-seat. Two or three officers in American uniforms were in the crowd next to the track. I recognized my friend Frank Martinek, of the Naval Intelligence. The train ground to a stop. Then they saw me and yelled a welcome.

Frank shouted up to me, 'We surrender. Will you accept our unconditional surrender?'

'I will!' I shouted back. 'And may God have pity on your miserable souls!'

I hurried to the back of the truck and scrambled down the little ladder. Martinek and my tried and true friends, Lieutenant-Colonel Bob Eichelberger and Major Sidney Graves, pounded me on the back.

'Young man,' Frank hilariously insisted, 'this is the first time in history that a war correspondent ever captured a town!' The others roared and pommelled me.

But a little later, when I sent off my story, I had to admit that the anti-Whites had pulled their *coup d'état* and taken over the town just before dawn, and that even the Japanese had been forced to accept the reverse.

I might have captured only a captured town, but at least I had my trousers on, and, as I have already said, that's something Kipling's Private Mulvaney lacked.

P.S. I was never able to find out whether or not that tow-headed machine-gunner got him to his wife before it thawed that spring. I've always hoped that he did.

THE PUBLICATION OF *ULYSSES*, February 1922

James Joyce

James Joyce had conceived the idea for his novel – now regarded by many as the greatest of the century – in 1906, but it was not until 1921 that he wrote the final word, battling desperately against poverty and failing eyesight. But this was not the end of the struggle. Episodes from *Ulysses* published in the States had been confiscated on the grounds of obscenity, and publication both there and in Britain was out of the question. Eventually Sylvia Beach, who owned a bookshop in Paris, published a limited edition – on 2 February 1922 (Joyce's fortieth birthday) – after the book had been reset six times, Joyce having almost entirely rewritten it in proof. It was not published in Britain until 1936.

Rue de l'Université 9, Paris VII
Dear Miss Weaver: Many thanks for your kind tele-gram. Two copies of *Ulysses* (nos. 901 and 902) reached Paris on 2 February and two further copies (nos. 251 and 252) on 5 February. One copy is on show, the other three were taken by subscribers who were leaving for different parts of the world. Since the announcement that the book was out the shop has been in a state of siege – buyers driving up two or three times a day and no copies to give them. After a great deal of telegraph-ing and telephoning it seems that 7 copies will come today and 30 tomorrow. A more nerveracking conclu-sion to the history of the book could scarcely have been

imagined! The first 10 copies of the *edition de luxe* will not be ready before Saturday so that you will not receive your copy (no. 1) before Tuesday of next week at the earliest. I am glad for my own sake (though hardly for yours) that you are advertising an English edition. I hope it will be possible in that event to correct the numerous misprints. [Ezra] Pound says it is . . .

Thanks also for the prompt return of the *Penelope* episode (the name of which by another strange coincidence is your own). It did not arrive too late. Your description of it also coincides with my intention – if the epithet 'posthuman' were added. I have rejected the usual interpretation of her as a human apparition – that aspect being better represented by Calypso, Nausikaa and Circe, to say nothing of the pseudo Homeric figures. In conception and technique I tried to depict the earth which is prehuman and presumably posthuman.

With kindest regards

yours very sincerely and to the end importunately.

GERMAN INFLATION, September 1922

Ernest Hemingway

Once across the muddy Rhine you are in Germany, and the German end of the bridge is guarded by a couple of the meekest and most discouraged looking German soldiers you have ever seen. Two French soldiers with fixed bayonets walk up and down and the two German soldiers, unarmed, lean against a wall and look on. The French soldiers are in full equipment and steel helmets, but the Germans wear the old loose tunics and high peaked, peace-time caps.

I asked a Frenchman the functions and duties of the German guard.

'They stand there,' he answered.

There were no marks to be had in Strasbourg, the mounting exchange had cleaned the bankers out days ago, so we changed some French money in the railway station at Kehl. For ten francs I received 670 marks. Ten francs amounted to about ninety cents in Canadian money. That ninety cents lasted Mrs Hemingway and me for a day of heavy spending and at the end of the day we had one hundred and twenty marks left!

Our first purchase was from a fruit stand beside the main street of Kehl where an old woman was selling apples, peaches and plums. We picked out five very good looking apples and gave the old woman a fifty-mark note. She gave us back thirty-eight marks in change. A very nice looking, white bearded old gentleman saw us buy the apples and raised his hat.

'Pardon me, sir,' he said, rather timidly, in German, 'how much were the apples?'

I counted the change and told him twelve marks.

He smiled and shook his head. 'I can't pay it. It is too much.'

He went up the street walking very much as white bearded old gentlemen of the old regime walk in all countries, but he had looked very longingly at the apples. I wish I had offered him some. Twelve marks, on that day, amounted to a little under two cents. The old man, whose life's savings were probably, as most of the non-profiteer classes are, invested in German pre-war and war bonds, could not afford a twelve-mark expenditure. He is a type of the people whose incomes do not increase with the falling purchasing value of the mark and the krone.

With marks at 800 to the dollar, or eight to a cent, we priced articles in the windows of the different Kehl shops. Peas were 18 marks a pound, beans 16 marks; a pound of Kaiser coffee, there are still many 'Kaiser' brands in the German republic, could be had for 34 marks. Gersten coffee, which is not coffee at all but roasted grain, sold for 14 marks a pound. Flypaper was 150 marks a package. A scythe blade cost 150 marks, too, or eighteen and three-quarters cents! Beer was ten marks a stein or one cent and a quarter.

Kehl's best hotel, which is a very well turned out place, served a five-course table d'hôte meal for 120 marks, which amounts to fifteen cents in our money. The same meal could not be duplicated in Strasbourg, three miles away, for a dollar.

Because of the customs regulations, which are very strict on persons returning from Germany, the French cannot come over to Kehl and buy up all the cheap goods they would like to. But they can come over and eat. It is a sight every afternoon to see the mob that storms the German pastry shops and tea places. The Germans make very good pastries, wonderful pastries, in fact, that, at the present tumbling mark rate, the French of Strasbourg can buy for a less amount apiece than the smallest French coin, the one sou piece. This miracle of exchange makes a swinish spectacle where the youth of the town of Strasbourg crowd into the German pastry shop to eat themselves sick and gorge on fluffy, cream-filled slices of German cake at five marks the slice. The contents of a pastry shop are swept clear in half an hour.

In a pastry shop we visited, a man in an apron, wearing blue glasses, appeared to be the proprietor. He was assisted by a typical 'boche' looking German with close cropped head. The place was jammed with French people of all ages and descriptions, all gorging cakes, while a young girl in a pink dress, silk stockings, with a pretty, weak face and pearl earrings in her ears took as many of their orders for fruit and vanilla ices as she could fill.

She didn't seem to care very much whether she filled the orders or not. There were soldiers in town and she kept going over to look out of the window.

The proprietor and his helper were surly and didn't seem

particularly happy when all the cakes were sold. The mark was falling faster than they could bake.

Meanwhile out in the street a funny little train jolted by, carrying the workmen with their dinner-pails home to the outskirts of the town, profiteers' motor cars tore by raising a cloud of dust that settled over the trees and the fronts of all the buildings, and inside the pastry shop young French hoodlums swallowed their last cakes and French mothers wiped the sticky mouths of their children. It gave you a new aspect on exchange.

As the last of the afternoon tea-ers and pastry eaters went Strasbourg-wards across the bridge the first of the exchange pirates coming over to raid Kehl for cheap dinners began to arrive. The two streams passed each other on the bridge and the two disconsolate looking German soldiers looked on. As the boy in the motor agency said, 'It's the way to make money.'

THE FASCISTS TAKE POWER, ITALY, October 1922

Benito Mussolini

The extreme right-wing Fascist party of Italy was formed by Benito Mussolini in 1919, taking a black shirt as its uniform and the slogan 'no discussion, only obedience' as its philosophical guide. The party thrived on the unrest and disillusion which swept Italy in the post-war period. In October Mussolini ordered his followers to march on Rome; the King gave way before this show of force, and called on Mussolini to form a government.

I was in a terrible state of nervous tension. Night after night I had been kept awake, giving orders, following the compact columns of the Fascisti, restraining the battle to the knightly practices of Fascism.

A period of greater responsibilities was going to begin for me. I must not fail in my duty or in my aims. I gathered all my strength to my aid, I invoked the memory of the dead, I asked the assistance of God, I called upon the living faithful to assist me in the great task that confronted me.

That night of 31 October 1922, I left the direction of the *Popolo d' Italia*, and turned my fighting journal over to my brother Arnaldo. In the 1 November number I published the following declaration:

'From now on, the direction of the *Popolo d' Italia* is entrusted to Arnaldo Mussolini.

'I thank and salute with brotherly love all the editors, collaborators, correspondents, employees, workers, all those who have assiduously and faithfully laboured with me for the life of this paper and for love of our Country.

MUSSOLINI.

ROME 30 October 1922.'

I parted with regret from the paper that had been the most constant and potent element of our Victory. I must add that my brother Arnaldo has been able to maintain the editorship in a capable, dignified way.

When I had entrusted the paper to my brother, I was off for Rome. To the zealous people who wanted to get me a special train to go to Rome to speak with the King, I said that for me a compartment in the usual train was quite enough. Engines and coal should not be wasted. Economize! That is the first and acid test of a true man of Government. And after all, I could only enter Rome at the head of my Black Shirts now camping at Santa Marinella in the atmosphere and the shining rays of the Capital.

The news of my departure sped all over Italy. In every station where the train stopped there had gathered the Fascisti and the masses who wanted to bring me, even through the pouring rain, their cheers and their goodwill.

Going from Milan was painful. That city had given me a home for ten years; to me it has been prodigal in its satisfactions; it had followed me in every stress; it had baptized the most wonderful squads of action of Fascism; it had been the scene of historical political struggles. Now I was leaving it, called by destiny and by a greater task. All Milan knew of my going, and I felt that even in the feeling of joy for a going that was a symbol of victory, there was also a shade of sadness.

But this was not the hour for sentimentality. It was the time for quick, sure decisions. After the kisses and farewells of my family, I said good-bye to many prominent Milanese; and then I went away, running into the night, to take counsel with myself, to refresh my soul, to listen to the echoes of voices of friends and to envisage the wide horizons of tomorrow's possibilities.

The minor episodes of that trip and of those days are not important. The train brought me into the midst of the Fascisti, I was in view of Rome at Santa Marinella. I reviewed the columns. I established the formalities for the entrance into Rome. I established connections between the Quadriumvirate and the authorities.

My presence redoubled the great enthusiasm. I read in the eyes of those young men the divine smile of triumph of an ideal. With such elements I would have been inspired to challenge, if need be, not only the base Italian ruling class, but enemies of any sort and race.

In Rome there was waiting for me an indescribable welcome. I did not want any delay. Even before making contacts with my political friends I motored to the Quirinal. I wore a black shirt. I was introduced without formalities to the presence of His Majesty the King. The Stefani agency and the great newspapers of the world gave stilted or speculative details about this interview. I will limit myself, for obvious reasons of reserve, to declare that the conference was characterized by great cordiality. I concealed no plans, nor did I fail to make plain my ideas of how to rule Italy. I obtained the Sovereign's approbation. I took up lodgings at the Savoy Hotel and began to work. First I made agreements with the general command of the army to bring a militia into Rome and file them off in proper formation in a review by the King. I gave detailed and precise orders. One hundred thousand Black Shirts paraded in perfect order before the Sovereign. They brought to him the homage of Fascist Italy!

THE GENERAL STRIKE, BRITAIN, May 1926

An Oxford undergraduate

The General Strike (4–12 May) was called by the Trades Union Congress in support of the mineworkers, who had been 'locked out' by the employers as a means of forcing a cut in wages. In the first days of the General Strike the country came to a standstill, but the TUC had little real stomach for a constitutional conflict with the government and quickly backed down. The effectiveness of the strike had also been undermined by troops and volunteers, especially students, running an emergency transport and supply service. For many undergraduates it made a pleasant change from their studies.

We set out from Oxford early in the evening in a vintage Bentley and drove at great speed through the lovely English countryside. At Doncaster our driver stood us dinner and a bottle of champagne. So far the drive had been uneventful, but from Doncaster onwards groups of strikers tried unsuccessfully to interrupt our progress by occasionally throwing stones or attempting to puncture our tyres. However, our driver remained unperturbed, and merely accelerated when he saw a hostile crowd – at times we reached eighty miles an hour . . .

On the following day those of us who were to work on the docks received our marching orders, while others went to drive trams or work the cranes. There were sentries on duty at the dock gates and a light cruiser, HMS *Enterprise*, was berthed near by in case of disturbances. We were under the supervision of a Cambridge don, Mr Owen Morshead, now librarian of Windsor Castle, and we worked from dawn to dusk with intervals for refreshment. Our method of obtaining alcoholic refreshment consisted in asking the sentry at the gate to give an order to a small pub just outside, the bottles of beer being suspended in a large basket over a wall bounding the dock. Money was then placed in the basket, which was hoisted back over the wall.

Some of the old hands who drifted back to work were surprised by the speed with which we unloaded the ships, but we realized that it was a different story working for a few days as an adventure, compared to regular work over a period of years.

AT A PARTY WITH SCOTT FITZGERALD, JUAN-LES-PINS, June 1926

Ernest Hemingway

Scott Fitzgerald, living on his royalties from *The Great Gatsby*, the quintessential Jazz Age novel, had found an inexpensive villa for Hemingway and his wife in the South of France that summer.

The single apéritif before lunch was very good and we had several more. That night there was a party to welcome us at the Casino, just a small party, the MacLeishes, the Murphys, the Fitzgeralds and we who were living at the villa. No one drank anything stronger than champagne and it was very gay and obviously a splendid place to write. There was going to be everything that a man needed to write except to be alone.

Zelda [Fitzgerald] was very beautiful and was tanned a lovely gold colour and her hair was a beautiful dark gold and she was very friendly. Her hawk's eyes were clear and calm. I knew everything was all right and was going to turn out well in the end when she leaned forward and said to me, telling me her great secret, 'Ernest, don't you think Al Jolson is greater than Jesus?'

Nobody thought anything of it at the time. It was only Zelda's secret that she shared with me, as a hawk might share something with a man. But hawks do not share. Scott did not write anything any more that was good until after he knew that she was insane.

THE END FOR SACCO AND VANZETTI, BOSTON, 23 August 1927

Louis Stark

Nicolò Sacco and Bartolomeo Vanzetti were Italian anarchist emigrants to America convicted of double murder during a 1920 payroll robbery. Their conviction was dubious, and the case became a *cause célèbre* around the world. After six years of appeals and stays of execution, the two Italian workmen (one was a fishmonger and the other a shoemaker) were electrocuted on 23 August 1927. In 1977 Sacco and Vanzetti were posthumously pardoned by the Governor of Massachusetts.

Police charged a crowd near the Bunker Hill Monument. The prison area was an armed camp. Searchlights swept glaring fingers over rooftops, revealing whole families gazing at the prison. All streets leading to the prison were roped off, and the public was banned from entering the prison zone.

Police horses stamped restlessly in the yellow glare of street lamps.

Mrs Sacco and Miss Vanzetti paid three visits to the prison on the last day and made their final appeal to the Governor in the evening.

Reporters were given special passes to the prison. Those of us who were to do the execution story were asked to present ourselves at the prison by ten o'clock if possible. Eddy remained on the streets observing the police and the crowds, and Gordon covered the last hours at the State House.

When I arrived at the prison, I found that telegraph wires had again been strung into the Prison Officers' Club. From ten o'clock we filed details of the preparations for the execution. The windows had been nailed down by a nervous policeman 'because somebody might throw something in'. The shades were drawn. The room was stuffy, and in an hour the heat was unbearable. We took off our coats, rolled up our shirt sleeves, and tried to be comfortable. The Morse operators were the coolest of the fifty men and women in the room. The noise of the typewriters and telegraph instruments made an awful din. Our nerves were stretched to the breaking-point. Had there not been a last minute reprieve on August 10? Might there not be one now? We knew of the personal appeal then being made by Mrs Sacco and Miss Vanzetti to the Governor.

W. G. Thompson, counsel for the two men, saw them for the last time. In an extraordinarily moving account of his final talks, later published in *The Atlantic Monthly*, Thompson described the attitude of the two Italians, their calmness in the face of death, their sincerity, their firm belief in their ideals:

'I told Vanzetti that although my belief in his innocence had all the time been strengthened both by my study of the evidence and by my increasing knowledge of his personality, yet there was a chance, however remote, that I might be mistaken; and that I thought he ought for my sake, in the closing hour of his life when nothing could save him, to give me his most solemn reassurance, both with respect to himself and with respect to Sacco. Vanzetti then told me quietly and calmly, and with a sincerity which I could not doubt, that I need have no anxiety about this matter; that both he and Sacco were absolutely innocent of the South Braintree crime and that he [Vanzetti] was equally innocent of the Bridgewater crime; that while, looking back, he now realized more clearly than he ever had the grounds of the suspicion against him and Sacco, he felt that no allowance had been made for his ignorance of American points of view and habits of thought, or for his fear as a radical and almost as an outlaw, and that in reality he was convicted on evidence which would not have convicted him had he not been an anarchist, so that he was in a very real sense dying for his cause. He said it was a cause for which he was prepared to die. He said it was the cause of the upward progress of humanity and the elimination of force from the world. He spoke with calmness, knowledge, and deep feeling.

'I was impressed by the strength of Vanzetti's mind, and by the extent of his reading and knowledge. He did not talk like a fanatic. Although intensely convinced of the truth of his own views, he was still able to listen with calmness and with understanding to the expression of views with which he did not agree. In this closing scene the impression of him which had been gaining ground in my mind for three years was deepened and confirmed – that he was a man of powerful mind, of unselfish disposition, of seasoned character and of devotion to high ideals. There was no sign of breaking down or of terror at approaching death. At parting he gave me a firm clasp of the hand and a steady glance, which revealed unmistakably the depth of his feeling and the firmness of his self-control . . .

'My conversation with Sacco was very brief. He showed

no sign of fear, shook hands with me firmly and bade me good-bye. His manner also was one of absolute sincerity.'

At quarter past eleven, Musmanno burst into Warden Hendry's office with a plea for a last talk with Vanzetti. The Warden, whose heart was touched by the young lawyer, had to refuse. It was too close to the hour set for the three executions.

Musmanno was on the verge of collapse.

'I want to tell them there is more mercy in their hearts than in the hearts of many who profess orthodox religion,' he said. 'I want to tell them I know they are innocent and all the gallows and electric chairs cannot change that knowledge. I want to tell them they are two of the kindest and tenderest men I have ever known.'

At the State House in the meantime, Governor Fuller talked with Mrs Sacco, Miss Vanzetti, Dr Edith B. Jackson and her brother Gardner, and Aldino Felicani of the Defense Committee.

The Governor was sorry. Everything had been done, the evidence had been carefully sifted. To prove it he called in State Attorney General Arthur K. Reading, whose legal explanations were lost on the three women. Reluctantly they left the Governor. Hope vanished.

Shortly after midnight, Warden Hendry rapped on the door leading to the interior of the prison and the death house. Musmanno, still in the Warden's office, laid a hand on Hendry's arm. 'Please, one last request.'

'No, no.'

Hendry, followed by the official witnesses, solemnly filed into the death chamber. The only reporter present at the execution was W. E. Playfair of the Associated Press. The rules limited the press to one representative, and Mr Playfair had been handed the assignment when the men were convicted in 1921.

Madeiros was the first to go. His cell was the nearest the chair. A messenger hurried to us with a bulletin.

Sacco walked the seventeen steps from his cell to the execution chamber slowly between two guards. He was calm.

'Long live anarchy,' he cried in Italian as he was strapped in the chair.

In English: 'Farewell my wife and child and all my friends.'

This was a slip probably due to his imperfect command of English. He had two children: Dante, fourteen, and Inez, six.

'Good evening, gentlemen,' he said.

Then his last words.

'Farewell, Mother.'

Vanzetti was the last to die. He shook hands with the two guards.

To Warden Hendry, he said, speaking slowly and distinctly: 'I want to thank you for everything you have done for me, Warden. I wish to tell you that I am innocent and that I have never committed any crime but sometimes some sin. [Almost the same words he had used when sentenced by Judge Thayer the previous April.] I thank you for everything you have done for me. I am innocent of all crime not only of this, but all. I am an innocent man.'

A pause.

'I wish to forgive some people for what they are now doing to me.'

The Warden was overcome. The current was turned on, and when Vanzetti was pronounced dead Hendry could scarcely whisper the formula required by law – 'Under the law I now pronounce you dead, the sentence of the court having been carried out.'

Mr Playfair lived up to his name. He dashed into our room with all the details of the last Sacco-Vanzetti story most of us were to write.

Governor Fuller remained at the State House until 12.12, a minute after Executioner Elliott had thrown the switch that ended the earthly existence of Sacco. Until a few minutes before midnight, Francis Fisher Kane had begged

Governor Fuller for a respite. Thompson, former attorney in the case, remained with the Governor until 11.45, making his final heart-rending plea for mercy.

When the Governor left the State House he knew that the Supreme Court had, on 22 August, docketed two appeals for writs of certiorari. He had a request pending before him that alienists be permitted to examine Sacco and Vanzetti, that execution be delayed until the matter of the Department of Justice's files had been cleared up. He had before him five new affidavits made by new witnesses found by the defense in the closing days. He had, or was presumed to have received from his secretary, the receipt for the eels which Vanzetti had purchased.

So that when the two men died in the electric chair the legal battle to save them was still under way and there was, in the opinion of many of the best minds in America, more than a 'reasonable doubt'. In the last hour a three- or four-hour reprieve was asked by Defense Attorney Hill so that he could fly to Williamstown in a chartered plane to consult Circuit Court Judge Anderson again.

At the naval airport Hill tried to get in touch with the Governor or the Attorney General, but without success. When a naval officer found out who Hill and his companions were, he ordered them off the grounds and told William Schuyler Jackson, a former New York Attorney General, that 'it would give me pleasure to shoot you'. Finally a reporter at the State House told them over the telephone that Sacco was in the death chamber. The long battle had ended.

BABE RUTH HITS HIS 60th HOME RUN, NEW YORK, September 1927

Mrs Babe Ruth

Legendary New York Yankees baseball player Babe Ruth (George

Herman) set the world record of 59 home runs in the 1920 season; in 1927 he hit 60 home runs.

The pennant race was over by 1 September, but Babe was fighting to break his 59 home-run record. He needed 17 to do it in the last month, or better than one every two days. He did it, of course. The 60th was made in Yankee Stadium against Washington. Tom Zachary, a left-hander, was the pitcher, and the homer came in the final game.

Babe had smashed out two home runs the day before to bring his total to 59 for the season, or the exact equal of his 1921 record. He had only this last game to set a new record. Zachary, a left-hander, was by the nature of his delivery a hard man for the Babe to hit. In fact Babe got only two homers in all his life against Tom.

Babe came up in the eighth and it was quite probable that this would be his very last chance to break his own record. My mother and I were at the game and I can still see that lovely, lovely home run. It was a tremendous poke, deep into the stands. There was never any doubt that it was going over the fence. But the question was, would it be fair? It was fair by only six glorious inches!

The Babe later professed himself to be unimpressed and unexcited and certainly not surprised by the blow. 'I knew I was going to hit it,' he insisted. I didn't, although I was now used to his rising to occasions.

What delighted him as much, more than the homer, was the spectacle of his pal, Charlie O'Leary, jumping and screaming on the coaching lines, his bald head glinting in the failing sun. Charlie had thrown away his cap in jubilation when the umps signalled the ball fair.

Babe knew the extent of Charlie's joy because he knew his little friend was almost psychopathic about his bald dome. They didn't play 'The Star-Spangled Banner' before every game then, only on festive occasions. On these occasions

Charlie would hide. The baring of Charlie's gleaming head was an appreciated tribute to the popularity of that historic homer.

I WATCH TELEVISION, LONDON, 1 August 1928

Sydney Moseley

Diary:
. . . I met a pale young man named Bartlett who is Secretary to the new Baird Television Company. *Television!* Anxious to see what it is all about . . . He invited me to go along to Long Acre where the new invention is installed. Now *that's* something! Television!

Met John Logie Baird; a charming man – a shy, quietly spoken Scot. He could serve as a model for the schoolboy's picture of a shock-haired, modest, dreamy, absent-minded inventor. Nevertheless shrewd. We sat and chatted. He told me he is having a bad time with the scoffers and sceptics – including the BBC and part of the technical press – who are trying to ridicule and kill his invention of television at its inception. I told him that if he would let me see what he has actually achieved – well, he would have to risk my damning it – or praising it! If I *were* convinced – I would battle for him. We got on well together and I have arranged to test his remarkable claim.

(Later) Saw television! Baird's partner, a tall, good-looking but highly temperamental Irishman, Captain Oliver George Hutchinson, was nice but very nervous of chancing it with me. He was terribly anxious that I should be impressed. Liked the pair of them, especially Baird, and decided to give my support . . . I think we really have what is called television. And so, once more into the fray!

THE WALL STREET CRASH, NEW YORK, 24 October 1929

Elliott V. Bell

Throughout the 1920s the USA had enjoyed a bubble of unparalleled prosperity; with the great stock-market crash of October 1929 the bubble burst, and the Great Depression was formally ushered in. The collapse of America's economy was soon followed by that of Europe's.

The day was overcast and cool. A light north-west wind blew down the canyons of Wall Street, and the temperature, in the low fifties, made bankers and brokers on their way to work button their topcoats around them. The crowds of market traders in the brokers' board rooms were nervous but hopeful as the ten o'clock hour for the start of trading approached. The general feeling was that the worst was over and a good many speculators who had prudently sold out earlier in the decline were congratulating themselves at having bought back their stocks a good deal cheaper. Seldom had the small trader had better or more uniform advice to go by.

The market opened steady with prices little changed from the previous day, though some rather large blocks, of 20,000 to 25,000 shares, came out at the start. It sagged easily for the first half-hour, and then around eleven o'clock the deluge broke.

It came with a speed and ferocity that left men dazed. The bottom simply fell out of the market. From all over the country a torrent of selling orders poured onto the floor of the Stock Exchange and there were no buying orders to meet it. Quotations of representative active issues, like Steel, Telephone, and Anaconda, began to fall two, three, five, and even ten points between sales. Less active stocks became unmarketable. Within a few moments the ticker service was hopelessly swamped and from then on no one knew what was really happening. By one-thirty the ticker tape was nearly two hours late; by two-thirty it was 147 minutes late. The last quotation was not printed on the tape until 7.08½ p.m., four hours, eight and one-half minutes after the close. In the meantime, Wall Street had lived through an incredible nightmare.

In the strange way that news of a disaster spreads, the word of the market collapse flashed through the city. By noon great crowds had gathered at the corner of Broad and Wall Streets where the Stock Exchange on one corner faces Morgan's across the way. On the steps of the Sub-Treasury Building, opposite Morgan's, a crowd of press photographers and newsreel men took up their stand. Traffic was pushed from the streets of the financial district by the crush.

It was in this wild setting that the leading bankers scurried into conference at Morgan's in a belated effort to save the day. Shortly after noon Mr Mitchell left the National City Bank and pushed his way west on Wall Street to Morgan's. No sooner had he entered than Albert H. Wiggin was seen to hurry down from the Chase National Bank, one block north. Hard on his heels came William C. Potter, head of the Guaranty Trust, followed by Seward Prosser of the Bankers Trust. Later George F. Baker, Jr, of the First National, joined the group.

The news of the bankers' meeting flashed through the streets and over the news tickers – stocks began to rally – but for many it was already too late. Thousands of traders, little and big, had gone 'overboard' in that incredible hour between eleven and twelve. Confidence in the financial and political leaders of the country, faith in the 'soundness' of economic conditions had received a shattering blow. The panic was on.

At Morgan's the heads of six banks formed a consortium – since known as the bankers' pool of October, 1929 – pledging a total of $240,000,000, or $40,000,000 each, to provide a 'cushion' of buying power beneath the falling market. In addition, other financial institutions, including James Speyer and Company and Guggenheim Brothers, sent over to Morgan's unsolicited offers of funds aggregating $100,000,000. It was not only the first authenticated instance of a bankers' pool in stocks but by far the largest concentration of pool buying power ever brought to bear on the stock market – but in the face of the panic it was pitifully inadequate.

After the bankers had met, Thomas W. Lamont, Morgan partner, came out to the crowd of newspaper reporters who had gathered in the lobby of his bank. In an understatement that has since become a Wall Street classic, he remarked:

'It seems there has been some disturbed selling in the market.'

It was at the same meeting that 'T.W.' gave to the financial community a new phrase – 'air pockets', to describe the condition in stocks for which there were no bids, but only frantic offers. (Mr Lamont said he had it from his partner, George Whitney, and the latter said he had it from some broker.)

After the meeting, Mr Lamont walked across Broad Street to the Stock Exchange to meet with the governors of the Exchange. They had been called together quietly during trading hours and they held their meeting in the rooms of the Stock Clearing Corporation so as to avoid attracting attention. Mr Lamont sat on the corner of a desk and told them about the pool. Then he said:

'Gentlemen, there is no man nor group of men who can buy all the stocks that the American public can sell.'

It seems a pretty obvious statement now, but it had a horrid sound to the assembled governors of the Exchange. It meant that the shrewdest member of the most powerful banking house in the country was telling them plainly that the assembled resources of Wall Street, mobilized on a scale never before attempted, could not stop this panic.

The bankers' pool, in fact, turned out a sorry fiasco. Without it, no doubt, the Exchange would have been forced to close, for it did supply bids at some price for the so-called pivotal stocks when, because of the panic and confusion in the market, there were no other bids available. It made a small profit, but it did not have a ghost of a chance of stemming the avalanche of selling that poured in from all over the country. The stock market had become too big. The days that followed are blurred in retrospect. Wall Street became a nightmarish spectacle.

The animal roar that rises from the floor of the Stock Exchange and which on active days is plainly audible in the Street outside, became louder, anguished, terrifying. The streets were crammed with a mixed crowd – agonized little speculators, walking aimlessly outdoors because they feared to face the ticker and the margin clerk; sold-out traders, morbidly impelled to visit the scene of their ruin; inquisitive individuals and tourists, seeking by gazing at the exteriors of the Exchange and the big banks to get a closer view of the national catastrophe; runners, frantically pushing their way through the throng of idle and curious in their effort to make deliveries of the unprecedented volume of securities which was being traded on the floor of the Exchange.

The ticker, hopelessly swamped, fell hours behind the actual trading and became completely meaningless. Far into the night, and often all night long, the lights blazed in the windows of the tall office buildings where margin clerks and bookkeepers struggled with the desperate task of trying to clear one day's business before the next began. They fainted at their desks; the weary runners fell exhausted on the marble floors of banks and slept. But within a few months they were to have ample time to rest up. By then thousands of them had been fired.

Agonizing scenes were enacted in the customers' rooms of the various brokers. There traders who a few short days before had luxuriated in delusions of wealth saw all their hopes smashed in a collapse so devastating, so far beyond their wildest fears, as to seem unreal. Seeking to save a little from the wreckage, they would order their stocks sold 'at the market', in many cases to discover that they had not merely lost everything but were, in addition, in debt to the broker. And then, ironic twist, as like as not the next few hours' wild churning of the market would lift prices to levels where they might have sold out and had a substantial cash balance left over. Every move was wrong, in those days. The market seemed like an insensate thing that was wreaking a wild and pitiless revenge upon those who had thought to master it.

The excitement and sense of danger which imbued Wall Street was like that which grips men on a sinking ship. A camaraderie, a kind of gaiety of despair, sprang up. The Wall Street reporter found all doors open and everyone snatched at him for the latest news, for shreds of rumour. Who was in trouble? Who had gone under last? Where was it going to end?

I remember dropping in to see a vice-president of one of the larger banks. He was walking back and forth in his office.

'Well, Elliott,' he said, 'I thought I was a millionaire a few days ago. Now I find I'm looking through the wrong end of the telescope.'

He laughed. Then he said: 'We'll get those bastards that did this yet.'

I never did find out whom he meant, but I learned later that he was not merely 'busted' but hopelessly in debt.

AN INTERVIEW WITH AL CAPONE, CHICAGO, 1930

Claud Cockburn

The Prohibition-era gangster Al(phonse) Capone was born in Brooklyn, but achieved his notoriety in Chicago.

The Lexington Hotel had once, I think, been a rather grand family hotel, but now its large and gloomy lobby was deserted except for a couple of bulging Sicilians and a reception clerk who looked at one across the counter with the expression of a speakeasy proprietor looking through the grille at a potential detective. He checked on my appointment with some superior upstairs, and as I stepped into the elevator I felt my hips and sides being gently frisked by the tapping hands of one of the lounging Sicilians. There were a couple of ante-rooms to be passed before you got to Capone's office and in the first of them I had to wait for a quarter of an hour or so, drinking whisky poured by a man who used his left hand for the bottle and kept the other in his pocket.

Except that there was a sub-machine-gun, operated by a man called MacGurn – whom I later got to know and somewhat esteem – poking through the transom of a door behind the big desk, Capone's own room was nearly indistinguishable from that of, say, a 'newly arrived' Texan oil millionaire. Apart from the jowly young murderer on the far side of the desk, what took the eye were a number of large, flattish, solid silver bowls upon the desk, each filled with roses. They were nice to look at, and they had another purpose too, for Capone when agitated stood up and dipped the tips of his fingers in the waters in which floated the roses.

I had been a little embarrassed as to how the interview was to be launched. Naturally the nub of all such interviews is somehow to get around to the question 'What makes you tick?' but in the case of this millionaire killer the approach to this central question seemed mined with dangerous impediments. However, on the way down to the Lexington Hotel I had had the good fortune to see, in I think the *Chicago Daily News*, some statistics offered by an insurance company which dealt with the average expectation of life of gangsters in Chicago. I forget exactly what the average expectation was, and also what the exact age of Capone at that time was – I think he was in his early thirties. The point was, however, that in any case he was four years older than the upper limit considered by the insurance company to be the proper average expectation of life for a Chicago gangster. This seemed to offer a more or less neutral and academic line of approach, and after the ordinary greetings I asked Capone whether he had read this piece of statistics in the paper. He said that he had. I asked him whether he considered the estimate reasonably accurate. He said that he thought that the insurance companies and the newspaper boys probably knew their stuff. 'In that case,' I asked him, 'how does it feel to be, say, four years over the age?'

He took the question quite seriously and spoke of the matter with neither more nor less excitement or agitation than a man would who, let us say, had been asked whether he, as the rear machine-gunner of a bomber, was aware of the average incidence of casualties in that occupation. He apparently assumed that sooner or later he would be shot despite the elaborate precautions which he regularly took. The idea that – as afterwards turned out to be the case – he would be arrested by the Federal authorities for income-tax evasion had not, I think, at that time so much as crossed his mind. And, after all, he said with a little bit of corn-and-ham somewhere at the back of his throat, supposing he had not gone into this racket? What would he have been doing? He would, he said, 'have been selling newspapers barefoot on the street in Brooklyn'.

He stood up as he spoke, cooling his finger-tips in the rose bowl in front of him. He sat down again, brooding and sighing. Despite the ham-and-corn, what he said was quite probably true and I said so, sympathetically. A little bit too sympathetically, as immediately emerged, for as I spoke I saw him looking at me suspiciously, not to say censoriously. My remarks about the harsh way the world treats barefoot boys in Brooklyn were interrupted by an urgent angry waggle of his podgy hand.

'Listen,' he said, 'don't get the idea I'm one of these

goddam radicals. Don't get the idea I'm knocking the American system. The American system . . .' As though an invisible chairman had called upon him for a few words, he broke into an oration upon the theme. He praised freedom, enterprise and the pioneers. He spoke of 'our heritage'. He referred with contemptuous disgust to Socialism and Anarchism. 'My rackets,' he repeated several times, 'are run on strictly American lines and they're going to stay that way.' This turned out to be a reference to the fact that he had recently been elected the President of the Unione Siciliano, a slightly mysterious, partially criminal society which certainly had its roots in the Mafia. Its power and importance varied sharply from year to year. Sometimes there did seem to be evidence that it was a secret society of real power, and at other times it seemed more in the nature of a mutual benefit association not essentially much more menacing than, say, the Elks. Capone's complaint just now was that the Unione was what he called 'lousy with black-hand stuff'. 'Can you imagine,' he said, 'people going in for what they call these blood feuds – some guy's grandfather was killed by some other guy's grandfather, and this guy thinks that's good enough reason to kill the other.' It was, he said, entirely unbusinesslike. His vision of the American system began to excite him profoundly and now he was on his feet again, leaning across the desk like the chairman of a board meeting, his fingers plunged in the rose bowls.

'This American system of ours,' he shouted, 'call it Americanism, call it Capitalism, call it what you like, gives to each and every one of us a great opportunity if we only seize it with both hands and make the most of it.' He held out his hand towards me, the fingers dripping a little, and stared at me sternly for a few seconds before reseating himself.

CIVIL DISOBEDIENCE, INDIA, 21 May 1930

Webb Miller

As part of their Civil Disobedience campaign to remove the British from India, the followers of Gandhi organized a protest against the Salt Tax in 1930.

After plodding about six miles across country lugging a pack of sandwiches and two quart bottles of water under a sun which was already blazing hot, inquiring from every native I met, I reached the assembling place of the Gandhi followers. Several long, open, thatched sheds were surrounded by high cactus thickets. The sheds were literally swarming and buzzed like a beehive with some 2,500 Congress or Gandhi men dressed in the regulation uniform of rough homespun cotton *dhotis* and triangular Gandhi caps, somewhat like American overseas soldiers' hats. They chattered excitedly and when I arrived hundreds surrounded me, with evidences of hostility at first. After they learned my identity, I was warmly welcomed by young college-educated, English-speaking men and escorted to Mme Naidu. The famous Indian poetess, stocky, swarthy, strong-featured, bare-legged, dressed in rough, dark homespun robe and sandals, welcomed me. She explained that she was busy martialling her forces for the demonstration against the salt pans and would talk with me more at length later. She was educated in England and spoke English fluently.

Mme Naidu called for prayer before the march started and the entire assemblage knelt. She exhorted them, 'Gandhi's body is in gaol but his soul is with you. India's prestige is in your hands. You must not use any violence under any circumstances. You will be beaten but you must not resist; you must not even raise a hand to ward off blows.' Wild, shrill cheers terminated her speech.

Slowly and in silence the throng commenced the half-mile march to the salt deposits. A few carried ropes for lassoing the barbed-wire stockade around the salt pans. About a score who were assigned to act as stretcher-bearers wore crude, hand-painted red crosses pinned to their breasts; their stretchers consisted of blankets. Manilal Gandhi, second son of Gandhi, walked among the foremost of the marchers. As the throng drew near the salt pans they commenced chanting the revolutionary slogan, *Inquilab zindabad*, intoning the two words over and over.

The salt deposits were surrounded by ditches filled with water and guarded by 400 native Surat police in khaki shorts and brown turbans. Half-a-dozen British officials commanded them. The police carried *lathis* – five-foot clubs tipped with steel. Inside the stockade twenty-five native riflemen were drawn up.

In complete silence the Gandhi men drew up and halted 100 yards from the stockade. A picked column advanced from the crowd, waded the ditches, and approached the barbed-wire stockade, which the Surat police surrounded, holding their clubs at the ready. Police officials ordered the marchers to disperse under a recently imposed regulation which prohibited gatherings of more than five persons in any one place. The column silently ignored the warning and slowly walked forward. I stayed with the main body about 100 yards from the stockade.

Suddenly, at a word of command, scores of native police rushed upon the advancing marchers and rained blows on their heads with their steel-shod *lathis*. Not one of the marchers even raised an arm to fend off the blows. They went down like ten-pins. From where I stood I heard the sickening whacks of the clubs on unprotected skulls. The waiting crowd of watchers groaned and sucked in their breaths in sympathetic pain at every blow.

Those struck down fell sprawling, unconscious or writhing in pain with fractured skulls or broken shoulders. In two or three minutes the ground was quilted with bodies. Great patches of blood widened on their white clothes. The survivors without breaking ranks silently and doggedly marched on until struck down. When every one of the first column had been knocked down stretcher-bearers rushed up unmolested by the police and carried off the injured to a thatched hut which had been arranged as a temporary hospital.

Then another column formed while the leaders pleaded with them to retain their self-control. They marched slowly toward the police. Although every one knew that within a few minutes he would be beaten down, perhaps killed, I could detect no signs of wavering or fear. They marched steadily with heads up, without the encouragement of music or cheering or any possibility that they might escape serious injury or death. The police rushed out and methodically and mechanically beat down the second column. There was no fight, no struggle; the marchers simply walked forward until struck down. There were no outcries, only groans after they fell. There were not enough stretcher-bearers to carry off the wounded; I saw eighteen injured being carried off simultaneously, while forty-two still lay bleeding on the ground awaiting stretcher-bearers. The blankets used as stretchers were sodden with blood . . .

In the middle of the morning V. J. Patel arrived. He had been leading the Swaraj movement since Gandhi's arrest, and had just resigned as President of the Indian Legislative Assembly in protest against the British. Scores surrounded him, knelt, and kissed his feet. He was a venerable gentleman of about sixty with white flowing beard and moustache, dressed in the usual undyed, coarse homespun smock. Sitting on the ground under a mango tree, Patel said, 'All hope of reconciling India with the British Empire is lost for ever. I can understand any government's taking people into custody and punishing them for breaches of the law, but I cannot understand how any government that calls itself civilized

could deal as savagely and brutally with non-violent,
unresisting men as the British have this morning.'

By eleven the heat reached 116 degrees in the shade and
the activities of the Gandhi volunteers subsided. I went back
to the temporary hospital to examine the wounded. They lay
in rows on the bare ground in the shade of an open, palm-
thatched shed. I counted 320 injured, many still insensible
with fractured skulls, others writhing in agony from kicks in
the testicles and stomach. The Gandhi men had been able to
gather only a few native doctors, who were doing the best
they could with the inadequate facilities. Scores of the
injured had received no treatment for hours and two had
died. The demonstration was finished for the day on account
of the heat.

I was the only foreign correspondent who had witnessed
the amazing scene – a classic example of *satyagraha* or non-
violent civil disobedience.

THE TEST MATCH, LORDS, 28–30 June 1930

E. W. Swanton

There were so many memorable things about the Lord's Test
Match of 1930 that the picture of it, in all its splendour and
excitement, remains fresh in the mind's eye to this day. It
contained some wonderful batsmanship by some of the
greatest players in the game's history, and for all four days
the sun poured down on what was then the largest crowd
(115,000) ever to see a cricket match in England.

There were four hundreds, by K. S. Duleepsinhji, Woodfull, Bradman, and Chapman. 'Duleep's' 173 came in his
first Test against Australia and Bradman's 254 was at the
moment of its making the highest score ever made by an
Australian in a Test. Yet England, whose two innings
totalled exactly 800, were brought, on the fourth and last

day, from the brink of defeat to a real prospect of a draw, and when finally the ending of their second innings at half past three meant that a definite result was certain it seemed for a palpitating half-hour that they might even defy all possibility and snatch a victory.

That did not happen, but when young McCabe made the winning hit in the evening sunshine to give Australia their first win in England in nine Test Matches there was such an aura of content at a battle bravely fought, such a sense of honour being satisfied all round, as characterises only the great sporting occasions.

This, however, was not only in itself a tremendous contest that put the emotions under the severest strain from first to last; it was also one that marked, and was seen to mark by all who were at Lord's on Saturday 28 and Monday 30 June, the arrival of a cricketer of unique gifts whose play would henceforth dominate the game as it had not been dominated since the era of W. G. Don Bradman had come to England two months before, a young man of twenty-one who, after being dropped for one match during the Australian series of 1928–29, had scored a hundred in the Fifth Test. Here he had opened the season in a burst of glory at Worcester, reached a thousand runs by the last day of May, and followed this with a hundred of rare skill and maturity that came near to denying England victory in the First Test at Trent Bridge. 'Plum' Warner was already announcing the arrival of a new star of extraordinary brightness. But it was this Lord's innings that clinched the matter.

When in Australia nearly seventeen years later, with almost every batting record then to his name, and his fame supreme, I asked Don what was the best innings he had ever played, he said at once 'My 254 at Lord's,' going on, characteristically, to give as his reasons 'because I never hit the ball anywhere but in the middle of the bat, and I never lifted one off the ground until the stroke from which I was out'. Bradman's innings turned the match and made the foundation from which Australia were to regain the Ashes. But before passing on to the story of the game let us make a brief survey of the company.

The England XI, led by Percy Chapman, contained Jack Hobbs, greatest of all professional batsmen, at the age of forty-seven playing in his *tenth* and final series against Australia. It contained in Maurice Tate probably the finest bowler of his type ever seen. It contained two of the greatest all-round cricketers of any country or generation, Frank Woolley and Walter Hammond. It contained 'Duleep', whose illness at the height of his powers was soon to deprive the game of a genius. It contained two of cricket's immortal characters, 'Patsy' Hendren and George Duckworth. Not least it contained as many as five past, present or future captains of England – Percy Chapman, Jack White, 'Gubby' Allen, Walter Robins and Walter Hammond.

Allow for the enthusiasm of youth, and the enchantment that time lends to the distant view, and it still seems an incomparable collection of talent and personality. Note, by the way, that Herbert Sutcliffe and Harold Larwood were missing, both because of injury. The latter, contrary to general belief, was as a rule expensive on the English Test wickets of his day, but Sutcliffe, of course, was and had been since 1924 the inseparable complement to Hobbs. How he might have relished England's long rearguard in the second innings!

If some of the Australian names by comparison suffer a little in lustre and tend to be dwarfed by Bradman, they likewise include a rich assortment of the great. When has Australia had a better opening pair than Woodfull and Ponsford, a finer wicket-keeper than Oldfield, a leg-spin bowler superior to Grimmett, batsmen more gracious in style than McCabe and Kippax?

Vic Richardson, Woodfull's successor as captain and for long a commanding figure on the Australian scene, and the bowlers Wall, Fairfax and Hornibrook complete the *dramatis personae* of the Lord's Test of 1930. It is, by the way, a rather sad coincidence that although the England team was senior in age to the Australian – only two of the latter, Woodfull and Fairfax, have passed on, whereas three only of their opponents, Allen, Robins and Woolley, have survived.

Frank Woolley, whose eightieth birthday will shortly be upon us! He it was who began this game on a note of such transcendent quality that though his innings was inconsiderable in the context of the final score it remains clear in the minds of anyone with whom one ever discusses the match – and not least the Australians. The circumstances of Woolley's opening the innings with Hobbs – the only time he went in first for England in 64 Test Matches – are worth a short digression. From 1909 to 1926 inclusive Woolley played for England 52 times successively. His omission at the age of forty-one from the M.C.C. side to Australia in 1928–29 led to what in those days of more reticent cricket writing passed for an uproar.

For Woolley was not only an idol in Kent, he was an institution among cricket crowds everywhere, a debonair, exciting punisher of every sort of bowling whose batting flourished in an atmosphere of charm and personality that set it right apart. Denis Compton had his army of devoted 'fans' and so did Walter Hammond, but neither even of these, I think, commanded quite such a following as Woolley. And among their number I was as a young man – and still am, in upper middle age – not the least ardent and faithful.

Woolley had been discarded for Australia, be it added, at the end of his most triumphant season. In 1928 he made 3,352 runs, an aggregate which then had been only once exceeded. The following summer, when the South Africans came, he was omitted from the first two drawn Tests wherein the English batting did not greatly distinguish itself. Recalled at this point he led the way with three characteristically easy, majestic innings of 83, 95 not out, and 154 which paved the way to the two victories that settled the series, and at the same time, as it was felt from Blackheath down to Dover, put the selectors in their places.

But in the first 1930 Test at Trent Bridge the great man had fallen for 0 and 5. Again he had been omitted, in favour this time of 'Duleep', and was only drafted back when Sutcliffe dropped out. This, then, was for Woolley and for all his array of worshippers the crucial appearance. He was forty-three, certainly, but these were not the days when a man was thought to be 'over the hill' in his middle thirties. Why, Hobbs, his only superior in terms of fame and achievement, who was now accompanying him to the wicket, was nearly five years older.

Wall, from the Pavilion end, began the game with a maiden to Hobbs. Fairfax bowled at the other, and Woolley simply leaned on his first ball and sent it flashing up the hill, to rattle among the seats under the Grand Stand balcony behind cover point. (I know because I was sitting there in the Press Box annexe.) The next three-quarters of an hour were pure heaven. Even the dismissal of Hobbs, soon caught behind off Wall, seemed a relatively minor incident as one watched the Australian attack plundered with a succession of strokes that held the crowd in wonder and fascination.

Forty minutes after he had received his first ball, his score now 41, Woolley faced Fairfax, who had taken over from Wall at the Pavilion end. Fairfax dropped one a little short and Woolley came down on the ball and cut it left-handed just behind square with the speed of light. No gully could conceivably have arrested the stroke, but Wall had retreated until he was almost a pitch's length from the bat. Instinctively he grabbed at something red hurtling straight at his boots, and incredibly the catch stuck. So ended one of the little masterpieces of batting, and the hundred before lunch – before one o'clock, I dare say – that never was.

Hammond batted hesitantly. At this stage of his career he was in Tests at home only a shadow of his great self, probably because he was trying to repeat the very cautious methods he had employed to make his huge scores on the flawless Australian wickets of 1928–9 when time was no object. When he was drawn forward by Grimmett and bowled off his pads England were 105 for three. But Woolley had lit the torch, and it was the batting from now on that held the stage throughout the game.

So far as the two England innings went this was despite the excellence of Grimmett. The wicket was particularly comfortable in pace but the little man kept pegging away from the Nursery end, using all his resources of spin and flight, bowling a little 'flatter' and faster to the quicker-footed, tossing the ball a little higher to the rest, and giving it an accordingly sharper tweak. He was the foundation of the Australian attack of 1930, and it was the punishment he took after lunch at the hands of Duleep and Hendren that put England, temporarily at least, on top. No one was more nimble at coming to meet slow bowling than little Patsy, while the lithe Duleep, with his oriental speed of eye, though he moved much more deliberately, achieved the same results.

These two made 104 together in an hour and a half. However, the new ball accounted not only for Hendren but also for Chapman and Allen, the latter playing in his first Test Match. For a second time the innings was set on its feet, thanks now to Tate. Many a great bowler fancies himself as a batsman but few of his kind have been as effective as Maurice, who in his youth used to open the Sussex innings and over his Test career had the more than useful average for a number eight bat of 25. No stylist, he played straight in defence and gave the half-volley a hearty thump. In a boyish way Maurice had a keen sense of theatre. The scene and the situation were just up his street. The seventh wicket added 98 in seventy minutes, and, when Tate left, Duleep embarked on an all-out assault.

There is some uncertainty over the tactical plan late in the day which at this distance cannot be exactly determined. This was only the second four-day Test to be contested in England, and the critics all had different ideas as to how it should be planned. At six o'clock, so legend has it, Archie Maclaren, the arch-pundit, was brandishing his umbrella in the Long Room and declaiming that 'Percy must be mad'. A declaration was the obvious policy, thought he, with the aim a couple of wickets before close of play.

Did Duleep receive a hurry-up signal from the dressing-room balcony? Evidence is conflicting, but when at quarter past six he was caught at long-off by Bradman off Grimmett, his uncle, 'Ranji', though expressing the greatest pride in his nephew's achievement, is said also to have exclaimed, 'the boy was always careless'. Well, the careless boy had made 173 in five hours, and, far from declaring, Chapman let the innings run its course next morning.

By close of play that hot, eventful Saturday everyone, including presumably Maclaren, was a little wiser about the waging of a four-day match, at any rate when Bradman was around. Who does not remember the Saturday of his first Lord's Test? With me the picture of this one stands clear: the crowd in baking heat, spilling out on to the grass, watching quietly while Woodfull and Ponsford laid their careful foundations, equally at home against all the English bowling except for an occasional tester from Tate; the inspection of troops by the King in mid-afternoon, the small, slight, bearded figure of King George with grey bowler hat, button-hole, and rather high walking-stick, moving up and down the lines of the teams while the crowd stood, thankfully taking the chance to stretch their legs; the fall of Ponsford to the first ball afterwards, caught Hammond, bowled White – the origin, this, of the tradition that the monarch's visit is generally worth a wicket to England; and finally the brilliant, relentless taking to pieces of the England bowling by Bradman.

Over his career Bradman was rarely a spectacular starter.

His innings tended to come gradually to full glory from quiet, methodical beginnings. But now he almost leapt down the pitch at White's first ball, reached it on the full-pitch and smacked it crisply to the boundary under the Nursery clock-tower. This was his first sight in England of 'Farmer' White, whose length and wonderful control had pegged down the Australians so completely on their own wickets the previous year. Bradman literally jumped at the chance of showing his mastery, and White was known afterwards to say that such was Don's speed of eye and foot he believed he need never have let him bounce unless he had wanted to. But Bradman was equally at home with everyone, and while Woodfull, almost unnoticed, pursued his worthy way the runs accrued at a remarkable rate at the other end.

In the last two hours forty minutes of play Australia went from 162 for one to 404 for two: 242 runs, of which Bradman's share was 155. In fact he caught up Woodfull who, having had three hours start, was stumped off Robins for 155 just before the close. The implications of Bradman's assault were quickly realized. My predecessor, Colonel Philip Trevor, remarked in Monday's *Daily Telegraph* that no one before had seen a side get more than 400 in a Test in England, 'and at the end of the second day's play have to ask themselves if they are going to be beaten'.

M. D. Lyon was contributing a daily piece to the news pages, and alongside a report of how a sun-bathing 'club' was attacked and beaten up by a crowd of outraged citizens at the Welsh Harp at Hendon, he glanced prophetically, and with the most accurate insight, into the immediate future. 'Suppose Australia add a further 330 runs by five o'clock,' he wrote, 'then Woodfull will be able to declare with perfect safety, for they have an innings in hand, and England will be batting under a severe psychological disadvantage, with only a draw or defeat the possible result.'

In fact Australia made 325 more and declared at the tea interval, with all sorts of records lying strewn in their wake:

notably, Bradman's 254, the highest Test score in England and the second highest in England-Australia matches, while 729 for six was the largest of all totals by either side in either country. And there was the somewhat grim comedy of the delay in finding the figure seven for the hundreds column on the Tavern score-board. Kippax, batting with the utmost polish, scored almost run for run with Bradman in their long partnership for the third wicket, whereafter all the Australians who got to the crease made runs and made them fast. This was despite a high standard of English fielding, wherein Chapman was the brightest ornament. It was a superb one-handed catch by the captain, wide to his right, at silly-mid-off that at last disposed of Bradman. The Australian run-rate over their innings was just over 70 an hour, probably the most rapid in the history of Anglo-Australian Tests – and be it noted that England in those less sophisticated days bowled their overs at only a fraction under 23 an hour. Twenty-three! The attack, well-assorted in method if expensive in result, comprised Allen, Tate, White, Robins, Hammond, and Woolley. Your modern cynic may remark that had the captain and his bowlers connived in 'going slow', and delivered, say, at the average rate of the recent series in Australia, the protraction of the Australian innings would have resulted in England easily saving the match. But let me not philosophise painfully about that!

As it was, England's task was in the highest degree formidable, and at nightfall it was still more so with Hobbs bowled round his legs sweeping at a ball that pitched in the follow-through marks and Woolley out hit wicket, having brushed the stumps with his leg as he forced Grimmett to the mid-wicket boundary. Hammond and Duleep lasted out and next morning took the score to 129, but with both of them, and Hendren also, out with 147 on the board England were apparently sliding fast to an innings defeat.

Now came the last of the batting episodes that lifts this game high among the classics. Allen, with a hitherto unsuccessful First Test behind him, joined Chapman around twelve o'clock, their side still 157 runs in arrear. The stand began inauspiciously, for Chapman, misreading Grimmett's googly, so his partner maintains, at once spooned the ball up into the covers where Richardson and Ponsford each left the catch to the other. Thus reprieved, Chapman turned his particular attention to Grimmett while Allen batted in an orthodox and attractive way.

At lunch both had reached 50, and only 42 were needed to make Australia bat again. We had seen some intelligent aggressive cricket, with Allen mostly at the Nursery end taking the faster bowling while Grimmett was attacked by the left-hander. But here is another curiosity. 'Gubby' Allen was under the impression all the morning that so far as possible this was the plan that was being followed, but when on going out again in the afternoon he asked whether they should carry on as before, Percy surprised him by saying, 'Oh, you can't do that in a Test Match.' Chapman had great personal qualities as a captain – indeed, in my time I doubt that England has had another as good when all virtues are weighed in the scales – but his make-up was an unusual mixture of the shrewd and the naïve.

As it happened, Allen was soon out, but Chapman went from strength to strength, hitting four sixes and 12 fours in an innings of 121 that lasted just over two hours and a half. There could be no clearer example of the old axiom about attack being so often the best mode of defence.

Chapman's play, sketchy at first and growing in power and certainty the longer he batted, was of course just the medicine the crowd were praying for. In particular they enjoyed his onslaught on Grimmett, who was in almost permanent occupation of the Nursery End, and whose spin down the Lord's 'hill' the right-handers found so difficult to confront. Here Chapman was at an advantage, for to him the ball turned in, towards the bat, not away, threatening its outer edge for a catch at slip or behind the wicket.

Chapman, thrusting out his right leg to cover the stumps –
and not incommoded, incidentally, by the present Law
which came to pass a few years later – either stunned the
ball with hands and handle well forward of the bottom of the
bat, or hit it with a full swing into the country down by the
Mound Stand and the Tavern.

After lunch he discarded the Cambridge Quidnunc cap of
blue with the vertical yellow stripes which was his normal
wear, and the change in appearance was symbolic. Bareheaded, literally, he went for the Australian bowling, hitting
Grimmett not only into the boundary fence but over it into
the crowd. Did not one such blow whistle through the
narrow aperture between the score-board and the Tavern
and land in St John's Wood Road? Such details are not easy
to confirm getting on for forty years later, but I fancy so. At
all events the bombardment in that quarter was pretty
severe, and it was fine disciplined hitting calling for a nice
coordination of cool head and eye attuned. This undoubtedly was Chapman's finest hour. When at last Chapman was
caught behind the wicket there was now a real chance of
saving the game, but Robins, with the impetuosity of youth,
called White for a hard hit to Bradman lying deep at mid-off,
and 'the Farmer', in his fortieth year, was easily beaten by a
fast return. This incident, followed as it was by an ill-judged
rebuke in the dressing-room between innings from 'Shrimp'
Leveson-Gower, the chairman of selectors, and a characteristically blunt rejoinder by Robins, caused the latter's
dropping for the subsequent Tests of the series – but he
still had a dramatic part to play in this one.

Australia went in half an hour before tea, needing only 72
to win, but the wicket after all the traffic of the four days and
having been baked by unusual heat was now definitely
dusty. Robins was brought on for the fifth over and at once
should have had Woodfull caught at mid-on. But with the
next ball Robins bowled Ponsford, while at the other end
Bradman was marvellously caught in the gully by Chapman

off a genuine late cut. Robins' wrist-spin for several overs continued to look infinitely dangerous, and the crowd was on the tip-toe of excitement. Duckworth caught Kippax off him (23 for three) and if the 'keeper could have taken a second chance offered by Woodfull, Australia would probably have been struggling for their lives. But the magic moment passed, Robins' length grew uncertain, and the placid Woodfull was sensibly supported by McCabe.

So Australia coasted home, and, though there was some grumbling afterwards about the poor state of English bowling, no one grudged the winners their success: certainly not Chapman, who after winning six successive Tests against Australia now found himself on the losing end for the one and only time. 'It has been a great match,' he said, 'and I think that the people who came each day to see it must have been well rewarded by the fine struggle they saw. Australia fully deserved their victory, for they played splendid cricket at every point.' Woodfull's comment was equally congratulatory and generous. Those were courteous days.

HUNGER MARCHERS, WASHINGTON, December 1931

John Dos Passos

The Great Depression, which had begun with the Wall Street Crash in 1929, was the worst this century. By the early 1930s over twelve million people were unemployed in the United States – more than a quarter of the workforce.

Washington has a drowsy look in the early December sunlight. The Greco-Roman porticoes loom among the bare trees, as vaguely portentous as phrases about democracy in the mouth of a Southern Senator. The Monument, a finger of light cut against a lavender sky, punctuates the antiquated rhetoric of the Treasury and the White House. On the hill, above its tall foundation banked with magnolia trees, the dome of the Capitol bulges smugly. At nine o'clock groups of sleepy-looking cops in well-brushed uniforms and shiny-visored caps are straggling up the hill. At the corner of Pennsylvania Avenue and John Marshall Place a few hunger marchers stand around the trucks they came in. They looked tired and frowzy from the long ride. Some of them are strolling up and down the avenue. That end of the avenue, with its gimcrack stores, boarded-up burlesque shows, Chinese restaurants and flophouses, still has a little of the jerkwater, out-in-the-sticks look it must have had when Lincoln drove up it in a barouche through the deep mud or Jefferson rode to his inauguration on his own quiet nag.

Two elderly labouring men are looking out of a cigar-store door at a bunch of Reds, young Jewish boys from New York or Chicago, with the white armbands of the hunger marchers. 'Won't get nutten that a-way,' one of them says. 'Whose payin' for it anyway, hirin' them trucks and gasoline . . . Somebody's payin' for it,' barks the clerk indignantly from behind the cash register. 'Better'd spent it on grub or to buy 'emselves overcoats,' says the older man. The man who first spoke shakes his head sadly. 'Never won't get nutten that a-way.' Out along the avenue a few Washingtonians look at the trucks and old moving vans with *Daily Worker* cartoons pasted on their sides. They stand a good way off, as if they were afraid the trucks would explode; they are obviously swallowing their unfavourable comments for fear some of the marchers might hear them. Tough eggs, these Reds.

At ten o'clock the leaders start calling to their men to fall in. Some tall cops appear and bawl out drivers of cars that get into the streets reserved for the marchers to form up in. The marchers form in a column of fours. They don't look as if they'd had much of a night's rest. They look quiet and serious and anxious to do the right thing. Leaders, mostly bareheaded youngsters, run up and down, hoarse and nervous, keeping everybody in line. Most of them look like city dwellers, men and women from the needle trades, restaurant workers, bakery or laundry employees. There's a good sprinkling of Negroes among them. Here and there the thick shoulders and light hair of a truck driver or farm hand stand out. Motorcycle cops begin to cluster around the edges. The marchers are receiving as much attention as distinguished foreign officials.

Up on the hill, cordons of cops are everywhere, making a fine showing in the late-fall sunshine. There's a considerable crowd standing around; it's years since Washington has been interested in the opening of Congress. They are roping off the route for the hunger marchers. They stop a taxicab that is discovered to contain a small white-haired Senator. He curses the cops out roundly and is hurriedly escorted under the portals.

Inside the Capitol things are very different. The light is amber and greenish, as in an aquarium. Elderly clerks white as termites move sluggishly along the corridors, as if beginning to stir after a long hibernation. The elevator boy is very pale. 'Here comes the army of the unfed,' he says, pointing spitefully out of the window. 'And they're carrying banners, though Charlie Curtis said they couldn't.' A sound of music comes faintly in. Led by a band with silvery instruments like Christmas-tree ornaments that look cheerful in the bright sunlight, the hunger marchers have started up Capitol Hill. Just time to peep down into the Senate Chamber where elderly parties and pasty-faced pages are beginning to gather. Ever seen a section of a termite nest under glass?

There's a big crowd in the square between the Capitol and the Congressional Library. On the huge ramps of the steps that lead to the central portico the metropolitan police have placed some additional statuary; tastefully arranged groups of cops with rifles, riot guns and brand-new tear-gas pistols that look as if they'd just come from Sears, Roebuck. People whisper

'machine-gun nests', but nobody seems to know where they
are. There's a crowd on the roof around the base of the dome,
faces are packed in all the windows. Everybody looks cheerful,
as if a circus had come to town, anxious to be shown. The
marchers fill the broad semicircle in front of the Capitol, each
group taking up its position in perfect order, as if the show had
been rehearsed. The band, playing 'Solidarity Forever'
(which a newspaper woman beside me recognizes as 'On-
ward Christian Soldiers'), steps out in front. It's a curious little
band, made up of martini-horns, drums, cymbals and a lyre
that goes tinkle, tinkle. It plays cheerfully and well, led by a
drum major with a red tasselled banner on the end of his staff,
and repeats again and again 'The Red Flag', 'Solidarity', and
other tunes variously identified by people in the crowd. Above
the heads of the marchers are banners with slogans printed out:
IN THE LAST WAR WE FOUGHT FOR THE BOSSES: IN THE NEXT WAR WE'LL
FIGHT FOR THE WORKERS . . . $150 CASH . . . FULL PAY FOR UNEMPLOYMENT
RELIEF. The squad commanders stand out in front like cheer-
leaders at a football game and direct the chanting: 'We
Demand – Unemployed Insurance, We Demand – Unemployed Insurance, WE DEMAND – UNEMPLOYED INSURANCE.'

A deep-throated echo comes back from the Capitol façade
a few beats later than each shout. It's as if the statues and the
classical-revival republican ornaments in the pediment were
shouting too.

A small group leaves the ranks and advances across the
open space towards the Senate side. All the tall cops drawn
up in such fine order opposite the hunger marchers stick out
their chests. Now it's coming. A tremor goes over the groups
of statuary so tastefully arranged on the steps. The tear-gas
pistols glint in the sun. The marchers stand in absolute
silence.

Under the portal at the Senate entrance the swinging
doors are protected by two solid walls of blue serge. Cameramen and reporters converge with a run. Three men are
advancing with the demands of the hunger marchers written

out. They are the centre of a big group of inspectors, sergeants, gold and silver braid of the Capitol and metropolitan police. A young fellow with a camera is hanging from the wall by the door. 'Move the officer out of the way,' he yells. 'Thank you . . . A little back, please lady, I can't see his face . . . Now hand him the petition.'

'We're not handing petitions, we're making demands,' says the leader of the hunger marchers. Considerable waiting around. The Sergeant at Arms sends word they can't be let in. Somebody starts to jostle, the cops get tough, cop voices snarl. The committee goes back to report while the band plays the 'Internationale' on marini-horns and lyre . . .

HITLER IS APPOINTED CHANCELLOR, GERMANY, 29–30 January 1933

Joachim von Ribbentrop

A wine merchant who became a member of Hitler's National Socialist Party, Ribbentrop, along with President Hindenburg and his ministers, principally Franz von Papen, played a key role in the backstairs dealings which saw Hitler placed in power.

Diary: Sunday, 29 January:
At eleven a.m. long Hitler-Papen talk. Hitler declared that on the whole everything was clear. But there would have to be general elections and an Enabling Law. Papen saw Hindenburg immediately. I lunched with Hitler at the Kaiserhof. We discussed the elections. As Hindenburg does not want these, Hitler asked me to tell the President that these would be the last elections. In the afternoon Göring and I went to Papen. Papen declared that all obstacles are removed and that Hindenburg expects Hitler tomorrow at eleven a.m.

Monday, 30 January: Hitler appointed Chancellor.

SIR MALCOLM CAMPBELL BREAKS THE LAND SPEED RECORD, DAYTONA BEACH, 22 February 1933

Daily Express *reporter*

Campbell's average speed in *Bluebird* was 273mph.

The beach was full of mist at first and he could not take the car out. Then the mist rose, and there was visibility for a few hundred yards.

The officials suggested that Campbell should give [only] an exhibition run.

But he refused to disappoint the thousands who had come to Daytona for a public holiday – today being Washington's birthday.

Nor was he deterred by the fact that today was the anniversary of the death of an American speed king while racing on these very sands.

Campbell's start had been delayed for three weeks by his own attack of influenza – with a temperature of 102 – and by the weather. And his achievement today was all the greater in that the course had been shortened from eleven miles to nine. It takes some miles to get up speed before passing over the electrical timing wires.

Thousands of people held their breath as the great car – a mere blur – flashed out of the mist half a mile away, zipped past and then was lost in the mist again.

At the end of the first run Campbell, with white overalls over his plus fours, stepped out of the car into a madly cheering throng of American mechanics.

He had a look round, changed tyres, and in half an hour sped off on the return trip.

At the end of the second trip, with the record definitely smashed, he lit a cigarette, examined the canvas stitching through his torn tyres and described his experiences.

Then it was seen that heavy bandaging covered his crippled arm.

'It was terrifying,' he said. 'I lost all sense of direction. Several times I thought I was heading for the sea on one side or the sand hills on the other. I was bounced around like a pea in a pod.

'It takes a lot to frighten me, but if I did not believe in Bluebird with all my heart I would never have faced that return run. Wobbling at 270 miles an hour is not too pleasant.

'I had to keep for safety to a strip 40 yards wide. That's very little when you're travelling at 146 yards a second. I'd find myself shooting out of some mist heading heaven knows where.'

THE REICHSTAG FIRE, BERLIN, 23 February 1933

D. Sefton Delmer

The arson of the German parliament building was allegedly the work of a Communist-sympathizing Dutchman, van der Lubbe. More probably, the fire was started by the Nazis, who used the incident as a pretext to outlaw political opposition and introduce dictatorship.

'This is a God-given signal! If this fire, as I believe, turns out to be the handiwork of Communists, then there is nothing that shall stop us now crushing out this murder pest with an iron fist.'

Adolf Hitler, Fascist Chancellor of Germany, made this dramatic declaration in my presence tonight in the hall of the burning Reichstag building.

The fire broke out at 9.45 tonight in the Assembly Hall of the Reichstag.

It had been laid in five different corners and there is no doubt whatever that it was the handiwork of incendiaries.

One of the incendiaries, a man aged thirty, was arrested by the police as he came rushing out of the building, clad only in shoes and trousers, without shirt or coat, despite the icy cold in Berlin tonight.

Five minutes after the fire had broken out I was outside the Reichstag watching the flames licking their way up the great dome into the tower.

A cordon had been flung round the building and no one was allowed to pass it.

After about twenty minutes of fascinated watching I suddenly saw the famous black motor car of Adolf Hitler slide past, followed by another car containing his personal bodyguard.

I rushed after them and was just in time to attach myself to the fringe of Hitler's party as they entered the Reichstag.

Never have I seen Hitler with such a grim and determined expression. His eyes, always a little protuberant, were almost bulging out of his head.

Captain Göring, his right-hand man, who is the Prussian Minister of the Interior, and responsible for all police affairs, joined us in the lobby. He had a very flushed and excited face.

'This is undoubtedly the work of Communists, Herr Chancellor,' he said.

'A number of Communist deputies were present here in the Reichstag twenty minutes before the fire broke out. We have succeeded in arresting one of the incendiaries.'

'Who is he?' Dr Goebbels, the propaganda chief of the Nazi Party, threw in.

'We do not know yet,' Captain Göring answered, with an ominously determined look around his thin, sensitive mouth. 'But we shall squeeze it out of him, have no doubt, doctor.'

We went into a room. 'Here you can see for yourself, Herr Chancellor, the way they started the fire,' said Captain

Göring, pointing out the charred remains of some beautiful oak panelling.

'They hung cloths soaked in petrol over the furniture here and set it alight.'

We strode across another lobby filled with smoke. The police barred the way. 'The candelabra may crash any moment, Herr Chancellor,' said a captain of the police, with his arms outstretched.

By a detour we next reached a part of the building which was actually in flames. Firemen were pouring water into the red mass.

Hitler watched them for a few moments, a savage fury blazing from his pale blue eyes.

Then we came upon Herr von Papen, urbane and debonair as ever.

Hitler stretched out his hand and uttered the threat against the Communists which I have already quoted. He then turned to Captain Göring. 'Are all the other public buildings safe?' he questioned.

'I have taken every precaution,' answered Captain Göring. 'The police are in the highest state of alarm, and every public building has been specially garrisoned. We are waiting for anything.'

It was then that Hitler turned to me. 'God grant', he said, 'that this is the work of the Communists. You are witnessing the beginning of a great new epoch in German history. This fire is the beginning.'

And then something touched the rhetorical spring in his brain.

'You see this flaming building,' he said, sweeping his hand dramatically around him. 'If this Communist spirit got hold of Europe for but two months it would be all aflame like this building.'

By 12.30 the fire had been got under control. Two Press rooms were still alight, but there was no danger of the fire spreading.

Although the glass of the dome has burst and crashed to the ground the dome still stands.

So far it has not been possible to disentangle the charred debris and see whether the bodies of any incendiaries, who may have been trapped in the building, are among it.

At the Prussian Ministry of the Interior a special meeting was called late tonight by Captain Göring to discuss measures to be taken as a consequence of the fire.

The entire district from the Brandenburg Gate, on the west, to the River Spree, on the east, is isolated tonight by numerous cordons of police.

ARMS TRADING, SHANGHAI, May 1934
'GH'

One of the facts that most impresses the visitor to Shanghai is that the importers of this city, no matter what goods they specialize in, are always quite ready to undertake to procure a consignment of arms, better, cheaper and deadlier than those of any competitor. On board cargo boats lying off Shanghai there are large cases, ostensibly marked 'Bibles', 'Pianos', 'Umbrellas', or 'Glassware'. In the language of slave traders in the Red Sea, everyone knows that when a pass is signed for 'Mules', human ones are referred to. So, in the dealer's language in Shanghai, 'Bibles' mean revolvers, 'Pianos' mean mitrailleuses, 'Umbrellas' mean rifles, and 'Glassware' bullets.

Often as China has received foreign loans, seldom has she ever had ready money in her hands. In the past, when loans were concluded with China, it was generally in order that they should be used for the purchase of arms from the countries floating the loans. Two Viennese banks, the Niederoesterreichische Escompte-Gesellschaft and the Oesterreichische Boden-Kreditanstalt, concluded three big loans in China just before the war, only on the condition that most of the loans should be spent on battleships constructed at the Cantiere Navale Triestino, and on munitions from the Skoda Works in Pilsen. Quite officially, today, English firms deliver tanks and steel plates; the French deliver big cannons, the Czechoslovakians deliver mitrailleuses; the Norwegians, explosives; the Belgians, revolvers; the Swedes, military searchlights; the Germans, poison gas; the Americans, nitrate and gun-cotton. Unofficially, this trade assumes bigger proportions, and everybody is ready to close an eye when it is a question of arms smuggling.

In 1919 the American Minister in Peking did propose to the other great powers an arms embargo agreement, by which the contracting parties should agree not to deliver arms and munitions to China until a stabilized form of government was formed. The great parties duly signed the agreement, which was later submitted to and signed by Italy, the Netherlands, Denmark and Belgium. The only important country not asked to sign the agreement was Germany, since in 1919 Germans were regarded by the Allies as mere 'Huns', not worthy to associate with other members of the concert of nations. Fortunately for the arms industry, gentlemen know how to keep a gentlemen's agreement. Thus, when the troops of Wu-Pei-Fu appeared wearing British trench helmets, the British Government declared that they only supplied China with these for decorative purposes to be used on parades.

The fact that Germany was not invited to sign the arms embargo agreement turned out to be of great benefit to her, because, in order to keep to the letter of the agreement, the gentlemen who signed it began very shortly afterwards to supply China with arms, using some German subject as a figure-head to sign the contract. The subsequent history of the delivery of arms to China by Germany would fill not an article, but several large books. In 1928 there was a fantastic story of the Czechoslovakian ship, *Praha*, with a German crew and German captain, and 100,000 rifles, munitions and tanks on board, which, unfortunately, had to stop in Manila Harbour to get water. The simple inhabitants of those islands were surprised to see a ship of the Republic of Czechoslovakia. She turned out to be German, the *Hedwig*, which had obtained from the Skoda works some kind of Czechoslovakian protection.

I was very anxious to meet one of these German arms dealers to hear myself his point of view. It was arranged for me by a mutual friend, to meet such a German, whom I shall call Herr Meyer. Amongst other things, he told me that he was engaged in a shipment of arms that were going to be sent to Vladivostok from China. I expressed surprise at this. 'To the Russians?' I inquired. 'Oh! well,' he answered, 'what happens to the arms I do not know. The chief thing is that they are paid for. Besides, you should not ask so many questions. What guarantee have we that the consignment will not be forced by storms, or lack of water, to enter a Japanese harbour?' 'Well,' I said, 'do you want to sell to the Japanese or the Chinese?' To this the man truthfully replied: 'It does not matter to whom I sell it, or whether the Chinks kill the Japs, or the Japs kill the Chinks; it does not matter a damn to me. The best thing those slant-eyes can do is to exterminate each other.'

Finding it difficult to answer this, I was silent. 'Prosit!' said Herr Meyer, lifting his glass. I lifted mine.

THE FIRST TELEVISION BROADCAST BY THE BBC, 1 February 1935

'Our Special Representative', London Daily Telegraph

A trial run for the BBC's new televison service, which was

introduced later in the year. The test broadcast, watched by about fifty people, was transmitted from the BBC's studios at Crystal Palace.

. . . Externally the television set resembles a slightly larger edition of the ordinary broadcast receiver. In front, however, is a panel for a televised picture measuring 12 inches by 9 inches. The picture, shown without any apparent noise and with practically no flicker, might have been likened to that obtained from a cinema film shown in miniature.

Miss Alma Taylor, displaying one new hat after another and describing them at the same time, was also able to answer us back when we spoke to her by telephone to the studio. Then came an exterior scene. Horses were shown jumping in the grounds of Crystal Palace and the announcer – seen on the screen as clearly as he was heard – explained that this was a scene comparable to that which might be seen in the future when the Derby is televised.

Other scenes were of a boxing match in the studio (as if the fight were taking place in Albert Hall); a lecture as from a school, with the lecturer drawing clear diagrams to illustrate points; and portions of popular sound films.

Definition was extraordinarily good. Always, however, the best results were obtained when the human figures were shown only at half length. Details smaller than this were not very satisfactory. One was conscious after a while that the necessity for concentration was a little trying to the eyes.

In yesterday's [1 February] demonstrations, television was through the medium of a film. The scenes were photographed by a cinema camera at Crystal Palace and developed so rapidly that they were being televised within 30sec, while still partially wet. The time lag of 30sec did not in any way spoil the transmission.

STALIN RIDES THE MOSCOW METRO, 23 April 1935

'Our Own Correspondent', London Daily Telegraph

M. Joseph Stalin, Dictator of Soviet Russia, has just taken his first journey by 'tube'.

Leaving the Kremlin after nightfall yesterday [23 April] he drove with his three principal lieutenants, M. Molotoff, M. Orgonokidze and M. Kaganovich to the Crimea Square terminal station, and from there travelled over the full eight miles of Moscow's new underground.

Properly to appreciate the wide interest this has caused here one must go back to the opening of the first steam railways in England.

Stalin, we are officially informed, was 'wildly cheered' when he inspected the grandiose multi-coloured marbles which, in Moscow, replace London's plain but practical Underground stations.

This new Tube, although virtually ready these last three months, has not yet begun selling tickets or conveying ordinary passengers to and from their work. It is hoped, however, to begin a regular service on Thursday.

Stalin closely inspected the new escalators. These moving stairs are the chief source of astonishment to Moscow residents. Today a number of women and children who had been granted special 'joy-riding tickets' could only be persuaded to scale the escalator when a policeman undertook to accompany them.

Yesterday and today queues of these privileged ticket-holders waited hours for their turn to have a free ride with more eagerness than any crowds ever waited for rides on a scenic railway at Wembley. Again, disconsolate youngsters loitered in a vain hope of begging or stealing a pass.

As expected, the gorgeous marble pillars, and the floodlit tiling in the stations, which would be worthy of a setting for a grand opera, made a special appeal. As one of Moscow's oldest foreign inhabitants said to me, 'This Metro is ultra-modern in technique, but its gorgeous stations are the most characteristically Russian thing done here since the Revolution'.

JOE LOUIS FIGHTS MAX BAER, NEW YORK, October 1935

Jonathan Mitchell

These people are here, 95,000 of them, because they have money. Down there on the field, men have paid $150 and more for a pair of tickets. Twenty thousand seats were stamped 'ringside', and the customers out beyond third base were bilked. They should have known that Mike Jacobs, who is running this fight, is a smart man. No one can do anything to him, because he has the support of Hearst.

It feels good to have money again. Everyone in this crowd has money. The people who were swindled by Jacobs can afford it. Happy days are here again. Of course, things aren't so good, with twenty million on relief. A man can be fired, and next morning there are ten men in line waiting for his job. But the unemployed have been around for a long time. No one can expect us to sit home and be sympathetic indefinitely.

It is a cold, clear night. The Stadium rises steeply around one half of the field. The floodlights on its upper edge are directed on the field and the bleachers, and the Stadium itself is black except for a steady row of red exit signs. Almost the whole of the immense field is covered with chairs. Jacobs has pushed the customers so closely together that all that can be seen of them, under the floodlights, is their microscopic, bright faces. They form neat rows, divided into plots by the aisles, like commercial Dutch tulip beds. There are acres of them, shining pinkly. Men in white, with high cardboard signs in their caps, move gravely about selling pop, like gardeners. The ring is at second base, and the movie operators' metal cage, high on a pole, that you used to see at fights is missing. The only movement comes from white tobacco smoke, rising in heavy waves. Through it you can see the American flags along the top of the Stadium, after the fashion of the opening verse of 'The Star-Spangled Banner'.

Near at hand the crowd is a respectable, bridge-playing one. About a fifth are Negroes, more carefully dressed and more mannerly than the whites. The little drunk with the long woollen muffler is certainly a Bronx dentist. He thinks correctly that the preliminary match now going on is poor, and keeps screaming, 'Lousy'. He brandishes a handful of crumpled bills and will give odds to anyone. There seems to be something painful in his past that he would like to explain, but the woollen muffler keeps blowing in his face, and communication between him and us is eternally frustrated.

There is a stirring in the aisles near the ring. The people who amount to something, and who are bowed through the police lines outside the Stadium, are entering. There are five state governors, the Republican National Committee, important business figures, and a large number of people whose press agents made them come so that their names would be in tomorrow's papers. Max Baer and his attendants are now at home plate. A dozen little pushing figures open up the crowd for him, and another dozen follow behind. Baer wears a white bathrobe, and has his hands on the shoulders of the state trooper in front of him. He nods to his many friends. Joe Louis, with another state trooper and other attendants, pushes in from third base. We learn afterwards that his bride, Marva Trotter, is in the first row in a bright-green dress and orchids. Louis seems to see no one.

The floodlights are extinguished. Nothing exists except the

brightly glowing ring. That is old Joe Humphries being lifted through the ropes, the man who announced fights before the depression. Since then he has been sick, and had a bad time. We have all been having a bad time, for that matter. Jack Dempsey squats in Baer's corner, but no one notices him. Humphries's assistant is bawling into the microphones: 'Although Joe Louis is coloured, he is a great fighter, in the class of Jack Johnson and the giants of the past.' His voice fades away, and returns. 'American sportsmanship, without regard to race, creed or colour, is the talk of the world. Behave like gentlemen, whoever wins.' Nearly 2,000 police at the entrances of the Stadium are there to break up a possible race riot.

Baer has stripped. He has made a lot of money, Baer has. From all reports, he has spent a lot. He has played Broadway, Miami, and the other hot spots. Why shouldn't he have done so? Joe Louis takes off his flashing silk bathrobe, blue with a vermilion lining. It is the only extravagant gesture he makes. For all his youth, he is thick under the jaws, thick around the waist. His face is earnest, thoughtful, unsmiling.

Max Baer hasn't been, I suppose, what you would call a good boy. Joe Louis has, though. This is his greatest advantage. He once was taken to a night club, and it is reported that within ten minutes he wanted to go home. He said he was sleepy. He is supposed to have saved his money. Louis's father died when he was only two years old, down in Alabama. Until she married again, his mother had a hard struggle to support the children, and they were very dear to her. Louis is fond of his mother. She is a Lily of the Valley at her church in Detroit, where the family now lives. The Lilies are having a supper, or some such event, in a few days. She wants him there, and he is going with his new wife.

We are too far away to hear the gong. They are out in the middle of the ring, with a stubby little man in a white sweater moving softly around them. Baer holds both hands, open, clumsily in front of him. Look at Joe Louis. He is leading with a straight left arm, his right hand before his face ready to block, and his right elbow tucked in to his ribs. That is scientific. That is what they teach in correspondence courses, or the night gymnasium classes of the YMCA. In the first thirty seconds, you can tell that he reeks of study, practice, study. Any romantic white person who believes that the Negro possesses a distinctive quality ought to see Louis. He suggests a gorilla or a jungle lion about as much as would an assistant professor at the Massachusetts Institute of Technology.

Baer stands flat-footed, with his great death-dealing right fist doubled by his side. He swings, and you can almost count three while the fist sails through the air. Louis moves sidewise and back, because he has been taught that if you move with a blow it can never hurt you. Baer's glove slides up the side of Louis's head harmlessly. He swings again and again, and, carefully and unhurriedly, Louis slips away. Look! Louis at last is going in. A left, a right and another left in close. Louis has pulled in his head, and with both arms up before him, he looks like a brown crayfish. All you can see is the twitching of his shoulders. So incredibly fast he is that the blows themselves are almost invisible. His hands cannot possibly move more than a few inches. Look! Baer is backing into a neutral corner. Louis is raining down blows. Baer's nose spurts blood, his lower lip bleeds, his face is red pulp.

Baer must have meant something to many people. He made wisecracks and went to parties and was a harbinger of the return of the old days. He was Broadway, he was California and Florida, he represented the possession of money once more and spending it. This saddle-coloured, dour-faced, tongue-tied, studious youth, who is punishing Baer, punishing him more cruelly than human flesh and bones can endure, what does he represent? Baer stands with his hands hanging at his sides. He is helpless. He cannot hit the dissolving form before him, and he has never learned to protect himself. He holds his fine head, with its sweep of tightly curled hair and its great, brooding nose, high above his torturer. Pride alone keeps his head up, pride that has no tangible justification whatever. It was the same pride that kept Colonel Baratieri at Adowa, twenty years before Joe Louis was born.

It is the first round, and the fight is as good as over. Maybe it was foolish to spend money going to a fight. There must be many people, even down there in the ringside seats, who couldn't afford to spend what they did on tickets. No one can be sure of his job with twenty million on relief. This is a crazy country, with people handing out a million dollars to Mike Jacobs and Hearst, while families right here in New York City are without enough to eat.

Round one is ended. Jack Dempsey vaults into the ring in a single, startling leap. Perhaps it is a trick. He must have vaulted from the ground to the edge of the ring platform, and from there into the ring itself. But from a distance, it seems one motion, and it is beautiful. Beside the man that Dempsey was, Baer and Louis and Schmeling are phonies. Nowadays everything, including men, is somehow different.

The next three rounds are slaughter. In the second, Baer makes a wild, swinging, purposeless attack. For probably fifteen seconds, he appears formidable, but his attack has no substance inside it. With the third round, he is beaten, but Louis does not rush in, as Dempsey would have, to kill. Deliberately he circles Baer, with his earnest, thoughtful face, seeking an opening through which to strike without possible risk of injury. He takes no chance of a last, desperate fling of Baer's prodigious right hand. He is a planner. He is a person who studies the basic aspects of a problem and formulates a programme. Apparently his studies are satisfactory, for he carefully steps up and knocks Baer down twice. Baer is on the canvas when time is called. Dempsey slides across the ring, picks Baer up like a mother, fusses over him until the fourth, and final, round. Baer once more is down. When the stubby referee, swinging his arm, reaches seven he tries to rouse himself. This turns out later to have been a fortunate gesture. The customers who suspected the honesty of the fight, and were unconvinced that a man could be half killed by fifty blows full on the jaw, were reassured as they watched Baer struggling to his feet. Had he been trying to throw the fight, they reasoned, he would have lain still. At the count of ten, Baer is on one knee, his swollen face wearing a comical expression of surprise.

The floodlights return us to time and space. Near at hand, there is remarkably little cheering, even from Negroes. They act as if, despite the police, they think it more prudent to restrain their feelings. There in the ring, placing his hand on Baer's shoulder in a stiff gesture, is the best fighter living, and the first Negro whose backers and trainer are men of his race. No white man shares in Louis's winnings. If the whites of the Boxing Commission will permit the match, he will be champion of the world.

All across the Stadium, the neat tulip beds are being broken up as tiny figures push into the aisles and towards the exits. A man with a small blond moustache is sobbing: 'Maxie, why didn't you hit him?' Downtown in the Forties and Fifties, redecorated speakeasies will quickly be crammed to the doors and customers turned away. In Lenox Avenue in Harlem, Negroes will be tap-dancing from kerb to kerb, and singing: 'The Baer goes over the mountain', and 'Who won the fight?' Tomorrow the financial sections of the newspapers will report that business leaders regard the fight as final proof that the country's economic worries are past and a comfortable and prosperous future is assured.

THE WORLD PREMIÈRE OF CHAPLIN'S
MODERN TIMES, NEW YORK, 6 February 1936

'Our Correspondent', London Daily Telegraph

There was pandemonium on Broadway last night when 1,800 people paid thirty shillings each to see the world première of Charlie Chaplin's new film, *Modern Times*.

Five thousand autograph-hunters collected outside the Rivoli Theatre and mobbed the celebrities – including Evelyn Laye, Tilly Losche, Gloria Swanson, Ginger Rogers, and Eddie Cantor – who attended the performance.

A riot call was issued, but the crowd stoutly resisted the violent attempts of hundreds of policemen to drive them from the entrance of the theatre.

Many celebrities, endeavouring to run the gauntlet from their cars through the crowd, were badly manhandled as college students enthusiastically thrust autograph books under their noses and curious women fingered and clutched the dresses worn by famous actresses and screen stars.

Traffic was halted for more than a quarter of an hour. Many persons slipped on the icy pavements and received minor injuries.

People had come from all over the world to see the first Chaplin picture for nearly five years, and to hear Chaplin's voice on the screen for the first time.

The film was given an enthusiastic reception, and there was tremendous applause when Chaplin uttered his first words. This solitary breach of his silent tradition comes when Charlie sings a song in a night club and reveals that he possesses an unusually pleasant voice.

Losing the detachable linen cuff, on which he had carefully written the words of his song, he has to improvise, with the result that the song deteriorates into extraordinary gibberish reminiscent of the Jabberwock in *Alice in Wonderland*.

We see the same old lovable clown, with the same cane, hat and oversize shoes, again cast as a brow-beaten tramp who, unable to find a niche for himself in modern society, is comforted by the companionship of an irrepressible girl waif, and pursued by the police as a vagrant. The same old 'gags' that Chaplin has used for the last twenty years are brought out and surprisingly enough, they stand the test of time. Last night's audience showed their whole-hearted amusement by practically unceasing and vociferous mirth.

The picture ends, as do all Chaplin pictures, with a long shot showing the comedian walking down the highway. On this occasion, however, he is accompanied for the first time by a girl, his little gamin friend, attractively played by Paulette Goddard.

Neither Chaplin nor his leading lady was at the première.

EMPEROR HAILE SELASSIE RETREATS, ETHIOPIA, 4 April 1936

Colonel Konovaloff

Benito Mussolini, the Italian dictator, invaded Ethiopia in October 1935, using machine-guns and mustard gas to defeat the barefoot and poorly armed Ethiopian Army of Emperor Haile Selassie. The writer of this account of the Emperor's withdrawal after his ill-starred attack on the Italians at Mai Chow was a military adviser with Selassie's army.

It was impossible to find a single man ready to obey an order or even in his proper place. Soldiers drifted about in every direction and in disorderly crowds: the mountain was full of them. The Emperor returned to his observation point after a late lunch, but there was a heavy mist and one could distinguish little. Before nightfall a new council. A little later they began to examine the objects which filled the cave to see what could be taken away; much opening of trunks and cases.

Near nightfall the Emperor began to distribute in person the things that he could not take with him: cartridges, oddments of clothing, liquor, preserved foods, supplies of all sorts. The cave filled up with soldiers who wished to profit from the occasion. When the Emperor wished to leave the cave he could force a passage only with the greatest difficulty. Beatings, shouts, gesticulations, and at last the mob left the place with their booty.

At 9.30 we left Aia and took the road for Korem.

Behind us they exploded all the artillery and rifle ammunition, the tins of petrol and drums of oil, which destroyed along with them all that remained of the piles of striped shirts and black satin capes with which we hoped to draw the Azebu Galla to our side.

The field radio station was abandoned with the rest.

The descent from our mountain was terrible, so dark was the night.

Every minute the road was jammed. When the Ethiopians march the main object of each man is to pass all the others. This mob of people trying to thread its way through donkeys, mules and hundreds of other Ethiopians created an incredible disorder.

We took the whole night to cover the ten kilometres or so which separated us from Lake Ashangi. I had lost sight of the Emperor and the sons of Ras Kassa with whom I had travelled before, and was marching now with a group of soldiers. It was only at dawn that two of the Emperor's pages joined me. They too had been separated in the crowd.

We hurried. At every moment the aeroplanes might appear.

These last days they had continually bombarded the shelterless borders of Lake Ashangi and the two passes to north and south of it, full of baggage trains and soldiers. After a moment's halt I decided to go on to Korem: my companions did not continue with me.

It was seven o'clock in the morning when the first aeroplane was seen. Bombs rained upon our troops in retreat. Other aeroplanes appeared. When I had crossed the pass and come down into the valley the bombardment was let loose in all ferocity.

Fourteen planes took turns to hurl their bombs upon the unbroken flood of humanity which surged towards Korem. I had to travel rather to the left of the crowd.

I shall never forget the picture that I saw.

The wide valley, which during the season of rains is inundated in part, lay level under the blazing African sun. To its side the blue surface of the lake was lightly ruffled by the breeze. Along the road the weary people dragged themselves, scattering for a moment in panic or massing together in groups. Four, six, eight bombs burst one after the other. They fell some distance from the road and hit nobody . . . The people quicken pace. Here is another aeroplane which seems to be choosing its victims as it flies just over their heads. One explosion . . . then another which raises a jet of earth clods, sand and stones.

People are hit this time. Everything round me disperses. I turn round and see someone dying on the ground. A form that slightly moves.

Fear pushes the survivors upon their road without attending to the wretch who cannot follow them, for he has lost his legs.

At the same moment our allies the Azebu Galla fire on us from the hilltops where their villages lie. When they see stragglers they kill them and strip the bleeding bodies of rifles, cartridges and clothes.

Before us there is a corner of hell which none of us can avoid. On one side of the road is the lake, on the other are the mountains. The pass is narrow, and the human flood finds it hard to press forward and through.

Everybody knows that in the bush and behind the rocks hide the treacherous Azebu, on the watch. A hail of bombs burst all over the pass wounding animals and men.

Poor little Ethiopian donkeys! . . . how often have I seen them on the road, their jaws smashed to pieces, their eyes blown from their sockets, their stomachs opened by a bomb.

We crossed the dangerous pass. Blot after dark blot along

our road. These were stains of blood dried quickly by the lively sun: they showed us the way.

We hurried on over bodies sprawled and tumbled. Once more I found myself in a wide open place where I tried to keep my distance from the crowd.

Behind a turn in the road a bomb has just burst. I see the Ethiopian in front of me bending over an extended body. '*Ato Gabre Mariam?*' he said. 'What has happened?'

'*Pomp, bakon madanit*' ('Bomb, please medicine'), answers the wounded man, turning his eyes in supplication to me. *And I do not want to be left behind. See us, me and the Ethiopian following me, running on along the road.*

As I go, I see again a face now no more than a pulp of bleeding flesh, over which a young boy hangs sobbing, trying his best to help the wounded. Others are falling around us . . . we run on and on . . . and at last we are near the caves of Korem which will shelter us from the Azebu bullets and the aeroplanes.

On a range of hills, covered with bush, there are *tukuls* and the characteristic small properties of the Ethiopians, surrounded by palisades. Farther off on a small mountain there is a larger property kept more tidily. It belongs to the local *shum*. I run down the hill and on towards the slope where the caves are dug.

At my feet, until lost to view, spreads the valley inhabited by the terrible Azebu Galla. It is time I reached my refuge – two planes are already flying over me . . .

JESSE OWENS TAKES GOLD IN THE 100-METRE DASH, BERLIN, 4 August 1936

New York Times *reporter*

The 1936 Berlin Olympics were intended by the Nazi regime to be a demonstration of the physical superiority of the Teuton. To

Hitler's ill-concealed disgust, however, the games were dominated by black American athlete Jesse James Cleveland Owens, who won four track and field gold medals, including the gold for the garland event, the men's 100-metre dash.

Owens won today because he is the world's fastest human. No one ever ran a more perfect race. His start was perfect, his in-between running perfect and his finish perfect.

The Buckeye Bullet ripped out of his starting holes as though slung by a giant catapult. He was ahead in his first stride and let Osendarp and Wykoff battle behind him for what was left of the race.

Metcalfe, hardly the best starter in the world, was off in atrocious fashion. He was sixth in the six-man field at the getaway, but once in his stride he certainly moved. By sixty metres he had drawn even with the Hollander and begun to cut down the two-yard advantage Owens had on him.

It was then a speed duel between a streamlined express and an old-fashioned steam engine that exuded sheer, rugged power. Metcalfe cut those two yards to one at the wire, but it was as close as he could get.

Owens's time was a new world record of 10.3 seconds. Ralph Metcalfe was also a black American. Hitler left the stadium rather than have to congratulate Owens on his victory.

JESSE OWENS WINS THE BROAD JUMP, BERLIN, 5 August 1936

Arthur J. Daley, **New York Times**

The broad jump was one of the most dramatic events of the entire day, surprising as that may sound. It started with an unusual flourish and ended the same way. In the morning the leapers had to beat 23 feet 5 inches to qualify.

Owens strolled over and, still in his pullovers, raced to the pit and ran through, a customary warm-up gesture. But the red flag was raised in a token greatly to the Buckeye Bullet's astonishment. That counted as one of his three jumps. On his second try, which he made in earnest, Jesse hit the take-off board cleanly and sailed through the air. Again the red flag was waved for some mysterious reason.

The situation was getting to the alarming by this time. Owens had only one jump left to stay in the competition. So, on his last attempt, he sprinted carefully, left the ground with a half-foot clearance at the take-off and went past 25 feet to safety.

In the afternoon Owens had no close calls of that nature. The pressure came from Long. The German, carried along on the wings of superhuman endeavour – the hallmark of every Reich athlete in this meet – was bounding right at Owens's heels. He was only little more than an inch behind the American's 7.87 metres as they went up for their last three jumps.

On his second in the final Long hit the nail exactly on the head; doing the same distance as the Ohian and tying him for the championship as the crowd went into frenzied ecstasies of applause. But his jubilation was short lived. Owens came thundering down the runway and drove out into space a moment later. He had taken the play away at 7.94 metres and then drove beyond Long's reach with his final jump that cemented the distinction of his becoming the first 26-footer in Olympic history.

A SPANISH CIVIL WAR DIARY, 1936

Franz Borkenau

The civil war between Franco's Nationalists and Spain's elected leftist Republican government lasted from July 1936 to April 1939, and ended in Nationalist victory.

Diary, 5 September
At about 1 p.m. we reached the headquarters of the northern sector of the Cordova front, and were billeted in a hospital, in a very pleasant sanatorium. The staff itself was less pleasant. I have seen a number of staffs now, of various degrees of competence and pleasantness, from very good ones (by existing standards) to more unsatisfactory ones, but I never saw anything like this. The first thing we learned was that the attack had failed; that instead, since six in the morning the enemy had been attacking heavily. The coincidence of the enemies' attack preceding by just a few hours the attempt to attack from the Government side was surprising, but it did not seem to be a subject for consideration by the staff. Neither was the failure of the intended operation itself, or, for that matter, the whole war. While, a few miles ahead, a heavy attack on an important position was proceeding and (affairs were not going in favour of the Government), the staff, officers, doctors, nurses (of a more than dubious quality), were sitting down quietly to a good lunch, chatting, flirting, telling dirty stories, and not caring a bit about their duty, not even trying to establish any contact with the fighting lines for many hours; the wounded who were brought in from time to time were neglected by the nurses in the most shameless and repugnant manner. Finally, by about three o'clock, we had passed through the ordeal of standing what the staff thought was good behaviour, and proceeded to the front, to the small village of Cerro Muriano.

There, at half-past three, we found pandemonium. A little way ahead of the village there is a low wooded ridge, from which occasional rifle and machine-gun fire was sounding. The wood was burning on the right side of the village, from shelling in the morning. The fighting was obviously not very heavy at the moment of our arrival. But we witnessed a scene such as before I only knew from stories of the Thirty Years' War, though probably similar things happened occasionally in the World War. The whole village was in flight; men, women, and children; on foot, by donkeys, by cars, and motor-lorries. The latter had been crowded at the entrance to the village opposite the front, for troop, munition, and food transport. These cars and lorries were simply stormed by the inhabitants, a few of whom knew how to drive, and did drive the vehicles away, or if ignorant of driving, forced the drivers at the rifle point to disobey orders, leave the battlefield, and carry off the fugitives. All that naturally in a hullabaloo. Women carrying their babies in their arms, and their cattle at rope-ends; they sobbing, the babies crying; men trying to carry on their arms and backs what small portion of their movable property they could bear away in their haste. The whole village, in a few minutes, was completely derelict. Many of the fleeing men wore the CNT initials on their caps (Cerro Muriano is just in the province of Cordova, which is much more anarchist than Jaen), and carried their rifles with them, not to use them against the enemy, but against whoever might try to stop their flight. The whole village guard, the local peasant militia, was running away, and even set the pace for the wild rush to the rear. At the moment, our war correspondents' car was the only one which did not move towards the rear but towards the front. We stopped, our driver and guard got down, and drew their revolvers. A few deserters from the Franco army, all of them old UGT and CNT members, who, by chance, found themselves in the village at the moment of the disaster, joined our guards. They stopped the flying cars and lorries, pointed their revolvers at the heads of the drivers, and, joining reproaches and imprecations to the menace of arms, ordered the cars and lorries to stop; women and children might proceed to a safer place, but all men except the drivers had to stay and defend the village. Wasn't it a shame that men armed with good rifles, and wearing the proud insignia of the CNT, were running away like cowards? 'Rifles are no good against bombs and shells,' the fugitives shouted back. Sometimes the menace of the drawn revolvers, closer and more immediate than that of the battle behind, succeeded for a moment; some lorries were stopped, some men descended. But as soon as the small group who tried to re-establish discipline had proceeded a few yards farther, to the next car or the next but one, the men mounted again and drove away in haste.

It was only hours later that I found out exactly what had happened. The village had been bombarded throughout the whole morning from the air, and occasionally with artillery fire too; then there had been the usual break in fighting during the siesta hours, from about one o'clock to half-past three, a ritual observed by both parties throughout the Spanish civil war; and just when we arrived the bombardment of the village had reopened, and the strained nerves of the inhabitants could stand it no longer. When we entered the village, it offered a sorry sight; all houses deserted; most doors locked; cats, dogs, pigs wandering helplessly in the streets and yards. But the front line, in contrast to the village guard, stood unshattered. The village, in spite of the panic, had suffered very little; nothing was either destroyed or burning.

The left flank of Cerro Muriano is protected by a railway bank, which proved to be very valuable cover. Occasionally bullets struck the streets, but on the whole we could proceed towards the lines unmolested. Directly behind the lines, at the front entry of the village, a sort of barrack, probably used in normal times for housing the railway personnel, had been transformed into a red-cross station. There we stopped. Casualties were few. The column fighting just ahead of us was the usual size of a militia column, about 300 to 400 men. There had been less than ten wounded back at the base hospital (the one where the staff were billeted), and now not more than ten men were being treated at the Red Cross station. Twenty casualties, 5 to 7 per cent of all the effectives, and these including casualties of every description from the slightest upwards, is certainly not a heavy list after more than seven hours' fighting; there were three or four dead. The panic became increasingly unintelligible. Meanwhile I watched the activity at the Red Cross station. It was queer to observe that all the militia-men treated had exactly the same attitude, whether they were brought in with simple nervous shock (as was very frequently the case) or with dangerous wounds; for them, the thing was over; they considered themselves as good as dead, or rather, played dead. The two doctors, swift and efficient, started every new case with a question about what was wrong, but never once did they get an answer; they had to find out for themselves, undressing the patients and looking for wounds. Suddenly there was a big crash, as near as could possibly be. A bomb had come down a few yards from the Red Cross station, which was flying the Red Cross flag in a way impossible to overlook. In a second all the men were flat on the ground, and only we three journalists still stood upright (it is, of course, not the slightest use to take cover against bombs *in a building*, but training had gone already far enough to make covering an instinctive reaction with the militia-men). The wounded did not move at all, but a nurse started sobbing hysterically. The behaviour of the doctors, in great contrast to the scene we had just watched, was brilliant; they did not interrupt for a moment the fulfilment of their duties – this was not the type of doctor we had met a few hours ago at staff headquarters. The enemy bomber, after launching a few bombs farther back in the village, went away, but returned after a few minutes. In the meantime I tried to get to the front line itself, but the fire was now too heavy to pass. I decided to take cover in a tunnel under the railway bank. To my great surprise I found that the bombs the enemy were dropping were no good at all. The holes made by them were only a few fingers deep; such bombs were obviously harmless, if one was not struck by one directly. Standing at the entry of the tunnel where I had taken cover I saw a bomb explode a few yards away; the air pressure drove me back, but nothing else happened. Much more awkward was the machine-gun fire. It definitely took a nasty turn. First it had been ahead only, but it was clearly approaching from the left flank, across the railway line; a few Moorish machine-gunners had turned the flank of the Government lines, unopposed. They might enter the village any minute.

Things gradually became unpleasant. If the Moors caught us in our shelter under the railway bank, there would be very little chance to explain that we were neutrals; they would kill us at once. Thus, dangerous as it might be, we had to leave cover, go into the open, and get out of the village as quickly as possible. But this was easier said than done. At first we were lucky and got out during a break in the bombing and machine-gunning. On the main road stood a captain with a few men, who examined our papers with admirable calm and courtesy – he was the one officer who behaved firmly on this day, and that night I learned that he had restored order and confidence in the front line and thus avoided catastrophe. Very soon, however, the machine-gun fire reopened, from very near, though we could not see the Moors, who were lying on the other side of the bank; and it was cross-fire, because besides the Moors flanking us from across the bank there was the main line of the insurgents, firing at the village from the right wing. We slipped from one house to the next during occasional breaks in the firing. Meantime, the bombing continued unchanged. There were two enemy planes now, alternately fetching bombs and bombing the village; they were completely unopposed. There had been talk during lunch of Government aircraft being ordered to come and take part in the fighting, but no Government plane appeared. The bombs were ridiculously inefficient; about 50 per cent did not explode at all, and the rest did very little damage; not a single one of the huts of which this miserable village consisted was burning when the bombardment stopped towards dusk. But the mere fact of standing in continual air bombardment for nearly three hours, unprotected and without aircraft to oppose the bombers, is nerve-shattering. Finally we got out of the village. A few hundred yards outside stood a number of cars and lorries, which, after having evacuated the village, had returned. But the scenes of flight of the afternoon were now repeated, only this time it was not the villagers but the militia from the front line, who went back, singly or in small groups, and forced the cars to drive them away. It was a scene of complete disorder. The officers, the men said, had run away first; why should they stay? One man got into our car, and when I asked him what business he had behind the lines he bluntly replied: 'To escape.'

We had to seek shelter once more, this time in a small tunnel under the road, before we could get away with our car. The bombing was too heavy and too near for us to take the risk of driving off. Our driver and guard had behaved admirably, going to fetch us in the bombarded and machine-gunned village. There was another journalists' car whose driver had ignominiously run away. There were similar differences between the various small units of militia. While the troops from Jaen and Valencia ran away before our eyes, a small group of militia from Alcoy, an old revolutionary centre in the province of Murcia, arrived. They stood the bombardment – which, I must repeat, did no real damage – with the proudest gallantry and unconcernedness; there were two girls among the group, more courageous even than the men. Discipline, however, was lacking to an almost incredible extent. The tunnel where we had taken shelter was far from being bomb-proof; at best it was a suitable hiding-place. but it became unavailing even for that, because every time the bombardment stopped for a moment the militia-men from Alcoy crawled out of cover to watch the enemy planes. Finally, we got safely back to headquarters, where they were as uninterested as at midday.

THE BATTLE OF CABLE STREET, LONDON, 7 October 1936

Phil Piratin

Following Mussolini's lead, Sir Oswald Mosley had founded the British Union of Fascists which advocated the abolition of free speech, greater interest in the Commonwealth, and anti-semitism.

It was obvious that the Fascists and the police would now turn their attention to Cable Street. We were ready. The moment this became apparent the signal was given to put up the barricades. We had prepared three spots. The first was near a yard where there was all kinds of timber and other oddments, and also an old lorry. An arrangement had been made with the owner that this old lorry could be used as a barricade. Instructions had been given about this, but when someone shouted 'Get the lorry!' evidently not explaining that it was in the nearby yard, some of the lads, looking up the street, saw a stationary lorry about 200 yards away. They went along, brought it back, and pushed it over on its side before anyone even discovered that it was not the lorry meant to be used. Still it was a lorry, and supplemented by bits of old furniture, mattresses, and every kind of thing you expect to find in box-rooms, it was a barricade which the police did not find it easy to penetrate. As they charged they were met with milk bottles, stones, and marbles. Some of the housewives began to drop milk bottles from the roof tops. A number of police surrendered. This had never happened before, so the lads didn't know what to do, but they took away their batons, and one took a helmet for his son as a souvenir.

Cable Street was a great scene. I have referred to 'the lads'. Never was there such unity of all sections of the working class as was seen on the barricades at Cable

Street. People whose lives were poles apart, though living within a few hundred yards of each other; bearded Orthodox Jews and rough-and-ready Irish Catholic dockers – these were the workers that the Fascists were trying to stir up against each other. The struggle, led by the Communist Party, against the Fascists had brought them together against their common enemies, and their lackeys.

Meanwhile, charges and counter-charges were taking place along 'the front' from Tower Hill to Gardner's Corner. Many arrests were made, many were injured. It was the police, however, who were carrying on the battle, while the Fascists lurked in the background, protected by a 'fence' of police. Mosley was late. As soon as he arrived, in a motor-car, a brick went clean through the window.

It was later rumoured that Sir Philip Game had been on the telephone to the Home Secretary, and had pleaded with Sir John Simon to forbid the march. Sir John was adamant. Sir Philip Game, however, made up his own mind. He forbade the march and told Mosley to argue it out with Sir John Simon. The Fascists lined up, saluted their leader, and marched through the deserted City to the Embankment, where they dispersed. The working class had won the day.

DUCKING A FASCIST BULLET, SPAIN, January 1937

George Orwell

The British writer George Orwell was one of the many thousands of leftist sympathizers from Europe and America who volunteered to fight for the Spanish Republic. The following incident took place on the Ebro front, in north-western Spain.

In the afternoon we did our first guard and Benjamin showed us round the position. In front of the parapet there ran a system of narrow trenches hewn out of the rock, with extremely primitive loopholes made of piles of limestone. There were twelve sentries, placed at various points in the trench and behind the inner parapet. In front of the trench was the barbed wire, and then the hillside slid down into a seemingly bottomless ravine; opposite were naked hills, in places mere cliffs of rock, all grey and wintry, with no life anywhere, not even a bird. I peered cautiously through a loophole, trying to find the Fascist trench.

'Where are the enemy?'

Benjamin waved his hand expansively. 'Over zere.' (Benjamin spoke English – terrible English.)

'But *where*?'

According to my ideas of trench warfare the Fascists would be fifty or a hundred yards away. I could see nothing – seemingly their trenches were very well concealed. Then with a shock of dismay I saw where Benjamin was pointing; on the opposite hill-top, beyond the ravine, 700 metres away at the very least, the tiny outline of a parapet and a red-and-yellow flag – the Fascist position. I was indescribably disappointed. We were nowhere near them! At that range our rifles were completely useless. But at this moment there was a shout of excitement. Two Fascists, greyish figurines in the distance, were scrambling up the naked hillside opposite. Benjamin grabbed the nearest man's rifle, took aim, and pulled the trigger. Click! A dud cartridge; I thought it a bad omen.

The new sentries were no sooner in the trench than they began firing a terrific fusillade at nothing in particular. I could see the Fascists, tiny as ants, dodging to and fro behind their parapet, and sometimes a black dot which was a head would pause for a moment, impudently exposed. It was obviously no use firing. But presently the sentry on my left, leaving his post in the typical Spanish fashion, sidled up to me and began urging me to fire. I tried to explain that at that range and with these rifles you could not hit a man except by accident. But he was only a child, and he kept motioning with his rifle towards one of the dots, grinning as eagerly as a dog that expects a pebble to be thrown. Finally I put my sights up to 700 and let fly. The dot disappeared. I hope it went near enough to make him jump. It was the first time in my life that I had fired a gun at a human being.

Now that I had seen the front I was profoundly disgusted. They called this war! And we were hardly even in touch with the enemy! I made no attempt to keep my head below the level of the trench. A little while later, however, a bullet shot past my ear with a vicious crack and banged into the parados behind. Alas! I ducked. All my life I had sworn that I would not duck the first time a bullet passed over me; but the movement appears to be instinctive, and almost everybody does it at least once.

THE BOMBING OF GUERNICA, SPAIN, 26 April 1937

Noel Monks

I passed through Guernica at about 3.30 p.m. The time is approximate, based on the fact that I left Bilbao at 2.30. Guernica was busy. It was market day. We passed through the town and took a road that Anton said would take us close to Marquina, where, as far as I knew, the front was. The front was there, all right, but Marquina was not. It had been smashed flat by bombers.

We were about eighteen miles east of Guernica when Anton pulled to the side of the road, jammed on the brakes and started shouting. He pointed wildly ahead, and my heart shot into my mouth when I looked. Over the tops of some hills appeared a flock of planes. A dozen or so bombers were flying high. But down much lower, seeming just to skim the treetops were six Heinkel 52 fighters. The bombers flew on towards Guernica, but the Heinkels, out for random plunder, spotted our car, and, wheeling like a flock of homing pigeons, they lined up the road – and our car.

Anton and I flung ourselves into a bomb hole, twenty yards to the side of the road. It was half filled with water, and we sprawled in mud. We half knelt, half stood, with our heads buried in the muddy side of the crater.

After one good look at the Heinkels, I didn't look up again until they had gone. That seemed hours later, but it was probably less than twenty minutes. The planes made several runs along the road. Machine-gun bullets plopped into the mud ahead, behind, all around us. I began to shiver from sheer fright. Only the day before Steer, an old hand now, had 'briefed' me about being strafed. 'Lie still and as flat as you can. But don't get up and start running, or you'll be bowled over for certain.'

When the Heinkels departed, out of ammunition I presumed, Anton and I ran back to our car. Nearby a military car was burning fiercely. All we could do was drag two riddled bodies to the side of the road. I was trembling all over now, in the grip of the first real fear I'd ever experienced. On occasions I'd been scared before – as when I'd crashed into the sea in the *Cutty Sark* – but here on the road to Guernica I was in a bad state of jitters indeed. Then suddenly the quaking passed and I felt exhilarated. These were the days in foreign reporting when personal experiences were copy, for there hadn't been a war for eighteen years, long enough for those who went through the last one to forget, and for a generation and a half who knew nothing of war to be interested. We used to call them 'I' stories, and when the Spanish war ended in 1939 we were as heartily sick of writing them as the public must have been of reading them.

At the foot of the hills leading to Guernica we turned off the main road and took another back to Bilbao. Over to our left, in the direction of Guernica, we could hear the crump of bombs. I thought the Germans had located reinforcements moving up from Santandar to stem the retreat. We drove on to Bilbao.

At the Presidencia, Steer and Holme were writing dispatches. They asked me to join them at dinner at Steer's hotel. They said they, too, had seen flights of bombers, but didn't know where the bombs had dropped. The Torrontegui Hotel where I started to dine with Steer, Holme, Captain Roberts of the *Seven Seas Spray* and his game little daughter Fifi, that night was peopled mostly by Franco sympathizers. President Aguirre and his Government knew they were there, but they remained unmolested.

We'd eaten our first course of beans and were waiting for our bully beef when a Government official, tears streaming down his face, burst into the dismal dining-room crying: 'Guernica is destroyed. The Germans bombed and bombed and bombed.'

The time was about 9.30 p.m. Captain Roberts banged a huge fist on the table and said: 'Bloody swine.' Five minutes later I was in one of Mendiguren's limousines speeding towards Guernica. We were still a good ten miles away when I saw the reflection of Guernica's flames in the sky. As we drew nearer, on both sides of the road, men, women and children were sitting, dazed. I saw a priest in one group. I stopped the car and went up to him. 'What happened, Father?' I asked. His face was blackened, his clothes in tatters. He couldn't talk. He just pointed to the flames, still about four miles away, then whispered: 'Aviones . . . bombas . . . mucho, mucho.'

In the good 'I' tradition of the day, I was the first correspondent to reach Guernica, and was immediately pressed into service by some Basque soldiers collecting charred bodies that the flames had passed over. Some of the soldiers were sobbing like children. There were flames and smoke and grit, and the smell of burning human flesh was nauseating. Houses were collapsing into the inferno.

In the Plaza, surrounded almost by a wall of fire, were about a hundred refugees. They were wailing and weeping and rocking to and fro. One middle-aged man spoke English.

He told me: 'At four, before the market closed, many aeroplanes came. They dropped bombs. Some came low and shot bullets into the streets. Father Aronategui was wonderful. He prayed with the people in the Plaza while the bombs fell.' The man had no idea who I was, as far as I know. He was telling me what had happened to Guernica.

Most of Guernica's streets began or ended at the Plaza. It was impossible to go down many of them, because they were walls of flame. Debris was piled high. I could see shadowy forms, some large, some just ashes. I moved round to the back of the Plaza among survivors. They had the same story to tell, aeroplanes, bullets, bombs, fire.

Within twenty-four hours, when the grim story was told to the world, Franco was going to brand these shocked, homeless people as liars. So-called British experts were going to come to Guernica, weeks afterwards, when the smell of burnt human flesh had been replaced by petrol dumped here and there among the ruins by Mola's men, and deliver pompous judgements: 'Guernica was set on fire wilfully by the Reds.'

No Government official had accompanied me to Guernica. I wandered round the place at will. I drove back to Bilbao and had to waken the cable operator – it was nearly two in the morning – to send my message. Censorship had been lifted completely. The man who sent my dispatch couldn't read English. If the 'Reds' had destroyed Guernica and hundreds of their fellow Basques, I could have blown the whole story for all they knew – as I certainly would have done. I told the facts about the bombing of Guernica in my message and described the terrible scenes I'd witnessed.

The only things left standing were a church, a sacred Tree, symbol of the Basque people, and, just outside the town, a small munitions factory. There hadn't been a single anti-aircraft gun in the town. It had been mainly a fire raid. Steer and Holme picked up some dud incendiary bombs. They were branded with the German eagle. Some were handed to British agents and positively identified.

A sight that haunted me for weeks was the charred bodies of several women and children huddled together in what had been the cellar of a house. It had been a refugio. Franco's British apologists were going to proclaim that these people had been locked in the cellar by their own men while the house was dynamited and set alight.

Later that day I was to get a bomb addressed to me, personally. So was Steer. So was Holme. It was in the form of a cable from my office: 'Berlin denies Guernica bombing. Franco says he had no planes up yesterday owing fog. Quiepo de Llano [Franco's foul-mouthed broadcasting general in Seville] says Reds dynamited Guernica during retreat. Please check up soonest.'

Please check up!

Back we went to Guernica, all three of us. We compared notes. We checked each other's experiences the day before. Refugees from Guernica were pouring into Bilbao now. With an interpreter I took one family for a car ride to calm them down, soothe their shattered nerves. Then gently, quietly, I got from them their story. It was the same as the others. We asked Mendiguren to collect the weather reports for us from all fronts. No one had seen fog for a week on our front.

CRASH OF THE *HINDENBURG*, NEW JERSEY, May 1937

Herb Morrison

The airship *Hindenburg* – 250 metres long and 40 metres wide – was the 118th airship to be built in Germany, and in its first year of service carried more than 1,200 passengers across the Atlantic. May marked the start of the 1937 service, and the *Hindenburg's* arrival in the USA was watched by Herb Morrison, a newscaster for a local radio station. The cause of the disaster which consumed the airship as she came in to land is unknown.

It's crashing! It's crashing terrible . . . oh my . . . get out of the way please . . . it's burning, bursting into flames and . . . it's falling on the mooring pad and all the folks can see that this [is] terrible, this is one of the worst catastrophes in the world . . . it's twenty, forty, oh, four or five hundred feet into the sky and it's a terrific great flame, ladies and gentlemen . . . oh, the humanity . . . I can't talk, ladies and gentlemen, honest, it's just laying there, a mass of smoking wreckage . . . I – I'm sorry . . . honestly I can hardly breathe . . . I – I'm going to step inside where I cannot see it . . . I tell you it's terrible . . . I – I – listen, folks, I'm going to have to stop for a minute because I've lost my voice . . . oh, this is the worst thing I've ever witnessed.

A MEETING WITH SIGMUND FREUD, VIENNA, 1938

Max Eastman

Berggasse 19 was a big roomy house full of books and pictures, the whole mezzanine floor padded with those thick rich rugs in which your feet sank like a camel's in the sand. I was not surprised to see hanging beside Rembrandt's *Anatomy Class*, without which no doctor's office would be recognizable, a picture of *The Nightmare* – a horrid monster with a semievil laugh or leer, squatting upon a sleeping maiden's naked breast. Freud's early specialty had been anatomy, and he had in him the hard scientific curiosity suggested by Rembrandt's picture. But he had too, in my belief, a streak of something closely akin to medieval superstition. He liked to talk about '*The* Unconscious', personifying the mere absence of a quality – and that the quality of awareness – and making it into a scheming demon for which anatomy certainly finds no place. Freud's discovery that impulses suppressed out of our thoughts can continue to control those thoughts, both waking and sleeping, and also our actions and bodily conditions, was certainly a major event in the history of science. But what a lot of purely literary mythology he built around it! Mental healing always did and always will run off into magic.

With such thoughts I sat there whetting my curiosity until the door opened and he came in.

Well – he was smaller than I thought, and slender-limbed, and more feminine. I have been surprised at the feminineness of all the great men I have met, including the Commander of the Red Army. Genius is a nervous phenomenon and, except for the steam-roller variety that struts the boards just now, it involves delicacy. Freud's nose was flatter than I expected, too, and more one-sided. It looked as if somebody with brass knuckles had given him a poke in the snoot. It made him, when he threw his head clear back and laughed softly, as he frequently did, seem quaint and gnomelike. His voice was gentle too, gentle and a little thin, as though he were purposely holding back half his breath in order to be mischievous.

'What did you want?' he said in perfect English as we shook hands.

'Not a thing,' I said. 'I just wanted to look you over.'

THE PRIVATE LIFE OF ADOLF HITLER, BERCHTESGADEN, 1938

Anon.

The author of this account of the German dictator at home was one of the maids at his mountain retreat.

I had read in the German newspapers that Hitler lived a simple, unostentatious life. In a few minutes I realized how the trusting German people were being misled.

Keitner [an SS guard] was quite cynical about it. As he showed me the main dining room he smiled and said, 'You see, of course, how the Führer appreciates comfort. Only the best is good enough for him.' This particular room is sixty feet long by forty feet wide. A massive oak table runs down the centre. A soft glow comes from cunningly concealed lighting. Four etchings by Dürer hang on the walls. A vast Persian carpet covers the floor. Later on it was part of my duty, together with another girl, to lay the table. When the dinner was an informal one the service was of magnificent Dresden china, but when important guests were present they ate off solid silver – most of it plate from the Jewish merchants of Nuremberg, stolen from them by Himmler's agents.

The room in which Hitler receives his guests overlooks the Austrian Alps. This room houses his aviary of rare birds. One day I counted them. There were seventy-eight – all chattering and screaming at the same time. He always fed them himself. The death of one of them brought tears to his eyes. Its little corpse was buried in a small plot of ground with a tiny headstone of bronze placed on the grave.

Berchtesgaden has fourteen bedrooms for guests. Each bedroom has a private bathroom. The marble of Hitler's own bath comes from Italy. It was a present from Mussolini.

Every bedroom has a signed copy of *Mein Kampf*, together with pornographic French books imported from Paris. And every room has a portrait of Hitler over the bed.

The kitchens at Berchtesgaden are magnificent. All cooking is done by electricity. A former head chef of the Adlon Hotel in Berlin is in charge, with four younger men under him. He himself cooks only for Hitler. A Gestapo man is present night and day to ensure that no poison is introduced into the food.

Many walls are covered with rare Gobelin tapestries. 'Actually they are priceless,' declared Keitner, 'but if they were offered for sale in America they would fetch several million dollars.'

'But how can the Führer afford them?' I gasped.

'Well, there are ways and means,' smiled Keitner. 'The Führer can, for example, request a museum to "loan" him a tapestry, or he can suggest to a wealthy industrialist that it would be wise of him to send him a present. Then, some of them were just stolen from one of the ex-Kaiser's many castles.'

There are five rooms in Berchtesgaden which have never been photographed. I saw them once and once only. They are called the Chambers of the Stars. They form a kind of penthouse on the roof. Only two people can enter them at any time – Hitler himself and his astrologer, one Karl Ossietz.

In the main room of this suite the ceiling is made of dark blue glass on which, by pressing a switch, the movements of the planets and constellations are shown. The best optical workers in Jena worked on this room for over a year before Hitler was satisfied with it. Designs of the zodiac form the patterns on the walls. In another of these rooms the only illumination comes from a brazier which burns night and day. Hitler often spends hours alone there, gazing into its angry glow or staring into a huge crystal globe.

In Germany no mention of Ossietz is allowed to be made, yet he is perhaps the most important man in the Third Reich outside Hitler himself. He just arrived at Berchtesgaden one day and has remained there ever since. He is the Rasputin of Nazi Germany.

Shortly after my arrival the Führer spent three days and nights in this suite alone with Ossietz. Göring arrived from Berlin with urgent news – but even the fat field marshal could not speak to Hitler until he emerged. He consults the stars before embarking upon any major activity. He would sooner listen to the advice of Ossietz than to counsel from his General Staff.

Every member of Hitler's staff hates Ossietz. They are all jealous of his influence. Göring, in particular, detests the man. He refused twice to stay in the same room with him. But Ossietz remains. Perhaps it is because he has told the Führer that he will still be ruling Germany when he himself dies, and he fixes the year of his death as 1962.

HITLER'S INSTRUCTIONS TO HIS GUESTS, BERCHTESGADEN, 1938

Instructions to Visitors:

1. Smoking is forbidden, except in this bedroom.
2. The guest must not talk to servants or carry any parcel or message from the premises for any servant.
3. At all times the Führer must be addressed and spoken of as such and never as 'Herr Hitler' or other title.
4. Women guests are forbidden to use excessive cosmetics and must on no account use colouring material on their fingernails.
5. Guests must present themselves for meals within two minutes of the announcing bell. No one may sit at table or leave the table until the Führer has sat or left.
6. No one may remain seated in a room when the Führer enters.
7. Guests must retire to their rooms at 11 p.m. unless expressly asked to remain by the Führer.
8. Guests must remain in this wing of the house and must on no account enter the domestic quarters, the offices or the quarters of the SS officers, or the political police bureau.
9. On leaving Berchtesgaden, guests are absolutely forbidden to discuss their visit with strangers or to mention any remark made to them by the Führer. The conveying of information about the Führer's private life in this way will be visited by the severest penalties.

THE ANSCHLUSS, AUSTRIA, 11 March 1938

George Clare

Austria was forced into union (anschluss) with Hitler's Germany on 11 March. The news was broken to the Austrian people in a radio announcement by their chancellor, Kurt von Schuschnigg.

The music stopped. It was about a quarter to eight. A breathless voice, more shouting than speaking, announced 'The Chancellor', and then Schuschnigg spoke, his voice trembling with emotion: 'Austrian men and women! This day has brought us face to face with a serious and decisive situation. It is my task to inform the Austrian people about the events of this day. The Government of the German Reich presented a time-limited ultimatum to the Federal President demanding that he appoint a candidate chosen by the Reich Government to the office of Chancellor and also follow its suggestions when selecting the ministers to serve in that cabinet. Should the Federal President not accept this ultimatum then German troops would begin to cross our frontiers this very hour.

'I wish to place on record before the world that the reports disseminated in Austria that the workers have revolted and that streams of blood have been shed, that the Government is incapable of mastering the situation and cannot ensure law and order, are fabrications from A to Z.

'The Federal President has instructed me to inform the nation that we are giving way to brute force. Because we refuse to shed German blood even in this tragic hour, we have ordered our armed forces, should an invasion take place, to withdraw without serious resistance, without resistance, and to await the decisions of the coming hours. The Federal President has asked the army's command over all troops. All further orders for the armed forces will be issued by him.

'So, in this hour, I bid farewell to the people of Austria with a German word and a wish from the bottom of my heart: "God save Austria!"'

They played the national anthem. After the last bars of Haydn's tune we all sat in the utter silence for a few moments. Then, before any of us had had a chance to say anything, the sounds of hundreds of men shouting at the top of their voices could be heard. Still indistinct, still distant, it sounded threatening none the less. Those raucous voices grew louder, were coming closer.

I rushed to the window and looked out into Nussdorferstrasse. It was still quite empty. A few moments. Then the first lorry came into sight. It was packed with shouting, screaming men. A huge swastika flag fluttered over their heads. Most of them had swastika armlets on their sleeves, some wore S. A. caps, some even steel helmets.

Now we could hear clearly what they were shouting: '*Ein Volk, ein Reich, ein Führer!*' they were chanting in chorus, followed by '*Ju-da verr-rrecke! Ju-da verr-rrecke!*' ('Per-ish Judah!') In English this sounds softer, less threatening, but in German, coming from a thousand throats, screaming it out in the full fury of their hate, as lorry after lorry with frenzied Nazis passed below our window, it is a sound one can never forget.

Father switched the light off so that the men on the lorries could not see us – my parents and the Ornsteins had joined me by the window – and we stood there for nearly twenty minutes watching the procession. Only when the last lorry had disappeared in the distance was the light switched on again. The others sat down, but I stayed by the window.

I was still looking out into Nussdorferstrasse when I suddenly heard a muffled shout from right below our window. I craned my neck and saw an Austrian policeman, a swastika brassard already over his dark green uniform sleeve, his truncheon in his fist, lashing out with beserk fury at a man writhing at his feet.

I immediately recognized that policeman. I had known him all my life. I had seen him on traffic duty at the nearby crossroads, had chatted with him when we occasionally met in the shops around the corner, had seen him give Father a polite salute in the street. Indeed, when I was much younger I had identified this policeman with Poldi's fictitious one, the one she had invented to get me to go to sleep in the dark. He had been, first the ogre of my childhood, then almost a friend, and now that I saw him club with all the strength of his powerful body some poor soul who had shouted out his anger at the ecstatic Nazis, not fiction but fact had made him an ogre again. Within minutes of Schuschnigg's farewell that policeman, yesterday's protector, had been transformed into tomorrow's persecutor and tormentor. That was more terrifying even than the frenzied *Ju-da, verr-rrecke!*' Nothing could have driven home more clearly what had happened on this one day than this single incident.

I turned back into Father's study and joined in the conversation. I said nothing about the scene I had witnessed. Now that all doubt had gone the talk had become more animated. The certainty must have given us all a feeling of relief. We did not know what was yet to come, but we all knew that our life in Austria and a family history linked so closely with that country for so long, were over. The radio, still on in the background, now played Hitler's favourite marches.

We finally parted at about two o'clock on the Saturday morning, and the words Selma Ornstein spoke to Mother as she was about to leave have remained in my mind through all these years. They illuminated so sharply the abyss that had opened between our past and our future. They were not at all profound. But the very simplicity of what she said was an unforgettable summing-up of 11 March 1938: Tell me, Stella, what on earth did we talk about before? Maids, children, dresses, food? What world did we think we were living in?'

Then we went to bed. Around us there still was the protective warmth and familiarity of my parents' flat.

But our home – it was no more.

HITLER SPEAKS AT THE NUREMBERG RALLY, 1938

Virginia Cowles

One night I went to the stadium with Jules Sauerwein to hear an address Hitler was making to Nazi political leaders gathered from all over Germany. The stadium was packed with nearly 200,000 spectators. As the time for the Führer's arrival drew near, the crowd grew restless. The minutes passed and the wait seemed interminable. Suddenly the beat of the drums increased and three motor-cycles with yellow standards fluttering from their wind-shields raced through the gates. A few minutes later a fleet of black cars rolled swiftly into the arena: in one of them, standing in the front seat, his hand outstretched in the Nazi salute, was Hitler.

The demonstration that followed was one of the most extraordinary I have ever witnessed. Hitler climbed to his box in the Grand Stand amid a deafening ovation, then gave a signal for the political leaders to enter. They came, a hundred thousand strong, through an opening in the far end of the arena. In the silver light they seemed to pour into the bowl like a flood of water. Each of them carried a Nazi flag and when they were assembled in mass formation, the bowl looked like a shimmering sea of swastikas.

Then Hitler began to speak. The crowd hushed into silence, but the drums continued their steady beat. Hitler's voice rasped into the night and every now and then the multitude broke into a roar of cheers. Some of the audience began swaying back and forth, chanting '*Seig Heil*' over and over again in a frenzy of delirium. I looked at the faces around me and saw tears streaming down people's cheeks. The drums had grown louder and I suddenly felt frightened. For a moment I wondered if it wasn't a dream; perhaps we were really in the heart of the African jungle. I had a sudden feeling of claustrophobia and whispered to Jules Sauerwein, asking if we couldn't leave. It was a silly question, for we were hemmed in on all sides, and there was nothing to do but sit there until the bitter end.

At last it was over. Hitler left the box and got back in the car. As soon as he stopped speaking the spell seemed to break and the magic vanish. That was the most extraordinary thing of all: for when he left the stand and climbed back into his car, his small figure suddenly became drab and unimpressive. You had to pinch yourself to realize that this was the man on whom the eyes of the world were riveted; that he alone held the lightning in his hands.

GAS-CONSCIOUSNESS IN ENGLAND, September 1938

Martha Gellhorn

Hitler's occupation of the German-speaking parts of Czechoslovakia brought Europe to the edge of war, and many prepared for the worst. In the event, Hitler was 'appeased' by Britain and France and the peace was maintained, if only for a year.

England is gas-conscious. There are 40 million gas masks already stored in government depots, and all over England people are being fitted with the ordinary civilian gas mask, which sells for about 75 cents and will be given away free in time of war. The ordinary gas mask is a small rubber affair, with isinglass over the eyes, a boxlike snout that contains the filter to keep out gas (but you can exhale tobacco smoke through the mask, which makes some people suspect that the masks are not exactly 100 per cent safe) and a narrow face-covering to keep the mask on. ('Of course you can get burned in it by mustard gas,' said the salesman, 'but then you can get burned in all of them.')

It is not sure at all that gas is a practical weapon against civilian populations, but it has been proved in Spain and China that a 500-pound bomb is a real horror. However, underground shelters against high-explosive bombs are not being built, because they are too expensive; and the main plan of ARP is dispersal, which means that when the sirens howl out the warning, the citizens of England are supposed to go home and wait and try to think about something else. The people are told that they can make their homes gasproof by sticking old rags and strips of adhesive tape over leaky walls, and can keep their window-panes from shattering when bombs fall in the neighbourhood by pasting three sheets of cellophane over their windows. They are sold (for $7.50) with a sand bucket and a shovel and a small fire hose: the idea is that you hurry forth (perhaps wearing dark glasses against the glare of burning London) with the shovel and scoop up an incendiary bomb and plop it into the sand bucket and then turn on the fire hose. Seven booklets are put out by the Home Office, to teach people how to behave during the air raids, easy lessons for beginners. Also, you are informed in advance that – if you work in ARP – you get $5,000 if you die or are blinded, or lose both feet or a hand and a foot. You get $2,500 if you are half blind or lose only one foot or hand, and so down the list of miseries.

Part IV

The Second World War
1939–45

GERMAN PANZERS INVADE POLAND,
1 September 1939

General Heinz Guderian

A leading tank expert and exponent of the *Blitzkrieg* ('lightning war') theory, Guderian created the Panzer armies which overran Poland in 1939, and the West in 1940.

On the 1 September at 04.45 hours the whole corps moved simultaneously over the frontier. There was a thick ground mist at first which prevented the air force from giving us any support. I accompanied the 3rd Panzer Brigade, in the first wave, as far as the area north of Zempelburg where the preliminary fighting took place. Unfortunately the heavy artillery of the 3rd Panzer Division felt itself compelled to fire into the mist, despite having received precise orders not to do so. The first shell landed fifty yards ahead of my command vehicle, the second fifty yards behind it. I reckoned that the next one was bound to be a direct hit and ordered my driver to turn about and drive off. The unaccustomed noise had made him nervous, however, and he drove straight into a ditch at full speed. The front axle of the half-tracked vehicle was bent so that the steering mechanism was put out of action. This marked the end of my drive. I made my way to my corps command post, procured myself a fresh vehicle and had a word with the over-eager artillerymen. Incidentally it may be noted that I was the first corps commander ever to use armoured command vehicles in order to accompany tanks on to the battlefield. They were equipped with radio, so that I was able to keep in constant touch with my corps headquarters and with the divisions under my command.

The first serious fighting took place north of Zempelburg in and around Gross-Klonia, where the mist suddenly lifted and the leading tanks found themselves face to face with Polish defensive positions. The Polish anti-tank gunners scored many direct hits. One officer, one officer cadet and eight other ranks were killed.

Gross-Klonia had once belonged to my great-grandfather, Freiherr Hiller von Gärtringen. Here, too, was buried my grandfather Guderian. My father had been born in this place. This was the first time I had ever set eyes on the estate, once so beloved by my family.

After successfully changing vehicles, I rejoined the 3rd Panzer Division whose most forward troops had now reached the Brahe. The bulk of the division was between Pruszcz and Klein-Klonia and was about to settle down for a rest. The divisional commander had been sent for by the Commander-in-Chief of the Army Group, Colonel-General von Bock, and was therefore absent. I asked the officers of the 6th Panzer Regiment who were there to tell me about the situation on the Brahe.

The regimental commander did not believe that a passage of the river could be forced on that day, and he was eager to carry out the welcome orders for a rest. The corps order – that the Brahe should be crossed during the first day of the attack – had been forgotten. I walked angrily away and tried to decide what measure I should take to improve this unhappy state of affairs. A young Lieutenant Felix came over to where I was standing. He had taken off his tunic, his shirt sleeves were rolled up, and his arms were black with powder. 'Herr General,' he said, 'I've just come from the Brahe. The enemy forces on the far bank are weak. The Poles set fire to the bridge at Hummermühle, but I put the fire out from my tank. The bridge is crossable. The advance has only stopped because there's no one to lead it. You must go there yourself, sir.' I looked at the young man in amazement. He made a very good impression and his eyes inspired confidence. Why should not this young lieutenant have done the trick of Columbus and the egg? I followed his advice and drove through a confusion of German and Polish vehicles along the narrow sandy track that led through the woods to Hummermühle, where I arrived between 16.00 and 17.00 hours. A group of staff officers were standing behind a stout oak tree about 100 yards from the water's edge. They greeted me with the cry: 'Herr General, they're shooting here!' They were indeed, both the tank guns of the 6th Panzer Regiment and the rifles of the 3rd Rifle Regiment blazing away. The enemy on the far bank sat in his trenches and was invisible. First of all I put a stop to the idiotic firing, in which I was ably assisted by the newly arrived commander of the 3rd Rifle Brigade, Colonel Angern. Then I ordered that the extent of the enemy's defensive positions be established. Motor-cycle Battalion 3, which had not yet been in action, was sent across the river in rubber boats at a point that was not under enemy fire. When they had crossed successfully, I ordered the tanks over the bridge. They took the Polish bicycle company, which was defending this sector of the stream, prisoner. Casualties were negligible.

THE HOUSE OF COMMONS DISCUSSES WAR AND PEACE, LONDON, 2 September 1939

Mr Ralph Glyn, MP

Diary: September 3

Last night in London was one of the great times in modern history. The half-hour in the Commons – 7.30 to 8 – was perhaps the most decisive half-hour that we have known.

All through the day the House had been in a schoolboyish, almost hysterical mood; they were laughing and shuffling. There was a feeling that something fishy was happening in Downing Street. The Cabinet was still sitting. Ministers were telephoning Paris – and the Germans were bombing Poland. *Why* were we not at war?

At half-past seven we met again, this time subdued and tense. Chamberlain we knew would declare war. The Ambassadors were looking down; Count Edward Raczijnsky pale and worn. Chamberlain came in looking grey – a kind of whitish-grey – and glum, dour. Captain Margesson, the Secretary to the Treasury, came behind him, purple with anxiety. Chamberlain's statement! . . . In the house we thought he was only halfway through when – he sat down. There was a gasp, first of horror, then anger. His own back-benchers leaned forward to cry, 'Munich, Munich!' The House seemed to rise to its feet with Mr Arthur Greenwood, the Labour leader.

Mr L. S. Amery, sitting very small near Anthony Eden, jumped up to shout at Greenwood – 'Speak for England.' Others took up the cry. Chamberlain white and hunched. Margesson with sweat pouring down his face, Sir John Simon, the Foreign Secretary, punctiliously looking holy.

Greenwood spoke slowly and very simply. He spoke for England and what is more he saved Chamberlain by most skilfully suggesting that it was the French who were delaying. Then one or two back-benchers, Chamberlain's own supporters, got up. It was not a joint Anglo-French pledge to Poland, they said, it was a *British* pledge – why were we not fulfilling it? The House swung against Chamberlain again. Winston Churchill, I saw, was getting whiter and grimmer. He turned round to look at Eden, who nodded as if to say, 'You speak, I'll follow.' I know that Churchill was about to move a vote of censure on the Government – which would have fallen. But Chamberlain looked across at Churchill: 'I'm playing straight,' his glance seemed to say, 'there really *are* reasons for delay.' Churchill sat back, relaxed, uneasy.

Then James Maxton, the pacifist, rose, gaunt, a Horseman from the Apocalypse, doom written across his face: 'Don't let's talk of national honour: what do such phrases mean? The plain fact is that war means the slaughter of millions. If the Prime Minister can still maintain the peace he will have saved those lives, he mustn't be rushed.' Again the House swung and was poised. We all thought in the curious hush: What if the gaunt figure of doom were right after all? Slaughter – misery – ruin – was he right? But the alternative: Hitler trading on our fears, Germany treading on freedom, Europe under terror. The whole House was swayed in unison with the drama which itself was living.

Another back-bencher spoke: 'We must keep our pledge – Hitler must be stopped.' Once again we were swinging against Chamberlain, when Margesson, damp and shapeless, rose to move the adjournment. In a kind of daze it was carried.

We broke up, some feeling sick from the reaction – two members *were* sick – all were uneasy and ashamed. I went home, lay awake all night, slept a bit towards morning, and was awakened by the air-raid warning. Had the Germans read the feelings of the country? Were they attacking first?

BRITAIN DECLARES WAR ON GERMANY, 3 September 1939

Neville Chamberlain

The text of the Prime Minister's announcement of war, broadcast on the fine, late summer's morning of Sunday, 3 September.

I am speaking to you from the Cabinet Room at 10, Downing Street.

This morning the British Ambassador in Berlin handed the German Government a final Note stating that, unless we heard from them by 11 o'clock that they were prepared at once to withdraw their troops from Poland, a state of war would exist between us.

I have to tell you now that no such undertaking has been received, and that consequently this country is at war with Germany. You can imagine what a bitter blow it is to me that all my long struggle to win peace has failed. Yet I cannot believe that there is anything more or anything different that I could have done and that would have been more successful.

Up to the very last it would have been quite possible to have arranged a peaceful and honourable settlement between Germany and Poland, but Hitler would not have it. He had evidently made up his mind to attack Poland whatever happened and although he now says he put forward reasonable proposals which were rejected by the Poles, that is not a true statement.

The proposals were never shown to the Poles, nor to us, and, though they were announced in a German broadcast on Thursday night, Hitler did not wait to hear comments on them, but ordered his troops to cross the Polish frontier. His action shows convincingly that there is no chance of expecting that this man will ever give up his practice of using force to gain his will. He can only be stopped by force.

We and France are today, in fulfilment of our obligations, going to the aid of Poland, who is so bravely resisting this wicked and unprovoked attack on her people. We have a clear conscience. We have done all that any country could do to establish peace. The situation in which no word given by Germany's ruler could be trusted and no people or country could feel themselves safe has become intolerable. And now that we have resolved to finish it, I know that you will all play your part with calmness and courage.

At such a moment as this the assurances of support that we have received from the Empire are a source of profound encouragement to us.

When I have finished speaking certain detailed announcements will be made on behalf of the Government. Give these your closest attention. The Government have made plans under which it will be possible to carry on the work of the nation in the days of stress and strain that may be ahead. But these plans need your help.

You may be taking your part in the fighting services or as a volunteer in one of the branches of Civil Defence. If so you will report for duty in accordance with the instructions you have received. You may be engaged in work essential to the prosecution of war for the maintenance of the life of the people – in factories, in transport, in public utility concerns, or in the supply of other necessaries of life. If so, it is of vital importance that you should carry on with your jobs.

Now may God bless you all. May He defend the right. It is the evil things that we shall be fighting against – brute force, bad faith, injustice, oppression and persecution – and against them I am certain that the right will prevail.

WAR IS ANNOUNCED IN BERLIN, 3 September 1939

William L. Shirer

The American correspondent William L. Shirer reported on Nazi Germany, mostly for CBS radio, until 1940.

I was standing in the Wilhelmplatz about noon when the loudspeakers suddenly announced that England had declared herself at war with Germany. Some 250 people were standing there in the sun. They listened attentively to the announcement. When it was finished there was not a murmur. They just stood there as they were before. Stunned. The people cannot realize yet that Hitler has led them into a world war. No issue has been created for them yet, though as this day wears on, it is plain that 'Albion's perfidy' will become the issue as it did in 1914. In *Mein Kampf* Hitler says the greatest mistake the Kaiser made was to fight England, and Germany must never repeat that mistake.

It has been a lovely September day, the sun shining, the air balmy, the sort of day the Berliner loves to spend in the woods or on the lakes nearby. I walked in the streets. On the faces of the people astonishment, depression. Until today they have been going about their business pretty much as usual. There were food cards and soap cards and you couldn't get any gasoline and at night it was difficult stumbling around in the black-out. But the war in the east has seemed a bit far away to them – two moonlight nights and not a single Polish plane over Berlin to bring destruction – and the papers saying that German troops have been advancing all along the line, that the Polish air force has been destroyed. Last night I heard Germans talking of the 'Polish thing' lasting but a few weeks, or months at the most. Few believed that Britain and France would move. Ribbentrop was sure they wouldn't and had told the Führer, who believed him. The British and French had been accommodating before. Another Munich, why not? Yesterday, when it seemed that London and Paris were hesitating, everyone, including those in the Wilshelmstrasse, was optimistic. Why not?

In 1914, I believe, the excitement in Berlin on the first day of the World War was tremendous. Today, no excitement, no hurrahs, no cheering, no throwing of flowers, no war fever, no war hysteria. There is not even any hate for the French and British – despite Hitler's various proclamations to the people, the party, the East Army, the West Army, accusing the 'English warmongers and capitalistic Jews' of starting this war. When I passed the French and British embassies this afternoon, the sidewalk in front of each of them was deserted. A lone *Schupo* paced up and down before each.

At lunch-time we gathered in the courtyard of the Adlon for drinks with a dozen members of the British Embassy staff. They seemed completely unmoved by events. They talked about *dogs* and such stuff. Some mystery about the French not acting in concert with the British today, Coulondre's ultimatum not running out until five p.m., six hours after Britain was at war. But the French tell us this was due to faulty communications with Paris.

The High Command lets it be known that on the western front the Germans won't fire *first* against the French.

Later. – Broadcast all afternoon and evening. Third night of the black-out. No bombs, though we rather expected the British and French. The newspapers continue to praise the decree against listening in to foreign broadcasts! What are they afraid of?

THE HOUSE OF COMMONS DISCUSSES EVACUATION, LONDON, September 1939

Harold Nicolson, MP

Diary: 14 September, 1939

The House is mainly concerned with the evacuation of children. It seems that where children have been evacuated along with their school-teachers everything has gone well. But when the mothers have come, there has been trouble. Many of the children are verminous and have disgusting habits. This horrifies the cottagers upon whom they have been billeted. Moreover, the mothers refuse to help, grumble dreadfully, and are pathetically homesick and bored. Many of them have drifted back to London. Much ill feeling has been caused. But the interesting thing is that this feeling is

not between the rich and the poor but between the urban
and the rural poor. This is a perplexing social event. One
thing that they say is that these children were evacuated at
the end of the holidays and were therefore more verminous
and undisciplined than if they had been taken in the middle
of the term. But the effect will be to demonstrate to people
how deplorable is the standard of life and civilization among
the urban proletariat.

THE *ROYAL OAK* IS TORPEDOED, SCAPA FLOW, 13 October 1939

Gunther Prien

The Second World War was barely six weeks old when German
submarine U-47, commanded by Gunther Prien, penetrated the
defences of the Royal Navy's base at Scapa Flow and sank the
battleship *Royal Oak*.

. . . We are in Scapa Flow.

14.10.39. It is disgustingly light. The whole bay is lit up. To
the south of Cava there is nothing. I go farther in. To port, I
recognize the Hoxa Sound coastguard, to which in the next
few minutes the boat must present itself as a target. In that
event all would be lost; at present south of Cava no ships are
to be seen, although visibility is extremely good. Hence
decisions:

South of Cava there is no shipping; so before staking
everything on success, all possible precautions must be
taken. Therefore, turn to port is made. We proceed north
by the coast. Two battleships are lying there at anchor, and
further inshore, destroyers. Cruisers not visible, therefore
attack on the big fellows.

Distance apart, 3,000 metres. Estimated depth, seven and

a half metres. Impact firing. One torpedo fired on northern ship, two on southern. After a good three and a half minutes, a torpedo detonates on the northern ship; of the other two nothing is to be seen.

About! Torpedo fired from stern; in the bow two tubes are loaded; three torpedoes from the bow. After three tense minutes comes the detonation on the nearer ship. There is a loud explosion, roar, and rumbling. Then come columns of water, followed by columns of fire, and splinters fly through the air. The harbour springs to life. Destroyers are lit up, signalling starts on every side, and on land, 200 metres away from me, cars roar along the roads. A battleship had been sunk, a second damaged, and the other three torpedoes have gone to blazes. All the tubes are empty. I decide to withdraw, because: (1) With my periscopes I cannot conduct night attacks while submerged . . . (2) On a bright night I cannot manoeuvre unobserved in a calm sea. (3) I must assume that I was observed by the driver of a car which stopped opposite us, turned around, and drove off towards Scapa at top speed. (4) Nor can I go farther north, for there, well hidden from my sight, lie the destroyers which were previously dimly distinguishable.

At full speed both engines we withdraw. Everything is simple until we reach Skildaenoy Point. Then we have more trouble. It is now low tide. The current is against us. Engines at slow and dead slow; I attempt to get away. I must leave by the south through the narrows, because of the depth of the water. Things are again difficult. Course, 058°, slow – ten knots. I make no progress. At full speed I pass the southern blockship with nothing to spare. The helmsman does magnificently. Full speed ahead both, finally three-quarter speed and full ahead all out. Free of the blockships – ahead a mole! Hard over and again about, and at 02.15 we are once more outside. A pity that only one was destroyed. The torpedo misses I explain as due to faults of course, speed and drift. In tube 4, a misfire. The crew behaved splendidly throughout the operation.

THE BREAKTHROUGH ON THE MEUSE, FRANCE, 13 May 1940

Erwin Rommel, Wehrmacht

After the months of 'phoney war', Hitler sent his army sweeping into France and the Low Countries. The breakthrough of German armour at the River Meuse, in which Rommel played the key role, allowed the Wehrmacht to by-pass France's heavily fortified Maginot Line.

On 13 May, I drove off to Dinant at about 04.00 hours with Captain Schraepler. The whole of the divisional artillery was already in position as ordered, with its forward observers stationed at the crossing points. In Dinant I found only a few men of the 7th Rifle Regiment. Shells were dropping in the town from French artillery west of the Meuse, and there were a number of knocked-out tanks in the streets leading down to the river. The noise of battle could be heard from the Meuse valley.

There was no hope of getting my command and signals vehicle down the steep slope to the Meuse unobserved, so Schraepler and I clambered down on foot through the wood to the valley bottom. The 6th Rifle Regiment was about to cross to the other bank in rubber boats, but was being badly held up by heavy artillery fire and by the extremely troublesome small arms fire of French troops installed among the rocks on the west bank.

The situation when I arrived was none too pleasant. Our boats were being destroyed one after the other by the French flanking fire, and the crossing eventually came to a standstill. The enemy infantry were so well concealed that they were impossible to locate even after a long search through glasses. Again and again they directed their fire into the area in which I and my companions – the commanders of the Rifle

Brigade and the Engineer Battalion – were lying. A smoke screen in the Meuse valley would have prevented these infantry doing much harm. But we had no smoke unit. So I now gave orders for a number of houses in the valley to be set alight in order to supply the smoke we lacked.

Minute by minute the enemy fire grew more unpleasant. From up river a damaged rubber boat came drifting down to us with a badly wounded man clinging to it, shouting and screaming for help – the poor fellow was near to drowning. But there was no help for him here, the enemy fire was too heavy.

Meanwhile the village of Grange [1¼ miles west of Houx (and the Meuse), and 3 miles north-west of Dinant] on the west bank had been taken by the 7th Motor-cycle Battalion, but they had not cleaned up the river bank as thoroughly as they should have done. I therefore gave orders for the rocks on the west bank to be cleared of the enemy.

With Captain Schraepler, I now drove south down the Meuse valley road in a Panzer IV to see how things were going with the 7th Rifle Regiment. On the way we came under fire several times from the western bank and Schraepler was wounded in the arm from a number of shell splinters. Single French infantrymen surrendered as we approached.

By the time we arrived the 7th Rifle Regiment had already succeeded in getting a company across to the west bank, but the enemy fire had then become so heavy that their crossing equipment had been shot to pieces and the crossing had had to be halted. Large numbers of wounded were receiving treatment in a house close beside the demolished bridge. As at the northern crossing point, there was nothing to be seen of the enemy who were preventing the crossing. As there was clearly no hope of getting any more men across at this point without powerful artillery and tank support to deal with the enemy nests, I drove back to Division Headquarters, where I met the Army commander, Colonel-General von Kluge and the Corps commander, General Hoth.

After talking over the situation with Major Heidkaemper and making the necessary arrangements, I drove back along the Meuse to Leffé [a village on the outskirts of Dinant] to get the crossing moving there. I had already given orders for several Panzer IIIs and IVs and a troop of artillery to be at my disposal at the crossing point. We left the signals vehicle for the time being at a point some 500 yards east of the river and went forward on foot through deserted farms towards the Meuse. In Leffé we found a number of rubber boats, all more or less badly damaged by enemy fire, lying in the street where our men had left them. Eventually, after being bombed on the way by our own aircraft, we arrived at the river.

At Leffé weir we took a quick look at the footbridge, which had been barred by the enemy with a spiked steel plate. The firing in the Meuse valley had ceased for the moment and we moved off to the right through some houses to the crossing point proper. The crossing had now come to a complete standstill, with the officers badly shaken by the casualties which their men had suffered. On the opposite bank we could see several men of the company which was already across, among them many wounded. Numerous damaged boats and rubber dinghies lay on the opposite bank. The officers reported that nobody dared show himself outside cover, as the enemy opened fire immediately on anyone they spotted.

Several of our tanks and heavy weapons were in position on the embankment east of the houses, but had seemingly already fired off almost all their ammunition. However, the tanks I had ordered to the crossing point soon arrived, to be followed shortly afterwards by two field howitzers from the Battalion Grasemann.

All points on the western bank likely to hold enemy riflemen were now brought under fire, and soon the aimed fire of all weapons was pouring into rocks and buildings. Lieutenant Hanke knocked out a pill-box on the bridge ramp with several rounds. The tanks, with turrets traversed left, drove slowly north at fifty yards' spacing along the Meuse valley, closely watching the opposite slopes.

Under cover of this fire the crossing slowly got going again, and a cable ferry using several large pontoons was started. Rubber boats paddled backwards and forwards and brought back the wounded from the west bank. One man who fell out of his boat on the way grabbed hold of the ferry rope and was dragged underwater through the Meuse. He was rescued by Private Heidenreich, who dived in and brought him to the bank.

I now took over personal command of the 2nd Battalion of the 7th Rifle Regiment and for some time directed operations myself.

With Lieutenant Most I crossed the Meuse in one of the first boats and at once joined the company which had been across since early morning. From the company command post we could see Companies Enkefort and Lichter were making rapid progress.

I then moved up north along a deep gully to the Company Enkefort. As we arrived an alarm came in: 'Enemy tanks in front'. The company had no anti-tank weapons, and I therefore gave orders for small arms fire to be opened on the tanks as quickly as possible, whereupon we saw them pull back into a hollow about 1,000 yards north-west of Leffé. Large numbers of French stragglers came through the bushes and slowly laid down their arms.

DUNKIRK: THE VIEW FROM THE BEACHES, May 1940

A British artillery officer

By 21 May the German army had reached the English Channel at Abbeville, encircling the Belgian army and British Expeditionary

Force sent to reinforce the Allied front. On 26 May Lord Gort, commander of the BEF, was authorized to re-embark his army back to Britain, and he began to concentrate the BEF and remnants of the French and Belgian armies – a total of some 400,000 men – at Dunkirk. The evacuation continued for nine days, from 26 May to June 3, all of them under ceaseless attack by the *Wehrmacht* and *Luftwaffe*.

Eventually we arrived at the spot on this side of the last canal separating us from the sea, where we had to abandon the vehicles. They were smashed up in the darkness and pushed into the canal. The men formed up by the roadside and the roll was called for the last time. A weird scene, the Troop sergeant-majors calling out the names of the gunners in loud whispers, and ticking them off on their lists by torch-light as the answers came back out of the darkness, from nowhere it seemed.

'All present and correct, sir.'

And once more the fifty of us started off, this time on foot, formed-up in threes, the Major and I walking at the head of the column. To our great joy we discovered that the bridge spanning the canal had not been smashed. Once over it, and another obstacle between us and the Unknown had been passed. We continued towards Malo-les-Bains, crossing the railway, and marching through the ruined street of Rösen-daal, whose skeleton walls stood around us like the ruins of some bygone civilization. The only sound was the crunching of the broken glass under our feet, as if we were marching over hard ice-crystals on a winter's day. Mysterious shadows flitted about the streets, in and out of broken doorways, and disappearing silently round corners. They were stray inha-bitants who had been cut off by the swift march of events and were living in cellars. And a few looters. And, probably, a few spies. The German gun-fire was now incessant, the flash of the explosions continually lighting up the scene for a second or two on every side of us.

Now we were no longer alone. We began to meet little batches of our infantry marching in the same direction. Often as we approached we would be hailed out of the darkness:

'Is that A Company, King's Own Scottish Borderers?' Or the name of some other unit would be shouted. These were bits of the rearguard coming back, and marching still in good formation down to the beaches.

We were now in the region of the dunes, which rose like humps of a deeper darkness. And these in their turn were dotted with the still blacker shapes of abandoned vehicles, half-sunk in the sand, fantastic twisted shapes of burned-out skeletons, and crazy-looking wreckage that had been heaped up in extraordinary piles by the explosions of bombs. All these black shapes were silhouetted against the angry red glare in the sky, which reflected down on us the agony of burning Dunkirk.

Slowly we picked our way between the wreckage, sinking ankle-deep in the loose sand, until we reached the gaunt skeletons of what had once been the houses on the promenade. The whole front was one long continuous line of blazing buildings, a high wall of fire, roaring and darting in tongues of flame, with the smoke pouring upwards and disappearing in the blackness of the sky above the roof-tops. Out seawards the darkness was as thick and smooth as black velvet, except for now and again when the shape of a sunken destroyer or paddle-steamer made a slight thickening on its impenetrable surface. Facing us, the great black wall of the Mole stretched from the beach far out into sea, the end of it almost invisible to us. The Mole had an astounding, terrifying background of giant flames leaping a hundred feet into the air from blazing oil tanks. At the shore end of the Mole stood an obelisk, and the high-explosive shells burst around it with monotonous regularity.

Along the promenade, in parties of fifty, the remnants of practically all the last regiments were wearily trudging

along. There was no singing, and very little talk. Everyone
was far too exhausted to waste breath. Occasionally out of
the darkness came a sudden shout:

'A Company, Green Howards . . .'

'C Company, East Yorks . . .'

These shouts came either from stragglers trying to find lost
units, or guides on the look-out for the parties they were to
lead on to the Mole for evacuation.

The tide was out. Over the wide stretch of sand could be
dimly discerned little oblong masses of soldiers, moving in
platoons and orderly groups down towards the edge of the
sea. Now and again you would hear a shout:

'Alf, where are you? . . .'

'Let's hear from you, Bill . . .'

'Over this way, George . . .'

It was none too easy to keep contact with one's friends in
the darkness, and amid so many little masses of moving men,
all looking very much alike. If you stopped for a few seconds
to look behind, the chances were you attached yourself to
some entirely different unit.

From the margin of the sea, at fairly wide intervals, three
long thin black lines protruded into the water, conveying the
effect of low wooden breakwaters. These were lines of men,
standing in pairs behind one another far out into the water,
waiting in queues till boats arrived to transport them, a score
or so at a time, to the steamers and warships that were filling
up with the last survivors. The queues stood there, fixed and
almost as regular as if ruled. No bunching, no pushing.
Nothing like the mix-up to be seen at the turnstiles when
a crowd is going into a football match. Much more orderly,
even, than a waiting theatre queue.

About this time, afraid that some of our men might be
tailing off, I began shouting, '2004th Field Regiment . . .
2004th Field Regiment . . .'

A group of dead and dying soldiers on the path in front of
us quickened our desire to quit the promenade. Stepping

over the bodies we marched down the slope on to the dark beach. Dunkirk front was now a lurid study in red and black; flames, smoke, and the night itself all mingling together to compose a frightful panorama of death and destruction. Red and black, all the time, except for an occasional flash of white low in the sky miles away to the left and right where big shells from coastal defence guns at Calais and Nieuport were being hurled into the town.

Down on the beach you immediately felt yourself surrounded by a deadly evil atmosphere. A horrible stench of blood and mutilated flesh pervaded the place. There was no escape from it. Not a breath of air was blowing to dissipate the appalling odour that arose from the dead bodies that had been lying on the sand, in some cases for several days. We might have been walking through a slaughter-house on a hot day. The darkness, which hid some of the sights of horror from our eyes, seemed to thicken this dreadful stench. It created the impression that death was hovering around, very near at hand.

We set our faces in the direction of the sea, quickening our pace to pass through the belt of this nauseating miasma as soon as possible.

'Water . . . Water . . .' groaned a voice from the ground just in front of us.

It was a wounded infantryman. He had been hit so badly that there was no hope for him. Our water-bottles had long been empty, but by carefully draining them all into one we managed to collect a mouthful or two. A sergeant knelt down beside the dying man and held the bottle to his lips. Then we proceeded on our way, leaving the bottle with the last few drains in it near the poor fellow's hand so that he could moisten his lips from time to time.

On either side, scattered over the sand in all sorts of positions, were the dark shapes of dead and dying men, sometimes alone, sometimes in twos and threes. Every now and then we had to pull ourselves up sharply in the darkness to avoid falling over a wooden cross erected by comrades on the spot where some soldier had been buried. No assistance that availed anything could be given to these dying men. The living themselves had nothing to offer them. They just pressed forward to the sea, hoping that the same fate would not be theirs. And still it remained a gamble all the time whether that sea, close though it was, would be reached in safety. Splinters from bursting shells were continually whizzing through the air, and occasionally a man in one of the plodding groups would fall with a groan.

DUNKIRK: THE VIEW FROM THE BOATS, 1 June 1940

Commander C. H. Lightoller, RNR (Retd)

The evacuation was carried by an armada of 222 naval units and 665 civilian craft. These vessels succeeded in bringing back to Britain 224,585 British and 112,546 French and Belgian troops. Among the civilian vessels was the yacht *Sundowner* owned by Commander Lightoller. Lightoller had already appeared in history; he was the senior surviving officer of the *Titanic*.

Half-way across we avoided a floating mine by a narrow margin, but having no firearms of any description – not even a tin hat – we had to leave its destruction to someone better equipped. A few minutes later we had our first introduction to enemy aircraft, three fighters flying high. Before they could be offensive, a British destroyer – *Worcester*, I think – overhauled us and drove them off. At 2.25 p.m. we sighted and closed the twenty-five-foot motor-cruiser *Westerly*; broken down and badly on fire. As the crew of two (plus three naval ratings she had picked up in Dunkirk) wished to abandon ship – and quickly – I went alongside and took them aboard, giving them the additional pleasure of again facing the hell they had only just left.

We made the fairway buoy to the Roads shortly after the sinking of a French transport with severe loss of life. Steaming slowly through the wreckage we entered the Roads. For some time now we had been subject to sporadic bombing and machine-gun fire, but as the *Sundowner* is exceptionally and extremely quick on the helm, by waiting till the last moment and putting the helm hard over – my son at the wheel – we easily avoided every attack, though sometimes near lifted out of the water.

It had been my intention to go right on to the beaches, where my second son, Second-Lieutenant R. T. Lightoller, had been evacuated some forty-eight hours previously; but those of the *Westerly* informed me that the troops were all away, so I headed up for Dunkirk piers. By now dive-bombers seemed to be eternally dropping out of the cloud of enemy aircraft overhead. Within half a mile of the pierheads a two-funnelled grey-painted transport had over-hauled and was just passing us to port when two salvoes were dropped in quick succession right along her port side. For a few moments she was hid in smoke and I certainly thought they had got her. Then she reappeared, still gaily heading for the piers and entered just ahead of us.

The difficulty of taking troops on board from the quay high above us was obvious, so I went alongside a destroyer (*Worcester* again, I think) where they were already embarking. I got hold of her captain and told him I could take about a hundred (though the most I had ever had on board was twenty-one). He, after consultation with the military C.O., told me to carry on and get the troops aboard. I may say here that before leaving Cubitt's Yacht Basin, we had worked all night stripping her down of everything movable, masts included, that would tend to lighten her and make for more room.

My son, as previously arranged, was to pack the men in and use every available inch of space – which I'll say he carried out to some purpose. On deck I detailed a naval rating to tally the troops aboard. At fifty I called below, 'How are you getting on?' getting the cheery reply, 'Oh, plenty of room yet.' At seventy-five my son admitted they were getting pretty tight – all equipment and arms being left on deck.

I now started to pack them on deck, having passed word below for every man to lie down and keep down; the same applied on deck. By the time we had fifty on deck I could feel her getting distinctly tender, so took no more. Actually we had exactly a hundred and thirty on board, including three *Sundowners* and five *Westerlys*.

During the whole embarkation we had quite a lot of attention from enemy planes, but derived an amazing degree of comfort from the fact that the *Worcester*'s A.A. guns kept up an everlasting bark overhead.

Casting off and backing out we entered the Roads again; there it was continuous and unmitigated hell. The troops were just splendid and of their own initiative detailed look-outs ahead, astern, and abeam for inquisitive planes, as my attention was pretty wholly occupied watching the steering and giving orders to Roger at the wheel. Any time an aircraft seemed inclined to try its hand on us, one of the look-outs would just call quietly, 'Look out for this bloke, skipper', at the same time pointing. One bomber that had been parti-cularly offensive, itself came under the notice of one of our fighters and suddenly plunged vertically into the sea just about fifty yards astern of us. It was the only time any man ever raised his voice above a conversational tone, but as that big black bomber hit the water they raised an echoing cheer.

My youngest son, Pilot Officer H. B. Lightoller (lost at the outbreak of war in the first raid on Wilhelmshaven), flew a Blenheim and had at different times given me a whole lot of useful information about attack, defence and evasive tactics (at which he was apparently particularly good) and I attribute in a great measure our success in getting across without a single casualty to his unwitting help.

On one occasion an enemy machine came up astern at about a hundred feet with the obvious intention of raking our decks. He was coming down in a gliding dive and I knew that he must elevate some ten to fifteen degrees before his guns would bear. Telling my son 'Stand by,' I waited till, as near as I could judge, he was just on the point of pulling up, and then 'Hard a-port.' (She turns 180 degrees in exactly her own length.) This threw his aim completely off. He banked and tried again. Then 'Hard a-starboard,' with the same result. After a third attempt he gave it up in disgust. Had I had a machine-gun of any sort, he was a sitter – in fact, there were at least three that I am confident we could have accounted for during the trip.

Not the least of our difficulties was contending with the wash of fast craft, such as destroyers and transports. In every instance I had to stop completely, take the way off the ship and head the heavy wash. The M.C. being where it was, to have taken one of these seas on either the quarter or beam would have at once put paid to our otherwise successful cruise. The effect of the consequent plunging on the troops below, in a stinking atmosphere with all ports and skylights closed, can well be imagined. They were literally packed like the proverbial sardines, even one in the bath and another on the WC, so that all the poor devils could do was sit and be sick. Added were the remnants of bully beef and biscuits. So that after discharging our cargo in Ramsgate at ten p.m., there lay before the three of us a nice clearing-up job.

WAITING FOR THE GERMANS, PARIS, 12 June 1940

Emmanuel d'Astier

I went first to the Invalides. The only officer I found there said: 'We are expecting them at any moment.' Beneath our feet, the Metro had fallen silent, the buses and taxis were no doubt with the Post Office and the other vehicles on the roads to the south. All traffic had ceased; the police had been withdrawn. I tried to get news from the houses of five or six friends: but the friends and their *concierges* had gone. I left Bordier near the Opera to attend to his business. He would have considerable difficulty in tracing his machines. Then I went home.

The house was empty. On the staircase, I heard a sound of sobbing. Seated on a step, a maidservant was weeping: 'I've been left behind; I've been left behind.' I sat down beside her, patted her on the back and promised to take her away. . . . When I got up to leave the house, nothing bound me any longer to the world which had come to an end. And yet, I looked round for some talisman to take with me. Even though I had conquered hope and desire for possessions, books remained my weakness. I put six in my pockets.

Bordier was waiting for me at a café in the rue Richer; it seemed to be the only one open for a kilometre around. Two metal merchants were sitting with him. A newsboy gave us the last copy of a half-sized paper; it looked like the newspaper of a besieged city. Two women at the bar were questioning the cashier.

'Where are they?'

'At Saint-Denis.'

'It's all over then?'

'Perhaps it's a trap.'

The panic-stricken had left Paris. Those who remained were on holiday, if somewhat bewildered. From the Boulevards to the Porte de Châtillon, I do not believe we passed a single car. The choice had been made. But for a few pedestrians in the deserted streets all was still.

Paris fell on 14 June.

FRANCE SURRENDERS, COMPIÈGNE, 21 June 1940

William L. Shirer

On 21 June France capitulated and signed a formal surrender to the Germans. The signing took place in the railway carriage at Compiègne, where Marshal Foch had dictated terms to the Germans in 1918.

On the exact spot in the little clearing in the Forest of Compiègne where, at five a.m. on 11 November 1918, the armistice which ended the World War was signed, Adolf Hitler today handed *his* armistice terms to France. To make German revenge complete, the meeting of the German and French plenipotentiaries took place in Marshal Foch's private [railway] car, in which Foch laid down the armistice terms to Germany twenty-two years ago. Even the same table in the rickety old *wagon-lit* car was used. And through the windows we saw Hitler occupying the very seat on which Foch had sat at that table when he dictated the other armistice.

The humiliation of France, of the French, was complete. And yet in the preamble to the armistice terms Hitler told the French that he had not chosen this spot at Compiègne out of revenge; merely to right an old wrong. From the demeanour of the French delegates I gathered that they did not appreciate the difference . . .

The armistice negotiations began at three-fifteen p.m. A warm June sun beat down on the great elm and pine trees, and cast pleasant shadows on the wooded avenues as Hitler, with the German plenipotentiaries at his side, appeared. He alighted from his car in front of the French monument to Alsace-Lorraine which stands at the end of an avenue about 200 yards from the clearing where the armistice car waited on exactly the same spot it occupied twenty-two years ago.

The Alsace-Lorraine statue, I noted, was covered with German war flags so that you could not see its sculptured work nor read its inscription. But I had seen it some years before – the large sword representing the sword of the Allies, and its point sticking into a large, limp eagle, representing the old Empire of the Kaiser. And the inscription underneath in French saying: 'TO THE HEROIC SOLDIERS OF FRANCE . . . DEFENDERS OF THE COUNTRY AND OF RIGHT . . . GLORIOUS LIBERATORS OF ALSACE-LORRAINE'.

Through my glasses I saw the Führer stop, glance at the monument, observe the Reich flags with their big swastikas in the centre. Then he strode slowly towards us, towards the little clearing in the woods. I observed his face. It was grave, solemn, yet brimming with revenge. There was also in it, as in his springy step, a note of the triumphant conqueror, the defier of the world. There was something else, difficult to describe, in his expression, a sort of scornful, inner joy at being present at this great reversal of fate – a reversal he himself had wrought.

Now he reaches the little opening in the woods. He pauses and looks slowly around. The clearing is in the form of a circle some 200 yards in diameter and laid out like a park. Cypress trees line it all round – and behind them, the great elms and oaks of the forest. This has been one of France's national shrines for twenty-two years. From a discreet position on the perimeter of the circle we watch.

Hitler pauses, and gazes slowly around. In a group just behind him are the other German plenipotentiaries: Göring, grasping his field-marshal's baton in one hand. He wears the sky-blue uniform of the air force. All the Germans are in uniform, Hitler in a double-breasted grey uniform, with the Iron Cross hanging from his left breast pocket. Next to Göring are the two German army chiefs – General Keitel, chief of the Supreme Command, and General von Brauchitsch, commander-in-chief of the German army. Both are just approaching sixty, but look younger, especially Keitel, who had a dapper appearance with his cap slightly cocked on one side.

Then there is Erich Raeder, Grand Admiral of the German Fleet, in his blue naval uniform and the invariable upturned collar which German naval officers usually wear. There are two non-military men in Hitler's suite – his Foreign Minister, Joachim von Ribbentrop, in the field-grey uniform of the Foreign Office; and Rudolf Hess, Hitler's deputy, in a grey party uniform.

The time is now three-eighteen p.m. Hitler's personal flag is run up on a small standard in the centre of the opening.

Also in the centre is a great granite block which stands some three feet above the ground. Hitler, followed by the others, walks slowly over to it, steps up, and reads the inscription engraved in great high letters on that block. It says: 'HERE ON THE ELEVENTH OF NOVEMBER 1918 SUCCUMBED THE CRIMINAL PRIDE OF THE GERMAN EMPIRE ... VANQUISHED BY THE FREE PEOPLES WHICH IT TRIED TO ENSLAVE.'

Hitler reads it and Göring reads it. They all read it, standing there in the June sun and the silence. I look for the expression on Hitler's face. I am but fifty yards from him and see him through my glasses as though he were directly in front of me. I have seen that face many times at the great moments of his life. But today! It is afire with scorn, anger, hate, revenge, triumph. He steps off the monument and contrives to make even this gesture a masterpiece of contempt. He glances back at it, contemptuous, angry – angry, you almost feel, because he cannot wipe out the awful, provoking lettering with one sweep of his high Prussian boot. He glances slowly around the clearing, and now, as his eyes meet ours, you grasp the depth of his hatred. But there is triumph there too – revengeful, triumphant hate. Suddenly, as though his face were not giving quite complete expression to his feelings, he throws his whole body into harmony with his mood. He swiftly snaps his hands on his hips, arches his shoulders, plants his feet wide apart. It is a magnificent gesture of defiance, of burning contempt for this place now and all that it has stood for in the twenty-two years since it witnessed the humbling of the German Empire . . .

It is now three-twenty-three p.m. and the Germans stride over to the armistice car. For a moment or two they stand in the sunlight outside the car, chatting. Then Hitler steps up into the car, followed by the others. We can see nicely through the car windows. Hitler takes the place occupied by Marshal Foch when the 1918 armistice terms were signed. The others spread themselves around him. Four chairs on the opposite side of the table from Hitler remain empty. The French have not yet appeared. But we do not wait long. Exactly at three-thirty p.m. they alight from a car. They have flown up from Bordeaux to a nearby landing field. They too glance at the Alsace-Lorraine memorial, but it's a swift glance. Then they walk down the avenue flanked by three German officers. We see them now as they come into the sunlight of the clearing.

General Huntziger, wearing a bleached khaki uniform, Air General Bergeret and Vice-Admiral Le Luc, both in dark blue uniforms, and then, almost buried in the uniforms, M. Nöel, French Ambassador to Poland. The German guard of honour, drawn up at the entrance to the clearing, snaps to attention for the French as they pass, but it does not present arms.

It is a grave hour in the life of France. The Frenchmen keep their eyes straight ahead. Their faces are solemn, drawn. They are the picture of tragic dignity.

They walk stiffly to the car, where they are met by two German officers, Lieutenant-General Tippelskirch, Quarter-master General, and Colonel Thomas, chief of the Führer's headquarters. The Germans salute. The French salute. The atmosphere is what Europeans call 'correct'. There are salutes, but no handshakes.

Now we get our picture through the dusty windows of that old *wagon-lit* car. Hitler and the other German leaders rise as the French enter the drawing-room. Hitler gives the Nazi salute, the arm raised. Ribbentrop and Hess do the same. I cannot see M. Noël to notice whether he salutes or not.

Hitler, as far as we can see through the windows, does not say a word to the French or to anybody else. He nods to General Keitel at his side. We see General Keitel adjusting his papers. Then he starts to read. He is reading the preamble to the German armistice terms. The French sit there with marble-like faces and listen intently. Hitler and Göring glance at the green table-top.

The reading of the preamble lasts but a few minutes. Hitler, we soon observe, has no intention of remaining very long, of listening to the reading of the armistice terms themselves. At three-forty-two p.m., twelve minutes after the French arrive, we see Hitler stand up, salute stiffly, and then stride out of the drawing-room, followed by Göring, Brauchitsch, Raeder, Hess, and Ribbentrop. The French, like figures of stone, remain at the green-topped table. General Keitel remains with them. He starts to read them the detailed conditions of the armistice.

Hitler and his aides stride down the avenue towards the Alsace-Lorraine monument, where their cars are waiting. As they pass the guard of honour, the German band strikes up the two national anthems, *Deutschland, Deutschland über Alles* and the *Horst Wessel* song. The whole ceremony in which Hitler has reached a new pinnacle in his meteoric career and Germany avenged the 1918 defeat is over in a quarter of an hour.

I MURDER LEON TROTSKY, MEXICO CITY, 29 August 1940

Ramon Mercader

Leon Trotsky had lost the power struggle in the USSR which followed the death of Lenin in 1924, and was exiled by the triumphant Josef Stalin. Trotsky's brand of democratic Communism continued to prove a thorn in Stalin's authoritarian side, however, and in 1940 Stalin arranged to have one of his agents assassinate Trotsky as he worked in his Mexico City study.

I put the raincoat on the table on purpose so that I could take out the ice axe which I had in the pocket . . . I took the pistolet out of my raincoat, took it in my fist and, closing my eyes, I gave him a tremendous blow on the head. The man screamed in such a way that I will never forget [it] as long as I live. His scream was . . . very long, infinitely long, and it still seems to me as if that scream was piercing my brains.

THE BATTLE OF BRITAIN, September 1940

Pilot Officer John Maurice Beard

After the fall of France, Britain stood alone against Germany. Hitler made a peace overture in June, which was dismissed by Winston Churchill, who had taken over from Chamberlain as Prime Minister. The blow against the island power came soon after with a full-scale air-attack by Göring's *Luftwaffe*: the Battle of Britain. Beginning in August, it lasted until November, although the peak of the fighting was in September. The RAF was outnumbered in planes and pilots four to one; John Beard was one of 'The Few', a 21-year-old Hurricane pilot.

I was supposed to be away on a day's leave but dropped back to the aerodrome to see if there was a letter from my wife. When I found out that *all* the squadrons had gone off into action, I decided to stand by, because obviously something big was happening. While I was climbing into my flying kit, our Hurricanes came slipping back out of the sky to refuel, reload ammunition, and take off again. The returning pilots were full of talk about flocks of enemy bombers and fighters which were trying to break through along the Thames Estuary. You couldn't miss hitting them, they said. Off to the east I could hear the steady roll of anti-aircraft fire. It was a brilliant afternoon with a flawless blue sky. I was crazy to be off.

An instant later an aircraftsman rushed up with orders for me to make up a flight with some of the machines then reloading. My own Hurricane was a nice old kite, though it had a habit of flying left wing low at the slightest provocation. But since it had already accounted for fourteen German aircraft before I inherited it, I thought it had some luck, and I was glad when I squeezed myself into the same old seat again and grabbed the 'stick'.

We took off in two flights [six fighters], and as we started to gain height over the station we were told over the R.T. [radiotelephone] to keep circling for a while until we were made up to a stronger force. That didn't take long, and soon there was a complete squadron including a couple of Spitfires which had wandered in from somewhere.

Then came the big thrilling moment: ACTION ORDERS. Distantly I heard the hum of the generator in my R.T. earphones and then the voice of the ground controller crackling through with the call signs. Then the order 'Fifty plus bombers, one hundred plus fighters over Canterbury at 15,000 heading northeast. Your vector [steering course to intercept] nine zero degrees. Over!'

We were flying in four V formations of three. I was flying No. 3 in Red flight, which was the squadron leader's and thus the leading flight. On we went, wing tips to left and right slowly rising and falling, the roar of our twelve Merlins drowning all other sound. We crossed over London, which, at 20,000 feet, seemed just a haze of smoke from its countless chimneys, with nothing visible except the faint glint of the barrage balloons and the wriggly silver line of the Thames.

I had too much to do watching the instruments and keeping formation to do much thinking. But once I caught a reflected glimpse of myself in the windscreen – a goggled, bloated, fat thing with the tube of my oxygen supply protruding gruesomely sideways from the mask which hid my mouth. Suddenly I was back at school again, on a hot afternoon when the Headmaster was taking the Sixth and droning on and on about the later Roman Emperors. The boy on my right was showing me surreptitiously some illustrations which he had pinched out of his father's medical books during the last holidays. I looked like one of those pictures.

It was an amazingly vivid memory, as if school was only yesterday. And half my mind was thinking what wouldn't I then have given to be sitting in a Hurricane belting along at 350 miles an hour and out for a kill. *Me* defending London! I grinned at my old self at the thought.

Minutes went by. Green fields and roads were now beneath us. I scanned the sky and the horizon for the first glimpse of the Germans. A new vector came through on the R.T. and we swung round with the sun behind us. Swift on the heels of this I heard Yellow flight leader call through the earphones. I looked quickly toward Yellow's position, and there they were!

It was really a terrific sight and quite beautiful. First they seemed just a cloud of light as the sun caught the many glistening chromium parts of their engines, their windshields, and the spin of their airscrew discs. Then, as our squadron hurtled nearer, the details stood out. I could see the bright-yellow noses of Messerschmitt fighters sandwiching the bombers, and could even pick out some of the types. The sky seemed full of them, packed in layers thousands of feet deep. They came on steadily, wavering up and down along the horizon. 'Oh, golly,' I thought, 'golly, golly . . .'

And then any tension I had felt on the way suddenly left me. I was elated but very calm. I leaned over and switched on my reflector sight, flicked the catch on the gun button from 'Safe' to 'Fire', and lowered my seat till the circle and dot on the reflector sight shone darkly red in front of my eyes.

The squadron leader's voice came through the earphones, giving tactical orders. We swung round in a great circle to attack on their beam – into the thick of them. Then, on the order, down we went. I took my hand from the throttle lever so as to get both hands on the stick, and my thumb played neatly across the gun button. You have to steady a fighter just as you have to steady a rifle before you fire it.

My Merlin screamed as I went down in a steeply banked dive on to the tail of a forward line of Heinkels. I knew the air was full of aircraft flinging themselves about in all directions, but, hunched and snuggled down behind my sight I was conscious only of the Heinkel I had picked out. As the angle of my dive increased, the enemy machine loomed larger in the sight field, heaved toward the red dot, and then he was there!

I had an instant's flash of amazement at the Heinkel proceeding so regularly on its way with a fighter on its tail. 'Why doesn't the fool *move*?' I thought, and actually caught myself flexing my muscles into the action *I* would have taken had I been he.

When he was square across the sight I pressed the button. There was a smooth trembling of my Hurricane as the eight-gun squirt shot out. I gave him a two-second burst and then another. Cordite fumes blew back into the cockpit making an acrid mixture with the smell of hot oil and the air-compressors.

I saw my first burst go in and, just as I was on top of him and turning away, I noticed a red glow inside the bomber. I turned tightly into position again and now saw several short tongues of flame lick out along the fuselage. Then he went down in a spin, blanketed with smoke and with pieces flying off.

I left him plummeting down and, horsing back on my

stick, climbed up again for more. The sky was clearing, but ahead toward London I saw a small, tight formation of bombers completely encircled by a ring of Messerschmitts. They were still heading north. As I raced forward, three flights of Spitfires came zooming up from beneath them in a sort of Prince-of-Wales's-feathers manoeuvre. They burst through upward and outward, their guns going all the time. They must have each got one, for an instant later I saw the most extraordinary sight of eight German bombers and fighters diving earthward together in flames.

I turned away again and streaked after some distant specks ahead. Diving down, I noticed that the running progress of the battle had brought me over London again. I could see the network of streets with the green space of Kensington Gardens, and I had an instant's glimpse of the Round Pond, where I sailed boats when I was a child. In that moment, and as I was rapidly overhauling the Germans ahead, a Dornier 17 sped right across my line of flight, closely pursued by a Hurricane. And behind the Hurricane came two Messerschmitts. He was too intent to have seen them and they had not seen me! They were coming slightly toward me. It was perfect. A kick at the rudder and I swung in toward them, thumbed the gun button, and let them have it. The first burst was placed just the right distance ahead of the leading Messerschmitt. He ran slap into it and he simply came to pieces in the air. His companion, with one of the speediest and most brilliant 'get-outs' I have ever seen, went right away in a half Immelmann turn. I missed him completely. He must almost have been hit by the pieces of the leader but he got away. I hand it to him.

At that moment some instinct made me glance up at my rear-view mirror and spot two Messerschmitts closing in on my tail. Instantly I hauled back on the stick and streaked upward. And just in time. For as I flicked into the climb, I saw the tracer streaks pass beneath me. As I turned I had a quick look round the 'office' [cockpit]. My fuel reserve was running out and I had only about a second's supply of ammunition left. I was certainly in no condition to take on two Messerschmitts. But they seemed no more eager than I was. Perhaps they were in the same position, for they turned away for home. I put my nose down and did likewise.

Only on the way back did I realize how hot I was. I had forgotten to adjust the ventilator apparatus in all the stress of the fighting, and hadn't noticed the thermometer. With the sun on the windows all the time, the inside of the 'office' was like an oven. Inside my flying suit I was in a bath of perspiration, and sweat was cascading down my face. I was dead tired and my neck ached from constantly turning my head on the lookout when going in and out of dogfights. Over east the sky was flecked with A. A. puffs, but I did not bother to investigate. Down I went, home.

At the station there was only time for a few minutes' stretch, a hurried report to the Intelligence Officer, and a brief comparing of notes with the other pilots. So far my squadron seemed to be intact, in spite of a terrific two hours in which we had accounted for at least thirty enemy aircraft.

But there was more to come. It was now about four p.m. and I gulped down some tea while the ground crew checked my Hurricane. Then, with about three flights collected, we took off again. We seemed to be rather longer this time circling and gaining height above the station before the orders came through on the R.T. It was to patrol an area along the Thames Estuary at 20,000 feet. But we never got there.

We had no sooner got above the docks than we ran into the first lot of enemy bombers. They were coming up in line about 5,000 feet below us. The line stretched on and on across the horizon. Above, on our level, were assorted groups of enemy fighters. Some were already in action, with our fellows spinning and twirling among them. Again I got that tightening feeling at the throat, for it really was a sight to make you gasp.

But we all knew what to do. We went for the bombers. Kicking her over, I went down after the first of them, a Heinkel 111. He turned away as I approached, chiefly because some of our fellows had already broken into the line and had scattered it. Before I got up he had been joined by two more. They were forming a V and heading south across the river.

I went after them. Closing in on the tail of the left one, I ran into a stream of crossfire from all three. How it missed me I don't know. For a second the whole air in front was thick with tracer trails. It seemed to be coming straight at me, only to curl away by the windows and go lazily past. I felt one slight bank, however, and glancing quickly, saw a small hole at the end of my starboard wing. Then, as the Heinkel drifted across my sights, I pressed the button – once – twice . . . Nothing happened.

I panicked for a moment till I looked down and saw that I had forgotten to turn the safety-catch knob to the 'Fire' position. I flicked it over at once and in that instant saw that three bombers, to hasten their getaway, had jettisoned all their bombs. They seemed to peel off in a steady stream. We were over the southern outskirts of London now and I remember hoping that most of them would miss the little houses and plunge into fields.

But dropping the bombs did not help my Heinkel. I let him have a long burst at close range, which got him right in the 'office'. I saw him turn slowly over and go down, and followed to give him another squirt. Just then there was a terrific crash in front of me. Something flew past my window, and the whole aircraft shook as the engine raced itself to pieces. I had been hit by A.A. fire aimed at the bombers, my airscrew had been blown off, and I was going down in a spin.

The next few seconds were a bit wild and confused. I remember switching off and flinging back the sliding roof almost in one gesture. Then I tried to vault out through the roof. But I had forgotten to release my safety belt. As I fumbled at the pin the falling aircraft gave a twist which shot me through the open cover. Before I was free, the air stream hit me like a solid blow and knocked me sideways. I felt my arm hit something, and then I was falling over and over with fields and streets and sky gyrating madly past my eyes.

I grabbed at the rip cord on my chute. Missed it. Grabbed again. Missed it. That was no fun. Then I remember saying to myself, 'This won't do. Take it easy, take it slowly.' I tried again and found the rip cord grip and pulled. There was a terrific wrench at my thighs and then I was floating still and peacefully with my 'brolly' canopy billowing above my head.

The rest was lovely. I sat at my ease just floating gradually down, breathing deep, and looking around. I was drifting across London again at about 2,000 feet.

A BURN VICTIM, BRITAIN, September 1940

Richard Hillary

Shot down in the Battle of Britain, Spitfire pilot Richard Hillary was badly burnt as he ejected from his plane.

I was falling. Falling slowly through a dark pit. I was dead. My body, headless, circled in front of me. I saw it with my mind, my mind that was the redness in front of the eye, the dully scream in the ear, the grinning of the mouth, the skin crawling on the skull. It was death and resurrection. Terror, moving with me, touched my cheek with hers and I felt the flesh wince. Faster, faster . . . I was hot now, hot, again one with my body, on fire and screaming soundlessly. Dear God, no! No! Not that, not again. The sickly smell of death was in my nostrils and a confused roar of sound. Then all was quiet. I was back.

Someone was holding my arms.

'Quiet now. There's a good boy. You're going to be all right. You've been very ill and you mustn't talk.'

I tried to reach up my hand but could not.

'Is that you, nurse? What have they done to me?'

'Well, they've put something on your face and hands to stop them hurting and you won't be able to see for a little while. But you mustn't talk: you're not strong enough yet.'

Gradually I realized what had happened. My face and hands had been scrubbed and then sprayed with tannic acid. The acid had formed into a hard black cement. My eyes alone had received different treatment: they were coated with a thick layer of gentian violet. My arms were propped up in front of me, the fingers extended like witches' claws, and my body was hung loosely on straps just clear of the bed.

I can recollect no moments of acute agony in the four days which I spent in that hospital; only a great sea of pain in which I floated almost with comfort. Every three hours I was injected with morphia, so while imagining myself quite coherent, I was for the most part in a semi-stupor. The memory of it has remained a confused blur.

Two days without eating, and then periodic doses of liquid food taken through a tube. An appalling thirst, and hundreds of bottles of ginger beer. Being blind, and not really feeling strong enough to care. Imagining myself back in my plane, unable to get out, and waking to find myself shouting and bathed in sweat. My parents coming down to see me and their wonderful self-control.

They arrived in the late afternoon of my second day in bed, having with admirable restraint done nothing the first day. On the morning of the crash my mother had been on her way to the Red Cross, when she felt a premonition that she must go home. She told the taxi-driver to turn about and arrived at the flat to hear the telephone ringing. It was our Squadron Adjutant, trying to reach my father. Embarassed by finding himself talking to my mother, he started in on a glamorized history of my exploits in the air and was bewildered by mother cutting him short to ask where I was. He managed somehow after about five minutes of incoherent stuttering to get over his news.

They arrived in the afternoon and were met by Matron. Outside my ward a twittery nurse explained that they must not expect to find me looking quite normal, and they were ushered in. The room was in darkness; I just a dim shape in one corner. Then the blinds were shot up, all the lights switched on, and there I was. As my mother remarked later, the performance lacked only the rolling of drums and a spotlight. For the sake of decorum my face had been covered with white gauze, with a slit in the middle through which protruded my lips.

We spoke little, my only coherent remark being that I had no wish to go on living if I were to look like Alice. Alice was a large country girl who had once been our maid. As a child she had been burned and disfigured by a Primus stove. I was not aware that she had made any impression on me, but now I was unable to get her out of my mind. It was not so much her looks as her smell I had continually in my nostrils and which I couldn't dissociate from the disfigurement.

They sat quietly and listened to me rambling for an hour. Then it was time for my dressings and they took their leave.

The smell of ether. Matron once doing my dressing with three orderlies holding my arms; a nurse weeping quietly at the head of the bed, and no remembered sign of a doctor. A visit from the lifeboat crew that had picked me up, and a terrible longing to make sense when talking to them. Their inarticulate sympathy and assurance of quick recovery. Their discovery that an ancestor of mine had founded the lifeboats, and my pompous and unsolicited promise of a subscription. The expectation of an American ambulance to drive me up to the Masonic Hospital (for Margate was used only as a clearing station). Believing that I was already in it and on my way and waking to the disappointment that I had not been moved. A dream that I was fighting to open my eyes and could not: waking in a sweat to realize it was a dream and then finding it to be true. A sensation of time slowing down, of words and actions, all in slow motion. Sweat, pain, smells, cheering messages from the Squadron, and an overriding apathy.

Finally I was moved. The ambulance appeared with a cargo of two somewhat nervous ATS women who were to drive me to London, and, with my nurse in attendance, and wrapped in an old grandmother's shawl, I was carried aboard and we were off. For the first few miles I felt quite well, dictated letters to my nurse, drank bottle after bottle of ginger beer, and gossiped with the drivers. They described the countryside for me, told me they were new to the job, expressed satisfaction at having me for a consignment, asked me if I felt fine. Yes, I said, I felt fine; asked my nurse if the drivers were pretty, heard her answer yes, heard them simpering, and we were all very matey. But after about half an hour my arms began to throb from the rhythmical jolting of the road. I stopped dictating, drank no more ginger beer, and didn't care whether they were pretty or not. Then they lost their way. Wasn't it awful and shouldn't they stop and ask? No, they certainly shouldn't: they could call out the names of the streets and I would tell them where to go. By the time we arrived at Ravenscourt Park I was pretty much all-in. I was carried into the hospital and once again felt the warm September sun burning my face. I was put in a private ward and had the impression of a hundred excited ants buzzing around me. My nurse said good-bye and started to sob. For no earthly reason I found myself in tears. It had been a lousy hospital, I had never seen the nurse anyway, and I was now in very good hands; but I suppose I was in a fairly exhausted state. So there we all were, snivelling about the place and getting nowhere. Then the charge nurse came up and took my arm and asked me what my name was.

'Dick,' I said.

'Ah,' she said brightly. 'We must call you Richard the Lion Heart.'

I made an attempt at a polite laugh but all that came out was a dismal groan and I fainted away. The house surgeon took the opportunity to give me an anaesthetic and removed all the tannic acid from my left hand.

At this time tannic acid was the recognized treatment for burns. The theory was that in forming a hard cement it protected the skin from the air, and encouraged it to heal up underneath. As the tannic started to crack, it was to be chipped off gradually with a scalpel, but after a few months of experience, it was discovered that nearly all pilots with third-degree burns so treated developed secondary infection and septicaemia. This caused its use to be discontinued and gave us the dubious satisfaction of knowing that we were suffering in the cause of science. Both my hands were suppurating, and the fingers were already contracting under the tannic and curling down into the palms. The risk of shock was considered too great for them to do both hands. I must have been under the anaesthetic for about fifteen minutes and in that time I saw Peter Pease killed.

He was after another machine, a tall figure leaning slightly forward with a smile at the corner of his mouth. Suddenly from nowhere a Messerschmitt was on his tail about 150 yards away. For two seconds nothing happened. I had a terrible feeling of futility. Then at the top of my voice I shouted, 'Peter, for God's sake look out behind!'

I saw the Messerschmitt open up and a burst of fire hit Peter's machine. His expression did not change, and for a moment his machine hung motionless. Then it turned slowly on its back and dived to the ground. I came to, screaming his name, with two nurses and the doctor holding me down on the bed.

'All right now. Take it easy, you're not dead yet. That must have been a very bad dream.'

I said nothing. There wasn't anything to say. Two days later I had a letter from Colin. My nurse read it to me. It was very short, hoping that I was getting better and telling me that Peter was dead.

Slowly I came back to life. My morphia injections were less frequent and my mind began to clear. Though I began to feel and think again coherently I still could not see. Two VADs fainted while helping with my dressings, the first during the day and the other at night. The second time I could not sleep and was calling out for someone to stop the beetles running down my face, when I heard my nurse say fiercely, 'Get outside quick: don't make a fool of yourself here!' and the sound of footsteps moving towards the door. I remember cursing the unfortunate girl and telling her to put her head between her knees. I was told later that for my first three weeks I did little but curse and blaspheme, but I remember nothing of it. The nurses were wonderfully patient and never complained. Then one day I found that I could see. My nurse was bending over me doing my dressings, and she seemed to me very beautiful. She was. I watched her for a long time, grateful that my first glimpse of the world should be anything so perfect. Finally I said:

'Sue, you never told me that your eyes were so blue.'

For a moment she stared at me. Then, 'Oh, Dick, how wonderful,' she said. 'I told you it wouldn't be long'; and she dashed out to bring in all the nurses on the block.

I felt absurdly elated and studied their faces eagerly, gradually connecting them with the voices that I knew.

THE BLITZ, September–November 1940

Thwarted in its attempt to destroy the RAF, the *Luftwaffe* switched its attention to mass-bombing raids on London. The first of the big raids came on 7 September, when 375 bombers unloaded their bombs on the capital.

Virginia Woolf

Diary: Thursday, 5 September

Hot, hot, hot. Record heat wave, record summer if we kept records this summer. At 2.30 a plane zooms: 10 minutes later air raid sounds; 20 later, all clear. Hot, I repeat; and doubt if I'm a poet. H. P. hard labour. Brain w— no, I can't think of the word – yes, wilts. An idea. All writers are unhappy. The picture of the world in books is thus too dark. The wordless are the happy: women in cottage gardens: Mrs Chavasse. Not a true picture of the world; only a writer's picture. Are musicians, painters, happy? Is their world happier?

Tuesday, 10 September

Back from half a day in London – perhaps our strangest visit. When we got to Gower Street a barrier with diversion on it. No sign of damage. But coming to Doughty Street a crowd. Then Miss Perkins at the window. Mecklenburgh Square roped off. Wardens there. Not allowed in. The house about 30 yards from ours struck at one in the morning by a bomb. Completely ruined. Another bomb in the square still unexploded. We walked round the back. Stood by Jane Harrison's house. The house was still smouldering. That is a great pile of bricks. Underneath all the people who had gone down to their shelter. Scraps of cloth hanging to the bare walls at the side still standing. A looking glass I think swinging. Like a tooth knocked out – a clean cut. Our house undamaged. No windows yet broken – perhaps the bomb has now broken them. We saw Bernal with an arm band jumping on top of the bricks. Who lived there? I suppose the casual young men and women I used to see from my window; the flat dwellers who used to have flower pots and sit in the balcony. All now blown to bits. The garage man at the back – blear eyed and jerky – told us he had been blown out of his bed by the explosion: made to take shelter in a church. 'A hard cold seat,' he said, 'and a small boy lying in my arms. I cheered when the all clear sounded. I'm aching all over.' He said the Jerries had been over for three nights

trying to bomb Kings Cross. They had destroyed half Argyll
Street, also shops in Grays Inn Road. Then Mr Pritchard
ambled up. Took the news as calm as a grig. 'They actually
have the impertinence to say this will make us accept peace
. . .!' he said: he watches raids from his flat roof and sleeps
like a hog. So, after talking to Miss Perkins, Mrs Jackson –
but both serene – Miss P. had slept on a camp bed in her
shelter – we went on to Grays Inn. Left the car and saw
Holborn. A vast gap at the top of Chancery Lane. Smoking
still. Some great shop entirely destroyed: the hotel opposite
like a shell. In a wine shop there were no windows left.
People standing at the tables – I think drink being served.
Heaps of blue-green glass in the road at Chancery Lane.
Men breaking off fragments left in the frames. Glass falling.
Then into Lincoln's Inn. To the *New Statesman* office:
windows broken, but house untouched. We went over it.
Deserted. Wet passages. Glass on stairs. Doors locked. So
back to the car. A great block of traffic. The Cinema behind
Madame Tussaud's torn open: the stage visible; some
decoration swinging. All the Regent's Park houses with
broken windows, but undamaged. And then miles and
miles of orderly ordinary streets – all Bayswater, and Sussex
Square as usual – streets empty – faces set and eyes bleared.
In Chancery Lane I saw a man with a barrow of music
books. My typist's office destroyed. Then at Wimbledon a
siren: people began running. We drove, through almost
empty streets, as fast as possible. Horses taken out of the
shafts. Cars pulled up. Then the all clear. The people I think
of now are the very grimy lodging house keepers, say in
Heathcote Street: with another night to face: old wretched
women standing at their doors; dirty, miserable. Well – as
Nessa said on the phone, it's coming very near. I had thought
myself a coward for suggesting that we should not sleep two
nights at 37. I was greatly relieved when Miss P. telephoned
advising us not to stay, and L. agreed.

Kathleen Box

Kathleen Box was a member of Mass-Observation (an unofficial 1930s-40s group which recorded British life and society).

Diary: Monday 14 October
Slept in basement again last night with Tibbles. Hear a good many bombs which don't sound very far off. After the loudest of these I hear movements next door where they sleep in the basement, their wall being also the wall of this house. I hear someone go to the front door – probably the elder Miss H – and she says to, I suppose, a passing warden – 'Was it a bomb?' I don't hear the reply, but the wardens and men from the fire station next door (the other side) as usual are out in the street, talking, laughing and sometimes whistling tunes. I sleep all right as usual.

5.20 Wakened by the H's coming back from next door. (They generally come back when there is an all clear, whatever time of night it is.) So I take pillow and eiderdown and go to my bed upstairs to finish the night there.

9.00 Miss H calls out good morning from the hall as I go into the bathroom. She says, 'Wasn't it a bad air-raid last night?' I say yes it was noisy and ask if she knows where the loudest crash came from. She says the old lady next door, who sleeps in the back basement room, was looking out of the window as she lay in bed and saw the bomb come down. She said it was glowing red hot and very large. When I ask if it was an incendiary she says no it was too big. She says she thinks it must have landed Parson's Green way, which is just round the back of these houses. I suggest that they are after Fulham Power Station, but she says they have already hit this some time ago and that we are getting our electricity from another power station now. She says it is the gas works (Chelsea way) that they are trying for.

10.40 Tobacconist opposite is in high spirits. He says, 'I was running round putting out fires at half past one in the morning.' He sleeps in the trench shelters near Edith Grove with his brother's family. They looked out and saw an incendiary bomb blazing away within about 5 feet of the trench. So out they went, he said 'Get the shovels' and they shovelled on sand from buckets, and when this was all used up they got some cinders from a pile outside a factory near by and threw them on and that put it out. 'My niece was the one. She was running round with a spade. She was as quick as I was. My brother he was asleep, and I didn't think to wake him, of course you don't when you've got something to do, he helped at the finish. We were all running round there. You don't think of the shrapnel falling when you've got something to do, we were working away in it. Then I saw a house blazing over that way (points) and I turned round and saw another house blazing over there (points opposite direction) so I says "Call the fire brigade – sound the fire alarm". So somebody did that and then the one over there went down. Then the fire brigade came and they were putting out the other house when the first one blazed up again. So I said, "Look over there. What about that one." They said "We can't do two things at once, you'll have to get some more help. Ring up the station." And then when we'd done that blowed if another fire didn't start out that way (pointing). Coo it was a night! And they were yelling at the people in the house, "Come out, there's a bloody fire on." Of course I fell over a great block of stone by the factory gate there, getting the cinders and skinned me bloomin' leg all up here. But that didn't matter. After it all we went back to the shelter and had a cup of tea and a fag.' F40 [a woman about 40] comes in whilst he is in the middle of the story and listens to the last part of it. She says, when he has finished, 'Fulham got it badly again last night, didn't it? They say they got it in Delvino Road, and in Munster Road and Horder Road, there's nothing left of it round that corner where the Labour Exchange is.'

Edward Murrow, American journalist

All the fires were quickly brought under control. That's a common phrase in the morning communiqués. I've seen how it's done; spent a night with the London fire brigade. For three hours after the night attack got going, I shivered in a sandbag crow's-nest atop a tall building near the Thames. It was one of the many fire-observation posts. There was an old gun barrel mounted above a round table marked off like a compass. A stick of incendiaries bounced off rooftops about three miles away. The observer took a sight on a point where the first one fell, swung his gun-sight along the line of bombs, and took another reading at the end of the line of fire. Then he picked up his telephone and shouted above the half gale that was blowing up there, 'Stick of incendiaries – between 190 and 220 – about three miles away.' Five minutes later a German bomber came boring down the river. We could see his exhaust trail like a pale ribbon stretched straight across the sky. Half a mile downstream there were two eruptions and then a third, close together. The first two looked as though some giant had thrown a huge basket of flaming golden oranges high in the air. The third was just a balloon of fire enclosed in black smoke above the house-tops. The observer didn't bother with his gun sight and indicator for that one. Just reached for his night glasses, took one quick look, picked up his telephone, and said, 'Two high explosives and one oil bomb,' and named the street where they had fallen.

There was a small fire going off to our left. Suddenly sparks showered up from it as though someone had punched the middle of a huge camp-fire with a tree trunk. Again the gun sight swung around, the bearing was read, and the report went down the telephone lines: 'There is something in high explosives on that fire at 59.'

There was peace and quiet inside for twenty minutes. Then a shower of incendiaries came down far in the distance. They didn't fall in a line. It looked like flashes from an electric train on a wet night, only the engineer was drunk and driving his train in circles through the streets. One sight at the middle of the flashes and our observer reported laconically, 'Breadbasket at 90 – covers a couple of miles.' Half an hour later a string of fire bombs fell right beside the Thames. Their white glare was reflected in the black, lazy water near the banks and faded out in midstream where the moon cut a golden swathe broken only by the arches of famous bridges.

We could see little men shovelling those fire bombs into the river. One burned for a few minutes like a beacon right in the middle of a bridge. Finally those white flames all went out. No one bothers about the white light, it's only when it turns yellow that a real fire has started.

I must have seen well over a hundred fire bombs come down and only three small fires were started. The incendiaries aren't so bad if there is someone there to deal with them, but those oil bombs present more difficulties.

As I watched those white fires flame up and die down, watched the yellow blazes grow dull and disappear, I thought, what a puny effort is this to burn a great city.

THE HOME FRONT: A CHILD'S VIEW, SHEFFIELD, Autumn 1940

George Macbeth

In the morning, I would walk along Clarkehouse Road with my eyes glued to the pavement for shrapnel. It became the fashion to make a collection of this, and there were few days when I came home without a pocketful of jagged, rusting bits, like the unintelligible pieces from a scattered jigsaw of pain and violence.

Of course we didn't see them as this at the time. They were simply free toys from the sky, as available and interesting as the horse chestnuts in the Botanical Gardens, or the nippled acorns in Melbourne Avenue.

It must have been about this time that the British Restaurants were opening, with their austerity jam roll and meat balls; and our own meals were beginning to rely rather more on rissoles and home-made apple sponge. But my mother was always a good manager, and I have no sense of any sudden period of shortage or of going hungry.

Sweets were the great loss. There was no longer an everlasting, teeth-spoiling fountain of sherbet and liquor-ice, or of Boy Blue cream whirls, or of Cadbury's Caramello. Sweets were hard to come by, and then limited to a fixed ration.

One of the worst casualties was chocolate. The traditional division into milk and plain disappeared, and an awful intervening variety known as Ration Chocolate was born, issued in semi-transparent grease-proof wrappers, and about as appetizing as cardboard. In spite of a lifelong sweet tooth, I could never eat it.

LUNCH WITH DE GAULLE, LONDON, 20 January 1941

Harold Nicolson, MP

Harold Nicolson records a meeting with General Charles de Gaulle, the leader of the Free French movement.

20 January 1941

I lunch with General de Gaulle at the Savoy. Attlee and Dalton are there. De Gaulle looks less unattractive with his hat off, since it shows his young hair and the tired and not wholly benevolent look in his eyes. He has the taut manner of a man who is becoming stout and is conscious that only the exercise of continuous muscle-power can keep his figure in shape. I do not like him. He accuses my Ministry of being 'Pétainiste.' [follower of Marshal Pétain, the leader of the puppet government set up in southern France by the Germans, which had its capital at Vichy] *'Mais non,'* I say, *'Monsieur le Général.' 'Enfin, Pétainisant.' 'Nous travaillons,'* I said, *'pour la France entière.' 'La France entière,'* he shouted, *'c'est la France Libre. C'est moi!'* Well, well. I admit he has made a great Boulangiste gesture. But the spectre of General Boulanger passes across my mind. He begins to abuse Pétain, saying that once again he has sold himself to Laval, saying that Weygand showed cowardice when bombed at the front. Osusky says that French opinion imagines that de Gaulle and Pétain are at heart as one. *'C'est une erreur,'* he says sharply. I am not encouraged.

To change the subject I say that I have received a letter from occupied France which I was surprised had passed the censor. De Gaulle says that he had received a long letter of the most Gaulliste nature, the writer of which had written on the top, 'I am sure the censor will stop this.' Underneath in violet ink was written, *'La censure approuve totalement.'* We discuss Darlan [Admiral of the Vichy French Fleet]. He says that Darlan loves his ships as a race-horse owner loves his horses. It does not matter to him whether he races at Longchamps or on Epsom Downs. What matters is that it should be a great race and that he should win it. *'Mais il manque d'estomac.'* Had he been a strong man, he would either have fought his fleet with us against the Italians or fought with the Germans against us. As it was, he was preserving his race-horses and they would become old, old, old.

I turn on Roosevelt's inaugural address from Washington. I am still young enough to be amazed at hearing a voice from Washington as if it were in my own room. It is a good speech. He recalls the great blows which America has struck for liberty. He reminds them that Washington created the American idea, that Lincoln saved it from disintegration, and that now they must save it from a menace from outside. 'We do not retreat,' he concludes. 'We are not content to stand still.' I enjoyed that part very much indeed.

DOGFIGHT OVER FRANCE, Summer 1941

Hugh 'Cocky' Dundas, RAF

It was hot in the garden, lying face down on the lawn, a pot of iced shandy by my hand, Robin (my golden retriever) huffing and puffing and panting at the ants. Odd to be lying there peacefully, listening to the click of croquet balls, the blur of voices, the gramophone. The shandy sharp, cold, stimulating.

'Hullo, Cocky.'

'Hullo, Johnnie.'

'Get a squirt this morning, Cocky?'

'Yes, Johnnie, I got a squirt. Missed the bastard as usual, though.'

'Another show this afternoon, Cocky. Take off 15.30.'

'Yes, I know; take off 15.30.' Three hours ago, over Lille. It happened yesterday, and last week, and last month. It will happen again in exactly two and a half hours, and tomorrow, and next month.

The grass smelt sweet in the garden, and the shandy was good, and Robin's panting, and the gramophone playing 'Momma may I go out dancing – yes, my darling daughter'.

It was hot at dispersal and the grass, what was left of it, brown and oil-stained. The Spitfires creaked and twanged in the sun.

'Everything under control, Hally?' [Flying Officer Hall was the squadron engineer officer.]

'Yes, Cocky, everything under control. DB's not ready yet, but it will be.' [DB were the identification letters of Douglas Bader's plane.]

'Well, for Christ's sake see that it is, or there'll be some laughing off to do.'

'It will be ready, Cocky.'

'OK. Hally.'

Inside is as hot as outside. The pilots, dressed almost as they like, lie about sweating.

'Chalk, please, Durham.'

They all watch as I chalk initials under the diagram of twelve aircraft in three sections of four. Nobody moves much until I have finished and written the time of take-off.

'Smith, you'll be with DB. Nip, you and I on his right. Johnnie, you with the CO and two of 'B' Flight. OK?'

'OK, Cocky.'

Here comes DB.

'Why the bloody hell isn't my aircraft ready? Cocky, my bloody aeroplane's not ready. We take off in 20 minutes. Where's that prick Hally?'

'It's OK, DB, it'll be ready. I've seen Hally.'

'Well, look at the bloody thing. They haven't even got the cowlings on yet. Oi, Hally, come here!'

Christ, I wish we could get going.

'Chewing-gum, Johnnie, please. Thanks, pal.'

'OK, DB?'

'Yes, Cocky, it's going to be OK.'

We walk together again, as far as the road.

'Well, good luck, Cocky. And watch my tail, you old bastard.'

'I'll do that, DB. Good luck.'

Just time for two or three more puffs before climbing into A for Apple.

'Everything OK, Goodlad?' [the fitter who looked after my plane].

'OK, sir.'

'Good show. Bloody hot.'

Climbing in, the hottest thing of all. The old girl shimmers like an oven, twangs and creaks.

'Good luck, sir.'

'Thanks.'

Up the line DB's motor starts. 610 have formed up and are beginning to move off across the airfield as we taxi out – DB, myself, Smithie, Nip, then two composite sections from both flights.

Straggle over the grandstand at Goodwood in a right-hand turn and set course east in a steady climb, Ken's twelve a little above and behind to the left, Stan's out to the right. Ten thousand feet over Shoreham. The old familiar, nostalgic taste in the mouth. Brighton – Maxim's last Saturday night; dancing with Diana in the Norfolk. Beachy, once a soft summer playground, now gaunt buttress sticking its chin bluntly out towards our enemies. Spread out now into wide semi-independent fours. Glint of perspex way out and above to the south shows Stan and his boys nicely placed between us and the sun. Dungeness slides slowly past to port and we still climb steadily, straight on, way out in front.

Twenty-five thousand.

'Levelling out.'

Puffs of black ten thousand feet below show where the bombers are crossing between Boulogne and Le Touquet. Six big cigars with tiers of protective fighters milling above them.

'Hello, Douglas, Woody calling. There are fifty plus gaining height to the east.'

'OK, Woody.'

'Put your corks in boys.' Stan.

Over the coast at Hardelot we nose ahead without altering course.

'DB, there's some stuff at three o'clock, climbing round to the south-west.'

'OK, I see it. Stan, you deal with them if necessary.'

'OK, OK. Don't get excited.'

Usual remarks. Usual shouts of warning. Usual bad language. Usual bloody Huns climbing round the usual bloody way.

St Omer on the left. We fly on, straight and steady in our fours, towards Lille. Stan's voice:

'They're behind us, Walker squadron. Stand by to break.'

Then: 'Look out, Walker. Breaking starboard.'

Looking over my shoulder to the right and above I see the specks and glints which are Stan's planes break up into the fight, a quick impression of machines diving, climbing, gyrating. Stan, Ian, Tony, Derek and the rest of them are fighting for their lives up there.

Close to the target area now. More black puffs below show where the bombers are running in through the flak.

'Billy here, DB. There's a lot of stuff coming round at three o'clock, slightly above.'

Quick look to the right. Where the hell? Christ, yes! There they are, the sods. A typical long, fast, climbing straggle of 109s.

'More below, DB, to port.'

'OK, going down. Ken, watch those buggers behind.'

'OK, DB.'

'Come on, Cocky.'

Down after DB. The Huns are climbing fast to the south. Have to get in quick before those sods up above get at us. Turn right, open up slightly. We are diving to two or three hundred feet below their level. DB goes for the one on the left. Nipple is on my right. Johnnie slides across beyond him. Getting in range now. Wait for it, wait for DB and open up all together. 250 yards . . . 200 . . . wish to Christ I felt safer behind . . . 150. DB opens up. I pull my nose up slightly to put the dot a little ahead of his orange spinner. Hold it and squeeze, cannon and machine guns together . . . correct slightly . . . you're hitting the bastard . . . wisp of smoke.

'BREAK, Rusty squadron, for Christ's sake BREAK!'

Stick hard over and back into tummy, peak revs and haul her round. Tracers curl past . . . orange nose impression not forty yards off . . . slacken turn for a second . . . hell of a mêlée . . . better keep turning, keep turning, keep turning.

There's a chance, now. Ease off, nose up, give her two lengths' lead and fire. Now break, don't hang around, break! Tracers again . . . a huge orange spinner and three little tongues of flame spitting at me for a second in a semi-head-on attack. Round, round, so that she judders and nearly spins. Then they're all gone, gone as usual as suddenly as they came.

'Cocky, where the hell are you? Are you with me, Cocky?'

There he is, I think. Lucky to find him after that shambles.

'OK, DB, coming up on your starboard now.'

'Right behind you, Cocky.' That's Johnnie calling.

'OK, Johnnie, I see you.'

Good show; the old firm's still together.

It was cooler, on the lawn, and still. The shadows from the tall trees stretched out to the east. Robin lay beside me pressing his muzzle into the grass, huffing at insects. The pint-pot of Pimms was cool in my hands and the ice clinked when I moved. The cucumber out of the drink was good and cold and sharp when I sucked it.

'Hullo, Cocky.'

'What-ho, Johnnie.'

'Tough about Derek.'

'Yes, Johnnie; and Mab.'

The croquet balls sounded loud to my ear, pressed in the grass. The distant gramophone started again on 'Momma, may I go out dancing'.

'Come on, you old bastard, let's drink up and get out of here.'

The tide washed up the creek to Bosham and splashed

against the balcony of the Old Ship. We sat and sipped our
good, warm, heartening brandy and watched the red sun dip
through the western haze, watched the stars light one by one,
watched the two swans gliding past like ghost ships.

'Cocky.'

'Yes, Johnnie.'

'Readiness at four a.m.'

'OK, let's go.'

MEDICAL EXPERIMENTS AT DACHAU, 1941–45

Franz Blaha

Dachau was one of the principal Nazi concentration camps for the
imprisonment – and frequently death – of 'undesirables', among
them Jews, Slavs, political opponents and gypsies.

I, Franz Blaha, being duly sworn, depose and state as
follows:

I was sent as a prisoner to the Dachau Concentration
Camp in April 1941, and remained there until the liberation
of the camp in April 1945. Until July 1941 I worked in a
Punishment Company. After that I was sent to the hospital
and subjected to the experiments in typhoid being conducted
by Dr Mürmelstadt. After that I was to be made the subject
of an experimental operation, and only succeeded in avoiding this by admitting that I was a physician. If this had been
known before I would have suffered, because intellectuals
were treated very harshly in the Punishment Company.
In October 1941 I was sent to work in the herb plantation, and later in the laboratory for processing herbs.
In June 1942, I was taken into the hospital as a surgeon.
Shortly afterwards I was directed to conduct a stomach
operation on twenty healthy prisoners. Because I would

not do this I was put in the autopsy room, where I stayed until April 1945. While there I performed approximately 7,000 autopsies. In all, 12,000 autopsies were performed under my direction.

From mid-1941 to the end of 1942 some 500 operations on healthy prisoners were performed. These were for the instruction of the SS medical students and doctors and included operations on the stomach, gall bladder, spleen and throat. These were performed by students and doctors of only two years' training, although they were very dangerous and difficult. Ordinarily they would not have been done except by surgeons with at least four years' surgical practice. Many prisoners died on the operating table and many others from later complications. I performed autopsies on all these bodies. The doctors who supervised these operations were Lang, Mürmelstadt, Wolter, Ramsauer and Kahr. *Standartenführer* Dr Lolling frequently witnessed these operations.

During my time at Dachau I was familiar with many kinds of medical experiments carried on there with human victims. These persons were never volunteers but were forced to submit to such acts. Malaria experiments on about 1,200 people were conducted by Dr Klaus Schilling between 1941 and 1945. Schilling was personally asked by Himmler to conduct these experiments. The victims were either bitten by mosquitoes or given injections of malaria sporozoites taken from mosquitoes. Different kinds of treatment were applied, including quinine, pyrifer, neosalvarsan, antipyrin, pyramidon and a drug called 2516 Behring. I performed autopsies on bodies of people who died from these malaria experiments. Thirty to forty died from the malaria itself. Three to four hundred died later from diseases which proved fatal because of the physical condition resulting from the malaria attacks. In addition there were deaths resulting from poisoning due to overdoses of neosalvarsan and pyramidon. Dr Schilling was present at the time of my autopsies on the bodies of his patients.

In 1942 and 1943 experiments on human beings were conducted by Dr Sigismund Rascher to determine the effects of changing air pressure. As many as twenty-five persons were put at one time into a specially constructed van in which pressure could be increased or decreased as required. The purpose was to find out the effects of high altitude and of rapid parachute descents on human beings. Through a window in the van I have seen the people lying on the floor of the van. Most of the prisoners who were made use of died as a result of these experiments, from internal haemorrhages of the lungs or brain. The rest coughed blood when taken out. It was my job to take the bodies out and to send the internal organs to Munich for study as soon as they were found to be dead. About 400 to 500 prisoners were experimented on. Those not dead were sent to invalid blocks and liquidated shortly afterwards. Only a few escaped.

Rascher also conducted experiments on the effect of cold water on human beings. This was done to find a way for reviving aviators who had fallen into the ocean. The subject was placed in ice-cold water and kept there until he was unconscious. Blood was taken from his neck and tested each time his body temperature dropped one degree. This drop was determined by a rectal thermometer. Urine was also periodically tested. Some men lasted as long as twenty-four to thirty-six hours. The lowest body temperature reached was nineteen degrees C., but most men died at twenty-five degrees C., or twenty-six degrees C. When the men were removed from the ice water attempts were made to revive them by artificial warmth from the sun, from hot water, from electro-therapy or by animal warmth. For this last experiment prostitutes were used and the body of the unconscious man was placed between the bodies of two women. Himmler was present at one such experiment. I could see him from one of the windows in the street between the blocks. I have personally been present at some of the cold-water experiments when Rascher was absent, and I have seen notes and diagrams on them in Rascher's laboratory. About 300 persons were used in these experiments. The majority died. Of those who lived many became mentally deranged. Those not killed were sent to invalid blocks and were killed, just as were the victims of the air-pressure experiments. I only know two who survived – a Jugoslav and a Pole, both of whom have become mental cases.

Liver-puncture experiments were performed by Dr Brachtl on healthy people, and on people who had diseases of the stomach and gall bladder. For this purpose a needle was jabbed into the liver of a person and a small piece of liver was extracted. No anaesthetic was used. The experiment is very painful and often had serious results, as the stomach or large blood vessels were often punctured and haemorrhage resulted. Many persons died of these tests, for which Polish, Russian, Czech and German prisoners were employed. Altogether these experiments were conducted on about 175 people.

Phlegmone experiments were conducted by Dr Schütz, Dr Babor, Dr Kieselwetter and Professor Lauer. Forty healthy men were used at a time, of whom twenty were given intra-muscular, and twenty intravenous, injections of pus from diseased persons. All treatment was forbidden for three days, by which time serious inflammation and in many cases general blood poisoning had occurred. Then each group was divided again into groups of ten. Half were given chemical treatment with liquid and special pills every ten minutes for twenty-four hours. The rest were treated with sulphanamide and surgery. In some cases all of the limbs were amputated. My autopsy also showed that the chemical treatment had been harmful and had even caused perforations of the stomach wall. For these experiments Polish, Czech and Dutch priests were ordinarily used. Pain was intense in such experiments. Most of the 600 to 800 persons who were used finally died. Most of the others became permanent invalids and were later killed.

In the autumn of 1944 there were sixty to eighty persons who were subjected to salt-water experiments. They were locked in a room and for five days were given nothing to swallow but salt water. During this time their urine, blood and excrement were tested. None of these prisoners died, possibly because they received smuggled food from other prisoners. Hungarians and gypsies were used for these experiments.

It was common practice to remove the skin from dead prisoners. I was commanded to do this on many occasions. Dr Rascher and Dr Wolter in particular asked for this human skin from human backs and chests. It was chemically treated and placed in the sun to dry. After that it was cut into various sizes for use as saddles, riding breeches, gloves, house slippers and ladies' handbags. Tattooed skin was especially valued by SS men. Russians, Poles and other inmates were used in this way, but it was forbidden to cut out the skin of a German. This skin had to be from healthy prisoners and free from defects. Sometimes we did not have enough bodies with good skin and Rascher would say, 'All right, you will get the bodies.' The next day we would receive twenty or thirty bodies of young people. They would have been shot in the neck or struck on the head so that the skin would be uninjured. Also we frequently got requests for the skulls or skeletons of prisoners. In those cases we boiled the skull or the body. Then the soft parts were removed and the bones were bleached and dried and reassembled. In the case of skulls it was important to have a good set of teeth. When we got an order for skulls from Oranienburg the SS men would say, 'We will try to get you some with good teeth.' So it was dangerous to have a good skin or good teeth.

THE GERMAN AMBASSADOR HANDS OVER THE DECLARATION OF WAR ON THE USSR, MOSCOW, 22 June 1941

Ivan Krylov

At six o'clock in the morning of 22 June 1941, the German Ambassador, Count von Schulenburg, handed Molotov a

Note of the German Government declaring war on the Soviet Union.

Both Count von Schulenburg and Molotov were pale with emotion. The Commissar for Foreign Affairs took the Note wordlessly, spat on it and then tore it up. He rang for his secretary Poskrebichev.

'Show this gentleman out through the back door.'

THE WEHRMACHT ADVANCES INTO RUSSIA, July 1941

General Blumentritt, Wehrmacht

Operation Barbarossa, Hitler's invasion of Russia launched on 22 June, was a three-pronged attack; one offensive under General von Leeb drove through the Baltic states towards Leningrad; the main offensive, under von Bock, headed towards Moscow; and the third, under von Rundstedt, headed through southern Poland towards the Black Sea. All three army groups initially made rapid progress, despite the difficult terrain and the tenacity – and elusiveness – of the Russian troops.

The infantry had a hard time keeping up. Marches of twenty-five miles in the course of a day were by no means exceptional, and that over the most atrocious roads. A vivid picture which remains of these weeks is the great clouds of yellow dust kicked up by the Russian columns attempting to retreat and by our infantry hastening in pursuit. The heat was tremendous, though interspersed with sudden showers which quickly turned the roads to mud before the sun reappeared and as quickly baked them into crumbling clay once again.

By 2 July the first battle was for all intents and purposes won. The haul was astounding. A hundred and fifty thousand prisoners taken, some 1,200 tanks and 600 guns captured or destroyed. First impressions revealed that the Russian was as tough a fighter as ever. His tanks, however, were not particularly formidable and his air force, so far as we could see, non-existent.

The conduct of the Russian troops, even in this first battle, was in striking contrast to the behaviour of the Poles and of the Western allies in defeat. Even when encircled, the Russians stood their ground and fought. The vast extent of the country, with its forests and swamps, helped them in this. There were not enough German troops available completely to seal off a huge encirclement such as that of Bialystok-Slonim. Our motorized forces fought on or near to the roads: in the great trackless spaces between them the Russians were left largely unmolested. This was why the Russians were able not infrequently to break out of our encirclements, whole columns moving by night through the forests that stretched away eastwards. They always attempted to break out to the east, so that the eastern side of each encirclement had to be held by our strongest troops, usually Panzer troops. Nevertheless, our encirclements were seldom entirely successful.

AN ENCOUNTER WITH RUSSIAN PRISONERS, EASTERN FRONT, July 1941

Benno Zieser, Wehrmacht

We suddenly saw a broad, earth-brown crocodile slowly shuffling down the road towards us. From it came a subdued hum, like that from a beehive. Prisoners of war. Russians, six deep. We couldn't see the end of the column. As they drew near the terrible stench which met us made us quite sick; it was like the biting stench of the lion house and the filthy odour of the monkey house at the same time.

But these were not animals, they were men. We made haste out of the way of the foul cloud which surrounded them, then what we saw transfixed us where we stood and we forgot our nausea. Were these really human beings, these grey-brown figures, these shadows lurching towards us, stumbling and staggering, moving shapes at their last gasp, creatures which only some last flicker of the will to live enabled to obey the order to march? All the misery in the world seemed to be concentrated here. There was also that gruesome barrage of shouts and wails, groans, lamentations and curses which combined with the cutting orders of the guards into a hideous accompaniment.

We saw one man shuffle aside from the ranks, then a rifle butt crash between his shoulder-blades and drive him gasping back into place. Another with a head wound lost in bloodstained bandages ran a few paces out with gestures almost ludicrous in their persuasiveness to beg one of the nearby local inhabitants for a scrap of bread. Then a leather thong fetched him a savage lash round his shoulders and yanked him, too, back into place. Another, a lanky fellow, a regular giant, stepped aside to pump ship, and when he too was forced back he could not stop nature and it all drenched the man in front, but he never even turned his head.

Stray dogs were legion, among them were the most unbelievable mongrels; the only thing they were all alike in was that they were thin. The Sheikh said one could have learned to play the harp on their ribs. That was no hindrance to the prisoners. They were hungry, so why not eat roast dog? They were always trying to catch the scary beasts. They would also beg us with gestures and *bow-wows* and *bang-bangs* to kill a dog for them. There it was, shoot it! And we almost always did; it was a bit of sport anyway, and at the same time it delighted those human skeletons. Besides, those wild dogs were a regular pest.

When we brought one down, there followed a performance that could make a man puke. Yelling like mad, the

Russkies would fall on the animal and tear it in pieces with their bare hands, even before it was quite dead. The pluck they would stuff their pockets with, like tobacco, whenever they got hold of any of that – it made a sort of iron ration. Then they would light a fire, skewer shreds of the dog's meat on sticks and roast it. There were always fights over the bigger bits. The burnt flesh stank frightfully; there was almost no fat in it.

But they did not have roast dog every day. Behind the huts there was a big midden, a regular mountain of stinking waste, and if we did not look out they would poke about in it and eat such things as decaying onions, the mere sight of which was enough to turn you up. If one of us came near they would scatter like dung-flies. I once found one roasting dried pig's dung.

SIEGE OF LENINGRAD, August 1941–July 1942

Alexander Werth

For almost a year Leningrad was completely encircled by the *Wehrmacht* and a Finnish army under Mannerheim. It is estimated that a million Leningraders lost their lives, mostly from starvation.

One of the greatest examples of how Leningrad fought for its life was when in the spring [of 1942] 300,000 or 400,000 people came out into the street with shovels – people who were scarcely standing on their feet, so weak and hungry were they – and proceeded to clean up the town. All winter the drains and sewers had been out of action; there was a great danger of epidemics spreading with the coming of the warm weather. And in a few days these 300,000 or 400,000 weak, hungry people – many of them were very old people who had never handled a shovel in their lives – had shovelled away and dumped into the river and the canals all those mountains of snow and filth which, had they remained there, would have poisoned Leningrad. And it was a joy to see the city streets a few days later all clean and tidy. It had a great moral effect . . .

It was our people and not the soldiers who built the fortifications of Leningrad. If you added up all the antitank trenches outside Leningrad, made by the hands of our civilians, they would add up to as much as the entire Moscow-Volga canal. During the three black months of 1941, 400,000 people were working in three shifts, morning, noon and night, digging and digging. I remember going down to Luga during the worst days, when the Germans were rapidly advancing on Luga. I remember there a young girl who was carrying away earth inside her apron. It made no sense. I asked her what she was doing that for. She burst into tears, and said she was trying to do at least that – it wasn't much, but her hands simply couldn't hold a shovel any longer. And, as I looked at her hands, I saw that they were a mass of black and bloody bruises. Somebody else had shovelled the earth on to her apron while she knelt down, holding the corners of the apron with the fingers of her bruised, bloodstained hands. For three months our civilians worked on these fortifications. They were allowed one day off in six weeks. They never took their days off. There was an eight-hour working day, but nobody took any notice of it. They were determined to stop the Germans. And they went on working under shellfire, under machine-gun fire and the bombs of the Stukas.

THE RUSSIAN WINTER ARRIVES,
13 November 1941

Heinrich Haape, Wehrmacht

Like another previous invader of Russia, Napoleon Bonaparte,

Hitler found that winter would undo his plans. Heinrich Haape
was a medical officer with the *Wehrmacht*.

On 13 November we awoke and shivered. An icy blast from
the north-east knifed across the snowy countryside. The sky
was cloudless and dark blue, but the sun seemed to have lost
its strength and instead of becoming warmer towards noon as
on previous days, the thermometer kept falling and by
sundown had reached minus twelve degrees Centigrade.

The soldiers, who up to now had not regarded the light
frosts too seriously, began to take notice. One man who had
been walking outside for only a short distance without his
woollen *Kopfschutzer* or 'head-saver' came into the sick bay.
Both ears were white and frozen stiff.

It was our first case of frost-bite.

We gently massaged the man's ears, taking care not to
break the skin, and they thawed out. We powdered them and
covered them with cotton-wool and made a suitable head-
dressing. Perhaps we had managed to save the whole of the
ears; we should have to wait and see.

This minor case of frost-bite was a serious warning. The
icy winds from Siberia – the breath of death – were blowing
across the steppes; winds from where all life froze, from the
Arctic ice-cap itself. Things would be serious if we could not
house ourselves in prepared positions and buildings, and I
stopped to think of the armies marching on Moscow across
open country at this very moment. All that those men had
received so far were their woollen *Kopfschutzers*; the winter
clothing had still not arrived. What was happening to the
men's feet, for the ordinary army boot retained very little
warmth?

Then, too, the thermometer showed only twelve degrees
below zero. Temperatures would drop to minus twenty-four
degrees – minus thirty-six degrees – minus forty-eight
degrees – perhaps even lower. It was beyond comprehension

– a temperature four times colder than a deep freezer. To attempt any movement without warm clothing in those conditions would be sheer suicide. Surely the older generals had been right when, after the battle of Vyasma and Bryansk, they had counselled: 'Dig in for the winter.' Some of them were men with experience of Russia during the 1914–1918 War. At the most they had said, continue the war through the winter only with a few thoroughly-equipped and well-provisioned divisions. Make the big push in the spring.

If only the battle for Moscow had started fourteen days earlier, the city would now have been in our hands. Or even if the rains had held off for fourteen days. If – if – if. If Hitler had started 'Barbarossa' six weeks earlier as originally planned; if he had left Mussolini on his own in the Balkans and had attacked Russia in May; if we had continued our sweeping advance instead of stopping at the Schutsche Lake; if Hitler had sent us winter clothing. Yes, if, if, if – but now it was too late.

Those Arctic blasts that had taken us by surprise in our protected positions had scythed through our attacking troops. In a couple of days there were 100,000 casualties from frost-bite alone; 100,000 first-class, experienced soldiers fell out because the cold had surprised them.

A couple of days later our winter clothing arrived. There was just enough for each company to be issued with four heavy fur-lined greatcoats and four pairs of felt-lined boots. Four sets of winter clothing for each company! Sixteen greatcoats and sixteen pairs of winter boots to be shared among a battalion of 800 men! And the meagre issue coincided with a sudden drop in the temperature to minus twenty-two degrees.

Reports reached us that the issue of winter clothing to the troops actually advancing on Moscow had been on no more generous scale. More and more reports were being sent to Corps and Army Headquarters recommending that the attack on Moscow by a summer-clad army be abandoned and that winter positions be prepared. Some of these reports were forwarded by Central Army Group to the Führer's Headquarters, but no reply or acknowledgement ever came. The order persisted: 'Attack!' And our soldiers attacked.

The attacks of the *Wehrmacht* brought them to within five miles of Moscow's city limits during the first week of December; a Red Army counter-attack on 6 December began to drive the Germans back, and they would never come so close to the prize again.

PEARL HARBOR, HAWAII, 7 December 1941

John Garcia

I was sixteen years old, employed as a pipe fitter apprentice at Pearl Harbor Navy Yard. On 7 December 1941, oh, around 8.00 a.m., my grandmother woke me. She informed me that the Japanese were bombing Pearl Harbor. I said, 'They're just practising.' She said, no, it was real and the announcer is requesting that all Pearl Harbor workers report to work. I went out on the porch and I could see the anti-aircraft fire up in the sky. I just said, 'Oh boy.'

I was four miles away. I got out on my motor-cycle and it took me five, ten minutes to get there. It was a mess.

I was working on the USS *Shaw*. It was on a floating dry dock. It was in flames. I started to go down into the pipe fitter's shop to get my toolbox when another wave of Japanese came in. I got under a set of concrete steps at the dry dock where the battleship *Pennsylvania* was. An officer came by and asked me to go into the *Pennsylvania* and try to get the fires out. A bomb had penetrated the marine deck, and that was three decks below. Under that was the magazines: ammunition, powder, shells. I said, 'There ain't no way I'm gonna go down there.' It could blow up any minute. I was young and sixteen, not stupid, not at sixty-two cents an hour. (Laughs.)

A week later, they brought me before a navy court. It was determined that I was not service personnel and could not be ordered. There was no martial law at the time. Because I was sixteen and had gone into the water, the whole thing was dropped.

I was asked by some other officer to go into the water and get sailors out that had been blown off the ships. Some were unconscious, some were dead. So I spent the rest of the day swimming inside the harbour, along with some other Hawaiians. I brought out I don't know how many bodies and how many were alive and how many dead. Another man would put them into ambulances and they'd be gone. We worked all day at that . . .

The following morning, I went with my tools to the *West Virginia*. It had turned turtle, totally upside down. We found a number of men inside. The *Arizona* was a total washout. Also the *Utah*. There were men in there, too. We spent about a month cutting the superstructure of the *West Virginia*, tilting it back on its hull. About 300 men we cut out of there were still alive by the eighteenth day. It took two weeks to get all the fires out. We worked around the clock for three days. There was so much excitement and confusion. Some of our sailors were shooting five-inch guns at the Japanese planes. You just cannot down a plane with a five-inch shell. They were landing in Honolulu, the unexploded naval shells. They have a ten-mile range. They hurt and killed a lot of people in the city.

When I came back after the third day, they told me that a shell had hit the house of my girl. We had been going together for, oh, about three years. Her house was a few blocks from my place. At the time, they said it was a Japanese bomb. Later we learned it was an American shell. She was killed. She was preparing for church at the time.

The surprise attack by Japan on the US Pacific Fleet sank ten ships and damaged many more. It also brought America into the Second World War.

THE SINKING OF *REPULSE* AND *PRINCE OF WALES*, 10 December 1941

O. D. Gallagher

Singapore, Britain's great naval base in the Far East, was vulnerable to the Japanese army which had begun advancing down through Indo-China and its coastal waters. In an effort to defeat the Japanese before they could reach Singapore, the British fleet dispatched the battlecruiser *Repulse* and the battleship *Prince of Wales* to intercept the Japanese. In the early hours of 10 December the warships were spotted and attacked by the Japanese airforce. The attacks continued throughout the morning.

A new wave of planes appeared at twelve-twenty p.m. The end was near, though we did not know it. *Prince of Wales* lay about ten cables astern of our port side. She was helpless. Not only was her steering-gear destroyed, but also her screws by that first torpedo. Unlike the German *Bismarck* caught by the Navy in the Atlantic, which lost only her steering-gear and was able to keep moving in a circle, *Prince of Wales* was a hulk.

All the aircraft made for her. I do not know how many there were in this last attack, but it was afterwards estimated that there were between fifty and eighty Japanese torpedo-bombers in operation during the entire action. *Prince of Wales* fought desperately to beat off the determined killers who attacked her like a pack of dogs on a wounded buck. *Repulse* and the destroyers formed a rough circle around her, to add our fire-power. All ships fired with the intention of protecting

Prince of Wales, and in doing so each neglected her own defences.

It was difficult to make out her outline through the smoke and flame from all her guns except the 14-inchers. I saw one plane drop a torpedo. It fell nose-heavy into the sea and churned up a thin wake as it drove straight at the immobile *Prince of Wales*. It exploded against her bows. A couple of seconds later another hit her – and another.

I gazed at her turning slowly over on her port side, her stern going under, and dots of men jumping into the sea, and was thrown against the bulkhead by a tremendous shock as *Repulse* was hit by a torpedo on her port side.

The sinking of the two warships was a catastrophe for the British, and spelled the end for Singapore.

THE HOME FRONT: THE GREAT MAN CHASE, December 1941

Anon. member of the British Women's Auxiliary Air Force

The main consequence of a lot of women living together seems to be that since everyone realizes that everyone else's emotions, aims and actions are similar to their own – conventional barriers and restraints are torn down and conversation gets down to bedrock.

The presence of both sexes always imposes restraint in conversation. The soldier's fumbling excuse for hard swearing is always 'Oh, well, when a lot of us lads get together [. . .]' Similarly when women are together in our circumstances, we use words we wouldn't think of bringing out in public.

Not only in choice of words, but also in choice of topic and depth of discussion is this new candour created. Even at women's tea parties . . . women are on their guard against each other and don't admit their basic feelings . . . But here we've got to know each other well: we're all in the same boat and we're all after the same thing. So why kid each other?

And what is this thing we're all after? Obviously, a man. Preferably an officer or a sergeant pilot. I should say that 85 per cent of our conversation is about men, dances (where we meet men), 15 per cent about domestic and shop matters and a negligible proportion on other matters.

But to get a man is not sufficient. It's easy to get a man. In fact it's difficult not to. Competitive factors in the Great Man-Chase are under the following headings:

1. Quality: The desirable qualities are rank, wings, looks, money, youth in that order. Rank is unbelievably important. There's a Wing-Commander here whose only redeeming feature is that he's young. He isn't good-looking, he's owned to be a great bore and he's extremely 'fast' (which is *not* a recommendation) yet he could go out with any woman on the station he cared to ask. No one would refuse . . . The height of sex-rank is commission and wings. Higher commission, the better. Sergeant pilots and ground commissions tie for second place. This includes army officers. Ground stripes come a poor third. For the rest as far as most Ops girls are concerned, there is little hunting-value. In the term 'looks' I include charm, personality, etc. This counts only as a narrow comparison viz P/O [Pilot Officer] A is better than P/O B because he is more charming, but we'd rather go out with P/O B who is *not* charming, than with Sergeant C who *is* (and he's good-looking too). Members of the Army without commissions don't get a look in at all . . .

2. Quantity: Naturally the more men one can fasten to one's train the more prestige one gains in the Chase.

3. Intensity – a deliberately vague term embodying length of affair, extent of ardour and its manifestations.

Of course the longer you can keep your man, the higher up

you are in the competition. It's better if he's madly in love with you. He shouldn't be seen in public with other women. And telegrams, chocolates, cigarettes and really 'classy' evenings out all put you one step higher on the ladder. As far as physical manifestations are concerned, the average Ops girl admittedly likes a man who can kiss well, eyes 'wandering' with suspicion and definitely abstains from actual immorality. Technique in kissing is of first importance . . . Further than kissing is not eyed favourably. 'I *like* Bill and he *is* a Squadron Leader and all that but I simply can't face the coping I have to do every evening'. ('Coping' having become the accepted term for dealing with unwanted passion.) So the eligible men are those who kiss well but 'know when to stop' . . .

It seems to me that practically the entire object of the Chase is a matter of vanity and prestige . . .

Becoming of necessity subjective: I allowed myself to drift into this chase for the past few months and have discovered:

a. That I am happiest when I am conducting two or three successful affairs with eligibles as above.

b. That I am second happiest when I am *pretending to other girls* that they are successful affairs as above . . .

A girl in our Control had been trying very hard to get a date with a new officer. She was sitting next to him in the Ops room one day full of concentration in her conversation when suddenly she smiled, looked across at me, and mouthed the words 'Got him!'

BATTLE OF MIDWAY, 7 June 1942

Captain Mitsuo Fuchida and Captain Masatake Okumiya, Imperial Japanese Navy

The naval struggle between Japan and the USA in the Pacific which culminated in the battle of Midway was the first in which the opposing fleets never saw each other: virtually all the fighting was done by carrier-based aircraft. The engagement cost the Americans the carrier Yorktown and 147 planes; the Japanese lost four fast carriers and a similar number of aircraft. Midway completely changed the balance of power in the Pacific.

As our fighters ran out of ammunition during the fierce battle they returned to the carriers for replenishment, but few ran low on fuel. Service crews cheered the returning pilots, patted them on the shoulder, and shouted words of encouragement. As soon as a plane was ready again the pilot nodded, pushed forward the throttle, and roared back into the sky. This scene was repeated time and again as the desperate air struggle continued.

Preparations for a counter-strike against the enemy had continued on board our four carriers throughout the enemy torpedo attacks. One after another, planes were hoisted from the hangar and quickly arranged on the flight deck. There was no time to lose. At 10.20 Admiral Nagumo gave the order to launch when ready. On *Akagi*'s flight deck all planes were in position with engines warming up. The big ship began turning into the wind. Within five minutes all her planes would be launched.

Five minutes! Who would have dreamed that the tide of battle would shift completely in that brief interval of time?

Visibility was good. Clouds were gathering at about 3,000 metres, however, and though there were occasional breaks, they afforded good concealment for approaching enemy planes. At 10.24 the order to start launching came from the bridge by voice-tube. The Air Officer flapped a white flag, and the first Zero fighter gathered speed and whizzed off the deck. At that instant a look-out screamed: 'Hell-Divers!' I looked up to see three black enemy planes plummeting towards our ship. Some of our machine-guns managed to fire a few frantic bursts at them, but it was too late. The plump silhouettes of the American Dauntless dive-bombers quickly grew larger, and then a number of black objects suddenly floated eerily from their wings. Bombs! Down they came straight towards me! I fell intuitively to the deck and crawled behind a command post mantelet.

The terrifying scream of the dive-bombers reached me first, followed by the crashing explosion of a direct hit. There was a blinding flash and then a second explosion, much louder than the first. I was shaken by a weird blast of warm air. There was still another shock, but less severe, apparently a near-miss. Then followed a startling quiet as the barking of guns suddenly ceased. I got up and looked at the sky. The enemy planes were already gone from sight.

The attackers had got in unimpeded because our fighters, which had engaged the preceding wave of torpedo planes only a few moments earlier, had not yet had time to regain altitude. Consequently, it may be said that the American dive-bombers' success was made possible by the earlier martyrdom of their torpedo planes. Also, our carriers had no time to evade because clouds hid the enemy's approach until he dived down to the attack. We had been caught flat-footed in the most vulnerable condition possible – decks loaded with planes armed and fuelled for an attack.

Looking about, I was horrified at the destruction that had been wrought in a matter of seconds. There was a huge hole in the flight deck just behind the amidship elevator. The elevator itself, twisted like molten glass, was dropping into the hangar. Deck plates reeled upwards in grotesque con-figurations, planes stood tail up, belching livid flame and jet-black smoke. Reluctant tears streamed down my cheeks as I watched the fires spread, and I was terrified at the prospect of induced explosions which would surely doom the ship. I heard Masuda yelling, 'Inside! Get inside! Everybody who isn't working! Get inside!'

Unable to help, I staggered down a ladder and into the

ready room. It was already jammed with badly burned victims from the hangar deck. A new explosion was followed quickly by several more, each causing the bridge structure to tremble. Smoke from the burning hangar gushed through passageways and into the bridge and ready room, forcing us to seek other refuge. Climbing back to the bridge, I could see that *Kaga* and *Soryu* had also been hit and were giving off heavy columns of black smoke. The scene was horrible to behold.

Akagi had taken two direct hits, one on the after rim of the amidship elevator, the other on the rear guard on the port side of the flight deck. Normally, neither would have been fatal to the giant carrier, but induced explosions of fuel and munitions devastated whole sections of the ship, shaking the bridge and filling the air with deadly splinters. As fire spread among the planes lined up wing to wing on the after flight deck, their torpedoes began to explode, making it impossible to bring the fires under control. The entire hangar area was a blazing inferno, and the flames moved swiftly towards the bridge.

Because of the spreading fire, our general loss of combat efficiency, and especially the severance of external communication facilities, Nagumo's Chief of Staff, Rear-Admiral Kusaka, urged that the flag be transferred at once to light cruiser *Nagara*. Admiral Nagumo gave only a half-hearted nod, but Kusaka patiently continued his entreaty: 'Sir, most of our ships are still intact. You must command them.'

The situation demanded immediate action, but Admiral Nagumo was reluctant to leave his beloved flagship. Most of all he was loath to leave behind the officers and men of *Akagi*, with whom he had shared every joy and sorrow of war. With tears in his eyes, Captain Aoki spoke up: 'Admiral, I will take care of the ship. Please, we all implore you, shift your flag to *Nagara* and resume command of the Force.'

At this moment Lieutenant-Commander Nishibayashi, the Flag Secretary, came up and reported to Kusaka: 'All passages below are on fire, sir. The only means of escape is by rope from the forward window of the bridge down to the deck, then by the outboard passage to the anchor deck. *Nagara*'s boat will come alongside the anchor deck port, and you can reach it by rope ladder.'

Kusaka made a final plea to Admiral Nagumo to leave the doomed ship. At last convinced that there was no possibility of maintaining command from *Akagi*, Nagumo bade the Captain good-bye and climbed from the bridge window with the aid of Nishibayashi. The Chief of Staff and other staff and headquarters officers followed. The time was 10.46.

On the bridge there remained only Captain Aoki, his Navigator, the Air Officer, a few ratings, and myself. Aoki was trying desperately to get in touch with the engine room. The Chief Navigator was struggling to see if anything could be done to regain rudder control. The others were gathered on the anchor deck fighting the raging fire as best they could. But the unchecked flames were already licking at the bridge. Hammock mantelets around the bridge structure were beginning to burn. The Air Officer looked back at me and said, 'Fuchida, we won't be able to stay on the bridge much longer. You'd better get to the anchor deck before it is too late.'

In my condition this was no easy task. Helped by some sailors, I managed to get out of the bridge window and slid down the already smouldering rope to the gun deck. There I was still ten feet above the flight deck. The connecting monkey ladder was red hot, as was the iron plate on which I stood. There was nothing to do but jump, which I did. At the same moment another explosion occurred in the hangar, and the resultant blast sent me sprawling. Luckily the deck on which I landed was not yet afire, for the force of the fall knocked me out momentarily. Returning to consciousness, I struggled to rise to my feet, but both of my ankles were broken.

Crewmen finally came to my assistance and took me to the anchor deck, which was already jammed. There I was strapped into a bamboo stretcher and lowered to a boat which carried me, along with other wounded, to light cruiser *Nagara*. The transfer of Nagumo's staff and of the wounded was completed at 11.30. The cruiser got under way, flying Admiral Nagumo's flag at her mast.

Meanwhile, efforts to bring *Akagi*'s fires under control continued, but it became increasingly obvious that this was impossible. As the ship came to a halt, her bow was still pointed into the wind, and pilots and crew had retreated to the anchor deck to escape the flames, which were reaching down to the lower hangar deck. When the dynamos went out, the ship was deprived not only of illumination but of pumps for combating the conflagration as well. The fireproof hangar doors had been destroyed, and in this dire emergency even the chemical fire extinguishers failed to work.

The valiant crew located several hand pumps, brought them to the anchor deck and managed to force water through long hoses into the lower hangar and decks below. Firefighting parties, wearing gas masks, carried cumbersome pieces of equipment and fought the flames courageously. But every induced explosion overhead penetrated to the deck below, injuring men and interrupting their desperate efforts. Stepping over fallen comrades, another damage-control party would dash in to continue the struggle, only to be mowed down by the next explosion. Corpsmen and volunteers carried out dead and wounded from the lower first-aid station, which was jammed with injured men. Doctors and surgeons worked like machines.

The engine rooms were still undamaged, but fires in the middle deck sections had cut off all communication between the bridge and the lower levels of the ship. Despite this the explosions, shocks and crashes above, plus the telegraph indicator which had rung up 'Stop', told the engine-room crews in the bowels of the ship that something must be wrong. Still, as long as the engines were undamaged and full propulsive power was available they had no choice but to stay at General Quarters. Repeated efforts were made to communicate with the bridge, but every channel of contact, including the numerous auxiliary ones, had been knocked out.

The intensity of the spreading fires increased until the heat-laden air invaded the ship's lowest sections through the intakes, and men working there began falling from suffocation. In a desperate effort to save his men, the Chief Engineer, Commander K. Tampo, made his way up through the flaming decks until he was able to get a message to the Captain reporting conditions below. An order was promptly given for all men in the engine spaces to come up on deck. But it was too late. The orderly who tried to carry the order down through the blazing hell never returned, and not a man escaped from the engine room.

As the number of dead and wounded increased and the fires got further out of control, Captain Aoki finally decided at 18.00 that the ship must be abandoned. The injured were lowered into boats and cutters sent alongside by the screening destroyers. Many uninjured men leapt into the sea and swam away from the stricken ship. Destroyers *Arashi* and *Nowaki* picked up all survivors. When the rescue work was completed, Captain Aoki radioed to Admiral Nagumo at 19.20 from one of the destroyers, asking permission to sink the crippled carrier. This enquiry was monitored by the Combined Fleet flagship, whence Admiral Yamamoto dispatched an order at 22.25 to delay the carrier's disposition. Upon receipt of this instruction, the Captain returned to his carrier alone. He reached the anchor deck, which was still free from fire, and there lashed himself to an anchor to await the end.

Meanwhile, uncontrollable fires continued to rage throughout *Kaga*'s length, and finally, at 16.40, Commander Amagai gave the order to abandon ship. Survivors were transferred to the two destroyers standing by. Two hours later the conflagration subsided enough to enable Commander Amagai to lead a damage-control party back on board in the hope of saving the ship. Their valiant efforts proved futile, however, and they again withdrew. The once crack carrier, now a burning hulk, was wrenched by two terrific explosions before sinking into the depths at 19.25 in position 30° 20′ N., 179° 17′ W. In this battle 800 men of *Kaga*'s crew, one-third of her complement, were lost.

Soryu, the third victim of the enemy dive-bombing attack, received one hit fewer than *Kaga*, but the devastation was just as great. When the attack broke, deck parties were busily preparing the carrier's planes for take-off, and their first awareness of the onslaught came when great flashes of fire were seen sprouting from *Kaga*, some distance off to port, followed by explosions and tremendous columns of black smoke. Eyes instinctively looked skyward just in time to see a spear of thirteen American planes plummeting down on *Soryu*. It was 10.25.

Three hits were scored in as many minutes. The first blasted the flight deck in front of the forward elevator, and the next two straddled the amidship elevator, completely wrecking the deck and spreading fire to petrol tanks and munition storage rooms. By 10.30 the ship was transformed into a hell of smoke and flames, and induced explosions followed shortly.

In the next ten minutes the main engines stopped, the steering system went out, and fire mains were destroyed. Crewmen, forced by the flames to leave their posts, had just arrived on deck when a mighty explosion blasted many of them into the water. Within twenty minutes of the first bomb hit the ship was such a mass of fire that Captain Ryusaku Yanagimoto ordered 'Abandon ship!' Many men jumped into the water to escape the searing flames and were picked up by destroyers *Hamakaze* and *Isokaze*. Others made more orderly transfers to the destroyers.

It was soon discovered, however, that Captain Yanagimoto had remained on the bridge of the blazing carrier. No ship commander in the Japanese Navy was more beloved by his men. His popularity was such that whenever he was going to address the assembled crew, they would gather an hour or more in advance to ensure getting a place up front. Now, they were determined to rescue him at all costs.

Chief Petty Officer Abe, a Navy wrestling champion, was chosen to return and rescue the Captain, because it had been decided to bring him to safety by force if he refused to come willingly. When Abe climbed to *Soryu's* bridge he found Captain Yanagimoto standing there motionless, sword in hand, gazing resolutely towards the ship's bow. Stepping forward, Abe said, 'Captain, I have come on behalf of all your men to take you to safety. They are waiting for you. Please come with me to the destroyer, sir.'

When this entreaty met with silence, Abe guessed the Captain's thoughts and started towards him with the intention of carrying him bodily to the waiting boat. But the sheer strength of will and determination of his grim-faced commander stopped him short. He turned tearfully away, and as he left the bridge he heard Captain Yanagimoto calmly singing *Kimigayo*, the national anthem.

THE DEFENCE OF HENDERSON FIELD, GUADALCANAL, 24 October 1942

Sergeant Mitchell Paige, USMC

On 7 August 1942 the Americans landed a division of Marines on Guadalcanal in the Eastern Solomons and seized the jungle-strip airfield the Japanese were building there. The Japanese counter-attacked vigorously, and both sides poured men and *matériel* into Guadalcanal. The island was ringed by a series of massive naval confrontations, while the battle on land centred on the struggle for the airbase, now renamed Henderson Field. The peak of the fighting came in October.

Before we could get set up darkness came and it started raining like hell. It was too black to see anything, so I crawled along the ridge-front until it seemed I had come to the nose. To make sure I felt around with my hands and the ridge seemed to drop away on all sides. There we set up.

With the guns set up and the watches arranged, it was time for chow. I passed the word along for the one can of 'Spam' and the one can of 'borrowed peaches' that we had with us. Then we found out some jerk had dropped the can of peaches and it had rolled down the ridge into the jungle. He had been too scared to tell us what he had done. I shared out the 'Spam' by feeling for a hand in the darkness and dropping into it. The next morning I sent out a couple of scouts to 'look over the terrain'. So we got our peaches back.

That night Smitty and I crawled out towards the edge of the nose and lay on our backs with the rain driving into our faces. Every so often I would lift up and call some of the boys by name to see if they were still awake and to reassure myself as well as them.

It must have been two o'clock in the morning when I heard a low mumbling. At once I got Smitty up. A few minutes later we heard the same noise again. I crawled over to the men and told them to stand by. I started figuring. The Japs might not know we were on the nose and might be preparing to charge us, or at any moment they might discover our positions. I decided to get it over with. As soon as the men heard the click of my pin coming out of the grenade, they let loose their grenades too.

Smitty was pulling out pins as I threw the grenades. The Japs screamed, so we knew we had hit them. We threw a few more grenades and then there was silence.

All that second day we dug in. We had no entrenching

tools so we used bayonets. As night came I told the men we would have a hundred per cent watch and they were not to fire until they saw a Jap.

About the same time as the night before we heard the Japs talking again. They were about a hundred yards from the nose. It was so damned quiet, you could hear anything. I crawled around to the men and told them to keep quiet, look forward and glue their ears to the ground. As the Japs advanced we could hear the bushes rustle. Suddenly all hell broke loose.

All of us must have seen the Japs at the same time. Grenades exploded everywhere on the ridge-nose, followed by shrieks and yells. It would have been death to fire the guns because muzzle flashes would have given away our positions and we could have been smothered and blasted by a hail of grenades. Stansbury, who was lying in the foxhole next to mine, was pulling out grenade-pins with his teeth and rolling the grenades down the side of the nose. Leipart, the smallest guy in the platoon, and my particular boy, was in his foxhole delivering grenades like a star pitcher.

Then I gave the word to fire. Machine-guns and rifles let go and the whole line seemed to light up. Pettyjohn yelled to me that his gun was out of action. In the light from the firing I could see several Japs a few feet away from Leipart. Apparently he had been hit because he was down on one knee. I knocked off two Japs with a rifle but a third drove his bayonet into Leipart. Leipart was dead; seconds later, so was the Jap. After a few minutes, I wouldn't swear to how long it was, the blitz became a hand-to-hand battle. Gaston was having trouble with a Jap officer, I remember that much. Although his leg was nearly hacked off and his rifle all cut up, Gaston finally connected his boot with the Jap's chin. The result was one slopehead with one broken neck.

Firing died down a little, so evidently the first wave was a flop. I crawled over to Pettyjohn, and while he and Faust covered me I worked to remove a ruptured cartridge and change the belt-feed pawl. Just as I was getting ready to feed in a belt of ammo, I felt something hot on my hand and a sharp vibration. Some damned slopehead with a light machine-gun had fired a full burst into the feeding mechanism and wrecked the gun.

Things got pretty bad on the second wave. The Japs penetrated our left flank, carried away all opposition and were possibly in a position to attack our ridge-nose from the rear. On the left, however, Grant, Payne and Hinson stood by. In the centre, Lock, Swanek and McNabb got it and were carried away to the rear by corpsmen. The Navy boys did a wonderful job and patched up all the casualties, but they were still bleeding like hell and you couldn't tell what was wrong with them, so I sent them back. That meant that all my men were casualties and I was on my own. It was lonely up there with nothing but dead slopeheads for company, but I couldn't tell you what I was thinking about. I guess I was really worrying about the guns, shooting as fast as I could, and getting a bead on the next and nearest Jap.

One of the guns I couldn't find because it wasn't firing. I figured the guys had been hit and had put the gun out of action before leaving. I was always very insistent that if for any reason they had to leave a gun they would put it out of action so that the Japs wouldn't be able to use it. Being without a gun myself, I dodged over to the unit on my right to get another gun and give them the word on what was going on. Kelly and Totman helped me bring the gun back towards the nose of the ridge and we zig-zagged under an enemy fire that never seemed to stop. While I was on the right flank I borrowed some riflemen to form a skirmish line. I told them to fix bayonets and follow me. Kelly and Totman fed ammo as I sprayed every inch of terrain free of Japs. Dawn was beginning to break and in the half-light I saw my own machine-gun still near the centre of the nose. It was still in working order and some Japs were crawling towards it.

We got there just in time. I left Kelly and Totman and ran over to it.

For too many moments it seemed as though the whole Japanese Army was firing at me. Nevertheless three men on the right flank thought I might be low on ammunition and volunteered to run it up to me. Stat brought one belt and he went down with a bullet in the stomach. Reilly came up with another belt. Just as he reached the gun, he was hit in the groin. His feet flew out and nearly knocked me off the gun. Then Jonjeck arrived with a belt and stopped a bullet in the shoulder. As I turned I saw a piece of flesh disappear from his neck. I told him to go back for medical aid, but he refused. He wanted to stay up there with me. There was not time to argue, so I tapped him on the chin, hard enough so that he went down. That convinced him that I wanted my order obeyed.

My ears rang when a Jap sighted in on me with his light machine-gun but luckily he went away to my left. Anyway, I decided it was too unhealthy to stay in any one place for too long, so I would fire a burst and then move. Each time I shifted, grenades fell just where I had been. Over the nose of the ridge in the tall grass, which was later burned for security, I thought I saw some movement. Right off the nose, in the grass, thirty Japs stood up. One of them was looking at me through field-glasses. I let them have it with a full burst and they peeled off like grass under a mowing machine.

After that, I guess I was so wound up that I couldn't stop. I rounded up the skirmish line, told them I was going to charge off the nose and I wanted them to be right behind me. I picked up the machine-gun, and without noticing the burning hot water jacket, cradled it in my arms. Two belts of ammo I threw around my shoulders. The total weight was about 150 pounds, but the way I felt I could have carried three more without noticing it. I fed one of the belts off my shoulders into the gun, and then started forward. A colonel dropped about four feet in front of me with his yellow belly full of good American lead. In the meantime the skirmish line came over the nose, whooping like a bunch of wild Indians. We reached the edge of the clearing where the jungle began and there was nothing left either to holler at or shoot at. The battle was over with that strange sort of quietness that always follows.

The first thing I did was to sit down. I was soaked in perspiration and steam was rising in a cloud from my gun. My hand felt funny. I looked down and saw through my tattered shirt a blister which ran from my fingertips to my forearm. Captain Ditta came running up, slapped me on the back and gave me a drink, from his canteen.

For three days after the battle, we camped around the nose. They estimated that there were 110 Japs dead in front of my sector. I don't know about that, but they started to smell so horribly that we had to bury them by blasting part of the ridge over on top of them. On the third day we marched twelve miles back to the airport. I never knew what day it was, and what's more I didn't care.

JEWS ARE ROUNDED UP, AMSTERDAM, 19 November 1942

Anne Frank

In pursuit of the 'final solution', the mass extermination of the Jews, the Nazis deported some 500,000 West European Jews to the SS death camps at Treblinka, Auschwitz, Belsen, Treblinka, Sobibor and Majdanek. These included 104,000 Jews from the Netherlands.

Thursday, 19 November 1942
Apart from that, all goes well. Dussel has told us a lot about the outside world, which we have missed for so long now. He had very sad news. Countless friends and acquaintances have

gone to a terrible fate. Evening after evening the green and grey army lorries trundle past. The Germans ring at every front door to enquire if there are any Jews living in the house. If there are, then the whole family has to go at once. If they don't find any, they go on to the next house. No one has a chance of evading them unless one goes into hiding. Often they go round with lists, and only ring when they know they can get a good haul. Sometimes they let them off for cash – so much per head. It seems like the slave hunts of olden times. But it's certainly no joke; it's much too tragic for that. In the evenings, when it's dark, I often see rows of good, innocent people accompanied by crying children, walking on and on, in charge of a couple of these chaps, bullied and knocked about until they almost drop. No one is spared – old people, babies, expectant mothers, the sick – each and all join in the march of death.

How fortunate we are here, so well cared for and undisturbed. We wouldn't have to worry about all this misery were it not that we are so anxious about all those dear to us whom we can no longer help.

I feel wicked sleeping in a warm bed, while my dearest friends have been knocked down or have fallen into a gutter somewhere out in the cold night. I get frightened when I think of close friends who have now been delivered into the hands of the cruellest brutes that walk the earth. And all because they are Jews!

Anne Frank was later taken to Belsen herself, where she died in 1945.

EL ALAMEIN, October–November 1942

The battle of El Alamein was the turning point of the war in North

Africa, a decisive victory for General Montgomery's British 8th Army over Erwin Rommel's Afrika Korps.

Erwin Rommel

On the afternoon of the 24th, I was rung up on the Semmering [Germany, where Rommel had been on leave for his health] by Field Marshal Keitel, who told me that the British had been attacking at Alamein with powerful artillery and bomber support since the previous evening. General Stumme was missing. He asked whether I would be well enough to return to Africa and take over command again. I said I would. Keitel then said that he would keep me informed of developments, and would let me know in due course whether I was to return to my command. I spent the next few hours in a state of acute anxiety, until the evening, when I received a telephone call from Hitler himself. He said that Stumme was still missing – either captured or killed – and asked whether I could start for Africa immediately. I was to telephone him again before I actually took off, because he did not want me to interrupt my treatment unless the British attack assumed dangerous proportions. I ordered my aircraft for seven o'clock next morning and drove immediately to Wiener Neustadt. Finally, shortly after midnight, a call came through from the Führer. In view of developments at Alamein he found himself obliged to ask me to fly back to Africa and resume my command. I took off next morning. I knew there were no more laurels to be earned in Africa, for I had been told in the reports I had received from my officers that supplies had fallen far short of my minimum demands. But just how bad the supply situation really was I had yet to learn.

On arriving at Rome at about 11.00 hours (25 October) I was met at the airport by General von Rintelen, Military

Attaché and German General attached to the Italian forces. He informed me of the latest events in the African theatre. After heavy artillery preparation, the enemy had taken part of our line south of Hill 31; several battalions of 164th Division and of Italians had been completely wiped out. The British attack was still in progress and General Stumme still missing. General von Rintelen also informed me that only three issues of petrol remained in the African theatre; it had been impossible to send any more across in the last weeks, partly because the Italian Navy had not provided the shipping and partly because of the British sinkings. This was sheer disaster, for with only 300 kilometres' worth of petrol per vehicle between Tripoli and the front, and that calculated over good driving country, a prolonged resistance could not be expected; we would be completely prevented from taking the correct tactical decisions and would thus suffer a tremendous limitation in our freedom of action. I was bitterly angry, because when I left there had been at least eight issues for the Army in Egypt and Libya, and even this had been absurdly little in comparison with the minimum essential of thirty issues. Experience had shown that one issue of petrol was required for each day of battle; without it, the army was crippled and could not react to the enemy's moves. General von Rintelen regretted the situation, but said that he had unfortunately been on leave and had consequently been unable to give sufficient attention to the supply question.

Feeling that we would fight this battle with but small hope of success, I crossed the Mediterranean in my Storch and reached headquarters at dusk (25 October). Meanwhile, General Stumme's body had been found at midday and taken to Derna. He had apparently been driving to the battlefield along the Alarm track when he had suddenly been fired on in the region of Hill 21 by British infantry using anti-tank and machine-guns. Colonel Buechting had received a mortal wound in the head. The driver, Corporal Wolf, had immediately swung the car round, and General Stumme had leapt out and hung on to the outside of it, while the driver drove at top speed out of the enemy fire. General Stumme must have suddenly had a heart attack and fallen off the car. The driver had noticed nothing. On Sunday morning the General had been found dead beside the Alarm track. General Stumme had been known to suffer from high blood-pressure and had not really been fit for tropical service.

We all deeply regretted the sudden death of Stumme. He had spared no pains to command the army well and had been day and night at the front. Just before setting off on his last journey on 24 October, he had told the acting Chief of Staff that he thought it would be wise to ask for my return, since with his short experience of the African theatre, and in view of the enormous British strength and the disastrous supply situation, he felt far from certain that he would be able to fight the battle to a successful conclusion. I, for my part, did not feel any more optimistic.

General von Thoma and Colonel Westphal reported to me that evening on the course of the battle to date, mentioning particularly that General Stumme had forbidden the bombardment of the enemy assembly positions on the first night of the attack, on account of the ammunition shortage. As a result the enemy had been able to take possession of part of our minefield and to overcome the occupying troops with comparatively small losses to himself. The petrol situation made any major movement impossible and permitted only local counter-attacks by the armour deployed behind the particular sector which was in danger. Units of the 15th Panzer Division had counter-attacked several times on 24 and 25 October, but had suffered frightful losses in the terrible British artillery fire and non-stop RAF bombing attacks. By the evening of the 25th, only 31 of their 119 tanks remained serviceable.

There were now only very small stocks of petrol left in

North Africa and a crisis was threatening. I had already – on my way through Rome – demanded the immediate employment of all available Italian submarines and warships for the transport of petrol and ammunition. Our own air force was still unable to prevent the British bombing attacks, or to shoot down any major number of British aircraft. The RAF's new fighter-bombers were particularly in evidence, as is shown by the fact that every one of the captured tanks belonging to the *Kampfstaffel* had been shot up by this new type of aircraft.

Our aim for the next few days was to throw the enemy out of our main defence line at all costs and to reoccupy our old positions, in order to avoid having a westward bulge in our front.

That night our line again came under a heavy artillery barrage, which soon developed into one long roll of fire. I slept only a few hours and was back in my command vehicle again at 05.00 hours [26 October], where I learnt that the British had spent the whole night assaulting our front under cover of their artillery, which in some places had fired as many as 500 rounds for every one of ours. Strong forces of the Panzer divisions were already committed in the front line. British night-bombers had been over our units continuously. Shortly before midnight the enemy had succeeded in taking Hill 28, an important position in the northern sector. [Called by the British 'Kidney Ridge'] He had then brought up reinforcements to this point ready to continue the attack in the morning with the object of extending his bridge-head west of the minefields.

Attacks were now launched on Hill 28 by elements of the 15th Panzer Division, the Littorio and a Bersaglieri Battalion, supported by the concentrated fire of all the local artillery and A.A. Unfortunately, the attack gained ground very slowly. The British resisted desperately. Rivers of blood were poured out over miserable strips of land which, in normal times, not even the poorest Arab would have bothered his head about. Tremendous British artillery fire pounded the area of the attack. In the evening part of the Bersaglieri Battalion succeeded in occupying the eastern and western edges of the hill. The hill itself remained in British hands and later became the base for many enemy operations.

I myself observed the attack that day from the north. Load after load of bombs cascaded down among my troops. British strength round Hill 28 was increasing steadily. I gave orders to the artillery to break up the British movement north-east of Hill 28 by concentrated fire, but we had too little to do it successfully. During the day I brought up the 90th Light Division and the *Kampfstaffel*, in order to press home the attack on Hill 28. The British were continually feeding fresh forces into their attack from Hill 28 and it was clear that they wanted to win through to the area between El Daba and Sidi Abd el Rahman. I therefore moved the Trieste into the area east of El Daba. Late in the afternoon German and Italian dive-bomber formations made a self-immolating attempt to break up the British lorry columns moving towards the north-west. Some 60 British fighters pounced on these slow machines and forced the Italians to jettison their bombs over their own lines, while the German pilots pressed home their attack with very heavy losses. Never before in Africa had we seen such a density of anti-aircraft fire. Hundreds of British tracer shells criss-crossed the sky and the air became an absolute inferno of fire.

British attacks supported by tanks tried again and again to break out to the west through our line south of Hill 28. Finally, in the afternoon, a thrust by 160 tanks succeeded in wiping out an already severely mauled battalion of the 164th Infantry Division and penetrated into our line towards the south-west. Violent fighting followed in which the remaining German and Italian tanks managed to force the enemy back. Tank casualties so far, counting in that day's, were 61 in the 15th Panzer Division and 56 in the Littorio, all totally destroyed. Following on their non-stop night attacks, the RAF sent over formations of 18 to 20 bombers at hourly intervals throughout the day, which not only caused considerable casualties, but also began to produce serious signs of fatigue and a sense of inferiority among our troops.

The supply situation was now approaching disaster. The tanker *Proserpina*, which we had hoped would bring some relief in the petrol situation, had been bombed and sunk outside Tobruk. There was only enough petrol left to keep supply traffic going between Tripoli and the front for another two or three days, and that without counting the needs of the motorized forces, which had to be met out of the same stocks. What we should really have done now was to assemble all our motorized units in the north in order to fling the British back to the main defence line in a concentrated and planned counter-attack. But we had not the petrol to do it. So we were compelled to allow the armoured formations in the northern part of our line to assault the British salient piecemeal.

Since the enemy was operating with astonishing hesitancy and caution, a concentrated attack by the whole of our armour could have been successful, although such an assembly of armour would of course have been met by the heaviest possible British artillery fire and air bombardment. However, we could have made the action more fluid by withdrawing a few miles to the west and could then have attacked the British in an all-out charge and defeated them in open country. The British artillery and air force could not easily have intervened with their usual weight in a tank battle of this kind, for their own forces would have been endangered.

But a decision to take forces from the southern front was unthinkable with the petrol situation so bad. Not only could we not have kept a mobile battle going for more than a day or two, but our armour could never have returned to the south if the British had attacked there. I did, however, decide to bring the whole of the 21st Panzer Division up north, although I fully realized that the petrol shortage would not

allow it to return. In addition, since it was now obvious that
the enemy would make his main effort in the north during
the next few days and try for a decision there, half the Army
artillery was drawn off from the southern front. At the same
time I reported to the Führer's HQ that we would lose the
battle unless there was an immediate improvement in the
supply situation. Judging by previous experience, there was
very little hope of this happening.

Relays of British bombers continued their attack throughout the night of the 26th. At about 02.00 hours a furious
British barrage by guns of every calibre suddenly began in
the northern sector. Soon it was impossible to distinguish
between gun-fire and exploding shells and the sky grew
bright with the glare of muzzle-flashes and shell-bursts.
Continuous bombing attacks seriously delayed the approach march of the 21st Panzer Division and a third of
the Ariete. By dawn the 90th Light Division and the Trieste
had taken up position round the southern side of Sidi Abd el
Rahman.

That morning [27 October] I gave orders to all formations
to pin down the British assault forces during their approach
by all-out fire from every gun they could bring to bear.

The tactics which the British were using followed from
their apparently inexhaustible stocks of ammunition. Their
new tank, the General Sherman, which came into action for
the first time during this battle, showed itself to be far
superior to any of ours.

Attacks against our line were preceded by extremely
heavy artillery barrages lasting for several hours. The
attacking infantry then pushed forward behind a curtain
of fire and artificial fog, clearing mines and removing
obstacles. Where a difficult patch was struck they frequently
switched the direction of their attack under cover of smoke.
Once the infantry had cleared lanes in the minefields, heavy
tanks moved forward, closely followed by infantry. Particular skill was shown in carrying out this manoeuvre at night

and a great deal of hard training must have been done before the offensive.

In contact engagements the heavily gunned British tanks approached to a range of between 2,000 and 2,700 yards and then opened concentrated fire on our anti-tank and anti-aircraft guns and tanks, which were unable to penetrate the British armour at that range. The enormous quantities of ammunition which the enemy tanks used – sometimes they fired over 30 rounds at one target – were constantly replenished by armoured ammunition carriers. The British artillery fire was directed by observers who accompanied the attack in tanks.

In the early hours of 27 October, the British attacked again towards the south-west at their old break-in point south of Hill 28. At about 10 a.m. I went off to Telegraph Track. Two enemy bomber formations, each of 18 aircraft, dropped their bombs inside ten minutes into our defence positions. The whole front continued to lie under a devastating British barrage.

Local counter-attacks were due to be launched that afternoon by the 90th Light Division on Hill 28 and by the 15th and 21st Panzer Divisions, the Littorio and a part of the Ariete, against the British positions between minefields L and I.

At 14.30 hours I drove to Telegraph Track again, accompanied by Major Ziegler. Three times within a quarter of an hour units of the 90th Light Division, which had deployed and were standing in the open in preparation for the attack, were bombed by formations of eighteen aircraft. At 15.00 hours our dive-bombers swooped down on the British lines. Every artillery and anti-aircraft gun which we had in the northern sector concentrated a violent fire on the point of the intended attack. Then the armour moved forward. A murderous British fire struck into our ranks and our attack was soon brought to a halt by an immensely powerful anti-tank defence, mainly from dug-in anti-tank guns and a large number of tanks. We suffered considerable losses and were obliged to withdraw. There is, in general, little chance of success in a tank attack over country where the enemy has been able to take up defensive positions; but there was nothing else we could do. The 90th Light Division's attack was also broken up by heavy British artillery fire and a hail of bombs from British aircraft. A report from the division that they had taken Hill 28 unfortunately turned out to be untrue.

That evening further strong detachments of the Panzer divisions had to be committed in the front to close the gaps. Several of the 90th Light Division's units also went into the line. Only 70 tons of petrol had been flown across by the *Luftwaffe* that day, with the result that the army could only refuel for a short distance, for there was no knowing when petrol would arrive in any quantity and how long the divisions would have to get along with the few tons we could issue to them. The watchword 'as little movement as possible' applied more than ever.

In the evening we again sent SOSs to Rome and the Führer's HQ. But there was now no longer any hope of an improvement in the situation. It was obvious that from now on the British would destroy us bit by bit, since we were virtually unable to move on the battlefield. As yet, Montgomery had only thrown half his striking force into the battle.

The end at El Alamein came on 2 November. The leader of the British forces describes how.

General Montgomery

At two a.m. I directed two hard punches at the 'hinges' of the final break-out area where the enemy was trying to stop us widening the gap which we had blown. That finished the battle.

The armoured car regiments went through as dawn was breaking and soon the armoured divisions got clean away into the open desert; they were now in country clear of minefields, where they could manoeuvre and operate against the enemy rear areas and retreating columns.

The armoured cars raced away to the west, being directed far afield on the enemy line of retreat.

THE END AT STALINGRAD, January 1943

The battle for Stalingrad opened on 15 September and was fought with the utmost ferocity, street by street, house by house, in what the Germans called the *Rattenkrieg* ('rat war'). The 270,000-strong German Sixth Army under von Paulus became completely surrounded by the Red Army, but Hitler refused to allow von Paulus to withdraw and ordered him to 'hedgehog' himself in. By the year's end the situation inside Stalingrad had deteriorated rapidly; rations had fallen below subsistence level, ammunition supplies had dwindled and cold and disease claimed thousands of *Wehrmacht* lives. On 10 January the Russians began a final assault on the doomed army.

Anon. German soldiers, letters home

To return to the present position. Of the division there are only sixty-nine men still fit for action. Bleyer is still alive, and Hartlieb as well. Little Degen has lost both arms; I expect he will soon be in Germany. Life is finished for him, too. Get him to tell you the details which you people think worth knowing. D. has given up hope. I should like to know what he thinks of the situation and its consequences. All we have left are two machine-guns and 400 rounds. And then a mortar and ten bombs. Except for that all we have are hunger and fatigue

For a long time to come, perhaps for ever, this is to be my last letter. A comrade who has to go to the airfield is taking it along with him, as the last machine to leave the pocket is taking off tomorrow morning. The situation has become quite untenable. The Russians are only two miles from the last spot from which aircraft can operate, and when that's gone not even a mouse will get out, to say nothing of me. Admittedly several hundred thousand others won't escape either, but it's precious little consolation to share one's own destruction with other men.

On 24 January the Führer sent the following communique to the Sixth Army, Stalingrad.

Adolf Hitler

Surrender is forbidden. 6th Army will hold their positions to the last man and the last round and by their heroic endurance will make an unforgettable contribution towards the establishment of a defensive front and the salvation of the Western world.

A week later, at five-forty-five, 31 January, the 6th Army HQ radio announced:

The Russians stand at the door of our bunker. We are destroying our equipment.
This station will no longer transmit.

Immediately after this transmission the Sixth Army laid down its arms and surrendered. Alongside von Paulus there surrendered 23 generals, 2,000 officers and 130,000 other ranks. Over 100,000 Germans were killed and wounded in the battle; many of the wounded were buried alive by the Red Army who dynamited their underground shelters.

CAPTURED GERMAN OFFICERS, STALINGRAD, January 1943

Alexander Werth

The most unforgettable of [the captured German soldiers] was Lieutenant-General von Arnim, a cousin of the other Arnim who was to be captured in Tunisia a few months later. He was enormously tall, with a long twisted nose, and a look of fury in his long horse-like face with its popping eyes. He had a stupendous display of crosses and orders and mantelpiece ornaments. He, no more than the others, had any desire to explain why they had allowed themselves to be trapped at Stalingrad, and why they had been licked. When somebody put the question, he snarled and said, 'The question is badly put. You should ask how did we hold out so long against such overwhelming numerical superiority?' And one of the sulking ones in the background said something about hunger and cold.

But how they all hated any suggestion that the Red Army was a better army and a better-led army than theirs! When somebody suggested it, Von Arnim snorted and went almost purple with rage.

. . . One thing astonished me about these generals: they had been captured only a couple of days ago – and they looked healthy, and not in the least undernourished. Clearly, throughout the agony of Stalingrad, when their soldiers were dying of hunger, they were continuing to have more or less regular meals. There could be no other explanation for their normal, or almost normal, weight and appearance.

The only man who looked in poor shape was Paulus himself. We weren't allowed to speak to him; he was only shown us. (We could then testify that he was alive and had not committed suicide.) He stepped out of a large cottage – it was more like a villa – gave us a look, then stared at the horizon, and stood on the steps for a minute or two, amid a rather awkward silence, together with two other officers; one was General Schmidt, his Chief of Staff, a sinister, Göring-like creature, wearing a strange fur cap made of imitation leopard skin. Paulus looked pale and sick, and has a nervous twitch in his left cheek. He had more natural dignity than any of the others, and wore only one or two decorations.

A SOVIET AVIATION FACTORY, 1943

Wendell Wilkie

I spent one entire day looking at a Soviet aviation plant. I saw other factories in Russia, candy factories, munition factories, foundries, canneries, and power plants. But this aviation plant, now located outside of Moscow, remains most vivid in my memory.

It was a big place. My guess would be that some 30,000 workers were running three shifts and that they were making a very presentable number of airplanes every day . . .

American aviation experts were with me on this inspection, and they confirmed my impression that the planes we saw wheeled from the end of the assembly line and tested on an airfield next to the factory were good planes. And, peculiarly enough, they pronounced the armoured protection for the pilots the best of any they knew on any plane anywhere in the world. I am no aviation expert, but I have inspected a good many factories in my life. I kept my eyes open, and I think my report is fair.

Parts of the manufacturing process were crudely organized. The wings of the Stormovik are made of plywood, compressed under steam pressure, and then covered with canvas. The woodworking shops seemed to me to rely too much on hand labour, and their product showed it. Also, some of the electrical and plating shops were on the primitive side.

With these exceptions, the plant would compare favourably in output and efficiency with any I have ever seen. I walked through shop after shop of lathes and punching presses. I saw machine tools assembled from all over the world, their trade-names showing they came from Chemnitz, from Skoda, from Sheffield, from Cincinnati, from Sverdlovsk, from Antwerp. They were being efficiently used.

More than thirty-five per cent of the labour in the plant was done by women. Among the workers we saw boys not more than ten years old, all dressed in blue blouses and looking like apprentice students, even though the officials of the factory pulled no punches in admitting that the children work, in many of the shops, the full sixty-six-hour week worked by the adults. Many of the boys were doing skilled jobs on lathes, and seemed to be doing them extremely well.

On the whole, the plant seemed to us Americans to be overstaffed. There were more workers than would be found in a comparable American factory. But hanging over every third or fourth machine was a special sign, indicating that its worker was a 'Stakhanovite', pledged to overfulfil his or her norm of production . . . The walls of the factory carried fresh and obviously honoured lists of those workers and those shops which were leading in what was apparently a ceaseless competition for more and better output. A fair conclusion would be that this extra incentive, which was apparent in the conversation of any worker we stopped to talk to at random, made up for a large part, but not all, of the handicap of relative lack of skill.

The productivity of each individual worker was lower than in the United States. Russian officials admitted this to me freely. Until they can change this by education and training, they explained, they must offset it by putting great emphasis on patriotic drives for output and by recruiting all the labour power, even that of children and old women, that they can find. Meanwhile, and there was nothing done with mirrors here, we could see the planes leaving the cavernous doors of the final assembly unit, testing their machine-guns and cannon on a target range, and then taking to the air over our heads.

THE DAMBUSTERS RAID, RUHR VALLEY, 16 May 1943

Guy Gibson, RAF

The famous 'bouncing bomb' attack on the Ruhr Valley dams by RAF 617 Squadron was intended to disrupt production in Germany's industrial heartland. Nineteen Lancaster bombers led by Wing Commander Guy Gibson took part in the raid, eight of which were lost. Two dams, the Möhne and Eder, were destroyed, bringing widespread flooding; a third dam, the Sorpe, survived the bomb that hit it. Here Guy Gibson describes the attack on the Möhne dam. He was killed in action a year later.

The minutes passed slowly as we all sweated on this summer's night, sweated at working the controls and sweated with fear as we flew on. Every railway train, every hamlet and every bridge we passed was a potential danger, for our Lancasters were sitting targets at that height and speed. We fought our way past Dortmund, past Hamm – the well-known Hamm which has been bombed so many times; we could see it quite clearly now, its tall chimneys, factories and balloons capped by its umbrella of flak like a Christmas tree about five miles to our right; then we began turning to the right in between Hamm and the little town of Soest, where I nearly got shot down in 1940. Soest was sleepy now and did not open up, and out of the haze ahead appeared the Ruhr hills.

'We're there,' said Spam.

'Thank God,' said I, feelingly.

As we came over the hill, we saw the Möhne Lake. Then we saw the dam itself. In that light it looked squat and heavy and unconquerable; it looked grey and solid in the moonlight, as though it were part of the countryside itself and just as immovable. A structure like a battleship was showering out flak all along its length, but some came from the powerhouse below it and nearby. There were no searchlights. It was light flak, mostly green, yellow and red, and the colours of the tracer reflected upon the face of the water in the lake. The reflections on the dead calm of the black water made it seem there was twice as much as there really was.

'Did you say these gunners were out of practice?' asked Spam, sarcastically.

'They certainly seem awake now,' said Terry.

They were awake all right. No matter what people say, the Germans certainly have a good warning system. I scowled to myself as I remembered telling the boys an hour or so ago that they would probably only be the German equivalent of the Home Guard and in bed by the time we arrived.

It was hard to say exactly how many guns there were, but tracers seemed to be coming from about five positions, probably making twelve guns in all. It was hard at first to tell the calibre of the shells, but after one of the boys had been hit, we were informed over the RT that they were either 20-mm type or 37-mm, which, as everyone knows, are nasty little things.

We circled around stealthily, picking up the various landmarks upon which we had planned our method of attack, making use of some and avoiding others; every time we came within range of those bloody-minded flak-gunners they let us have it.

'Bit aggressive, aren't they?' said Trevor.

'Too right they are.'

I said to Terry, 'God, this light flak gives me the creeps.'

'Me, too,' someone answered.

For a time there was a general blind on the subject of light flak, and the only man who didn't say anything was Hutch, because he could not see it and because he never said anything about flak, anyway. But this was not the time for talking. I called up each member of our formation and found, to my relief, that they had all arrived, except, of course, Bill Astell. Away to the south, Joe McCarthy had just begun his diversionary attack on the Sorpe. But not all of them had been able to get there; both Byers and Barlow had been shot down by light flak after crossing the coast; these had been replaced by other aircraft of the rear formation. Bad luck, this being shot down after crossing the coast, because it could have happened to anybody; they must have been a mile or so off track and had got the hammer. This is the way things are in flying; you are either lucky or you aren't. We, too, had crossed the coast at the wrong place and had got away with it. We were lucky.

Down below, the Möhne Lake was silent and black and deep, and I spoke to my crew.

'Well boys, I suppose we had better start the ball rolling.' This with no enthusiasm whatsoever. 'Hello, all Cooler aircraft. I am going to attack. Stand by to come in to attack in your order when I tell you.'

Then to Hoppy: 'Hello, "M Mother". Stand by to take over if anything happens.'

Hoppy's clear and casual voice came back. 'OK, Leader. Good luck.'

Then the boys dispersed to the pre-arranged hiding-spots in the hills, so that they should not be seen either from the ground or from the air, and we began to get into position for our approach. We circled wide and came around down moon, over the high hills at the eastern end of the lake. On straightening up we began to dive towards the flat, ominous water two miles away. Over the front turret was the dam silhouetted against the haze of the Ruhr Valley. We could see the towers. We could see the sluices. We could see everything. Spam, the bomb-aimer, said, 'Good show. This is wizard.' He had been a bit worried, as all bomb-aimers are, in case they cannot see their aiming points, but as we came in over the tall fir trees his voice came up again rather quickly. 'You're going to hit them. You're going to hit those trees.'

'That's all right, Spam. I'm just getting my height.'

To Terry: 'Check height, Terry.'

To Pulford: 'Speed control, Flight-Engineer.'

To Trevor: 'All guns ready, gunners.'

To Spam: 'Coming up, Spam.'

Terry turned on the spotlights and began giving directions – 'Down – down – down. Steady – steady.' We were then exactly sixty feet.

Pulford began working the speed; first he put on a little flap to slow us down, then he opened the throttles to get the air-speed indicator exactly against the red mark. Spam began lining up his sights against the towers. He had turned the fusing switch to the 'ON' position. I began flying.

The gunners had seen us coming. They could see us coming with our spotlights on for over two miles away. Now they opened up and the tracers began swirling towards us; some were even bouncing off the smooth surface of the lake. This was a horrible moment: we were being dragged along at four miles a minute, almost against our will, towards the things we were going to destroy. I think at that moment the boys did not want to go. I know I did not want to go. I thought to myself, 'In another minute we shall all be dead – so what?' I thought again, 'This is terrible – this feeling of fear – if it is fear.' By now we were a few hundred yards away, and I said quickly to Pulford, under my breath, 'Better leave the throttles open now and stand by to pull me out of the seat if I get hit.' As I glanced at him I thought he looked a little glum on hearing this.

The Lancaster was really moving and I began looking through the special sight on my windscreen. Spam had his eyes glued to the bombsight in front, his hand on his button; a special mechanism on board had already begun to work so that the mine would drop (we hoped) in the right spot. Terry was still checking the height. Joe and Trev began to raise their guns. The flak could see us quite clearly now. It was not exactly inferno. I have been through far worse flak fire than that; but we were very low. There was something sinister and slightly unnerving about the whole operation. My aircraft was so small and the dam was so large; it was thick and solid, and now it was angry. My aircraft was very small. We skimmed along the surface of the lake, and as we went my gunner was firing into the defences, and the defences were firing back with vigour, their shells whistling past us. For some reason, we were not being hit.

Spam said, 'Left – little more left – steady – steady – steady – coming up.' Of the next few seconds I remember only a series of kaleidoscopic incidents.

The chatter from Joe's front guns pushing out tracers which bounced off the left-hand flak tower.

Pulford crouching beside me.

The smell of burnt cordite.

The cold sweat underneath my oxygen mask.

The tracers flashing past the windows – they all seemed the same colour now – and the inaccuracy of the gun positions near the power-station; they were firing in the wrong direction.

The closeness of the dam wall.

Spam's exultant, 'Mine gone.'

Hutch's red Very lights to blind the flak-gunners.

The speed of the whole thing.

Someone was saying over the RT, 'Good show, leader. Nice work.'

Then it was all over, and at last we were out of range, and there came over us all, I think, an immense feeling of relief and confidence.

Trevor said, 'I will get those bastards,' and he began to spray the dam with bullets until at last he, too, was out of range. As we circled round we could see a great 1000-feet column of whiteness still hanging in the air where our mine had exploded. We could see with satisfaction that Spam had been good, and it had gone off in the right position. Then, as we came closer, we could see that the explosion of the mine had caused a great disturbance upon the surface of the lake and the water had become broken and furious, as though it were being lashed by a gale. At first we thought that the dam itself had broken, because great sheets of water were slopping over the top of the wall like a gigantic basin. This caused some delay, because our mines could only be dropped in calm water, and we would have to wait until all became still again.

We waited.

We waited about ten minutes, but it seemed hours to us. It must have seemed even longer to Hoppy, who was the next to attack. Meanwhile, all the fighters had now collected over our target. They knew our game by now, but we were flying too low for them; they could not see us and there were no attacks.

At last – 'Hello, "M Mother". You may attack now. Good luck.'

'OK. Attacking.'

Hoppy, the Englishman, casual, but very efficient, keen now on only one thing, which was war. He began his attack.

He began going down over the trees where I had come from a few moments before. We could see his spotlights quite clearly, slowly closing together as he ran across the water.

We saw him approach. The flak, by now, had got an idea from which direction the attack was coming, and they let him have it. When he was about 100 yards away someone said, hoarsely, over the RT: 'Hell! He has been hit.'

'M Mother' was on fire; an unlucky shot had got him in one of the inboard petrol tanks and a long jet of flame was beginning to stream out. I saw him drop his mine, but his bomb-aimer must have been wounded, because it fell straight on to the power-house on the other side of the dam. But Hoppy staggered on, trying to gain altitude so that his crew could bale out. When he had got to about 500 feet there was a vivid flash in the sky and one wing fell off; his aircraft disintegrated and fell to the ground in cascading, flaming fragments. There it began to burn quite gently and rather sinisterly in a field some three miles beyond the dam.

Someone said, 'Poor old Hoppy!'

Another said, 'We'll get those bastards for this.'

A furious rage surged up inside my own crew, and Trevor said, 'Let's go in and murder those gunners.' As he spoke, Hoppy's mine went up. It went up behind the power-house with a tremendous yellow explosion and left in the air a great ball of black smoke; again there was a long wait while we watched for this to clear. There was so little wind that it took a long time.

Many minutes later I told Mickey to attack; he seemed quite confident, and we ran in beside him and a little in front; as we turned, Trevor did his best to get those gunners as he had promised.

Bob Hay, Mickey's bomb-aimer, did a good job, and his mine dropped in exactly the right place. There was again a gigantic explosion as the whole surface of the lake shook, then spewed forth its cascade of white water. Mickey was all right; he got through. But he had been hit several times and one wing-tank lost all its petrol. I could see the vicious tracer from his rear-gunner giving one gun position a hail of bullets as he swept over. Then he called up, 'Okay. Attack completed.' It was then that I thought that the dam wall had moved. Of course we could not see anything, but if Jeff's theory had been correct, it should have cracked by now. If only we could go on pushing it by dropping more successful mines, it would surely move back on its axis and collapse.

Once again we watched for the water to calm down. Then in came Melvyn Young in 'D Dog'. I yelled to him, 'Be careful of the flak. It's pretty hot.'

He said, 'Okay.'

I yelled again, 'Trevor's going to beat them up on the other side. He'll take most of it off you.'

Melvyn's voice again. 'Okay. Thanks.' And so as 'D Dog' ran in we stayed at a fairly safe distance on the other side, firing with all guns at the defences, and the defences, like the stooges they were, firing back at us. We were both out of range of each other, but the ruse seemed to work, and we flicked on our identification lights to let them see us even more clearly. Melvyn's mine went in, again in exactly the right spot, and this time a colossal wall of water swept right over the dam and kept on going. Melvyn said, 'I think I've done it. I've broken it.' But we were in a better position to see than he, and it had not rolled down yet. We were all getting pretty excited by now, and I screamed like a schoolboy over the RT: 'Wizard show, Melvyn. I think it'll go on the next one.'

Now we had been over the Möhne for quite a long time, and all the while I had been in contact with Scampton Base. We were in close contact with the Air Officer Commanding and the Commander-in-Chief of Bomber Command, and with the scientist, observing his own greatest scientific experiment in Damology. He was sitting in the operations room, his head in his hands, listening to the reports as one after another the aircraft attacked. On the other side of the room the Commander-in-Chief paced up and down. In a way their job of waiting was worse than mine. The only difference was that they did not know that the structure was shifting as I knew, even though I could not see anything clearly.

When at last the water had all subsided I called up No. 5 – David Maltby – and told him to attack. He came in fast, and I saw his mine fall within feet of the right spot; once again the flak, the explosion and wall of water. But this time we were on the wrong side of the wall and could see what had happened. We watched for about five minutes, and it was rather hard to see anything, for by now the air was full of spray from these explosions, which had settled like mist on our windscreens. Time was getting short, so I called up Dave Shannon and told him to come in.

As he turned I got close to the dam wall and then saw what had happened. It had rolled over, but I could not believe my eyes. I heard someone shout, 'I think she has gone!' Other voices took up the cry and quickly I said, 'Stand by until I make a recce.' I remembered that Dave was going in to attack and told him to turn away and not to approach the target. We had a closer look. Now there was no doubt about it; there was a great breach 100 yards across, and the water, looking like stirred porridge in the moonlight, was gushing out and rolling into the Ruhr Valley towards the industrial centres of Germany's Third Reich.

Nearly all the flak had now stopped, and the other boys came down from the hills to have a closer look to see what had been done. There was no doubt about it at all – the Möhne Dam had been breached and the gunners on top of the dam, except for one man, had all run for their lives towards the safety of solid ground; this remaining gunner was a brave man, but one of the boys quickly extinguished his flak with a burst of well-aimed tracer. Now it was all quiet, except for the roar of the water which steamed and hissed its way from its 150-foot head. Then we began to shout and scream and act like madmen over the RT, for this was a tremendous sight, a sight which probably no man will ever see again.

Quickly I told Hutch to tap out the message, 'Nigger', to my station, and when this was handed to the Air Officer Commanding there was (I heard afterwards) great excitement in the operations room. The scientist jumped up and danced round the room.

Then I looked again at the dam and at the water, while all around me the boys were doing the same. It was the most amazing sight. The whole valley was beginning to fill with fog from the steam of the gushing water, and down in the foggy valley we saw cars speeding along the roads in front of this great wave of water, which was chasing them and going faster than they could ever hope to go. I saw their headlights burning and I saw water overtake them, wave by wave, and then the colour of the headlights underneath the water changing from light blue to green from green to dark purple, until there was no longer anything except the water bouncing down in great waves. The floods raced on, carrying with them as they went – viaducts, railways, bridges and everything that stood in their path. Three miles beyond the dam the remains of Hoppy's aircraft were still burning gently, a dull red glow on the ground. Hoppy had been avenged.

Then I felt a little remote and unreal sitting up there in the warm cockpit of my Lancaster, watching this mighty power which we had unleashed; then glad, because I knew that this was the heart of Germany, and the heart of her industries, the place which itself had unleashed so much misery upon the whole world.

We knew, as we watched, that this flood-water would not win the war; it would not do anything like that, but it was a catastrophe for Germany.

I circled round for about three minutes, then called up all aircraft and told Mickey and David Maltby to go home and the rest to follow me to Eder, where we would try to repeat the performance.

MASS BOMBING, HAMBURG, Summer 1943

During the spring and summer of 1943 Hamburg, Berlin, and the Ruhr Valley were bombed by the RAF and USAAF in a series of night raids the intensity of which was unparalleled in the history of warfare. Hamburg was almost obliterated by the bombing and the fire-storm it set off. A secret report prepared by the German government recorded that:

Trees three feet thick were broken off or uprooted, human beings were thrown to the ground or flung alive into the flames by winds which exceeded a hundred and fifty miles an hour. The panic-stricken citizens knew not where to turn. Flames drove them from the shelters, but high-explosive bombs sent them scurrying back again. Once inside, they were suffocated by carbon-monoxide poisoning and their bodies reduced to ashes as though they had been placed in a crematorium, which was indeed what each shelter proved to be. The fortunate were those who jumped into the canals and waterways and remained swimming or standing up to their necks in water for hours until the heat should die down.

B-17 RAID ON REGENSBURG, 1943

John Muirhead, USAAF

The town of Regensburg was a major centre of German war production, the site of the massive Messerschmitt works. It was thus a major target for the Allied bomber forces.

'Flak! Flak at ten o'clock.'
We were passing Klagenfurt. The bursts were high and to

our left, edging toward us as the batteries corrected their fire. It was closing on us. Crystal fragments of steel burned the air around us while we blundered through the greasy traces of brown and black smoke. Our squadron lead plane suddenly showed a stream of flaming oil from his number-two engine. I watched curiously to see how quickly the pilots could shut down the engine and feather the prop. It was secured within minutes. The flames subsided, but a mist of smoking oil trailed the plane, leaving a widened, curling ribbon of black behind us. The damaged plane didn't waver but held the lead steady, not yielding our course. It was a violent passage of about ten minutes before we were out of the range of the guns. It was an eternity, a second-by-second deliverance from each exploding shell. And there was no end, only another beginning.

'Top turret to pilot. They're back. Three o'clock level.' Pete hesitated, as though he were puzzled. 'Queer – For Christ's sake! They're JU-88s, a string of them! I make out six. Off about a thousand yards, on our course. The rest of you guys? Do you see anything else?' Each gunner reported in negative; no other enemy planes in sight. It didn't seem possible that they were throwing these old bombers at us. They were slow and not heavily armed, easy targets for our packed firepower.

'They're turning – Rockets! Jesus, they're shootin' fuckin' rockets at us!'

A cluster of white tracks moved gracefully toward us, arcing away from the bombers like the start of a fireworks display. Each rocket was followed by a core of pulsing orange light that refracted through the exhaust vapours, making shimmering circles of yellow and red. They passed about fifty yards in front of the lead squadron, and their auras faded as their vapour tracks blended together to form a thin cloud through which we passed, spilling the curves of whiteness over our wings and engines.

'Bandits. Twelve o'clock.' It was Andy's voice, our navi-

gator. The words were spoken quietly. I could barely hear
him on the intercom. He knew there was no need to shout, no
need to summon us with a brave rallying cry; it was only a
matter of making it known – they had returned.

Two waves were coming straight in, ten in each line. They
were ME-210s, two-engine fighters with plenty of firepower.
One line was attacking level, heading for the lead squadron;
the other line of ten was slightly higher, and were sliding over
the top of their comrades, positioning for an attack on our
squadron.

'Ten coming in. Eleven o'clock high.'

The top turret and the nose open fired. I could see the
blinking wing guns of the incoming fighters, and I watched
the white lines of tracers merge before me. Black bursts of
twenty-millimetre shells stitched a line over our left wing.
Our squadron leader began to go to pieces: large chunks of
metal blew away from the lower part of the nose; the chin
turret was hanging at a strange angle; the end of his right
wing blew away, and the plane flipped over. It continued to
turn, performing a looping barrel roll of flame before it fell
from us in an almost vertical dive. The fighters broke to our
right except for one flaming coffin that continued through
our formation, miraculously missing the left wing of the lead
flight by inches.

As the frenzy of the battle raged, my terror faded and I
waited for my death. I no longer saw them: the 109s, the
410s, the 210s, and the 190s, coming at us from all directions.
I no longer saw the horror of my comrades burning and
dying. I shut my soul to everything but the plane ahead of
me. I held *Laura* steady under the tail guns as though she
were nailed there.

Sweat covered me: it ran down my back and between my
buttocks; it streamed down my chest; my eyes burned with it.
My crotch and thighs were soaked with urine. I crouched in
my small seat, strapped to it so I could barely move. Life-
giving air came into my lungs from a slender rubber tube

that could be severed with a boy's jackknife. Goggles shielded my eyes from the blasts of ice-cold air pouring through the ragged holes in the windshield. A band of rubber plastic around my throat with two small diaphragms pressed against my vocal cords allowed me to speak; but there were no words: the maelstrom roared around me, and only my gasping breath pulsed through the unmindful slender strands of wire.

After a long, long time, some words were spoken to me, words I could barely comprehend.

'Bombardier to pilot. We're coming up on the IP. Bomb-bay doors are coming open.'

We had made it! We had made it to Regensburg!

The group wheeled in a shallow turn, settling in on the angle of attack. We were on the bomb run. The fighters were gone, but ahead of us loomed a wall of flak. It was more than enough for our ragged band of fourteen bombers. We had lost seven, and were now down to five in the lead, five in the left, and four in my right squadron. We plunged into the darkness.

Laura was rocked by near explosions. She was vibrating, trying to fall off on her right wing: Paul's voice came on the intercom. 'Number three – number three. Manifold pressure's gone. Oil pressure's dropping.'

'Shutting down number three.' I hit the feathering button.

Paul's hands moved fast: throttle, off; fuel, off; oil pump, off; switches, off. 'Number three, secure.'

The vibration lessened. Paul and I watched the blades slow down, and we waited for them to rotate with their edges facing into the wind. If the blades failed to feather, we would have an almost impossible drag on our plane: the broad area of the three blades, flat in the wind, would be a barrier, slowing *Laura* down. We would be forced to fall behind the formation, and the German fighters would make short work of us.

Paul's hand pounded my knee. 'It's okay. She's feathered. Okay to trim.'

I advanced power slightly on the other inboard, then adjusted the rudder and aileron trim to compensate for the dead engine. Paul came back to me. 'I'll give you a damage report when we're out of this stuff.'

The flak engulfed us. It was so intense we could only feel the turbulence from the near bursts; we were in a swirling torrent that obscured the individual explosions except when they came close and fire blazed out of the shadows. Something slammed into the armour plate on the back of my seat; a gaping hole appeared in the Plexiglas over my head.

A plane was falling out of the lead squadron. I watched for chutes. Suddenly she blew; a tremendous explosion of flame and debris leaped outward. The shock wave rocked the squadron, and we struggled to recover. We had to keep the formation tight; we couldn't fail now. As we fought to control our planes, the group leader's voice came in on a command frequency. 'Steady. Steady. Hold it steady.'

Laura lurched upward.

'Bombs away! Bombs away!'

Three tons of bombs had dropped out of the racks. The group started a wide turn to the left, nosing down in a shallow dive to clear the inferno. We levelled off at 22,000 feet and began our long journey home.

We were mauled on our return. The battle was a series of violent sporadic attacks by German fighters now disorganized and without the concentrated fury they had been able to throw at us on our way in. They were rising in smaller numbers. Some of them couldn't get back to us: the time it took them to land, refuel, climb to 22,000 feet, and search for us as we pushed hard for the coast made interception more a matter of luck than anything else. But those who found us fought with a ferocity that our reduced numbers and battle-damaged planes could barely endure. They slashed at our formation with an abandoned savagery to make us pay for the rubble and corpses of Regensburg, for their comrades blasted out of the air; they slashed at us in their rage against an onslaught they knew would never end. We lost two more bombers to these furious attacks, and by the time we reached the Adriatic the original group strength was reduced to ten aircraft.

Ten B-17s crossed the coastline, ten torn machines carrying exhausted men, wounded and dead men. And those who lived watched the calm sea pass beneath them; they watched the towering cumulus along the coast swell upward in a billowing stream, forming great castles of purple-and-white fleece. They watched and saw nothing. Their vision still held the battle, and they stared with unseeing eyes at the splendour of the sky and sea.

I RESCUE MUSSOLINI, GRAN SASSO, 23 September 1943

Otto Skorzeny

Otto Skorzeny, the Chief of the *Waffen* SS Special Troops, brought off one of the most improbable exploits of the war in rescuing Benito Mussolini from the mountain fastness of Gran Sasso, where the dictator had been imprisoned by Italian forces intent on surrender to the Allies.

September 10 1943. We had not been out of our uniforms for two nights and days, and though our general was in the same case it was essential that I should see him with a view to making the great decision.

But first I discussed all the possibilities with Radl. We both fully realized that speed was absolutely vital. Every day, every hour that we delayed increased the danger that the Duce might be removed elsewhere, nay even worse, delivered over to the Allies. This supposition subsequently turned out to be most realistic. One of the terms of the armistice agreed by General Eisenhower was that the Duce should be handed over.

A ground operation seemed hopeless from the start. An attack on the steep, rocky slopes would have cost us heavy losses, as well as giving good notice to the enemy and leaving them time to conceal their prisoner. To forestall that eventuality, the whole massif would have to be surrounded by good mountain troops. A division at least would be required. So a ground operation was ruled out.

The factor of surprise could be our only trump as it was to be feared that the prisoner's guards had orders to kill him if there was any danger of rescue. This supposition later proved well founded. Such an order could only be frustrated by lightning intervention.

There remained only two alternatives – parachute landings or gliders.

We pondered long over both and then decided in favour of the second. At such altitudes, and in the thin air, a parachute drop would involve too rapid a rate of descent for anyone equipped with the normal parachute only. We also feared that in this rocky region the parachutists would be scattered too widely, so that an immediate attack by a compact detachment would not be possible.

So a glider remained the only solution. The final decision was in the hands of the Parachute Corps experts and General Student.

What were the prospects of success with glider landings? When we took our air photographs to the big laboratory at Frascati on the afternoon of the 8th, we had found it completely destroyed. I asked one of my officers to look somewhere else and he eventually found an emergency laboratory at an airstrip. Unfortunately, we could not have the usual big stereos which would have shown up all the details of the mountain zone. We would have to be content with ordinary prints approximately 14 by 14 cm.

These proved good enough to enable me to recognize the

triangular meadow which I had noticed as we flew over. On the suitability of this meadow as a landing-ground we based our whole plan and I accordingly drew up detailed orders for the individual parties.

General Student suggested that a parachute battalion infiltrate by night into the valley and seize the lower station of the funicular at the hour appointed for the landing. In that way we should have cover on that side and also a line of retreat if withdrawal became necessary after the operation was complete.

The talk with General Student had the desired result. Of course he realized that there were many most serious objections but he agreed that there was only one possible way short of abandoning the enterprise altogether. Then the experts in air landings – the Chief-of-Staff and the Ia Air of the Parachute Corps – were called in to give their reactions.

These two officers were at first wholly adverse to the plan. They objected that an air landing of this kind at such an altitude and without a prepared landing-ground had never been attempted before. In their view the projected operation would result in the loss of at least 80 per cent of the troops employed. The survivors would be too few to have any chance of success.

My answer was that I was fully aware of this danger, but every novel venture must have a beginning. We knew the meadow was flat and a careful landing should enable us to avoid serious casualties. 'Of course, gentlemen, I am ready to carry out any alternative scheme you may suggest.'

After careful consideration, General Student gave his final approval and issued his orders: 'The twelve gliders required are to be flown from the south of France to Rome at once. I fix six a.m. on 12 September as zero-hour. At that moment the machines must land on the plateau and the funicular station be seized by our battalion. We can assume that at that early hour the dangerous air currents so common in Italian mountain regions will be relatively weak. I will instruct the pilots personally and impress upon them the importance of the utmost care in landing. I am sure you are right, Captain Skorzeny. The operation cannot be carried out in any other way!'

After this decision had been given Radl and I worked out the details of our plan. We had to make careful calculations of the distances, make up our minds as to what arms and equipment the men should carry and, above all, prepare a large-scale plan showing the exact landing-place for each of the twelve gliders. Each glider could take ten men, i.e., a group, in addition to the pilot. Each group must know exactly what it had to do. I decided that I would go myself in the third glider so that the immediate assault by my own and the fourth group could be covered by the two groups already landed.

At the conclusion of these labours we spent a little time discussing our chances. We did not bluff ourselves that they were other than very slim. No one could really say whether Mussolini was still on the mountain and would not be spirited away elsewhere before we arrived. There was the further question whether we could overpower the guards quickly enough to prevent anyone killing him first, and we had not forgotten the warning given by the staff officers.

We must, in any event, allow for casualties in the landings. Even without any casualties we should only be 108 men and they could not all be available at the same moment. They would have to tackle 150 Italians who knew the ground perfectly and could use the hotel as a fortress. In weapons the two opponents could be regarded as approximately equals, as our parachutists' tommy-guns gave us an advantage, compensating to some extent for the enemy's superiority in numbers, particularly if we had not suffered too badly at the outset.

While we were immersed in these calculations Radl interrupted: 'May I suggest, sir, that we forget all about figures and trying to compute our chances; we both know that they are very small, but we also know that, however small, we shall stake our lives on success!'

One more thought occurred to me: how could we increase the effect of surprise, obviously our most potent weapon? We racked our brains for a long time and then Radl suddenly had a bright idea: 'Why not take with us an Italian officer, someone who must be reasonably well known to the Carabinieri up there? His very presence will bluff the guards for a short time and restrain them from immediately reacting to our arrival by violence against the Duce. We must make the best possible use of the interval.'

This was an excellent idea, which I promptly approved and considered how best to exploit. General Student must confer with the officer in question during the evening before the operation and somehow persuade him to come with us. To prevent leakage or betrayal, he must remain with us until the following morning.

We discussed the choice of the most suitable person with someone who knew the situation in Rome and decided upon some high-ranking officer of the former Italian headquarters in that city who had adopted a substantially neutral attitude during the recent disturbances. He must be invited to a conference at Frascati after General Student had approved the idea.

Fresh troubles now descended upon us. The reports we received during 11 September about the movement of the gliders was very unsatisfactory. Owing to enemy air activity they had had to make various detours and bad weather had not helped. Despite these misfortunes, we hoped to the last that they would arrive in time, but we hoped in vain.

The selected Italian officer, a general, appeared punctually, but had to be politely put off till the next day and invited to a conference with General Student for eight p.m. at the Practica di Mare airfield. Zero-hour had to be postponed, as we received news that the gliders could not arrive in Rome before the early hours of the 12th. General

Student fixed it for two o'clock on the Sunday (12 September) as we certainly could not wait another twenty-four hours. This postponement involved awkward changes in our plans and further prejudiced our chances. Owing to the air currents and local winds to be anticipated in the middle of the day the landing would be more dangerous, and the fact that the assault was to be made at two p.m. (i.e., in broad daylight) set a difficult task for the detachment operating in the valley. Various changes were necessary and had to be made with the utmost speed.

In the afternoon of the Saturday I visited the garden of a monastery in Frascati where my own men and the Mors battalion had pitched their tents. For this enterprise I meant to take volunteers only, and I had no intention of keeping them in the dark as to the dangers involved. I had them paraded and made a short speech: 'The long waiting-time is over. We have an important job to do tomorrow. Adolf Hitler has ordered it personally. Serious losses must be anticipated and, unfortunately, cannot be avoided. I shall of course lead you and can promise you that I will do my utmost. If we all stick together the assault will and must succeed. Anyone prepared to volunteer take one step forward!'

It gave me the greatest pleasure to see that not one of my men wanted to be left behind. To my officers and von Berlepsch commanding the one parachute company, I left the disagreeable task of refusing some of them, as the party must not exceed 108 in all. I myself selected 18 of my *Waffen SS* men. A small special commando was chosen for the valley detachment and another for an operation to rescue the Duce's family. I remained at the camp a little longer and was delighted with the spirit and enthusiasm everywhere displayed.

At that moment we got a terrible shock from an Allied wireless message which came through. It was to the effect that the Duce had arrived as a prisoner in Africa on board an

Italian man-of-war which had come from Spezia. When I recovered from the fright I took a map and compasses. As we knew the exact moment when part of the Italian fleet left Spezia I could easily calculate that even the fastest ship could not possibly have reached Africa so soon. The wireless message must, therefore, be a hoax. Was I not justified in regarding all news from enemy sources with the greatest suspicion ever after?

Sunday, 12 September, 1943. At five a.m. we marched in close order to the airfield. There we learned that the gliders were expected at ten a.m.

I again inspected the equipment of my men, who were all wearing parachute uniform. Parachute rations for five days had been issued. I had arranged that several boxes of fruit should be sent up and we sat about, pleasantly idle, in the shade of the buildings and trees. There was an atmosphere of tension, of course, but we took care to prevent any manifestation of apprehension or nerves.

By eight o'clock, the Italian officer had not showed up so I had to send Radl off to Rome, telling him that the man had to be produced, alive, in double quick time. The trusty Radl duly produced him, though he had the greatest difficulty in finding him in the city.

General Student had a short talk with him in my presence, Lieutenant Warger acting as interpreter. We told him of Adolf Hitler's request for his participation in the operation, with a view to minimizing the chance of bloodshed. The officer was greatly flattered by this personal request from the head of the German state and found it impossible to refuse. He agreed, thereby placing an important trump in our hands.

About eleven the first gliders came in. The towing planes were quickly refuelled and the coupled aircraft drawn up in the order in which they were to start. General Student dismissed the men of Berlepsch's company and then my men. The pilots and the twelve group commanders were summoned to an inner room, where General Student made a short speech in which he again laid great stress on the absolute necessity for a smooth landing. He categorically forbade crash landings, in view of the danger involved.

I gave the glider commanders detailed instructions and drew a sketch on a blackboard showing the exact landing-place of each craft, after which I cleared up all outstanding points with the commanders of each group and explained the tasks allotted to them. The men had decided on their password, something guaranteed to shift all obstacles. It was 'Take it easy', and the battle cry remained the watch-word of the SS commandos right up to the end of the war.

Flying times, altitudes, and distances were then discussed with the Ic (Intelligence officer) of the Parachute Corps, who had been on the photographic expedition with us. He was to take his place in the first towing plane as, apart from Radl and myself, he alone knew the appearance of the ground from the air. The flying time for the 100 kilometres to be covered would be approximately one hour, so it was essential that we should start at one o'clock prompt.

At twelve-thirty, there was a sudden air-raid warning. Enemy bombers were reported and before long we were hearing bomb bursts quite near. We all took cover and I cursed at the prospect of the whole enterprise being knocked on the head at the last moment. Just when I was in the depths of despair, I heard Radl's voice behind me: 'Take it easy!' and confidence returned in a flash. The raid ended just before one o'clock. We rushed out to the tarmac and noticed several craters, though our gliders were unharmed. The men raced out to their aircraft and I gave the order to emplane, inviting the Italian General to sit in front of me on the narrow board, which was all that was available in the cramped space into which we were packed like herrings. There was in fact hardly any room for our weapons. The General looked as if he were already regretting his decision and had already shown some hesitation in following me into the glider. But I felt it was too late to bother about his feelings. There was no time for that sort of thing!

I glanced at my watch. One o'clock! I gave the signal to start. The engines began to roar and we were soon gliding along the tarmac and then rising into the air. We were off.

We slowly gained altitude in wide circles and the procession of gliders set course towards the north-east. The weather seemed almost ideal for our purpose. Vast banks of white cloud hung lazily at about 3,000 metres. If they did not disperse we should reach our target practically unobserved and drop out of the sky before anyone realized we were there.

The interior of the glider was most unpleasantly hot and stuffy. I suddenly noticed that the corporal sitting behind me was being sick and that the general in front had turned as green as his uniform. Flying obviously did not suit him; he certainly was not enjoying himself. The pilot reported our position as best he could and I carefully followed his indications on my map, noting when we passed over Tivoli. From the inside of the glider we could see little of the country. The cellophane side-windows were too thick and the gaps in the fabric (of which there were many) too narrow to give us any view. The German glider, type DFS 230, comprised a few steel members covered with canvas. We were somewhat backward in this field, I reflected, thinking enviously of an elegant aluminium frame.

We thrust through a thick bank of clouds to reach the altitude of 3,500 metres which had been specified. For a short time we were in a dense grey world, seeing nothing of our surroundings, and then we emerged into bright sunshine, leaving the clouds below us. At that moment the pilot of our towing machine, a Hentschel, came through on the telephone to the commander of my glider: 'Flights 1 and 2 no longer ahead of us! Who's to take over the lead now?'

This was bad news. What had happened to them? At that time I did not know that I also had only seven machines instead of nine behind me. Two had fallen foul of a couple of bomb craters at the very start. I had a message put through: 'We'll take over the lead ourselves!'

I got out my knife and slashed right and left in the fabric to make a hole big enough to give us something of a view. I changed my mind about our old-fashioned glider. At least it was made of something we could cut!

My peephole was enough to let us get our bearings when the cloud permitted. We had to be very smart in picking up bridges, roads, river bends, and other geographical features on our maps. Even so, we had to correct our course from time to time. Our excursion should not fail through going astray. I did not dwell on the thought that we should be without covering fire when we landed.

It was just short of zero-hour when I recognized the valley of Aquila below us and also the leading vehicles of our own formation hastening along it. It would clearly be at the right place at the right time, though it must certainly have had its troubles too. We must not fail it!

'Helmets on!' I shouted as the hotel, our destination, came in sight, and then: 'Slip the tow-ropes!' My words were followed by a sudden silence, broken only by the sound of the wind rushing past. The pilot turned in a wide circle, searching the ground – as I was doing – for the flat meadow appointed as our landing-ground. But a further, and ghastly, surprise was in store for us. It was triangular all right, but so far from being flat it was a steep, a very steep hillside! It could even have been a ski-jump.

We were now much nearer the rocky plateau than when we were photographing it and the conformation of the ground was more fully revealed. It was easy to see that a landing on this 'meadow' was out of the question. My pilot, Lieutenant Meyer, must also have realized that the situation was critical, as I caught him looking all round. I was faced with a ticklish decision. If I obeyed the express orders of my General I should abandon the operation and try to glide down to the valley. If I was not prepared to do so, the forbidden crash-landing was the only alternative.

It did not take me long to decide. I called out: 'Crash landing! As near to the hotel as you can get!' The pilot, not hesitating for a second, tilted the starboard wing and down we came with a rush. I wondered for a moment whether the glider could take the strain in the thin air, but there was little time for speculation. With the wind shrieking in our ears we approached our target. I saw Lieutenant Meyer release the parachute brake, and then followed a crash and the noise of shattering wood. I closed my eyes and stopped thinking. One last mighty heave, and we came to rest.

The bolt of the exit hatch had been wrenched away, the first man was out like a shot and I let myself fall sideways out of the glider, clutching my weapons. We were within fifteen metres of the hotel! We were surrounded by jagged rocks of all sizes, which may have nearly smashed us up but had also acted as a brake so that we had taxied barely twenty metres. The parachute brake now folded up immediately behind the glider.

The first Italian sentry was standing on the edge of a slight rise at one corner of the hotel. He seemed lost in amazement. I had no time to bother about our Italian passenger, though I had noticed him falling out of the glider at my side, but rushed straight into the hotel. I was glad that I had given the order that no one must fire a shot before I did. It was essential that the surprise should be complete. I could hear my men panting behind me. I knew that they were the pick of the bunch and would stick to me like glue and ask no explanations.

We reached the hotel. All the surprised and shocked sentry required was a shout of 'mani in alto' (hands up). Passing through an open door, we spotted an Italian soldier engaged in using a wireless set. A hasty kick sent his chair flying from under him and a few hearty blows from my machine-pistol wrecked his apparatus. On finding that the room had no exit into the interior of the hotel we hastily retraced our steps and went outside again.

We raced along the façade of the building and round the corner to find ourselves faced with a terrace two and a half metres high. Corporal Himmel offered me his back and I was up and over in a trice. The others followed in a bunch.

My eyes swept the façade and lit on a well-known face at one of the windows of the first storey. It was the Duce! Now I knew that our effort had not been in vain! I yelled at him: 'Away from the window!' and we rushed into the entrance hall, colliding with a lot of Italian soldiers pouring out. Two machine-guns were set up on the floor of the terrace. We jumped over them and put them out of action. The Carabinieri continued to stream out and it took a few far from gentle blows from my weapon to force a way through them. My men yelled out '*mani in alto*'. So far no one had fired a shot.

I was now well inside the hall. I could not look round or bother about what was happening behind me. On the right was a staircase. I leaped up it, three steps at a time, turned left along a corridor and flung open a door on the right. It was a happy choice. Mussolini and two Italian officers were standing in the middle of the room. I thrust them aside and made them stand with their backs to the door. In a moment my Untersturmführer Schwerdt appeared. He took the situation in at a glance and hustled the mightily surprised Italian officers out of the room and into the corridor. The door closed behind us.

We had succeeded in the first part of our venture. The Duce was safely in our hands. Not more than three or four minutes had passed since we arrived!

At that moment the heads of Holzer and Benz, two of my subordinates, appeared at the window. They had not been able to force their way through the crowd in the hall and so had been compelled to join me via the lightning-conductor. There was no question of my men leaving me in the lurch. I sent them to guard the corridor.

I went to the window and saw Radl and his SS men running towards the hotel. Behind them crawled Obersturmführer Merzel, the company commander of our Friedenthal special unit and in charge of glider No. 4 behind me. His glider had grounded about 100 metres from the hotel and he had broken his ankle on landing. The third group in glider No. 5 also arrived while I was watching.

I shouted out: 'Everything's all right! Mount guard everywhere!'

I stayed a little while longer to watch gliders 6 and 7 crashland with Lieutenant Berlepsch and his parachute company. Then before my very eyes followed a tragedy. Glider 8 must have been caught in a gust; it wobbled and then fell like a stone, landed on a rocky slope and was smashed to smithereens.

Sounds of firing could now be heard in the distance and I put my head into the corridor and shouted for the officer-in-command at the hotel. A colonel appeared from nearby and I summoned him to surrender forthwith, assuring him that any further resistance was useless. He asked me for time to consider the matter. I gave him one minute, during which Radl turned up. He had had to fight his way through and I assumed that the Italians were still holding the entrance, as no one had joined me.

The Italian colonel returned, carrying a goblet of red wine which he proffered to me with a slight bow and the words: 'To the victor!'

A white bedspread, hung from the window, performed the functions of a white flag.

After giving a few orders to my men outside the hotel I was able to devote attention to Mussolini, who was standing in a corner with Untersturmführer Schwerdt in front of him. I introduced myself: 'Duce, the Führer has sent me! You are free!'

Mussolini embraced me: 'I knew my friend Adolf Hitler would not leave me in the lurch,' he said.

The surrender was speedily carried out. The Italian other ranks had to deposit their arms in the dining-room of the hotel but I allowed the officers to keep their revolvers. I learned that we had captured a general in addition to the colonel.

I was informed by telephone that the station of the funicular had also fallen undamaged into our hands. There had been little fighting, but the troops had arrived to the second and the surprise had been complete.

Lieutenant von Berlepsch had already replaced his monocle when I called to him from the window and gave orders that reinforcements must be sent up by the funicular. I wanted to make insurance doubly sure and also show the Italian colonel that we had troops in the valley also. I then had our wireless truck in the valley called up on the telephone with instructions to send out a message to General Student that the operation had succeeded.

The first to arrive by the funicular was Major Mors, commanding the parachute formation in the valley. Of course the inevitable journalist put in an appearance. He immediately made a film to immortalize the hotel, the damaged gliders and the actors in the drama. He made a mess of it and later on I was very annoyed that the pictures in the magazine suggested that he had himself taken part in the operation. We certainly had too much to do in the first moments to find time to pose for reporters.

Major Mors then asked me to present him to the Duce, a request I was very pleased to comply with.

I was now responsible for Mussolini and my first anxiety was how we were to get him to Rome. Our plan had provided for three possibilities.

Both he and I considered that it would be too dangerous to travel 150 kilometres by road through an area which had not been occupied by German troops since the defection of Italy. I had therefore agreed with General Student that Plan A should be the sudden *coup de main* against the Italian airfield of Aquila de Abruzzi, at the entrance to the valley. We should hold it only a short time. I would give the zero-hour for this attack by wireless and a few minutes later three German He 1 1 ls would land. One of them would pick up the Duce and myself and leave at once, while the two others gave us cover and drew off any aircraft pursuing.

Plan B provided that a Fieseler-Storch should land in one of the meadows adjoining the valley station. Plan C was for Captain Gerlach to attempt a landing with the Fieseler-Storch on the plateau itself.

Our wireless truck got through to Rome with the report of our success, but when I had fixed up a new timetable with Lieutenant Berlepsch and tried to give the parachutists the zero-hour, 4 o'clock, for the attack on the airfield we found we could not make contact. That was the end of Plan A.

I had watched the landing of one of the Fieseler-Storchs in the valley through my glasses. I at once used the telephone of the funicular to have the pilot instructed to prepare to take off again at once. The answer came back that the aircraft had suffered some damage on landing and could not be ready straight away. So only the last and most dangerous alternative, Plan C, remained.

After they had been disarmed, the Italian other ranks showed themselves extremely helpful and some of them had joined with the men we had sent out to rescue the victims of the glider crash. Through our glasses we had seen some of them moving, so that we could hope that it had not been fatal to all its occupants. Other Carabinieri now helped in clearing a small strip. The biggest boulders were hastily removed, while Captain Gerlach circled overhead and waited for the agreed signal to land. He proved himself a master in the art of emergency landing, but when I told him how we proposed to make a getaway with his help he was anything but pleased with the prospect, and when I added that there would be three of us he said bluntly that the idea was impracticable.

I had to take him aside for a short but tense discussion. The strength of my arguments convinced him at last. I had indeed considered every aspect of the matter most carefully and fully realized my heavy responsibility in joining the other two. But could I possibly justify letting the Duce go alone with Gerlach? If there was a disaster, all that was left for me was a bullet from my own revolver: Adolf Hitler would never forgive such an end to our venture. As there was no other way of getting the Duce safely to Rome it was better to share the danger with him, even though my presence added to it. If we failed, the same fate would overtake us all.

In this critical hour I did not fail to consult my trusty friend, Radl. I then discussed with him and Major Mors the question of how we were to get back. The only men we wanted to take with us were the general and the colonel, and we must get them to Rome as soon as possible. The Carabinieri and their officers could be left at the hotel. The Duce had told me that he had been properly treated, so that there was no reason not to be generous. My pleasure at our success was so great that I wanted to spare my opponents.

To guard against sabotage to the cable railway I ordered that two Italian officers should ride in each cage and that after we had got away the machinery should be damaged sufficiently to prevent its being put in working order again for some time. All other details I left to Major Mors.

Now at last, I had time to pay a little attention to the Duce. I had seen him once before, in 1943, when he was addressing the crowd from the balcony of the Palazzo Venezia. I must admit that the familiar photographs of him in full uniform bore little resemblance to the man in the ill-fitting and far from smart civilian suit who now stood before me. But there was no mistaking his striking features, though he struck me as having aged a lot. Actually he looked very ill, an impression intensified by the fact that he was unshaved and his usually smooth, powerful head was covered with short, stubbly hair.

But the big, black, burning eyes were unmistakably those of the Italian dictator. They seemed to bore right into me as he talked on in his lively, southern fashion.

He gave me some intensely interesting details about his fall and imprisonment. In return I managed to give him some pleasant news: 'We have also concerned ourselves with the fate of your family, Duce. Your wife and the two youngest children were interned by the new government in your country place at Bocca della Caminata. We got in touch with Donna Rachele some weeks ago. While we were landing here another of my commandos, under Hauptsturmführer Mandel, was sent to fetch your family. I'm sure they are free by now!'

The Duce shook my hand warmly. 'So everything's all right. I'm very grateful to you!'

Donning a loose winter overcoat and a dark, soft hat, the Duce came out of the door. I went ahead to the waiting Storch. Mussolini took the rear seat and I stowed myself in behind. I noticed a slight hesitation before he climbed in and recollected that he was a pilot himself and could well appreciate the risks he was running.

The engine worked up to full speed and we nodded to the comrades we were leaving behind. I seized a stay in each hand and by moving my body up and down, tried to give the aircraft more thrust or lessen the weight. Gerlach signalled the men holding the wings and tail to let go and the airscrew drew us forward. I thought I heard a mixture of 'Eviva's' and 'Heil's' through the cellophane windows.

But, although our speed increased and we were rapidly approaching the end of the strip, we failed to rise. I swayed about madly and we had hopped over many a boulder when a yawning gully appeared right in our path. I was just thinking that this really was the end when our bird suddenly rose into the air. I breathed a silent prayer of thanksgiving!

Then the left landing-wheel hit the ground again, the machine tipped downwards and we made straight for the gully. Veering left, we shot over the edge. I closed my eyes, held my breath and again waited the inevitable end. The wind roared in our ears.

It must have been all over in a matter of seconds, for when I looked around again Gerlach had got the machine out of its dive and almost on a level keel. Now we had sufficient airspeed, even in this thin air. Flying barely thirty metres above the ground, we emerged in the Arrezzano valley.

All three of us were decidedly paler than we had been a few minutes earlier, but no words were wasted. In most unsoldierly fashion I laid my hand on the shoulder of Benito Mussolini whose rescue was now beyond doubt.

Having recovered his composure, he was soon telling me stories about the region through which we were flying at an altitude of 100 metres, carefully avoiding the hilltops. 'Just here I addressed a huge crowd twenty years ago.' . . . 'Here's where we buried an old friend' . . . the Duce reminisced.

At length Rome lay below us, on our way to Practica di Mare. 'Hold tight! Two-point landing,' Gerlach shouted, reminding me of the damage to our landing-gear. Balancing on the right front and tail landing-wheels, we carefully touched down. Our trip was over.

Captain Melzer welcomed us in the name of General Student and congratulated us warmly on our success. Three He 111s were waiting for us, and after the conventions had been observed by my formally presenting their crews to the Duce, I gratefully shook Gerlach's hand on parting. There was no time to lose if we were to reach Vienna before dark.

JUNGLE WARFARE, NEW GUINEA, December 1943

Pat Robinson

The rainy season was now on in earnest and the daily downpours made life miserable for everybody, turned streams into raging torrents, wiped out bridges, transformed swamps into lakes and make the few existing roads impassable. Most of the boys were unshaven, and it was not long before they all became hollow-eyed. They had cold bully beef and biscuits to eat and wet mud for a bed.

The Japs were trapped with their backs to the sea in a triangular area that stretched from Cape Endaiadere, three miles below Buna, to a point beyond Gona, fourteen miles above Buna, and inland for distances that varied from mere yards to a mile or more. Americans formed the spearhead of the thrust against Buna, while Australians concentrated on knocking out the Japs entrenched at Gona.

It was difficult to distinguish our own and the Japs' positions at any time because there was no such thing as a front line. But there were pockets of resistance everywhere. Sometimes the enemy were in foxholes or machine-gun pits only ten yards from us. For instance, around Sanananda Point the Japs were along the shore. Farther inland there was a strong force of Australians. Still farther inland was still another force of Japs, who in turn were sandwiched in between two groups of Americans . . .

The main body of our forces, laying direct siege to Buna itself, encountered a heavy barrage of enemy artillery and mortar fire. Our own 75 mm guns replied in kind. Jap barrages often appeared pointless, but they were effective nevertheless. They would try to knock out our artillery, of course, but they also seemed to fire aimlessly all over the landscape. And enemy planes, taking advantage of the thick weather which held our own airmen on the other side of the mountains, swooped down on our positions in strafing attacks. At one point seven Zeros raked our positions with machine-gun fire. There is nothing more trying than to face a plane travelling more than 300 miles an hour only twenty feet over your head with all its guns spraying the earth with bullets.

The enemy troops were as quick to take advantage of

weather conditions as were their brothers in the Jap Air Corps, and they repeatedly sought to infiltrate our positions with small guerrilla bands. Once along the Giriwu River near Saputs they tried to slip in under cover of a fog to wipe out an Australian company in a surprise attack, but the Australians had long since become wise to every Jap trick; they met the Japs this time with a withering blast of rifle fire . . .

By 3 December the Australians and Yanks had cut off Gona and had infiltrated into the defences around Buna. The end was in sight for the Japs, but they never stopped trying to land reinforcements. They made their fifth attempt on 9 December, when six destroyers tried to send troops ashore on barges. Our bombers and pursuit planes suddenly swooped down on them, sank all the barges and routed the destroyers.

The Japs were being trapped in an ever-narrowing beach-head and they made repeated attempts to break through the encircling ring of steel. Near Sanananda Point a large force of Australians surrounded ninety-five Japs and called on them to surrender. It was a case of surrender or die. These Japs, all tough Marines, chose death. They not only would not surrender but they wouldn't even dig in. They attacked, and every one of them was killed . . .

Gona fell to the Australians on 10 December, and the next day the Japs were hemmed in on a thin fringe of beach and coastal jungle around Buna. Every foot of that defence line bristled with guns.

Then the torrential rains came. The fighting almost ceased for a day or two, and we took advantage of the weather-enforced truce to bury 638 Japs. These dead men had been lying outside Jap positions for days and the enemy had had no chance to bury them under the constant avalanche of mortar, machine-gun and artillery fire from our side, to say nothing of a steady downpour of bombs and bullets from our airmen. The stench was unbearable, and we wondered how the live Japs had borne it until we discovered they were wearing gas masks as protection against their own dead.

D-DAY: EMBARKATION, 4 June 1944

Alan Moorehead

The Allied invasion of Normandy, 6 June 1944, was the greatest seaborne invasion in history. Some 160,000 troops – British, American, French, Polish and Canadian – embarked 5,000 craft in southern England to make the journey to 'the far shore'.

At three o'clock we were standing in a line on the path leading up to the gate. The young naval officer came by festooned with his explosives and rather surprisingly took up a position behind me. As each new group of troops turned up they exchanged wisecracks with the others already arrived. 'Blimey, 'ere's the Arsenal' . . . ''Ome for the 'olidays' . . . 'Wot's that, Arthur?' 'Them's me water-wings, dearie.' Even after waiting another hour there was still optimism in the ranks. Then we marched out through the gate and got on to the vehicles. An officer was running down the line making sure everyone was on board. He blew a whistle and we started off. Five miles an hour. Down Acacia Avenue. Round the park into High Street; a mile-long column of ducks and three-ton lorries, of Jeeps and tanks and bulldozers. On the sidewalk one or two people waved vaguely. An old man stopped and mumbled, 'Good luck.' But for the most part the people stared silently and made no sign. They knew we were going. There had been rehearsals before but they were not deceived. There was something in the way the soldiers carried themselves that said all too clearly 'This is it. This is the invasion.' And yet they were cheerful still. It was a relief to be out of the camp and moving freely in the streets again. Every now and again the column halted. Then we crept on slowly again towards the hards.

Two hours went by and the soldiers began to grow bored. They seized on anything for amusement. When a girl came by on a bicycle she was cheered with salacious enthusiasm from one end of the column to the other. An athlete dressed in a pink suit began to pace round the cricket field. The soldiers watched him with relish for a minute. Then, 'Hyah, Pinkie.' 'Careful, dearie.' Derisive shouting followed him round the ground. Towards the end of the column a soldier who was trained as a sniper took down his rifle with its telescopic sights and fixed them upon two lovers who were embracing at the farther end of the park. His friends gathered round him while he gave them a lewd commentary on what he saw. The soldiers were becoming very bored. It grew dark and the cricket match ended. Every hour or so a tea-waggon came round and the men ran towards it with their enamel mugs. One after another the lights in the houses were blacked out and the soldiers, left alone in the empty street, lapsed into complete listlessness and tiredness. Rumours kept passing back and forth from vehicle to vehicle. 'Our ship has fouled its anchor.' 'There has been a collision in the harbour.' Or more spectacularly, 'We have already made a landing on the Channel Islands.'

Towards ten o'clock the officers began running down the column shouting for the drivers to start. We began to edge forward slowly and presently came out on the dark promenade along the sea. There were many ships, both those moving in the sound and those which had brought their bows up on to the hard and had opened their gates to receive the vehicles. We were marked down for the Landing Ship Tank 816. A clamour of light and noise was coming out of its open bows. One after another the vehicles crept down the ramp and on to the great lift that took them to the upper deck. The sailors kept shouting to one another as they lashed down the trucks on the upper deck. All night the thump of army boots against the metal deck went on.

D-DAY: A PARATROOPER LISTS HIS KIT, WELFORD AERODROME, 5 June 1944

Donald Burgett, US 101st Airborne Division

The seaborne invasion of Normandy was preceded by an airborne assault by the US 101st, US 82nd and the British 6th Airborne divisions. This airborne assault was intended to protect the flanks of the five Normandy beaches where the infantry would land. In the darkness of the evening of 5 June these airborne divisions emplaned in airfields all over the south of England. These paratroopers had to carry fantastic quantities of kit into battle.

My personal equipment consisted of: one suit of ODs, worn under my jump suit – this was an order for everyone – helmet, boots, gloves, main chute, reserve chute, Mae West, rifle, .45 automatic pistol, trench knife, jump knife, hunting knife, machete, one cartridge belt, two bandoliers, two cans of machine-gun ammo totalling 676 rounds of .30 ammo, 66 rounds of .45 ammo, one Hawkins mine capable of blowing the track off a tank, four blocks of TNT, one entrenching tool with two blasting caps taped on the outside of the steel part, three first-aid kits, two morphine needles, one gas mask, a canteen of water, three days' supply of K rations, two days' supply of D rations (hard tropical chocolate bars), six fragmentation grenades, one Gammon grenade, one orange smoke and one red smoke grenade, one orange panel, one blanket, one raincoat, one change of socks and underwear, two cartons of cigarettes and a few other odds and ends.

Unsurprisingly, Burgett could hardly walk and had to be helped into the plane by Air Corps personnel. On the flight over, Burgett and his comrades knelt on the floor and rested the weight of the gear and parachutes on the seat behind. The British paratroopers were only slightly less encumbered.

D-DAY: THE AIRBORNE LANDINGS, 6 June 1944

Guy Remington

At the airfield [on the evening of 5 June], we were directed to the planes that were to carry us over the Channel. I had seen some action before, so I had at least an idea of what to expect. Not many of the other men were so fortunate. The only thing that worried me, as we sat in the dark waiting for the takeoff, was the thought that I might break a leg in my jump. I tried not to think about that. We took off at ten-thirty, just as the moon was coming up. There appeared to be very little ground wind, and the weather seemed ideal for a night jump. Through the open door of my plane, I watched the other transports lifting heavily off the ground. They looked like huge, black bats as they skimmed slowly over the treetops and fell into formation. Before long, we took off too. Presently, near the coast of England, a squadron of fighters appeared below us. They flashed their lights on and off, and then wheeled away. That was *adiós*.

We had a two-hour run ahead of us, so I settled down in my seat. A major, sitting directly across from me, smiled, his teeth startlingly white in the dark. I smiled back. The noise of the plane made it impossible to talk. Suddenly the jump master shouted, 'Stand up and hook up!' I realized that I had been asleep, hard as it was to believe. The plane was rocking and bucking, trying to dodge the occasional bursts of flak from the dark, anonymous countryside below. A small red light gleamed in the panel by the door. We hooked up our parachutes, lined up close together, and waited. Then we stood there, waiting, for twelve and a half minutes. It seemed a long and terrible time.

The green light flashed on at seven minutes past midnight. The jump master shouted, 'Go!' I was the second man out. The black Normandy pastures tilted and turned far beneath me. The first German flare came arching up, and instantly machine-guns and forty-millimetre guns began firing from the corners of the fields, striping the night with yellow, green, blue, and red tracers. I pitched down through a wild Fourth of July. Fire licked through the sky and blazed around the transports heaving high overhead. I saw some of them go plunging down in flames. One of them came down with a trooper, whose parachute had become caught on the tail-piece, streaming out behind. I heard a loud gush of air: a man went hurtling past, only a few yards away, his parachute collapsed and burning. Other parachutes, with men whose legs had been shot off slumped in the harness, floated gently toward the earth.

I was caught in a machine-gun cross-fire as I approached the ground. It seemed impossible that they could miss me. One of the guns, hidden in a building, was firing at my parachute, which was already badly torn; the other aimed at my body. I reached up, caught the left risers of my parachute, and pulled on them. I went into a fast slip, but the tracers followed me down. I held the slip until I was about twenty-five feet from the ground and then let go the risers. I landed up against a hedge in a little garden at the rear of a German barracks. There were four tracer holes through one of my pants legs, two through the other, and another bullet had ripped off both my breast pockets, but I hadn't a scratch.

D-DAY: THE AIRBORNE LANDINGS, 6 June 1944

Major Friedrich Hayn, Wehrmacht Staff Officer

At 01.11 hours – an unforgettable moment – the field telephone rang. Something important was coming through: while listening to it the General stood up stiffly, his hand gripping the edge of the table. With a nod he beckoned his chief of staff to listen in. 'Enemy parachute troops dropped east of the Orne estuary. Main area Bréville-Ranville and the north edge of the Bavent forest. Counter-measures are in progress.' This message from 716 Intelligence Service struck like lightning.

Was this, at last, the invasion, the storming of '*Festung Europa*'? Someone said haltingly, 'Perhaps they are only supply troops for the French Resistance?' . . . The day before, in the St Malo area, many pieces of paper had been passing from hand to hand or had been dropped into the letterboxes; they all bore a mysterious announcement: *La carotte rouge est quittée*. Furthermore, our wireless operators had noticed an unusually large volume of coded traffic. Up till now, however, the Resistance groups had anxiously avoided all open action; they were put off by the danger of premature discovery and consequent extermination.

Whilst the pros and cons were still being discussed, 709 Infantry Division from Valognes announced: 'Enemy parachute troops south of St Germain-de-Varreville and near Ste Marie-du-Mont. A second drop west of the main Carentan–Valognes road on both sides of the Merderet river and along the Ste Mère-Eglise–Pont-l'Abbé road. Fighting for the river crossings in progress.' It was now about 01.45 hours.

Three dropping zones near the front! Two were clearly at important traffic junctions. The third was designed to hold the marshy meadows at the mouth of the Dives and the bridge across the canalized Orne near Ranville. It coincided with the corps boundary, with the natural feature which formed our northern flank but would serve the same purpose for an enemy driving south. It is the task of parachute troops, as advance detachments from the air, to occupy tactically important areas and to hold them until ground troops, in this case landing forces, fight their way through to them and incorporate them into the general front. Furthermore in Normandy they could, by attacking the strongpoints immediately west of the beach, paralyse the coastal defences. If it really was the task of the reported enemy forces to keep open the crossings, it meant that a landing would soon take place and they were really in earnest!

D-DAY: THE LANDINGS, 6 June 1944

Throughout the night of 5 June the Allied armada made its way across the Channel, arriving off the Normandy coast in the steely dawn of the 6th, when the troops were ordered into the assault craft in which they would make the final approach.

Lieutenant H.T. Bone, East Yorkshire Regiment

In the Mess decks we blacked our faces with black Palm Olive cream and listened to the naval orders over the loud-hailer. Most of us had taken communion on the Sunday, but the padre had a few words to say to us. Then the actual loading into craft – swinging on davits – the boat lowering and finally 'Away boats'. While this was going on, all around could be seen the rest of the convoy, with battleships and cruisers firing their big guns every few minutes and destroyers rushing round. One had been hit by something and only the up-ended part of its bows remained in view. As our flotilla swung into line behind its leader we raised our flag, a black silk square with the white rose of Yorkshire in the centre . . . It was some distance to the beaches, and it was a wet trip. All of us had a spare gas-cape to keep us dry and we chewed our gum stolidly. Mine was in my mouth twelve or fourteen hours later and I usually hate the stuff and never touch it. Shielding ourselves from the spray and watching the fire going down from all the supporting arms and the Spits [Spitfires] overhead, the time soon passed . . . Suddenly there was a jarring bump on the left, and looking up from our boards we saw one of the beach obstacles about two feet above our left gunwale with a large mine on top of it, just as photographs had shown us. Again a bump, on the right, but still we had not grounded. The Colonel and the flotilla leader were piloting us in, and for a few brief minutes nothing happened except the music of the guns and the whang of occasional bullets overhead, with the sporadic explosions of mortar bombs and the background of our own heavy machine-gun fire. The doors opened as we grounded and the Colonel was out. The sea was choppy and the boat swung a good bit as one by one we followed him. Several fell in and got soaked through. I was lucky. I stopped for a few seconds to help my men with their wireless sets and to ensure they kept them dry. As we staggered ashore we dispersed and lay down above the water's edge.

The bloodiest fighting of the day came at Omaha beach, where the US 1st and 29th Infantry Divisions had the ill luck to encounter a crack *Wehrmacht* division, the 352nd, on a training manoeuvre. Omaha was also the most topographically difficult of the beaches, dominated as it is by a high cliff.

Captain Joseph T. Dawson, US 1st Infantry Division

We landed at H + 30 minutes [7.00 am] and found . . . both the assault units rendered ineffective because of the enormous casualties they suffered. Fortunately, when we landed there was some let-up in the defensive fire from the Germans. Even so the boat containing assault unit Company G, which I commanded, took a direct hit from the artillery of the Germans, and I suffered major casualties. I lost about twenty men out of a total complement of 250 from that hit on my boat, and this included my naval officer who was communications link with the Navy, who were to support us with their fire from the battleships and cruisers some 8,000 yards out in the water.

As soon as we were able to assemble we proceeded off the beach through a minefield which had been identified by some of the soldiers who had landed earlier. We knew this because two of them were lying there in the path I selected. Both men had been destroyed by the mines. From their position, however, we were able to identify the path and get through the minefield without casualties and proceed up to the crest of the ridge which overlooked the beach. We got about halfway up when we met the remnants of a platoon of E Company, commanded by Lieutenant Spalding. This was the only group – somewhere less than twenty men – we encountered who had gotten off the beach. They had secured some German prisoners, and these were sent to the beach under escort. Above me, right on top of the ridge, the Germans had a line of defences with an excellent field of fire. I kept the men behind and, along with my communications sergeant and his assistant, worked our way slowly up to the crest of the ridge. Just before the crest was a sharp perpendicular drop, and we were able to get up to the crest without being seen by the enemy. I could now hear the Germans talking in the machine-gun nest immediately above me. I then threw two grenades, which were successful in eliminating the enemy and silencing the machine-gun which had been holding up our approach. Fortunately for me this action was done without them having any awareness of my being there, so it was no hero . . . it was an act of God, I guess.

D-DAY: MEETING THE LIBERATORS, VER-SUR-MER, 6 June 1944

Anne de Vigneral, civilian

Diary: 6 June
12 noon. Relative calm, but we all run to find boards and branches to cover our trench. We fetch rugs, mattresses etc. On the last foray we meet a German officer who says to me, 'The sleep is ended.' He was naive! We try to have a disjointed lunch, but it is interrupted continually. The German officer stations himself in a farmer's hedge and forbids them to betray him . . . In any case bursts of fire are everywhere, the children run back into the house. I hadn't realized that in the field where we collected our wood the English were in one hedge, the Germans in the hedge opposite and they were shooting at each other!

1 p.m. I beg everyone to eat, but the noise gets worse and when I open the window I see all the Germans bent double going over the village bridge. We take our plates out, scuttle across the terrace and fall into the trench. The terrace is covered with bullets, the little maid feels one scrape her leg . . . we found it afterwards . . . We see lots of Germans in the area between the property and the river. We don't know what to think.

1.15. We pop our heads out of the trench and see soldiers, but we can't recognize them. Is the uniform khaki or green? They are on their stomachs in the leaves . . .

1.30. To reassure myself I go to the kitchen to get some coffee (we had lunched in the trench) and come back quietly but very obviously carrying a coffee pot . . . and then the soldiers hidden in the laurels by the bridge come out. Hurrah, they are Canadians. We have lumps in our throats, we all speak at once, it is indescribable. Some laugh, some cry. They give the children chocolate; they are of course delighted. Themselves, they arrive calmly, chewing gum. (Isn't that typically English.)

2.00. Their officer arrives and tours the house with me looking for delayed action bombs. I, without a thought of danger, and all in a rush, open doors and cupboards. We find some bottles of champagne which we bring down. We sit on the steps and all drink. Even Jacques, seven years old, has a glass and drinks a toast with us. We all have already been given Capstan and Gold Flake cigarettes. Oh, don't they smell lovely!

D-DAY: A SOLDIER'S DIARY

Corporal G. E. Hughes, 1st Battalion, Royal Hampshire Regiment

Diary: 6 June
06.00 Get in LCA. Sea very rough. Hit the beach at 7.20 hours. Murderous fire, losses high. I was lucky T[hank] God. Cleared three villages. Terrible fighting and ghastly sights.

THE ATTEMPTED ASSASSINATION OF ADOLF HITLER, EASTERN GERMANY, 20 July 1944

Heinrich Bucholz

Dismayed by Hitler's conduct of the war, a group of senior officers decided to assassinate him during a conference at his Eastern Front HQ, the 'Wolf's Lair'. A briefcase containing a bomb with a time fuse was placed under the map table by Colonel Count von Stauffenberg. Bucholz was a stenographer at the Wolf's Lair.

I remember it as a clap of thunder coupled with a bright yellow flash and clouds of thick smoke. Glass and wood splintered through the air. The large table on which all the situation maps had been spread out and around which the participants were standing – only we stenographers were sitting – collapsed. After a few seconds of silence I heard a voice, probably Field Marshal Keitel, shouting: 'Where is the Führer?' Then further shouts and screams of pain arose.

The Führer survived the bomb attempt. His injuries and subsequent medical treatment were noted by Theo Morell, his private physician.

Right forearm badly swollen, prescribed acid aluminium acetate compresses. Effusion of blood on right shinbone has subsided. On back of third or fourth finger of left hand there is a large burn blister. Bandage. Occiput partly and hair completely burned, a palm-size second degree skin burn on the middle of the calf and a number of contusions and open flesh wounds. Left forearm has effusion of blood on interior aspect and is badly swollen, can move it only with difficulty – He is to take two Optalidons at once, and two tablespoons of Brom-Nervacit before going to sleep.

'DOODLEBUGS' LAND ON LONDON, July 1944

Vere Hodgson

In June 1944, German V1 rockets – or 'Doodlebugs' – began landing on London and South East England, fired from bases in France and Holland.

Diary:
. . . These Robot Planes go on after daybreak, which the old raids never did. I could hear the wretched thing travelling overhead at 6 a.m. They did not fall on us – but they fell on someone. Our guns barked out and spat and fussed until they

had gone. They travel quickly and on Thursday night were low over Kensington. In fact everyone of us was perfectly convinced the thing was exactly three inches above the roof.

Nothing is said on the wireless or in the papers except . . . Southern England! That is us – and we are all fed-up.

Monday was our fire-watch. Mrs Hoare light-heartedly remarked: 'I don't think there will be any more air-raids.' And in my heart I agreed with her. But not a bit of it! Hitler has still got a sting in his Nasty Tail. At 4 a.m. we were amazed to be roused by a Warning. We all got up. In 20 minutes All Clear. Just as I had bedded down another went. I sat on the steps. It was just getting light. Mr Bendall reported to the Street Leader.

In the morning much discussion, for no one knew about Robot Planes. Cannot remember all the events of Thursday night. We had little sleep. I was in my flat – something trundled across the sky. In the morning nothing on the wireless, and we felt injured – as we needed the sympathy of our friends! On and off all day we had Warnings and gunfire. One Robot fell in Tooley St in the City. One of the women from our Printing Works rang up to say at Eltham they had had a terrible night – all her windows and doors blown out. It all pointed to Kent.

By Saturday we all felt very cheap. I longed to go and see the Invasion pictures, but did not feel equal to cope with queues – so went to a local Cinema and saw a little. All through we had across the screen – Air Raid Warning. Then All Clear. Three times. But the audience was in a light-hearted mood and laughed aloud. We had not learned then to take the Robots seriously . . .

Went to cheer up Auntie. She was not well and had slept little. She had heard something had fallen on St Mary Abbots Hospital. All night long they came. By dawn I could not believe it could continue. But it did. So got myself a cup of tea. Did jobs. Later felt sick from lack of sleep, and to the sound of the Brains Trust dozed off. Later went for a walk. Felt better in the air. Every other person carrying a tin hat. Went along Marloes Road ... great piles of glass marked the route. Heavy Rescue lorries were driving in and out gathering up the débris. All one roof of the Hospital gone ... about 4 a.m. Saturday. One woman said twelve children were brought out dead. But I don't know, as my informant was too agitated to be coherent.

They may have to evacuate the Hospital. Many nurses killed. Heard another had fallen at Marble Arch, and in Putney. As I walked back through the Park I pondered on these things, and decided to sleep tonight at the Sanctuary. London is in a chastened mood after the last three nights.

PARIS CELEBRATES LIBERATION, September 1944

Simone de Beauvoir

The German forces in Paris surrendered on 25 August 1944, after attack from the Americans and Free French without and an uprising by the citizens from within. The celebrations continued for a week or more.

We were liberated. In the streets, the children were singing:

> Nous ne les reverrons plus,
> C'est fini, ils sont foutus.

And I kept saying to myself: It's all over, it's all over. It's all over: everything's beginning. Patrick Walberg, the Leirises' American friend, took us for a jeep ride through the suburbs; it was the first time in years that I'd been out in a car. Once again I wandered after midnight in the mild September air. The bistros closed early, but when we left the terrace of the Rhumerie or the smoky little red inferno of the Montana, we had the sidewalks, the benches, the streets. There were still snipers on the roofs, and my heart would grow heavy when I sensed the vigilant hatred overhead. One night, we heard sirens. An airplane, whose nationality we never discovered, was flying over Paris; V-1s fell on the suburbs and blew houses to bits. Walberg, usually well-informed, said that the Germans were putting the finishing touches to new and even more terrifying secret weapons. Fear returned, and found its place still warm. But joy quickly swept it away. With our friends, talking, drinking, strolling, laughing, night and day we celebrated our deliverance. And all the others who were celebrating too, near or far, became our friends. An orgy of brotherhood! The shadows that had immured France exploded. The tall soldiers, dressed in khaki and chewing their gum, were living proof that you could cross the seas again. They ambled past, and often they stumbled. Singing and whistling, they stumbled along the sidewalks and the subway platforms; stumbling, they danced at night in the bistros and laughed their loud laughs, showing teeth white as children's. [Jean] Genet, who had no sympathy with the Germans but who detested idylls, declared loudly on the terrace of the Rhumerie that these costumed civilians had no style. Stiff in their black and green carapaces, the occupiers had been something else! For me, these carefree young Americans were freedom incarnate: our own and also the freedom that was about to spread – we had no doubts on this score – throughout the world.

SURVIVAL IN AUSCHWITZ, October 1944

Primo Levi

Primo Levi was a member of the Italian anti-Fascist resistance, who was deported to the SS death camp at Auschwitz in 1944. He survived to write, amongst other books, memoirs of prison camp life, including *Survival in Auschwitz* from which the following is taken.

We fought with all our strength to prevent the arrival of winter. We clung to all the warm hours, at every dusk we tried to keep the sun in the sky for a little longer, but it was all in vain. Yesterday evening the sun went down irrevocably behind a confusion of dirty clouds, chimney stacks and wires, and today it is winter.

We know what it means because we were here last winter; and the others will soon learn. It means that in the course of these months, from October till April, seven out of ten of us will die. Whoever does not die will suffer minute by minute, all day, every day: from the morning before dawn until the distribution of the evening soup we will have to keep our muscles continually tensed, dance from foot to foot, beat our arms under our shoulders against the cold. We will have to spend bread to acquire gloves, and lose hours of sleep to repair them when they become unstitched. As it will no longer be possible to eat in the open, we will have to eat our meals in the hut, on our feet, everyone will be assigned an area of floor as large as a hand, as it is forbidden to rest against the bunks. Wounds will open on everyone's hands, and to be given a bandage will mean waiting every evening for hours on one's feet in the snow and wind.

Just as our hunger is not that feeling of missing a meal, so our way of being cold has need of a new word. We say 'hunger'. we say 'tiredness', 'fear', 'pain', we say 'winter' and they are different things. They are free words, created and used by free men who lived in comfort and suffering in their homes. If the Lagers had lasted longer a new, harsh language would have been born; and only this language could express what it means to toil the whole day in the wind, with the temperature below freezing, wearing only a shirt, underpants, cloth jacket and trousers, and in one's body nothing but weakness, hunger and knowledge of the end drawing nearer.

In the same way in which one sees a hope end, winter arrived this morning. We realized it when we left the hut to go and wash: there were no stars, the dark cold air had the smell of snow. In roll-call square, in the grey of dawn, when we assembled for work, no one spoke. When we saw the first flakes of snow, we thought that if at the same time last year they had told us that we would have seen another winter in Lager, we would have gone and touched the electric wire-fence; and that even now we would go if we were logical, were it not for this last senseless crazy residue of unavoidable hope.

Because 'winter' means yet another thing.

Last spring the Germans had constructed huge tents in an open space in the Lager. For the whole of the good season each of them had catered for over 1,000 men: now the tents had been taken down, and an excess 2,000 guests crowded our huts. We old prisoners knew that the Germans did not like these irregularities and that something would soon happen to reduce our number.

One feels the selections arriving. '*Selekcja*': the hybrid Latin and Polish word is heard once, twice, many times, interpolated in foreign conversations; at first we cannot distinguish it, then it forces itself on our attention, and in the end it persecutes us.

This morning the Poles had said '*Selekcja*'. The Poles are the first to find out the news, and they generally try not to let it spread around, because to know something which the others still do not know can always be useful. By the time that everyone realizes that a selection is imminent, the few possibilities of evading it (corrupting some doctor or some prominent with bread or tobacco; leaving the hut for Ka-Be or vice-versa at the right moment so as to cross with the commission) are already their monopoly.

In the days which follow, the atmosphere of the Lager and the yard is filled with 'Selekcja': nobody knows anything definite, but all speak about it, even the Polish, Italian, French civilian workers whom we secretly see in the yard. Yet the result is hardly a wave of despondency: our collective morale is too inarticulate and flat to be unstable. The fight against hunger, cold and work leaves little margin for thought, even for this thought. Everybody reacts in his own way, but hardly anyone with those attitudes which would seem the most plausible as the most realistic, that is with resignation or despair.

All those able to find a way out, try to take it; but they are the minority because it is very difficult to escape from a selection. The Germans apply themselves to these things with great skill and diligence.

Whoever is unable to prepare for it materially, seeks defence elsewhere. In the latrines, in the washroom, we show each other our chests, our buttocks, our thighs, and our comrades reassure us: 'You are all right, it will certainly not be your turn this time . . . *du bist kein Muselmann* . . . more probably mine . . .' and they undo their braces in turn and pull up their shirts.

Nobody refuses this charity to another: nobody is so sure of his own lot to be able to condemn others. I brazenly lied to old Wertheimer; I told him that if they questioned him, he should reply that he was forty-five, and he should not forget to have a shave the evening before, even if it cost him a quarter-ration of bread; apart from that he need have no fears, and in any case it was by no means certain that it was a selection for the gas chamber; had he not heard the *Block-ältester* say that those chosen would go to Jaworszno to a convalescent camp?

It is absurd of Wertheimer to hope: he looks sixty, he has enormous varicose veins, he hardly even notices the hunger any more. But he lies down on his bed, serene and quiet, and replies to someone who asks him with my own words; they are the command-words in the camp these days: I myself repeated them just as – apart from details – Chajim told them to me, Chajim, who has been in Lager for three years, and being strong and robust is wonderfully sure of himself; and I believed them.

On this slender basis I also lived through the great selection of October 1944 with inconceivable tranquillity. I was tranquil because I managed to lie to myself sufficiently. The fact that I was not selected depended above all on chance and does not prove that my faith was well-founded.

Monsieur Pinkert is also, *a priori*, condemned: it is enough to look at his eyes. He calls me over with a sign, and with a confidential air tells me that he has been informed – he cannot tell me the source of information – that this time there is really something new: the Holy See, by means of the International Red Cross . . . in short, he personally guarantees both for himself and for me, in the most absolute manner, that every danger is ruled out; as a civilian he was, as is well known, attaché to the Belgian embassy at Warsaw.

Thus in various ways, even those days of vigil, which in the telling seem as if they ought to have passed every limit of human torment, went by not very differently from other days.

The discipline in both the Lager and Buna is in no way relaxed: the work, cold and hunger are sufficient to fill up every thinking moment.

Today is working Sunday, *Arbeitssonntag*: we work until one p.m., then we return to camp for the shower, shave and general control for skin diseases and lice. And in the yards, everyone knew mysteriously that the selection would be today.

The news arrived, as always, surrounded by a halo of contradictory or suspect details: the selection in the infirmary took place this morning; the percentage was seven per cent of the whole camp, thirty, fifty per cent of the patients. At

Birkenau, the crematorium chimney has been smoking for ten days. Room has to be made for an enormous convoy arriving from the Poznan ghetto. The young tell the young that all the old ones will be chosen. The healthy tell the healthy that only the ill will be chosen. Specialists will be excluded. German Jews will be excluded. Low Numbers will be excluded. You will be chosen. I will be excluded.

At one p.m. exactly the yard empties in orderly fashion and for two hours the grey unending army files past the two control stations where, as on every day, we are counted and recounted, and past the military band which for two hours without interruption plays, as on every day, those marches to which we must synchronize our steps at our entrance and our exit.

It seems like every day, the kitchen chimney smokes as usual, the distribution of the soup is already beginning. But then the bell is heard, and at that moment we realize that we have arrived.

Because this bell always sounds at dawn, when it means the reveille; but if it sounds during the day, it means 'Blocksperre', enclosure in huts, and this happens when there is a selection to prevent anyone avoiding it, or when those selected leave for the gas, to prevent anyone seeing them leave.

Our Blockältester knows his business. He has made sure that we have all entered, he has the door locked, he has given everyone his card with his number, name, profession, age and nationality and he has ordered everyone to undress completely, except for shoes. We wait like this, naked, with the card in our hands, for the commission to reach our hut. We are hut 48, but one can never tell if they are going to begin at hut 1 or hut 60. At any rate, we can rest quietly at least for an hour, and there is no reason why we should not get under the blankets on the bunk and keep warm.

Many are already drowsing when a barrage of orders, oaths and blows proclaims the imminent arrival of the commission. The Blockältester and his helpers, starting at the end of the dormitory, drive the crowd of frightened, naked people in front of them and cram them in the *Tagesraum* which is the Quartermaster's office. The *Tagesraum* is a room seven yards by four: when the drive is over, a warm and compact human mass is jammed into the *Tagesraum*, perfectly filling all the corners, exercising such a pressure on the wooden walls as to make them creak.

Now we are all in the *Tagesraum*, and besides there being no time, there is not even any room in which to be afraid. The feeling of the warm flesh pressing all around is unusual and not unpleasant. One has to take care to hold up one's nose so as to breathe, and not to crumple or lose the card in one's hand.

The *Blockältester* has closed the connecting door and has opened the other two which lead from the dormitory and the *Tagesraum* outside. Here, in front of the two doors, stands the arbiter of our fate, an SS subaltern. On his right is the *Blockältester*, on his left, the quartermaster of the hut. Each one of us, as he comes naked out of the *Tagesraum* into the cold October air, has to run the few steps between the two doors, give the card to the SS man and enter the dormitory door. The SS man, in the fraction of a second between two successive crossings, with a glance at one's back and front, judges everyone's fate, and in turn gives the card to the man on his right or his left, and this is the life or death of each of us. In three or four minutes a hut of 200 men is 'done', as is the whole camp of 12,000 men in the course of the afternoon.

Jammed in the charnel-house of the *Tagesraum*, I gradually felt the human pressure around me slacken, and in a short time it was my turn. Like everyone, I passed by with a brisk and elastic step, trying to hold my head high, my chest forward and my muscles contracted and conspicuous. With the corner of my eye I tried to look behind my shoulders, and my card seemed to end on the right.

As we gradually come back into the dormitory we are allowed to dress ourselves. Nobody yet knows with certainty his own fate, it has first of all to be established whether the condemned cards were those on the right or the left. By now there is no longer any point in sparing each other's feelings with superstitious scruples. Everybody crowds around the oldest, the most wasted-away, and most 'muselmann'; if their cards went to the left, the left is certainly the side of the condemned.

Even before the selection is over, everybody knows that the left was effectively the 'schlechte Seite', the bad side. There have naturally been some irregularities: René, for example, so young and robust, ended on the left; perhaps it was because he has glasses, perhaps because he walks a little stooped like a myope, but more probably because of a simple mistake: René passed the commission immediately in front of me and there could have been a mistake with our cards. I think about it, discuss it with Alberto, and we agree that the hypothesis is probable; I do not know what I will think tomorrow and later; today I feel no distinct emotion.

It must equally have been a mistake about Sattler, a huge Transylvanian peasant who was still at home only twenty days ago; Sattler does not understand German, he has understood nothing of what has taken place, and stands in a corner mending his shirt. Must I go and tell him that his shirt will be of no more use?

There is nothing surprising about these mistakes: the examination is too quick and summary, and in any case, the important thing for the Lager is not that the most useless prisoners be eliminated, but that free posts be quickly created, according to a certain percentage previously fixed.

The selection is now over in our hut, but it continues in the others, so that we are still locked in. But as the soup-pots have arrived in the meantime, the Blockältester decides to proceed with the distribution at once. A double ration will be given to those selected. I have never discovered if this was a ridiculously charitable initiative of the Blockältester, or an explicit disposition of the SS, but in fact, in the interval of two or three days (sometimes even much longer) between the selection and the departure, the victims at Monowitz-Auschwitz enjoyed this privilege.

Ziegler holds out his bowl, collects his normal ration and then waits there expectantly. 'What do you want?' asks the *Blockältester*: according to him, Ziegler is entitled to no supplement, and he drives him away, but Ziegler returns and humbly persists. He was on the left, everybody saw it, let the *Blockältester* check the cards; he has the right to a double ration. When he is given it, he goes quietly to his bunk to eat.

Now everyone is busy scraping the bottom of his bowl with his spoon so as not to waste the last drops of the soup; a confused, metallic clatter, signifying the end of the day. Silence slowly prevails and then, from my bunk on the top row, I see and hear old Kuhn praying aloud, with his beret on his head, swaying backward and forward violently. Kuhn is thanking God because he has not been chosen.

Kuhn is out of his senses. Does he not see Beppo the Greek in the bunk next to him, Beppo who is twenty years old and is going to the gas chamber the day after tomorrow and knows it and lies there looking fixedly at the light without saying anything and without even thinking any more? Can Kuhn fail to realize that next time it will be his turn? Does Kuhn not understand that what has happened today is an abomination, which no propitiatory prayer, no pardon, no expiation by the guilty, which nothing at all in the power of man can ever clean again?

If I were God, I would spit at Kuhn's prayer.

THE SUICIDE OF FIELD MARSHAL ERWIN ROMMEL, GERMANY, 14 October 1944

Manfred Rommel

The field marshal was implicated in the outer edges of the plot to assassinate Hitler. In October the Führer decided on revenge.

Manfred Rommel, a young artillery officer at the time, is the field marshal's son.

At about twelve o'clock a dark-green car with a Berlin number stopped in front of our garden gate. The only men in the house apart from my father, were Captain Aldinger, a badly wounded war-veteran corporal and myself. Two generals – Burgdorf, a powerful florid man, and Maisel, small and slender – alighted from the car and entered the house. They were respectful and courteous and asked my father's permission to speak to him alone. Aldinger and I left the room. 'So they are not going to arrest him,' I thought with relief, as I went upstairs to find myself a book.

A few minutes later I heard my father come upstairs and go into my mother's room. Anxious to know what was afoot, I got up and followed him. He was standing in the middle of the room, his face pale. 'Come outside with me,' he said in a tight voice. We went into my room. 'I have just had to tell your mother,' he began slowly, 'that I shall be dead in a quarter of an hour.' He was calm as he continued: "To die by the hand of one's own people is hard. But the house is surrounded and Hitler is charging me with high treason. "In view of my services in Africa,"' he quoted sarcastically, 'I am to have the chance of dying by poison. The two generals have brought it with them. It's fatal in three seconds. If I accept, none of the usual steps will be taken against my family, that is against you. They will also leave my staff alone.'

'Do you believe it?' I interrupted.

'Yes,' he replied. 'I believe it. It is very much in their interest to see that the affair does not come out into the open. By the way, I have been charged to put you under a promise of the strictest silence. If a single word of this comes out, they will no longer feel themselves bound by the agreement.'

I tried again. 'Can't we defend ourselves . . .' He cut me off short.

'There's no point,' he said. 'It's better for one to die than for all of us to be killed in a shooting affray. Anyway, we've practically no ammunition.' We briefly took leave of each other. 'Call Aldinger, please,' he said.

Aldinger had meanwhile been engaged in conversation by the generals' escort to keep him away from my father. At my call, he came running upstairs. He, too, was struck cold when he heard what was happening. My father now spoke more quickly. He again said how useless it was to attempt to defend ourselves. 'It's all been prepared to the last detail. I'm to be given a state funeral. I have asked that it should take place in Ulm. In a quarter of an hour, you, Aldinger, will receive a telephone call from the Wagnerschule reserve hospital in Ulm to say that I've had a brain seizure on the way to a conference.' He looked at his watch. 'I must go, they've only given me ten minutes.' He quickly took leave of us again. Then we went downstairs together.

We helped my father into his leather coat. Suddenly he pulled out his wallet. 'There's still 150 marks in there,' he said. 'Shall I take the money with me?'

'That doesn't matter now, Herr Field Marshal,' said Aldinger.

My father put his wallet carefully back in his pocket. As he went into the hall, his little dachshund which he had been given as a puppy a few months before in France, jumped up at him with a whine of joy. 'Shut the dog in the study, Manfred,' he said, and waited in the hall with Aldinger while I removed the excited dog and pushed it through the study door. Then we walked out of the house together. The two generals were standing at the garden gate. We walked slowly down the path, the crunch of the gravel sounding unusually loud.

As we approached the generals they raised their right hands in salute. 'Herr Field Marshal,' Burgdorf said shortly and stood aside for my father to pass through the gate. A knot of villagers stood outside the drive. Maisel turned to me, and asked: 'What battery are you with?'

'36/7, Herr General,' I answered.

The car stood ready. The SS driver swung the door open and stood to attention. My father pushed his Marshal's baton under his left arm and with his face calm, gave Aldinger and me his hand once more before getting in the car.

The two generals climbed quickly into their seats and the doors were slammed. My father did not turn again as the car drove quickly off up the hill and disappeared round a bend in the road. When it had gone Aldinger and I turned and walked silently back into the house. 'I'd better go up and see your mother,' Aldinger said. I went upstairs again to await the promised telephone call. An agonizing depression excluded all thought.

I lit a cigarette and tried to read again, but the words no longer made sense. Twenty minutes later the telephone rang. Aldinger lifted the receiver and my father's death was duly reported. That evening we drove into Ulm to the hospital where he lay. The doctors who received us were obviously ill at ease, no doubt suspecting the true cause of my father's death. One of them opened the door of a small room. My father lay on a camp-bed in his brown Africa uniform, a look of contempt on his face.

It was not then entirely clear what had happened to him after he left us. Later we learned that the car had halted a few hundred yards up the hill from our house in an open space at the edge of the wood. Gestapo men, who had appeared in force from Berlin that morning, were watching the area with instructions to shoot my father down and storm the house if he offered resistance. Maisel and the driver got out of the car, leaving my father and Burgdorf inside. When the driver was permitted to return ten minutes or so later, he saw my father sunk forward with his cap off and the marshal's baton fallen from his hand. Then they drove off at top speed to Ulm, where the body was unloaded at the hospital; afterwards General Burgdorf drove on to Ulm *Wehrmacht* Headquarters where he first telephoned to Hitler to report my father's death and then to the family of one of his escort officers to compose the menu for that night's dinner. General Burgdorf, who was hated for his brutality by ninety-nine per cent of the Officer Corps, ended his own life in Berlin in April 1945, after staggering round drunk with Bormann for several days in the Führer's bunker.

Perhaps the most despicable part of the whole story was the expressions of sympathy we received from members of the German Government, men who could not fail to have known the true cause of my father's death and in some cases had no doubt themselves contributed to it, both by word and deed. I quote a few examples:

> *In the Field*
> *16 October 1944*

Accept my sincerest sympathy for the heavy loss you have suffered with the death of your husband. The name of Field Marshal Rommel will be for ever linked with the heroic battles in North Africa.

> ADOLF HITLER

> *Führer's Headquarters*
> *26 October 1944*

The fact that your husband, Field Marshal Rommel, has died a hero's death as the result of his wounds, after we had all hoped that he would remain to the German people, has deeply touched me. I send you, my dear Frau Rommel, the heartfelt sympathy of myself and the German *Luftwaffe*.

In silent compassion, Yours,

> GÖRING, *Reichsmarschall des Grossdeutschen Reiches*

THE US ARMY SLOGS UP ITALY, Winter, 1944

Ernie Pyle

Although Italy had been invaded by the Allies in July 1943, their progress up the long 'boot' of Italy had been painfully slow, hindered by inclement weather, mountainous terrain and determined German resistance. Here the American war correspondent Ernie Pyle describes the war the GIs fought in the Appenine mountains in the winter of 1944.

The war in Italy was tough. The land and the weather were both against us. It rained and it rained. Vehicles bogged down and temporary bridges washed out. The country was shockingly beautiful, and just as shockingly hard to capture from the enemy. The hills rose to high ridges of almost solid rock. We couldn't go around them through the flat peaceful valleys, because the Germans were up there looking down upon us, and they would have let us have it. So we had to go up and over. A mere platoon of Germans, well dug in on a high, rock-spined hill, could hold out for a long time against tremendous onslaughts.

I know the folks back home were disappointed and puzzled by the slow progress in Italy. They wondered why we moved northward so imperceptibly. They were impatient for us to get to Rome. Well, I can say this – our troops were just as impatient for Rome. But on all sides I heard: 'It never was this bad in Tunisia.' 'We ran into a new brand of Krauts over here.' 'If it would only stop raining.' 'Every day we don't advance is one day longer before we get home.'

Our troops were living in almost inconceivable misery. The fertile black valleys were knee-deep in mud. Thousands of the men had not been dry for weeks. Other thousands lay at night in the high mountains with the temperature below freezing and the thin snow sifting over them. They dug into the stones and slept in little chasms and behind rocks and in half-caves. They lived like men of prehistoric times, and a club would have become them more than a machine-gun. How they survived the dreadful winter at all was beyond us who had the opportunity of drier beds in the warmer valleys.

That the northward path was a tedious one was not the fault of our troops, nor of their direction either. It was the weather and the terrain and the weather again. If there had been no German fighting troops in Italy, if there had been merely German engineers to blow the bridges in the passes, if never a shot had been fired at all, our northward march would still have been slow. The country was so difficult that we formed a great deal of cavalry for use in the mountains. Each division had hundreds of horses and mules to carry supplies beyond the point where vehicles could go no farther. On beyond the mules' ability, mere men – American men – took it on their backs.

On my way to Italy, I flew across the Mediterranean in a cargo plane weighted down with more than a thousand pounds beyond the normal load. The cabin was filled with big pasteboard boxes which had been given priority above all other freight. In the boxes were packboards, hundreds of them, with which husky men would pack 100, even 150, pounds of food and ammunition, on their backs, to comrades high in those miserable mountains.

But we could take consolation from many things. The air was almost wholly ours. All day long Spitfires patrolled above our fighting troops like a half-dozen policemen running up and down the street watching for bandits.

What's more, our artillery prevailed – and how! We were prodigal with ammunition against those rocky crags, and well we might be, for a $50 shell could often save ten lives in country like that. Little by little, the fiendish rain of explosives upon the hillsides softened the Germans. They always were impressed by and afraid of our artillery, and we had concentrations of it there that were demoralizing.

And lastly, no matter how cold the mountains, or how wet the snow, or how sticky the mud, it was just as miserable for the German soldier as for the American.

Our men were going to get to Rome all right. There was no question about that. But the way was cruel. No one who had not seen that mud, those dark skies, those forbidding ridges and ghostlike clouds that unveiled and then quickly hid the enemy, had the right to be impatient with the progress along the road to Rome.

The mountain fighting went on week after dreary week. For a while I hung around with one of the mule-pack outfits. There was an average of one mule-packing outfit for every infantry battalion in the mountains. Some were run by Americans, some by Italian soldiers.

The pack outfit I was with supplied a battalion that was fighting on a bald, rocky ridge nearly 4,000 feet high. That battalion fought constantly for ten days and nights, and when the men finally came down less than a third of them were left.

All through those terrible days every ounce of their supplies had to go up to them on the backs of mules and men. Mules took it the first third of the way. Men took it the last bitter two-thirds, because the trail was too steep even for mules.

The mule skinners of my outfit were Italian soldiers. The human packers were mostly American soldiers. The Italian mule skinners were from Sardinia. They belonged to a mountain artillery regiment, and thus were experienced in climbing and in handling mules. They were bivouacked in an olive grove alongside a highway at the foot of the mountain. They made no trips in the daytime, except in emergencies, because most of the trail was exposed to artillery fire. Supplies were brought into the olive grove by truck during the day, and stacked under trees. Just before dusk they would start loading the stuff on to mules. The Americans who actually managed the supply chain liked to get the mules loaded by dark, because if there was any shelling the Italians instantly disappeared and could never be found.

There were 155 skinners in this outfit and usually about eighty mules were used each night. Every mule had a man to lead it. About ten extra men went along to help get mules up if they fell, to repack any loads that came loose, and to unpack at the top. They could be up and back in less than three hours. Usually a skinner made just one trip a night, but sometimes in an emergency he made two.

On an average night the supplies would run something like this – 85 cans of water, 100 cases of K ration, 10 cases of D ration, 10 miles of telephone wire, 25 cases of grenades and rifle and machine-gun ammunition, about 100 rounds of heavy mortar shells, 1 radio, 2 telephones, and 4 cases of first-aid packets and sulfa drugs. In addition, the packers would cram their pockets with cigarettes for the boys on top; also cans of Sterno, so they could heat some coffee once in a while.

Also, during that period, they took up more than 500 of the heavy combat suits we were issuing to the troops to help keep them warm. They carried up cellophane gas capes for some of the men to use as sleeping bags, and they took extra socks for them too.

Mail was their most tragic cargo. Every night they would take up sacks of mail, and every night they'd bring a large portion of it back down – the recipients would have been killed or wounded the day their letters came.

On the long man-killing climb above the end of the mule trail they used anywhere from 20 to 300 men a night. They rang in cooks, truck drivers, clerks, and anybody else they could lay their hands on. A lot of stuff was packed up by the fighting soldiers themselves. On a big night, when they were building up supplies for an attack, another battalion which was in reserve sent 300 first-line combat troops to do the packing. The mule packs would leave the olive grove in bunches of twenty, starting just after dark. American soldiers were posted within shouting distance of each other all along the trail, to keep the Italians from getting lost in the dark.

Those guides – everybody who thought he was having a tough time in this war should know about them. They were men who had fought all through a long and bitter battle at the top of the mountain. For more than a week they had been far up there, perched behind rocks in the rain and cold, eating cold K rations, sleeping without blankets, scourged constantly with artillery and mortar shells, fighting and ducking and growing more and more weary, seeing their comrades wounded one by one and taken down the mountain.

Finally sickness and exhaustion overtook many of those who were left, so they were sent back down the mountain under their own power to report to the medics there and then go to a rest camp. It took most of them the better part of a day to get two-thirds of the way down, so sore were their feet and so weary their muscles.

And then – when actually in sight of their haven of rest and peace – they were stopped and pressed into guide service, because there just wasn't anybody else to do it. So there they stayed on the mountainside, for at least three additional days and nights that I know of, just lying miserably alongside the trail, shouting in the darkness to guide the mules.

They had no blankets to keep them warm, no beds but the rocks. And they did it without complaining. The human spirit is an astounding thing.

THE GENERAL SAYS 'NUTS', BASTOGNE, 22 December 1944

Colonel S.L.A. Marshall

In a last desperate gamble to win the war in the West, Hitler launched a counter-offensive in the Ardennes in December 1944.

The counter-offensive made dramatic gains, although the Germans failed to take the town of Bastogne, where the Americans – including the famous 101st Airborne Division – held grimly on. The Germans, however, desperately needed the American petrol stored at Bastogne. Hopefully, on 22 December they offered surrender terms to the besieged Americans, commanded by Brigadier-General McAuliffe. Colonel Marshall was a member of McAuliffe's staff.

McAuliffe asked someone what the paper contained and was told that it requested a surrender.

The General laughed and said, 'Aw, nuts!' It really seemed funny to him at the time. He figured he was giving the Germans 'one hell of a beating' and that all of his men knew it. The demand was all out of line with the existing situation.

But McAuliffe realized that some kind of reply had to be made and he sat down to think it over. Pencil in hand, he sat there pondering a few minutes and then he remarked, 'Well, I don't know what to tell them.' He asked the staff what they thought, and Colonel Kinnard, his G-3, replied, 'That first remark of yours would be hard to beat.'

General McAuliffe didn't understand immediately what Kinnard was referring to. Kinnard reminded him, 'You said "Nuts".' That drew applause all around. All members of the staff agreed with much enthusiasm and because of their approval McAuliffe decided to send that message back to the Germans.

Then he called Colonel Harper in and asked him how he would reply to the message. Harper thought for a minute but before he could compose anything, General McAuliffe gave him the paper on which he had written his one word reply and asked, 'Will you see that it's delivered?'

'I will deliver it myself,' answered Harper. 'It will be a lot of fun.' McAuliffe told him not to go into the German lines.

Colonel Harper returned to the command post of Company F. The two Germans were standing in the wood blindfolded and under guard. Harper said, 'I have the American commander's reply.'

The German captain asked, 'Is it written or verbal?'

'It is written,' said Harper. And then he said to the German major, 'I will stick it in your hand.'

The German captain translated the message. The major then asked: 'Is the reply negative or affirmative? If it is the latter I will negotiate further.'

All of this time the Germans were acting in an upstage and patronizing manner. Colonel Harper was beginning to lose his temper. He said, 'The reply is decidedly not affirmative.' Then he added, 'If you continue this foolish attack your losses will be tremendous.' The major nodded his head.

Harper put the two officers in the jeep and took them back to the main road where the German privates were waiting with the white flag.

He then removed the blindfold and said to them, speaking through the German captain: 'If you don't understand what "nuts" means, in plain English it is the same as "Go to Hell". And I will tell you something else – if you continue to attack, we will kill every goddam German that tries to break into this city.'

The German major and captain saluted very stiffly. The captain said, 'We will kill many Americans. This is war.'

'On your way, bud,' said Colonel Harper.

The small party of the enemy, carrying their white flag, disappeared down the snowy road in the direction of their own lines. The USA troops climbed back into their foxholes.

And the threatened artillery barrage failed to materialize.

Four days later the US 4th Armoured Division fought its way through to relieve Bastogne. The Ardennes offensive had been broken.

IWO JIMA, 19 February 1945

A US Marine Corps correspondent

Iwo Jima is a small volcanic island which lies at the southern end of a chain which stretches into Tokyo Bay. The Americans wanted to build an airbase on the island – which, in early 1945, was Japanese-held and heavily fortified – mainly to enable American fighters to support B29s in their raids over Japan. The invasion of Iwo Jima was launched on 19 February 1945. The fighting was expected to take eight days; it lasted five weeks.

When the 24th Marine Regiment's 2nd Battalion reached the scene, they called it 'the Wilderness', and there they spent four days on the line, with no respite from the song of death sung by mortars among those desolate crevices and gouged shell holes. The Wilderness covered about a square mile inland from Blue Beach 2, on the approaches to Airfield no. 2, and there was no cover. Here and there stood a blasted dwarf tree; here and there a stubby rock ledge in a maze of volcanic crevices.

The 2nd Battalion attacked with flame throwers, demolition charges, 37-millimetre guns, riflemen. A tank advancing in support was knocked out by a mortar shell. After every Japanese volley, Corsair fighter planes streamed down on the mortar positions, ripping their charges of bombs into the Wilderness. But after every dive was ended, the mortars started their ghastly song again.

Cracks in the earth run along the open field to the left of the Wilderness, and hot smoke seeped up through the cracks. Gains were counted in terms of 100 or 200 yards for a day, in terms of three or four bunkers knocked out. Losses were counted in terms of three or four men suddenly turned to bloody rags after the howl of a mortar shell, in terms of a flame-thrower man hit by a grenade as he poured his flame into a bunker. The assault platoon of flame throwers and demolitionists, spearheading the regiment's push through the Wilderness, lost two assistant squad leaders killed.

The Japs were hard to kill. Cube-shaped concrete blockhouses had to be blasted again and again before the men inside were silenced. Often the stunned and wounded Japs continued to struggle among the ruins, still trying to fire back. A sergeant fired twenty-one shots at a semi-concealed Jap before the latter was killed. Another Marine assaulting a pillbox found a seriously wounded Jap trying to get a heavy machine gun into action. He emptied his clip at him but the Jap kept reaching. Finally, out of ammunition, the Marine used his knife to kill him.

Forty-eight hours after the attack began, one element of the Third Division moved into the line under orders to advance at all costs.

Behind a rolling artillery barrage and with fixed bayonets, the unit leaped forward in an old-fashioned hell-bent-for-leather charge and advanced to the very mouths of the fixed Jap defences. Before scores of pillboxes the men flung themselves at the tiny flaming holes, throwing grenades and jabbing with bayonets. Comrades went past, hurdled the defences and rushed across Airfield no. 2. In three minutes one unit lost four officers. Men died at every step. That was how we broke their line.

Across the field we attacked a ridge. The enemy rose up out of holes to hurl our assault back. The squads re-formed and went up again. At the crest they plunged on the Japs with bayonets. One of our men, slashing his way from side to side, fell dead from a pistol shot. His comrade drove his bayonet into the Jap who had killed him. The Japs on the ridge were annihilated.

And now behind those proud and weary men, our whole previously stalled attack poured through. Tanks, bazookas and demolition men smashed and burned the by-passed fortifications. In an area 1,000 yards long and 200 deep, more than 800 enemy pillboxes were counted.

The survivors of this bold charge covered 800 yards in an hour and a half. Brave men had done what naval shelling, aerial bombardment, artillery and tanks had not been able to do in two days of constant pounding. What was perhaps the most intensively fortified small area ever encountered in battle had been broken.

Six thousand Americans died on Iwo Jima. Another 12,500 died in April in the seizure of Okinawa, an island in the Ryukyu chain, also designated as a USAAF fighter base. The Japanese dead numbered 21,000 on Iwo Jima, and around 100,000 on Okinawa.

CROSSING THE GERMAN BORDER, 9 February 1945

John Foley

After crushing Hitler's December offensive, the Allies made rapid progress in the West. By early February they had reached the border of Germany.

. . . 'What's this striped pole across the road, sir?' said Pickford.

'The frontier!' I said, pointing to the deserted hut which had housed the frontier police and customs men.

I stared curiously at my first German civilian. He was an old man, dressed in shabby serge and an engine-driver's sort of cap. His grizzled face regarded us from above a bushy white moustache as we clattered over the broken frontier barrier. And then I heard *Angler*'s driver's hatch being thrown open, and when I looked over my shoulder I saw Smith 161 leaning out and staring questioningly at the old German.

'We on the right road for Berlin, mate?' asked Smith 161, with a perfectly straight face.

I swear the old blue eyes winked, as the man tugged at his grizzled moustache and said: *'Berlin? Ja, ja! Gerade aus!'*

'I thought the Germans had no sense of humour,' said Pickford, when we got moving again.

'I know,' I said. 'But he can remember Germany before Hitler, and probably before the Kaiser, too.'

A BOMB HITS THE PROPAGANDA MINISTRY, BERLIN, 13 March 1945

Joseph Goebbels

Joseph Goebbels was one of the principal ring-leaders of Nazism and head of the Nazi's Ministry of Public Enlightenment and Propaganda.

This evening's Mosquito raid was particularly disastrous for me because our Ministry was hit. The whole lovely building on the Wilhelmstrasse was totally destroyed by a bomb. The throne-room, the Blue Gallery and my newly rebuilt theatre hall are nothing but a heap of ruins. I drove straight to the Ministry to see the devastation for myself. One's heart aches to see so unique a product of the architect's art, such as this building was, totally flattened in a second. What trouble we have taken to reconstruct the theatre hall, the throne-room and the Blue Gallery in the old style! With what care have we chosen every fresco on the walls and every piece of furniture! And now it has all been given over to destruction. In addition fire has now broken out in the ruins, bringing with it an even greater risk since 500 bazooka missiles are stored underneath the burning wreckage. I do my utmost to get the fire brigade to the scene as quickly and in as great strength as possible, so as at least to prevent the bazooka missiles exploding.

As I do all this I am overcome with sadness. It is twelve years to the day – 13 March – since I entered this Ministry as Minister. It is the worst conceivable omen for the next twelve years.

THE BEHEADING OF LOOTERS, BERLIN, 4 April 1945

Joseph Goebbels

The ringleaders [of the looting of a bakery by starving Berliners] were sentenced by the People's Court this very afternoon. Three were condemned to death – one man and two women. The case of one of the women is less serious so that I have decided to pardon her. The other two who were condemned to death I shall have beheaded during the night. The people of Rahnsdorf will be informed by placard that these two ringleaders have been sentenced and executed; the rest of the Berlin population will be told over the wired broadcast with appropriate comment. I think that this will have a most sobering effect. In any case I am of the opinion that no more bakeries in Berlin will be looted in the immediate future. This is how one must proceed if one is to keep order in a city with millions of inhabitants – and order is a prerequisite for continuation of our resistance.

A MEETING WITH HITLER, BERLIN, April 1945

Gerhard Boldt

The author was a junior *Wehrmacht* officer seconded to Hitler's Berlin HQ to prepare war maps.

It was now four p.m. and most of those who are to take part
in the conference have assembled in the ante-room. They
stand or sit together in groups, talk and eat sandwiches while
drinking real coffee or brandy. The Chief beckons me
forward to introduce me. He is surrounded by Field-Marshal Keitel, General Jodl, Grand-Admiral Dönitz, and
Bormann. Next to them are grouped their ADCs. In one
corner, near a small table holding a telephone, Himmler is
talking to the General of the SS Fegelein, the permanent
representative of Himmler with Hitler. Fegelein is married to
a sister of Eva Braun, the future wife of Hitler. His whole
attitude now already displays the brazen assurance of a
brother-in-law of the head of the German Reich. Kaltenbrunner, the dreaded head of the Supreme Reich Security
Office, stands apart, alone and reading a document. The
permanent Deputy of the Reich Press Chief with Hitler,
Lorenz, makes conversation with the Standard Leader
Zander, Bormann's deputy. Reich Marshal Göring is sitting
at a round table in the centre of the ante-room, together with
the officers of his staff, the Generals Koller and Christians.
Hitler's chief ADC, General Burgdorf, now crosses the ante-
room and disappears into the studio. Shortly afterwards he
reappears in the open doorway:

'The Führer requests your presence!' Göring leads and all
the others follow behind him in their order of rank.

Hitler stands alone in the centre of the huge room, turned
towards the ante-room. They approach in their order of
entry, and he greets nearly everyone by a handshake,
silently, without a word of welcome. Only once in a while
he asks a question, which is answered by 'Yes, Führer' or
'No, Führer.' I remain standing near the door and wait for
the things that are bound to come. It is certainly one of the
most remarkable moments of my life. General Guderian
speaks with Hitler apparently concerning myself, for he
looks in my direction. Guderian beckons, and I approach
Hitler. Slowly, heavily stooping, he takes a few shuffling steps

in my direction. He extends his right hand and looks at me with a queerly penetrating look. His handshake is weak and soft without any strength. His head is slightly wobbling. (This struck me later on even more, when I had the leisure to observe him.) His left arm hangs slackly and his hand trembles a good deal. There is an indescribable flickering glow in his eyes, creating a fearsome and totally unnatural effect. His face and the parts round his eyes give the impression of total exhaustion. All his movements are those of a senile man.

A SPITFIRE PILOT ENCOUNTERS A GERMAN JET FIGHTER, April 1945

Johnnie Johnson

The world's first operational jet fighter, the German Messerschmitt 262, was introduced by the *Luftwaffe* in the dying days of the war and far outclassed any Allied plane.

During the following days we were often attacked by the 262s, and more airmen were killed and more Spitfires damaged. The enemy jets came in very fast from the east, and in order to protect our airfield we carried out standing patrols at 20,000 feet, the favourite attacking height of the intruders. But the Spitfires were far too slow to catch the 262s, and although we often possessed the height advantage we could not bring the jets to combat. Suddenly we were outmoded and out-dated. Should the enemy possess reasonable numbers of these remarkable aircraft, it would not be long before we lost the air superiority for which we had struggled throughout the war.

The complete superiority of the Messerschmitt 262 was well demonstrated to us one evening when we carried out a dusk patrol over Grave. Kenway had told us that the jets were active over Holland, but although we scanned the skies we could see nothing of them. Suddenly, without warning, an enemy jet appeared about one hundred yards ahead of our Spitfires. The pilot must have seen our formation, since he shot up from below and climbed away at a high speed. Already he was out of cannon range, and the few rounds I sent after him were more an angry gesture at our impotence than anything else. As he soared into the darkening, eastern sky, he added insult to injury by carrying out a perfect upward roll.

A VISIT TO BELSEN DEATH CAMP, 19 April 1945

Richard Dimbleby

Alongside the 500,000 Jews from Western Europe (see p.332) who were killed by the SS, 5.5 million Jews from Eastern Europe were also executed. Some of these were shot on the spot by special SS squads; most, however, were shipped to the extermination camps, Belsen among them, to be gassed.

I picked my way over corpse after corpse in the gloom, until I heard one voice raised above the gentle undulating moaning. I found a girl, she was a living skeleton, impossible to gauge her age for she had practically no hair left, and her face was only a yellow parchment sheet with two holes in it for eyes. She was stretching out her stick of an arm and gasping something, it was 'English, English, medicine, medicine', and she was trying to cry but she hadn't enough strength. And beyond her down the passage and in the hut there were the convulsive movements of dying people too weak to raise themselves from the floor.

In the shade of some trees lay a great collection of bodies. I walked about them trying to count, there were perhaps 150 of them flung down on each other, all naked, all so thin that their yellow skin glistened like stretched rubber on their bones. Some of the poor starved creatures whose bodies were there looked so utterly unreal and inhuman that I could have imagined that they had never lived at all. They were like polished skeletons, the skeletons that medical students like to play practical jokes with.

At one end of the pile a cluster of men and women were gathered round a fire; they were using rags and old shoes taken from the bodies to keep it alight, and they were heating soup over it. And close by was the enclosure where 500 children between the ages of five and twelve had been kept. They were not so hungry as the rest, for the women had sacrificed themselves to keep them alive. Babies were born at Belsen, some of them shrunken, wizened little things that could not live, because their mothers could not feed them.

One woman, distraught to the point of madness, flung herself at a British soldier who was on guard at the camp on the night that it was reached by the 11th Armoured Division; she begged him to give her some milk for the tiny baby she held in her arms. She laid the mite on the ground and threw herself at the sentry's feet and kissed his boots. And when, in his distress, he asked her to get up, she put the baby in his arms and ran off crying that she would find milk for it because there was no milk in her breast. And when the soldier opened the bundle of rags to look at the child, he found that it had been dead for days.

There was no privacy of any kind. Women stood naked at the side of the track, washing in cupfuls of water taken from British Army trucks. Others squatted while they searched themselves for lice, and examined each other's hair. Sufferers from dysentery leaned against the huts, straining helplessly, and all around and about them was this awful drifting tide of exhausted people, neither caring nor watching. Just a few held out their withered hands to us as we passed by, and blessed the doctor, whom they knew had become the camp commander in place of the brutal Kramer.

I have never seen British soldiers so moved to cold fury as the men who opened the Belsen camp this week.

THE FUNERAL OF PRESIDENT ROOSEVELT, GEORGIA, 20 April 1945

Douglas B. Cornell

Franklin Delano Roosevelt, US President, had died on the morning of 12 April. He was buried at his family home in Georgia. He was succeeded as US President by Harry S. Truman, the Vice-President.

As President Truman looked on with a face frozen in grief, Franklin D. Roosevelt was committed today to the warm brown earth of his native soil.

Under a cloudless, spring sky, the body of the late Chief Executive was lowered solemnly into a grave in the flower garden of his family estate.

Watching with strained faces were members of the family, dignitaries of government and little sad-faced groups of plain people – the employees on the place and neighbours from the countryside.

A detail of grey-clad cadets from the US Military Academy at West Point fired a volley of three farewell salutes. A bugler played 'Taps', its sweet but still sad notes echoing through the wooded estate.

Soldiers, sailors and marines, who had held an American flag over the casket, folded it and handed it to Mrs Roosevelt.

The garden where Mr Roosevelt rests lies between the family home where he was born sixty-three years ago and the library which houses his state papers and the gifts of a world which recognized him as one of its pre-eminent leaders.

It was exactly ten a.m. when the first gun of a presidential salute was fired from a battery in the library grounds to the east of the quarter-acre garden. They boomed at solemnly spaced intervals.

An honour guard lining the hemlock hedge around the garden stood at attention.

A few moments later, the distant melody of a bugle came to those within the garden. A flight of bombers and another of training planes droned overhead.

The beat of muffled drums in slow cadence rolled through the wooded hills above the Hudson. In the distance, gradually drawing nearer, a band played a funeral dirge.

Promptly at ten-thirty a.m., the National Anthem sounded and, as the wheels of the caisson noisily ground the gravel of the roadway, the notes of 'Nearer, My God, to Thee', were played softly. Through a passageway at one corner, the elderly, grey-bearded rector of the President's Episcopal Church at Hyde Park walked across the newly clipped grass toward the grave.

The Rev. George W. Anthony was wearing the black and white surplice and stole of the clergy. He removed a black velvet skull-cap and took his position at the head of the grave, toward the west.

'All that the father giveth me shall come to me,' the Rev. Mr Anthony said.

A lone plane circling above almost drowned his words as he declared that unto Almighty God 'we commit his body to the ground; earth to earth, ashes to ashes, dust to dust.'

There was a stirring in the crowd.

'Blessed are the dead who die in the Lord,' the rector intoned. 'Lord, have mercy upon us. Christ, have mercy upon us. Lord, have mercy upon us.'

The pastor repeated the words of the Lord's Prayer. Elliott's lips moved with him.

The services followed the ordinary Episcopal burial rites

for the dead. There were no words of eulogy, only the word of God.

Near its conclusion the Rev. Mr Anthony recited the poem written by John Ellerton in 1870: 'Now the labourer's task is o'er; now the battle-day is past.'

'Father, in Thy gracious keeping we now leave Thy servant sleeping,' the rector continued.

The services were brief. They were over by ten-forty-five. The flag which Mrs Roosevelt clutched tightly was handed to Elliott, and the family filed out.

THE MARCH ON BERLIN, 21 April 1945

Soviet war correspondent

A vivid glimpse of the Red Army's final push on the German capital.

None of us will ever forget that night. Twenty-three bridges had been thrown across the swollen Oder. Engines roared in unison. Pillars of heavy dust hung in the air.

The glow on the western horizon grew bigger and bigger as our parachute flares exposed every nook and cranny of the German lines. Shell-bursts lit up the sky. The earth trembled, and over the German positions rose an immense fountain of smoke, earth and rocks . . .

The Guards advanced over the level plain, tanks and self-propelled guns spitting fire ahead of them and leaving a dense trail of dust behind. Flails, or 'trawler tanks' as the Red Army men call them, cut lanes through the minefields . . .

By seven in the morning it was fully light. Dust and smoke lay over us like a blanket, getting thicker every moment. Ahead of us a red flag waved from a hilltop, planted by Senior Lieutenant Nikolai Derevenko . . .

I have never seen anything to equal the density of the German trench system on the Berlin approaches. Each village, each railway station squats inside a closely meshed web of trenches. Single buildings are elaborately girdled with them . . .

The Germans are floundering in dust and smoke as Soviet guns burn them out of their nests. The sun is hot. The great toilers of war, the sappers, pass by us. They blow up everything the Germans can build, even their trickiest fortifications, lying underground to a depth of two hundred feet, like those in the Oder zone of the Berlin fortified area.

There is a cloud of dust over the Berlin autobahn. Russia, the Ukraine, Byelorussia, Georgia, Armenia, Azerbaidjan, Uzbekistan, Kazakhstan, Kirghizia, Lithuania, Latvia and Esthonia are marching on Berlin . . .

Dust, dust, dust . . . Nothing to drink, everything dried up, burnt out. But nothing matters. We are going on to Berlin with lips black and parched. The distance grows less and less on the signposts. The heavy guns go by on their way to fire their first salvos into Berlin.

SOVIET GUNS OPEN FIRE ON BERLIN, 22 April 1945

Soviet war correspondent

On the walls of the houses we saw Goebbels' appeals, hurriedly scrawled in white paint: 'Every German will defend his capital. We shall stop the Red hordes at the walls of our Berlin.' Just try and stop them!

Steel pillboxes, barricades, mines, traps, suicide squads with grenades clutched in their hands – all are swept aside before the tidal wave.

Drizzling rain began to fall. Near Bisdorf I saw batteries preparing to open fire.

'What are the targets?' I asked the battery commander.

'Centre of Berlin, Spree bridges, and the northern and Stettin railway stations,' he answered.

Then came the tremendous words of command: 'Open fire at the capital of Fascist Germany.'

I noted the time. It was exactly 8.30 a.m. on 22 April. Ninety-six shells fell in the centre of Berlin in the course of a few minutes.

The German capital fell to the Red Army on 2 May. Hitler was already dead, having committed suicide in his underground bunker on 30 April.

THE GERMANY ARMY SURRENDERS, LUNEBERG HEATH, 3 May 1945

Field Marshal Montgomery

On 3 May Field Marshal Keitel sent a delegation to my headquarters on Lüneburg Heath, with the consent of Admiral Dönitz, to open negotiations for surrender. This party arrived at eleven-thirty hours and consisted of:

General-Admiral von Friedeburg, C.-in-C. of the German Navy.

General Kinzel, Chief of Staff to Field Marshal Busch, who was commanding the German land forces on my northern and western flanks.

Rear-Admiral Wagner.

Major Freidel, a staff officer.

This party of four was later joined by Colonel Pollek, another staff officer.

They were brought to my caravan site and were drawn up under the Union Jack, which was flying proudly in the breeze. I kept them waiting for a few minutes and then came out of my caravan and walked towards them. They all saluted, under the Union Jack. It was a great moment; I knew the Germans had come to surrender and that the war was over. Few of those in the signals and operations caravans at my Tac Headquarters will forget the thrill experienced when they heard the faint 'tapping' of the Germans trying to pick us up on the wireless command link – to receive the surrender instructions from their delegation.

I said to my interpreter, 'Who are these men?' He told me. I then said, 'What do they want?'

Admiral Friedeburg then read me a letter from Field Marshal Keitel offering to surrender to me the three German armies withdrawing in front of the Russians between Berlin and Rostock. I refused to consider this, saying that these armies should surrender to the Russians. I added that, of course, if any German soldiers came towards my front with their hands up they would automatically be taken prisoner. Von Friedeburg said it was unthinkable to surrender to the Russians as they were savages, and the German soldiers would be sent straight off to work in Russia.

I said the Germans should have thought of all these things before they began the war, and particularly before they attacked the Russians in June 1941.

Von Friedeburg next said that they were anxious about the civilian population in Mecklenburg, who were being overrun by the Russians, and they would like to discuss how these could be saved. I replied that Mecklenburg was not in my area and that any problems connected with it must be discussed with the Russians. I said they must understand that I refused to discuss any matter connected with the situation on my eastern flank between Wismar and Domitz; they must approach the Russians on such matters. I then asked if they wanted to discuss the surrender of their forces on my western flank. They said they did not. But they were anxious about the civilian population in those areas, and would like to arrange with me some scheme by which their troops could withdraw slowly as my forces advanced. I refused.

I then decided to spring something on them quickly. I said to von Friedeburg:

'Will you surrender to me all German forces on my western and northern flanks, including all forces in Holland, Friesland with the Frisian Islands and Heligoland, Schleswig-Holstein, and Denmark? If you will do this, I will accept it as a tactical battlefield surrender of the enemy forces immediately opposing me, and those in support of Denmark.'

He said he could not agree to do this. But he was anxious to come to some agreement about the civilian population in those areas; I refused to discuss this. I then said that if the Germans refused to surrender unconditionally the forces in the areas I had named, I would order the fighting to continue; many more German soldiers would then be killed, and possibly some civilians also from artillery fire and air attack. I next showed them on a map the actual battle situation on the whole western front; they had no idea what this situation was and were very upset. By this time I reckoned that I would not have much more difficulty in getting them to accept my demands. But I thought that an interval for lunch might be desirable so that they could reflect on what I had said. I sent them away to have lunch in a tent by themselves, with nobody else present except one of my officers. Von Friedeburg wept during lunch and the others did not say much.

After lunch I sent for them again, and this time the meeting was in my conference tent with the map of the battle situation on the table. I began this meeting by delivering an ultimatum. They must surrender unconditionally all their forces in the areas I had named; once they had done this I would discuss with them the best way of occupying the areas and looking after the civilians; if they refused, I would go on with the battle. They saw at once that

I meant what I said. They were convinced of the hope-
lessness of their cause but they said they had no power to
agree to my demands. They were, however, now prepared to
recommend to Field Marshal Keitel the unconditional
surrender of all the forces on the western and northern
flanks of 21 Army Group. Two of them would go back to
OKW, see Keitel, and bring back his agreement.

I then drew up a document which summarized the
decisions reached at our meeting, which I said must be
signed by myself and von Friedeburg, and could then be
taken to Flensburg, and given to Keitel and Dönitz.

The instrument of surrender was signed on 7 May 1945. The war
in Europe was over. Eisenhower sent the following laconic dispatch
to the Allied Chiefs of Staff.

The mission of this Allied Force was fulfilled at three a.m.,
local time, 7 May 1945. Eisenhower.

VICTORY IN EUROPE CELEBRATIONS, 7 May 1945

Mollie Panter-Downes, London

The big day started off here with a coincidence. In the last
hours of peace, in September, 1939, a violent thunderstorm
broke over the city, making a lot of people think for a
moment that the first air raid had begun. Early Tuesday
morning, VE Day, nature tidily brought the war to an end
with an imitation of a blitz so realistic that many Londoners
started awake and reached blurrily for the bedside torch.
Then they remembered, and, sighing with relief, fell asleep
again as the thunder rolled over the capital, already waiting
with its flags. The decorations had blossomed on the streets

Monday afternoon. By six that night, Piccadilly Circus and all the city's other focal points were jammed with a cheerful, expectant crowd waiting for an official statement from Downing Street. Movie cameramen crouched patiently on the rooftops. When a brewer's van rattled by and the driver leaned out and yelled 'It's all over', the crowd cheered, then went on waiting. Presently word spread that the announcement would be delayed, and the day, which had started off like a rocket, began to fizzle slowly and damply out. Later in the evening, however, thousands of Londoners suddenly decided that even if it was not yet VE Day, it was victory, all right, and something to celebrate. Thousands of others just went home quietly to wait some more.

When the day finally came, it was like no other day that anyone can remember. It had a flavour of its own, an extemporaneousness which gave it something of the quality of a vast, happy village fête as people wandered about, sat, sang, and slept against a summer background of trees, grass, flowers, and water. It was not, people said, like the 1918 Armistice Day, for at no time was the reaction hysterical. It was not like the Coronation, for the crowds were larger and their gaiety, which held up all through the night, was obviously not picked up in a pub. The day also surprised the prophets who had said that only the young would be resilient enough to celebrate in a big way. Apparently the desire to assist in London's celebration combusted spontaneously in the bosom of every member of every family, from the smallest babies, with their hair done up in red-white-and-blue ribbons, to beaming elderly couples who, utterly without self-consciousness, strolled up and down the streets arm in arm in red-white-and-blue paper hats. Even the dogs wore immense tricoloured bows. Rosettes sprouted from the slabs of pork in the butcher shops, which, like other food stores, were open for a couple of hours in the morning. With their customary practicality, housewives put bread before circuses. They waited in the long bakery queues, the string bags of the common round in one hand and the Union Jack of the glad occasion in the other. Even queues seemed tolerable that morning. The bells had begun to peal and, after the night's storm, London was having that perfect, hot, English summer's day which, one sometimes feels, is to be found only in the imaginations of the lyric poets.

The girls in their thin, bright dresses heightened the impression that the city had been taken over by an enormous family picnic. The number of extraordinarily pretty young girls, who presumably are hidden on working days inside the factories and government offices, was astonishing. They streamed out into the parks and streets like flocks of twittering, gaily plumaged cockney birds. In their freshly curled hair were cornflowers and poppies, and they wore red-white-and-blue ribbons around their narrow waists. Some of them even tied ribbons around their bare ankles. Strolling with their uniformed boys, arms candidly about each other, they provided a constant, gay, simple marginal decoration to the big, solemn moments of the day. The crowds milled back and forth between the Palace, Westminster, Trafalgar Square, and Piccadilly Circus, and when they got tired they simply sat down wherever they happened to be – on the grass, on doorsteps, or on the kerb – and watched the other people or spread handkerchiefs over their faces and took a nap. Everybody appeared determined to see the King and Queen and Mr Churchill at least once, and few could have been disappointed. One small boy, holding on to his father's hand, wanted to see the trench shelters in Green Park too. 'You don't want to see shelters today,' his father said. 'You'll never have to use them again, son.' 'Never?' the child asked doubtfully. 'Never!' the man cried, almost angrily. '*Never!* Understand?' In the open space before the Palace, one of the places where the Prime Minister's speech was to be relayed by loudspeaker at three o'clock, the crowds seemed a little intimidated by the nearness of that symbolic block of grey stone. The people who chose to open their lunch baskets and munch sandwiches there among the flower beds of tulips were rather subdued. Piccadilly Circus attracted the more demonstrative spirits.

By lunchtime, in the Circus, the buses had to slow to a crawl in order to get through the tightly packed, laughing people. A lad in the black beret of the Tank Corps was the first to climb the little pyramidal Angkor Vat of scaffolding and sandbags which was erected early in the war to protect the pedestal of the Eros statue after the figure had been removed to safekeeping. The boy shinnied up to the top and took a tiptoe Eros pose, aiming an imaginary bow, while the crowd roared. He was followed by a paratrooper in a maroon beret, who, after getting up to the top, reached down and hauled up a blonde young woman in a very tight pair of green slacks. When she got to the top, the Tank Corps soldier promptly grabbed her in his arms and, encouraged by ecstatic cheers from the whole Circus, seemed about to enact the classic role of Eros right on the top of the monument. Nothing came of it, because a moment later a couple of GIs joined them and before long the pyramid was covered with boys and girls. They sat jammed together in an affectionate mass, swinging their legs over the sides, wearing each other's uniform caps, and calling down wisecracks to the crowd. 'My God,' someone said, 'think of a flying bomb coming down on this!' When a firecracker went off, a hawker with a tray of tin brooches of Monty's head happily yelled that comforting, sometimes fallacious phrase of the blitz nights, 'All right, mates, it's one of ours!'

All day long, the deadly past was for most people only just under the surface of the beautiful, safe present, so much so that the Government decided against sounding the sirens in a triumphant 'all clear' for fear that the noise would revive too many painful memories. For the same reason, there were no salutes of guns – only the pealing of the bells, and the whistles of tugs on the Thames sounding the doot, doot, doot, dooooot of the 'V', and the roar of the planes, which swooped back and forth over the city, dropping red and green signals toward the blur of smiling, upturned faces.

It was without any doubt Churchill's day. Thousands of King George's subjects wedged themselves in front of the Palace throughout the day, chanting ceaselessly 'We want the King' and cheering themselves hoarse when he and the Queen and their daughters appeared, but when the crowd saw Churchill there was a deep, full-throated, almost reverent roar. He was at the head of a procession of Members of Parliament, walking back to the House of Commons from the traditional St Margaret's Thanksgiving Service. Instantly, he was surrounded by people – people running, standing on tiptoe, holding up babies so that they could be told later they had seen him, and shouting affectionately the absurd little nurserymaid name, 'Winnie, Winnie!' One of two happily sozzled, very old, and incredibly dirty cockneys who had been engaged in a slow, shuffling dance, like a couple of Shakespearean clowns, bellowed, 'That's 'im, that's 'is little old lovely bald 'ead!' The crowds saw Churchill again later, when he emerged from the Commons and was driven off in the back of a small open car, rosy, smiling, and looking immensely happy. Ernest Bevin, following in another car, got a cheer too. One of the throng, an excited East Ender, in a dress with a bodice concocted of a Union Jack, shouted, 'Gawd, fancy me cheering Bevin, the chap who makes us work!' Herbert Morrison, sitting unobtrusively in a corner of a third car, was hardly recognized, and the other Cabinet Ministers did no better. The crowd had ears, eyes, and throats for no one but Churchill, and for him everyone in it seemed to have the hearing, sight, and lungs of fifty men. His slightly formal official broadcast, which was followed by buglers sounding the 'cease firing' call, did not strike the emotional note that had been expected, but he hit it perfectly in his subsequent informal speech ('My dear friends, this is your victory . . .') from a Whitehall balcony.

All day long, little extra celebrations started up. In the Mall, a model of a Gallic cock waltzed on a pole over the heads of the singing people. 'It's the Free French,' said someone. The Belgians in the crowd tagged along after a Belgian flag that marched by, its bearer invisible. A procession of students raced through Green Park, among exploding squibs, clashing dustbin lids like cymbals and waving an immense Jeyes Disinfectant poster as a banner. American sailors and laughing girls formed a conga line down the middle of Piccadilly and cockneys linked arms in the Lambeth Walk. It was a day and night of no fixed plan and no organized merriment. Each group danced its own dance, sang its own song, and went its own way as the spirit moved it. The most tolerant, self-effacing people in London on V E Day were the police, who simply stood by, smiling benignly, while soldiers swung by one arm from lamp standards and laughing groups tore down hoardings to build the evening's bonfires. Actually, the police were not unduly strained. The extraordinary thing about the crowds was that they were almost all sober. The number of drunks one saw in that whole day and night could have been counted on two hands – possibly because the pubs were sold out so early. The young service men and women who swung arm in arm down the middle of every street, singing and swarming over the few cars rash enough to come out, were simply happy with an immense holiday happiness. They were the liberated people who, like their counterparts in every celebrating capital that night, were young enough to outlive the past and to look forward to an unspoilt future. Their gaiety was very moving.

Just before the King's speech, at nine Tuesday night, the big lamps outside the Palace came on and there were cheers and ohs from children who had never seen anything of that kind in their short, blacked-out lives. As the evening wore on, most of the public buildings were floodlighted. The night was as warm as midsummer, and London, its shabbiness now hidden and its domes and remaining Wren spires warmed by lights and bonfires, was suddenly magnificent. The handsomest building of all was the National Gallery, standing out honey-coloured near a ghostly, blue-shadowed St Martin's and the Charles I bit of Whitehall. The illuminated and floodlighted face of Big Ben loomed like a kind moon. Red and blue lights strung in the bushes around the lake in St James's Park glimmered on the sleepy, bewildered pelicans that live there.

By midnight the crowds had thinned out some, but those who remained were as merry as ever. They went on calling for the King outside the Palace and watching the searchlights, which for once could be observed with pleasure . . .

James Byrom, soldier, Germany

On VE night the victorious armies got drunk according to a long-cherished plan. I think I must have been on duty, for I was as sober as a judge and I remember standing at a dormer window in the great *Luftwaffe* hospital at Wismar, looking at the magnificent sunset and thinking that I had now come almost full circle, back to the sea that washed the shores of Sweden.

On a ward balcony below me wounded Germans were talking quietly. Presently, as the glow of their cigarettes confirmed that it was dark, the victory celebrations began. Up from the British lines came brilliant flares, singly and in clusters, but without pattern or prodigality, as if one soldier in each platoon had been given an official coloured hat and told to fling it in the air. But farther away, in the Russian lines, the glow of bonfires steadily lit up the sky. Distance subdued the flickering, making static cones that were slightly blurred by smoke or mist; and I could fancy that they were ghost fires, the fires of other historic triumphs, so strongly did I feel them as a symbol of the unreality of victory in relation to the recurring failure to keep the peace.

'A Correspondent', *The* **Hereford Times**

Passing through the village of Stoke Lacy early on Tuesday afternoon one was startled to see an effigy of Hitler in the car park at the Plough. That evening a crowd began to gather, and word went round that Hitler was to be consumed in flames at 11 p.m. At that hour excitement was intense, when Mr W. R. Symonds called upon Mr S. J. Parker, the Commander of No. 12 Platoon of the Home Guard, to set the effigy alight. In a few minutes the body of Hitler disintegrated as this 1,000-year empire had done. First his arm, poised in the Hitler salute, dropped as smartly as it was ever raised in real life . . . then a leg fell off, and the flames burnt fiercely to the strains of 'Rule Britannia', 'There'll Always be an England', and 'Roll Out the Barrel'. The crowd spontaneously linked hands and in a circle 300-strong sang the National Anthem.

If the war in Europe had ended, the war in the Far East was still being fought. The Allies, however, had developed a secret and deadly weapon.

THE WORLD'S FIRST ATOM BOMB TEST, LOS ALAMOS, 17 July 1945

Sir Geoffrey Taylor

Code-named 'The Manhattan Project', the world's first atomic bomb was built by the Allies and detonated at a test in the New Mexico desert. The world had entered the nuclear age.

I was one of the group of British scientific men who worked at Los Alamos in New Mexico, where most of the recent experimental work on atomic bombs was carried out, and I saw the first bomb explode. Before I tell you about this; I ought to say that I have witnessed many ordinary bomb trials. In such trials the kind of result to be expected is always known beforehand, and the trial is designed to find out just how much damage the bomb will do. The first atomic bomb test had to be approached with a totally different outlook because it was not possible to make any previous experiment on a smaller scale. None of us knew whether we were going to witness an epoch-making experiment or a complete failure. The physicists had predicted that a self-propagating reaction involving neutrons was possible and that this would lead to an explosion. The mathematicians had calculated what mechanical results were to be expected. Engineers and physicists had set up an apparatus rather like that used in testing ordinary bombs, to measure the efficiency of the explosion. But no one knew whether this apparatus would be needed, simply because nobody knew whether the bomb would go off.

Our uncertainty was reflected in the bets which were made at Los Alamos on the amount of energy to be released. These ranged from zero to the equivalent of 80,000 tons of TNT. Those of us who were to witness the test assembled during a late afternoon in July at Los Alamos for the 230-mile drive to the uninhabited and desolate region where the test was to be made. We arrived about three o'clock in the morning at a spot twenty miles from the hundred-foot tower on which the bomb was mounted. Here we were met by a car containing a radio receiver. Round this we assembled, listening for the signal from the firing point which would tell us when to expect the explosion. We were provided with a strip of very dark glass to protect our eyes. This glass is so dark that at midday it makes the sun look like a little undeveloped dull green potato. Through this glass I was unable to see the light which was set on the tower to show us where to look. Remember, it was still dark. I therefore fixed my eyes on this light ten seconds before the explosion was due to occur. Then I raised the dark glass to my eyes two seconds before, keeping them fixed on the spot where I had last seen the light. At exactly the expected moment, I saw through the dark glass a brilliant ball of fire which was far brighter than the sun. In a second or two it died down to a brightness which seemed to be about that of the sun, so, realizing that it must be lighting up the country-side, I looked behind me and saw the scrub-covered hills, twenty-two miles from the bomb, lighted up as though by a midday sun. Then I turned round and looked directly at the ball of fire. I saw it expand slowly, and begin to rise, growing fainter as it rose. Later it developed into a huge mushroom-shaped cloud, and soon reached a height of 40,000 feet.

Though the sequence of events was exactly what we had calculated beforehand in our more optimistic moments, the whole effect was so staggering that I found it difficult to believe my eyes, and judging by the strong ejaculations from my fellow-watchers other people felt the same reaction. So far we had heard no noise. Sound takes over one and a half minutes to travel twenty miles, so we next had to prepare to receive the blast wave. We had been advised to lie on the ground to receive the shock of the wave, but few people did so, perhaps owing to the fact that it was still dark, and rattle-snakes and tarantulas were fairly common in the district. When it came it was not very loud, and sounded like the crack of a shell passing overhead rather than a distant high-explosive bomb. Rumbling followed and continued for some time. On returning to Los Alamos, I found that one of my friends there had been lying awake in bed and had seen the light of the explosion reflected on the ceiling of his bedroom, though the source of it was over 160 miles away in a straight line.

THE ALLIES DECIDE TO DROP THE ATOMIC BOMB ON JAPAN, POTSDAM, 25 July 1945

President Harry S. Truman

Diary: Potsdam 25 July 1945

We met at eleven today. That is Stalin, Churchill, and the US President. But I had a most important session with Lord Mountbatten and General Marshall before that. We have discovered the most terrible bomb in the history of the world. It may be the fire destruction prophesied in the Euphrates Valley Era, after Noah and his fabulous Ark.

Anyway we 'think' we have found the way to cause a disintegration of the atom. An experiment in the New Mexican desert was startling – to put it mildly. Thirteen pounds of the explosive caused the complete disintegration of a steel tower 60 feet high, created a crater 6 feet deep and 1,200 feet in diameter, knocked over a steel tower ½ mile away and knocked men down 10,000 yards away. The explosion was visible for more than 200 miles and audible for 40 miles and more.

This weapon is to be used against Japan between now and August 10th. I have told the Sec. of War, Mr Stimson, to use it so that military objectives and soldiers and sailors are the target and not women and children. Even if the Japs are savages, ruthless, merciless and fanatic, we as the leader of the world for the common welfare cannot drop this terrible bomb on the old capital or the new.

He and I are in accord. The target will be a purely military one and we will issue a warning statement asking the Japs to surrender and save lives. I'm sure they will not do that, but we will have given them the chance. It is certainly a good thing for the world that Hitler's crowd or Stalin's did not discover this atomic bomb. It seems to be the most terrible thing ever discovered, but it can be made the most useful.

The following day, 26 July, the Allies called upon Japan to surrender. The alternative they said was 'prompt and utter destruction'. Japan did not surrender.

HIROSHIMA, 6 August 1945

Colonel Tibbets, USAAF

The destruction promised by the Allies came on 6 August, when three B29s of the US air force took off from Tinian and flew to Hiroshima, the eighth largest city in Japan. One of the planes, the Enola Gay, carried an atomic bomb. The commander of the mission was Colonel Tibbets.

Up to this point it was common practice in any theatre of war to fly straight ahead, fly level, drop your bombs, and keep right on going, because you could bomb several thousands of feet in the air and you could cross the top of the place that you had bombed with no concern whatsoever. But it was determined by the scientists that, in order to escape and maintain the integrity of the aircraft and the crew, that this aeroplane could not fly forward after it had dropped the bomb. It had to turn around and get away from that bomb as fast as it could. If you placed this aeroplane in a very steep angle of bank to make this turn, if you turned 158 degrees from the direction that you were going, you would then begin to place distance between yourself and that point of explosion as quickly as possible. You had to get away from the shock wave that would be coming back from the ground in the form of an ever expanding circle as it came upwards. It's necessary to make this turn to get yourself as far as possible from an expanding ring and 158 degrees happened to be the turn for that particular circle. It was difficult. It was something that was not done with a big bomber aeroplane. You didn't make this kind of a steep turn – you might almost call it an acrobatic manoeuvre – and the big aircraft didn't do these things. However, we refined it, we learned how to do it. It had been decided earlier that there was a possibility that an accident could occur on take-off, and so therefore we would not arm this weapon until we had left the runway and were out to sea. This of course meant that had there been an accident there would have been an explosion from normal powder charges but there would not have been a nuclear explosion. As I said this worried more people than it worried me because I had plenty of faith in my aeroplane. I knew my engines were good. We started our take-off on time which was somewhere about two-forty-five I think, and the aeroplane went on down the runway. It was loaded quite heavily but it responded exactly like I had anticipated it would. I had flown this aeroplane the same way before and there was no problem and there was nothing different this night in the way we went. We arrived over the initial point and started in on the bomb run which had about eleven minutes to go, rather a long type of run for a bomb but on the other hand we felt we needed this extra time in straight and level flight to stabilize the air speed of the aeroplane, to get everything right down to the last-minute detail. As I indicated earlier the problem after the release of the bomb is not to proceed forward but to turn away. As soon as the weight had left the aeroplane I immediately went into this steep turn and we tried then to place distance between ourselves and the point of impact. In this particular case that bomb took fifty-three seconds from the time it left the aeroplane until it exploded and this gave us adequate time of course to make the turn. We had just made the turn and rolled out on level flight when it seemed like somebody had grabbed a hold of my aeroplane and gave it a real hard shaking because this was the shock wave that had come up. Now after we had been hit by a second shock wave not quite so strong as the first one I decided we'll turn around and go back and take a look. The day was clear when we dropped that bomb, it was a clear sunshiny day and the visibility was unrestricted. As we came back around again facing the direction of Hiroshima we saw this cloud coming up. The cloud by this time, now two minutes old, was up at our altitude. We were 33,000 feet at this time and the cloud was up there and continuing to go right on up in a boiling fashion, as if it was rolling and boiling. The surface was nothing but a black boiling, like a barrel of tar. Where before there had been a city with distinctive houses, buildings and everything that you could see from our altitude, now you couldn't see anything except a black boiling debris down below.

The first atomic bomb to be dropped in warfare killed 80,000 inhabitants – a quarter of Hiroshima's inhabitants.

NAGASAKI, 9 August 1945

Tatsuichiro Akizuki

Three days after Hiroshima a second atomic bomb was dropped, this time on Nagasaki. Tatsuichiro Akizuki was working in Nagasaki as a doctor when the bomb landed.

On Thursday, 9 August, the boundless blue sky, the loud shrilling of cicadas, promised another day as hot and as sultry as the day before.

At eight-thirty I began the medical examination and

treatment of out-patients. Nearly thirty had turned up by ten o'clock. Some were patients requiring artificial pneumo-thorax (the temporary collapsing of a lung); they had been entrusted to us by Takahara Hospital, 5,000 metres away. Miss Yoshioka, a woman doctor in her mid-thirties who came from there, arrived to assist me with the operations, as well as two nurses also belonging to Takahara Hospital. Our hospital was in something of a turmoil.

During the morning Mr Yokota turned up to see his daughter, who was one of our in-patients. He lived at the foot of Motohara Hill, and was an engineer in the research department of the Mitsubishi Ordnance Factory, then one of the centres of armament manufacture in Japan. The torpe-does used in the attack on Pearl Harbor had been made there. Mr Yokota always had something interesting to say. He used to visit me now and again, often passing on some new piece of scientific information.

He said: 'I hear Hiroshima was very badly damaged on the sixth.'

Together we despaired over the destiny of Japan, he as an engineer, I as a doctor.

Then he said gloomily: 'I don't think the explosion was caused by any form of chemical energy.'

'What then?' I inquired, eager to know about the cause of the explosion, even though my patients were waiting for me.

He said: 'The power of the bomb dropped on Hiroshima is far stronger than any accumulation of chemical energy produced by the dissolution of a nitrogen compound, such as nitro-glycerine. It was an *atomic* bomb, produced by atomic fission.'

'Good heavens! At last we have atomic fission!' I said, though somewhat doubtfully.

Just then the long continuous wail of a siren arose.

'Listen . . . Here comes the regular air-raid.'

'The first warning . . . The enemy are on their way.'

Mr Yokota hurried back down the hill to his factory and

all at once I began to feel nervous. It was now about ten-thirty. When such a warning sounded we were supposed to make sure our patients took refuge in our basement air-raid shelter. We were meant to do likewise. But recently I had become so accustomed to air-raids that, even though it was somewhat foolhardy, I no longer bothered with every precaution. In any case, breakfast was about to begin. At the time our diet at the hospital consisted of two meals a day of unpolished rice. The patients were waiting for their breakfast to be served, and so remained on the second and third floors.

I went out of the building. It was very hot. The sky had clouded over a little but the familiar formation of B29 bombers was neither to be seen nor heard. I asked myself: 'What route will our dear enemies choose to take today?'

I went in again to warn my patients to stay away from the windows – they could be swept by machine-gun fire. Recently we had been shot up once or twice by fighter-planes from American aircraft carriers in neighbouring waters.

About thirty minutes later the all-clear sounded. I said to myself: In Nagasaki everything is still all right. *Im Westen Nichts Neues* – All quiet on the Western Front.

I went down to the consulting room, humming cheerfully. Now that the all-clear had been given I felt free from danger. I entered the room and found Dr Yoshioka about to carry out an artificial pneumo-thorax operation on one of the male out-patients. 'You ought to stop working when the air-raid warning goes, at least for a little while,' I told her.

'Thank you,' she replied. 'But there were so many patients waiting.'

She looked tired. She had come to the hospital that morning on foot, walking 5,000 metres across Nagasaki, and since then she had been very busy treating the patients who needed attention.

'Please have a rest,' I said. 'I'll carry on in your place.'

'Well . . . Thank you for your kindness,' she said, and went upstairs to her room to rest. I began the pneumo-thorax. Miss Sugako Murai, one of our few trained nurses, was there by my side to help me. She was two years younger than me and came from Koshima in Nagasaki; she had been at Urakami Hospital for about four months, since April.

It was eleven o'clock. Father Ishikawa, who was Korean, aged about thirty-six and the hospital chaplain, was listening in the hospital chapel to the confessions of those Catholics who had gone to him to confess, one after the other, before the great festival, on 15 August, of the Ascension of the Virgin Mary, which was only a week away. Brother Joseph Iwanaga was toiling outside the hospital with some farm workers, digging another air-raid shelter in the shrubbery in the centre of the hospital yard. Mr Noguchi had just begun to repair the apparatus used to lift water from the well. Other members of staff were busy providing a late breakfast. Some were filling big bowls with miso soup; others were carrying them through the corridors or up the stairs. The hospital was a hive of activity after the all-clear.

'Well, we'll soon be getting our breakfast,' I said to Miss Murai. 'The patients must be hungry.'

So was I, but before we had our breakfast we would have to finish treating all the out-patients.

I stuck the pneumo-thorax needle into the side of the chest of the patient lying on the bed. It was just after eleven a.m.

I heard a low droning sound, like that of distant aeroplane engines.

'What's that?' I said. 'The all-clear has gone, hasn't it?'

At the same time the sound of the plane's engines, growing louder and louder, seemed to swoop down over the hospital.

I shouted: 'It's an enemy plane! Look out – take cover!'

As I said so, I pulled the needle out of the patient and threw myself beside the bed.

There was a blinding white flash of light, and the next moment – *Bang! Crack!* A huge impact like a gigantic blow smote down upon our bodies, our heads and our hospital. I lay flat – I didn't know whether or not of my own volition. Then down came piles of debris, slamming into my back.

The hospital has been hit, I thought. I grew dizzy, and my ears sang.

Some minutes or so must have passed before I staggered to my feet and looked around. The air was heavy with yellow smoke; white flakes of powder drifted about; it was strangely dark.

Thank God, I thought – I'm not hurt! But what about the patients?

As it became brighter, little by little our situation grew clearer. Miss Murai, who had been assisting me with the pneumo-thorax, struggled to her feet beside me. She didn't seem to have been seriously injured, though she was completely covered with white dust. 'Hey, cheer up!' I said. 'We're not hurt, thank God!'

I helped her to her feet. Another nurse, who was also in the consulting room, and the patient, managed to stand up. The man, his face smeared white like a clown and streaked with blood, lurched towards the door, holding his bloody head with his hands and moaning.

I said to myself over and over again: Our hospital has suffered a direct hit – We've been bombed! Because the hospital stood on a hill and had walls of red brick, it must, I thought, have attracted the attention of enemy planes. I felt deeply and personally responsible for what had happened.

The pervading dingy yellow silence of the room now resounded with faint cries – 'Help!' The surface of the walls and ceiling had peeled away. What I had thought to be clouds of dust or smoke was whirling brick-dust and plaster. Neither the pneumo-thorax apparatus nor the microscope on my desk were anywhere to be seen. I felt as if I were dreaming.

I encouraged Miss Murai, saying: 'Come on, we haven't been hurt at all, by the grace of God. We must rescue the in-patients.' But privately I thought it must be all over with them – the second and third floors must have disintegrated, I thought.

We went to the door of the consulting room which faced the main stairway, and there were the in-patients coming down the steps, crying: 'Help me, doctor! Oh, help me, sir.' The stairs and the corridor were heaped with timbers, plaster, debris from the ceiling. It made walking difficult. The patients staggered down towards us, crying: 'I'm hurt! Help me!' Strangely, none seemed to have been seriously injured, only slightly wounded, with fresh blood dripping from their faces and hands.

If the bomb had actually hit the hospital, I thought, they would have been far more badly injured.

'What's happened to the second and third floors?' I cried. But all they answered was – 'Help me! Help!'

One of them said: 'Mr Yamaguchi has been buried under the debris. Help him.'

No one knew what had happened. A huge force had been released above our heads. What it was, nobody knew. Had it been several tons of bombs, or the suicidal destruction of a plane carrying a heavy bomb-load?

Dazed, I retreated into the consulting room, in which the only upright object on the rubbish-strewn floor was my desk. I went and sat on it and looked out of the window at the yard and the outside world. There was not a single pane of glass in the window, not even a frame – all had been completely blown away. Out in the yard dun-coloured smoke or dust cleared little by little. I saw figures running. Then, looking to the south-west, I was stunned. The sky was as dark as pitch, covered with dense clouds of smoke; under that blackness, over the earth, hung a yellow-brown fog. Gradually the veiled ground became visible, and the view beyond rooted me to the spot with horror.

All the buildings I could see were on fire: large ones and small ones and those with straw-thatched roofs. Further off along the valley, Urakami Church, the largest Catholic church in the east, was ablaze. The technical school, a large two-storeyed wooden building, was on fire, as were many houses and the distant ordnance factory. Electricity poles were wrapped in flame like so many pieces of kindling. Trees on the nearby hills were smoking, as were the leaves of sweet potatoes in the fields. To say that everything burned is not enough. It seemed as if the earth itself emitted fire and smoke, flames that writhed up and erupted from underground. The sky was dark, the ground was scarlet, and in between hung clouds of yellowish smoke. Three kinds of colour – black, yellow and scarlet – loomed ominously over the people, who ran about like so many ants seeking to escape. What had happened? Urakami Hospital had not been bombed – I understood that much. But that ocean of fire, that sky of smoke! It seemed like the end of the world.

I ran out into the garden. Patients who were only slightly hurt came up to me, pleading for aid.

I shouted at them: 'For heaven's sake! You're not seriously wounded!'

One patient said: 'Kawaguchi and Matsuo are trapped in their rooms! They can't move. You must help them!'

I said to myself: Yes, we must first of all rescue those seriously ill tubercular patients who've been buried under the ruins.

I looked southwards again, and the sight of Nagasaki city in a sea of flames as far as the eye could reach made me think that such destruction could only have been caused by thousands of bombers, carpet-bombing. But not a plane was to be seen or heard, although even the leaves of potatoes and carrots at my feet were scorched and smouldering. The electricity cables must have exploded underground, I thought.

And then at last I identified the destroyer – 'That's it!' I cried. 'It was the new bomb – the one used on Hiroshima!'

'Look – there's smoke coming from the third floor!'

exclaimed one of the patients, who had fled for safety into the hospital yard.

I turned about and looked up at the roof.

The hospital was built of brick and reinforced concrete, but the main roof was tiled, sloping in the Japanese style, and in the middle of the roof was another small, ridged roof, from whose end a little smoke was issuing, as if something was cooking there. Almost all the tiles had fallen off, leaving the roof timbers exposed.

That's odd, I said to myself, not heeding what I saw.

The smoke from the hospital looked just like that of a cigarette in comparison with the masses billowing above the technical school, Urakami Church, nearby houses, and the Convent of the Holy Cross, which were now blazing with great ferocity. The sky was dark, as if it were threatening to rain.

'As soon as we have some rain,' I said, 'these fires will quickly be extinguished.' So saying, I began to dash about in the confusion.

The fire in the hospital roof spread little by little. It was rather strange how the roof was the first thing in the hospital to catch fire. But the temperature at the instant the bomb exploded would have been thousands of degrees Centigrade at the epicentre and hundreds of degrees Centigrade near the hospital. Wooden buildings within 1,500 metres of the epicentre instantly caught fire. Within 1,000 metres, iron itself melted. The hospital stood 1,800 metres away from the epicentre. Probably, coming on top of the scorching heat of the sun, which had shone for more than ten days running, the blasting breath of hundreds of degrees Centigrade had dried out the hospital timbers and ignited them. The attics under the roof were wooden and used as a store-house; the fire now spread through them. Upset as I was, at first I wasn't too concerned, thinking it was only a small fire. But before long the main roof of the building was enveloped in flames.

'Doctor! Doctor!' people shouted. 'There are still many patients on the third floor!'

I went up to the third floor many times, and ran down just as often. As I rushed about like a madman, the damage sustained by the hospital became much clearer. Brother Iwanaga and Mr Noguchi, who were both fit and well, also raced up and down in the work of rescue.

'Dr Yoshioka has been badly hurt. I'm afraid she's going to die.'

That cry was heard several times, and it so discouraged me that, for a while, my feet would hardly move.

I also heard someone say: 'Brother Iwanaga is taking Dr Yoshioka to the hill opposite the hospital, carrying her on his back. Please come quickly, sir!'

Another voice cried from somewhere a bit later: 'The chief nurse has been injured, and is being taken to the hill where Dr Yoshioka is.'

Meanwhile we were carrying those patients who were seriously ill down from the third floor, even as the fire was spreading along the hospital roof. But thanks to the unselfish devotion of the nurses and the co-operation of the in-patients, we were able to bring out all the serious tubercular cases, until only two remained. Pinned under fallen beams, they could not be pulled away, despite all our efforts. At that point I came close to running away myself, to giving them up in despair. But something had to be tried to rescue them. Brother Iwanaga and Mr Noguchi brought a saw with which we cut through the beams until at last the two could be freed.

Miss Murai wept with happiness, overjoyed that no patients would now be burnt to death in the hospital.

'We have rescued every one of them!' she cried.

Ten or twenty minutes after the smoke had cleared outside, people began coming up the hill from the town below, crying out and groaning: 'Help me, help!' Those cries and groans seemed not to be made by human voices; they sounded unearthly, weird.

About ten minutes after the explosion, a big man, half-naked, holding his head between his hands, came into the yard towards me, making sounds that seemed to be dragged from the pit of his stomach.

'Got hurt, sir,' he groaned; he shivered as if he were cold. 'I'm hurt.'

I stared at him, at the strange-looking man. Then I saw it was Mr Zenjiro Tsujimoto, a market-gardener and a friendly neighbour to me and the hospital. I wondered what had happened to the robust Zenjiro.

'What's the matter with you, Tsujimoto?' I asked him, holding him in my arms.

'In the pumpkin field over there – getting pumpkins for the patients – got hurt . . .' he said, speaking brokenly and breathing feebly.

It was all he could do to keep standing. Yet it didn't occur to me that he had been seriously injured.

'Come along now,' I said. 'You are perfectly all right, I assure you. Where's your shirt? Lie down and rest somewhere where it's cool. I'll be with you in a moment.'

His head and his face were whitish; his hair was singed. It was because his eyelashes had been scorched away that he seemed so bleary-eyed. He was half-naked because his shirt had been burned from his back in a single flash. But I wasn't aware of such facts. I gazed at him as he reeled about with his head between his hands. What a change had come over this man who was stronger than a horse, whom I had last seen earlier that morning. It's as if he's been struck by lightning, I thought.

After Mr Tsujimoto came staggering up to me, another person who looked just like him wandered into the yard. Who he was and where he had come from I had no idea. 'Help me,' he said, groaning, half-naked, holding his head between his hands. He sat down, exhausted. 'Water . . . Water . . .' he whispered.

'What's the trouble? What's wrong with you? What's become of your shirt?' I demanded.

'Hot – *hot* . . . Water . . . I'm burning.' They were the only words that were articulate.

As time passed, more and more people in a similar plight came up to the hospital – ten minutes, twenty minutes, an hour after the explosion. All were of the same appearance, sounded the same. 'I'm hurt, *hurt!* I'm burning! Water!' They all moaned the same lament. I shuddered. Half-naked or stark naked, they walked with strange, slow steps, groaning from deep inside themselves as if they had travelled from the depths of hell. They looked whitish; their faces were like masks. I felt as if I were dreaming, watching pallid ghosts processing slowly in one direction – as in a dream I had once dreamt in my childhood.

These ghosts came on foot uphill towards the hospital, from the direction of the burning city and from the more easterly ordnance factory. Worker or student, girl or man, they all walked slowly and had the same mask-like face. Each one groaned and cried for help. Their cries grew in strength as the people increased in number, sounding like something from the Buddhist scriptures, re-echoing everywhere, as if the earth itself were in pain.

One victim who managed to reach the hospital yard asked me, 'Is this a hospital?' before suddenly collapsing on the ground. There were those who lay stiffly where they fell by the roadside in front of the hospital; others lay in the sweet-potato fields. Many went down to the steep valley below the hospital where a stream ran down between the hill of Motohara and the next hill. 'Water, water,' they cried. They went instinctively down to the banks of the stream, because their bodies had been scorched and their throats were parched and inflamed; they were thirsty. I didn't realize then that these were the symptoms of 'flash-burn'.

Many times I met with and separated from Brother Iwanaga as each of us toiled wherever we happened to be. Earlier, Brother Iwanaga had rescued a farmer, Mr Yamano, by sawing through the boughs of a tree that had fallen upon him in the yard. Now Brother Iwanaga said to me: 'Father Ishikawa has been hurt, some part of his head.'

After mass that morning Father Ishikawa had listened to the confessions of the Catholics, who had grown in number as the festival of the Ascension of the Virgin Mary approached. Towards eleven o'clock, he had returned to his room on the third floor to fetch a book he needed, and then hurried back to the chapel. He was passing along the corridor in the middle of the first floor when a sudden white flash filled the corridor with light; there was a great roar and he was hurled head over heels through the air, striking his head against a concrete post. But although he was in some pain, he returned to the chapel, where such thick yellowish smoke and white dust hung over the broken furnishings he could hardly tell where he was. Not a person was in sight. It was there that Brother Iwanaga found him. When I saw Father Ishikawa, lying down in a shaded part of the yard, one of his eyes had swollen purple. Fortunately, the bleeding from his injured head had stopped.

Black smoke was now billowing up from the hospital roof. By the time the rescue of all the patients had been achieved, the top floor was enveloped in smoke and the fire in the roof burned furiously.

'Ah, the X-ray machines will be burnt!' I exclaimed, in spite of myself.

Miss Murai and some of the patients took up my cry. We had thought the fire would be held back by the ceiling of the third floor, which was made of thick concrete. But when a lift was installed in the hospital, a shaft three metres square had been built in the middle of the building, from the basement to the third floor. Into that shaft burning timbers now fell, crashing down into the basement, where three of the most up-to-date X-ray machines were stored, Half of the best X-ray machines in Nagasaki city were, in fact, in the care of our hospital, thought to be the safest place for them. In the transformer of every X-ray machine there was a quantity of insulation oil. The transformers blew up in the intense heat and the machines caught fire.

'There they go,' I murmured sadly.

The sun shone dim and reddish through the south-westerly veil of black smoke over the city. It seemed a long time since the explosion. I thought it must now be evening, but only three hours had passed. It was just two o'clock and still broad daylight. I had completely lost any sense of time. And I was not alone – it was a timeless day for everyone. It seemed as if years had passed, maybe because so many houses continued to burn and because so many badly injured people appeared one after another before my eyes. On the other hand, it felt as if only a moment had passed, because all around us people and houses and fields seemed unbelievably changed.

Not every part of the hospital was beset with fire. Brother Iwanaga and I went in and out of the building many times, for I still had to make sure that all the patients and staff were safe and to check for any dead or wounded. We couldn't imagine how everything had looked before the explosion – rooms, corridors, furniture and the rest. The ceilings had all been stripped of their planks and plaster, the walls of their panelling. Desks, cupboards, bookcases, instrument boxes, medicine chests had all been overturned. Whatever had escaped the onslaught had been emptied – drawers were open and their contents lost. I never found out what happened to the contents of my desk. A gigantic wind had struck the hospital, shattered the windows, torn through every room, swept along the corridors and ravaged everything inside the hospital with a force beyond human comprehension.

It is the mark of the devil, I thought – of the devil's claw.

Clothes which the chief nurse and the nurses once wore were lying about as if torn off their bodies. The mere sight of them made me afraid that they had been killed. But in fact it was only that the door of the wardrobe in the room had been torn off and the clothing inside blown out.

I noticed other unusual facts. The ceremonial robes usually kept by the altar in the chapel were discovered far away, torn to shreds. The books from the library were scattered in unimaginable places. As for my own office, where many important records and instruments were kept – the whole room had been wrecked. I couldn't find a thing. The clothes I had put on that morning were all that remained of my possessions. My shoes were straw sandals. I felt uneasy about them. There had been three pairs of fine leather shoes in my room, but I couldn't find any of them, hard as I tried. In the end I ran about for several days with only straw sandals on my feet. My soles must have been infected by radioactivity but I was unaware of the danger.

In the afternoon a change was noticeable in the appearance of the injured people who came up to the hospital. The crowd of ghosts which had looked whitish in the morning were now burned black. Their hair was burnt; their skin, which was charred and blackened, blistered and peeled. Such were those who now came toiling up to the hospital yard and fell there weakly.

'Are you a doctor? Please, if you wouldn't mind, could you examine me?' So said a young man.

'Cheer up!' I said. It was all I could say.

He died in the night. He must have been one of the many medical students who were injured down at the medical college. His politeness and then his poor blackened body lying dead on the concrete are things I shall never forget.

Neither shall I ever forget the countenance of a father who came stumbling up to me, carrying his baby in his arms. The father begged me to try to do something for his baby. I examined the child. The wall of its stomach had been sliced open and part of its intestines protruded. The baby's face was purple. No pulse could be felt.

I said, 'It's hopeless.'

The father, laying his baby on the grass in the yard, sat down exhausted and said: 'Would you do what you can?'

I shook my head. There was nothing that I could do. I had neither medical instruments nor medicine. He wouldn't leave the child.

The brick wall around the hospital was in ruins, blown down by the blast. The wall, hundreds of metres long, had like everything else been crushed by a devilish force. A child who had been playing near the wall lay beneath it on the road, his skull broken like a pomegranate.

Gradually the severity of cases increased: a person whose body had been riven by pieces of glass or splinters blown by the colossal force of the blast; a person who had been battered by heavy objects falling upon him; a person who had been blown off his feet and thrown against something hard – people with such serious injuries appeared one after the other. None of them, however, knew how they had come to be so badly injured. They all trembled with fear and pain, each thinking that the bomb had fallen only on them.

The southern sky was still dark. After the strange clouds caused by the explosion had thinned, smoke from the burning city obscured the sky. Through it the sun shone redly now and again. Sometimes the sound of aeroplane engines could be heard overhead – not Japanese planes, but those of the enemy. Because of the smoke, we couldn't see them. The droning sound of the enemy's low-altitude flights was repeated several times, and every time the sound was heard the injured trembled, fled and hid, fearing that another bomb would be dropped or that machine-gun fire would sweep through them. Whenever the sound of the engines was heard we stopped whatever we were doing and hid, thinking the enemy were about to attack again with even greater ferocity.

I thought it unlikely, however, that they would drop any more bombs on us after the new bomb. Possibly the planes were flying over on reconnaissance, checking on the damage the bomb had done. But the injured who ran about below, seeking to survive any further attack, and the people caring

for the injured could not reason as objectively as I. The throb
of engines made all of us tremble and cower, and the hateful
sound continued off and on, endlessly, as it would do even
through the night, droning above the city where the black
smoke hung in heavy clouds.

'Isn't all this destruction enough?' I cried, and bit my lip
in mortification.

The atomic explosion at Nagasaki killed an estimated 90,000
people, including those who died later of radiation sickness. Japan
surrendered the next day.

ANNOUNCING THE END OF THE SECOND WORLD WAR, 10 August 1945

Maxine Andrews

Maxine Andrews was one of the Andrews Sisters, a popular singing
group during the 1940s. The Sisters entertained troops all over the
world, including in August 1945 a glum group of GIs in Italy who
were about to be shipped out to fight in the Far East.

Our last date was in Naples. We were billeted in Caserta,
eighteen miles away. We did all our shows at repo depots,
where all the guys were being shipped out. We had one more
show to do. It was loaded with about eight thousand of the
most unhappy-looking audience you'd ever seen. They were
hanging from the rafters. All these fellas were being shipped
out to the South Pacific. They hadn't been home for four
years, and it was just their bad luck. We were trying to get
them into good spirits.

We were pretty well through with the show when I heard
someone offstage calling me: 'Pssst. Pssst.' Patty was doing a

little scene with Arthur Treacher. The soldier said to me, 'I have a very important message for Patty to tell the audience.' I started to laugh, because they were always playing tricks on us. He said, 'I'm not kidding. It's from the CO.' I said, 'I can't do it in the middle of the show.' He said, 'You're gonna get me in trouble.' So I took the piece of paper. I didn't read it. I walked out on the stage, saying to myself I'm gonna get in trouble with Patty, with Arthur, with the CO. I waited until the skit was over. Patty said, 'Stop your kidding. We can't read that here. We've got to finish the show.' I shoved the note at her. She finally said, 'All right, I'll go along with the gag.'

So she said to the fellas, 'Look, it's a big joke up here. I have a note supposedly from the CO.' Without reading it first, she read it out loud. It announced the end of the war with Japan. There wasn't a sound in the whole auditorium. She looked at it again. She looked at me. It was serious. So she said, 'No, fellas, this is from the CO. This is an announcement that the war is over, so you don't have to go.' With that, she started to cry. Laverne and I were crying. Still there was no reaction from the guys. So she said it again: 'This is the end, this is the end.'

All of a sudden, all hell broke loose. They yelled and screamed. We saw a pair of pants and a shirt come down from above. Following it was a body. He came down and fell on the guys sitting downstairs. Patty said, 'You want to go out and get drunk? Or you want to see the show?' 'No, no, no, we want to see the rest of the show.' We made it very short.

We got into the jeep, and all of a sudden it hit us. Oh heavens, if this is a joke, they're gonna tar and feather us. We'll have to swim all the way back to the States. We suffered until we got to Caserta. They reassured us that the announcement was true.

A few years ago, Patty was working someplace in Cleveland. She checked into the hotel and was in the elevator.

This elevator man said, 'Don't you remember me?' He was a short, bald-headed guy. She said, 'Should I?' He said, 'Yeah, remember Naples? Remember the guy that fell off the rafter? That was me.'

Part V

Our Times
1946–94

EXECUTION OF NAZI WAR CRIMINALS, NUREMBERG, 16 October 1946

Kingsbury Smith

The trials held by the International Military Tribunal at Nuremberg found twelve of the surviving leaders of Nazi Germany guilty of crimes against humanity. The twelve, who included Martin Bormann, tried *in absentia*, were sentenced to death by hanging. Kingsbury Smith represented the American press at the hangings.

Hermann Wilhelm Göring cheated the gallows of Allied justice by committing suicide in his prison cell shortly before the ten other condemned Nazi leaders were hanged in Nuremberg gaol. He swallowed cyanide he had concealed in a copper cartridge shell, while lying on a cot in his cell.

The one-time Number Two man in the Nazi hierarchy was dead two hours before he was scheduled to have been dropped through the trapdoor of a gallows erected in a small, brightly lighted gymnasium in the gaol yard, thirty-five yards from the cell block where he spent his last days of ignominy.

Joachim von Ribbentrop, foreign minister in the ill-starred regime of Adolf Hitler, took Göring's place as first to the scaffold.

Last to depart this life in a total span of just about two hours was Arthur Seyss-Inquart, former *Gauleiter* of Holland and Austria.

In between these two once-powerful leaders, the gallows claimed, in the order named, Field Marshal Wilhelm Keitel; Ernst Kaltenbrunner, once head of the Nazis' security police; Alfred Rosenberg, arch-priest of Nazi culture in foreign lands; Hans Frank, *Gauleiter* of Poland; Wilhelm Frick, Nazi minister of the interior; Fritz Sauckel, boss of slave labour; Colonel General Alfred Jodl; and Julius Streicher, who bossed the anti-Semitism drive of the Hitler Reich.

As they went to the gallows, most of the ten endeavoured to show bravery. Some were defiant and some were resigned and some begged the Almighty for mercy.

All except Rosenberg made brief, last-minute statements on the scaffold. But the only one to make any reference to Hitler or the Nazi ideology in his final moments was Julius Streicher.

Three black-painted wooden scaffolds stood inside the gymnasium, a room approximately 33 feet wide by 80 feet long with plaster walls in which cracks showed. The gymnasium had been used only three days before by the American security guards for a basketball game. Two gallows were used alternately. The third was a spare for use if needed. The men were hanged one at a time, but to get the executions over with quickly, the military police would bring in a man while the prisoner who preceded him still was dangling at the end of the rope.

The ten once great men in Hitler's Reich that was to have lasted for a thousand years walked up thirteen wooden steps to a platform eight feet high which also was eight feet square.

Ropes were suspended from a crossbeam supported on two posts. A new one was used for each man.

When the trap was sprung, the victim dropped from sight in the interior of the scaffolding. The bottom of it was boarded up with wood on three sides and shielded by a dark canvas curtain on the fourth, so that no one saw the death struggles of the men dangling with broken necks.

Von Ribbentrop entered the execution chamber at 1.11 a.m. Nuremberg time. He was stopped immediately inside the door by two Army sergeants who closed in on each side of him and held his arms, while another sergeant who had followed him in removed manacles from his hands and replaced them with a leather strap.

It was planned originally to permit the condemned men to walk from their cells to the execution chamber with their hands free, but all were manacled immediately following Göring's suicide.

Von Ribbentrop was able to maintain his apparent stoicism to the last. He walked steadily toward the scaffold between his two guards, but he did not answer at first when an officer standing at the foot of the gallows went through the formality of asking his name. When the query was repeated he almost shouted, 'Joachim von Ribbentrop!' and then mounted the steps without any sign of hesitation.

When he was turned around on the platform to face the witnesses, he seemed to clench his teeth and raise his head with the old arrogance. When asked whether he had any final message he said, 'God protect Germany,' in German, and then added, 'May I say something else?'

The interpreter nodded and the former diplomatic wizard of Nazidom spoke his last words in loud, firm tones: 'My last wish is that Germany realize its entity and that an understanding be reached between the East and the West. I wish peace to the world.'

As the black hood was placed in position on his head, von Ribbentrop looked straight ahead.

Then the hangman adjusted the rope, pulled the lever, and von Ribbentrop slipped away to his fate.

Field Marshal Keitel, who was immediately behind von Ribbentrop in the order of executions, was the first military leader to be executed under the new concept of international law – the principle that professional soldiers cannot escape punishment for waging aggressive wars and permitting crimes against humanity with the claim they were dutifully carrying out orders of superiors.

Keitel entered the chamber two minutes after the trap had dropped beneath von Ribbentrop, while the latter still was at the end of his rope. But von Ribbentrop's body was concealed inside the first scaffold; all that could be seen was the taut rope.

Keitel did not appear as tense as von Ribbentrop. He held his head high while his hands were being tied and walked erect toward the gallows with a military bearing. When asked his name he responded loudly and mounted the gallows as he might have mounted a reviewing stand to take a salute from German armies.

He certainly did not appear to need the help of guards who walked alongside, holding his arms. When he turned around atop the platform he looked over the crowd with the iron-jawed haughtiness of a proud Prussian officer. His last words, uttered in a full, clear voice, were translated as 'I call on God Almighty to have mercy on the German people. More than 2 million German soldiers went to their death for the fatherland before me. I follow now my sons – all for Germany.'

After his black-booted, uniformed body plunged through the trap, witnesses agreed Keitel had showed more courage on the scaffold than in the courtroom, where he had tried to shift his guilt upon the ghost of Hitler, claiming that all was the Führer's fault and that he merely carried out orders and had no responsibility.

With both von Ribbentrop and Keitel hanging at the end

of their ropes there was a pause in the proceedings. The American colonel directing the executions asked the American general representing the United States on the Allied Control Commission if those present could smoke. An affirmative answer brought cigarettes into the hands of almost every one of the thirty-odd persons present. Officers and GIs walked around nervously or spoke a few words to one another in hushed voices while Allied correspondents scribbled furiously their notes on this historic though ghastly event.

In a few minutes an American army doctor accompanied by a Russian army doctor and both carrying stethoscopes walked to the first scaffold, lifted the curtain and disappeared within.

They emerged at 1.30 a.m. and spoke to an American colonel. The colonel swung around and facing official witnesses snapped to attention to say, 'The man is dead.'

Two GIs quickly appeared with a stretcher which was carried up and lifted into the interior of the scaffold. The hangman mounted the gallows steps, took a large commando-type knife out of a sheath strapped to his side and cut the rope.

Von Ribbentrop's limp body with the black hood still over his head was removed to the far end of the room and placed behind a black canvas curtain. This all had taken less than ten minutes.

The directing colonel turned to the witnesses and said, 'Cigarettes out, please, gentlemen.' Another colonel went out the door and over to the condemned block to fetch the next man. This was Ernst Kaltenbrunner. He entered the execution chamber at 1.36 a.m., wearing a sweater beneath his blue double-breasted coat. With his lean haggard face furrowed by old duelling scars, this terrible successor to Reinhard Heydrich had a frightening look as he glanced around the room.

He wet his lips apparently in nervousness as he turned to

mount the gallows, but he walked steadily. He answered his name in a calm, low voice. When he turned around on the gallows platform he first faced a United States Army Roman Catholic chaplain wearing a Franciscan habit. When Kaltenbrunner was invited to make a last statement, he said, 'I have loved my German people and my fatherland with a warm heart. I have done my duty by the laws of my people and I am sorry my people were led this time by men who were not soldiers and that crimes were committed of which I had no knowledge.'

This was the man, one of whose agents – a man named Rudolf Hoess – confessed at a trial that under Kaltenbrunner's orders he gassed 3 million human beings at the Auschwitz concentration camp!

As the black hood was raised over his head Kaltenbrunner, still speaking in a low voice, used a German phrase which translated means, 'Germany, good luck.'

His trap was sprung at 1.39 a.m.

Field Marshal Keitel was pronounced dead at 1.44 a.m. and three minutes later guards had removed his body. The scaffold was made ready for Alfred Rosenberg.

Rosenberg was dull and sunken-cheeked as he looked around the court. His complexion was pasty-brown, but he did not appear nervous and walked with a steady step to and up the gallows.

Apart from giving his name and replying 'no' to a question as to whether he had anything to say, he did not utter a word. Despite his avowed atheism he was accompanied by a Protestant chaplain who followed him to the gallows and stood beside him praying.

Rosenberg looked at the chaplain once, expressionless. Ninety seconds after he was swinging from the end of a hangman's rope. His was the swiftest execution of the ten.

There was a brief lull in the proceedings until Kaltenbrunner was pronounced dead at 1.52 a.m.

Hans Frank was next in the parade of death. He was the

only one of the condemned to enter the chamber with a smile on his countenance.

Although nervous and swallowing frequently, this man, who was converted to Roman Catholicism after his arrest, gave the appearance of being relieved at the prospect of atoning for his evil deeds.

He answered to his name quietly and when asked for any last statement, he replied in a low voice that was almost a whisper, 'I am thankful for the kind treatment during my captivity and I ask God to accept me with mercy.'

Frank closed his eyes and swallowed as the black hood went over his head.

The sixth man to leave his prison cell and walk with handcuffed wrists to the death house was 69-year-old Wilhelm Frick. He entered the execution chamber at 2.05 a.m., six minutes after Rosenberg had been pronounced dead. He seemed the least steady of any so far and stumbled on the thirteenth step of the gallows. His only words were, 'Long live eternal Germany,' before he was hooded and dropped through the trap.

Julius Streicher made his melodramatic appearance at 2.12 a.m.

While his manacles were being removed and his hands bound, this ugly, dwarfish little man, wearing a threadbare suit and a well-worn bluish shirt buttoned to the neck but without a tie (he was notorious during his days of power for his flashy dress), glanced at the three wooden scaffolds rising up menacingly in front of him. Then he glared around the room, his eyes resting momentarily upon the small group of witnesses. By this time, his hands were tied securely behind his back. Two guards, one on each arm, directed him to Number One gallows on the left of the entrance. He walked steadily the six feet to the first wooden step but his face was twitching.

As the guards stopped him at the bottom of the steps for identification formality he uttered his piercing scream: 'Heil Hitler!'

The shriek sent a shiver down my back.

As its echo died away an American colonel standing by the steps said sharply, 'Ask the man his name.' In response to the interpreter's query Streicher shouted, 'You know my name well.'

The interpreter repeated his request and the condemned man yelled, 'Julius Streicher.'

As he reached the platform, Streicher cried out, 'Now it goes to God.' He was pushed the last two steps to the mortal spot beneath the hangman's rope. The rope was being held back against a wooden rail by the hangman.

Streicher was swung around to face the witnesses and glared at them. Suddenly he screamed, *'Purim Fest 1946.'* [Purim is a Jewish holiday celebrated in the spring, commemorating the execution of Haman, ancient persecutor of the Jews described in the Old Testament.]

The American officer standing at the scaffold said, 'Ask the man if he has any last words.'

When the interpreter had translated, Streicher shouted, 'The Bolsheviks will hang you one day.'

When the black hood was raised over his head, Streicher said, 'I am with God.'

As it was being adjusted, Streicher's muffled voice could be heard to say, 'Adele, my dear wife.'

At that instant the trap opened with a loud bang. He went down kicking. When the rope snapped taut with the body swinging wildly, groans could be heard from within the concealed interior of the scaffold. Finally, the hangman, who had descended from the gallows platform, lifted the black canvas curtain and went inside. Something happened that put a stop to the groans and brought the rope to a standstill. After it was over I was not in a mood to ask what he did, but I assume that he grabbed the swinging body and pulled down on it. We were all of the opinion that Streicher had strangled.

Then, following removal of the corpse of Frick, who had

been pronounced dead at 2.20 a.m., Fritz Sauckel was brought face to face with his doom.

Wearing a sweater with no coat and looking wild-eyed, Sauckel proved to be the most defiant of any except Streicher.

Here was the man who put millions into bondage on a scale unknown since the pre-Christian era. Gazing around the room from the gallows platform he suddenly screamed, 'I am dying innocent. The sentence is wrong. God protect Germany and make Germany great again. Long live Germany! God protect my family.'

The trap was sprung at 2.26 a.m. and, as in the case of Streicher, there was a loud groan from the gallows pit as the noose snapped tightly under the weight of his body.

Ninth in the procession of death was Alfred Jodl. With the black coat-collar of his *Wehrmacht* uniform half turned up at the back as though hurriedly put on, Jodl entered the dismal death house with obvious signs of nervousness. He wet his lips constantly and his features were drawn and haggard as he walked, not nearly so steady as Keitel, up the gallows steps. Yet his voice was calm when he uttered his last six words on earth: 'My greetings to you, my Germany.'

At 2.34 a.m. Jodl plunged into the black hole of the scaffold. He and Sauckel hung together until the latter was pronounced dead six minutes later and removed.

The Czechoslovak-born Seyss-Inquart, whom Hitler had made ruler of Holland and Austria, was the last actor to make his appearance in this unparalleled scene. He entered the chamber at 2.38 ½ a.m., wearing glasses which made his face an easily remembered caricature.

He looked around with noticeable signs of unsteadiness as he limped on his left clubfoot to the gallows. He mounted the steps slowly, with guards helping him.

When he spoke his last words his voice was low but intense. He said, 'I hope that this execution is the last act of the tragedy of the Second World War and that the lesson taken from this world war will be that peace and understanding should exist between peoples. I believe in Germany.'

He dropped to death at 2.45 a.m.

With the bodies of Jodl and Seyss-Inquart still hanging, awaiting formal pronouncement of death, the gymnasium doors opened again and guards entered carrying Göring's body on a stretcher.

He had succeeded in wrecking plans of the Allied Control Council to have him lead the parade of condemned Nazi chieftains to their death. But the council's representatives were determined that Göring at least would take his place as a dead man beneath the shadow of the scaffold.

The guards carrying the stretcher set it down between the first and second gallows. Göring's big bare feet stuck out from under the bottom end of a khaki-coloured United States Army blanket. One blue-silk-clad arm was hanging over the side.

The colonel in charge of the proceedings ordered the blanket removed so that witnesses and Allied correspondents could see for themselves that Göring was definitely dead. The Army did not want any legend to develop that Göring had managed to escape.

As the blanket came off it revealed Göring clad in black silk pyjamas with a blue jacket shirt over them, and this was soaking wet, apparently the result of efforts by prison doctors to revive him.

The face of this twentieth-century freebooting political racketeer was still contorted with the pain of his last agonizing moments and his final gesture of defiance.

They covered him up quickly and this Nazi warlord, who like a character out of the days of the Borgias, had wallowed in blood and beauty, passed behind a canvas curtain into the black pages of history.

ISRAEL DECLARES INDEPENDENCE, TEL AVIV, 14 May 1948

James Cameron

The Jews had been displaced from their homeland in Palestine in the second century AD by the Romans. Nearly two thousand years later, following Nazi persecution, many Jews began to emigrate to their ancient homeland, which caused friction with the Arab peoples who had since settled there. In 1947 the United Nations proposed that Palestine should be divided into Jewish and Arab states, with Jerusalem as a neutral zone. This plan was rejected by the Arabs but accepted by the Jews who, in May 1948, proclaimed the independent state of Israel.

In Rothschild Boulevard in the middle of Tel-Aviv stood the Museum Hall, a building as undistinguished as all others in the town; it had once been the home of Meir Dizengoff, first Mayor of Tel-Aviv. It was to be undistinguished no longer.

Outside the hall was drawn up a guard of honour of cadets from the Jewish Officers' School. A strong detachment of Haganah military police meticulously scrutinised the credentials of every soul entering up the steps from the Boulevard. In the steaming heat of that afternoon the atmosphere of crisis was almost tangibly neurotic. The Yishuv had waited six hundred generations for this day; Jewry had trod a long hard road from Babylon and Pharaoh's Egypt and the deserts and the ghettos of the world; what had seemed endless was now at last to have an end. The moment could not and must not be wrecked now by a chance intruding enemy. Security was tense. Every arrival passed the cordons of guards who were men from Berlin and London and Cracow and South Africa and Iraq and Egypt, from the death-camps of Germany and Poland, from the farms of Galilee. No museum had ever been harder to enter.

The hall was crowded to suffocation, the heat magnified by the film-camera lights, the shadows broken by the flashbulbs. Above it all, against the blue and white hangings, looked down the portrait of the sombre-bearded Viennese journalist Theodor Herzl, who had dreamed it all how long ago? Just over fifty years.

Below the portrait of Herzl sat the eleven of the National Administration and the secretary. At the centre table sat the fourteen members of the National Council. Around them in a semi-circle were the Rabbis, Mayors, elders of the Yishuv, officers of the Haganah command, councillors, fund-raisers, the Zionist General Council. But from Jerusalem none could come, nor from Haifa and the north. Tel-Aviv was still an enclave in a hostile land.

At exactly four o'clock David Ben-Gurion, wearing a necktie for the only time in living memory, rapped his gavel on the table. The whole hall rose to its feet. The Philharmonic Orchestra concealed upstairs drew up its bows – but they were too late, already the crowd was singing the 'Hatikvah'.

It faded out, and Ben-Gurion said: 'The land of Israel was the birthplace of the Jewish people. Here their spiritual, religious and national identity was formed. In their exile from the land of Israel the Jews remained faithful to it in all the countries of their dispersal, never ceasing to hope and pray for the restoration of their national freedom.'

His white woolly halo danced, his face glistened in the heat, his eloquence mounted to a Hebraic fervour; he was speaking for Joshua and David, Nehemiah and Ezra the Writer, for the fugitives from the Crusaders and Saladin and Spain, for the survivors of Dachau and Ravensbruck, for the sabra Yishuv who had drained the Hulah swamps, the founders of Rehovot, the builders of Tel-Aviv itself, for the immigrant bus-drivers and the waiters in the cafés of Dizengoff Square, and those who were yet to come.

'Therefore by virtue of the natural and historic right of the

Jewish people to be a nation as other nations, and of the Resolution of the General Assembly of the United Nations, we hereby proclaim the establishment of the Jewish nation in Palestine, to be called the Medinat Yisrael: the State of Israel.'

It was far from over; he had now to read the Articles arising from the declaration, the setting up of provisional authorities, the principles of 'social and political equality of all citizens distinguishing not between religions, races or sexes, providing freedom of religion, conscience, education, language and culture, the safeguarding of the Holy Places of all faiths.

'We appeal to the United Nations for help to the Jewish people in building their State, and to admit Israel into the family of nations. We offer only peace and friendship to all neighbouring states and people . . .'

And finally: 'With trust in God, we set our hand to this declaration, at this session of the Provisional State Council, on the soil of the Homeland, in the city of Tel-Aviv, on this Sabbath eve, the fifth of Iyar 5708, the fourteenth day of May 1948.'

It had taken exactly thirty-two minutes. Plus, of course, 2,000 years.

MARILYN MONROE IN HOLLYWOOD, 1950

Arthur Miller

The playwright – and future husband of Marilyn Monroe – describes his first meeting with the movie icon of the century.

A few days earlier I had gone to the Twentieth Century Fox studio with Kazan, who was under contract there and had many friends working on the sound stages. One of them, his former film editor, was now directing *As Young As You Feel*, a comedy with my father's *bête noire* Monty Woolley and, in a bit part, Marilyn. Moviemaking was still an exotic and fantastic affair for me, and full of mysteries. We had just arrived on a nightclub set when Marilyn, in a black open-work lace dress, was directed to walk across the floor, attracting the worn gaze of the bearded Woolley. She was being shot from the rear to set off the swivelling of her hips, a motion fluid enough to seem comic. It was, in fact, her natural walk: her footprints on a beach would be in a straight line, the heel descending exactly before the last toeprint, throwing her pelvis into motion.

When the shot was finished she came over to Kazan, who had met her with Hyde on another visit some time before. From where I stood, yards away, I saw her in profile against a white light, with her hair coiled atop her head; she was weeping under a veil of black lace that she lifted now and then to dab her eyes. When we shook hands the shock of her body's motion sped through me, a sensation at odds with her sadness amid all this glamour and technology and the busy confusion of a new shot being set up. She had been weeping, she would explain later, while telling Kazan that Hyde had died calling her name in a hospital room she had been forbidden by his family to enter. She had heard him from the corridor, and had left, as always, alone.

THE KOREAN WAR: THE STAND OF THE GLOSTERS AT IMJIN RIVER 23 April 1951

Anthony Farrar-Hockley

The Communist regime of North Korea launched a major offensive in the Korean War on 22 April 1951, breaking through the line held by the United Nations west of Chungpyong Reservoir. The situation for the UN was saved only by the stand of the

Gloucestershire Regiment at Imjin River against a much larger enemy force, consisting mainly of Chinese Communist troops. Although the Glosters were defeated, their action broke one arm of the Korean advance. Anthony Farrar-Hockley was a junior officer with the Glosters.

Below John's trenches on the Castle Site, a tin can holding stones is rattling; another sounds close by. The watchers, listeners all, respond without a sound to this first warning. The barbed wire rattles, barb scrapes barb and locks; the tin can sound again. A whispered word and all safety catches are released. Here and there, the split pins of grenades are eased across the cast-iron shoulders.

A faint, incomprehensible sound is heard in the night; the air is ruffled lightly; an object falls near, by a slit trench, smoking. Less than two seconds pass in which the occupants regard it, understand its nature, duck and take cover as it explodes. This is the first grenade: the first of many.

Echoing now, the hill is lit with flame that flickers from above and below. Mortars begin to sound down near the Imjin and the call is taken up by those that lie to the south behind C Company. Slowly, like a fire, the flames spread east and west around Castle Hill; and east again across the village of Choksong, as the enemy from Gloster Crossing, tardily launched at last, meets and is repulsed by D Company.

Now, almost hand to hand, the Chinese and British soldiers meet. Figures leap up from the attacking force, run forward to new cover and resume their fire upon the men of the defence who, coolly enough, return their fire, as targets come to view, as the attackers close with them. Occasionally an individual climax may be reached in an encounter between two men when, only a few feet apart, each waits to catch the other unawares, sees a target, fires, and leaps across to follow his advantage.

And now, to the defenders' aid, the carefully planned

defensive fire is summoned. The Vickers guns cut across the cliffs and slopes by which the Chinese forces climb to the attack. Long bursts of fire – ten, twenty, thirty, forty rounds – are fired and fired again: the water in the cooling jackets warms, the ground is littered with spent cases. The mortars and the gunners drop their high explosive in amongst the crowded ranks that press on to the hill slopes from the river crossings.

Such are the enemy's losses that now and then there is a brief respite for the defence as the attackers are withdrawn for reinforcement. The weight of defensive fire is so great that the enemy has realized he must concentrate his strength in one main thrust up to each hilltop. As the night wanes, fresh hundreds are committed to this task, and the tired defenders, much depleted, face yet one more assault.

Mike commands D Company – Lakri is fuming in Japan, moving heaven and earth to get a plane to bring him back from leave. Victors of their first encounters, D Company are sadly weakened by the ceaseless blows rained on them. One of Mike's platoons has been withdrawn right to the hilltop and they form a close defensive ring about the high ridge line which constitutes the vital ground of the position. Ever and again by weight of small-arms fire, by sorties, and as a result of many concentrations fired by mortars and guns, the assault waves are forced back. But still they reappear. For every casualty suffered by the enemy, two, three, four more Chinese will appear to take his place. Yet D Company is holding its ground.

From Castle Hill, the news is grave. John's platoon, now decimated, has been withdrawn by Pat before they are over-run completely. Their officer dead, so many others of their comrades dead or wounded, they go back to Phil's platoon position where they wait for dawn.

The Castle Site, the highest point of our defences forward, is taken after six hours fighting.

The dawn breaks. A pale, April sun is rising in the sky. Take any group of trenches here upon these two main hill positions looking north across the river. See, here, the weapon pits in which the defenders stand: unshaven, wind-burned faces streaked with black powder, filthy with sweat and dust from their exertions, look towards their enemy with eyes red from fatigue and sleeplessness; grim faces, yet not too grim that they refuse to smile when someone cracks a joke about the sunrise. Here, round the weapons smeared with burnt cordite, lie the few pathetic remnants of the wounded, since removed: cap comforters; a boot; some cigarettes half-soaked with blood; a photograph of two small girls; two keys; a broken pencil stub. The men lounge quietly in their positions, waiting for the brief respite to end.

'They're coming back, Ted.'

A shot is fired, a scattered burst follows it. The sergeant calls an order to the mortar group. Already they can hear the shouting and see, here and there, the figures moving out from behind cover as their machine-guns pour fire from the newly occupied Castle Site. Bullets fly back and forth; overhead, almost lazily, grenades are being exchanged on either side; man meets man; hand meets hand. This tiny corner of the battle that is raging along the whole front, blazes up and up into extreme heat, reaches a climax and dies away to nothingness – another little lull, another breathing space.

Phil is called to the telephone at this moment; Pat's voice sounds in his ear.

'Phil, at the present rate of casualties we can't hold on unless we get the Castle Site back. Their machine-guns up there completely dominate your platoon and most of Terry's. We shall never stop their advance until we hold that ground again.'

Phil looks over the edge of the trench at the Castle Site, two hundred yards away, as Pat continues talking, giving him the instructions for the counter attack. They talk for a minute or so; there is not much more to be said when an instruction is given to assault with a handful of tired men across open ground. Everyone knows it is vital: everyone knows it is appallingly dangerous. The only details to be fixed are the arrangements for supporting fire; and, though A Company's Gunners are dead, Ronnie will support them from D Company's hill. Behind, the machine-gunners will ensure that they are not engaged from the open eastern flank. Phil gathers his tiny assault party together.

It is time, they rise from the ground and move forward up to the barbed wire that once protected the rear of John's platoon. Already two men are hit and Papworth, the Medical Corporal, is attending to them. They are through the wire safely – safely! – when the machine-gun in the bunker begins to fire. Phil is badly wounded: he drops to the ground. They drag him back through the wire somehow and seek what little cover there is as it creeps across their front. The machine-gun stops, content now it has driven them back; waiting for a better target when they move into the open again.

'It's all right, sir,' says someone to Phil. 'The Medical Corporal's been sent for. He'll be here any minute.'

Phil raises himself from the ground, rests on a friendly shoulder, then climbs by a great effort on to one knee.

'We must take the Castle Site,' he says; and gets up to take it.

The others beg him to wait until his wounds are tended. One man places a hand on his side.

'Just wait until Papworth has seen you, sir – '

But Phil has gone: gone to the wire, gone through the wire, gone towards the bunker. The others come out behind him, their eyes all on him. And suddenly it seems as if, for a few breathless moments, the whole of the remainder of that field of battle is still and silent, watching amazed, the lone figure that runs so painfully forward to the bunker holding the approach to the Castle Site: one tiny figure, throwing grenades, firing a pistol, set to take Castle Hill.

Perhaps he will make it – in spite of his wounds, in spite of the odds – perhaps this act of supreme gallantry may, by its sheer audacity, succeed. But the machine-gun in the bunker fires directly into him: he staggers, falls, is dead instantly; the grenade he threw a second before his death explodes after it in the mouth of the bunker. The machine-gun does not fire on three of Phil's platoon who run forward to pick him up; it does not fire again through the battle: it is destroyed; the muzzle blown away, the crew dead.

Before dawn, the Battalion Command Post had moved up the hill to the ridge between Guido's platoon and Paul's company headquarters. From here, in a bunker constructed under RSM Hobbs's supervision some days before, the Colonel could overlook the battle on the two hill positions north of us. The desperate nature of the struggle was manifest before the morning sun rose. By night, the calls for fire support, each fresh report from A or D Company Headquarters, and the Gunner wireless links had made it all too clear that this attack was in strength. If this was feinting, it was a costly, realistic feint!

Just after dawn, Walters, at his wireless, said that Pat wanted me on the set. I sat down on the reverse slope of the hill behind the bunker and spoke into the handset. Pat replied:

'I'm afraid we've lost Castle Site. I am mounting a counter-attack now but I want to know whether to expect to stay here indefinitely or not. If I am to stay on, I must be reinforced as my numbers are getting very low.'

I told him to wait and went back into the bunker. The Colonel was standing in the Observation Post at the far end. I told him what Pat had said and asked what he intended to do. He looked through his glasses at D Company's hill and then said:

'I'll talk to him myself.'

We both went back to the wireless set. I stood watching the Colonel as he spoke to Pat, the distant crackle of rifle and light-machine-gun fire in my ears, and the long tack-tack-tack of the Vickers mingling with the hollow boom of the mortars firing from just below us. The Colonel had stopped talking; from the headset came the buzz of Pat's voice. Then the Colonel replied. He said:

'You will stay there at all costs until further notice.'

At all costs.

Pat knew what that order meant, and I knew – and the Colonel knew. As he got up I saw that he was pale and that his hand shook a little as he relit his pipe.

I watched the Colonel go back to the bunker as I put on the headset to speak to Pat again. The next half-hour would tell how the day would go for us.

There were two questions in the Colonel's mind as he stood at the open end of the bunker, viewing the action fought by his two forward companies: would the Chinese continue to press their attack in daylight with the threat of intervention by our aircraft; and, secondly, how long would it be before the Chinese discovered that both our flanks were completely open – that the ROKs were two and a half miles to the west, the Fifth Fusiliers two to the east – and encircle us? Yet, whatever the answer to these questions, his orders were to hold the road between Choksong and Solma-ri. Very well, the Battalion would hold it. And the Battalion would remain disposed as at present just as long as each sub-unit retained its integrity; for our present disposition was un-questionably well-suited to fighting an action designed to hold the road firmly.

I began talking to Pat again, discussing the prospect of reinforcements, and telling him that his ammunition repla-cement was already going forward in Oxford carriers under Henry's supervision. We spoke only very briefly and he ended by saying:

'Don't worry about us; we'll be all right.'

I said: 'Good luck.'

I did not speak to Pat again; he was killed a quarter of an hour later.

There were no planes that day; there were targets and more elsewhere. The Gunner Colonel spoke to me twice, and I knew from his voice how desperately he wanted to help us. So the Chinese were pushed unceasingly over the Gloster and Western Crossings. The guns and mortars fired all day but the Rifles and Fusiliers – to say nothing of the brave Belgians – needed support too. There were so many of them. Really, for a force reputedly bent on 'imperialist aggression' we must have seemed pathetically thin on the ground to the Chinese Commissars.

At about half past eight it became apparent that the positions of A and D Companies had become untenable; little by little they were being swamped by a tide of men. Each minute was widening the gaps between the little fighting groups – as yet still organized platoons and companies. The time had come when the advantage of holding the ground forward would be outweighed by the loss of much or all of two rifle-company groups. The order to withdraw was given over the wireless.

Watching from the Command Post, I saw the men withdrawing, step by step, down the reverse hill slopes: D Company and A Company leaving the ground they had fought for so well, that had cost the enemy such a price.

I went down the hill a little later and there, by the ford, the survivors of the night battle were coming in: a long, straggling line of men; for all were heavily laden with arms and ammunition. To me they looked cheerful, though tired – but something more than that: they looked surprised. I think, above all, it was a surprise to many of them that they had been withdrawn – grave though they had known their position to be, and dangerous their surroundings.

Unquestionably, it was difficult for them to understand that, in holding their ground for so long, they had made a priceless contribution to the battle: but a soldier engaged in a fight that may be to the death has no time for the appreciation of such things. He is, to say the least, otherwise engaged.

Just north of the ford, along the roadsides; around the cook-house and the Regimental Aid Post, they rested now, as Watkins issued tea as fast as he could make it, and all the bread, bacon and sausages he had to hand. Comrade passed mess tin to comrade, who drank and passed in turn to his next neighbour. Men lay back, without removing their haversacks, their heads resting in the ditches, smoking, talking quietly, resting. Yes, it had been a long night.

The Colonel came down the hill. He had just moved B Company back fifteen hundred yards to the very base of Kamak-San to conform with A and D Companies' withdrawal. He had now to fit the latter two into the revised defence disposition. With Mike and Jumbo he looked over the map and pointed out their new positions on the ground. Jumbo was to take the much-reduced A Company to man the key ridge to the west which Spike's Pioneers now held. Behind, looked down upon by this long feature – marked Hill 235 – was a small, square, almost flat-topped hill, where Mike would deploy D Company. As Mike and Jumbo went outside again, Henry was marking the map afresh. The old, blue lines that circled Castle Hill, Choksong, the hill D Company had held, soon vanished from the shiny talc. Now two new rings marked their positions; the symbols were completed by the moving chinagraph. The operations map was fitted back into its place and Henry soon descended to correct his own in the Intelligence Office. I put out my hand to the telephone to tell the remainder of the Battalion how our new line stood, taking it from its rest without looking down. For I was looking at the tiny group of marks upon the talc; and as I looked I realized that this was what the Chinese would attack next – tonight!

When I recall that day, it rises in my memory as a series of incidents, clear in themselves, but joined by a very hazy thread of continuity.

I remember Colour-Sergeant Buxcey organising his Korean porters with mighty loads for the first of many ascents to their new positions. Nine, I think, he made. Nine times up the hill; and so, poor devils, nine times down a path at once precipitous and rough. On coming down, one wished for the easier journey of the upward climb; and upwards, sweating, breathless, weary, one envied those who went the opposite way.

When Buxcey's anxious face has left my mind, I can see Bob working at the Regimental Aid Post, one hand still wet with blood as he turns round, pausing for a moment to clean himself before he begins to minister to yet another wounded man. The ambulance cars are filled; the jeep that Bounden drives has been out time and again with the stretchers on its racks. Baxter, Brisland, Mills, the whole staff of the RAP, is hard at work with dressings, drugs, instruments. This is the reckoning they pay for basking in the sun down by the stream when times are quiet. It is a price they pay willingly and to the full.

I remember watching the slow, wind-tossed descent of a helicopter that came down for some casualties to whom the winding, bumpy road back south would have meant certain death. I saw Bob and the Padre standing back as the plane lifted, their hair blown wildly by the slipstream from the rotors as she lifted into the sky.

Shaw and Mr Evans, the Chief Clerk, went off to Seoul in my jeep. I watched them until they disappeared round the road-bend down by Graham's mortar pits. Richard was down by the ford, and Carl, the Counter-Mortar Officer.

'I'm sending my vehicles back, except for my jeep,' said Carl. 'I've decided I'll stay with you to make up your number of Forward Observation Officers. I've seen the Colonel.'

The lumbering half-tracks disappeared along the road and Carl settled down to chat to Guy on Gunner matters. I wondered what the Gunner Colonel was going to say on finding that his radar specialist had stayed with us. And I thanked God that the latter was a real Gunner as well as a boffin.

We were certainly going to discover that he had not forgotten how to shoot.

Donald, the Assistant Adjutant, came into the Command Vehicle. We had various things to discuss – welfare cases – two men had to go from the Battalion on a Field Hygiene course – there were messages from Freddie, who had thought of them as he rode back to B Echelon after his visit earlier in the day. Afterwards, we had some coffee and over it I told him that he had better stay forward to reinforce A Company, just for the time being. He went off happily to climb the slopes to Jumbo's Hill, as pleased as Punch that he could take command of a platoon – if only for the forthcoming engagement – before he was packed back to Rear HQ and his Assistant Adjutancy.

Jumbo had come forward that morning to find Pat and two of his platoon commanders, John and Philip, dead; only Terry left to lead fifty-seven fit men out of the original body nearly one hundred strong. The arrival of Donald would give him two platoon commanders. I put the phone back after telling him the news, and walked out on to the grass to get some sleep.

That morning the Padre said a funeral service for Pat, whose body had been sent back from Company Headquarters on the ammunition-laden Oxford Carrier which Henry had driven through a hail of fire descending on the pass to Choksong. Pat's body was the only one to which we could pay our last respects – but we did not forget the others. Three of us stood by while the solemn words were quietly said; then we saluted and walked away, each busy with his own thoughts.

Pat lay at rest beside the soft-voiced stream, quiet in the morning sunlight, the noise of last night's battle gone forever in the wind.

'The Second-in-Command is here, sir,' said Judkins, my batman. 'And are you going to have anything to eat?'

I opened my eyes to blue sky and huge white clouds. It was afternoon; I had slept for two hours. Judkins stood on the grass by the edge of my blanket, a mug and plate in one hand, a knife, fork, and spoon in the other.

I hated getting up; and I was a fool to refuse the hot stew Watkins had cooked. How little one learns by experience! I asked Judkins for some tea and had a cigarette with Digby, the Second-in-Command. He had come forward from Rear HQ some time before but had been unwilling to awaken me.

'The Colonel has told me to go back in view of this attack on Rear HQ,' he said. We settled a point or two before he got into his jeep and drove off with Bainbridge at the wheel, for all the world as if he was on his way to a dinner party. They were going to a party all right. Four hours before a sizeable force, which had circled us, had attacked Rear HQ. The road was cut, and the route forward that might bring us relief or reinforcement was – at that very moment – closing.

It is dark, the moon obscured by cloud. Night is the time for their attack. Although we have had no planes during the day, our Gunners have inflicted too much damage to permit them to press their advance. Released from concern about our troops, hitherto so closely engaged on the hills forward, the Gunners delivered concentration after concentration on the almost endless series of targets before them before the enemy called a halt and went to ground.

But now it is dark. Already their stealthy infantry will

have left the little holes in which they have kept hidden from the sun and our observers.

We sit in a battle Command Post. Walters is there at his wireless: nearby sit Richard, Henry, and Guy. Frank is laying a line from the Mortar Troop Headquarters where Sergeant-Major Askew keeps his solitary vigil; somewhere about is Smythe, the Signal Sergeant; Lucas, the Operations Clerk, is making yet another cup of coffee; the Colonel is sitting with his head against the earthen wall, taking advantage of the quiet to doze. I sit by Walters, and, in the glow of red light from the wireless, see that his eyelids are drooping, heavy with an unsatisfied need for sleep. My eyes are heavy, too. How marvellous, what luxury, to find oneself suddenly in a bed with nothing to wake up for until, say, breakfast on a silver tray, in thirty hours' time. Well, why ask a bed? A blanket on that grass outside . . .

Frank is talking to me, and I realize that I have been dropping off into a doze. It is better that I get up and walk about outside for a little. Richard follows me as Frank departs for his Headquarters, a hundred yards away. We hear the stream rushing over the little waterfall; the light wind cools our cheeks, hot from the close atmosphere of the dug-out. The radiance of the moon is widening in the sky above us. Beneath our feet, the old year's grass rustles as we stroll up and down, talking.

Suddenly, Richard pauses in mid-sentence. We both look up, quickly, to the eastern end of C Company's ridge. The battle has started.

In the Command Post dug-out, the telephone is ringing.

In the original Battalion defensive layout, Denis's Company – B Company – were on the far right flank, holding the approaches to the great Kamak-San feature – itself too vast for us to hold – at the same time constituting the right rear base of the Battalion. Unlike C Company, they had never been absolutely in reserve, inasmuch as there had been nothing except the river between them and the enemy; although, of course, to their north-west, A and D Companies had been in closer proximity to an often evanescent foe. Now, with both A and D Companies withdrawn, their prospect of a major engagement became a certainty.

Whilst the battle had raged around Choksong village for the possession of A and D Companies' hills, B Company had been little more than spectators. A few Chinese patrols had bumped them during the hours of darkness, but they had held their fire, except at one post where a complete patrol of fifteen men was destroyed by an LMG of Geoff's platoon. Thus the Chinese did not know B Company's positions on the morning of the 23rd; for all they knew, their contact on the previous night might well have been with one of our patrols, instead of with a position in our main defences. Thus, expecting to renew the attack that night, they had sent a further series of patrols forward towards B Company during the morning; and these patrols were all in strength, designed to produce, at all costs, reaction from us.

Denis was determined not to reveal his positions unless absolutely compelled to; but, faced with a number of strong armed parties along his front, he realized that, sooner or later he would be forced to engage them. In these circumstances, he made up his mind to do so by sortie, by which means the enemy could not be certain either of the main position or – equally important – the strength of the force from which they had sprung.

Sergeant Petherick took out a force in this connection, expecting to engage, at most, twenty men: he returned after meeting two hundred. Backwards and forwards, all among the battle knolls that lay below the peak of Kamak-San, engagements flared up and died, only to be renewed elsewhere.

The daylight waned, the evening shadows deepened, merged and grew into one, to form the darkness of another night.

Below great Kamak-San, Denis's Company prepared themselves for what they knew the darkness would bring forth.

To the west, that night, the 1st ROK Division was to repulse, with great tenacity, a strong and vigorous attack by two divisions attempting to open up the road that ran from Munsan-Ni to Seoul – a part of the western highway that ran up from the south to the border on the Yalu River. Eastwards, the Fifth Fusiliers would fight desperately against attacks across the river in great strength; and beyond, the Belgians and the Rifles, Puerto Ricans, Turks, Americans would be engaged in increasing intensity.

Here, near Choksong, lay the centre of the attack upon the western sector; here ran the road which was, historically, the main route of invasion from the north.

Already one full day behind their time-plan for the advance, the Chinese now prepared to end the resistance once and for all, and surge along the road to Seoul through Uijong-bu, catching, perhaps, the whole left flank of the UN 3rd Division unawares.

Their problem now was, at what point should they attack? Last night's experience made it plain that one vast, human wave would never serve to overwhelm the sturdy wall of the defence. Further, the British left flank, on Hill 235, would not be easy to attack. They could not know of Jumbo's dangerous weakness on the ridge.

Then, too, attack upon the west might leave us time and opportunity to make a second withdrawal, on to Kamak-San, from which we should not easily be dislodged. The choice fell, therefore, upon the approaches to Kamak-San, and thus upon B Company and part of C, whose right flank lay across the western spur leading to the final, jagged crest.

I run into the dugout: Walters has answered the telephone, which he hands to me. Denis says:

'Well, we've started. They're attacking Beverly's platoon now – about 150, I should think.'

My torch is on the map; and I examine the exact location of the attack as the Colonel begins to talk to Denis. Nearby, I hear the heavier sound of shells exploding above the noisy small-arms fire and mortars. Recce is shooting along B Company's front.

Paul is on the other telephone; his news from C Company is the same: parties of enemy attempting to infiltrate, while others assault our positions in great strength, trying again to engulf us. Jack's platoon and David's are engaged; Guido's platoon is under machine-gun fire from D Company's former position.

It is ten minutes to twelve: the battle is warming.

Here they come again: a screaming mob of cotton-suited soldiers, their yellow faces gleaming in the light of the trip flares they have sprung and the mortar flares drifting slowly down beneath their parachutes.

An hour after midnight, the whole of B and C Companies are engaged; the guns, the mortars, the machine-guns once again deliver their supporting fire with all their might.

In character, the battle much resembles that of the previous night: wave after wave of men armed with grenades and burp guns storm the positions under cover of mortar and machine-gun fire, are halted, engaged in a short desperate struggle, and driven back. A lull follows. Both sides reorganize. The attack recommences. The character of the battle is the same, too, in that these ceaseless blows, delivered in such strength, inevitably reduce our numbers speedily. Their casualties are high – much higher than ours; but in this battle of attrition they can afford them; we cannot.

It is in the nature of the ground that the battle differs; and the Chinese have made the mistake of attacking obliquely across our front – perhaps because they did not really know where B Company lay. Thus for the first two hours, much of the weight of their attack was spent fruitlessly. Only after

great loss have they redirected their line of assault. Old
Kamak-San looks down upon a ring of intermittent flame
across his northern base. Last night the flames were further
off. Now they are nearer; growing nearer, hour by hour.

It is three o'clock. In the Command Post we are drinking
coffee and talking. The telephone is quiet for the moment but
the noise of the battle reaches us clearly. As I sit talking to
Richard, I wonder if he realizes how gravely we are situated:
a vast body of the enemy pushing south; our flanks open; the
road cut behind us. It is a great comfort to reflect that,
though they can take Kamak-San without firing a shot –
they have only to travel round our unguarded flanks, after
all – it will do them no good. We hold the road; and we shall
continue to hold it.

The telephone is ringing again: Paul is speaking:

'I'm afraid they've overrun my top position,' he says, 'and
they're reinforcing hard. They're simply pouring chaps in up
above us. Let me know what the Colonel wants me to do, will
you?'

This is, immediately, disaster. The enemy has forced his
way up on to Paul's highest defensive post by overwhelming
his men with their numbers. The result of this is that the
Chinese now command most of C Company's ground, have
forced a wedge between C and B Company, and dominate
the valley in which the mortars lie – heavy and medium –
and the entire Headquarters. If we are not quick, we may be
caught by the enemy who has only to fire over open sights
straight down into us.

Already, however, the Colonel, who is listening, has made
up his mind.

'Pack the Headquarters up,' he says, 'and get everyone out
of the valley up between D Company and the Anti-Tank
Platoon position. I'm going to withdraw C Company in ten
minutes; and I shall move B over to join us after first light.'

He picks up the telephone and starts to speak to Paul as I

give Richard and Henry their instructions. They need but a few words: speed is the requirement here. Foolishly, I forget Frank has laid a line to the Command Post, and waste precious time going to his Headquarters. He is not there. I give a message to Sergeant-Major Askew and go on: Graham's mortars are warned – Sam's Headquarters – the Regimental Aid Post – the Regimental Sergeant-Major. Before I return to the Command Post, the first party of signallers is moving up the gorge towards D Company's hill.

Back at the Command Post I burn those papers that must *not* be taken. Lucas and I pick up Jennings, the Rear Link Wireless commander: together we smash the fixed radio-equipment. Again, I go around the area. Overhead, along the ridge C Company is holding, there is a sudden ominous quiet. I wonder if they are already mounting a machine-gun at the head of the valley; if they are already descending to the stream, crossing by the mortar pits which I am now approaching. It is no good wondering: I shall know soon enough what they are doing. The mortar pits stand silent, strangely deserted after the bustle of the earlier part of the night. Turning back along the road, I see a mug of steaming tea standing on a box at the entrance to Sam's HQ. The RAP has gone, too; Bob's jeep is in wild disorder; packages, web equipment, an old coffee tin are scattered across the seats, flung there in haste after he had removed the other contents. Everyone has gone.

Not quite everyone. There is a murmur of voices from the signals office; a metallic rasping catches my ear. As I step down from the bank on the edge of the road, two signallers appear. They have come back for space batteries, quite unaware that the sands in the hour-glass are fast running out. Indeed, I cannot be sure if there is even one grain left to fall: the Chinese have held the head of the valley for nearly forty minutes.

Anthony-Farrar Hockley was captured shortly afterwards by the North Vietnamese, and was interned in a POW camp.

APPEARING BEFORE THE HOUSE UN-AMERICAN ACTIVITIES COMMITTEE, WASHINGTON, 21 May 1952

Lillian Hellman

The internal politics of the USA in the early 1950s were conditioned by the fears of the Cold War with the USSR. A witch-hunt led by Senator McCarthy attacked citizens suspected of left-wing views, many of whom were 'blacklisted', prevented from working. A particular target for the attentions of McCarthyism was the entertainment industry; playwright Lillian Hellman was only one of many writers and artists to be asked to appear before Congress's House Un-American Activities Committee to admit their political belief and 'name names' of other suspected Communists.

The Committee room was almost empty except for a few elderly, small-faced ladies sitting in the rear. They looked as if they were permanent residents and, since they occasionally spoke to each other, it was not too long a guess that they came as an organized group or club. Clerks came in and out, put papers on the rostrum, and disappeared. I said maybe we had come too early, but Joe [Rauh, Hellman's lawyer] said no, it was better that I get used to the room.

Then, I think to make the wait better for me, he said, 'Well, I can tell you now that in the early days of seeing you, I was scared that what happened to my friend might happen to me.'

He stopped to tell Pollitt [Rauh's assistant] that he didn't understand about the press – not one newspaperman had appeared.

I said; 'What happened to your friend?'

'He represented a Hollywood writer who told him that he would under no circumstances be a friendly witness. That was why my friend took the case. So they get here, in the same seats we are, sure of his client, and within ten minutes the writer is one of the friendliest witnesses the Committee has had the pleasure of. He throws in every name he can think of, including his college roommate, childhood friend.'

I said, 'No, that won't happen and for more solid reasons than your honour or even mine. I told you I can't make quick changes.'

Joe told Pollitt that he thought he understood about no press and the half-empty room: the Committee had kept our appearance as quiet as they could. Joe said, 'That means they're frightened of us. I don't know whether that's good or bad, but we want the press here and I don't know how to get them.'

He didn't have to know. The room suddenly began to fill up behind me and the press people began to push toward their section and were still piling in when Representative Wood began to pound his gavel. I hadn't seen the Committee come in, don't think I had realized that they were to sit on a raised platform, the government having learned from the stage, or maybe the other way around. I was glad I hadn't seen them come in – they made a gloomy picture. Through the noise of the gavel I heard one of the ladies in the rear cough very loudly. She was to cough all through the hearing. Later I heard one of her friends say loudly, 'Irma, take your good cough drops.'

The opening questions were standard: what was my name, where was I born, what was my occupation, what were the titles of my plays. It didn't take long to get to what really interested them: my time in Hollywood, which studios had I worked for, what periods of what years, with some mysterious emphasis on 1937. (My time in Spain, I thought, but I was wrong.)

Had I met a writer called Martin Berkeley? (I had never, still have never, met Martin Berkeley, although Hammett* told me later that I had once sat at a lunch table of sixteen or seventeen people with him in the old Metro-Goldwyn-Mayer commissary.) I said I must refuse to answer that question. Mr Tavenner said he'd like to ask me again whether I had stated I was abroad in the summer of 1937. I said yes, explained that I had been in New York for several weeks before going to Europe, and got myself ready for what I knew was coming: Martin Berkeley, one of the Committee's most lavish witnesses on the subject of Hollywood, was now going to be put to work. Mr Tavenner read Berkeley's testimony. Perhaps he is worth quoting, the small details are nicely formed, even about his 'old friend Hammett', who had no more than a bowing acquaintance with him.

MR TAVENNER: . . . I would like you to tell the committee when and where the Hollywood section of the Communist Party was first organized.

MR BERKELEY: Well, sir, by a very strange coincidence the section was organized in my house . . . In June of 1937, the middle of June, the meeting was held in my house. My house was picked because I had a large living room and ample parking facilities . . . And it was a pretty good meeting. We were honoured by the presence of many functionaries from downtown, and the spirit was swell . . . Well, in addition to Jerome and the others I have mentioned before, and there is no sense in me going over the list again and again . . . Also present was Harry Carlisle, who is now in the process of being deported, for which I am very grateful. He was an English subject. After Stanley Lawrence had stolen what funds there were from the party out here, and to make amends had gone to Spain and gotten himself killed, they

* Dashiell Hammett. The detective story writer, author of such private eye classics as *The Maltese Falcon*, was Hellman's long-time partner.

sent Harry Carlisle here to conduct Marxist classes . . . Also
at the meeting was Donald Ogden Stewart. His name is
spelled Donald Ogden S-t-e-w-a-r-t. Dorothy Parker, also a
writer. Her husband Allen Campbell, C-a-m-p-b-e-l-l; my
old friend Dashiell Hammett, who is now in jail in New York
for his activities; that very excellent playwright, Lillian
Hellman . . .

And so on.

When this nonsense was finished, Mr Tavenner asked me
if it was true. I said that I wanted to refer to the letter I had
sent, I would like the Committee to reconsider my offer in the
letter.

MR TAVENNER: In other words, you are asking the committee
not to ask you any questions regarding the participation of
other persons in the Communist Party activities?

I said I hadn't said that.

Mr Wood said that in order to clarify the record
Mr Tavenner should put into the record the correspondence
between me and the Committee. Mr Tavenner did just that,
and when he had finished Rauh sprang to his feet, picked up
a stack of mimeographed copies of my letter, and handed
them out to the press section. I was puzzled by this – I hadn't
noticed he had the copies – but I did notice that Rauh was
looking happy.

Mr Tavenner was upset, far more than the printed words
of my hearing show. Rauh said that Tavenner himself had
put the letters in the record, and thus he thought passing out
copies was proper. The polite words of each as they read on
the page were not polite as spoken. I am convinced that in
this section of the testimony, as in several other sections –
certainly in Hammett's later testimony before the Senate
Internal Security Subcommittee – either the court stenographer missed some of what was said and filled it in later, or the
documents were, in part, edited. Having read many exam-

ples of the work of court stenographers, I have never once
seen a completely accurate report.

Mr Wood told Mr Tavenner that the Committee could
not be 'placed in the attitude of trading with the witnesses as
to what they will testify to' and that thus he thought both
letters should be read aloud.

Mr Tavenner did just this, and there was talk I couldn't
hear, a kind of rustle, from the press section. Then
Mr Tavenner asked me if I had attended the meeting
described by Berkeley, and one of the hardest things I ever
did in my life was to swallow the words, 'I don't know him,
and a little investigation into the time and place would have
proved to you that I could not have been at the meeting he
talks about.' Instead, I said that I must refuse to answer the
question. The 'must' in that sentence annoyed Mr Wood – it
was to annoy him again and again – and he corrected me:
'You might refuse to answer, the question is asked, do you
refuse?'

But Wood's correction of me, the irritation in his voice,
was making me nervous, and I began to move my right hand
as if I had a tic, unexpected, and couldn't stop it. I told
myself that if a word irritated him, the insults would begin to
come very soon. So I sat up straight, made my left hand hold
my right hand, and hoped it would work. But I felt the sweat
on my face and arms and knew that something was going to
happen to me, something out of control, and I turned to Joe,
remembering the suggested toilet intermission. But the clock
said we had only been there sixteen minutes, and if it was
going to come, the bad time, I had better hang on for a
while.

Was I a member of the Communist Party, had I been,
what year had I stopped being? How could I harm such
people as Martin Berkeley by admitting I had known them,
and so on. At times I couldn't follow the reasoning, at times I
understood full well that in refusing to answer questions
about membership in the Party I had, of course, trapped

myself into a seeming admission that I once had been.

But in the middle of one of the questions about my past, something so remarkable happened that I am to this day convinced that the unknown gentleman who spoke had a great deal to do with the rest of my life. A voice from the press gallery had been for at least three or four minutes louder than the other voices. (By this time, I think, the press had finished reading my letter to the Committee and were discussing it.) The loud voice had been answered by a less loud voice, but no words could be distinguished. Suddenly a clear voice said, 'Thank God somebody finally had the guts to do it.'

It is never wise to say that something is the best minute of your life, you must be forgetting, but I still think that unknown voice made the words that helped to save me. (I had been sure that not only did the elderly ladies in the room disapprove of me, but the press would be antagonistic.) Wood rapped his gavel and said angrily, 'If that occurs again, I will clear the press from these chambers.'

'You do that, sir,' said the same voice.

Mr Wood spoke to somebody over his shoulder and the somebody moved around to the press section, but that is all that happened. To this day I don't know the name of the man who spoke, but for months later, almost every day I would say to myself, I wish I could tell him that I had really wanted to say to Mr Wood: 'There is no Communist menace in this country and you know it. You have made cowards into liars, an ugly business, and you made me write a letter in which I acknowledged your power. I should have gone into your Committee room, given my name and address, and walked out.' Many people have said they liked what I did, but I don't much, and if I hadn't worried about rats in jail, and such . . . Ah, the bravery you tell yourself was possible when it's all over, the bravery of the staircase.

In the Committee room I heard Mr Wood say, 'Mr Walter does not desire to ask the witness any further questions. Is there any reason why this witness should not be excused from further attendance before the Committee?'

Mr Tavenner said, 'No, sir.'

My hearing was over an hour and seven minutes after it began. I don't think I understood that it was over, but Joe was whispering so loudly and so happily that I jumped from the noise in my ear.

He said, '*Get up. Get up.* Get out of here immediately. Pollitt will take you. Don't stop for any reason, to answer any questions from anybody. Don't run, but walk as fast as you can and just shake your head and keep moving if anybody comes near you.'

Some years later Hellman asked Rauh why she was not prosecuted by the Committee:

He said, 'There were three things they wanted. One, names which you wouldn't give. Two a smear by accusing you of being a 'Fifth Amendment Communist'. They couldn't do that because in your letter you offered to testify about yourself. And three, a prosecution which they couldn't do because they forced us into taking the Fifth Amendment. They had sense enough to see that they were in a bad spot. We beat them, that's all.'

HOW MOSCOW BROKE THE NEWS OF STALIN'S DEATH, 7 March 1953

Victor Zorza, BBC

There was a spluttering and an odd, incomprehensible noise issuing from the radio receiver which was tuned in to the Moscow home service. The one o'clock news bulletin had just been broadcast. It was a repeat of the bulletin that went out at midnight, and that in turn had been a repeat of the evening broadcast.

I waited. The news of Stalin's death had just been released to the outside world by Moscow's foreign services. Now, surely, was the moment for the Russians to be told. But they were not told anything – except perhaps by implication. Solemn orchestral music brimmed out of the loudspeaker, filling the night with an eerie atmosphere of tragedy and sorrow. The Russians who were listening in at that moment – the broadcast was beamed to Siberia, where it was morning by then – had not been told; but they must have surmised the truth.

As time went on and the customary news bulletins, the early morning broadcast of the physical training instructor, and the talks on political subjects, failed to materialize, the surmise in the minds of the listeners must have turned to a dimly apprehended certainty. There were those, I am sure, who were still hoping against hope. The dread word had not been uttered yet. A crisis perhaps – but surely not death!

At 2.55 the music ceased. For a moment there was stillness in the air, silence in the room – and in the rooms of all the Russians whose sets were tuned to Moscow. Then came the bells. They pealed neither joyfully nor sorrowfully, and yet managed to impart to the waiting minds and straining ears a sense of foreboding something akin to fear – the feeling that overcomes most people at a crisis in life.

At 0300 the bells stopped, suddenly. Again silence. And then the majestic strains of the Soviet national anthem, which replaced the 'Internationale' during the war. The broad melody swept the vast expanses of Russia, of which it is intended to be descriptive. It penetrated into the little huts in the mountain settlements of Central Asia. And far in the North, where the snow and ice never thaw, it was heard by the camp guards who had just come back into the warmth of the guardroom, having been relieved by their comrades on the stroke of three. But the camp inmates – of whom I was once one – probably did not know and, if they knew, were hardly in a condition to care. They had just done a twelve-hour stretch of hard, back-breaking work, some in the forests where they had been felling trees, others in the goldmines of the Soviet Far East.

Five minutes, and the anthem came to a close. Would the ordinary news bulletin now be broadcast? Would it be a repeat of an earlier bulletin? Or would the news, which was by now in all the newspaper offices of the outside world, be told at last to the Russians?

Yuri Levitan, the announcer who during the war brought the Russians the news of victories – but never of defeats – was at the microphone. Slowly, solemnly, with a voice brimming over with emotion, he read:

'The Central Committee of the Communist party, the Council of Ministers and the Praesidium of the Supreme Soviet of the USSR, announce with deep grief to the party and all workers that on 5 March at 9.50 p.m., Josef Vissarionovich Stalin, Secretary of the Central Committee of the Communist party and Chairman of the Council of Ministers, died after a serious illness. The heart of the collaborator and follower of the genius of Lenin's work, the wise leader and teacher of the Communist party and of the Soviet people, stopped beating.'

The blow was a heavy one, he said. The news would bring pain to the hearts of all men. 'But in these dark days all the peoples of our country are becoming more united in the great brotherly family led by the Communist party, founded and educated by Lenin and Stalin. The Soviet people is united in its confidence and inspired with warm love for the Communist party, knowing that the supreme law governing all activity of the party is to serve the interests of the people.'

The Soviet people, he went on, would follow the guidance of the party, the rightness of whose policy had been demonstrated over and over again. Now, under the party's continued leadership, they would look forward to new successes. They knew, he said, quoting a recent statement of Stalin's without attributing it to the dead leader, that the improvement of the people's material well-being was the party's special concern. They also knew – and here his voice became firm and self-assured – that the defensive powers of the Soviet State were growing in strength, that the party was doing everything to prepare a crushing blow for any possible aggressor.

In foreign policy the party and the Government would strive to consolidate and preserve peace, oppose the preparations for the unleashing of new wars, and work for international collaboration – familiar words, these, coming from Moscow radio. Can there be any more substance in them than on the thousand previous occasions when Soviet spokesmen uttered them?

And then came the first intimate note with another, harder, note superimposed upon it. 'Dear friends and comrades,' Levitan said, 'the great directing and leading force of the Soviet Union in the struggle for the building of Communism is our Communist party. Steel-like unity and a monolithic cohesion of the ranks of the party are the main conditions for strength and power.'

CONQUERING EVEREST, HIMALAYAS, 29 May 1953

Edmund Hillary

Mount Everest, at 29,028 feet the highest mountain in the world, was finally conquered in 1953, by New Zealander Edmund Hillary and Nepalese Sherpa, Tenzing Norgay. Here Hillary describes their assault on the final ridge.

Leaving Tenzing to belay me as best he could I jammed my

way into this crack, then kicking backwards with my crampons I sank their spikes deep into the frozen snow behind me and levered myself off the ground. Taking advantage of every little rock-hold and the force of knee, shoulder and arms I could muster, I literally cramponed backwards up the crack with a fervent prayer that the cornice would remain attached to the rock. Despite the considerable effort involved, my progress although slow was steady, and as Tenzing paid out the rope I inched my way upwards until I could finally reach over the top of the rock and drag myself out of the crack on to a wide ledge. For a few moments I lay regaining my breath and for the first time really felt the fierce determination that nothing now could stop us reaching the top. I took a firm stance on the ledge and signalled to Tenzing to come on up. As I heaved hard on the rope Tenzing wriggled his way up the crack and finally collapsed exhausted at the top like a giant fish when it has just been hauled from the sea after a terrible struggle.

This great effort, at around 29,000ft had come near to breaking both of them; but they went on, flanked by huge cornices.

I had been cutting steps continuously for two hours, and Tenzing too, was moving very slowly. As I chipped steps around still another corner, I wondered rather dully just how long we could keep it up. Our original zest had now quite gone and it was turning more into a grim struggle. I then realized that the ridge ahead, instead of still monotonously rising, now dropped sharply away, and far below I could see the North Col and the Rongbuk Glacier (on the Tibetan side). I looked upwards to see a narrow snow ridge running up to a snowy summit. A few more whacks of the ice-axe in the firm snow and we stood on the top. My initial feelings were of relief – relief that there were no more steps to cut – no more ridges to traverse and no more humps to tantalize us with hopes of success. I looked at Tenzing and in spite of the balaclava, goggles and oxygen mask all encrusted with long icicles that concealed his face, there was no disguising his infectious grin of pure delight as he looked around him. We shook hands and then Tenzing threw his arm around my shoulders and we thumped each other on the back until we were almost breathless. It was 11.30 am. The ridge had taken us two and a half hours, but it seemed like a lifetime.

BANNISTER BREAKS THE FOUR-MINUTE MILE, OXFORD, 6 May 1954

Athletics Correspondent, The Times

R. G. Bannister accomplished at Oxford yesterday what a whole world of milers had recently been bracing themselves to achieve first – the four-minute mile. He did so in conditions which were far from promising, and he did better than even time, for he finished weary but triumphant and mobbed by an encircling crowd, in 3 min. 59.4 sec. – three-fifths of a second less than the magic four minutes. On the way, at 1500 metres he had equalled another world record, shared by Gundhar Haegg, the previous holder of the world record of 4 min. 1.4 sec. over the mile, Lennart Strand, another Swede and Walther Lueg, of Germany.

The occasion was the annual match between the University [Oxford] and the Amateur Athletics Association which one fears was rather forgotten in the general excitement. For the record, the A.A.A. won by 64 points to 34 in the 16 events. The crowd might have been larger but at least it did all it could to make up for the lack of numbers by an intelligent enthusiasm which enabled many among them to realize when the last lap was being run and Bannister raced well ahead that something big was about to be recorded by the time-keeper – almost certainly a world record – perhaps even the four-minute mile itself.

The conditions have been described as unpromising because a strong gusty wind was bound to handicap the runners part of the time as they ran round the Iffley Road track and one or two early showers threatened worse things still. Actually, the weather was fine for the race. The match itself was not started until five o'clock in the evening and an uneasy hour passed with little success for Oxford. C.E.F Higham's excellent time of 14.8 sec. in the high hurdles only inches behind P.H. Hildreth, the A.A.A. champion, in spite of a slow start, was the best thing seen so far. H. H. Boyd's victory in the half-mile to a great extent made up for his failures through unfitness in the university sports.

But all this was quickly forgotten when the mile was announced and the six runners lined up. Bannister, C. J. Chataway, W. T. Hulatt, and C. W. Brasher represented the A.A.A and G. F. Dole and A. D. Gordon ran for Oxford. Bannister's great time of 4 min. 3.6. sec. last year was well in mind and Chataway started as a university record holder, but nothing dramatic enough happened during the first two laps to excite more than the actual time-keepers.

Brasher, always a gallant and willing runner – or steeplechaser – set the pace and the first quarter was completed with Brasher a stride or two in front of Bannister and Chataway about the same distance away, third.

Chataway went ahead about half-way down the back-stretch during the third lap and Bannister went after him. Brasher dropped back and, one fears, became forgotten though he had deserved well of all concerned. At the bell, Chataway was still a little in front of Bannister and one had to wait again for the back-stretch to see a new and decisive phase in the race unfold itself. Bannister now lengthened his magnificent stride and, obviously going very fast, passed Chataway and raced farther and farther ahead.

Spectators now really sensed a triumph of above the average and as Bannister broke the tape some 50 yards ahead of Chataway there was a general swoop on the centre of the field. Bannister was encircled and disappeared from view, but somehow the news leaked out. There was a scene of the wildest excitement and what miserable spectators they would have been if they had not waved their programmes, shouted, even jumped in the air a little. It is hard not to believe that Bannister's time will not be accepted by the world authorities, for whatever else could be said the wind was at least as much a handicap as occasionally it was a help. Chataway's time of 4 min.7.2 sec. was his own personal best.

The following are Bannister's times for each quarter mile: 57.7 sec., 60.6 sec., 62.4 sec., and 58.7 sec.

ELVIS PRESLEY, 1956

Albert Goldman

Rock'n'roll was developed from the music of the black American south, and became the adopted sound of newly affluent white American 'teenagers' in the 1950s. By 1956 Elvis Aaron Presley (1935–77), the 'king' of rock'n'roll, was the most popular singing artist in America.

The Elvis of 1956 looks like a traffic signal: bright green or red sports jacket over navy blue slacks with red socks, white bucks (with blue soles), and sometimes a cummerbund. His guitar is encased in tan hand-tooled leather with his full name carved conspicuously across the skin.

The moment he reaches centre stage, he collars the mike and shouts, '*Wellll!*' Just as every girl in the house leans forward in expectation of ecstasy, he suddenly stops – and laughs at the kids for having been taken in. Then he rears back and starts again with another '*Wellll!*' This childish game continues until he finally releases the band to go into 'Heartbreak Hotel'.

Meantime, girls bolt from their seats all over the theatre and run down the aisles to the orchestra pit, where they snap their hero's picture. There must be a million fading flashes of Elvis taken in this year alone. What do the girls see that drives them wild? It sure isn't the All-American Boy. Elvis looks nothing like the young movie stars of the day, all those white-buck, crisp-cut, dumb schmucks with names like Tab, Rock, and Bob. Elvis Presley is the flip side of the boy next door. His fish-belly complexion; his brooding Latin eyes, heavily outlined with mascara; his Greek nose and thick, twisted lips; his long greasy hair, thrown forward into his face by his jerking motions – God! what a freak he looks to those little girls peering through their finders. And what a turn-on! After the show, they blither: 'I like him 'cause he looks so mean!' 'He's fascinating – like a snake.' 'I hear he peddles dope.' 'He's been in and out of jail.' 'He's gonna die of cancer in six months.' Oh, those teenyboppers wailing for their demon lover.

Like the gospel acts who are his inspiration, Elvis onstage is busy, busy, busy! From the moment he hits the boards until he ducks off twenty minutes later, he never stops moving. Though he is not a dancer and must lash his body to make it move, he understands instinctively that his kind of music demands action.

His famous 'gyrations' put him in a class by himself, distinct not only from the white rock 'n' rollers but from the black R & B acts.

Elvis's challenge is to create the effect of spectacular movement with just the three or four steps he can cut. He starts off positioned squarely before the mike in his straddle-legged gunslinger's stance. Then he starts shaking both limbs at once, 'wearing out his britches from inside,' as the band quips. Suddenly, he goes into his gospel bag. Throwing down his left hand, with its long shapely fingers, he sets it fluttering

like a hummingbird's wing. At the same moment, a pained
ecstatic expression crosses his face. Obviously, he's possessed.
Then he loses control of his limbs. The spirit that has seized
him is making those loosely trousered legs flail like rubber
hoses. Then they start snapping like scissors, one-two! one-
two! His knees knock like the Camel Walk. Then, just as
abruptly as it began, the fit stops. Elvis is left standing, like a
suddenly arrested bicyclist, with one foot on toepoint.

The local papers are always reporting that Elvis does
'bumps and grinds'. They're right on the money identifying
him as a burlesque dancer. No image could be more apt. But
their terminology is wrong. What they are pointing at is the
kind of move Elvis makes at the end of 'I Got A Sweetie'.
Bringing the tempo way down to the stripper's bump-and-
grind drag, Elvis snaps into profile, while supporting himself
by holding on with one hand to the standing mike. Then he
shoots out his legs in a series of knee-jerk hot shots that are the
pimp-walkin' daddy's answer to the stripper's pussy pumping.
The moves are totally different – but the message is the same.

JERRY LEE LEWIS CUTS HIS FIRST RECORD, MEMPHIS, 1956

Jack Clement

Jack Clement was a record producer at Sun Records, the company
owned by Sam Phillips, the man who discovered Elvis Presley.
Jerry Lee Lewis ('Killer') went on to become one of the great
originals of rock'n'roll with songs like 'Great Balls of Fire'.

Jerry Lee just walked into Sun Records one day. I was back
in the control room when Sally Wilburn, who worked up
front, came back and said, 'There's this guy out there who
says he plays piano like Chet Atkins'.

I said, 'I'd like to hear that – send him on back.' So he came in and said he could play 'Wildwood Flower' and stuff like that. So he sang me some wonderful country songs and I said, 'Hey, let me tape some of this.' It was mostly the George Jones stuff like 'Seasons Of My Heart', 'Window Up Above' – that's where he was at. But at this time country music wasn't really happening, everybody was rockin' and rollin'. We did cut some country at Sun but it wasn't Nashville-style – mostly it was rock 'n' roll. So I asked him if he did any rock 'n' roll. He told me no but he would go back home and work something up. So he left and I had that tape of him. Later, Sam came in and I played it for him. He loved it and asked where the guy on the tape was. I told him he was back down in Louisiana, and Sam said, 'Why didn't you sign him up?' Actually, we didn't really sign anybody up, we'd just make some tapes until we got something we liked then we'd put it out – then they'd sign up. I'd played that tape to everybody that walked in there. I loved him singing that George Jones stuff. George Jones was really the only country guy that was really happening, the rest was dead as shit, but I loved the way he sang country. Jerry Lee had written a rock 'n' roll song called 'End Of The Road'. Then he played me a version of 'You're The Only Star In My Blue Heaven' in 4/4 time rather than 3/4 and I loved it. That's what we cut – those songs and 'Crazy Arms' which didn't have anything on it but piano – a spinnet piano, and a cymbal – that's all. It was his first release and although the song had already been a hit for six months by Ray Price, it sold around a hundred and twenty thousand.

GRACE KELLY WEDS PRINCE RAINIER, MONTE CARLO, 19 April 1956

Donald Edgar

It was a sparkling morning on Thursday as I got into my stiff shirt, tied my white tie and put on my tail-coat for the final act of the Monte Carlo spectacular – the nuptial mass in the Cathedral which would add the blessing of the Church to the marriage of Grace and Rainier. There had been much discussion – even passionate at times – among the British and American male guests whether to wear morning coats or to conform to the European custom and appear in what we know as evening dress. I did not trouble to argue. If they wanted me to wear evening dress at a morning ceremony, well and good, for by this time I would have been quite willing to hire the full-dress uniform of Napoleon's Old Guard.

Helen Hamer arrived in the *Express* Rolls to pick me up. She looked delightful and as stylish as any of the daughters of the rich and famous. The Rolls idea did not turn out too good, except for the photographers, for we had to walk most of the way up the hill to the Cathedral.

It was certainly an impressive sight! There was a carefully swept red carpet and on either side were naval detachments from the visiting warships – American, French and Italian sailors and a party of Royal Marines from HMS *Dalrymple*. There were squads of photographers, TV camera crews and a film unit. I noted some new names to add to my list – Somerset Maugham looking absolutely immaculate, a credit to his tailor and valet, Lady Diana Cooper, the widow of Duff Cooper who after the war had been a renowned ambassador to France, and the enormously tall Conrad Hilton, who was there as President Eisenhower's representative, not as the immensely rich hotel proprietor whose hotels now proclaim American influence, if not elegance, throughout the world.

I took Helen's arm and we found our places in the Cathedral. There was a long wait and I had time to look around and admire the efficiency of the MGM technicians. Everything had been organized to make a great film sequence. Finally, to solemn organ music Grace came up the aisle on the arm of her father. Once more one could not but admire her loveliness. Rainier followed, beetle-browed as ever, once more laden with medals and decorations. The arc-lamps came on; the photographers and cameramen behind and on each side of the altar began their work.

Even in that theatrical setting, even with that sort of a congregation, the beauty of the nuptial mass with noble music, well-rehearsed choir and the ritual Latin phrases of the priests wove its spell. They say that in the film, which I did not see, tears fell down Grace's cheeks as she knelt before the altar. Were they sincere? Were they the final proof of professionalism? I incline to the former.

After the ceremony I guided Helen along a narrow, picturesque lane to the courtyard of the Palace where tables were laden with salmon, chicken and every sort of delicacy and where champagne flowed bountifully. The wedding-cake was an enormous work of art.

The now indubitable Princess Grace of Monaco showed herself with her husband to the crowds lining the streets of the town in an open Rolls, loaned by the millionaire Scottish draper, Hugh Fraser. She prayed, according to the tradition of newly wed Princesses of Monaco, at the shrine of the local patron saint, Dévote, in the tiny church dedicated to her.

Grace appeared on the Palace balcony in all her splen-dour, smiling and waving. Rainier, by her side, managed an uneasy grin. I think our Helen enjoyed it all though she only nervously sipped her champagne and nibbled at a sandwich. I delivered her back safely to the yacht and Eve Perrick and went back to the hotel to get out of my stiff collar and think about the story I would be writing.

In the afternoon Grace and Rainier embarked on the *Deo Juvante* for their honeymoon cruise and sailed out of the harbour with crowds waving and ships and yachts sounding their sirens.

It was over! It was finally over! The bar of the Hôtel de Paris filled up with men and women journalists stretching themselves at ease, even smiling at each other as the consciousness grew that the struggle was over – even with Rainier's officials. In the evening there was dancing in the streets, wine flowed and rockets soared once more in the sky – no doubt, once more at the expense of Mr Onassis.

THE HUNGARIAN REVOLUTION, BUDAPEST, 23 October 1956

D. Sefton Delmer, London **Daily Express**

The Communists – with Russian backing – had taken power in Hungary in 1947, and made the country a one-party Stalinist state. Throughout the 1950s discontent with the regime grew, causing dissension within the Communists' ranks themselves, with a popular, liberal wing growing up around prime minister Imre Nagy. On 23 October an anti-Stalinist insurrection broke out in Budapest.

I have been the witness today of one of the great events of history. I have seen the people of Budapest catch the fire lit in Poznan and Warsaw and come out into the streets in open rebellion against their Soviet overlords. I have marched with them and almost wept for joy with them as the Soviet emblems in the Hungarian flags were torn out by the angry and exalted crowds. And the great point about the rebellion is that it looks like being successful.

As I telephone this dispatch I can hear the roar of delirious crowds made up of student girls and boys, of Hungarian soldiers still wearing their Russian-type uniforms, and over-alled factory workers marching through Budapest and shouting defiance against Russia. 'Send the Red Army home,' they roar. 'We want free and secret elections.' And then comes the ominous cry which one always seems to hear on these occasions: 'Death to Rakosi.' Death to the former

Soviet puppet dictator – now taking a 'cure' on the Russian Black Sea Riviera – whom the crowds blame for all the ills that have befallen their country in eleven years of Soviet puppet rule.

Leaflets demanding the instant withdrawal of the Red Army and the sacking of the present Government are being showered among the street crowds from trams. The leaflets have been printed secretly by students who 'managed to get access', as they put it, to a printing shop when newspapers refused to publish their political programme. On house walls all over the city primitively stencilled sheets have been pasted up listing the sixteen demands of the rebels.

But the fantastic and, to my mind, really superingenious feature of this national rising against the Hammer and Sickle, is that it is being carried on under the protective red mantle of pretended Communist orthodoxy. Gigantic portraits of Lenin are being carried at the head of the marchers. The purged ex-Premier Imre Nagy, who only in the last couple of weeks has been readmitted to the Hungarian Communist Party, is the rebels' chosen champion and the leader whom they demand must be given charge of a new free and independent Hungary. Indeed, the Socialism of this ex-Premier and – this is my bet – Premier-soon-to-be-again, is no doubt genuine enough. But the youths in the crowd, to my mind, were in the vast majority as anti-Communist as they were anti-Soviet – that is if you agree with me that calling for the removal of the Red Army is anti-Soviet.

In fact there was one tricky moment when they almost came to blows on this point. The main body of students and marchers had already assembled outside their university in front of the monument to the poet-patriot Petofi who led the 1848 rebellion against the Austrians. Suddenly a new group of students carrying red banners approached from a side street. The banners showed them to be the students of the Leninist-Marxist Institute, which trains young teachers of Communist ideology and supplies many of the puppet rulers' civil servants.

The immediate reaction of the main body, I noticed, was to shout defiance and disapproval of the oncoming ideologists.

But they were quickly hushed into silence and the ideologues joined in the march with the rest of them, happily singing the *Marseillaise* . . .

THE CRUSHING OF THE HUNGARIAN REVOLUTION, BUDAPEST, 4 November 1956

In response to the uprising, Soviet tanks and troops invaded Hungary, setting up a pro-Russian, orthodox Stalinist regime. These Soviet forces crushed the revolt, but only after bloody street-fighting in Budapest.

Alain de Sedouy, **Paris-Presse** *journalist*

To achieve their purpose the Red Army launched elementary manoeuvres, taught in all the military schools throughout the world: how to take a hill. The Russians are good pupils. First an artillery barrage, followed by the attack of tanks with supporting groups in the rear, then followed by infantry encirclement at the bottom of the hill, in order to pick up survivors attempting to escape.

But this classic plan was to be upset by a child's trick. The 'children' poured oil on the narrow roads leading to the castle. The tractors skidded and the tanks had to give up. There were a few hours of respite.

But then files of 'Molotova' lorries could be seen advancing to the attack on the left, up a road behind the hill. At six p.m. the fate of the War Ministry was sealed. Thirty survivors who came out, hands raised above their heads, were shot on the spot, one after the other . . .

George Paloczi-Horvath, London Daily Herald *journalist*

It was dawn . . . the day the Russians struck again.

We were awakened by the roar of heavy guns. The radio was a shambles. All we got was the national anthem, played over and over again, and continual repetition of Premier Nagy's announcement that after a token resistance we must cease fighting and appeal to the free world for help.

After our ten days' war of liberty, after the pathetically short period of our 'victory', this was a terrible blow. But there was not time to sit paralysed in despair. The Russians had arrested General Maleter, head of the Central Revolutionary Armed Forces Council. The Army had received ceasefire orders. But what of the fighting groups of workers and students?

These courageous civilian units now had to be told to put up only token resistance in order to save bloodshed. They had been instructed not to start firing.

I called up the biggest group, the 'Corvin regiment.' A deputy commander answered the phone. His voice was curiously calm:

'Yes, we realized we should not open fire. But the Russians did. They took up positions around our block and opened fire with everything they had. The cellars are filled with 200 wounded and dead. But we will fight to the last man. There is no choice. But inform Premier Nagy that we did not start the fight.'

This was just before seven in the morning. Premier Nagy, alas, could not be informed any more. He was not to be found.

The situation was the same everywhere. Soviet tanks rolled in and started to shoot at every centre of resistance which had defied them during our first battle for freedom.

This time, the Russians shot the buildings to smithereens.

Freedom fighters were trapped in the various barracks, public buildings and blocks of flats. The Russians were going to kill them off to the last man. And they knew it. They fought on till death claimed them.

This senseless Russian massacre provoked the second phase of armed resistance. The installation of Kadar's puppet government was only oil on the fire. After our fighting days, after our brief span of liberty and democracy, Kadar's hideous slogans and stupid lies, couched in the hated Stalinite terminology, made everyone's blood boil. Although ten million witnesses knew the contrary, the puppet government brought forward the ludicrous lie that our war of liberty was a counter-revolutionary uprising inspired by a handful of Fascists.

The answer was bitter fighting and a general strike throughout the country. In the old revolutionary centres – the industrial suburbs of Csepel, Ujpest and the rest – the workers struck and fought desperately against the Russian tanks.

Posters on the walls challenged the lies of the puppet Government: '*The 40,000 aristocrats and fascists of the Csepel works strike on!*' said one of them.

'*The general strike is a weapon which can be used only when the entire working class is unanimous – so don't call us Fascists,*' said another.

Armed resistance stopped first. The Russians bombarded to rubble every house from which a single shot was fired. The fighting groups realized that further battles would mean the annihilation of the capital. So they stopped fighting.

But the strike went on.

The Workers' Councils, the Writers' Association and the Revolutionary Council of the Students decided at last that the general strike must be suspended if Hungary were not to commit national suicide . . .

THE SUEZ INVASION, EGYPT, 5–6 November 1956

Donald Edgar, London Daily Express

The nationalization of the Suez canal led to military intervention in Egypt by Britain and France, with airborne troops landing at Port Said on 5 November. Donald Edgar accompanied the seaborne troops, who landed at Port Said on the following day.

It was a sunny morning with a blue sky and our ship was in the centre of a great array of warships and transports which covered a great arc of sea from Port Fuad to the left of the Canal to Port Said in the centre and Gamil airfield on the right. Our ship was nearly stationary about three miles off shore, distant enough to reduce the scene to the size of a coloured picture postcard and the warships to toys on the Round Pond in Kensington Gardens.

It was only with an effort of will I could grasp that it was all for real, not a sequence from a film. It was really happening.

To the left of the Canal entrance a great cloud of black smoke from burning oil tanks was drifting over the city forming a sinister cloud. Along the sea-front puffs of white smoke were rising from shell-fire and red flames were taking hold on the right where the shanty town lay. Just off shore a line of elegant destroyers were moving along the beach firing into the city. As they had guns of only small calibre the reports at this distance were no more disturbing than the muffled woofs of a sleeping dog.

But to the extreme left, off Port Fuad, the French sector, lay a great battleship, the *Jean Bart*, and from time to time it fired a heavy shell from its great guns which made the air tremble a little where I stood.

Around us and further out to sea were cruisers and an aircraft carrier or two, waiting in ominous silence. Helicopters were ferrying back and forth from the beach. I learned later they had carried the 45 Royal Marine Commando in to support 40 and 42 Commandos which had earlier landed in their Buffalos together with C Sqdn of the 6 Royal Tank Regiment. I watched one helicopter fall into the sea and a ship nearby suddenly leaped forward to the rescue with the speed of a greyhound. I learned it was HMS *Manxman*, the fastest ship in the Royal Navy at the time.

I took in everything I could and asked questions of the Captain, who tried to be helpful within his limits. He told us with a wry smile that there had been trouble with the American Sixth Fleet which was in the area, escorting a shipload of American refugees from Alexandria. In fact, I gathered the Anglo-French convoy was being closely shadowed by the Americans and the air had been filled with tough, rude radio exchanges. Hanson Baldwin smiled – but in somewhat wintry fashion. I did not really believe that Eisenhower would give orders to the Sixth Fleet to blow us out of the water, but I knew the political situation was so tense that even the impossible might happen.

I was busy making notes, drawing rough sketch-maps and then began to feel somewhat dispirited as the first excitement wore off.

I kept telling myself how lucky I was – standing on the bridge watching the most impressive military operation the British had put on for many a year, with parachutists, Marine Commandos, tanks, aircraft and a naval bombardment. What is more I was looking at it all in safety. In the cussed way of the English I think this last factor was beginning to have its effect on me. I was beginning to feel sorry for the people of Port Said who were on the receiving end.

I remembered only too well what it felt like. In 1940 in France it was the Germans who had the tanks, the aircraft and the overwhelming force and I was at the receiving end, taking shelter in ditches and cellars.

However, I fought these feelings back. A few miles away British troops were fighting their way through a city, perhaps against heavy opposition, suffering casualties. What is more in a few hours I could well be in danger myself.

The captain went to the radio room and came back to say that as it was taking longer than expected to clear the area round the jetties of the Canal we should not be landing until the afternoon. He suggested we had lunch.

It was a lunch to remember. A steward served us imperturbably with a drink while we studied the menu. Another took our order with the same solicitude as a head-waiter in the Savoy Grill. A wine-waiter suggested an excellent Burgundy. Outside, not far away, the marine Commandos with the Centurion tanks were fighting their way through the wrecked buildings of Port Said. No doubt men, women and children were dying in fear and anguish. Yet here was I sitting down to an excellent lunch as if I was a first-class passenger on a luxury Mediterranean cruise.

But I ate the lunch and drank the wine with enjoyment. All my instincts as an old soldier came to my aid – eat and drink whilst you can, you never know where the next meal is coming from. Whilst we were finishing our coffee and brandy the ship started to move gently towards the Canal.

We went up again to the bridge. The ship was easing its way towards the jetty on the right-hand of the entrance to the Canal and the scene of destruction along the water-front cleared through the smoke. Crumbled masonry, blackened walls still standing with nothing behind, burnt-out vehicles, debris scattered over the road. A few soldiers hurried to and fro, but the firing – rifle and machine-gun and mortar – seemed to be concentrated a few hundred yards down the Canal. The captain had a radio set on the bridge tuned to the BBC and we heard a bland voice announcing that all resistance had ceased in Port Said. It was just then when with a great scream that froze me in terror, a section of naval fighter-bombers dived down over us dropping their rockets and firing their cannon just ahead of us. Almost quicker than sight they wheeled away into the sky while clouds of grey smoke rose into the air. We were all silent on the bridge for a minute or two. This was the attack by Sea Furies on Navy House where 40 Commando had encountered tough resistance from a hundred-odd Egyptians who had barricaded themselves in. Even the tanks, firing at point-blank range had been unable to dislodge them so the Navy was called in to help with an air-strike. The Navy complied, but with some regret for the building had become over the years part of the Royal Navy's heritage. Even after this devastating attack, however, the Egyptians fought on and a Marine officer told me they had to clear them out room by room. 'They didn't know how to fight professionally,' he said to me. 'But by God they fought to the end.'

It was not until the next day that twenty survivors gave themselves up. Their bravery was another proof that the Egyptians, often abandoned by their officers, can fight magnificently.

By now it was late afternoon. In front of us a transport was unloading more tanks and paratroops who moved off down the Canal road. There were two barges from the *Jean Bart* filled with French paratroops lying down philosophically in the open holds. I noticed with a certain surprise, some female contours among the camouflage uniforms. I had not known till then that the French paratroops had women in their ranks among whose duties were cooking and first-aid. It was an imaginative re-creation of the traditional *vivandières*!

As I was looking at the quayside I saw a group of senior officers who seemed to be waiting for transport while snipers' bullets seemed to me to be getting uncomfortably close. Campbell recognized the leader – Lt General Sir Hugh Stockwell, the Allied Commander, who cheerily waved his swagger-stick at the passing troops. He had been spending a few hours looking at the situation and was trying to get back to the headquarters ship, HMS *Tyne*. I was not to know then that he had a hazardous journey back in a landing-craft which was nearly swamped and when he finally got aboard was greeted with the fateful order to cease-fire at midnight (two a.m. local time).

It grew dark and we were told that no one would be allowed to disembark until the morning to avoid confusion. Then Baldwin and I had a stroke of luck. The Brigadier in charge of Medical Services was a passenger and brusquely said he was going ashore whatever anyone said. He was determined to contact the airborne medical team which had landed the day before. He had seen stretchers going into the damaged Casino Palace Hotel about fifty yards away from us by the side of the Canal. Baldwin and I asked him if we could go along. He nodded and we picked up our bags and followed him ashore.

There were fires enough around to light our way across ropes, hose-pipes and debris to the hotel. The entrance-hall was filled with stretcher-cases. A big reception-room on the right had been cleared for the medical team. In another room along a passage an operating-room had been fixed up with emergency lighting and surgeons stripped to the waist wearing leather aprons were at their tasks. The British casualties had for the most part been flown back by helicopter to an aircraft-carrier. This team was dealing now with Egyptian casualties – some military, most civilian – men, women and children.

The dead were being carried out to the garden in the back to be buried in a shallow grave temporarily.

It was a sombre scene with few words spoken. The surgeons looked to me very young and very tired. They were working in relays, coming back to the main room to sit down and drink a glass of whisky in between operating.

Baldwin had dumped his bag and disappeared. He knew exactly where he was going – to the American consulate whose position further along the Canal he had pin-pointed on a street map before he had landed.

I went out to the road. Night had fallen and the fires had dimmed. Sentries had been posted. Out at sea there was not a light to give a hint of the great convoy and its accompanying warships. A few shots sounded in the distance, but silence was enveloping the stricken city.

The Anglo-French Suez expedition was called off after joint pressure from Washington and Moscow. It marked a humiliating climb-down for the British, and many date 6 November 1956 as the day when Britain ceased to be a world power.

CASTRO SAILS TO CUBA IN THE *GRANMA*, 25 November 1956

Ernesto 'Che' Guevara

The Cuban Revolution began on 25 November 1956 when Fidel Castro and eighty-two supporters – including Che Guevara – sailed from exile in Mexico back to Cuba in the yacht *Granma*.

With our lights extinguished we left the port of Tuxpan amid an infernal mess of men and all sorts of material. The weather was very bad and navigation was forbidden, but the river's estuary was calm. We traversed the entrance into the Gulf and a little later turned on our lights. We began a frenzied search for the anti-seasickness pills, which we did not find. We sang the Cuban national anthem and the 'Hymn of 26 July' for perhaps five minutes and then the entire boat took on an aspect both ridiculous and tragic: men with anguished faces holding their stomachs, some with their heads in buckets, others lying in the strangest positions, immobile, their clothing soiled with vomit.

Apart from two or three sailors and four or five other

people, the rest of the eighty-three crew members were seasick. But by the fourth or fifth day the general panorama had improved a little. We discovered that what we had thought was a leak in the boat was actually an open plumbing faucet. We had thrown overboard everything superfluous in order to lighten the load.

The route we had chosen made a wide circuit south of Cuba, windward of Jamaica and the Grand Cayman islands, in order to reach the point of disembarkation somewhere near the town of Niquero, in the province of Oriente. The plan was carried out quite slowly. On the 30th we heard over the radio the news of riots in Santiago de Cuba, which our great Frank País had organized, hoping to coincide with the arrival of our expedition. The following night, 1 December, without water, fuel, and food, we were pointing our bow on a straight course towards Cuba, desperately seeking the lighthouse at Cabo Cruz. At two in the morning, on a dark and tempestuous night, the situation was worrisome. The watches moved about, looking for the beam of light which did not appear on the horizon. Roque, an ex-lieutenant in the Navy, once again mounted the small upper bridge looking for the light at Cabo. He lost his footing and fell into the water. A while later, as we set out once again, we did see the light, but the wheezing progress of our yacht made the last hours of the trip interminable. It was already daylight when we landed in Cuba, at a place known as Belic, on the Las Coloradas beach.

A coastguard cutter spotted us and telegraphed Batista's Army. No sooner had we disembarked and entered the swamp, in great haste and carrying only the indispensable, when we were attacked by enemy planes. Since we were walking through mangrove-covered marshes, we were not visible, nor were we hit by the planes, but the army of the dictatorship was now on our trail.

We took several hours to get through the swamp. We were delayed in this by the lack of experience and irresponsibility of a comrade who had claimed he knew the way. We were on solid ground, disoriented and walking in circles, an army of shadows, of phantoms, walking as if moved by some obscure psychic mechanism. We had had seven days of continual hunger and sickness at sea, followed by three days on land which were even more terrible. Exactly ten days after leaving Mexico, at dawn on 5 December, after a night's march interrupted by fainting, exhaustion, and rest stops, we reached a place known – what a paradox! – as Alegría [Happiness] de Pío.

At noon we became aware of unusual activity. Piper Cub planes as well as other military and private aircraft began to circle in the vicinity. Some of our men were calmly cutting and eating cane as the planes passed overhead, without thinking how visible they were to the low-flying aircraft.

As the troop's doctor, it was my job to treat the men's blisters. I think I remember my last patient on that day. He was Humberto Lamotte, and as it turned out it was his last day on earth. I can still see his tired and anxious face as he moved from our primitive clinic towards his post, carrying the shoes he could not wear.

Comrade Montané and I were leaning against a tree, talking about our respective children; we were eating our meagre rations – half a sausage and two crackers – when we heard a shot. In a matter of seconds a hurricane of bullets – or at least this is what it seemed to my anxious mind during that trial by fire – rained on the troop of eighty-two men. My rifle was not of the best – I had deliberately asked for it because a long asthma attack during the crossing had left me in a deplorable state and I did not want to waste a good weapon. I do not know exactly when or how things happened; the memories are already hazy. I do remember that during the cross-fire, Almeida – Captain in those days – came to ask for orders, but there was no longer anyone there to give them. As I found out later, Fidel tried in vain to regroup his men in the nearby cane field, which could be reached simply by crossing a small clearing. The surprise attack had been too massive, the bullets too abundant. Almeida went back to take charge of his group. At that moment a comrade dropped a cartridge box at my feet. I pointed questioningly to it and the man answered me with a face I remember perfectly, for the anguish it reflected seemed to say, 'It's too late for bullets,' and he immediately left along the path through the cane field (he was later murdered by Batista's thugs). This was perhaps the first time I was faced with the dilemma of choosing between my dedication to medicine and my duty as a revolutionary soldier. At my feet were a pack full of medicines and a cartridge box; together, they were too heavy to carry. I chose the cartridge box, leaving behind the medicine pack, and crossed the clearing which separated me from the cane field. I distinctly remember Faustino Perez kneeling on the edge of the field, firing his machine pistol. Near me a comrade named Arbentosa was walking towards the plantation. A burst of gun fire, nothing special about it, hit us both. I felt a terrible blow on the chest and another in the neck, and was sure I was dead. Arbentosa, spewing blood from his nose, mouth and an enormous wound from a .45 bullet, shouted something like, 'They've killed me', and began to fire wildly although no one was visible. From the ground I said to Faustino, 'They've got me' (but I used a stronger expression). Still firing, Faustino glanced at me and told me it was nothing, but in his eyes I read a sentence of death from my wound.

I stayed on the ground; following the same obscure impulse as Faustino, I fired once towards the forest. I immediately began to wonder what would be the best way to die, now that all seemed lost. I remembered an old story of Jack London's in which the hero, knowing that he is condemned to freeze to death in the icy reaches of Alaska, leans against a tree and decides to end his life with dignity. This is the only image I remember. Someone, crawling near me, shouted that we'd better surrender, and behind me I heard a voice, which I later learned belonged to Camilo

Cienfuegos, shouting back: 'Here no one surrenders . . .'
followed by an oath. Agitated and short of breath, Ponce
approached me. He had a wound, apparently through the
lung. He told me he was wounded and, indifferently, I
showed him that I was also. Ponce continued dragging
himself towards the cane field, together with the un-
wounded men. For a moment I was alone, stretched out
waiting for my death.

Almeida came over to me and urged me to move. In spite
of my pain, I did so and we entered a field . . . after this
everything became confused. The light planes flew low over
us, firing a few shots from their machine guns. This only
added to the Dantesque and grotesque scenes around us: a
stout *guerillo* trying to hide behind a single stalk of sugar
cane; and another, without really knowing why, crying for
silence in the midst of the tremendous uproar.

A group was formed, led by Almeida, and including
Lieutenant Ramiro Valdes (now a major), comrades Chao
and Benitez, and myself. With Almeida at the head, we
crossed the last row in the cane field in order to reach a small
sheltering forest. At that moment we heard the first shouts of
'Fire!' from the cane field, and columns of smoke and flames
arising from it; I am not sure of this, for I was thinking more
of the bitterness of our defeat and the imminence of my death
than of the specific incidents of the battle. We walked until
night prevented us from going any further and we decided to
sleep huddled together. We were attacked by mosquitoes,
tortured by thirst and by hunger. Such was our baptism of
fire on 5 December 1956, in the district of Niguero. Such was
the beginning of what would become the Rebel Army.

In all twelve guerrillas escaped the ambush; a group led by Fidel
Castro also got away. Only two years later the rebels, after their
inexorable guerrilla war in the Sierra Maestra, would overthrow
the regime of Fulgencio Batista.

A PARTY WITH ELVIS PRESLEY, MEMPHIS, December 1956

Jerry Lee Lewis

I could go and see Elvis, or he'd come and see me, and he'd say 'Come on Jerry, play the piano, just play a couple of songs', and he'd get me down at that piano and he wouldn't let me get up. He begged me to keep playing. He loved it. He said 'You've got more talent in your little finger than I've got in my whole body'. He said that to Sam Phillips too – he recognized that, he knew it. The first time I heard an Elvis Presley record I was living in Louisiana. He was singing 'Blue Moon of Kentucky', and I thought, 'I don't know who this dude is, but somebody done opened the door.' He was something else.

We had some good times together. I went to a party at Jack Clement's house with Elvis and we rode our motorcycles down the street. Buck naked. And this policeman on a horse sees us. It was three o'clock in the morning. He never caught us. If anybody had seen us, they never would have bought another record!

LITTLE ROCK, ARKANSAS, 23 September 1957

Relman Morin, Associated Press

Passions erupted throughout the American south in the 1950s as black Americans sought equal educational opportunities. The most famous of the clashes between segregationists and anti-segregationists came at Little Rock, where Governor Orval E. Faubus used National Guard troops at Central High School to prevent integration. The troops were withdrawn after a federal court ruling, but replaced by a large crowd which declared its intention of keeping black children out. Relman Morin won a Pulitzer Prize for this dispatch from Little Rock.

It was exactly like an explosion, a human explosion.

At 8.35 a.m., the people standing in front of the high school looked like the ones you see every day in a shopping centre.

A pretty, sweet-faced woman with auburn hair and a jewel-green jacket. Another holding a white portable radio to her ear. 'I'm getting the news of what's going on at the high school,' she said. People laughed. A grey-haired man, tall and spare, leaned over the wooden barricade. 'If they're coming,' he said, quietly, 'they'll be here soon.' 'They better,' said another, 'I got to get to work.'

Ordinary people – mostly curious, you would have said – watching a high school on a bright blue-and-gold morning.

Five minutes later, at 8.40, they were a mob.

The terrifying spectacle of 200-odd individuals, suddenly welded together into a single body, took place in the barest fraction of a second. It was an explosion, savagery chain-reacting from person to person, fusing them into a white-hot mass.

There are three glass windowed telephone booths across the street from the south end of the high school.

At 8.35, I was inside one of them, dictating.

I saw four Negroes coming down the centre of the street, in twos. One was tall and big shouldered. One was tall and thin. The other two were short. The big man had a card in his hat and was carrying a Speed Graphic, a camera for taking news pictures.

A strange, animal growl rose from the crowd.

'Here come the Negroes.'

Instantly, people turned their backs on the high school and ran toward the four men. They hesitated. Then they turned to run.

I saw the white men catch them on the sidewalk and the lawn of a home, a quarter-block away. There was a furious, struggling knot. You could see a man kicking at the big Negro. Then another jumped on his back and rode him to the ground, forearms deep in the Negro's throat.

They kicked him and beat him on the ground and they smashed his camera to splinters. The other three ran down the street with one white man chasing them. When the white man saw he was alone, he turned and fled back toward the crowd.

Meanwhile, five policemen had rescued the big man.

I had just finished saying, 'Police escorted the big man away – '

At that instant, a man shouted, 'Look, the niggers are going in.'

Directly across from me, three Negro boys and five girls were walking toward the side door at the south end of the school.

It was an unforgettable tableau.

They were carrying books. White bobby-sox, part of the high school uniform, glinted on the girls' ankles. They were all neatly dressed. The boys wore open-throat shirts and the girls ordinary frocks.

They weren't hurrying. They simply strolled across perhaps fifteen yards from the sidewalk to the school steps. They glanced at the people and the police as though none of this concerned them.

You can never forget a scene like that.

Nor the one that followed.

Like a wave, the people who had run toward the four Negro men, now swept back toward the police and the barricades.

'Oh, God, the niggers are in the school,' a man yelled.

A woman – the one with the auburn hair and green jacket – rushed up to him. Her face was working with fury now.

Her lips drew back in a snarl and she was screaming, 'Did they go in?'

'The niggers are in the school,' the man said.

'Oh, God,' she said. She covered her face with her hands. Then she tore her hair, still screaming.

She looked exactly like the women who cluster around a

mine head when there has been an explosion and men are trapped below.

The tall, lean man jumped up on one of the barricades. He was holding on to the shoulders of others nearby.

'Who's going through?' he roared.

'We all are,' the people shrieked.

They surged over and around the barricades, breaking for the police.

About a dozen policemen, in short-sleeved blue shirts, swinging billy clubs, were in front of them.

Men and women raced toward them and the policemen raised their clubs, moving this way and that as people tried to dodge around them.

A man went down, pole-axed when a policeman clubbed him.

Another, with crisp curly black hair, was quick as a rat. He dodged between two policemen and got as far as the schoolyard. There the others caught him.

With swift, professional skill, they pulled his coat half-way down his back, pinning his arms. In a flash they were hustling him back toward the barricades.

A burly, thick-bodied man wearing a construction worker's 'hard hat' charged a policeman. Suddenly, he stopped and held both hands high above his head.

I couldn't see it, but I assume the officer jammed a pistol in his ribs.

Meanwhile, the women – the auburn-haired one, the woman with the radio, and others – were swirling around the police commanding officers.

Tears were streaming down their faces. They acted completely distraught.

It was pure hysteria.

And they kept crying, 'The niggers are in our school. Oh, God, are you going to stand here and let the niggers stay in school?'

Then, swiftly, a line of cars filled with state troopers rolled toward the school from two directions. The flasher-signals on the tops of the cars were spurting red warnings.

REVOLUTION IN HAVANA, 31 December 1958–1 January 1959

Edwin Tetlow

After fighting for two years in the mountains, Fidel Castro's revolutionaries reached the Cuban capital on the last day of 1958.

The approaches to the city from the airport seemed normal enough as viewed from a big old Buick taxi which I shared with the young American, who confided to me that he expected to find 'a lovely young thing' among those welcoming him to Cuba. The dark-complexioned driver hummed softly to the music from his radio as he piloted us skilfully through the turbulent traffic. The Hotel Nacional, a great oblong block of a place, had a few rooms available, at a hefty rate for those days. I settled in and had a leisurely dinner from an expansive menu in the hotel restaurant, which was filled with well-dressed, and obviously well-heeled, Cubans and a minority of foreigners. Feeling comfortable, I set out to stroll in the warm evening air, dropping in on some of the tourist haunts of suburban Vedado and upper midtown Havana, amassing material for the feature article I should be writing the following morning.

Eventually, around 11 p.m. [31 December 1958], I strolled into the Casino at the Hotel Nacional to await midnight. I noted that the bar was being heavily patronized. A four-piece band was playing in one corner of the ornate salon, accompanying a lusty and busty Cuban contralto who was singing at full strength to make herself heard above the band and the hubbub from the bar, and the softer, sleeker noises from the casino itself, so different from the rattle, slap and clap made by dice-players as they thumped down their leathern cups on tables in the humbler haunts of the city. As the time passed towards midnight the noise became unbelievably piercing. How Cubans love noise! Eventually neither band nor contralto could be heard as separate entities.

Around the gaming tables, under glittering chandeliers bigger and more fanciful than any I had seen for years, guests both Cuban and foreign gambled with deep concentration. Only occasionally did heads turn and envious smiles appear round tight-lipped mouths when somebody shrieked in ecstasy after hitting the jackpot at one of the fruit machines lining the walls of the casino. Also along the walls were several armed policemen stationed like sentries. I asked once or twice of seemingly knowledgeable guests why they were there. One man just shrugged and said languidly: 'Who knows?' One other man told me they had appeared for the first time only a few evenings earlier.

At midnight there came a token acknowledgement that 1959 had arrived. The intense proceedings at the gaming tables and the fruit machines were halted for but a few moments. A few men and women kissed and some people shook hands and smiled at each other before resuming the serious business of the night. At about 12.30 a.m. the members of the band quietly packed their instruments, the singer folded up her microphone stand, and she and the musicians walked off into the night. Only the bar and the gaming tables continued operations, the former being sustained mainly by a party of American and other foreigners, who, growing more disarrayed almost by the minute, still managed to keep the tiring bartenders busy. At that hour I decided I had seen enough. I wanted to go to bed. Once there, I spent a few minutes jotting down facts and reminders for the writing I expected to be doing next morning. Satisfied that I had my assignment under control, I settled down and went to sleep.

I was awakened before 8 a.m. by an excited phone call from Robert Perez, my local correspondent, an energetic Puerto Rican who had lived for some years in Havana. 'He's gone,' he spluttered into the phone. 'Who's gone?' I asked, still half-asleep. 'Batista! Batista!' came the galvanizing answer from Perez. 'He went in the night.'

So he had. At about the time I was settling down to sleep he and a party of about forty, including many members of his family, had motored over to a military airfield at Camp Columbia, on the fringe of Havana, and – excessively heavily laden with baggage – had boarded an Army plane for a short hop eastwards across the water to the Dominican Republic, then still in the grip of Batista's fellow-dictator, General-issimo Rafael Trujillo, later assassinated.

Pure luck had landed me in the very centre of a revolution while it was happening and being won. No hasty packing of a suitcase this time, no mad rush to catch the first plane to the scene of action, no hectic chase after news which was already growing old! This was a foreign correspondent's dream come true, and I was determined to make the most of it. First, on the sound recommendation of Robert Perez, I moved out of the lordly but isolated Hotel Nacional and into the Hotel Colina, a small and well-placed observation-post giving a view from my third-floor window of the approaches to the University of Havana, where Fidel Castro had been edu-cated and where he was said to have substantial secret support.

The city was eerily quiet at about 8.45 a.m. as Perez and I made our cautious way to the Colina, not at all sure what might happen as we did so. Weren't revolutions affairs of wild shooting and melodramatic action? Not this one – yet. I felt as if I were in the eye of a hurricane, the centre where everything is still while furious winds whirl all around. Hardly anybody was moving. Perez told me as we inched our way towards the Colina that Cubans in the capital had done exactly what people in most countries of the Caribbean did when, as happens all too often in that steamy region, trouble threatened. They closed and locked their shutters, bolted all their doors, and holed up.

Once installed in my new strategic headquarters I implemented my plan of campaign. I despatched Perez on a mission of news-gathering in the city, asking him to phone me as often as seemed necessary with any information he had. I calculated that because of his intimate knowledge of the city, contacts he had, plus his command of his native Spanish, he would have no trouble about keeping me in touch with what was happening. And he did so with great efficiency. As for myself, I stayed as a willing prisoner in my hotel room. I put in a telephone call to my newspaper after having been told by the local exchange that there was, predictably, 'long delay' in calls to the outside world, including distant London. While I waited I began assembling the story I would telephone as soon as the call came through. I listened to Radio Havana as it broadcast messages from Fidel Castro telling the populace to keep calm while it waited for him to take control of the nation. 'Don't worry, I shall come to you,' he said. I took messages from the assiduous Perez and as best I could I kept an eye on what was happening in the streets leading to the University.

In fact, very little happened all that morning. Only a very few people were to be seen hurrying along in order to carry out missions which presumably could not be put off. I noticed that almost all these scurrying pedestrians kept as close as possible to any nearby wall or other cover they were afforded. However, my heaven-sent story was shaping up well. It was helped greatly by word from Robert Perez that Fidel Castro had sent an amplified message to the people of Havana. Speaking from his field camp near Santa Clara, the last sizeable city between him and the capital, he said he did not accept as a bargaining agent a three-man junta of 'so-called neutrals' whom Batista had left behind to represent him. 'I shall be coming into Havana soon,' Castro promised.

'Keep the peace until then. I am sending a company of Barbudos [bearded ones] to administer Havana until I get there. They will preserve Havana – and you.'

This message galvanized the nervous population of the city. Reassured, thousands of them opened their shutters and doors and got into their cars, to celebrate their unexpected liberation. They staged a fantastic crawl-around of the city streets. They draped their vehicles, almost all of them American-made, with Cuban flags. If the car was a convertible, they wound down the top and then joined the follow-my-leader procession of their neighbourhood. As they did so, more and more people climbed up on and into the cars until, as I counted from my observation-point in the Hotel Colina, there were often as many as ten persons in one car. As each individual procession made its slow progress along the old, narrow streets, the ecstatic celebrants chanted the word *Li-ber-tad* and most of them added emphasis by pounding with their fists their car's side or roof in rhythm with the three syllables of the word for liberty. Very soon the din became hard to stand. I was staggered by the intensity, emotion and, I must add, childlike character of the manifestation of happy relief. Nobody could possibly foresee the tribulations in store for Cuba for the next forty years . . .

My telephone call to London came through at last in the early afternoon, in time for me to dictate over fifteen hundred words, many of them forming impromptu sentences, as thoughts occurred to me, across the bed of the Atlantic Ocean. Even my vigil the previous evening in the casino of the Hotel Nacional was not wasted; indeed, the languid scene around the gaming tables and the jollity in the bar on the eve of one of the most startling and profound revolutionary upheavals of the century in Latin America added to the impact of the story I was able to tell. This was by far the most vivid first-hand report I had written in fifty years, during war as well as peace; and now that it was safely in the hands of my editors in Fleet Street, I was free to leave my bedroom at the Hotel Colina. I could spend the next couple of hours before my second phone call seeing for myself what was going on in the liberated city.

I permitted myself one substantial tot of Bacardi rum before I set out on the long walk from Vedado to midtown Havana. I had to thrust my way through the thick ranks of people watching, some with tears of joy coursing down their faces, the motorized crawl-around. But just as I was making the last turn into the Prado, which roughly marks the boundary between respectable bourgeois Havana and the livelier but sleazy down-town, I saw that something had happened to cut short the touching celebration. Panic was spreading among both Cubans in their cars and the onlookers who had been cheering them on. Vehicles were peeling off from the processions, screeching away into side-streets, and the crowds were scurrying for cover as quickly as their feet would race. In a matter of minutes I found myself uncomfortably alone in the mid-section of the broad Prado. What had happened?

The answer was forthcoming almost as soon as I asked myself the question. The underworld was taking over. One by one a party of dirty and ruffianly-looking young Cubans emerged from Calle Neptuno and other side-streets. Each was carrying a rifle or shotgun across his chest. They walked warily along the street, their gaze darting everywhere as they made sure that nobody was going to challenge them. Nobody did. Batista's hated armed policemen had fled into hiding once they heard that their protector had gone. (It transpired that by no means all of them escaped vengeance. Stories of beatings and murders of these men abounded during the next twenty-four hours.) The small-time gangsters now taking over central Havana were organized and ingenious. Some took up positions as watchdogs at strategic points, ordering away at gunpoint people such as myself, while their comrades went on a rampage of looting. Their first targets were parking-meters. These were smashed apart so that their contents could be rattled out and pocketed. Then came the turn of pinball machines and other gaming devices in arcades and deserted casinos which could easily be entered, including an especially lucrative one close to the Sevilla Biltmore Hotel. Here, from a discreet distance, I watched one gang of looters drag a slot-machine into the street and batter it open with jagged pieces of metal from a destroyed parking-meter. It struck me as a remarkable and possibly unique confirmation of the validity of the old saying that money makes money.

The physical hazards of remaining outdoors grew as the bandits got their hands on rum. They started shooting. Mostly it was the wildest kind of exhibitionism, but even so it claimed victims. Ambulances soon began making screaming runs through the streets on journeys to and from hospitals – and mortuaries. Late in the afternoon I went into one hospital and found it in chaos, overflowing with wounded persons and roughly bandaged out-patients. 'Some have been in street accidents, but mostly they seem to have been hit by flying bullets,' said one nurse to me.

There appeared to be no reason for most of the shooting. Indeed, one series of incidents which I ran into on my way back to the Colina tended to show that Cubans just weren't to be trusted with weapons. A man's rifle would go off either because it was defective or because he had forgotten his finger was on the trigger, or even because of a need – common in Latin America – to show off. The trouble was that very often a haphazard shot would start a chain reaction. Men who heard the shot would start firing their own weapons, with the result that shotgun pellets and bullets began flying around an area, ricocheting off walls, smashing windows and occasionally hitting an unlucky pedestrian. Rarely did there seem to be a justifiable tar- get. Alas, this kind of irresponsibility seemed to be occurring mostly near the University, and I was disturbed to deduce that the perpetrators were not underworld bandits of the kind I had met in the Prado but students who were supporters of Fidel Castro and were apparently obeying his broadcast admonitions to preserve the peace in Havana until he arrived. They were probably earnest enough in their devotion to his cause, but they wouldn't be much use if Batista's police and troops rallied. I reasoned that Fidel Castro would be well advised to get his trained Barbudos into Havana as quickly as he could. If they didn't come soon, there would probably be a confrontation between his amateur followers and the downtown bandits, and if the latter won, which seemed likely, unimaginable bloody chaos would follow.

The most senseless shooting spree of all happened on the afternoon of 2 January, the second day of the revolution. I was standing in the shelter of a shopping arcade near the Parque Centrale, in the centre of Havana, and was looking at the debris of splintered windows and doors and ransacked shelves left by yesterday's looters when I became aware of a noisy commotion on a street corner close to the Sevilla Biltmore. The cracks made by ragged rounds of gunshots were coming from somewhere close at hand. I crept cautiously forward to investigate. A squad of about half a dozen young men wearing armbands to show that they were members of a pro-Castro group which had come out of hiding during the past forty-eight hours were firing rifles and automatic pistols from the west side of the Prado at an upper window of a building on the opposite side of the wide thoroughfare. Their collective aim was atrocious. I could see bullets squelching into stonework far above, below and around the window, and only one or two were flying through it into the room beyond. The attack lasted at least half an hour, without, as I noted most carefully, a single shot coming back in reply. This one-sided 'battle' was happening so close to the Sevilla Biltmore that a party of American tourists, wisely obeying a recommendation from the US Embassy not to venture outdoors, could hear all the shooting but had no more idea of what it all meant than, it emerged, did the men involved.

The facts came to me eventually. Word had reached a volunteer unit of Castro supporters that some fugitives of the Batista regime were hiding in a room on the top floor of the building now being attacked. There were said to be at least a dozen armed followers of Rolando Masferrer, a notorious henchman of Batista, locked inside the room. When the shooting ended, one militiaman said gloatingly to me: 'We got the lot.' In truth, as I was able to confirm for myself a little later, there had been nobody at all in the whole building.

As taxis had vanished from the streets, we were walking on foot when we ran into trouble. A voice called out suddenly in grating Spanish from somewhere in the darkness a few feet ahead of us: 'Halt. Hands up!' Peering ahead, I could see three men with rifles pointed straight at us. Two of them were kneeling side by side on the pavement while the third, their leader, stood barring the way directly ahead. He had a revolver in his right hand – and an armed Cuban was not a man to be trifled with. His gun might very well go off by chance.

But I have never had much time for amateur warriors anywhere. Tonight, also, I was tired, hungry and consequently bad-tempered and of fallible judgement. I was tempted to bluff my way through and I was slow to comply with the orders of our interceptors. My American companions were perhaps wiser. They all raised their hands and one of them muttered impatiently to me as he did so: 'Come on, man. You'll get us all shot!' Unwillingly, I complied.

Our captors motioned us into the passageway of an apartment house. There, blocking the way, sat an unshaven young fellow at a desk. We were in the unit's rough-and-ready headquarters. The man at the desk started questioning the two Americans nearest to him. I was very hot indeed in that passageway. I sidled back into the street, leaving it to others who spoke far better Spanish than I to argue and protest against this unwarranted interference with the free movement of foreign civilians pursuing their daily task in extremely difficult circumstances, and so on. As I breathed the welcome fresh air I mentally assessed the odds about being able to make a dash for it and go up the hill to my hotel. I decided against trying to do so. Several of these amateur gunmen were still around, for I could hear them talking close to me. Even though there was a good chance that if they fired after me as I ran away they might very well miss me, I considered the risk not worth taking. If I were wounded or killed, my newspaper would be the innocent loser.

Meanwhile our negotiators were making no impression whatever on the man at the desk. He told them he was chief of one of the paramilitary units which had been ordered by Fidel Castro to keep the city peaceful, and he couldn't in good conscience let us go on our way. 'My authority doesn't extend very far,' he confessed. 'There are a lot of bandits still roaming around out there. You might get robbed – or worse – if I let you go off into the night.' It availed nothing that our spokesman told him we were well able to take care of ourselves and anyway intended to hole up in our hotels as soon as we got there. 'Sorry, you'll have to spend tonight under our protection,' the man insisted.

We were bundled into two cars and driven to a dingy-looking house in one of the streets running diagonally off the Malecon boulevard on the sea front. It turned out to have been a 'safe' house used by revolutionary agents and couriers as well as by fugitives from Batista's police. I was shown to a small and none-too-savoury bedroom immediately underneath a rooftop water cistern. Dumping my typewriter, my only luggage, resignedly in a corner of the room, I obeyed my captors' order to go down to the desk, sign my name in a register and claim a key.

As I did so, the good fortune which had sent me to Havana

in the first place and had attended me for forty-eight hours thereafter worked again. I was walking away from the hotel desk when I noticed a big utility truck standing in the street outside the hotel entrance. Half a dozen laughing soldiers – real soldiers this time – were unloading their kit and other baggage from it. I was astonished to observe that two of them standing with their backs facing me had black hair hanging down so long below their shoulders that I should have said they were girls if they obviously had not been blessed with thick black beards. I walked forward and began talking with them. They were, they said, the very first detachment of Barbudos which Castro had promised to send into Havana.

So the seeming ill-luck that had landed me into being arrested had also brought me another lively segment for the morrow's story. This is yet another example of how compensations have so frequently offset what seemed initially to be setbacks in my profession as a journalist. A missed train or plane, failure to establish contact by phone or cable with London, somebody's refusal to tell me something, were irritating when encountered, but so often were followed by a piece of unexpected good fortune. Perhaps this helps to explain my perennial optimism.

The Barbudos were among the fittest and happiest young warriors I have ever seen. They had good reason for being so. They had had very little serious fighting and, as the never-robust morale had seeped away from Batista's conscripts during the past few months in the Sierra Maestra, an astonishingly easy victory had fallen to them. They told me that they had enjoyed a leisurely, unchallenged, advance upon the capital from the eastern province of Oriente, through Camagüey and Las Villas. The peasants in these mostly rural areas had welcomed them with increasing ardour as the reality of Castro's total victory had become manifest. People had been eager to give them anything they wanted. One Barbudo told me he couldn't remember when he had been last paid. 'The one thing we didn't need was money,' he said. 'People couldn't do enough for us. They lavished everything, especially food, on us.'

Proof of this was forthcoming as some of the contents of the truck were arrayed on the counter of the hotel reception desk. There were hams, strings of sausages, cottage-made bread, butter, beer and many other such good provender. We were all invited to tuck into a midnight feast – rebel soldiers, our captors, American reporters, including one lone Englishman, and anybody else who happened to be about. Good fellowship bloomed with every mouthful. There was much hearty back-slapping, joking, talk and toasting of international understanding, and some glowing forecasts from the Barbudos of the future Cuba once Fidel Castro took charge.

MASSACRE AT SHARPEVILLE, SOUTH AFRICA, 21 March 1960

Humphrey Tyler, Drum *magazine*

A demonstration by black South Africans against the Apartheid law which required them to carry a pass, or ID card, was fired upon by police, killing 56, wounding 152, at the township of Sharpeville. Humphrey Tyler was the only journalist to witness the shootings.

We went into Sharpeville the back way, around lunch time last Monday, driving along behind a big grey police car and three Saracen armoured cars.

As we went through the fringes of the township many people were shouting the Pan Africanist slogan '*Izwe Lethu*' (Our Land). They were grinning and cheerful. Some kids waved to the policemen sitting on the Saracens and two of the policemen waved back.

It was like a Sunday outing – except that Major A. T. T. Spengler, head of the Witwatersrand Security Branch, was in the front car and there were bullets in the Saracens' guns.

At the main gates of the fenced-off location, policemen were stopping all cars coming in from the outside. Spengler and the Saracens headed for the police station which is deep inside the settlement, and we followed. The policemen were by now all inside the Saracens, with the hatches battened down, looking at Sharpeville through chinks of armour plating. Yet the Africans did not appear to be alarmed by the cars. Some looked interested and some just grinned.

There were crowds in the streets as we approached the police station. There were plenty of police, too, well armed.

A constable shoved the butt of his rifle against my windshield. Another pointed his rifle at my chest. Another leaned into the car, shouting: 'Have you got a permit to be in this location?'

I said no, whereupon he bellowed: 'Then get out, get out, get out! or I will arrest you on the spot. Understand?'

He had a police gun in his holster and a black pistol tucked into his belt. We decided to go around the other side of the police station, where we parked in a big field.

We could see a couple of the Saracens, their tops poking starkly above the heads of the crowd, just over 100 yards away from us. This was about seven minutes before the police opened fire.

The crowd seemed to be loosely gathered around them and on the fringes people were walking in and out. The kids were playing. In all there were about 3,000 people. They seemed amiable.

I said to Ian Berry, *Drum*'s chief photographer: 'This is going to go on all day.' He replied: 'Let's hang on for a bit.'

Suddenly there was a sharp report from the direction of the police station.

'That's a shot,' Berry said.

There were shrill cries of *Izwe Lethu* – women's voices, I

thought. The cries came from the police station and I could see a small section of the crowd swirl around the Saracens. Hands went up in the Africanist salute.

Then the shooting started. We heard the chatter of a machine-gun, then another, then another.

'Here it comes,' said Berry. He leaped out of the car with two cameras and crouched in the grass, taking pictures.

The first rush was on us, then past.

There were hundreds of women, some of them laughing. They must have thought that the police were firing blanks.

One woman was hit about ten yards from our car. Her companion, a young man, went back when she fell. He thought she had stumbled.

Then he turned her over and saw that her chest had been shot away. He looked at the blood on his hand and said: 'My God, she's gone!'

Hundreds of kids were running, too. One little boy had on an old black coat which he held up behind his head, thinking perhaps that it might save him from the bullets. Some of the children, hardly as tall as the grass, were leaping like rabbits. Some of them were shot, too.

Still the shooting went on. One of the policemen was standing on top of a Saracen, and it looked as though he was firing his sten gun into the crowd. He was swinging it around in a wide arc from his hip as though he were panning a movie camera. Two other police officers were on the truck with him, and it looked as though they were firing pistols.

Most of the bodies were strewn in the road running through the field in which we were. One man who had been lying still, dazedly got to his feet, staggered a few yards then fell in a heap. A woman sat with her head cupped in her hands.

One by one the guns stopped. Nobody was moving in our field except Berry. The rest were wounded – or dead. There was no longer a crowd and it was very quiet.

Berry ran back to the car, saying: 'Let's go before they get my film.' We drove out through the main gate, looking straight ahead.

Before the shooting, I heard no warning to the crowd to disperse. There was no warning volley. When the shooting started, it did not stop until there was no living thing on the huge compound in front of the police station.

The police have claimed they were in desperate danger because the crowd was stoning them. Yet only three policemen were reported to have been hit by stones – and more than 200 Africans were shot down.

The police also have said that the crowd was armed with 'ferocious weapons' which littered the compound after they fled.

I saw no weapons, although I looked very carefully, and afterwards studied the photographs of the death scene. While I was there I saw only shoes, hats and a few bicycles left among the bodies.

It seemed to me that tough stuff was behind the killings at Sharpeville. The crowd gave me no reason to feel scared, though I moved among them without any distinguishing mark to protect me, quite obvious with my white skin.

I think the police were scared, though, and I think the crowd knew it.

That final shrill cry from the women before the shooting started certainly sounded much more like a jeer than a battle-cry. And the first Africans who fled past me after the shooting started were still laughing.

A VISIT TO THE WHITE HOUSE, WASHINGTON, 25 January 1961

J. K. Galbraith

Just appointed US ambassador to India by President Kennedy, Galbraith writes in his diary:

After the meeting, Mac Bundy told me 'The Boss' (a new term) had been asking for me. I went into Ken O'Donnell's office and presently the President came through, grabbed me by the arm, and we had an hour-and-a-half chat which included a tour of the upstairs of the White House. We saw where Ike's golf shoes had poked innumerable holes in his office floor. When we left the office in the West Wing for the house proper, we went headlong into a closet. The President turned over furniture to see where it was made, dismissed some as Sears, Roebuck and expressed shock that so little – the Lincoln bed apart – consisted of good pieces. Only expensive reproductions. The effect is indeed undistinguished although today the house was flooded with sunlight and quite filled with flowers.

THE BERLIN WALL, November 1961

Mark Arnold-Foster, London Observer

In August 1961 the Soviet authorities began the building of a massive concrete wall to divide off their sector of conquered Berlin from those occupied by the Western powers. Ostensibly, the wall was to prevent spying by the West; more truthfully, it was to prevent the mass escape to the West of East Germans disaffected with Stalinism.

The wall starts in a bird sanctuary on the banks of a stream called the Tegeler Fliess. It flows through a marshy valley 200 yards from the village of Lubars, which has four big farms, a policeman, a duck pond – now frozen – and an inn called The Merry Finch. The village is reputed to be the coldest place in Berlin. It might have been moved here from Wiltshire.

It belongs, all the same, to the French sector of the city and the high road leading out of it leads only to the Russian sector. The barrier is seven minutes from The Merry Finch, but the East German People's Police can see you sooner. Here, as everywhere along the wall, they operate in pairs, one man with field glasses, the other with a gun.

At this point the barrier consists of three barbed-wire fences supported on concrete posts seven feet high and six inches thick. The first fence is on the border itself; the second is ten feet behind the first; the third is 150 yards behind the second. Each fence has up to ten strands of barbed wire and the ground between the first and second is obstructed with more barbed wire coiled over wooden supports consisting of two crosses linked together and resembling, but for the wire, gigantic devices for keeping carving knives off table-cloths.

The ground between the second and third fences has been cleared and can be lit at night. A line of poles thirty feet high, spaced thirty yards apart, carries a power line; each pole has a cluster of electric lights. There is a line of watchtowers twenty feet high spaced 600 yards apart which has been manned throughout this week.

Farther south, where the suburbs become denser, the border is marked by a railway embankment. In Berlin, as in Surrey, railway lines in leafy suburbs tend to be flanked by gardens. By this week the People's Police had managed to get rid of most of the gardens that were in their way on the east side of the tracks. On Wednesday they were burning the rubbish, the tool sheds along with cherry trees, at the Bornholmerstrasse Station, four and three-quarter miles south of the point at which the railway becomes the frontier.

Five hundred yards further south, at the back of the Hertha football stadium, the wall itself begins.

For most of its length it is eight feet high. It is made of pink prefabricated concrete slabs measuring three feet four inches by three feet eight inches. They are one foot thick. Smaller prefabricated concrete blocks, the size of four English bricks, have been used to fill in awkward corners.

In most places the wall has now been capped with one or two rows of grey cement posts, eleven feet eight inches long and a foot square and laid on their sides. Cemented into them are Y-shaped welded rods carrying seven strands of barbed wire, two of which overhang the wall on the Western side and two on the other. In the city the People's Police have cleared as much ground as they can on their side of the wall and have, in places, reinforced it with fences.

At one point in the south-eastern borough of Neukolln they have planted two seven-foot fences on the Western side of the wall – the first four feet from it and the second four feet from the first – and a third fence, only five feet high, 100 feet behind the wall. The power line and the lights run down the middle of the open ground.

This kind of clearance is neither necessary nor possible in most places. A mile south of the Hertha football stadium is the Bernauerstrase, in the borough of Wedding, where the sector boundary runs east and west and coincides with the building line on the south side of the street. Here, as in other places, the People's Police have made their wall out of houses. At first they bricked up the front door and the ground-floor windows: people who lived on the south side of the street were talking to people who lived on the north side.

Some of them were doing more than that. At a bus stop opposite No. 44 neighbours have put a cross in memory of a student called Bernd Lunser who, pursued by the People's Police, jumped off the roof on 4 October. The West Berlin Fire department tried, but failed, to catch him in a jumping sheet. No. 44 is five storeys high. This week, all the roofs on the southern side of the Bernauerstrasse have been fenced with barbed wire.

Two hundred yards down the road from No. 44 the wall has been heightened to ten feet. Behind it, at this point, is the graveyard of the Church of Reconciliation, Wedding. Farther west again the graveyard of the Church of St Sophia has also been walled in to a height of ten feet.

Neither section carries the usual barbed wire superstructure. Churchyards get broken glass instead.

The new wall round the French cemetery in the Lisenstrasse has barbed wire, but is even higher. It was the highest section of wall I saw.

Round the corner in the Invalidesstrase is a crossing point for the 500-odd West Berliners still allowed to visit East Berlin. A poster across the road says: THE STRONGER THE GERMAN DEMOCRATIC REPUBLIC GETS THE GREATER IS THE CERTAINTY OF PEACE IN GERMANY. It was here that an East German railway policeman shot and killed an unknown man who had dived into the neighbouring Humboldt Dock from the grounds of the Charite Hospital.

From the Humboldt Dock the wall follows the bank of the Spree to skirt the Reichstag building (at present occupied, in part, by the Durham Light Infantry) and to join this week's new works at the Brandenburg Gate. Here the wall is now thicker than anywhere else and its construction is more solid.

When they built it the East Germans began by sinking a row of steel posts into the roadway and cementing them in. They then laid slotted prefabricated concrete slabs over the posts, which projected through the slabs and held them steady. They then poured wet cement over the slabs and laid another layer on top, repeating the process until they had made a multi-decker sandwich in which slabs of concrete had been substituted for bread, the wet cement for butter.

The wall follows to the inch the western boundary of East Berlin which, in front of the Gate, bulges out into the roadway in a segment of a circle 100 yards wide and fifty deep. The East German construction workers – few, so it is said, come from Berlin began the job at half-past five last Sunday evening and finished at half past ten on Tuesday night. They were heavily guarded by People's Police, dressed for the most part in camouflaged combat uniforms. They ate at a field kitchen parked beneath the Gate.

From the gate down the Ebertstrasse to the Potsdamerplatz they added, in the same period, two rows of heavy welded steel tripods, fixed in the roadway with cement. These have been camouflaged, ineffectively, with the sort of netting used round tennis courts. Their military purpose seems to be to deter the Western Powers from attacking with tanks the site of the Wertheim department store, an undertaking once regarded here as Germany's answer to Harrods.

From the Potsdamerplatz the wall runs south to include the ruins of the Potsdam Station, then north again, then east towards the Spree. It bisects the Wilhelmstrasse immediately south of what used to be Göring's Air Ministry. This week, early on Tuesday morning, about 200 young West Berliners gathered here to protest against the reinforcement of the wall. Some of them threw burning torches into the Russian sector. The People's Police replied with a jet of water and ninety-seven tear-gas bombs. The West Berlin replied, in turn, with 107.

The next street east is Friedrichstrasse where foreigners may cross the border. It is a narrow place of tension where only one tank can operate at a time. Here, for a day and two nights last month, the United States and Russia faced each other with their guns loaded. The whole might and purpose of Nato was represented by the gunner of a single Patton tank, Private Baker, aged twenty, of Michigan.

The next gap in the wall is at the Heinrich Heine Strasse. Coffins are exchanged here on Wednesdays. The Wall runs thence along the northern boundary of the borough of Kreuzberg round the back of the Bethany Hospital to the banks of the River Spree.

From the Spree for rather more than half a mile the border follows the Landwehrkanal, forty yards wide and a once-useful waterway.

In Neukolln, the wall twists between blocks of flats, shops, houses, gardens. In two streets the boundary follows the building line, but here the situation that obtains in the Bernauerstrasse is reversed. The houses belong to the West, the pavement to the East.

Where this happens the People's Police have built their wall in the gutter. A notice at the end of one such street reads: CITIZENS OF SEBASTIANSTRASSE! WE DRAW YOUR ATTENTION TO THE FACT THAT THE PAVEMENT YOU USE BELONGS TO THE TERRITORY OF THE GERMAN DEMOCRATIC REPUBLIC AND THAT THE BUILDING LINE IS THE STATE FRONTIER. WE EXPECT YOU TO REFRAIN FROM ANY PROVOCATION ON THE TERRITORY BECAUSE OTHERWISE WE WILL TAKE THE SECURITY MEASURES THAT ARE NECESSARY.

There is an artificial mound in a children's playground in the courtyard between the two blocks of flats in the Wildenbruch-strasse in Neukolln which provides a better view across the wall than any other eminence in the borough. The People's Police across the way have once or twice reacted angrily to sightseers watching from its grassy summit. The people in the flats complain that the gas still lingers in their children's sandpit.

The wire ends four miles on in Rudow, a distant, pleasant southern suburb on State Highway 179, the road that leads to East Berlin Airport and to the site of Hitler's most powerful broadcasting station. Under its local name, Waltersdorfer Chausee, the road now ends in two rows of barbed wire and a slit-trench.

The last house in West Berlin is No. 197: small, neat and loved. What must have been No. 199 has been bulldozed away. It was, by all accounts, as neat and modest as 197. In the place where it used to stand the earth has been cleared away and flattened. The cherry trees have been flung aside to make way for the wire.

CASSIUS CLAY BEATS LISTON IN 60 SECONDS, LEWISTON, MAINE, 26 May 1963

Daily Telegraph *correspondent*

Cassius Clay retained the heavyweight championship of the world at St Dominic's Arena here tonight when he knocked out Sonny Liston in the first round with just about the first hard punch thrown throughout the brief encounter.

Liston, once known as the Iron Man, lasted exactly one minute of a sensational contest. He was floored by a short, right to the jaw, went down in a heap, and was unable to beat the count. At eight he tried to get up, but stumbled back, while the referee, Jersey Joe Walcott, temporarily lost control of the situation.

Walcott at first stood staring helplessly towards the time-keeper. Then he hurried across the ring to find out whether the full count had been tolled. Meanwhile Clay went hammering away with both hands at a man he had already beaten.

Walcott rushed back across the ring to restrain him and then, realizing that he had won so easily, Clay jumped for joy and raised his arms in triumph.

It was the fastest recorded knockout in the history of the world heavyweight championship.

CASSIUS CLAY BEATS HENRY COOPER IN THE FIFTH, LONDON, 19 June 1963

Donald Saunders, London Daily Telegraph

Cassius Clay, the Louisville Lip, added another accurate prediction to his long list at Wembley Stadium last night, when he stopped Henry Cooper, the British heavyweight champion, in the fifth round, just as he said he would.

But victory did not come in quite the fashion the young American had expected. Tommy Little, the referee, was forced to intervene midway through the round, because blood was streaming from cuts over Cooper's so-often-injured left eye.

And a few minutes earlier, Clay had looked anything but 'the greatest' as he landed in an untidy heap on the canvas after taking a left hook flush in the jaw.

The cocksure American, taking one chance too many, had walked into that punch in the dying seconds of the fourth round.

He slumped to the boards and came to a rest with his head against the bottom rope. The roar of the crowd prevented even those of us at the ringside hearing the bell. At all events, Mr Little continued the count under the new rule, until Clay heaved himself up at five, and walked poker-faced to his corner.

What might have happened had the round not ended then no one can say. Clay looked more surprised than hurt, but who knows what might have been the outcome had he been obliged to meet the full fury of Cooper instead of being able to walk to the safety of his stool?

In my view, Clay could have finished this fight in the third or fourth round, but instead kept things going so that he could stupidly hold up his five fingers triumphantly for the cameramen later.

As it happened, he got away with it, but perhaps when tempted henceforth he will remember the end of that fourth round against Cooper, and wonder whether the bell will always toll in his favour.

But let us now turn away from the future and go back over those five memorable rounds.

No one on this blustery, chilly night could accuse Cooper of being worried. The British champion has not for years made so aggressive a start.

He charged forward repeatedly trying to nail the poker-faced Clay with his left hook. Sometimes he got through, sometimes he missed badly, but never could he persuade his opponent that he was a potential menace.

Then, as Cooper walked back to his corner at the end of the round blood began to trickle from a cut over his left eye. Despite urgent attention during the interval, that trickle changed into a stream early in the third.

Clay, more and more confident with every second, just punched when and where he chose.

I thought it might end in the fourth when Clay once or twice cut loose with both hands. But then the 'Louisville Lip' remembered that he was supposed to be the greatest and pranced contemptuously in front of the half-blinded Cooper.

Desperately Cooper let go a left hook and a split second later Clay, now looking like a spanked child, was sitting wide-eyed against the ropes.

But any hopes we had that Clay might have overstepped the mark ended when he walked off to his stool. A minute later he came storming out of his corner, tore into his opponent with both hands, and as blood spurted from perhaps the worst eye injury Cooper has ever suffered, Mr Little had no alternative but to step between them.

THE GREAT TRAIN ROBBERY, BUCKINGHAMSHIRE, 8 August 1963

Ronald ('Ronnie') Arthur Biggs

Ronnie Biggs was a member of the 15-strong gang which committed one of Britain's most audacious crimes, a raid on a mail train in which £2.5 million was stolen. Although caught and sentenced for the crime, Biggs escaped from prison and fled abroad, eventually settling in Brazil.

I was in the Land-Rover which led our little convoy, and the driver was the big man who didn't get caught. Behind, the truck was driven by the smaller of the other two men who got away, with all the heavies in the back: Hussey, Welch, that mob. With me were Reynolds, Daly, Roger Cordrey and old Peter [a retired train driver brought along by the gang], while the rearguard were Charlie Wilson and Roy James. The idea of dressing up as soldiers to and from the robbery was that if we were stopped by a police car we could pretend we were an army patrol on manoeuvres, and we had paper to back up the story. Reynolds was dressed as an officer, John Daly as a corporal, while the rest of us were privates. Once at the scene of the robbery we had blue overalls to put over the uniforms, so that anybody seeing us would describe us as wearing blue boiler suits. We left our own clothes at the farm, keeping only our own shoes with us. Some of the guys had made masks out of black cloth and a couple had nylon stockings.

It took a little more than half an hour to get to the railway track, as we were not going too fast. I remember very clearly dropping John Daly off at the point where the distant signal was, for he had to do a bit of a job on the yellow. We then drove on to Bridego Bridge. We pulled up, switched the headlights off and pulled off the road. The old man was very relaxed, even lighting up his pipe, which made Charlie Wilson comment: 'Look at the old fucker. You'd think he was on his holiday.' It was my job to keep Peter happy, not let him get nervous, but it wasn't necessary. I too was happy and relaxed, pleased to be working with the gang, for it was the first time I had ever worked at such a high professional level and I was content to be shown how it was done.

The mail train was stopped in Buckinghamshire after the gang tampered with the signals. A train fireman, Whitby, and the driver, Mills, were overpowered by the gang, who disconnected the engine and two coaches – including the 'high-value package coach' – from the rest of the train, and drove the train to Bridego Bridge. There Mills and Whitby were taken out of the engine and handcuffed together.

While Mills and Whitby were lying on the grass, Bobby Welch was watching them. Meanwhile, I had been told to take Peter back to the Land-Rover and look after him, in case he panicked. While we were walking towards the Land-Rover we heard the sounds of breaking glass and the axe smashing through the side of the HVP coach as Charlie Wilson led the rest of the gang in the assault. A brief struggle ensued, but the sorters soon realised that they were out-numbered and that resistance was pointless. One of the gang, I know not who, asked Frank Dewhurst 'Are you all right?' This, and the way Charlie Wilson mopped the blood off Mills, clearly showed that we were not violent men by nature and that we were concerned for the condition of our victims. By the time that Peter and I were seated in the Land-Rover the unloading of the mailbags had commenced, and as we sat watching this scene unfold in the moonlight, I felt that I was seeing history in the making.

When 120 of the 128 mailbags had been passed by a human chain from the HVP coach to our truck, it was decided that it was time to leave. Mills and Whitby were taken to the mail coach and told to 'Keep your mouths shut. There are some right bastards here.'

The gang then took their 'loot' back to their HQ, the isolated Leatherslade Farm, in the village of Oakley.

I had thought that the news of the raid would have broken sooner, but we were back at the farm already opening the sacks, and old Peter was making the tea, when the first announcement came over the police radio, something like an hour after the robbery. It was to the effect that a train had been stopped at Cheddington by a group of men, an unknown amount of money had been stolen, and few details were available.

Bruce Reynolds and I cut open the mailbags, and the big man who wasn't caught, the one who attacked the train driver, opened up the packages and passed the money to

Charlie Wilson and Roger Cordrey, who stacked the bundles of notes. While this was going on there was another announcement over the radio saying that the thieves had gone to cover. The police said that they knew where we were hiding, they were searching the area and road blocks were being set up. In future all messages would be in code. The police announcements did not worry us but Gordon Goody was concerned lest there might have been a homing device in one of the sacks, so we started opening them at a feverish pace. Even so it took about five hours to open them all, pile up the wads of money and make sure that Goody's fears were unfounded. We didn't finish until 9.30 am. For me it was a wonderful birthday present.

When the count reached £1 million we were invited to take a look at it, just so that we could have the pleasure of knowing what a million looked like. Charlie Wilson was dancing the twist, Gordon Goody singing the Gerry and the Pacemakers song 'I Like It', in fact all of us at that moment were behaving as if we hadn't a care in the world.

Ronnie Biggs's share of the proceeds from the Great Train Robbery was around £148,000.

THE CIVIL RIGHTS MARCH ON WASHINGTON, 29 August 1963

Vincent Ryder and David Shears, London Daily Telegraph

The Great Negro March on Washington yesterday turned out to be an orderly, good-humoured stroll around the Lincoln Memorial by the 200,000 Civil Rights demonstrators.

Only two arrests were made. One was of a follower of

George Rockwell, the United States Nazi leader. Police hustled him away when he tried to make a speech.

Before the 200,000-strong Civil Rights march in Washington today was half over, Mr Bayard Rustin, deputy organizer and the real moving spirit, spoke of the next move.

He said: 'Already one of our objectives has been met. We said we would awaken the conscience of the nation and we have done it.'

The next move would be a 'counter-filibuster' if opponents in the Senate tried to talk the proposed Civil Rights Bill to death. On every day of this 'filibuster' 1,000 Negroes would be brought into Washington to stage a demonstration.

A great roar of approval met the warning by the Rev. Martin Luther King, the integrationist leader, that America was in for 'a rude awakening' if she thought she could go back to business as usual.

'Let us not seek to satisfy our thirst for freedom by drinking from the cup of hatred and bitterness,' said Mr King. Negroes would go on with the struggle until 'justice flows like water and righteousness like a stream'.

The cheers rolled over the crowd, jammed in front of the Lincoln Memorial and along the shallow reflecting pool.

It was a day of quiet triumph, a mingling of fervent demands with a show of orderly, relaxed calm. Earlier fears of disorder seemed almost laughably out of place.

Personalities in the march included Marlon Brando, Burt Lancaster, Lena Horne, Judy Garland, Sammy Davis, Sidney Poitier and Josephine Baker, who flew from Paris.

For two hours the marchers' numbers swelled around the monument within sight of the White House and the Capitol, which houses Congress.

They were entertained by singers and by brief speeches from their heroes, Jackie Robinson, the baseball player, and a man who roller-skated all the way from Chicago, and admitted his legs were tired.

The organizers expected that this sort of distraction would

be necessary to keep tempers under control. They need not have worried. The crowd seemed almost as determined to be respectable as to demand civil rights.

Black suits and dresses predominated. A group of poor Negroes from Parksville, Mississippi, were in well-pressed overalls.

There were clerical collars by the dozen. Clergymen of every denomination joined the demonstration.

THE ASSASSINATION OF PRESIDENT JOHN F. KENNEDY, DALLAS, 23 November 1963

Merriman Smith

It was a balmy, sunny noon as we motored through downtown Dallas behind President Kennedy. The procession cleared the centre of the business district and turned into a handsome highway that wound through what appeared to be a park.

I was riding in the so-called White House press 'pool' car, a telephone company vehicle equipped with a mobile radio-telephone. I was in the front seat between a driver from the telephone company and Malcom Kilduff, acting White House press secretary for the President's Texas tour. Three other pool reporters were wedged in the back seat.

Suddenly we heard three loud, almost painfully loud cracks. The first sounded as if it might have been a large firecracker. But the second and the third blasts were unmistakable. Gunfire.

The President's car, possibly as much as 150 or 200 yards ahead, seemed to falter briefly. We saw a flurry of activity in the secret service follow-up car behind the chief executive's bubble-top limousine.

Next in line was the car bearing Vice-President Lyndon B. Johnson. Behind that, another follow-up car bearing agents assigned to the vice-president's protection. We were behind that car.

Our car stood still for probably only a few seconds, but it seemed like a lifetime. One sees history explode before one's eyes and for even the most trained observer, there is a limit to what one can comprehend.

I looked ahead at the President's car but could not see him or his companion, Gov. John Connally. Both had been riding on the right side of the limousine. I thought I saw a flash of pink that would have been Mrs Jacqueline Kennedy.

Everybody in our car began shouting at the driver to pull up closer to the President's car. But at this moment, we saw the big bubbletop and a motorcycle escort roar away at high speed.

We screamed at our driver, 'get going, get going'. We careened around the Johnson car and its escort and set out down the highway, barely able to keep in sight of the President's car and the accompanying secret service car.

They vanished around a curve. When we cleared the same curve we could see where we were heading – Parkland Hospital. We spilled out of the pool car as it entered the hospital driveway.

I ran to the side of the bubbletop.

The President was face down on the back seat. Mrs Kennedy made a cradle of her arms around the President's head and bent over him as if she were whispering to him.

Gov. Connally was on his back on the floor of the car, his head and shoulders resting in the arms of his wife, Nellie, who shook with dry sobs. Blood oozed from the front of the governor's suit. I could not see the President's wound. But I could see blood spattered around the interior of the rear seat and a dark stain spreading down the right side of the President's dark grey suit.

From the telephone car, I had radioed the Dallas UPI

Bureau that three shots had been fired at the Kennedy motorcade.

Clint Hill, the secret service agent in charge of the detail assigned to Mrs Kennedy, was leaning over into the rear of the car.

'How badly was he hit, Clint?' I asked.

'He's dead,' Hill replied curtly.

BEATLEMANIA HITS AMERICA, NEW YORK, 7 February 1964

Tom Wolfe, New York Herald Tribune

John, Paul, Ringo and George arrive in New York on their first US tour.

By six-thirty a.m. yesterday [7 February], half the kids from South Orange, NJ to Seaford LI, were already up with their transistors plugged in their skulls. It was like a civil defence network or something. You could turn anywhere on the dial, WMCA, WCBS, WINS, almost any place, and get the bulletins: 'It's B-Day! Six-thirty a.m.! The Beatles left London thirty minutes ago! They're thirty minutes out over the Atlantic Ocean! Heading for New York!'

By one p.m. about 4,000 kids had finished school and come skipping and screaming into the international terminal at Kennedy Airport. It took 110 police to herd them. At one-twenty p.m., the Beatles' jet arrived from London.

The Beatles left the plane and headed for customs inspection and everybody got their first live look at the Beatles' hair style, which is a mop effect that covers the forehead, some of the ears and most of the back of the neck. To get a better look, the kids came plunging down the observation deck, and some of them already had their combs out, raking their hair down over their foreheads as they ran.

Then they were crowding around the plate-glass windows overlooking the customs section, stomping on the floor in unison, some of them beating time by bouncing off the windows.

The Beatles – George Harrison, 20; John Lennon, 23; Ringo Starr, 23; and Paul McCartney, 21 – are all short, slight kids from Liverpool who wear four-button coats, stovepipe pants, ankle-high black boots with Cuban heels. And droll looks on their faces. Their name is a play on the word 'beat'.

They went into a small room for a press conference, while some of the girls tried to throw themselves over a retaining wall.

Somebody motioned to the screaming crowds outside. 'Aren't you embarrassed by all this lunacy?'

'No,' said John Lennon. 'It's crazy.'

'What do you think of Beethoven?'

'He's crazy,' said Lennon. 'Especially the poems. Lovely writer.'

In the two years in which they have risen from a Liverpool rock-and-roll dive group to the hottest performers in the record business, they had seen much of this wildness before. What really got them were the American teenage car sorties.

The Beatles left the airport in four Cadillac limousines, one Beatle to a limousine, heading for the Plaza Hotel in Manhattan. The first sortie came almost immediately. Five kids in a powder blue Ford overtook the caravan on the expressway, and as they passed each Beatle, one guy hung out the back window and waved a red blanket.

A white convertible came up second, with the word BEETLES scratched on both sides in the dust. A police car was close behind that one with the siren going and the alarm light rolling, but the kids, a girl at the wheel and two guys in the back seat, waved at each Beatle before pulling over to the exit with the cops gesturing at them.

In the second limousine, Brian Sommerville, the Beatle's press agent, said to one of the Beatles, George Harrison: 'Did you see that, George?'

Harrison looked at the convertible with its emblem in the dust and said, 'They misspelled Beatles.'

But the third sortie succeeded all the way. A good-looking brunette, who said her name was Caroline Reynolds, of New Canaan, Conn., and Wellesley College, had paid a cab driver $10 to follow the caravan all the way into town. She cruised by each Beatle, smiling faintly, and finally caught up with George Harrison's limousine at a light at Third Avenue and 63rd St.

'How does one go about meeting a Beatle?' she said out of the window.

'One says hello,' said Harrison out of the window.

'Hello!' she said. 'Eight more will be down from Wellesley.' Then the light changed and the caravan was off again.

At the Plaza Hotel, there were police everywhere. The Plaza, on Central Park South just off Fifth Avenue, is one of the most sedate hotels in New York. The Plaza was petrified. The Plaza accepted the Beatles' reservations months ago, before knowing it was a rock-and-roll group that attracts teenage riots.

About 500 teenagers, most of them girls, had shown up at the Plaza. The police herded most of them behind barricades in the square between the hotel and the avenue. Every entrance to the hotel was guarded. The screams started as soon as the first limousine came into view.

The Beatles jumped out fast at the Fifth Avenue entrance. The teenagers had all been kept at bay. Old ladies ran up and touched the Beatles on their arms and backs as they ran up the stairs.

After they got to the Plaza the Beatles rested up for a round of television appearances (the Ed Sullivan Show Sunday), recordings (Capitol Records), concerts (Carnegie Hall, Wednesday) and a tour (Washington, Miami). The kids were still hanging around the Plaza hours after they went inside.

One group of girls asked everybody who came out, 'Did you see the Beatles? Did you touch them?'

A policeman came up, and one of them yelled, 'He touched a Beatle! I saw him!'

The girls jumped on the cop's arms and back, but it wasn't a mob assault. There were goony smiles all over their faces.

WINSTON CHURCHILL DIES, LONDON, 24 January 1965

Derek Lambert

Churchill was ninety-one at the time of his death.

Diary: January 24
Sir Winston Churchill, the greatest Englishman of our time, perhaps all time, died today. I report to Hyde Park Gate at ten a.m. A huddle of people, mostly Pressmen, are gathered at the end of the cul-de-sac, besieged for nine days, leading into Kensington Gore. I, like everyone else, treasure my evocation of Churchill. For me it is the voice, swaggering, sardonic and steely, summoning me as a child from the garden in the sunlit summers of the war. Vapour trails lace the sky, the stirrup pump sprays wilting lettuce, an air-raid siren moans fretfully. I join my parents beside the wireless and listen to him snarling defiance at Herr Hitler and the 'Narzis'. He was an alchemist of words who burnished us ordinary people with the golden glow of patriotism. It is not difficult for an adult to strike awe into a child: it is a miracle to inspire devotion. Churchill performed this miracle with his Victory Vs, his colossal nerve, his voice which transformed a classroom into an embattled outpost. He was the greatest man we kids had ever encountered. The children of

today are the poorer that they never knew his voice in those
Spitfire summer days that are now history.

THE KILLING OF GEORGE CORNELL AT THE BLIND BEGGAR PUBLIC HOUSE, LONDON, 9 March 1966

Ronald Kray

The Kray twins, Ronnie and Reggie, ran a Mafia-type gang or
'firm' in the East End of London in the 1960s. George Cornell was
a member of the rival Richardson firm, and had been implicated in
the shooting of a Kray associate, Richard Hart.

Richard Hart had to be avenged. No one could kill a
member of the Kray gang and expect to get away with it.
The problem was, both of the Richardsons and Mad Frankie
Fraser were in custody and likely to remain so. That left
Cornell. He would have to be the one to pay the price. And,
let's face it, who better? All I had to do was find him. The
next night, 9 March, I got the answer. He was drinking in
the Blind Beggar.

Typical of the yobbo mentality of the man. Less than
twenty-four hours after the Catford killing and here he was,
drinking in a pub that was officially on our patch. It was as
though he wanted to be killed.

I unpacked my 9mm Mauser automatic. I also got out a
shoulder holster. I called Scotch Jack Dickson and told him
to bring the car round to my flat and to contact Ian Barrie,
the big Scot, and to collect him on the way. As we drove
towards the Blind Beggar, I checked that Barrie was carrying
a weapon, just in case.

At eight-thirty p.m. precisely we arrived at the pub and
quickly looked around to make sure that this was not an

ambush. I told Dickson to wait in the car with the engine running, then Ian Barrie and I walked into the Blind Beggar. I could not have felt calmer, and having Ian Barrie alongside me was great. No general ever had a better right-hand man.

It was very quiet and gloomy inside the pub. There was an old bloke sitting by himself in the public bar and three people in the saloon bar: two blokes at a table and George Cornell sitting alone on a stool at the far end of the bar. As we walked in the barmaid was putting on a record. It was the Walker Brothers and it was called 'The Sun Ain't Gonna Shine Any More'. For George Cornell that was certainly true.

As we walked towards him he turned round and a sort of sneer came over his face. 'Well, look who's here,' he said.

I never said anything. I just felt hatred for this sneering man. I took out my gun and held it towards his face. Nothing was said, but his eyes told me that he thought the whole thing was a bluff. I shot him in the forehead. He fell forward on to the bar. There was some blood on the counter. That's all that happened. Nothing more. Despite any other account you may have read of this incident, that was what happened.

It was over very quickly. There was silence. Everyone had disappeared – the barmaid, the old man in the public and the blokes in the saloon bar. It was like a ghost pub. Ian Barrie stood next to me. He had said nothing.

I felt fucking marvellous. I have never felt so good, so bloody alive, before or since. Twenty years on and I can recall every second of the killing of George Cornell. I have replayed it in my mind millions of times.

After a couple of minutes we walked out, got into the car and set off for a pub in the East End run by a friend called Madge. On the way there we could hear the screaming of the police car sirens. When we got to the pub I told a few of my friends what had happened. I also told Reg, who seemed a bit alarmed.

Then we went to a pub at Stoke Newington called the Coach and Horses. There I gave my gun to a trusted friend

we used to call the Cat and told him to get rid of it. I
suddenly noticed my hands were covered in gunpowder
burns, so I scrubbed them in the washroom. I showered
and put on fresh clothing – underwear, a suit, a shirt and tie.
(We had spare sets of 'emergency' clothes at several places.)
All my old clothing was taken away to be burned. Upstairs in
a private room I had a few drinks with some of the top
members of the firm – Reg, Dickson, Barrie, Ronnie Hart
and others. We listened to the radio and heard that a man
had been shot dead in the East End. As the news was
announced I could feel everyone in the room, including
Reg, looking at me with new respect. I had killed a man. I
had got my button, as the Yanks say. I was a man to be
feared. I was now the Colonel.

ENGLAND WIN THE WORLD CUP, LONDON, 30 July 1966

David Miller

They had fetched him, three and a half years ago, from quiet
Ipswich, a taciturn, shy, deeply reserved man, and calmly
leading with his chin, as they say, he had promised to win
them the World Cup. There were those who laughed, and
some were still laughing when the tournament began. Yet by
the finish, with a relentless inflexibility of will, with sterling
courage, with efficiency that brought unbounded admiration, his team, England's team, helped to keep that promise.

   They did it, Alf Ramsey and England, after just about the
worst psychological reverse possible on an unforgettable
afternoon. With victory dashed from their grasp, cruelly,
only seconds from the final whistle, they came again in extra
time, driving weary limbs across the patterned turf beyond
the point of exhaustion, and crowned the ultimate achievement with a memorable goal with the last kick of all by

Hurst, making him the first player to score a hat-trick in the World Cup Final.

We had all often talked of the thoroughness of preparation of the deposed champions, Brazil, but England's glory this day, to be engraved on that glinting, golden trophy, was the result of the most patient, logical, painstaking, almost scientific assault on the trophy there had perhaps ever been – and primarily the work and imagination of one man.

For those close to him through the past three exciting seasons, Ramsey's management had been something for unending admiration, and the unison cry of the 93,000 crowd, 'Ram-sey, Ram-sey' as his side mounted the steps to collect Jules Rimet's statuette from the Queen was the final rewarding vindication for one who had unwaveringly pursued his own, often lonely, convictions.

As the crowd stood in ovation, Greaves looked on wistfully. Injury had cost him his place, and though he recovered, Ramsey had resisted the almost overpowering temptation to change a winning side. This, too, was vindication, his whole aim since 1963 having been to prepare not a team but a squad, so that at any moment he might replace an out of form or injured man without noticeable deterioration in the side. When the time came, the luckless Greaves's omission caused hardly a stir of pessimism.

At the start of the tournament, I had written that if England were to win, it would be with the resolution, physical fitness and cohesion of West Germany in 1954, rather than with the flair of Brazil in the two succeeding competitions. And so it proved, with the added coincidence that it was the Germans themselves, as usual bristling with all these same characteristics in profusion, who were the unlucky and brave victims of England's methodical rather than brilliant football. Before the semi-finals I said that the deciding factor of this World Cup, when all others had cancelled out in the modern proficiency of defensive systems, would be character, and now the character of every

England player burned with a flame that warmed all those who saw it. The slightest weakening, mentally or physically, in any position, could have lost this match a hundred times over, but the way in which Ball, undoubtedly the man of the afternoon, Wilson, Stiles, Peters, Bobby Charlton and above all Moore, impelled themselves on, was something one would remember long after the tumult of excitement and the profusion of incidents had faded. Justifiably, Moore was voted the outstanding player of the competition; his sudden, surging return to form on tour beforehand had helped cement the castle at the critical hour.

All assessments of great events should be measured by absolute standards along with the quality of contemporaries, and therefore one had to say that England were not a great team, probably not even at that moment the best team in the world, depending on what you mean by best.

What matters is that they were the best there at Wembley in July, on that sunny, showery afternoon, best when the chips were down in open combat, and that, after all, is what counts – the result, rather than its manner, goes into the record books. Besides, Ramsey had not set about producing the most entertaining but the most successful team. Could he afford to be the one romantic in a world of hard-headed, win-at-all-costs efficiency? Could he favour conventional wingers who promised much and produced little? A manager is ultimately only as good as the players at his disposal; handicapped by a shortage of world class, instinctive players of the calibre of the South Americans, Italians, Hungarians, or his own Bobby Charlton, and by an over-abundance of average competence, Ramsey had slowly eliminated all those who lacked what he needed for cohesion. What greater demonstration of unity of purpose could there have been than the insistence of the winners, for all the emotion of the moment, that the eleven reserves join them on the lap of honour, and after share equally the £22,000 bonus.

Some complained England were helped by playing all

their matches at Wembley, yet certainly in that mood and form they could and would have won anywhere in the country. Besides, under Ramsey, England had had more success abroad than ever before. If nothing else, this World Cup, penetrating almost every home in the land, should have persuaded the doubters, the detractors and the cynics that this is the greatest spectator sport there is, and the Final was a fitting climax.

At the start England asserted themselves – Bobby Charlton exerting a telling influence in midfield, even though closely watched by Beckenbauer sent Peters streaming through with fine anticipation, into spaces behind the German midfield trio. Suddenly, however, in the thirteenth minute, England found themselves a goal down for the first time in the competition. It was not an error under pressure, it was unforced. As a centre from the left came over, Wilson stood alone, eyes riveted on the dropping ball. He made to head it down to Moore, but his judgement betrayed him, sending it instead straight to Haller, who whipped in a low skidding shot past an unsighted, helpless Banks.

The strapping Germans and their flag-waving supporters bounced with joy, but within six minutes England were level. Midway inside the German half, on the left, Overath tripped Moore, and even before the referee had finished wagging his finger at Overath, Moore had spotted a gaping hole in the German rearguard. He placed the ball and took the kick almost in one move, a dipping floater that carried thirty-five yards and was met by Hurst, streaking in from the right, with another graceful, expertly-timed header like that which beat Argentina.

The pattern swung once more in the ten minutes before half-time. The three German strikers, nosing in and out like carnivorous fish, began to create havoc that was only averted after extreme anxiety. In between, Hunt, from a glorious pass by Bobby Charlton, hammered a thundering shot, a difficult one running away to his left, straight at Tilkowski.

On the stroke of half-time, it was England who were desperately lucky, when a fast dipper by Seeler was tipped over by Banks, arched in mid-air like a stalling buzzard.

Little happened for nearly twenty-five minutes after half-time, the lull punctuated only by 'Oh, oh, what a referee,' as Mr Dienst went fussily about his business. Then, with twenty minutes to go, England's rhythm began to build up again, Bobby Charlton, Ball and Peters stretching the Germans to the extreme of their physical endurance with passes that again and again almost saw Hurst and Hunt clear. With eleven minutes to go, Ball won a corner, put it across, the ball was headed out, and hit back first-time by Hurst. It struck a defender, fell free, and Peters swooped to lash it home.

England, sensing victory, played it slow, slow, but Hunt wasted a priceless chance when it was three red England shirts to one white German on the edge of the penalty area, by misjudging his pass. With a minute left, all was disaster as Jack Charlton was most harshly penalized for 'climbing' over the top of Held. Emmerich blasted the free kick. A German in the penalty area unquestionably pulled the ball down with his hand, and after a tremendous scramble, Weber squeezed the ball home to level the match.

You could see England's spirits sink as the teams changed over for extra time but, quickly calmed and reassured by the emotionless Ramsey, they rallied themselves instantly. Ball, still unbelievably dynamic, going like the wind right to the finish, had a shot tipped over, Bobby Charlton hit a post and with twelve minutes gone, England were once more in front as Stiles slipped the ball up the wing to Ball, whose cross was thumped hard by Hurst. The ball hit the bar, bounced down and came out, and after consultation with the Russian linesman, Bakhramov, a goal was given. I had my doubts, doubled after later seeing television, but that surely had to be the winner, for now, socks rolled down, both teams were physically in distress. Again England sought economy with gentle passes, keeping precious possession, wearing the Ger-

mans down yet further. Poor Wilson hardly knew where he
was after a blow on the head. Slowly the minutes ticked
away, agonisingly, until with the referee looking at his
watch, Hurst staggered on alone from yet one more of
Moore's perceptive passes, to hit the ball into the roof of
the net with what little strength he had left, and make
England's victory, like their football, solid and respectable.
Whether Ramsey, as silent in victory as defeat, could achieve
the impossible and adapt these same characteristics to win in
Mexico in 1970 was a chapter that would unfold over the
next four years.

ENGLAND: – Banks (*Leicester*); Cohen (*Fulham*), Charlton J.
(*Leeds*), Moore (*W. Ham*), Wilson (*Everton*); Stiles (*Manchester
United*), Charlton R. (*Manchester United*), Peters (*W. Ham*);
Ball (*Blackpool*), Hunt (*Liverpool*), Hurst (*W. Ham*).

WEST GERMANY: – Tilkowski: Hoettges, Schulz, Weber,
Schnellinger; Beckenbauer, Haller, Overath; Seeler, Held,
Emmerich.

Referee: – G. Dienst (Switzerland).

Linesmen: – K. Galba (Czechoslovakia), T. Bakhramov
(USSR).

THE LAST JOURNEY OF CHE GUEVARA, VALLEGRANDE, 10 October 1967

Richard Gott, Guardian

After playing a leading role in the Cuban Revolution, the Argen-
tinian-born Guevara left Cuba in 1965 to lead a guerrilla movement
in Bolivia. He was captured and executed by government troops
and the American CIA while trying to foment a revolt.

The body of Che Guevara was flown into this small hill town
in south-eastern Bolivia at five o'clock last night.

From the moment the helicopter landed bearing the small figure strapped in a stretcher to the landing rails, the succeeding operation was to a large extent left in the hands of a man in battledress, who, all the correspondents here agree, was unquestionably a representative of one of the United States intelligence agencies.

He was probably a Cuban exile and so Che Guevara, who in life had declared war almost singlehanded on the United States, found himself in death face to face with his major enemy.

The helicopter purposely landed far from where a crowd had gathered and the body of the dead guerilla leader was hastily transferred to a van. We commandeered a jeep to follow it and the driver managed to get through the gates of the hospital grounds where the body was taken to a small colour-washed hut that served as a mortuary.

The doors of the van burst open and the American agent leapt out, emitting a war cry of 'Let's get the hell out of here.' One of the correspondents asked him where he came from. 'Nowhere,' was the surly response.

The body, dressed in olive green fatigues with a zippered jacket, was carried into the hut. It was undoubtedly that of Che Guevara. Ever since I first reported in January that Che was probably in Bolivia I have not shared the general scepticism about his whereabouts.

I am probably one of the few people here who have seen him alive. I saw him in Cuba at an Embassy reception in 1963 and there is no doubt in my mind that this body was that of Che. It had a black wispy beard, long matted hair, and the shadow of a scar on the right temple, probably the result of an accident in July when he was grazed by a rifle shot.

On his feet he wore moccasins as though he had been shot down while running fleet-footed through the jungle. He had two wounds in the lower part of the neck and possibly one in the stomach. It is believed that he was captured when seriously wounded, but died before a helicopter could arrive to take him out of the battle zone.

My only doubts about the identity arose because Che was much thinner and smaller than I had recalled, but it is hardly surprising that after months in the jungle he had lost his former heavy appearance.

As soon as the body reached the mortuary the doctors began to pump preservative into it, and the American agent made desperate efforts to keep off the crowds. He was a very nervous man and looked furious whenever cameras were pointed in his direction. He knew that I knew who he was and he also knew that I knew that he should not be there, for this is a war in which the Americans are not supposed to be taking part. Yet here was this man, who has been with the troops in Vallegrande, talking to the senior officers on familiar terms.

One can hardly say that this was the factor with which Che failed to reckon, for it was his very purpose to provoke United States intervention in Latin America as a way of bringing help and succour to the embattled Vietnamese. But he certainly did fail to estimate correctly the strength and pervasiveness of the US intelligence agencies in this continent, and this more than anything else has been the cause of his downfall and that of the Bolivian guerrillas.

And so he is dead. As they pumped preservative into his half-naked, dirty body and as the crowd shouted to be allowed to see, it was difficult to recall that this man had once been one of the great figures of Latin America.

It was not just that he was a great guerrilla leader, he had been a friend of Presidents as well as revolutionaries. His voice had been heard and appreciated in inter-American councils as well as in the jungle. He was a doctor, an amateur economist, once Minister of Industries in revolutionary Cuba, and Fidel Castro's right-hand man. He may well go down in history as the greatest continental figure since Bolivar. Legends will be created around his name.

He was a Marxist but impatient of the doctrinal struggles between the Russians and the Chinese. He was perhaps the last person who tried to find a middle way between the two and attempted to unite radical forces everywhere in a concerted campaign against the US. He is now dead, but it is difficult to feel that his ideas will die with him.

VIETNAM WAR: THE CITADEL OF HUE, February 1968

Michael Herr

On 30 January 1968, the North Vietnamese marked the beginning of the Tet (lunar new year) by launching an offensive against 125 locations held by the South Vietnamese and US troops, including Khe Sahn, Saigon and Hue. This account of Hue during the fighting of February 1968 is from Michael Herr's classic of war journalism, *Dispatches*.

Going in, there were sixty of us packed into a deuce-and-a-half, one of eight trucks moving in convoy from Phu Bai, bringing in over 300 replacements for the casualties taken in the earliest fighting south of the Perfume River. There had been a harsh, dark storm going on for days, and it turned the convoy route into a mudbed. It was terribly cold in the trucks, and the road was covered with leaves that had either been blown off the trees by the storm or torn away by our artillery, which had been heavy all along the road. Many of the houses had been completely collapsed, and not one had been left without pitting from shell fragments. Hundreds of refugees held to the side of the road as we passed, many of them wounded. The kids would laugh and shout, the old would look on with that silent tolerance for misery that made so many Americans uneasy, which was usually misread as indifference. But the younger men and women would often look at us with unmistakable contempt, pulling their cheering children back from the trucks.

We sat there trying to keep it up for each other, grinning at the bad weather and the discomfort, sharing the first fear, glad that we weren't riding point or closing the rear. They had been hitting our trucks regularly, and a lot of the convoys had been turned back. The houses that we passed so slowly made good cover for snipers, and one B-40 rocket could have made casualties out of a whole truckload of us. All the grunts were whistling, and no two were whistling the same tune, it sounded like a locker room before a game that nobody wanted to play. Or almost nobody. There was a black Marine called Philly Dog who'd been a gang lord in Philadelphia and who was looking forward to some street fighting after six months in the jungle, he could show the kickers what he could do with some city ground. (In Hue he turned out to be incredibly valuable. I saw him pouring out about a hundred rounds of .30-calibre fire into a breach in the wall, laughing, 'You got to bring some to get some'; he seemed to be about the only man in Delta Company who hadn't been hurt yet.) And there was a Marine correspondent, Sergeant Dale Dye, who sat with a tall yellow flower sticking out of his helmet cover, a really outstanding target. He was rolling his eyes around and saying, 'Oh, yes, oh yes, Charlie's got his shit together here, this will be *bad*,' and smiling happily. It was the same smile I saw a week later when a sniper's bullet tore up a wall two inches above his head, odd cause for amusement in anyone but a grunt.

Everyone else in the truck had that wild haunted going-West look that said it was perfectly correct to be here where the fighting would be the worst, where you wouldn't have half of what you needed, where it was colder than Nam ever got. On their helmets and flak jackets they'd written the names of old operations, of girlfriends, their war names (FAR FROM FEARLESS, MICKEY'S MONKEY, AVENGER V, SHORT TIME SAFETY

MOE), their fantasies (BORN TO LOSE, BORN TO RAISE HELL, BORN TO KILL, BORN TO DIE), their ongoing information (HELL SUCKS, TIME IS ON MY SIDE, JUST YOU AND ME GOD – RIGHT?). One kid called to me, 'Hey man! You want a story, man? Here man, write this: I'm up there on 881, this was May, I'm just up there walkin' the ridgeline like a movie star and this Zip jumps up smack into me, lays his AK-47 fucking right *into* me, only he's so *amazed* at my *cool* I got my whole clip off 'fore he knew how to thank me for it. Grease one.' After twenty kilometres of this, in spite of the black roiling sky ahead, we could see smoke coming up from the far side of the river, from the Citadel of Hue.

The bridge was down that spanned the canal dividing the village of An Cuu and the southern sector of Hue, blown the night before by the Viet Cong, and the forward area beyond the far bank wasn't thought to be secure, so we bivouacked in the village for the night. It had been completely deserted, and we set ourselves up in empty hootches, laying our poncho liners out over broken glass and shattered brick. At dusk, while we all stretched out along the canal bank eating dinner, two Marine gunships came down on us and began strafing us, sending burning tracers up along the canal, and we ran for cover, more surprised than scared. 'Way to go, motherfucker, way to pinpoint the fuckin' enemy,' one of the grunts said, and he set up his M-60 machine-gun in case they came back. 'I don't guess we got to take *that* shit,' he said. Patrols were sent out, guards posted, and we went into the hootches to sleep. For some reason, we weren't even mortared that night.

In the morning we crossed the canal on a two-by-four and started walking in until we came across the first of the hundreds of civilian dead that we were to see in the next weeks: an old man arched over his straw hat and a little girl who'd been hit while riding her bicycle, lying there with her arm up like a reproach. They'd been lying out like that for a week; for the first time we were grateful for the cold.

Along the Perfume River's south bank there is a long, graceful park that separates Hue's most pleasant avenue, Le Loi, from the river-front. People will talk about how they'd sit out there in the sun and watch the sampans moving down the river, or watch the girls bicycling up Le Loi, past the villas of officials and the French-architected University buildings. Many of those villas had been destroyed and much of the University permanently damaged. In the middle of the street a couple of ambulances from the German Mission had been blown up, and the Cercle Sportif was covered with bullet holes and shrapnel. The rain had brought up the green, it stretched out cased in thick white fog. In the park itself, four fat green dead lay sprawled around a tall, ornate cage, inside of which sat a small, shivering monkey. One of the correspondents along stepped over the corpses to feed it some fruit. (Days later, I came back to the spot. The corpses were gone, but so was the monkey. There had been so many refugees and so little food then, and someone must have eaten him.) The Marines of 2/5 had secured almost all of the central south bank and were now fanning out to the west, fighting and clearing one of the major canals. We were waiting for some decision on whether or not US Marines would be going into the Citadel itself, but no one had any doubts about what that decision would be. We sat there taking in the dread by watching the columns of smoke across the river, receiving occasional sniper rounds, infrequent bursts of .50-calibre, watching the Navy LCUs on the river getting shelled from the wall. One Marine next to me was saying that it was just a damned shame, all them poor people, all them nice-looking houses, they even had a Shell station there. He was looking at the black napalm blasts and the wreckage along the wall. 'Looks like the Imperial City's had the schnitz,' he said.

THE VIETNAM WAR: THE PACIFICATION OF MY LAI, 16 March 1968

Time *magazine correspondent*

Throughout the 1960s the USA became steadily more embroiled in the civil war in Vietnam between the Communist North and non-Communist South, and in 1965 took the fateful decision of committing troops to help the embattled South Vietnamese regime. The My Lai massacre, committed by C Company of the US 11th Infantry Brigade, resulted in the court martial of Lieutenant William Calley for the murder of 109 Vietnamese citizens.

West, a squad leader in a platoon commanded by Lieutenant Jeffrey La Cross, followed Calley's platoon into My Lai. 'Everyone was shooting,' he said. 'Some of the huts were torched. Some of the *yanigans* [young soldiers] were shooting kids.' In the confusion, he claims, it was hard to tell 'mama-sans from papa-sans', since both wore black pyjamas and conical hats. He and his squad helped round up the women and children. When one of his men protested that 'I can't shoot these people', West told him to turn a group over to Captain Medina. On the way out of the village, West recalls seeing a ditch filled with dead and dying civilians. His platoon also passed a crying Vietnamese boy, wounded in both a leg and an arm. West heard a GI ask, 'What about him?' Then he heard a shot and the boy fell. 'The kid didn't do anything,' said West, 'He didn't have a weapon' . . .

Another soldier in the group following Calley's was SP4 Varnado Simpson, twenty-two. 'Everyone who went into the village had in mind to kill,' he says. 'We had lost a lot of buddies and it was a VC stronghold. We considered them either VC or helping the VC.' His platoon approached from the left flank. 'As I came up on the village there was a woman, a man and a child running away from it towards some huts. So I told them in their language to stop, and they didn't, and I had orders to shoot them down and I did this. This is what I did. I shot them, the lady and the little boy. He was about two years old.'

A detailed account came from Paul David Meadlo, twenty-two, a member of Calley's platoon . . . Meadlo says his group ran through My Lai, herding men, women, children and babies into the centre of the village – 'like a little island'.

'Lieutenant Calley came over and said, "You know what to do with them, don't you?" And I said, "Yes." And he left and came back about ten minutes later, and said, 'How come you ain't killed them yet?' And I told him that I didn't think he wanted us to kill them, that he just wanted us to guard them. He said, "No, I want them dead." So he started shooting them. And he told me to start shooting. I poured about four clips [68 shots] into them. I might have killed ten or fifteen of them.

'So we started to gather more people, and we had about seven or eight, and we put them in the hootch [hut] and then we dropped a hand grenade in there with them. And then they had about seventy to seventy-five people all gathered up by a ravine, so we threw ours in with them and Lieutenant Calley told me, "Meadlo, we got another job to do." And so he walked over to the people, and he started pushing them off and started shooting. We just pushed them all off and just started using automatics on them.'

According to SP5 Jay Roberts, the rampaging GIs were not interested solely in killing, although that seemed foremost in their minds. Roberts told *Life*, 'Just outside the village there was this big pile of bodies. This really tiny kid – he had only a shirt on, nothing else – he came over to the pile and held the hand of one of the dead. One of the GIs behind me dropped into a kneeling position thirty metres from this kid and killed him with a single shot.' Roberts also watched while troops accosted a group of women, including a teenage girl. The girl was about thirteen, wearing black pyjamas: 'A GI grabbed the girl and with the help of others started stripping her,' Roberts related. 'Let's see what she's made of,' a soldier said. 'VC boom-boom,' another said, telling the thirteen-year-old girl that she was a whore for the Vietcong. 'I'm horny,' said a third. As they were stripping the girl, with bodies and burning huts all around them, the girl's mother tried to help her, scratching and clawing at the soldiers.

Continued Roberts: 'Another Vietnamese woman, afraid for her own safety, tried to stop the woman from objecting. One soldier kicked the mother, and another slapped her up a bit. Haeberle [the photographer] jumped in to take a picture of the group of women. The picture shows the thirteen-year-old girl hiding behind her mother, trying to button the top of her pyjamas. When they noticed Ron, they left off and turned away as if everything was normal. Then a soldier asked, "Well, what'll we do with 'em?" "Kill 'em," another answered. I heard an M60 go off, a light machine-gun, and when we turned all of them and the kids with them were dead.'

THE NIGHT OF THE *PAVÉ*, PARIS, 7 May 1968

Anne Symonds, Daily Telegraph

A small dispute involving students at Nanterre and Sorbonne Universities grew into a mass student revolt in favour of reform of the centralized, authoritarian educational system. On 7 May the students, after being charged by riot police, responded by throwing *pavé* – the cobbles which surfaced the roads of Paris's Latin Quarter.

The worst street fighting since the Liberation of Paris in 1944 shook the Left Bank tonight as students and police fought for control of the Boulevard St Germain.

Smashed cars and overturned buses used as barricades littered the street, while riot police charged again and again, trying to force some 10,000 students into side streets.

As they were bombarded with tear gas grenades the students, at least half of them mini-skirted girls, replied with bricks, cobbles, firecrackers and chairs snatched from cafés. The heavy pall of smoke from the grenades and street fires, together with reports from the tear gas guns, added to the illusions that this was Paris in August 1944.

The Boulevard St Germain, main artery of the student quarter, was totally blocked when 1,500 rioters overturned two buses and pushed them across the road. Several other buses were abandoned by drivers and passengers.

By eleven-thirty p.m. the authorities reported that well over 150 people had been injured, some seriously during clashes. Student 'commando squads' ambushed police whose helicopters were circling overhead.

Water cannon, a new police weapon, were brought in, but within minutes students had smashed the vehicles' windscreens, forcing the drivers to flee.

Fighting had raged all day. The Sorbonne students were protesting against university conditions and against last week's closure of the Faculty of Letters in suburban Nanterre.

They were also protesting against alleged police violence during previous demonstrations on Friday over the Nanterre decision which followed persistent student rioting there.

Demonstrators were joined tonight by a contingent of university professors who this afternoon sent a delegation to demand the resignation of the Rector of the Sorbonne. It is estimated that tomorrow four university professors out of five will be on strike.

M. Maurice Grimaud, the Prefect of Police, said one

demonstrator, hit directly by a tear-gas bomb, may lose an eye.

There were violent clashes at the Place Maubert and in the Boulevard St Germain, in the heart of the Latin Quarter, where students tore up paving stones to use as weapons, and built barricades from vehicles and street gratings.

Police at first succeeded in driving back demonstrators at the Sorbonne, where Daniel Cohn-Bendit, left-wing student ringleader, appeared this morning before a university disciplinary council.

At one point several thousand students were driven across the Seine by pursuing police. They continued their march through the Opera district, on the Right Bank, before crossing back to the student quarter.

NIGHT OF THE BARRICADES, PARIS, 10 May 1968

Hans Koning

The Quartier Latin on the left bank of the Seine is a marvellously thick soup of college buildings, France's more famous middle schools, parks, cafés, boulevards and little streets: perfect headquarters for a new French revolution. There is nothing like that in American cities. I remember sitting in a Paris Left Bank café on the evening of 10 May which was going to be the Night of the Barricades: the night of 10 May to 11 May was to turn the tide against the police and put the students well-nigh in control of that part of the city. Before it had got really dark, there was already a wild excitement in the air. You could almost taste it; it affected everyone. Waiters distractedly put coffees and drinks down and didn't bother to check the money. As the evening wore on, tourist types and older people from other areas looked around, got their things together, and left in a hurry. But don't think that there was fear in the air, that people felt threatened. There was elation, not worry.

Some future rightist French government may bulldoze the Latin Quarter into wide-open spaces with scattered glass-and-concrete high rises – just as in the nineteenth century Baron Haussmann got rid of all the narrow workmen's streets and alleyways for Louis Napoleon and replaced them by the star pattern of the great boulevards, each one as straight as the path of a cannonball. When I got back to Paris in 1970, I found that the city had already asphalted over the paving stones of many streets and squares. The cobblestoned touristy charm had gone, but no future students would have paving stones to hand to heave at the cops.

The fighting of the 10–11 May night was astounding. It was astounding to watch the students being unafraid of police with tear gas and CS gas, concussion grenades, nightsticks, pistols, helmets, visors, shields, grenade rifles, and the famous leaded capes. It was equally astounding to find their courage 'rewarded', so to speak, by sympathy and even admiration not only from the radio reporters of the independent radio stations (Europe One and Radio Luxembourg) but also from the public at large. The fight was so unequal, the police so brutal that you had to be a very determined Law & Order person to feel sympathy for the authorities.

The students had made three demands: that the police get out of the Sorbonne, that the university be reopened, and that the arrested students and other demonstrators be released. They decided to try to enforce their case not 'by writing letters to the papers' but by protest marches. That night, with the police barring their way wherever they went, they built their barricades where they found themselves stuck, in the Rue St-Jacques, the Rue Gay-Lussac, and some other narrower streets south of the Panthéon. They dug in. It was the police, the CRS, and the Gardes Mobiles from the army who attacked.

Through the night various professors, famous scientists, and men of letters appealed (often on the radio) for the police to let up. When a statement of the Sorbonne rector blamed the students for not negotiating, Radio Luxembourg put an almost immediate student reaction on the air, repeating the three basic demands and inviting Rector Roche to answer them. The only answer was a repeat of Roche's original statement. When dawn came, the last barricades fell to the police, and the remaining young men, and some young women, were dragged, often clubbed, into the police vans. An unknown number was taken to the hospital by volunteers who had to fight the police to get through.

It was a cold morning. The streets were littered with stones, with debris of all sorts, burned-out cars, shoes, and lost pieces of clothing. A restless crowd of young people, probably mostly students too, filled the streets. It looked as if the police had won, but actually they had lost. The mood of the city and the country had turned against them.

By the end of May, workers too had launched a vast movement of strikes, paralysing the country. Eventually General De Gaulle, after securing the backing of the army, succeeded in re-establishing his authority and the revolution petered out.

THE SHOOTING OF ROBERT KENNEDY, LOS ANGELES, 5 June 1968

Alistair Cooke

At the time of his assassination by Sirhan Sirhan, Senator Robert Kennedy was running for the Democratic Party presidential nomination.

It was just after midnight. A surge of cheers and a great swivelling of lights heralded him, and soon he was up on the rostrum with his eager, button-eyed wife and Jesse Unruh, his massive campaign manager. It took minutes to get the feedback boom out of the mikes but at last there was a kind of subdued uproar and he said he first wanted to express 'my high regard to Don Drysdale for his six great shut-outs'. (Drysdale is a baseball pitcher whose Tuesday night feat of holding his sixth successive opposing teams to no runs has made him a legend.)

It was the right, the wry Kennedy note. He thanked a list of helpers by name. He thanked 'all those loyal Mexican Americans' and 'all my friends in the black community'. Then he stiffened his gestures and his style and said it only went to show that 'all those promises and all those party caucuses have indicated that the people of the United States want a change'.

He congratulated McCarthy on fighting for his principles. He hoped that now there might be 'a debate between the Vice-President and perhaps myself.' He flashed his teeth again in his chuckling, rabbity smile and ended, 'My thanks to all of you – and now it's on to Chicago and let's win there.'

A delirium of cheers and lights and tears and a rising throb of 'We want Bobby! We want Bobby! We want Bobby!'

He tumbled down from the rostrum with his aides and bodyguards about him. He would be with us in twenty seconds, half a minute at most. We watched the swinging doors of the kitchen. Over the gabble of the television there was suddenly from the direction of the kitchen a crackle of sharp sounds. Like a balloon popping.

An exploded flash bulb maybe, more like a man banging a tray several times against a wall. A half-dozen or so of us trotted to the kitchen door and at that moment time and life collapsed. Kennedy and his aides had been coming on through the pantry. It was now seen to be not a kitchen but a regular serving pantry with great long tables and racks of plates against the wall.

He was smiling and shaking hands with a waiter, then a

chef in a high white hat. Lots of Negroes, naturally, and they were glowing with pride for he was their man. Then those sounds from somewhere, from a press of people on or near a steam table. And before you could synchronize your sight and thought, Kennedy was a prone bundle on the greasy floor, and two or three others had gone down with him. There was an explosion of shouts and screams and the high moaning cries of mini-skirted girls.

The doors of the pantry swung back and forth and we would peek in on the obscene disorder and reel back again to sit down, then to glare in a stupefied way at the nearest friend, to steady one boozy woman with black-rimmed eyes who was pounding a table and screaming, 'Goddam stinking country!' The fat girl was babbling faintly like a baby, like someone in a motor accident.

Out of the chaos of the ballroom, Kennedy's brother-in-law was begging for doctors. And back in the pantry they were howling for doctors. It was hard to see who had been badly hit. One face was streaming with blood. It was that of Paul Schrade, a high union official, and it came out that he got off lightly.

A woman had a purple bruise on her forehead. Another man was down. Kennedy was looking up like a stunned choirboy from an open shirt and a limp huddle of limbs. Somehow, in the dependable fashion of the faith, a priest had appeared.

We were shoved back and the cameramen were darting and screaming and flashing their bulbs. We fell back again from the howling pantry into the haven of the press room.

Suddenly, the doors opened again and six or eight police had a curly black head and a blue-jeaned body in their grip. He was a swarthy, thick-featured unshaven little man with a tiny rump and a head fallen over, as if he had been clubbed or had fainted perhaps.

He was lifted out into the big lobby and was soon off in some mysterious place 'in custody'. On the television Huntley and Brinkley were going on in their urbane way about the 'trends' in Los Angeles and the fading McCarthy lead in Northern California.

A large woman went over and beat on the screen, as if to batter these home-screen experts out of their self-possession. We had to take her and say, 'Steady' and 'Don't do that'. And suddenly the screen went berserk, like a home movie projector on the blink. And the blurred, whirling scene we had watched in the flesh came wobbling in as a movie.

Then all the 'facts' were fired or intoned from the screen. Roosevelt Grier, a 300 lb. coloured football player and a Kennedy man, had grabbed the man with the gun and overwhelmed him. A Kennedy bodyguard had taken the gun, a .22 calibre. The maniac had fired straight at Kennedy and sprayed the other bullets around the narrow pantry.

Kennedy was now at the receiving hospital and soon transferred to the Good Samaritan. Three neurologists were on their way. He had been hit in the hip, perhaps, but surely in the shoulder and 'the mastoid area'. There was the first sinister note about a bullet in the brain.

In the timelessness of nausea and dumb disbelief we stood and sat and stood again and sighed at each other and went into the pantry again and looked at the rack of plates and the smears of blood on the floor and the furious guards and the jumping-jack photographers.

It was too much to take. The only thing to do was to touch the shoulder of the Kennedy man who had let you in and get out on to the street and drive home to the top of the silent Santa Monica Hills, where pandemonium is rebroadcast in tranquillity and where a little unshaven guy amuck in a pantry is slowly brought into focus as a bleak and shoddy villain of history.

MAN LANDS ON THE MOON, 20 July 1969

Neil Armstrong

At 10.56 p.m., EDT, on 20 July 1969, Neil A. Armstrong stepped down from the bottom rung of Apollo II's landing craft and became the first person to walk on the moon. Seconds later he was followed by his crewmate, Buzz Aldrin. Through the miracle of modern communications, hundreds of millions of people witnessed the event via TV. Below is Armstrong and Aldrin's commentary on the landing, as spoken to mission control at Houston.

ARMSTRONG: I'm at the foot of the ladder. The LM [lunar module] foot beds are only depressed in the surface about one or two inches, although the surface appears to be very, very fine grained as you get close to it. It's almost like a powder. It's very fine. I'm going to step off the LM now.

That's one small step for man, one giant leap for mankind.

The surface is fine and powdery. I can pick it up loosely with my toe. It does adhere in fine layers like powdered charcoal to the sole and the sides of my boots. I only go in a small fraction of an inch, maybe an eighth of an inch but I can see the footprints of my boots and the treads in the fine sandy particles.

There seems to be no difficulty in moving around this and we suspect that it's even perhaps easier than the simulations of 1/6 G that we performed in various simulations on the ground. Actually no trouble to walk around. The descent engine did not leave a crater of any size. It has about one-foot clearance on the ground. We're essentially on a very level place here. I can see some evidence of rays emanating from the descent engine, but a very insignificant amount.

HOUSTON: Neil, this is Houston did you copy about the contingency sample? Over.

ARMSTRONG: Roger. Going to get to that just as soon as I finish these picture series.

ALDRIN: Are you going to get the contingency sample? Okay. That's good.

ARMSTRONG: The contingency sample is down and it's up. Like it's a little difficult to dig through the crust. It's very interesting. It's a very soft surface but here and there where I plug with the contingency sample collector I run into very hard surface but it appears to be very cohesive material of the same sort. I'll try to get a rock in here.

HOUSTON: Oh, that looks beautiful from here, Neil.

ARMSTRONG: It has a stark beauty all its own. It's like much of the high desert of the United States. It's different but it's very pretty out here. Be advised that a lot of the rock samples out here, the hard rock samples have what appear to be vesicles in the surface. Also, as I look at one now that appears to have some sort of feenacres [spelled phonetically].

HOUSTON: Roger. Out.

ARMSTRONG: This has been about six or eight inches into the surface. It's easy to push on it. I'm sure I could push it in farther but it's hard for me to bend down farther than that.

ALDRIN: I didn't know you could throw so far, Neil.

ARMSTRONG: See me throw things? Is my pocket open?

ALDRIN: Yes it is. It's not up against your suit, though. Hit it back once more. More toward the inside. Okay that's good.

ARMSTRONG: Put it in the pocket.

ALDRIN: Yes. Push down. Got it? No it's not all the way in. Push. There you go.

ARMSTRONG: The sample is in the pocket. My oxygen is 81 per cent. I have no flags and I'm in minimum flow.

HOUSTON: Roger, Neil.

ALDRIN: How far are my feet from the . . .

ARMSTRONG: Okay, you're right at the edge of the porch.

ALDRIN: Now I want to back up and partially close the hatch – making sure not to lock it on my way out.

ARMSTRONG: . . . Good thought.

ALDRIN: That's our home for the next couple hours; we want to take good care of it. Okay, I'm on the top step and I can look down over the ICU and landing-gear pad. It's a very simple matter to hop down from one step to the next.

ARMSTRONG: Yes, I found that to be very comfortable, and walking is also very comfortable, Houston.

ARMSTRONG: You've got three more steps and then a long one.

ALDRIN: Okay. I'm going to leave that one foot up there and both hands down to about the fourth rung up.

ARMSTRONG: Now I think I'll do the same.

A little more. About another inch. There you got it. That's a good step.

About a three footer.

Beautiful view.

Ain't that somethin'?

TROOPS GO INTO NORTHERN IRELAND, August 1969

Anon. Lieutenant, 1st Royal Regiment of Wales

After fighting between the Protestant and minority Catholic communities in Northern Ireland, the British government sent in troops to restore order.

On the Friday afternoon we were moved up to Belfast, to Girdwood Park. The decision had been made to try and drive a wedge down the Falls Road between the two communities, and my company commander gave us a briefing on what we as a company were going to do. He said: 'I'm afraid I can't give you much information on what to expect. We've just to be ready for the worst. We know that there are quite a lot of weapons on the street, we know they're being actively used, and we have information that the place is burning quite badly. That's why it's been decided that we get in there tonight before anything worse happens.' I remember that my hands started to shake as I was taking down notes. The company sergeant major was sitting next to me, a hardbitten old bugger who'd been in Korea, and I can actually remember stopping writing and tapping his hand to stop mine shaking. I looked at him from time to time and I could see he was thinking the same – we were all slightly glassy-faced. I think the fear of the unknown is always the worst, and the information was so limited that we had to be prepared for everything.

So in we drove, and I remember the commuter traffic of Belfast going home that evening, all aware of what had been happening in the city for the past couple of days, all sticking their thumbs up in the air as if to say, 'Right. Long overdue. The Army's going in to sort this problem out.' I led my company along the Shankill and then down to the Falls, and the dear old Protestant ladies came out of their houses thinking we were going to sort out the troublesome Catholics. There were lots of shouts of encouragement: 'Get in there and smash the bastards.' We went down in box formation, as though we were putting down a riot in some banana republic, complete with our furled banner – I saw a film of it recently, and it certainly looks more than twenty years ago.

I halted my platoon because a double-decker bus was blocking the street and dashed forward to see what was happening. Beyond in the Falls Road was a burning garage and a shirt factory on fire, all six or seven storeys absolutely alight. The streets were strewn with stones and pebbles and cars on fire. The whole place was a nightmare. The houses on either side of the Falls Road probably going six houses deep into the side streets had all been burnt out, from petrol bombs through the front windows. There was the odd crack in the background, but one couldn't be sure whether it was from the fires or whether some actual shooting was going on. I think all our faces just showed disbelief.

The boys knew where they were supposed to go in terms of sealing off streets, so it was then a question of getting men down to the corners and road junctions and giving them cover in case there was shooting. We hadn't a clue what was going on really, but the feeling I got within half an hour was one of relief, on both sides. The Irish are terribly curious and they came out of all sorts of corners, and I think both Protestants and Catholics were relieved that there might be some stability, because when you live through that sort of thing as a civilian you're dreading another night. I think there was particular relief on the Catholic side because they were under tremendous pressure, and I think the first cups of tea we were given were Catholic tea.

As darkness came down it was mostly the Protestants trying to get down at the Catholics and do some stoning, and so we fired tear gas, maybe six canisters in all. The other impression that comes back strongly is small boys, who have been one of the perpetual problems of Northern Ireland ever since: you know, the hooligans that emerge from nowhere just to cause trouble. I think that night we had more problems from them than from anything else. The company sergeant major gave a couple of these lads the biggest bollocking of all time. Normally he would have frightened anybody, but they just went off down the road whistling. I don't think he could believe it himself.

Having worked out some sort of guard system for the night, my platoon sergeant and I unrolled our sleeping bags on a bit of grass in somebody's garden on the Falls Road. It was August, and we were both lying there looking up at the stars with this shirt factory still smouldering away, and I said to him: 'Do you think if that lot fell down in the night it'd reach us?' And with that I remember him standing up, rolling up his sleeping bag and going to the garden edge.

Apart from the odd incursion in the night, in most cases

people trying to throw stones, and the occasional crack of gunfire, nothing more came our way.

The following day was interesting. All the boys had offers of breakfast from the Catholics, to go into their homes. It was the quietest night they'd known for a long time. And then the most amazing sight: the regimental sergeant major came down the Falls Road, pace stick under arm, followed by the regimental police with wheelbarrows and brushes, and yelled at my platoon sergeant: 'Come on, let's get this place cleaned up, get it sorted out.' The whole of the road was littered with broken glass and bottles and smashed-up paving stones, and within half an hour the lads had all got brushes and were sweeping the pavement, tidying the place up. The irony was that there was a general feeling, which I remember so vividly, of: 'Let's get this place cleaned up and hand it back to them and then we'll be back off home.' And of course the other irony is the subsequent feeling that the whole problem might have been removed if the Army hadn't gone in until the following Monday: expensive on lives and property, but perhaps that might have been the end of it all, because at that stage a number of Catholics were quite prepared to cross the border.

Not having had a clue what to expect – which is not the first time the Army's been in that position – I think we all found it rather more difficult to accept because here were people who actually spoke English. They were obviously different, but you only have to travel a hundred miles in England and people are different, aren't they? So we had no real understanding of why on earth all this had happened, and it was only in the next three days or so that we actually started to learn of the problems of the Catholic community, how the two religions had managed to co-exist, and how matters had been handled in the past. So one started to get a certain sense of what Bernadette Devlin was all about.

There was probably an early perception of something wrong, that these sorts of things didn't just happen for nothing, and I think that when the soldiers discovered a little more about how votes were allocated in the Province, heard about job restrictions at Harland and Wolff, and learned that, basically, if you were a Catholic your chances weren't quite so good, then probably their sympathy lay with the Catholic people. But within ten days or so we'd started to get information on both sides and there was a quick realisation among the lads who hadn't met too many Ulstermen before that everything should be taken with a pinch of salt. They were very much in the middle getting both stories, and I think they just made up their own minds about what the truth was. They probably thought, 'What a mad bunch this lot is,' and I think within quite a short space of time they'd rather lost patience: reason and good sense and fair play and the idea of co-existence didn't seem to apply.

The other strong feeling was that the IRA had found the pressure too much for them at that stage. IRA was daubed everywhere, of course, but it stood for I Ran Away. The potential terrorists were, I think, completely discredited at that stage because under Protestant pressure they'd just found it too much and they had no standing in the Catholic community whatsoever. The Catholic community felt very let down, which in retrospect is such a pity, because the Army having come in and restored a physical situation, the only long-term solution had to be of a political nature. If only the political wheels had moved a bit faster: that couldn't have happened in weeks, but when you think that the first shot fired in anger at a British soldier was something like a year later, there was some time.

THE WOODSTOCK FESTIVAL, September 1969

Greil Marcus, **Rolling Stone** *correspondent*

Friday was the first day of the Woodstock Music and Arts Fair, now moved to White Lake near Bethel, New York, a hundred miles from New York City and fifty miles from Woodstock proper. The intrepid *Rolling Stone* crew thought it would be bright to beat the traffic, so we left the city early in the morning and headed up. When we got to Monticello, a little town eight miles from the festival, the traffic was light. Then we hit it. Eight miles of two-lane road jammed with thousands of cars that barely moved. Engines boiling over, people collapsed on the side of the road, everyone smiling in common bewilderment.

Automotive casualties looked like the skeletons of horses that died on the Oregon Trail. People began to improvise, driving on soft shoulders until they hit the few thousand who'd thought of the same thing, then stopping again. Finally the two lanes were transformed into four and still nothing moved. Bulbous vacationers (for this was the Catskills, laden with chopped liver and bad comedians) stared at the cars and the freaks and the nice kids, their stomachs sticking out into the road. Here we were, trying to get to the land of Hendrix and the Grateful Dead, all the while under the beady eyes of Mantovani fans.

There wasn't any traffic control. We sat still in our car and figured out all sorts of brilliant solutions to the transportation problem, everything from one-way roads to hired buses (a plan that failed at the last minute), but we still weren't getting anywhere, and it had been four hours now. This was the road on the map, right? No other way to get there? A lot of kids were pulling over and starting to walk through the fields. We had six miles to go. It was a cosmic traffic jam, where all the cars fall into place like pieces in a jigsaw puzzle and stay there for ever.

The police estimated that there were a million people on the road that day trying to get to the festival. A million people; 186,000 tickets had been sold; the promoters figured that maybe 200,000, tops, would show. That seemed outlandish, if believable. But no one was prepared for what happened, and no one could have been.

Perhaps a quarter of a million never made it. They gave
up and turned back, or parked on the highway and set up
tents on the divider strip and stuck it out. Shit, they'd come
to camp out for three days, and they were gonna do it. Many
had walked fifteen miles in the rain and the mud, only to give
up a mile or so before the festival and turn back, but they
were having fun. Camped on the highway with no idea
where White Lake was or what was going on, they were
making friends, dancing to car radios and making their own
music on their own guitars.

'Isn't it pretty here, all the trees and the meadows? And
whenever it gets too hot, it rains and cools everyone off. Wow.'
'Yeah, but you paid eighteen dollars and drove all the way
from Ohio and you can't even get to the festival. Aren't you
disappointed? Or pissed off?' 'No, man. Everyone is so
friendly, it's like being stuck in an elevator with people when
the power goes off. But it's much nicer here than in an elevator.

It was an amazing sight, the highway to White Lake: it
looked, as someone said, like Napoleon's army retreating
from Moscow. It looked like that for three days. Everywhere
one looked one saw tents and campfires, cars rolled into
ditches, people walking, lying down, drinking, eating, reading, singing. Kids were sleeping, making love, wading in the
marshes, trying to milk the local cows and trying to cook the
local corn. The army of New York State Quickway 17B was
on manoeuvres.

Thinking back to Saturday, one image sticks in my mind, an
image that I doubt is shared by many but one that I will
never forget. Friday night, folk music had been played –
Joan Baez, Arlo Guthrie, Sweetwater and Ravi Shankar. But
by the next morning the future was unclear, and rumours
that the area had been declared an official disaster seemed
quite credible. Many left Saturday morning, oppressed by
water shortages, ninety-degree heat, ninety-nine per cent
humidity and the crush of bodies.

'I love all these people,' said a young girl, 'they're all beautiful, and I never thought I'd be hassled by so many beautiful people, but I am, and I'm going home.' Faces were drawn and tired, eyes blank, legs moving slowly on blistered and sore feet. The lack of water, food and toilets was becoming difficult, though everyone shared, and many simply roamed the area with provisions with the sole purpose of giving them away. But it got hotter and hotter, and a boy was running toward the lake in a panic, cradling his little puppy in his arms. The dog was unconscious, its tongue out of its mouth but not moving. The boy thought the dog was going to die, and he was scared. He kept running, and I stared after him, and then I left the festival and decided to go home. I couldn't get a plane, and I was lucky to stay, but that scene was real, and it too was part of the festival at White Lake.

Everyone in the country has seen pictures of the crowd. Was it bigger than it looked? Whoever saw so many people in the same spot, all with the same idea? Well, Hitler did, and General MacArthur, and Mao, but this was a somewhat better occasion. They came to hear the music, and they stayed to dig the scene and the people and the countryside. Any time, no matter who was playing, one could see thousands moving in every direction and more camped on every hill and all through the woods. The magnificent sound system was clear and audible long past the point at which one could no longer see the bands.

The outstanding thing was the unthinkable weight of the groups that played. Take Saturday night and Sunday morning (the music was scheduled to begin at one in the afternoon and run for twelve hours, but it began at three or four and went until the middle of the next morning). Here's the line-up: Joe Cocker, Country Joe and the Fish, Ten Years After, the Band, Johnny Winter, Blood, Sweat and Tears, Crosby, Stills, Nash and Young, the Paul Butterfield

Blues Band, Sha Na Na and Jimi Hendrix. It's like watching God perform the Creation. 'And for My next number . . .'

Sometime around four in the morning the stage crew began to assemble the apparatus for the festival's most unknown quantity, Crosby, Stills, Nash and Young. This was not exactly their debut – they'd played once or twice before – but this was a national audience, both in terms of the composition of the crowd and the press and because of the amazing musical competition with which they were faced.

It took a very long time to get everything ready, and the people onstage crowded around the amplifiers and the nine or ten guitars and the chairs and mikes and organ, more excited in anticipation than they'd been for any other group that night. A large semicircle of equipment protected the musicians from the rest of the people. The band was very nervous. Neil Young was stalking around, kissing his wife, trying to tune his guitar off in a corner, kissing his wife again, staring off away from the crowd. Stills and Nash paced back and forth and tested the organ and the mikes, and drummer Dallas Taylor fiddled with his kit and kept trying to make it more than perfect. Finally, they went on.

They opened with 'Suite Judy Blue Eyes', stretching it out for a long time, exploring the figures of the song for the crowd, making their quiet music and flashing grimaces at each other when something went wrong. They strummed and picked their way through other numbers, and then began to shift around, Crosby singing with Stills, then Nash and Crosby, back and forth. They had the crowd all the way. They seemed like several bands rather than one.

Then they hit it. Right into 'Long Time Gone', a song for a season if there ever was one: Stills on organ, shouting out the choruses; Neil snapping out lead; Crosby aiming his electric twelve-string out over the edge of the stage, biting off his words and stretching them out – lyrics as strong as any we are likely to hear.

> There's something, something, something
> Goin' on around here
> That surely, surely, surely
> Won't stand
> The light of day
> Ooooooohhh!
> And it appears to be a long time . . .

I have never seen a musician more involved in his music. At one point Crosby nearly fell off the stage in his excitement.

Deep into the New York night they were, early Sunday morning in the dark after three days of chaos and order, and it seemed like the last of a thousand and one American nights. Two hundred thousand people covered the hills of a great natural amphitheatre, campfires burning in the distance, the lights shining down from the enormous towers on to the faces of the band. Crosby, Stills, Nash and Young were just one of the many acts at this festival, and perhaps they wouldn't top the bill if paired with Hendrix or the Airplane or Creedence Clearwater or the Who or the Band, but this was their night. Their performance was scary, brilliant proof of the magnificence of music, and I don't believe it could have happened with such power anywhere else. This was a festival that had triumphed over itself, as Crosby and his band led the way toward the end of it.

ALTAMONT, December 1969

Paul Cox

At the Rolling Stones free concert at Altamont Speedway, California, the Hell's Angel security force ran amok, beating and stabbing – and killing a black fan, Meredith Hunter. The hopes of the 1960s, the decade of peace and love, were dashed in that moment. Paul Cox was standing near Meredith Hunter in the crowd at Altamont.

An Angel kept looking over at me and I tried to keep ignoring him and I didn't want to look at him at all, because I was very scared of them and seeing what they were doing all day and because he kept trying to cause a fight or something and kept staring at us. He kept on looking over, and the next thing I know he's hassling this Negro boy on the side of me. And I was trying not to look at him, and then he reached over and shook this boy by the side of the head, thinking it was fun, laughing, and I noticed something was going to happen so I kind of backed off.

The boy yanked away, and when he yanked away, next thing I know he was flying in the air, right on the ground, just like all the other people it happened to. He scrambled to his feet, and he's backing up and he's trying to run from the Angels, and all these Angels are – a couple jumped off the stage and a couple was running alongside the stage, and his girlfriend was screaming to him not to shoot, because he pulled out his gun. And when he pulled it out, he held it in the air and his girlfriend is like climbing on him and pushing him back and he's trying to get away and these Angels are coming at him and he turns around and starts running. And then some Angel snuck up from right out of the crowd and leaped up and brought this knife down in his back. And then I saw him stab him again, and while he's stabbing him, he's running. This Negro boy is running into the crowd, and you could see him stiffen up when he's being stabbed.

He came running toward me. I grabbed on to the scaffold, and he came running kind of toward me and fell down on his knees, and the Hell's Angel grabbed onto both of his shoulders and started kicking him in the face about five times or so and then he fell down on his face. He let go and he fell down on his face. And then one of them kicked him on the side and he rolled over, and he muttered some words. He said, 'I wasn't going to shoot you.' That was the last words he muttered.

If some other people would have jumped in I would have

jumped in. But nobody jumped in and after he said, 'I wasn't going to shoot you,' one of the Hell's Angels said, 'Why did you have a gun?' He didn't give him time to say anything. He grabbed one of those garbage cans, the cardboard ones with the metal rimming, and he smashed him over the head with it, and then he kicked the garbage can out of the way and started kicking his head in. Five of them started kicking his head in. Kicked him all over the place. And then the guy that started the whole thing stood on his head for a minute or so and then walked off. And then the one I was talking about, he wouldn't let us touch him for about two or three minutes. Like, 'Don't touch him, he's going to die anyway, let him die, he's going to die.'

Chicks were just screaming. It was all confusion. I jumped down anyway to grab him and some other dude jumped down and grabbed him, and then the Hell's Angel just stood over him for a little bit and then walked away. We turned him over and ripped off his shirt. We rubbed his back up and down to get the blood off so we could see, and there was a big hole in his spine and a big hole on the side and there was a big hole in his temple. A big open slice. You could see all the way in. You could see inside. You could see at least an inch down. And then there was a big hole right where there's no ribs on his back – and then the side of his head was just sliced open – you couldn't see so far in – it was bleeding quite heavily – but his back wasn't bleeding too heavy after that – there – all of us were drenched in blood.

'BLOODY SUNDAY' IN LONDONDERRY, NORTHERN IRELAND, 30 January 1972

Sean Collins

Soldiers from the British Paratroop Regiment opened fire on a civil rights protest by Irish Catholics, killing thirteen.

Oh at the time of Bloody Sunday I was only a wain, a child of nine. There were seven in our family: my mother, my father, and five of us kids. We all lived in a two-bedroomed flat on the eighth floor of one of the blocks in Rossville Street. We didn't know then of course, but that was going to be right overlooking where the shootings were. The flats had been built to be occupied by Catholic families: there was a strict policy of segregation of areas on a religious basis in Derry, and the one we were in was called Bogside. Everybody more or less knew everyone else there, and everyone was poor.

The police used to patrol the Bogside a lot. I remember the police from the beginning, they were part of the everyday scenery. I don't recall much animosity towards them though. As a kid you knew there were occasions when there was trouble, protests and riots and all that, but you'd no idea what it was really about.

Sometimes the police'd appear in armoured cars which were called 'pigs': you'd see them firing gas or rubber bullets at people if there was a crowd. But it was something which had nothing to do with you: that was the adults' world, and what happened in it was what happened, that's all. I remember one of our favourite games we played was to imitate it: we didn't play 'cowboys and indians', we played 'cops and rioters'. Today it was your turn to be one, then the next day you were the other.

We'd never any understanding at all what it was about. My family wasn't Republican: all they cared for was we should keep out of trouble and not get hurt. They always told us if we saw something going on anywhere, we were to come straight home and stop inside. 'Course we never did though: we used to try and find good places to watch from, then afterwards we'd run round all the streets to see if we could find rubber bullets as souvenirs. An empty gas canister, well that'd be a great prize.

I remember it clearly when the soldiers came: our parents told us they were there to protect us and they were our friends. The first ones I ever saw were standing around in the street, and women were going up to them and talking to them and giving them cups of tea. To us wains they soon became sort of like hero figures: they gave us sweets, and asked our names, talked to us about different places in the world they'd been. The biggest thrill of all would be if one specially liked you and would let you touch his rifle, and hold it while you had a look along its sights. To me the soldiers were fascinating. I thought they were wonderful. None of us feared them at all in any way: grown-ups as well, we were all pleased and glad they were there.

The day of Bloody Sunday itself, all kids were told that after morning Mass we had to be home by 12 o'clock latest, and afterwards there'd be no going out playing for the rest of the day. Our parents said there was going to be a big march, it was going to come down from the Creggan and go to the Guildhall. If we were good we could go out on the balcony of the flat to watch it in the distance, but that was all. No one knew beforehand it was going to be diverted down Rossville Street and come right towards us. So there was great excitement then when it was, when it started to come right in our direction.

At first it looked peaceful enough. There was some shouting but only a little: but then after a while we began to hear some shooting from somewhere towards the back. I thought it was going to be an ordinary riot, and the police'd try to contain it as they usually did, by shooting off some rubber bullets and perhaps sending in some gas. But then suddenly I realized there was something different about the sound. It wasn't like one I'd ever heard before. When rubber bullets are fired, you hear 'Bang, bang, bang' like that. This wasn't that noise: it was much sharper, going 'Crack, Crack, Crack'. Then somebody on the balcony said, it was one of the adults I think, 'Jesus, that's rifle fire, they're using real bullets they are!' And we saw the marching column start to break up, people beginning to run away from it as hard as they could.

What I saw next after that I couldn't believe, not really at first at all. An army troop carrier appeared, and it started coming slowly towards us down the street. A man was running away from it and they were chasing him and trying to pin him against the wall. He escaped somehow, I think he dodged off somehow to the side. So then the troop carrier stopped, and out of it, or from out of another one that'd come along by its side, half a dozen soldiers jumped out. They stood by the vehicle a minute: and then slowly and deliberately each one of them went down on one knee and started to fire steadily into the crowd. It was like as if they were doing a sort of training demonstration, that's the only way I can describe it.

People were falling hit, and there was complete pandemonium. Some were stopping to try and help those who'd been hurt to get up, and others had for their only thought to get away. I saw a priest crouching down at the end of a wall: and when I looked at him I knew him, he was our own priest, Father Daly. He crawled from behind the wall to go to a man who was lying in the open a few yards away from him. I looked back where the soldiers were, and I saw one of them look up and he saw us watching from the balcony. He brought his gun up and took aim, but I didn't wait to see if he was really going to shoot or not; like everyone else there I ducked down. So whether that soldier fired or not, I don't know. Afterwards though nine bullet holes were found in the brickwork of the front of the flats, some of them as high up as the floor above ours.

Most of all what comes clearly back to me was my feeling of surprise. It was surprise that these men, the soldiers who I'd liked so much and admired – suddenly they weren't good people or heroes like I'd thought. They were cruel and heartless causing death and panic, putting terror into the hearts of the ordinary people of the community I lived in. It's difficult to judge the effect of it afterwards, but I'd say for me it was like the smashing up of a dream: sort of the end to my innocence somehow, the innocence of a child who till then had thought there was something noble and romantic about soldiers. I didn't think that afterwards, not ever again.

THE MILITARY ROUND UP THEIR OPPONENTS, CHILE, September 1973

Jim Ritter

A military coup, headed by General Pinochet, overthrew the elected Marxist government of Chile in September 1973. Among the many subsequently rounded up by the military as it searched out opponents was Jim Ritter, an American professor of physics at the Catholic University in Santiago.

We were driven off in an army truck. They loaded me in with another prisoner they had taken from the same group of buildings and drove through the streets of Santiago after curfew. That was a very interesting sight – completely dead. No people whatsoever around because you were shot for going out after curfew. Every night you heard shots ring out all the time. They were getting people who were out in the streets.

Finally we arrived at the Tacna Regiment and we were brought to a sort of waiting room where we were guarded by two soldiers, just like something out of the movies. Then we were told we were going to be interrogated. I turned over my passport to the officer in charge. My name was printed in a ledger and I was told to wait. We waited a few hours; it was not yet eight-thirty at night. Finally a little officer came into the room. There were now three of us prisoners. There was an Argentine leather worker who had been living with his Chilean girlfriend in the housing project and had had the misfortune of not having destroyed some Russian literature in translation. You know, novels. He was taken for that. There was a Chilean with us who was the administrator of one of the buildings. He had been taken because they had found a lot of Marxist literature in one of the eighty apartments in the building. So they took him prisoner, because he was the superintendent of the building – he swept the floor.

Then this little officer in paratroop outfit – with a black beret on his head – came in. He came over to each of us in turn. And now the whole atmosphere began to change. Up to now I had been treated either with friendliness by the private soldiers or at least with some sort of official abruptness – but nothing worse – by the officers. This guy came up screaming at us, 'Get up. What's your name? What are you doing here?' And finally, when you explained for the 105th time that you were a professor, and so on and so forth, he said, 'What do you know about the plot to assassinate major Chilean military leaders?' I said, 'What???' He said to me, 'All right, I'm going away now. I'll be back in a few minutes. I'll give you some time to refresh your memory. You had better commend your soul to God if there is a God for you.' And he stomped over to the next one, where he repeated the same act. It was sort of funny. I almost laughed. Luckily I cancelled that. Finally he went out and slammed the lights off like something from a bad film, and so you waited for him to come back. I was thinking, 'Gee, I wonder what he's going to do next? How's this going to come out?'

And then another officer comes in. This was the hard-soft routine that I remembered seeing so often on television. He comes up to ask us the same questions as the other guy, but he asks in a soft voice. We don't have to get up: 'No, no, keep on sitting.' And at the end of every answer we gave, he'd say, 'Perfect, great, great,' as though it were just a stupid little administrative mix-up and we'd be out of there in no time. That sort of approach. He left the lights on for us so we could read, and then half an hour after he left, the little guy comes in again. This time he doesn't say a word. He just goes over to each of us in reverse order, and while we're sitting there, he brings his hand up with an open palm and slaps us about four or five times across the face and then kicks us – still without saying a word. And then passes on to the next one and does precisely the same routine. Well, this was a bit frightening for me but it still was somehow unreal. I mean, it didn't really hurt all that much, and it was all part of the same 'hard guy-soft guy' routine and you felt that nothing more was going to happen. They're not going to shoot me, certainly. I mean, they would never shoot an American. This was before I knew about Frank Teruggi and Charley Horman, two Americans who were shot. I still felt absolutely safe. They could do that amount of nastiness to me but no more, and it still would make an interesting story for later.

We waited another half-hour and finally were taken out and loaded onto the trucks. I assumed we were going to the National Stadium. And I still felt, well, you got through that stage. Pretty soon you're going to get out.

And then things really started changing. We got up on the truck. And we were told to lie down on our stomachs, hands clasped behind our necks, and to spread our legs. I assumed this was to prevent escape or something. About ten soldiers got on the truck after us. And the truck still didn't start. It just stayed there. And then they started beating us. Now it was for real. The whole comic opera aspect of it was gone. I remember they would do each of us in turn. First they would kick the Chilean on my left. They'd kick him in the stomach five or six times. His whole body would sort of jump in the air with each kick. And then you knew it was going to be your turn. They were going to kick you in the stomach. There was nothing you could do. Then they'd pass on to the guy behind you, the next guy in the row. Then they would take the butts of the submachine-guns and start hitting you on the back of the head and on the kidneys. They'd do this to each of us in turn. I remember my legs weren't spread wide enough for them so they kicked them more and more apart. When I finally had them all the way out, one guy stomped very hard on my ankles, about ten times total on each ankle, which really hurt. Then he kicked me in the crotch. Now I began to get scared. I still didn't think they were going to kill me, but I did think they might really damage me. I really was afraid of being maimed. That they might do. And with that, the whole thing became very real. The pain didn't allow you to play the kind of safe game I'd been playing up to then – just being an observer, a coolly detached observer, of my own plight. I began to realize that this was for real and that I was not quite as immune as I thought I would be.

Finally they started the truck and they drove very slowly to the National Stadium – about a twenty-minute ride. And the entire time they kept working us over. I remember they kept yelling at us: 'Goddamn foreigners. Came down here to kill Chileans. Well, we're going to kill you. You'll see.'

We got to our destination and they said, 'All right, you bastards. Here we are at the stadium. This is Wonderland. Now, you're really going to see something.' And they prodded us into the stadium with their machine-guns, the muzzle-end this time, and stood us up against the wall. Having been beaten for the first time in my life, I now realized that it hurts for the moment and then the hurt seems to go away. You think it isn't so bad after all, but when you try to do something physically, you realize just how badly you've been hurt. We had to stand up and lean against the wall. They started kicking our feet further and further apart, all the time with the muzzles of their submachine guns at our backs. And you felt that they weren't going to shoot Americans on purpose, but maybe, just maybe, if you did something they might misinterpret, they might shoot you, you know, on the spur of the moment and worry about figuring it out later. I also realized that I couldn't stand up as well as I thought I could. I was really worried that if I slipped they might kill me.

This is a period where it's hard for me to reconstruct my own feelings because I'm removed. I'm safe. I'm out of Chile. I'm unhurt. But it had a sort of psychological effect that was perhaps the real point of it. What this maltreatment did to you before you got there was to strip away your dignity as an individual. This really did work. I felt completely powerless, completely and utterly powerless. They could do anything they wanted to you. No one would come. No big hero was going to save you. The American cowboy was not going to come over the hill. You were in there and they could do whatever they wanted to you. That might include maiming you, it might include killing you, it might include torturing you. There was nobody who was going to make it all better and fix it up. You could not even take refuge in yelling back at them, making a wisecrack, because as I found out later from people who had seen this happen, one guy who sort of broke finally was just shot dead where he was. You sort of felt this was a real possibility even before you knew about it concretely. You just accepted whatever they did to you, and it was this acceptance even more than the physical pain that really broke you down as an individual. You had to accept everything.

Finally I was taken over to another part of the stadium – inside the stadium, not where the bleachers are, but underneath the bleachers where the locker rooms are. We were put against the wall again but this time we were searched. I had not even been searched before. This 'up against the wall' was simply another minor physical maltreatment. But now the guy took all my stuff: ripped my wallet open to see what I was holding, checked inside of my boots to see if I had anything incriminating on me. I had gotten rid of my money when I went back to my apartment so they didn't get to keep that as they did with other people. My name was again entered in a ledger, again I had to go through the same rigmarole about what I was doing and so on and so forth. They gave me back my passport and I was taken to the prison section.

Now in the section I was in, they were using locker rooms. There were six in my section, each large enough to hold perhaps eleven men comfortably, and these were filled with about 180 people. You could count them when the people came out. In fact when I arrived they couldn't even physically fit any more people in the locker room. You looked inside and it was packed, a sea of people, mostly just standing or sitting very hunched up. There was simply no more room physically to put us in, so they put us in a new section they were starting, which was where the bleachers met the wall. Each of us was given one blanket and told to go there. I arrived very late – twelve-thirty or one in the morning – so I just went to sleep. The lights were always on. There were armed guards with cocked submachine-guns all the time, mainly pointing at you or around you. This was the type of existence you simply had to learn to live with. At this point I realized that this was not going to be a one-day little piece of administrative nonsense I'd have to go through. This was a bit more serious.

Prison routine is hard to talk about because it is the most incredibly boring thing in the world. There is absolutely nothing to do. You get up in the morning and it's cold. It was a very cold spring in Chile this year. And you sit huddled in your blanket and you wait, just wait. The lights are on all the time; the guards are there. They move around a bit but they don't actually do much. They talk together quietly. You can talk to other prisoners and, of course, you want to. You want to feel somehow identified with other people. You want to have some feeling of support. The big event is breakfast, because it's something that happens. You're taken out. For breakfast we were given a cup of coffee with milk and sugar and a little piece of dry bread. It was nice because you got in line. You picked up your piece of bread and you got your coffee. You sat and drank and ate – or you stood up and drank and ate – and you began to talk again. And then breakfast was over. You rinsed out your little plastic dish and gave it back and left the cup. And then you just sat there again. Then at about five or six in the afternoon we were given a little bowl of beans – hard lima beans – and noodles and another piece of bread. That was the diet you were on. It very quickly began to take its effect and make you weak. It was enough to keep you alive and to keep real intense hunger pains off, but you were always hungry, silently hungry. And you were debilitated so that you sat and couldn't even talk after a while. It was too much effort. If somebody new came in, you'd ask how he was, what happened to him, how was he tortured, and so forth. Then you just sat there.

NIXON RESIGNS AS US PRESIDENT, WASHINGTON, 8 August 1974

Richard Nixon

Richard Milhous Nixon, 37th President of the USA, resigned office under the threat of impeachment, when several leading members of his government were found guilty of organizing a break into the Democratic National Committee's headquarters in the Watergate Hotel, Washington.

Two minutes before nine o'clock I went into the Oval Office. I sat in my chair behind the desk while the technicians adjusted the lighting and made their voice check.

At forty-five seconds after nine, the red light on the camera facing my desk went on – it was time to speak to America and the world.

I began by saying how difficult it was for me to leave the battle unfinished, but my lack of congressional support would paralyse the nation's business if I decided to fight on.

> In the past few days . . . it has become evident to me
> that I no longer have a strong enough political base in
> the Congress to justify continuing that effort. As long as
> there was such a base, I felt strongly that it was
> necessary to see the constitutional process through to
> its conclusion, that to do otherwise would be unfaithful
> to the spirit of that deliberately difficult process, and a
> dangerously destabilizing precedent for the future.
>
> But with the disappearance of that base, I now
> believe that the constitutional purpose has been
> served, and there is no longer a need for the process
> to be prolonged.

Then I came to the most difficult sentence I shall ever have
to speak. Looking directly into the camera, I said,

> Therefore, I shall resign the presidency effective at
> noon tomorrow.

I continued:

> By taking this action, I hope that I will have hastened
> the start of that process of healing which is so despe-
> rately needed in America.
>
> I regret deeply any injuries that may have been done in
> the course of the events that led to this decision. I would
> say only that if some of my judgements were wrong – and
> some were wrong – they were made in what I believed at
> the time to be in the best interest of the nation.

I talked briefly about America and about the world. I talked
about my own attempts in twenty-five years of public life to
fight for what I believed in. I recalled that in my first
inaugural address I had pledged to consecrate myself and
my energies to the cause of peace among nations. I went on:

I have done my very best in all the days since to be true to that pledge. As a result of these efforts, I am confident that the world is a safer place today, not only for the people of America, but for the people of all nations, and that all of our children have a better chance than before of living in peace rather than dying in war.

This, more than anything, is what I hoped to achieve when I sought the presidency. This, more than anything, is what I hope will be my legacy to you, to our country, as I leave the presidency.

Throughout the speech I looked down at the pages of the text, but I did not really read it. That speech was truly in my heart. At the end, I said: 'To have served in this office is to have felt a very personal sense of kinship with each and every American. In leaving it, I do so with this prayer: May God's grace be with you in all the days ahead.'

The red light blinked off. One by one the blinding television lights were switched off. I looked up and saw the technicians respectfully standing along the wall, pretending that they were not waiting for me to leave so that they could dismantle their equipment. I thanked them and left the Oval Office.

Kissinger was waiting for me in the corridor. He said, 'Mr President, after most of your major speeches in this office we have walked together back to your house. I would be honoured to walk with you again tonight.'

As we walked past the dark Rose Garden, Kissinger's voice was low and sad. He said that he thought that historically this would rank as one of the great speeches and that history would judge me one of the great Presidents. I turned to him and said, 'That depends, Henry, on who writes the history.' At the door of the Residence I thanked him and we parted.

I quickly headed for the elevator that would take me to the

Family Quarters. The long hall was dark and the police and Secret Service had mercifully been removed or were keeping out of sight. When the doors opened on the second floor, the family was all waiting there to meet me. I walked over to them. Pat put her arms around me. Tricia. Julie. Ed. David. Slowly, instinctively, we embraced in a tender huddle, drawn together by love and faith.

We sat talking for a few minutes about the day and the speech. Suddenly I began to shake violently, and Tricia reached over to hold me. 'Daddy!' she exclaimed, 'the perspiration is coming clear through your coat!' I told them not to worry. I had perspired heavily during the speech, and I must have caught a chill walking over from the office. In a minute it had passed.

SAIGON: THE FINAL DAY, 29 April 1975

John Pilger

As the victorious Communist forces closed in on Saigon, the last Americans were being evacuated from the compound of the US embassy. Also awaiting a helicopter out was Australian journalist John Pilger.

People were now beginning to come over the wall. The Marines, who had orders not to use their guns, had been up all night and were doped with 'speed' – methedrine – which provides a 'high' for twenty-four hours before the body craves sleep. But methedrine also whittles the nerve ends, and some of the young Marines were beginning to show the effects. As the first Chinook helicopter made its precarious landing, its rotors slashed into a tree, and the snapping branches sounded like gunfire. '*Down! Down!*' screamed a corporal to the line of people crouched against the wall, waiting their turn to be evacuated, until an officer came and calmed him.

The helicopter's capacity was fifty, but it lifted off with seventy. The pilot's skill was breathtaking as he climbed vertically to two hundred feet, with bullets pinging against the rotors and shredded embassy documents playing in the downdraft. However, not all the embassy's documents were shredded and some were left in the compound in open plastic bags. One of these I have. It is dated 25 May, 1969 and reads, 'Top Secret . . . memo from John Paul Vann, counter insurgency':

. . . 900 houses in Chau Doc province were destroyed by American air strikes without evidence of a single enemy being killed . . . the destruction of this hamlet by friendly American firepower is an event that will always be remembered and never forgiven by the surviving population . . .

From the billowing incinerator on the embassy roof rained twenty, fifty and one hundred dollar bills. Most were charred; some were not. The Vietnamese waiting around the pool could not believe their eyes; former ministers and generals and torturers scrambled for their bonus from the sky or sent their children to retrieve the notes. An embassy official said that more than five million dollars were being burned. 'Every safe in the embassy has been emptied and locked again,' said the official, 'so as to fool the gooks when we've gone.'

The swishing of rotors now drowned the sounds of the dusk: the crump of artillery, the cries of women attempting to push young children over the wall. Two Marines watched a teenage girl struggle through the barbed wire. At first they did nothing, then as her hands clawed the last few inches one of them brought his rifle butt down on one hand, while the other brought his boot down on the other. The girl fell, crying, back into the mob. Somehow, most of one family had managed to get over the wall: a man, his wife, and her father. Their sons and his grandmother were next, but the barrel of an M-16 spun them back to the other side. The wife pleaded with a Marine to let the rest of her family over, but he did not hear her.

At least a thousand people were still inside the embassy, waiting to be evacuated, although most of the celebrities, like 'Giggles' Quang, had seen themselves on to the first helicopters; the rest waited passively, as if stunned. Inside the embassy itself there was champagne foaming on to polished desks, as several of the embassy staff tried systematically to wreck their own offices: smashing water coolers, pouring bottles of Scotch into the carpets, sweeping pictures from the wall. In a third-floor office a picture of the late President Johnson was delivered into a wastepaper basket, while a framed quotation from Lawrence of Arabia was left on the wall. The quotation read:

Better to let them do it imperfectly, than to do it perfectly yourself, for it is their country, their war, and your time is short.

From the third floor I could see the British embassy across the road. It was being quietly ransacked now. The Union Jack, which had been spread across the main entrance, perhaps to ward off evil spirits, had been torn away and looters were at work with little interference from the police. I derived some small satisfaction from the sight of this. It was there, a few days earlier, that the British Ambassador, a spiffy chap called John Bushell, had shredded his own papers and mounted his own little evacuation without taking with him a dozen very frightened British passport holders. Before he drove away, Mr Bushell gave an impromptu press conference.

'We are pulling out for reasons of safety,' he said. 'Our main responsibility is the safety of the British community in Saigon.'

I asked him about people who were waving their British passports outside the gates of the British embassy. Why were they not even allowed into the compound?

'Look here,' he replied, 'we gave ample warning. We put advertisements in the local papers. The trouble with these people, as I understand it, was that they didn't have tax clearance, which takes ten days, as well as exit visas from the Vietnamese government.'

Exit visas? Tax clearances? But wasn't this an emergency evacuation for reasons, as he had just said, of protecting life?

'Well, yes,' he replied, 'but we really can't break the rules laid down by government, can we?'

But surely this government had ceased to exist and there might be anarchy and a great deal of danger, which was why he was getting out?

'That may be true,' said the Ambassador, 'but we gave these people a reasonable time to get the paperwork done, and you really can't expect us to help them at such short notice . . . look here, the Americans surely will pick up any stray palefaces.'

But 'these people' were Indians and Chinese. The Ambassador looked confused.

'Oh, you mean Hong Kongers,' he said. 'They should have heeded our warnings . . . they'll have just to work hard at it, won't they?' At this, he turned to another British official and said, 'How many coolies . . . Vietnamese . . . are we leaving, do you know?'

The official replied, 'Coolies? Oh, about thirty-six in all.'

At six-fifteen p.m. it was my turn for the Jolly Green Giant as it descended through the dark into the compound. The loadmaster stopped counting at sixty; people were in each other's arms. The helicopter tilted, rose, dropped sharply, then climbed as if laden with rocks; off to the starboard there

were shots. We flew low over the centre of the city, over the
presidential palace where 'Big' Minh awaited his fate, and
the Caravelle Hotel, where I owed for two days, then out
along the Saigon River, over the Rung Sat, the 'swamp of
death' which lay between the city and the sea. The two
gunners scanned the ground, as they always used to, looking
for 'Charlie'. Some of us had on our minds the heat-seeking
missile which had brought a helicopter down as we watched
in the early hours. There was small arms fire around us, but
they were letting us go; and when the South China Sea lay
beneath us, the pilot, who was red-eyed with fatigue and so
young he had acne, lit up a cigarette and handed the packet
around. In the back of the helicopter there was a reminder of
what we had left: a woman, who had left her daughter on the
other side of the wall, cried softly.

A MEMBER OF THE MANSON GANG TRIES TO KILL PRESIDENT FORD, CALIFORNIA, 6 September 1975

George Frank

The day was sunny and beautiful, and the tiny woman in red
waited with other spectators for President Ford to walk by.

Most of the well-wishers wanted to shake Ford's hand.

The woman in red had a gun.

Lynette Alice Fromme, 27, known as 'Squeaky' in the
terrorist Charles Manson family to which she belongs, stood
quietly behind the spectators on the grounds of the state
capitol, eyewitnesses said.

'Oh, what a beautiful day,' she told a girl in the crowd,
Karen Skelton, 14.

'She looked like a gypsy,' Karen said later.

Squeaky wore a long red gown and red turban, and
carried a large, red purse. They matched her red hair.

On her forehead was a red 'X' carved during the 1971 Los Angeles trial in which Manson and three women followers were convicted of murder.

Squeaky, who had moved to Sacramento in northern California to be closer to the imprisoned Manson, 41, waited patiently for President Ford.

In her purse was a loaded .45 calibre automatic.

The sun beat down. The spectators squirmed in the 90-plus-degree morning heat.

Then, suddenly, the crowd perked up. Ford had emerged from the Senator Hotel and was coming up a sidewalk through the park of the Capitol grounds. Secret Service agents accompanied him.

He stopped to return greetings from the crowd.

The spectators, restrained by a rope, pressed forward to say hello.

He faced to his left and reached out for the extended hands.

'Good morning,' he said to the well-wishers, one after the other.

Squeaky made her move.

She lunged forward from the rear of the spectators, splitting them away on both sides.

Now she was only two feet from the President and, said police, aimed the gun at him.

Ford saw the revolver and 'the colour went out of his face,' said Karen Skelton.

He looked 'alarmed, frightened, and he hunched over,' said another spectator, Roy Miller, 50.

At that moment Secret Service Agent Larry Buendorf took the action that may have saved the President's life. Risking his own life, he lunged forward and threw himself between Squeaky and Ford.

He wrestled Squeaky to the ground, and he and police disarmed her.

Squeaky screamed, 'He's not your servant.'

Then she told police, 'Easy, guys, don't batter me. The gun didn't go off.'

Four or five agents threw themselves around the President and pushed him away from the crowd.

Ford's knees, troubled in the past, buckled in the crush, and he almost stumbled. But he stood up quickly.

'The country is in a mess,' shouted Squeaky as officers handcuffed her. 'The man is not your President.'

Moments later, as a police car drove her away, she had a faint smile on her face and appeared calm.

THE SEX PISTOLS PLAY THEIR FIRST CONCERT, LONDON, 6 November 1975

Adam Ant

The harbingers of punk rock played for the first time in public at St Martins School of Art, London. The band was formed by entrepreneur Malcom McLaren initially as a means of publicizing a clothes shop he ran with designer Vivienne Westwood.

'For their first ever gig . . . the Sex Pistols were support group to the band I was in, Bazooka Joe. I'll never forget it. They came in as a gang: they looked like they couldn't give a fuck about anybody. John had baggy pinstripe trousers with braces and a ripped-up T-shirt saying 'Pink Floyd' with 'I Hate' over it. Jonesy was tiny, he looked like a young Pete Townshend. Matlock had paint-spattered trousers and a woman's pink leather top. Paul Cook looked like Rod Stewart, like a little Mod really.

I watched them play: Malcolm was at the front, orchestrating them, telling them where to stand. Viv was there. There weren't many there: maybe a dozen of their people –

Jordan, Michael Collins, Andy Czezowski. They did 'Sub-stitute', and 'Whatcha Gonna Do About It' with the lyrics changed: 'I want you to know that I *hate* you baby.' Then John lost interest. He'd eat sweets, pull them out and suck them and just spit them out: he just looked at the audience, glazed.

There were no guitar solos, it was just simple songs. They did five and that was it: goodnight. The rest of my band hated them because they thought they couldn't play: in fact somebody said as much to Glen and he said: 'So what?' But I thought they were very tight. It was only John who hadn't learned how to make the voice last, but over a fifteen-minute burst, he was very clear. At the end Rotten slagged off Bazooka Joe as being a bunch of fucking cunts and our guitarist Danny Kleinman leapt from the front row and pinned John against the back wall: he made him apologize.

The impression they left on me was total . . . They had a certain attitude I'd never seen: they had bollocks and they had very expensive equipment and it didn't look like it belonged to them. They had the look in their eyes that said: 'We're going to be massive.' I stood there transfixed. When Danny jumped John, I didn't jump in to help him. I left Bazooka Joe the next day: I came out of that gig thinking, 'I'm tired of Teddy Boys' and it seemed to me that the Sex Pistols were playing simple songs that I could play. I just wanted to go away and form my own band.

BJORN BORG WINS WIMBLEDON FOR THE SECOND TIME, 27 June 1978

Geoffrey Green

The centre court clock stood at a quarter to four. It was windy and cold and overhead the clouds made a woollen blanket for the sun. It was at that precise moment that Borg of Sweden, sorely pressed by Amaya, the American giant, found his singles title slipping from his grasp.

Two sets to one down, 1–3 behind in the fourth and standing perilously at 15–40 on his own service, the championship seemed to be slowly ebbing away. But just when it appeared that he was about to depart before his appointed time the champion touch within him was reborn, so that at the end of two and a half hours he snatched a dramatic 8–9, 6–1, 1–6, 6–3, 6–3 victory.

This was probably the sort of pipe opener Borg needed as he chases Fred Perry's three successive Wimbledon triumphs of 1934–35–36. His recovery reflected the quality of a true champion. For nearly two hours he had sought a larger piece of the action against a towering American, a Flash Gordon of a young man, 6ft 7in of height, 15 st in weight, broad of shoulder and narrow at the hips, a powerful outsider standing thirty-first in the American rankings, who had once been the United States junior champion.

From that point of crisis Borg dug his way out of a dark hole, to go from 1–3 to 6–3 and two sets apiece. Amaya, within sight of victory, sadly saw it all slip away. Sympathy for him was balanced by a warmth of heart as the crowd came to life on a wintry afternoon, while Borg fed the flames of his recovery.

This was Borg's first competitive match on grass since his last Wimbledon win and he needed just such a battle. Amaya tested him fully up to the last furlong, unleashing a heavy left-handed service, many a fast, flat-hit passing shot down each wing and a penetrating backhand cross-court volley that had the Swede wrong-footed too often for comfort.

Borg never gave out in his best vein, but at the same time never gave in, and that was important. He showed character and a deep belief in himself, as he fought out of the fog of doubt into the light of certainty. In the end a packed gallery had a confectionery of good things.

Having broken back to 3–3 to win that critical fourth set

and then breaking again for 4–3 in the fifth with two glorious dipping backhand cross-court passes, it became as certain as day will follow night that he was home. If he played the waiting game on purpose it proved a dangerous ploy. Amaya, with his vast height and wide reach, often covered the net like an octopus, as he brought out the worst and the best in the champion. What failed the American in the final analysis was his serving of double faults – 12 of them in all as against nine by Borg. But it was the severity of his first service that weighed heavy on Borg's return, almost to unhinge the rhythm of his game on a court as well laundered as a bowling green but with a slippery quality in its spring.

Borg, with ice in his veins and balance in his feet, was able to take care of himself in the end – after losing the tiebreak 9–7 in a tough opening set of fifty minutes. At three o'clock a rustle of mackintoshes and umbrellas in the crowd signalled the arrival of a gentle drizzle as the champion reeled off the second set at 6–1, to draw level. Just as we sat back for the expected coup de grace, the unexpected happened. Amaya swept to 6–1 himself for the lead as he broke for 3–1 and again 5–1. When he went to 2–0 in the fourth he had taken seven games in a row; the champion wore a Strindberg gloom.

At 1–3 and 15–40 down, however, the ice broke and the tide suddenly turned in Borg's favour. What would have happened had Amaya taken that single point for a 4–1 lead is something for the mentally unemployed to ponder. Once at three-all in the final set Amaya hit a vertical shot off the wood that almost steepled to the skies, only to fall in court. That had the gallery in a paroxysm of laughter and I could swear that somewhere a voice murmured, 'We have lift off.' Borg and Amaya exchanged smiles that could have wounded others.

JACK NICKLAUS WINS THE BRITISH GOLF OPEN, 16 July 1978

Donald Steel

In the end there was no dream come true for Simon Owen, no victory for Peter Oosterhuis, no first triumph for the Japanese in the most traditional of all golf's settings – and no multiple play-off.

Instead, the multiple tie was for second place, and the 107th Open Championship produced the message which Jack Nicklaus has been delivering on and off these past sixteen years – a reminder that when it comes to winning major championships there has never been anyone to touch him in modern times – although it is three years since his last.

His latest, achieved with two strokes in hand with a last-round 69 and a total of 281, is his 15th as a professional; and he joined Bob Martin, J. H. Taylor and James Braid as the winner of two Opens at St Andrews. He also won, of course, at Muirfield in 1966.

His first at St Andrews was achieved in a never to be forgotten play-off with Doug Saunders, but his second yesterday was as fine as any. And, what is more, he had to contend with a challenge from his playing partner, New Zealander Simon Owen, who at the beginning of the week never crossed anyone's mind as a winner – not least his own.

By getting down in two at the 14th and holing a chip for a three at the 15th, he crept ahead of Nicklaus, who had hardly made an error all afternoon; but with three holes to play it was the implacable approach of Nicklaus and not the inexperience of Owen which prevailed.

After a superb, high pitch to the 16th had settled within five feet of the flag, Owen's second careered through the back of the green. His putt from one of the tees at the 17th failed to rise out of the swale at the back of the green, so that he was condemned to a five, and Nicklaus's brave putt for a birdie made a swing of two strokes.

The 17th has a chapter of accidents to tell from the past, but not for Nicklaus. A 3-wood split the fairway, his second with a 6-iron was expertly placed and his long approach putt up the bank was a model of judgement, nerve and skill.

Nicklaus knows better than most what can happen at the 18th. Consequently he took a 3-wood and no chances from the tee, but after pitching to the back of the green – Saunders country – there remained the possibility of Nicklaus taking three putts and Owen holing from about ten feet for a three.

As it was both took two putts, Nicklaus was re-enthroned and neither Oosterhuis, a gallant pursuer, nor anyone else had time to change things.

Oosterhuis failed narrowly with a birdie putt on the 17th, sadly missed the return and almost the final sight was of Tom Watson, the defending champion, putting his second into the Valley of Sin. Those on whom the gods smiled at Turnberry had reversed their allegiance; and nobody could ask fairer than that.

It was a pulsating climax, different from most and bewildering in how the pattern chopped and changed, but Nicklaus, for all the suggestions (quietly voiced) that he might have left the winning of Opens behind him, had the perfect answer, hitting the ball solidly and keeping his game together when he needed to most of all.

It is true that the finishing holes were easier than they had been in the earlier rounds, but no finishing holes are ever easy, and it required the world's supreme golfer for the last ten years to give his best at the critical moment.

He said afterwards that he had rarely played better and was proud of himself for reacting as he did and achieving what he came to do.

His third victory completes an amazing record over the last fifteen years in which he has rarely been out of the first six. But spare a thought for Owen, an unsuspecting hero, and

Oosterhuis, whose play was as relaxed as I have seen from him for some years.

Yesterday's wind was more the one that blew in practice last Saturday and, as if to answer the prayers of those who like to see the wind exert its influence on a seaside links, it stiffened appreciably as the leaders set out.

The long anxious morning had passed and the hour of reckoning had come. A combination of the wind and the ever-quickening greens put as much emphasis on prudence as it did on attack, and there was only an odd splash of red – indicating birdies – on the hole by hole scoreboard for the leaders in the early stages.

Ben Crenshaw, a professional with an unusual awareness and knowledge of the game's history, made one at the third but sandwiched it with a five at the second and a thoroughly unwelcome six at the fourth.

Tom Watson, defending the title he won in very different circumstances last year, must have felt it slipping away after hooking into the rough off the fourth tee and dropping another stroke by taking three putts on the fifth, admittedly from very long range after he had cut his second shot perilously near the crowds.

This had reverted to a genuine par five, with most of the principal contenders playing an iron short of the Spectacle bunkers, and Nicklaus had to work like mad on the enormous green to save his par five.

Having holed a useful putt for a birdie on the third, he played a wonderful pitch to a yard at the fourth to escape with a four, then needed a good twelve-footer which toppled in at the side after he had putted short on the fifth.

Every golfer needs reassurance in important rounds, no matter how many championships he has won, and when Oosterhuis, who had opened as solidly as anyone, dropped his first stroke at the sixth Nicklaus got that assurance. He was in the lead for the first time in the week.

By this stage, however, the threat to him was coming from a

quarter that he may not entirely have expected. Tom Kite, a member of the losing American Walker Cup team at St Andrews in 1971 – though himself winning both singles – went five under with a birdie at the fifth, and Bob Shearer, the best of the Australians and playing a few holes ahead, advanced with birdies at the sixth and the more perilous 11th.

Kite fell back by taking a five at the 10th, an infuriating hole at which to do such a thing, and Watson dropped his third stroke in a row at the sixth. Nicklaus got past the sixth, seventh and eighth without mishap and was once again very much the man everybody had to catch.

And let's not forget the gallant Isao Aoki, of Japan. He has been in the thick of it right from the start, and what could have been more uncompromising than the 10 straight par figures he turned out before heading for home with the wind now a bit of a help?

By contrast to last year, when the result had long since depended upon the epic battle between Nicklaus and Watson, the picture was repeatedly changing. And as Nicklaus turned for home as many as eight or nine still had a chance.

Owen was one of the few to birdie the 9th and 10th; Raymond Floyd launched his spectacular late run with five birdies in six holes from the 10th; Aoki continued his remarkably consistent string of pars; and Nick Faldo made his intentions clear with a birdie at the 12th, only to fall back at the 13th where he bunkered his second, and then sprang to life again with a four at the 14th.

Meanwhile, as Kite and Shearer, the latter no doubt encouraged by partnering Peter Thomson, recorded hard-working fives at the 14th, Oosterhuis drew level with Nicklaus with a birdie at the 9th and the chase was on.

Ahead, the famous skyline of the old town beckoned and thoughts were filled with victory. Now was the time for dreams to become reality, although in fact the story was only just beginning.

The final day of the Open is always something special, and the umpteenth battalion of the record crowd was filing into the Old Course as the milk and papers were being delivered around the town.

They were not quite as early as John Salvesen and Walter Woods, who start their daily tour of the course, cutting new holes, at 4.30. This is a subtle art anywhere; at St Andrews it is the key to the contest.

However, the early-comers were only just in time to see Andy Bean, who having started with a marker at eight-five holed out on the 18th at ten-twenty, there to be whipped promptly to Edinburgh Airport to catch the shuttle service to London and the afternoon flight back home.

As an accompaniment to the fastest round played in the championship for many years his 73 was good enough, but it didn't match Hale Irwin, who undoubtedly left his best until last.

It is strange that for such a fine player his best finish in several appearances in our Open was ninth when Tom Watson scored his first victory in 1975.

HOW THE OPEN WAS WON

69: Nicklaus (US) OUT: 443 454 434 (35), IN: 433 454 344 (34).
71: Owen (NZ) OUT: 444 555 433 (37), IN: 333 443 554 (34).
68: Floyd (US) OUT: 444 554 434 (37), IN: 325 343 443 (31).
70: Kite (US) OUT: 344 444 434 (34), IN: 533 454 444 (36).
71: Crenshaw (US) OUT: 453 654 434 (38) IN: 533 453 433 (33).

AYATOLLAH KHOMEINI FLIES BACK TO IRAN, 1 February 1979

John Simpson

After fourteen years in exile, the fundamentalist Shi'ite Muslim Ayatollah Khomeini returned to Iran to lead his supporters in their revolution against the Shah. John Simpson of the BBC was among the journalists who accompanied Khomeini aboard the Air France 747 jet which flew the Ayatollah from Paris to Tehran.

There was, fortunately, no shortage of space on the plane. Khomeini and his supporters and advisers were taking over the first-class section, which left us with two or three seats each. The discreet curtain dividing first-class passengers from the lower orders was kept firmly drawn. A regular undertone of prayer filtered through it, and those Iranians who had not been able to get seats in first-class stood or knelt in the aisles. I struck up a conversation with a British acquaintance of mine, who was based in Paris. He was not happy to be on the plane. 'I'm their Paris correspondent,' he kept saying. 'The only reason I'm here is because this whole thing is starting from Paris. What do I know about Iran? Nothing. So why did they send me? Because I'm their Paris correspondent.' The litany continued, and I moved away.

A little later in the flight I fell into conversation with a returning Iranian student. 'I am hoping with great sincerity,' he said, 'that this plane will be shot down.' Another student interrupted. 'That wouldn't be right at all. I want to sacrifice my life too, but I want us to land and take part in the Revolution. That would be a far better sacrifice.' With such difficult moral choices under discussion, I envied Bill Handford's ability, the inheritance of an old campaigner, to remain firmly asleep.

The Air France steward, an amusing, phlegmatic man, brought us dinner. There was no alcohol on the drinks trolley, by the express wish of the Ayatollah. For me, purely practical anxieties were beginning to take over: assuming that our flight landed safely, some pictures from it would be needed. Television is a literal medium: if you talk about someone flying from Paris to Tehran, you need to show him doing so. I applied at the dividing curtain, and was told that my request, like that of every other television correspondent on board (there were, apparently, fifteen of us) would be considered. I settled down for an uneasy sleep, nervous about what the morning might bring.

Three hours later it was light outside the aircraft, and coffee and croissants had put a little life back into me. There was a stir at the front end of the plane, and Sadeq Qotbzadeh emerged from behind the curtain, like Chorus in a Shakespeare play. He climbed on the foremost row of seats in our section, his back to the place where the film would have been projected if the Ayatollah had permitted such a thing on his flight.

'I have a serious announcement to make,' he said in French, and glanced at a piece of paper he was holding. Everyone went extremely quiet. 'We have just received a warning over the aircraft radio that the Iranian Air Force has orders to shoot us down directly we enter Iranian airspace.' Someone – it may have been the correspondent based in Paris – asked nervously if we would be turning round. 'Certainly not,' said Sadeq Qotbzadeh. 'What's he saying?' I heard Bill's voice ask me, quietly. 'You don't want to know,' I said.

Qotbzadeh, meanwhile, had climbed off his seat and was walking along the aisle with the practised skill of a public relations man, seeking out the television cameraman and the photographers. 'You can film the Imam now. But be brief.' I picked up the sound-recordist's gear and hurried forward with Bill. 'No journalists, just cameramen,' Qotbzadeh said, trying to hold me back. I reminded him that we had been allocated only two tickets, and had been forced to leave our sound-recordist in Paris, to follow us on a scheduled flight. He smiled and let me pass.

The Ayatollah was sitting at the front of the first-class compartment, on the left-hand side, looking out of the window: there were no impurities to be seen at this height. The whirring of the camera – we were still using film then, rather than video – caught his attention, and he turned to face us. He was utterly calm and passionless. I asked him a question, a routine enough one about his emotions on returning; his son Ahmad, sitting next to him, translated it into Farsi. The Ayatollah lowered his head without answering, and looked out of the window again.

A few minutes later, a better-phrased question from a French correspondent elicited the most famous remark of the trip.

'We are now over Iranian territory. What are your emotions after so many years of exile?'

'*Hichi*,' was the answer: 'Nothing.' Question and answer exemplified a mutual incomprehension. To Westerners, and to westernized Iranians, it sounded as though he cared nothing for the country he was about to plunge into revolution; perhaps we would have preferred him to break down and weep. But weeping was not much in Khomeini's line. He had spent his entire life ridding himself of false, personal, human emotions. It is permissible for a Muslim to express his love for Allah through the love of a person or a place, but not to love them strictly speaking for their own sake. Ayatollah Khomeini did not. The prophet Mohammed returned from his *Heigra*, the flight to Mecca, in order to carry out the first Islamic Revolution: Khomeini, too, was returning from a *Heigra*. Such moments were not to be debased with common emotions. But news of his reply to the French journalist's question was passed incredulously from one journalist to another at the back of the aircraft, and as we took note of it each of us remembered, no doubt, what Sadeq Qotbzadeh had warned might happen when we reached Iranian territory.

But nobody shot us down, and we continued our flight to Tehran, seeing at last the snowy peaks of the Elburz Mountains below us. Then, indeed, many of the Iranians in our part of the plane gave way to an unIslamic outburst of rejoicing, though some of them may have cast an anxious glance at the curtain to check that they were not being overheard and disapproved of. A thin yellowish sunshine cut through the cloud cover as we descended.

Tehran lay spread out below us, as peaceable and featureless as any city looks from the air. People were crowding together in their hundreds of thousands, their millions even, waiting for us to land; but from this height they were invisible. The pilot's voice came over the loudspeaker: 'We have not received permission to land. Until we receive this permission we shall be obliged to circle over the city. You may experience some discomfort.'

We experienced discomfort in fairly large quantities. A passenger aircraft like a Boeing 747 is stable and pleasant enough when it flies in a straight line, but when it circles at low altitude for half an hour or more it can induce airsickness and earache in the most seasoned travellers. Bill Handford caught my glance and winked; but the gloomy British journalist of my acquaintance was in an ecstasy of unhappiness. 'I am the Paris correspondent,' I could imagine him intoning. 'What am I doing here?'

At last it was over. The revolutionary welcoming committee on the ground had completed its negotiations with the airforce men who were running Mehrabad Airport, and the Boeing's agony of circling was at an end. We set a straight course for the runway and the wheels touched the ground of the country the Ayatollah felt nothing about returning to. The exile was back, his *Heigra* over; the final phase of the Revolution was about to begin.

THE SAS RELIEVE THE SIEGE AT PRINCE'S GATE, LONDON, 5 May 1980

Anon. SAS Trooper

The Iranian embassy in London had been taken over on 30 April 1980 by six Arab gunmen, who had held the staff hostage as a means of forcing Iran to concede to their demand for the liberation of Khuzestan. When Iran had failed to make any concessions, the gunmen had shot one of the male hostages. At that point, 5 May, the British government ordered a waiting unit of Special Air Service soldiers to storm the embassy building.

We took up a position behind a low wall as the demolition call sign ran forward and placed the explosive charge on the Embassy french windows. It was then that we saw the abseiler swinging in the flames on the first floor. It was all noise, confusion, bursts of submachine-gun fire. I could hear women screaming. Christ! It's all going wrong, I thought. There's no way we can blow that charge without injuring the abseiler. Instant change of plans. The sledge-man ran forward and lifted the sledge-hammer. One blow, just above the lock, was sufficient to open the door. They say luck shines on the brave. We were certainly lucky. If that door had been bolted or barricaded, we would have had big problems.

'Go. Go. Go. Get in at the rear.' The voice was screaming in my ear. The eight call signs rose to their feet as one and then we were sweeping in through the splintered door. All feelings of doubt and fear had now disappeared. I was blasted. The adrenalin was bursting through my blood-stream. Fearsome! I got a fearsome rush, the best one of my life. I had the heavy body armour on, with high-velocity plates front and back. During training it weighs a ton. Now it felt like a T-shirt. Search and destroy! We were in the library. There were thousands of books. As I adjusted my eyes to the half-light – made worse by the condensation on my respirator eyepieces – the thought occurred to me that if we had blown that explosive charge we might have set fire to the books. Then we would really have had big problems: the whole Embassy would have been ablaze in seconds.

The adrenalin was making me feel confident, elated. My mind was crystal clear as we swept on through the library and headed for our first objective. I reached the head of the cellar stairs first, and was quickly joined by Sek and two of the call signs. The entry to the stairs was blocked by two sets of step-ladders. I searched desperately with my eyes for any signs of booby-traps. There wasn't time for a thorough check. We had to risk it. We braced ourselves and wrenched the ladders out of the way.

Mercifully there was no explosion. The stairs were now cleared and we disappeared into the gloom of the basement. I fished a stun grenade out of my waistcoat and pulled the pin. Audio Armageddon, I thought as I tossed the grenade down into the darkness. We descended the stairs, squinting into the blinding flashes for any unexpected movement, any sign of the enemy, and then we were into the corridor at the bottom. We had no sledge, no Remington with us, so we had to drill the locks with 9-milly, booting the doors in, clearing the rooms methodically as we went along. Minutes turned into seconds; it was the fastest room clearance I'd ever done.

It was when I entered the last room that I saw the dark shape crouched in the corner. Christ! This is it, I thought. We've hit the jackpot. We've found a terrorist. I jabbed my MP 5 into the fire position and let off a burst of twenty rounds. There was a clang as the crouched figure crumpled and rolled over. It was a dustbin!

Nothing, not a thing. The cellars were clear. I was now conscious of the sweat. It was stinging my eyes, and the rubber on the inside of the respirator was slimy. My mouth was dry and I could feel the blood pulsing through my temples. And then we were off again, no time to stop now, up the cellar stairs and into the Embassy reception area. As we advanced across the hallway, there was smoke, confusion, a tremendous clamour of noise coming from above us. The rest of the lads, having stormed over the balcony at the front and blasted their way into the first floor of the building with a well-placed explosive charge, were now systematically cleaving the upper rooms, assisted by a winning combination of the stunning effect of the initial explosion, the choking fumes of CS gas, the chilling execution of well-practised manoeuvres and the sheer terror induced by their sinister, black-hooded appearance. We were intoxicated by the situation. Nothing could stop us now.

Through the gloom I could see the masked figures of the other team members forming into a line on the main staircase. My radio earpiece crackled into life. 'The hostages are coming. Feed them out through the back. I repeat, out through the back.'

I joined a line with Sek. We were six or seven steps up from the hallway. There were more explosions. The hysterical voices of the women swept over us. Then the first hostages were passed down the line. I had my MP 5 on a sling around my neck. My pistol was in its holster. My hands were free to help the hostages, to steady them, to reassure them, to point them in the right direction. They looked shocked and disorientated. Their eyes were streaming with CS gas. They stumbled down the stairs looking frightened and dishevelled. One woman had her blouse ripped and her breasts exposed. I lost count at fifteen and still they were coming, stumbling, confused, heading towards the library and freedom.

'This one's a terrorist!' The high-pitched yell cut through the atmosphere on the stairs like a screaming jet, adding to the confusion of the moment. A dark face ringed by an Afro-style haircut came into view; then the body, clothed in a green combat jacket, bent double, crouched in an unnatural pose, running the gauntlet of black-hooded figures. He was punched and kicked as he made his descent of the stairs. He was running afraid. He knew he was close to death.

He drew level with me. Then I saw it – a Russian fragmentation grenade. I could see the detonator cap protruding from his hand. I moved my hands to the MP 5 and slipped the safety-catch to 'automatic'. Through the smoke and gloom I could see call signs at the bottom of the stairs in the hallway. Shit! I can't fire. They are in my line of sight, the bullets will go straight through the terrorist and into my mates. I've got to immobilize the bastard. I've got to do something. Instinctively, I raised the MP 5 above my head and in one swift, sharp movement brought the stock of the weapon down on the back of his neck. I hit him as hard as I could. His head snapped backwards and for one fleeting second I caught sight of his tortured, hate-filled face. He collapsed forward and rolled down the remaining few stairs, hitting the carpet in the hallway, a sagging, crumpled heap. The sound of two magazines being emptied into him was deafening. As he twitched and vomited his life away, his hand opened and the grenade rolled out. In that split second my mind was so crystal clear with adrenalin it zoomed straight in on the grenade pin and lever. I stared at the mechanism for what seemed like an eternity, and what I saw flooded the very core of me with relief and elation. The pin was still located in the lever. It was all over, everything was going to be okay.

But this was no time to rest, this was one of the most vulnerable periods of the operation, the closing stages. This is where inexperienced troops would drop their guard. The radio crackled into life. 'You must abandon the building. The other floors are ablaze. Make your way out through the library entrance at the rear. The Embassy is clear. I repeat, the Embassy is clear.'

I joined Sek and we filed out through the library, through the smoke and the debris. We turned left and headed back for number 14, past the hostages, who were laid out and trussed up on the lawn ready for documentation, past the unexploded explosive charge, past the discarded sledge-hammer and other pieces of assault equipment – all the trappings of battle in the middle of South Kensington. It was 8.07 p.m.

As we made our way through the french windows of number 14, the Gonze, ex-Para, a new boy in the regiment from one of the other call signs, removed his respirator and asked the Irish police sergeant on duty at the door what the Embassy World snooker score was. A look of total disbelief spread across the policeman's face and he just stood there shaking his head from side to side.

I crossed the room to my holdall and as I began pulling off my assault equipment I could feel the tiredness spreading through my limbs. It wasn't just the energy expended on the assault, it was the accumulation of six days of tension and high drama, of snatched sleep in a noisy room, of anxiety and worry over the outcome of the operation. I looked to my left. The Toad had just returned. He looked tired, his face was flushed and he was out of breath. He looked at me and shook his head. 'I'm getting too old for this sort of thing.'

'So am I,' I replied.

Within fifteen minutes most of the team members had stripped off their assault kit, packed it into their holdalls and parcelled their MP 5s into plastic bags to be taken away for forensic examination. Before moving out through the front door of number 14 to the waiting Avis hire van, we had a dramatic visit from Home Secretary William Whitelaw, old Oyster Eyes himself. He stood before us, tears of joy unashamedly running down his cheeks, wringing his hands in relief. He thanked the assembled team members for what they had done for the country that day. 'This operation will show that we in Britain will not tolerate terrorists. The world must learn this.' It was a fine personal gesture and rounded the operation off perfectly.

LECH WALESA LEADS THE STRIKE AT THE GDANSK SHIPYARDS, POLAND, 14–23 August 1980

Anon. Gdansk shipyard worker

Lech Walesa, an electrician, led the strike at the Lenin shipyard in Gdansk which gave birth to the independent trade union Solidarity. With the later collapse of Stalinism in Poland, Walesa would become state president.

After director Gniech had given his brief explanations, this Leszek W. [i.e. Lech Walesa] appeared again. He, too, climbed up on to the bulldozer and told us he'd got in over the fence. I'm certain it was the first time that most of the workforce standing round that bulldozer had set eyes on Leszek. After all, it had been quite a time now since he'd been dismissed from the yard. Some of the people started asking who the fellow with the moustache was. Leszek took over the leadership of the strike. He wanted a reply to our demands and he insisted that A. Walentynowicz be allowed into the shipyard.* Leszek W. reached decisions very quickly though I must say that, to begin with, he appeared to be very tense indeed – I thought so, anyway. Leszek W. announced that all the sections would choose their own representatives to serve on the strike committee. The committee would start operating forthwith and would go to the conference hall with director Gniech. The workforce was to reassemble at a specified time to hear what the response of the management and the authorities might be. We assembled again at one in the afternoon and A. Walentynowicz was brought in. However, the explanations we were given proved unsatisfactory. Then Leszek proclaimed a sit-in strike which would last indefinitely. Only a small percentage of the workforce went home . . .

I remember clearly how, on the second day of the strike, Leszek W. spoke through the microphone at No. 2 Gate and said: 'I will keep the workers of the shipyard informed of any important developments through this microphone here by No. 2 Gate. When the time comes, I will announce the end of the strike through this microphone at No. 2 Gate.'

* The dismissal of Anna Walentynowicz had been one of the management's more unpopular decisions in the days prior to the strike.

There were no great changes or any conclusive decisions from the management during the second day. The Strike Committee started talks with the management between nine and ten o'clock. A large part of the workforce gathered outside the conference hall, reacting to the management's announcements and greeting Leszek Wałęsa with an ovation. They sang 'A Hundred Years' for Leszek and then they sang the National Anthem.

. . . On the third day of the strike . . . in the afternoon, the agreement was signed. The shipyard workers were supposed to leave the compound by six o'clock . . . I saw Leszek W. at No. 2 Gate. He was up on an electric truck and he was exhorting the people; he was explaining that they must stay in the yard, that we had to continue the strike as a sign of solidarity with the other factories and plants in the Three Towns (Gdansk, Gdynia and Sopot). I'm sorry to have to say that when Leszek asked the workers who were on their way out to stay in the yard, they didn't listen. They poured out like a river. I'll never forget that sight, or the workers' indifference. But Leszek's appeals did bring some results. People started to stop at No. 3 Gate and, after a while, some started to go back to their sections. But there were very few of them . . . In the evening Leszek came down to us and we all swore that we would stay there for as long as it took . . . Monday, 18 August . . . Leszek came down to No. 2 Gate at six. We sang the National Anthem and 'Boże, coś Polskę'. And then Leszek chatted with us for a bit. Another ordinary strike day had started . . . All the days from the 20th right to the end had exactly the same timetable. I'd be at No. 2 Gate by six, we'd all sing the National Anthem and 'Boże, coś Polskę' – Leszek always took part in the singing. From time to time there'd be rumours that some section leaders were forcing people to go back to work. Whenever that happened Leszek would pick up a flag and climb up on to the electric truck. Then he would lead the rest of us in a procession round the yard, making sure that there were no blacklegs.

On 31 August, at about five in the afternoon, Leszek Wałęsa came to No. 2 Gate. We welcomed him with smiles and cheers. In a short speech he explained that the strike was finished. Then the gates were thrown open as wide as they could go . . .

THE FALKLANDS WAR: THE FIRST MAN INTO PORT STANLEY, 14 June 1982

Max Hastings

The war between Britain and Argentina for the South Atlantic Falkland Islands (Malvinas) came to an end on 14 June 1982, with the surrender of the Argentine forces led by General Menendez. The first Briton into Port Stanley, the Falkland's capital, was the war correspondent, Max Hastings.

British forces are in Port Stanley. At 2.45 p.m. British time today, men of the 2nd Parachute Regiment halted on the outskirts at the end of their magnificent drive on the capital pending negotiations.

There, we sat on the racecourse until, after about twenty minutes I was looking at the road ahead and there seemed to be no movement. I thought, well I'm a civilian so why shouldn't I go and see what's going on because there didn't seem to be much resistance.

So I stripped off all my combat clothes and walked into Stanley in a blue civilian anorak with my hands in the air and my handkerchief in my hand.

The Argentinians made no hostile movement as I went by the apparently undamaged but heavily bunkered Government House.

I sort of grinned at them in the hope that if there were any Argentinian soldiers manning the position they wouldn't shoot at me.

Nobody took any notice so I walked on and after a few minutes I saw a group of people all looking like civilians a hundred yards ahead and I shouted at them.

I shouted: 'Are you British?' and they shouted back: 'Yes, are you?' I said 'Yes.'

They were a group of civilians who had just come out of the civil administration building where they had been told that it looked as if there was going to be a ceasefire.

We chatted for a few moments and then I walked up to the building and I talked to the senior Argentinian colonel who was standing on the steps. He didn't show any evident hostility.

They were obviously pretty depressed. They looked like men who had just lost a war but I talked to them for a few moments and I said: 'Are you prepared to surrender West Falkland as well as East?'

The colonel said: 'Well, maybe, but you must wait until four o'clock when General Menendez meets your general.'

I said: 'May I go into the town and talk to civilians?' He said: 'Yes,' so I started to walk down the main street past Falklanders who were all standing outside their houses.

They all shouted and cheered and the first person I ran into was the Catholic priest, Monsignor Daniel Spraggon, who said: 'My God, it's marvellous to see you.'

That wasn't directed at me personally but it was the first communication he had had with the British forces.

I walked on and there were hundreds, maybe thousands, of Argentinian troops milling around, marching in columns through the streets, some of them clutching very badly wounded men and looking completely like an army in defeat with blankets wrapped around themselves.

There were bits of weapons and equipment all over the place and they were all moving to central collection points before the surrender or ceasefire.

Eventually I reached the famous Falklands hotel, the Upland Goose. We had been dreaming for about three months about walking into the Upland Goose and having a drink, and I walked in and again it was marvellous that they all clapped and cheered.

They offered me gin on the assumption that this is the traditional drink of British journalists, but I asked if they could make it whisky instead and I gratefully raised my glass to them all.

Owner of the Upland Goose, Desmond King said: 'We never doubted for a moment that the British would turn up. We have just been waiting for the moment for everybody to come.'

The last few days had been the worst, he said, because Argentinian guns had been operating from among the houses of Stanley and they had heard this terrific, continuous battle going on in the hills.

They were afraid that it was going to end up with a house-to-house fight in Stanley itself. The previous night when I had been with the Paras we were getting a lot of shell fire coming in on us and eventually we sorted out the co-ordinates from which it was firing. Our observation officer tried to call down to fire on the enemy batteries and the word came back that you could not fire on them because they are in the middle of Stanley.

So the battalion simply had to take it and suffer some casualties.

Anyway, there we were in the middle of the Upland Goose with about twenty or thirty delighted civilians who said that the Argentinians hadn't done anything appalling. It depends what one means by appalling, but they hadn't shot anybody or hung anybody up by their thumbs or whatever.

They had looted a lot of houses that they had taken over. At times they got very nervous and started pushing people around with submachine guns in their backs and the atmosphere had been pretty unpleasant.

Robin Pitaleyn described how he had been under house arrest in the hotel for six weeks, since he made contact by radio with the *Hermes*. He dismissed criticism of the Falkland Island Company representatives who had sold goods to the occupiers.

'We were all selling stuff,' he said. 'You had a simple choice – either you sold it or they took it. I rented my house to their air force people. They said – either you take rent or we take the house. What would you have done?'

Adrian Monk described how he had been compulsorily evicted from his own house to make way for Argentinian soldiers who had then totally looted it. There appears to have been widespread looting in all the houses of Stanley to which the Argentinians had access.

The houses on the outskirts of the town in which the Argentinians had been living were an appalling mess full of everything from human excrement all over the place to just property lying all over the place where soldiers had ransacked through it. But they were all alive and they all had plenty of food and plenty to drink and they were all in tremendous spirits.

It wasn't in the least like being abroad. One talks about the Falklanders and yet it was as if one had liberated a hotel in the middle of Surrey or Kent or somewhere.

It was an extraordinary feeling just sitting there with all these girls and cheerful middle-age men and everybody chatting in the way they might chat at a suburban golf club after something like this had happened.

I think everybody did feel a tremendous sense of exhilaration and achievement. I think the Paras through all their tiredness knew they had won a tremendous battle.

It was the Paras' hour and, after their heavy losses and Goose Green and some of the fierce battles they had fought, they had made it all the way to Stanley and they were enjoying every moment of their triumph.

A question that has to be answered is how the Argentinian troops managed to maintain their supplies of food and ammunition.

I think it's one of the most remarkable things. I think intelligence hasn't been one of our strong points throughout the campaign.

Even our commanders and people in London agree that we have misjudged the Argentinians at several critical points in the campaign.

Our soldiers have been saying in the last couple of days how astonished they were when they overran enemy positions. We have been hearing a great deal about how short of food and ammunition they were supposed to be but whatever else they lacked it certainly was not either of those.

They had hundreds of rounds of ammunition, masses of weapons and plenty of food.

The civilians told me they had been running Hercules on to the runway at Port Stanley despite all our efforts with Naval gunnery, with Vulcans, with Harriers up to and including last night and, above all, at the beginning of May they ran a very big container ship called the *Formosa* through the blockade and got her back to Buenos Aires again afterwards. She delivered an enormous consignment of ammunition which really relieved the Argentinians' serious problems on that front for the rest of the campaign.

I think in that sense we have been incredibly lucky. The British forces have been incredibly lucky.

Considering the amount of stuff the Argentinians got in, we have done incredibly well in being able to smash them when they certainly had the ammunition and equipment left to keep fighting for a long time.

So why did they surrender? I think their soldiers had simply decided that they had had enough. Nobody likes being shelled and even well-trained troops find it an ordeal.

Even the Paras freely admit that it's very, very unpleasant being heavily shelled.

The last two nights, the Argentinian positions had been enormously heavily shelled by our guns. They gave them a tremendous pounding and when an Army starts to crumble and collapse it's very, very difficult to stop it.

I think that the Argentinian generals simply had to recognize that their men no longer had the will to carry on the fight.

This story of the fall of Port Stanley begins last night, when men of the Guards and the Gurkhas and the Parachute Regiment launched a major attack supported by an overwhelming British bombardment on the last line of enemy positions on the high ground above the capital.

Three civilians died in British counter-battery fire the night before last, as far as we know the only civilian casualties of the war. Mrs Doreen Burns, Mrs Sue Whitney and 82-year-old Mrs Mary Godwin were all sheltering together in a house hit by a single shell. Altogether only four or five houses in Stanley have been seriously damaged in the battle.

At first light the Paras were preparing to renew their attack in a few hours after seizing all their objectives on Wireless Ridge under fierce shell and mortar fire. Suddenly, word came that enemy troops could be seen fleeing for their lives in all directions around Port Stanley. They had evidently had enough. The decision was taken to press on immediately to complete their collapse.

Spearheaded by a company of the Parachute Regiment commanded by Major Dare Farrar-Hockley, son of the regiment's colonel, British forces began a headlong dash down the rocky hills for the honour of being first into Stanley.

I marched at breakneck speed with Major Farrar-Hockley through the ruins of the former Royal Marine base at Moody Brook, then past the smoking remains of buildings and strong-points destroyed by our shelling and bombing.

Our route was littered with the debris of the enemy's utter defeat.

We were already past the first houses of the town, indeed up to the War Memorial beside the sea, when the order came through to halt pending negotiations and to fire only in self-defence.

The men, desperately tired after three nights without sleep, exulted like schoolboys in this great moment of victory.

The Parachute Regiment officer with whom I was walking had been delighted with the prospect that his men who had fought so hard all through this campaign were going to be the first British troops into Stanley. But they were heartbroken when, just as we reached the racecourse the order came to halt.

Major Farrar-Hockley ordered off helmets, on red berets. Some men showed their sadness for those who hadn't made it all the way, who had died even during the last night of bitter fighting.

The Regiment moved on to the racecourse and they tore down the Argentinian flag flying from the flagpole. Afterwards they posed for a group photograph . . . exhausted, unshaven but exhilarated at being alive and having survived a very, very bitter struggle.

After half an hour with the civilians I began to walk back to the British lines. Scores of enemy were still moving through the town, many assisting badly wounded comrades, all looking at the end of their tether.

Damaged enemy helicopters were parked everywhere among the houses and on the racecourse. Argentine officers still looked clean and soldierly, but they made no pretence of having any interest in continuing the struggle.

Each one spoke only of 'four o'clock', the magic moment at which General Moore was scheduled to meet General Menendez and the war presumably come to a halt.

Back in the British lines, Union Jacks had been hoisted and Brigadier Julian Thompson and many of his senior officers had hastened to the scene to be on hand for the entry into the capital.

Men asked eagerly about the centre of Stanley as if it was on the other side of the moon.

By tomorrow, I imagine, when everyone has seen what little there is of this little provincial town to be seen, we shall all be asking ourselves why so many brave men had to die because a whimsical dictator, in a land of which we knew so little, determined that his nation had at all costs to possess it.

MASSACRE AT CHATILA CAMP, BEIRUT, 16–17 September 1982

Robert Fisk

After the Israeli army invaded South Lebanon in June, PLO (Palestine Liberation Organization) forces were evacuated to Syria. Many Palestinian refugees and non-combatants, however, remained behind in their camps. At the end of August, control of the camps was passed by the Israelis over to the Lebanese Christian militia.

What we found inside the Palestinian Chatila camp at ten o'clock on the morning of 18 September 1982 did not quite beggar description, although it would have been easier to re-tell in the cold prose of a medical examination. There had been massacres before in Lebanon, but rarely on this scale and never overlooked by a regular, supposedly disciplined army. In the panic and hatred of battle, tens of thousands had been killed in this country. But these people, hundreds of them, had been shot down unarmed. This was a mass killing, an incident – how easily we used the word 'incident' in Lebanon – that was also an atrocity. It went beyond even what the Israelis would have in other circumstances called a *terrorist* atrocity. It was a war crime.

Jenkins and Tveit and I were so overwhelmed by what we found in Chatila that at first we were unable to register our own shock. Bill Foley of AP had come with us. All he could say as he walked round was 'Jesus Christ!' over and over again. We might have accepted evidence of a few murders; even dozens of bodies, killed in the heat of combat. But there were women lying in houses with their skirts torn up to their waists and their legs wide apart, children with their throats cut, rows of young men shot in the back after being lined up at an execution wall. There were babies – blackened babies because they had been slaughtered more than twenty-four hours earlier and their small bodies were already in a state of decomposition – tossed into rubbish heaps alongside discarded US army ration tins, Israeli army medical equipment and empty bottles of whisky.

Where were the murderers? Or, to use the Israelis' vocabulary, where were the 'terrorists'? When we drove down to Chatila, we had seen the Israelis on the top of the apartments in the Avenue Camille Chamoun but they made no attempt to stop us. In fact, we had first driven to the Bourj al-Barajneh camp because someone told us that there was a massacre there. All we saw was a Lebanese soldier chasing a car thief down a street. It was only when we were driving back past the entrance to Chatila that Jenkins decided to stop the car. 'I don't like this,' he said. 'Where is everyone? What the fuck is that smell?'

Just inside the southern entrance to the camp, there used to be a number of single-storey concrete-walled houses. I had conducted many interviews inside these hovels in the late 1970s. When we walked across the muddy entrance of Chatila, we found that these buildings had all been dynamited to the ground. There were cartridge cases across the main road. I saw several Israeli flare canisters, still attached to their tiny parachutes. Clouds of flies moved across the rubble, raiding parties with a nose for victory.

Down a laneway to our right, no more than fifty yards from the entrance, there lay a pile of corpses. There were more than a dozen of them, young men whose arms and legs had been wrapped around each other in the agony of death.

All had been shot at point-blank range through the cheek, the bullet tearing away a line of flesh up to the ear and entering the brain. Some had vivid crimson or black scars down the left side of their throats. One had been castrated, his trousers torn open and a settlement of flies throbbing over his torn intestines.

The eyes of these young men were all open. The youngest was only twelve or thirteen years old. They were dressed in jeans and coloured shirts, the material absurdly tight over their flesh now that their bodies had begun to bloat in the heat. They had not been robbed. On one blackened wrist, a Swiss watch recorded the correct time, the second hand still ticking round uselessly, expending the last energies of its dead owner.

On the other side of the main road, up a track through the debris, we found the bodies of five women and several children. The women were middle-aged and their corpses lay draped over a pile of rubble. One lay on her back, her dress torn open and the head of a little girl emerging from behind her. The girl had short, dark curly hair, her eyes were staring at us and there was a frown on her face. She was dead.

Another child lay on the roadway like a discarded doll, her white dress stained with mud and dust. She could have been no more than three years old. The back of her head had been blown away by a bullet fired into her brain. One of the women also held a tiny baby to her body. The bullet that had passed through her breast had killed the baby too. Someone had slit open the woman's stomach, cutting sideways and then upwards, perhaps trying to kill her unborn child. Her eyes were wide open, her dark face frozen in horror.

Tveit tried to record all this on tape, speaking slowly and unemotionally in Norwegian. 'I have come to another body, that of a woman and her baby. They are dead. There are three other women. They are dead . . .' From time to time, he would snap the 'pause' button and lean over to be sick, retching over the muck on the road. Foley and Jenkins and I explored one narrow avenue and heard the sound of a tracked vehicle. 'They're still here,' Jenkins said and looked hard at me. They were still there. The murderers were still there, in the camp. Foley's first concern was that the Christian militiamen might take his film, the only evidence – so far as he knew – of what had happened. He ran off down the laneway.

Jenkins and I had darker fears. If the murderers were still in the camp, it was the witnesses rather than the photographic evidence that they would wish to destroy. We saw a brown metal gate ajar; we pushed it open and ran into the yard, closing it quickly behind us. We heard the vehicle approaching down a neighbouring road, its tracks clanking against pieces of concrete. Jenkins and I looked at each other in fear and then knew that we were not alone. We *felt* the presence of another human. She lay just beside us, a young, pretty woman lying on her back.

She lay there as if she was sunbathing in the heat, and the blood running from her back was still wet. The murderers had just left. She just lay there, feet together, arms outspread, as if she had seen her saviour. Her face was peaceful, eyes closed, a beautiful woman whose head was now granted a strange halo. For a clothes line hung above her and there were children's trousers and some socks pegged to the line. Other clothes lay scattered on the ground. She must have been hanging out her family's clothes when the murderers came. As she fell, the clothes pegs in her hand sprayed over the yard and formed a small wooden circle round her head.

Only the insignificant hole in her breast and the growing stain across the yard told of her death. Even the flies had not yet found her. I thought Jenkins was praying but he was just cursing again and muttering 'Dear God' in between the curses. I felt so sorry for this woman. Perhaps it was easier to feel pity for someone so young, so innocent, someone whose body had not yet begun to rot. I kept looking at her face, the neat way she lay beneath the clothes line, almost expecting her to open her eyes.

She must have hidden in her home when she heard the shooting in the camp. She must have escaped the attention of the Israeli-backed gunmen until that very morning. She had walked into her yard, heard no shooting, assumed the trouble was over and gone about her daily chores. She could not have known what had happened. Then the yard door must have opened, as quickly as we had just opened it, and the murderers would have walked in and killed her. Just like that. They had left and we had arrived, perhaps only a minute or two later.

We stayed in the yard for several more minutes. Jenkins and I were very frightened. Like Tveit, who had temporarily disappeared, he was a survivor. I felt safe with Jenkins. The militiamen – the murderers of this girl – had raped and knifed the women in Chatila and shot the men but I rather suspected they would hesitate to kill Jenkins, an American who would try to talk them down. 'Let's get out of here,' he said, and we left. He peered into the street first, I followed, closing the door very slowly because I did not want to disturb the sleeping, dead woman with her halo of clothes pegs.

Foley was back in the street near the entrance to the camp. The tracked vehicle had gone, although I could still hear it moving on the main road outside, moving up towards the Israelis who were still watching us. Jenkins heard Tveit calling from behind a pile of bodies and I lost sight of him. We kept losing sight of each other behind piles of corpses. At one moment I would be talking to Jenkins, at the next I would turn to find that I was addressing a young man, bent backwards over the pillar of a house, his arms hanging behind his head.

I could hear Jenkins and Tveit perhaps a hundred yards away, on the other side of a high barricade covered with earth and sand that had been newly erected by a bulldozer.

It was perhaps twelve feet high and I climbed with difficulty up one side of it, my feet slipping in the muck. Near the top, I lost my balance and for support grabbed a hunk of dark red stone that protruded from the earth. But it was no stone. It was clammy and hot and it stuck to my hand and when I looked down I saw that I was holding a human elbow that protruded, a triangle of flesh and bone, from the earth.

I let go of it in horror, wiping the dead flesh on my trousers, and staggered the last few feet to the top of the barricade. But the smell was appalling and at my feet a face was looking at me with half its mouth missing. A bullet or a knife had torn it away and what was left of the mouth was a nest of flies. I tried not to look at it. I could see, in the distance, Jenkins and Tveit standing by some more corpses in front of a wall but I could not shout to them for help because I knew I would be sick if I opened my mouth.

I walked on the top of the barricade, looking desperately for a place from which to jump all the way to the ground on the other side. But each time I took a step, the earth moved up towards me. The whole embankment of muck shifted and vibrated with my weight in a dreadful, springy way and, when I looked down again, I saw that the sand was only a light covering over more limbs and faces. A large stone turned out to be a stomach. I could see a man's head, a woman's naked breast, the feet of a child. I was walking on dozens of corpses which were moving beneath my feet.

The bodies had been buried by someone in panic. They had been bulldozed to the side of the laneway. Indeed, when I looked up, I could see a bulldozer – its driver's seat empty – standing guiltily just down the road.

I tried hard but vainly not to tread on the faces beneath me. We all of us felt a traditional respect for the dead, even here, now. I kept telling myself that these monstrous cadavers were not enemies, that these dead people would approve of my being here, would want Tveit and Jenkins and me to see all this and that therefore I should not be frightened. But I had never seen so many corpses before.

I jumped to the ground and ran towards Jenkins and Tveit. I think I was whimpering in a silly way because Jenkins looked around, surprised. But the moment I opened my mouth to speak, flies entered it. I spat them out. Tveit was being sick. He had been staring at what might have been sacks in front of a low stone wall. They formed a line, young men and boys, lying prostrate. They had been executed, shot in the back against the wall and they lay, at once pathetic and terrible, where they had fallen.

This wall and its huddle of corpses were reminiscent of something we had all seen before. Only afterwards did we realize how similar it was to those old photographs of executions in occupied Europe during the Second World War. There may have been twelve or twenty bodies there. Some lay beneath others. When I leaned down to look at them closely, I noticed the same dark scar on the left side of their throats. The murderers must have marked their prisoners for execution in this way. Cut a throat with a knife and it meant the man was doomed, a 'terrorist' to be executed at once.

As we stood there, we heard a shout in Arabic from across the ruins. 'They are coming back,' a man was screaming. So we ran in fear towards the road. I think, in retrospect, that it was probably anger that stopped us leaving, for we now waited near the entrance to the camp to glimpse the faces of the men who were responsible for all this. They must have been sent in here with Israeli permission. They must have been armed by the Israelis. Their handiwork had clearly been watched – closely observed – by the Israelis, by those same Israelis who were still watching us through their field-glasses.

Another armoured vehicle could be heard moving behind a wall to the west – perhaps it was Phalangist, perhaps Israeli – but no one appeared. So we walked on. It was always the same. Inside the ruins of the Chatila hovels, families had retreated to their bedrooms when the militiamen came through the front door and there they lay, slumped over the beds, pushed beneath chairs, hurled over cooking pots. Many of the women here had been raped, their clothes lying across the floor, their naked bodies thrown on top of their husbands or brothers, all now dark with death.

'SLIM': AIDS IN UGANDA, February 1987

Peter Murtagh

Around 10 million people are expected to die from Acquired Immune Deficiency Syndrome by the end of the century, most of them in Africa where the disease is thought to have originated.

Josephine Nnagingo lives in a mud and wattle farmhouse in the middle of her family's field of banana trees not far from Kyotera, a few miles from the shores of Lake Victoria in southern Uganda.

Nearby is a small building, used by the local Elim Pentecostal Church where, two Sundays ago, the congregation of women sang praise the Lord to the beat of homemade skin-covered drums. We made our way to Josephine's home as the chorus of happy voices in beautiful harmony wafted gently through the banana trees.

The church women believe that faith in God and adherence to his Gospel will protect them from Aids. Perhaps it will; but not Josephine.

She is dying from what her people call Slim, the Uganda word for Aids. It was coined in late 1984 by the district medical officer of Masaka, Dr Anthony Lergaba, who noticed the appearance of a new disease which appeared to waste people away.

Josephine, who is 27, first felt ill about three years ago

shortly after the birth of her fifth child. She got cramps in her stomach, began to vomit and developed chronic diarrhoea. She also has pains in her throat and chest and a skin rash covers much of her body. 'I have rashes which I scratch they are so painful. The disease came slowly and then started to weaken me,' she explained through an interpreter.

Because of the vomiting and diarrhoea, Josephine's body is not able to get the nourishment to keep it alive. She is slowly starving to death and does not expect to survive much longer.

The wasting of her shrunken body has made her head appear outsized, and her dress is now too big for her. Her arms and legs are desperately thin, and she moves only with pain.

Josephine is not unique in her family. Her sister died of Aids three years ago, as did Josephine's first husband the year before that. He fathered her first two children but her second husband, who fathered the other three, vanished after the birth of their last child. The baby was vomiting and had diarrhoea when it was born but appears now to be all right.

Behind the house and beneath a mound of stones is the grave of Josephine's grandfather whom the family believe also died of Aids. Josephine's mother, Folomela, says that he had the symptoms of Slim and lost a lot of weight before fading away seven years ago. A similarly appalling catalogue of death can be heard in almost every home in the Masaka and Rakai districts of southern Uganda. The disease has so devastated some of the tiny ports on the western shores of Lake Victoria that houses have been abandoned.

In some cases the occupants have returned to their family homes to die, while in others, deaths in the houses have prompted the survivors to flee in the belief that the buildings themselves are in some way responsible for the illness.

According to a doctor in Kyotera, five people a day died of Aids last December. The day before I visited the village there were three funerals, and two more on the day we were there. 'The situation is bad, very bad,' said the doctor. 'At the beginning, it used to be a young man's disease, but now it is no longer age specific. My landlord has lost four people in the last year, three brothers and a nephew. People have stopped working. Their job now is burying every day. Every day.'

About one million people live in the Masaka and Rakai districts, and the Aids virus is conservatively estimated to have infected 50,000 of them, or five per cent of the population. People are aware of the fatal consequences of the disease and many no longer bother to go to hospital when they fall ill.

One result is that a fatalistic approach has developed to all illnesses. Some people who contract curable tropical diseases are dying because they no longer seek medical help in the belief that they have Aids.

In a desperate search for help, people in the area have turned to witchdoctors and herbalists. Some of the men around Kyotera who believe that Aids is witchcraft have sex with the widows of victims. The widows almost certainly have the virus as well but, tragically, the men hope that the mysterious power which has apparently kept the widow alive will be transferred to them.

'They look at this good-looking woman and say why is she so good-looking and still alive? She must have some special power,' said the doctor.

When people go to witchdoctors, they are asked first if there is any person with whom they have ever had a row. Invariably there is and this person is then identified as the source of evil making the patient sick.

Herbs are prescribed and the patient is given talismans to wear. Animal bones may be hung on the front door of the patient's home, and the witchdoctor may prescribe dog soup. One witchdoctor made his patient throw out all the goods he had bought from the man identified as the source of his troubles. It did not work, however, and the patient died.

However, village faith in the witchdoctors was shaken recently. One of them had proudly put up a notice outside his home proclaiming that he had the cure for Slim. People believed it until he too contracted the disease.

THE SHOOTING OF THE STUDENTS AT TIANANMEN SQUARE, BEIJING, CHINA, 7 June 1989

Anon. Beijing student

I am a student at Qinghua University. I am twenty years old. I spent last night sitting on the steps of the Monument to the Heroes of the People. I witnessed from start to finish the shooting and suppression by the army of students and citizens.

Many of my fellow students have already been shot dead. My clothes are still stained with their blood. As a lucky survivor and an eyewitness, I want to tell peace-loving and good people across the world about the massacre.

Frankly speaking, we knew early on in the evening that the troops intended to suppress us. Someone whose status I can't reveal phoned us at four o'clock on Saturday afternoon. (The call was to a neighbourhood phone station in an alley near the Square.) The caller told us that the Square was about to be invaded and cleared. We went on to the alert. After a discussion we took some measures. We did our best to alleviate contradictions and avoid a bloodbath.

We had twenty-three submachine-guns and some incendiary bombs that we'd snatched from soldiers during the previous two days. The Autonomous Students' Union called a meeting and decided to return these weapons forthwith to the martial law troops to show that we intended to promote democracy by non-violent means. On the rostrum at Tiananmen Square beneath the portrait of Chairman Mao we liaised with troops about this, but an officer said that he was under higher orders not to accept the weapons.

So the negotiations failed. At around one in the morning, when things had become really critical, we destroyed the guns and dismantled the bombs. We poured away the petrol so that bad people couldn't use it and the authorities couldn't point to it as 'proof' that we were out to kill soldiers. After that, the Union told everyone in the Square that the situation was extremely grave, that bloodshed seemed inevitable, and that they wanted students and citizens to leave the Square. But there were still 40,000–50,000 students and about 100,000 citizens determined not to go. I, too, decided not to go.

The mood was extraordinarily tense. This was the first time we'd ever experienced such danger. I'd be lying if I said we weren't afraid, but everyone was psychologically braced and tempered. (Some students, of course, didn't believe that the troops would shoot to kill.) In a word, we were imbued with a lofty sense of mission. We were prepared to sacrifice ourselves for China's democracy and progress.

After midnight, after two armoured cars had sped down each side of the Square from the Front Gate, the situation became increasingly serious. Official loudspeakers repeatedly blared out 'notices'. Dense lines of steel-helmeted troops ringed the Square. Despite the darkness, you could clearly see the machine-guns mounted on top of the History Museum. There was not the slightest attempt to hide them.

We students crowded round the Monument to the Heroes of the People. I carefully estimated the crowd. Two-thirds were men, one-third were women; about 30 per cent from universities and colleges in Beijing. Most were students from other cities.

At four o'clock sharp, just before daybreak, the lights in the Square suddenly went out. The loudspeakers broadcast another order to 'clear the Square'. I suddenly had a tight feeling in my stomach. There was only one thought in my head: the time has come, the time has come.

The hunger-striker Hou Dejian (a Taiwan pop-singer now working on the mainland) and some other people negotiated with the troops and agreed to get the students to leave peacefully. But just as they were about to go, at 4.40 am, a cluster of red signal flares rose into the sky above the Square and the lights came on again.

I saw that the front of the Square was packed with troops. A detachment of soldiers came running from the east entrance of the Great Hall of the People. They were dressed in camouflage. They were carrying light machine-guns and wearing steel helmets and gas-masks.

As soon as these troops had stormed out, they lined up a dozen or so machine-guns in front of the Monument to the Heroes of the People. The machine-gunners lay down on their stomachs. Their guns pointed toward the Monument. The rostrum was behind them. When all the guns were properly lined up, a great mass of soldiers and armed police, wielding electric prods, rubber truncheons, and some special weapons of a sort I'd never seen before suddenly rushed us. We were sitting quietly. There were two differences between the troops and the armed police: their uniforms were different, and so were their helmets. The police helmets were bigger than the troops' and had steel flaps going down over the ears. The soldiers and the policemen started violently laying about us. They split our ranks down the middle and opened up a path to the Monument. They stormed up to its third tier. I saw forty or fifty students suddenly spurt blood. Armoured troop carriers and an even greater number of troops that had been waiting in the Square joined the siege. The troop carriers formed a solid blockade, except for a gap on the museum side.

The troops and policemen who had stormed the monument smashed our loudspeaker installations, our printing equipment, and our supply of soda water. Then they beat and threw down the steps the students still occupying the third tier. We'd stayed put all along, holding hands and singing the Internationale. We'd been shouting 'The people's army won't attack the people'. The students packing the third tier had no choice but to retreat under the blows and kicks of such a large body of men. While this was going

on, the sound of machine-guns started up. Some troops were
kneeling down and firing. Their bullets whizzed above our
heads. The troops lying on their stomachs shot up into the
students' chests and faces. We had no choice but to retreat
back up onto the Monument. When we reached it the
machine-guns stopped. But the troops on the Monument
beat us back down again. As soon as we'd been beaten down,
the machine-guns started up again.*

The dare-to-die brigade of workers and citizens picked up
anything that served as a weapon – bottles, pieces of wood –
and rushed towards the troops to resist them. The Students'
Union gave the order to retreat to places outside the Square.
It was not yet five o'clock.

A great crowd of students rushed toward the gap in the
line of troop carriers. The heartless drivers closed the gap.
Thirty-odd carriers drove into the crowd. Some people were
crushed to death. Even the flagpole in front of the Monument was snapped off. The whole Square was in massive
chaos. I'd never thought my fellow-students could be so
brave. Some started to push at the troop carriers. They were
mown down. Others clambered over their corpses and
pushed too. Finally they managed to push one or two
carriers aside and open up a gap. I and 3,000 other students
rushed through under a hail of fire. We ran across to the
entrance to the History Museum.

There were large numbers of citizens in front of the
Museum. We joined up with them. Seeing how bad things
were, we immediately ran off to the north in the direction of the
Gate of Heavenly Peace. But we'd only gone a few steps when
rifle fire broke out from a clump of bushes alongside the road.
We saw no people – just the bursts of fire from the gun-barrels.
So we turned and ran off south towards the Front Gate.

---

* This manoeuvre was plainly designed to avoid troops firing directly
onto the Monument, and chipping or pocking the stone fresco of heroes
(though, as television news has shown, they did hit a few).

I was running and weeping. I saw a second batch of students running off under machine-gun fire. I saw lots of people lying on their stomachs on the road that we were trying to escape along. We were all crying – running and crying. When we reached the Front Gate, we were suddenly confronted by a batch of troops. They didn't open fire. They were armed with big wooden staves. They beat us furiously.

Then a large crowd of citizens came pouring out of the Front Gate. They clashed violently with these troops. They protected us while we escaped in the direction of Beijing railway station. The troops pursued us. It was five o'clock. Dawn was breaking. The gunfire on the Square seemed to have died down a little.

THE FALL OF THE BERLIN WALL,
11 November 1989

Peter Millar and Richard Ellis, Sunday Times

After days of protest, the East German Communist regime was forced to open the country's borders, including the infamous Wall in Berlin.

More than one million Germans from East and West held the world's biggest non-stop party in Berlin yesterday, as their sober leaders tried in vain to dampen the euphoria by warning that a united Germany was not yet on the political agenda.

East Berliners poured into West Berlin to celebrate their liberty on free beer and wine, and late last night one 24-year-old visitor from the East gave birth to a baby girl on one of the city's bustling streets, to the delight of the partying crowds.

The new life seemed symbolic. Berlin was itself a city reborn. The party clogged the streets as the barriers that divided Germany melted like the ice of the cold war. Officials said well over a million people had passed the frontiers from East Germany into West Berlin and West Germany in a matter of hours.

After nightfall, as the party proved unstoppable, police shut off traffic from several main streets, and sealed off the Wall at the Brandenburg Gate to prevent demonstrators from dancing on it. West Berlin police said they were in constant touch with their East German colleagues on the other side of the wall.

Tension gave way to heated but good-natured banter between West Berliners and the normally sullen East German guards standing on the wall.

'I'm not here talking to you because I have to or because I've been told to,' one policeman said. 'I'm here because I want to (be).'

'What's your name, what's your name?' shouted the crowd.

'Call me Karl-Heinz,' he answered.

'Tell me, what will happen when there's no more use for the wall?' he was asked.

'Well, if it goes that far, I suppose we'll get to know each other.'

Along the Kurfurstendamm, tens of thousands of East and West Berliners linked their arms to sing songs celebrating their newly gained solidarity.

To the tune of Glory Glory Hallelujah, they chorused *Berlin ist ein Stadt, Deutschland is ein Land* (Berlin is one city, Germany is one country). As they sang, people held up cigarette lighters, matches and candles and sparklers to demonstrate their feelings.

For the benefit of American television crews, there were songs even in English: 'We shall overcome' and 'This land is my land'.

Street poets regaled the crowds with jokes and verses that concentrated on the collapse of the Berlin Wall. 'Die Maur', as the wall is known in German, is in two, said one, but no longer is Berlin.

Sales of beer and champagne soared as East Berliners continued to come over to the West to join the festivities, and traffic in West Berlin was at a standstill . . .

The first new border crossing point came into use just after dawn after a night of activity by workmen with bulldozers. East Berliners filed on foot from Bernauer Strass into the West.

This had been the scene of some of the most dramatic and emotional events of August 1961 when the wall was built – East Berliners dropping from upper storey windows while troops bricked up their front doors. Several died.

On Potsdamer Platz, once the Piccadilly Circus of the German empire and a hundred yards from the unmarked site of Hitler's bunker, the bulldozers were creating a crossing to be opened this morning.

Elsewhere, official teams were knocking down the wall to create eighteen new crossing points. At one new site, East Berlin engineers shook hands with their western counterparts through the gap they had created in the six-inch thick, steel-reinforced concrete.

Tourists watched in amazement, their cameras recording the historic moments. One American borrowed a hammer from a Berliner and told his wife: 'Get one of me hitting the wall, honey.'

Every small piece chipped off was seized as a souvenir. At one partly destroyed section near the Tiergarten, young West Berliners sold off chunks of the wall for DM10.

In the gift shops, newly printed T-shirts were selling well, the most popular bearing the slogan *Der Letze Macht Das Licht Aus!* (the last one turns out the light).

'THE MUSEUM OF MADNESS': A TOUR OF CEAUSESCU'S PALACE, BUCHAREST, December 1989

Simon Haydon

Nicolae Ceausescu was among the many East European Stalinist dictators to fall in 1989. As Simon Haydon found on visiting Ceausescu's palace after his execution, the Romanian leader lived in a style far at odds with his simple working man image.

Nicolae Ceausescu lived in a dream house dripping with gold and silver and packed with art treasures, while his nation starved. Even his nuclear bunker was lined with marble.

The new Romanian leadership yesterday gave Western journalists their first view of the Ceausescu home since he was deposed. The sprawling two-storey villa with forty rooms stands at the centre of a compound of a dozen houses for Ceausescu's ministers, generals and friends in northern Bucharest.

'I cannot even imagine a billionaire in the West living in such style,' said Octavio Badea, a musician who has joined about 500 soldiers and civilians guarding the house, which was briefly plundered last weekend during battles between Ceausescu loyalists and government troops.

The Ceausescus slept in separate apartments – and Elena's bore startling similarities to that of Imelda Marcos, unveiled after she and her husband fled their Manila palace in 1986. Rows of shoes were on display, some with diamond-encrusted heels made by Charles Jourdan. Elena's fur coats, part of a wardrobe that also included hundreds of dresses, were strewn over her large unmade bed.

Her husband's pyjamas still lay on the bed he last slept in a week ago. Three telephones stood on his bedside tables. 'It is almost too hard to understand. I hope one day this place will be turned into a museum of madness,' said Major Stancu Valentin, who escorted the journalists.

The visitors to the villa were met in an entry hall decorated with precious vases, topped by a golden dome. Further inside the ground floor was the piano room, with a Vienna-made Buchner grand piano, badly out of tune. All the rooms were crammed with paintings, valuable ornaments and gilded furniture. 'They had amazingly good taste considering he was not much more than a tyrannical peasant,' said Mr Badea.

One Christmas card was from the Ceausescus' daughter, Zoia, who was caught as she tried to flee with large sums of money – since stored upstairs for safe keeping. 'Happy Christmas to my dearly beloved parents from your daughter Zoia,' the card read.

Mrs Ceausescu had been learning English. BBC English-language videotapes were scattered round her room. And her husband was apparently a fan of Western films. Every room boasted a West German television set, on which he could show French or American films from a stack piled high in one of his flats.

Warm water flowed from gold-plated taps in the Italian-tiled bathrooms. On the balcony downstairs, where exquisite fountains once splashed, a soldier had left his dirty boots, exchanged for a pair of Ceausescu's.

Soldiers, fearing the Securitate may try to recapture the house, have taken up residence in the marble-lined nuclear bunker, which can sleep sixteen and has enough provisions for a long wait.

Major Valentin said the Ceausescus kept a relatively small staff because the dictator was mean. Documents in the kitchen showed he sent unused fruit and meat back to the markets to reclaim his money. The couple kept to a strict diet, with the ruler's daily food intake and calorie intake specially printed out for him.

Outside the house, the couple and their children – Nicu,

Zoia and Valentin – enjoyed a swanky fitness centre for the compound's residents, with a swimming pool, boxing ring, volleyball court and several tennis courts.

Ceausescu's 102-year-old mother, who lived in a bunga-low near the main house, was taken to hospital when her home was overrun last Friday. Her house is now a barracks for the troops protecting the plush residence.

THE GULF WAR: THE BOMBING OF BAGHDAD, 17 January 1991

John Simpson

John Simpson, Foreign Affairs Editor of the BBC was in the Iraqi capital when Operation Desert Storm, the Allied operation against Saddam Hussein and his occupation of Kuwait, began.

It had taken us much too long to get our gear together. I was angry with myself as we ran across the marble floor of the hotel lobby, scattering the security men and Ministry of Information minders.

A voice wailed after us in the darkness: 'But where are you going?' 'There's a driver here somewhere,' said Anthony Wood, the freelance cameraman we had just hired. When I saw which driver it was, I swore. He was the most cowardly of them all. The calmer, more rational voice of Eamonn Matthews, our producer, cut in: 'We'll have to use him. There's no one else.' It was true. The other drivers knew there was going to be an attack, and had vanished.

We had no idea where we wanted to go. There was no high ground, to give us a good shot of the city. We argued as the car screeched out of the hotel gate and down into the underpass. 'No bridges,' I said. 'He's heading for 14 July Bridge. If they bomb that we'll never get back.'

The driver swerved alarmingly, tyres squealing. At that moment, all round us, the anti-aircraft guns started up. Brilliant red and white tracers arched into the sky, then died and fell away. There was the ugly rumble of bombs. I looked at my watch: 2.37 a.m. The bombing of Baghdad had begun twenty-three minutes earlier than we had been told to expect. For us, those minutes would have made all the difference.

The sweat shone on the driver's face in the light of the flashes. 'Where's he going now?' He did a wild U-turn, just as the sirens started their belated wailing. Anthony wrestled with the unaccustomed camera. 'I'm getting this,' he grunted. The lens was pointing at a ludicrous angle into the sky as another immense burst of fireworks went off beside us. It was hard not to flinch at the noise.

'The bloody idiot – he's heading straight back to the hotel.' The driver had had enough. He shot in through the gates and stopped. We had failed ignominiously in our effort to escape the control of the authorities and now we were back.

I had become obsessed with getting out of the Al Rasheed Hotel. It smelled of decay, and it lay between five major targets: the presidential palace, the television station, an airfield, several Ministries. I had no desire to be trapped with 300 people in the underground shelters there, and I wanted to get away from the government watchers. Television requires freedom of action, and yet we were trapped again.

In the darkness of the lobby angry hands grabbed us and pushed us downstairs into the shelter. The smell of frightened people in a confined space was already starting to take over. Anthony held the camera over his head to get past the sobbing women who ran against us in the corridor. Children cried. Then the lights went out, and there was more screaming until the emergency power took over. Most of the Western journalists were hanging round the big shelter. I was surprised to see one of the cameramen there: he had a reputation for courage and independence, but now he was just looking at the waves of frightened people with empty red eyes. Anthony, by contrast was neither worried nor elated. He was mostly worried about getting his equipment together.

Not that it *was* his equipment. Anthony had stepped in to help us because our own cameramen had to leave. It had been a difficult evening. As more and more warnings came in from New York, Paris and London, about the likelihood of an attack, almost every news organization with people in Baghdad was instructing them to leave. The personal warnings President Bush had given to American editors suggested that the coming onslaught would be the worst since the Second World War.

I remembered my grandfather's stories of men going mad under the bombardment at the Somme and Passchendaele. This would be the first high-tech war in history and most newspapers and television companies were reluctant to expose their employees to it. The BBC, too, had ordered us out. Some wanted to; others didn't. In the end it came to a four-three split: Bob Simpson, the radio correspondent and a good friend of mine for years, decided to stay; so did Eamonn Matthews. I was the third. In our cases the BBC, that most civilized of British institutions, came up with a sensible formula: it was instructing us to leave, but promised to take no action against us if we refused.

We still needed a cameraman. But by now there were several people whose colleagues had decided to move out, but who were determined to stay themselves. We found two who were prepared to work with us: Nick Della Casa and Anthony Wood.

There seemed to be no getting out of the shelter. Guards, some of them armed with Kalashnikovs, stood at each of the exits from the basement. They had orders to stop anyone leaving. The main shelter was now almost too full to sit or lie down. Some people seemed cheerful enough, and clapped and sang or watched Iraqi television. Children were crying, and guests and hotel staff were still arriving all the time from the upper floors.

In the general panic, the normal patterns of behaviour were forgotten. A woman in her thirties arrived in a coat and bath towel, and slowly undressed and put on more clothes in front of everyone. Nobody paid her the slightest attention. The heavy metal doors with their rubber linings and the wheel for opening and closing them, as in a submarine, stayed open.

Even so, I felt pretty bad. From time to time it seemed to me that the structure of the hotel swayed a little as if bombs were landing around us. Perhaps it was my imagination. To be stuck here, unable to film anything except a group of anxious people, was the worst thing I could imagine. Anthony and I got through the submarine door and tried to work our way up the staircase that led to the outside world. A guard tried to stop us, but I waited till the next latecomer arrived and forced my way through. Anthony followed.

The upper floors were in darkness. We laboured along the corridor, trying to work out by feel which was our office. Listening at one door, I heard the murmur of voices and we were let in. The sky was lit up by red, yellow and white flashes, and there was no need for us to light torches or candles. Every explosion had us cowering and ducking. I wandered round a little and asked a friendly cameraman to film what's called in the trade 'a piece to camera' for me.

Despite the crash and the whine of bombs and artillery outside we whispered to each other. By now, though, I was acclimatizing to the conditions, and sorted out the words in my head before I started. You are not popular with cameramen if you need too many takes under such circumstances.

Back in the corridor there was a flash from a torch, and an Iraqi called out my name. A security man had followed me up from the shelter. In order to protect the others I walked down towards him in the yellow torchlight. I had no idea what I was going to do, but I saw a partly open door to my left and slipped inside. I was lucky. The vivid flashes through the window showed I was in a suite of rooms which someone was using as an office.

I worked my way past the furniture and locked myself in the bedroom at the end. Lying on the floor, I could see the handle turning slowly in the light from the battle outside. When the security man found the door was locked he started banging on it and calling out my name, but these doors were built to withstand rocket attacks; a mere security man had no chance.

Close by, a 2,000-pound penetration bomb landed, but contrary to the gossip in the hotel neither my eyeballs nor the fillings in my teeth came out. I switched on the radio I found by the bed and listened to President Bush explaining what was going on. It was 5.45, and I was soon asleep.

At nine o'clock there was more banging on the door, and more calling of my name. It was Eamonn, who had tracked me down to tell me he had got our satellite telephone to work. Smuggling the equipment through the airport two weeks before had been a smart piece of work, and in a city without power and without communications we now had both a generator and the means to broadcast to the outside world.

Eamonn moved the delicate white parasol of the dish around until it locked on to the satellite. It was hard to think that something so complex could be achieved so easily. We dialled up the BBC and spoke to the pleasant, cool voice of the traffic manager. It was just as if we were somewhere sensible, and not sheltering against a brick wall from the air raids. I gave a brief account to the interviewer at the other end about the damage that the raids had caused in the night: the telecommunications tower damaged, power stations destroyed. I had less idea what was happening on the streets. Directly the broadcast was over, I headed out with Anthony for a drive around. 'Not good take picture now, Mr John,' said the driver. He was an elderly crook but I had an affection for him all the same. 'Got to work, I'm afraid, Ali.' He groaned.

It was extraordinary: the city was in the process of being deprived of power and communications, and yet the only sign of damage I could see was a broken window at the Ministry of Trade. The streets were almost empty, except for soldiers trying to hitch a lift. 'Going Kuwait, Basra,' said Ali. Some were slightly wounded, and their faces seemed completely empty.

Iraqis are normally animated and sociable, but there was no talking now, even in the bigger groups. A woman dragged her child along by its arm. A few old men squatted with a pile of oranges or a few boxes of cigarettes in front of them. An occasional food shop or a tea-house was open; that was all.

'Allah.' A white car was following us. 'He see you take picture.' I told Ali to take a sudden right turn, but he lacked the courage. The security policeman waved us down. 'Just looking round,' I said, as disarmingly as I could. 'He say you come with him.' 'Maybe,' said Anthony.

We got back into the car, and followed the white car for a little. The Al Rasheed Hotel was in the distance. 'Go there,' I said loudly, and Ali for once obeyed. The policeman waved and shouted, but by now the sirens were wailing again and the Ministry of Defence, on the left bank of the river, went up in a column of brown and grey smoke.

Ali put his foot down, and made it to the hotel. The policeman in his white car arrived thirty seconds after us, but obediently searched for a place in the public car park while the three of us ran into the hotel and lost ourselves in the crowd which filled the lobby.

In a windowless side office, where our minders sat for safety, I spotted a face I knew: Jana Schneider, an American war photographer, completely fearless. Throughout the night she had wandered through Baghdad filming the falling missiles. Near the Sheraton she had watched a 'smart' bomb take out a Security Ministry building while leaving the houses on either side of it undamaged.

I found it hard to believe, and yet it tied in with my own observation. This extraordinary precision was something new in warfare. As the day wore on, Baghdad seemed to me to be suffering from an arteriosclerosis – it appeared unchanged, and yet its vital functions were atrophying with each new air raid. It was without water, power and communication.

I was putting together an edited report for our departing colleagues to smuggle out when someone shouted that a cruise missile had just passed the window. Following the line of the main road beside the hotel and travelling from southwest to north-east, it flashed across at 500 miles an hour, making little noise and leaving no exhaust. It was twenty feet long, and was a good hundred yards from our window. It undulated a little as it went, following the contours of the road. It was like the sighting of a UFO.

Another air raid began, and I ran down the darkened corridor to report over our satellite phone. Lacking the navigational sophistication of the cruise missile, I slammed into a heavy mahogany desk where the hotel security staff sometimes stationed themselves. I took the corner in the lower ribs and lay there for a little.

When I reported soon after that I was the only known casualty of the day's attacks among the Al Rasheed's population and explained that I had cracked a couple of ribs, this was taken in London to be a coded message that I had been beaten up.

I was deeply embarrassed. Having long disliked the journalist-as-hero school of reporting, I found myself a mild celebrity for something which emphatically hadn't taken place. An entire country's economic and military power was being dismantled, its people were dying, and I was broadcasting about cracked ribs. Each time they hurt I felt it was a punishment for breaking the basic rule: don't talk about yourself.

In the coffee shop, a neat but exhausted figure was reading from a thick sheaf of papers. Naji Al-Hadithi was a figure of power for the foreign journalists in Baghdad, since he was Director-General of the Information Ministry. Some found him sinister: a *New York Times* reporter took refuge in the US embassy for four nights after talking to him. I thought he was splendid company, a considerable Anglophile, and possessed of an excellent sense of humour. Once I took a colleague of mine to see him, and he asked where we'd been. 'We went to Babylon, to see what the whole country will look like in a fortnight's time,' I said. For a moment I thought I'd gone much too far, then I saw Al-Hadithi was rocking with silent laughter.

Now he looked close to exhaustion, and his clothes were rumpled. He read out some communiqués and a long, scarcely coherent letter from Saddam Hussein to President Bush. Afterwards we talked about the censorship the Ministry planned to impose. In the darkened lobby of the hotel, with the candlelight glinting on glasses and rings and the buttons of jackets, we argued amicably about the new rules. It seemed to me that it was the Security Ministry, not his own, that was insisting on them.

That evening Brent Sadler, the ITN correspondent, rang me. CNN had warned him that our hotel was to be a target that evening. I told the others. No one wanted to go down to the shelter. We decided instead to do what Jana Schneider had done the previous night, and roam the streets.

I cleared out my safety deposit box, and gathered the necessities of my new life: identification in case of arrest, money for bribes, a hairbrush in case I had to appear on television, a notebook and pen. No razor, since without water shaving was impossible. But we were unlucky again.

The sirens wailed early, at eight o'clock, and the automatic doors of the hotel were jammed shut. Once again, we were taken down into the shelter.

The whole cast of characters who inhabited our strange new world was there: Sadoun Jenabi, Al-Hadithi's deputy, a large, easy-going man who had spent years in Britain and stayed in the shelter most of the time now; and English peace campaigner, Edward Poore, who was a genuine eccentric, carried a cricket bat everywhere and had knotted a Romanian flag round his neck to remind himself of the time he spent there in the revolution; most of our minders and security men; just about all the journalists; and a large number of the hotel staff and their families, settling down nervously for the night. It was cold. I put a flak-jacket over me for warmth and used my bag as a pillow.

THE GULF WAR: SCUD MISSILES OVER ISRAEL, 19 January 1991

Ian Black, Guardian

It looked, said a man who saw it seconds before the first blast, just like a falling star.

For nearly five million Israelis, unusually experienced in adversity, the Iraqi missiles that landed yesterday were a terrible warning that this war may be very different from any they have known.

Most people were asleep when it happened. Air raid sirens wailed in Tel Aviv and Haifa only after the explosions, and in some parts of Jerusalem the job was left to civil defence loudspeaker vans touring the deserted streets.

It was a bad end to what had looked like being an encouraging day.

Initial euphoria at the allied pounding of Iraq had given way, as dusk fell on Thursday, to caution that not all

President Saddam Hussein's missiles had been destroyed.

The missiles came suddenly: only minutes separate the enhanced Scud-Bs' camouflaged launching sites in the south-western Iraqi desert from Tel Aviv.

Direct casualties were astonishingly low. Only twelve people suffered superficial injuries from the blast and shrapnel produced by conventional high explosives.

In Tel Aviv, a textile factory and two homes were destroyed. In Haifa there was little damage and no injuries. A three-yard-wide crater in an empty lot was all that was left of one missile.

Fifty other people were admitted to hospital, several – including newly arrived immigrants from the Soviet Union – as a result of prematurely injecting themselves with an anti-nerve gas agent.

'There was a big flash and a boom,' said Mani Barkan, one of the injured. 'It was like something from the movies.' Another Tel Aviv man said simply: 'It was a miracle no one was killed.'

But three elderly people died because they forgot – I did too, briefly, before I started choking – to remove the plastic stopper that protects the gas mask's screw-on filter when it is not being used.

An Arab girl, aged three, suffocated as her parents struggled to force her to wear the breathing hood for infants.

Precise locations of the seven or eight Scud hits were not revealed, to prevent the Iraqis from improving their aim if there is a second salvo.

Israelis were ready for an attack. A state of emergency had been declared early on Thursday, but at that stage people were told not to open their sealed gas mask kits.

Not since 1940, when Italian planes bombed Tel Aviv and killed forty-two, had civilians been in the front line.

As the news flowed in from Baghdad, Dhahran and Washington, it had seemed that the Jewish state, for once in its short and eventful history, was to be a spectator cheering from the sidelines in a war against a country that had threatened it long before Kuwait was conquered.

It was not to be. The moment the alert was sounded, people tumbled out of bed and into their safe rooms, windows sealed with plastic masking tape, bleach-soaked towel stuffed under the door.

Even the keyhole had to be blocked.

For many, the worst part was the uncertainty. In our flat in central Jerusalem, my wife and I entered the sealed spare bedroom, donned our masks easily enough, but took several agonizsing minutes to adjust the black rubber straps.

It was an unnerving experience. As aircraft roared overhead, the radio offered only repeated warnings to stay put and listen to civil defence instructions in a babel of languages – Hebrew and Arabic were followed by English, Russian and Romanian.

The telephone was a lifeline. Friends and relatives rang each other constantly, reassuring, offering advice and expressing a solidarity and warmth that briefly took the rough edge off a country where brusqueness is the social norm.

Children vomited: my nine-year-old son worried about his dog, which had run off as the alert sounded.

And he was unable to use the special rubber drinking straw attached to the mask issued to his age-group. Babies were placed in transparent protective infant carriers.

After the all-clear, people ventured out into the winter sunshine to buy milk and bread, carrying their gas masks naturally now, no longer with the sheepish is-this-all-really-necessary look they had when they collected them from the distribution centres. The longest queues were for newspapers.

No one knew what another night would bring, but the sealed rooms were ready and the masks at hand. And no one knew whether or how Israel's government would respond under immense international pressure to stay out, but also buffeted by domestic fury at the Iraqi attack.

One effect of the missile salvo was a wave of international sympathy. Get hit by a Scud, someone quipped bitterly, and suddenly you are an underdog again. After years of being cast as the Middle East's Goliath – with others playing plucky little David – it was an unfamiliar role.

THE GULF WAR: ALLIED FORCES CROSS INTO KUWAIT, 25 February 1991

Robert Fisk

We crossed the infamous berms before midday. Half-filled with black sludge, the ditches and earthworks ran guiltily across the Kuwaiti desert, the sand dark and soggy with oil. The allied armies were supposed to have been incinerated on these front lines.

But, instead, they left behind them the litter of burned-out Iraqi armour and ammunition trucks ripped in half by precision bombs.

The Iraqis were routed. In their place along the road to Kuwait City ran mile after mile of Kuwaiti and Saudi convoys – interspersed with the occasional US Marines patrol – their radio aerials adorned with red, white, black and green Kuwaiti banners and Saudi flags with their ubiquitous assertion: 'There is no God but God (Allah) and His Prophet is Muhammad.'

'Kuwait City' the road signs beckoned to us. By the time we stopped beneath lowering clouds of burning oil, the air pressure changing with the artillery blasts, the prize was only forty-five miles away, the suburbs scarcely thirty, half an hour's drive before the war.

Behind us, the Kuwaiti army's Ninth Battalion was hunting through the villas of the old bathing resort of Khiran. In front of us, at one end of az-Zawr – now also a hunting ground for the Kuwaiti troops in search of

Saddam Hussein's encircled soldiery – stood Colonel Fouad Haddad, his massive beard and shades almost totally obscuring his smile.

'Truly, I am happy,' he said. 'How long I have waited for this. Today is my country's independence day. I feel I am dreaming.'

It was difficult to shake the feelings of euphoria. After so many months and so much planning and personal fear – and, let us be frank – ruthlessness – the allied armies had cracked right through the Iraqi frontline and had driven thirty-five miles into Kuwait, up the desert highway from the frontier post, just as armies do in war films.

The Kuwaiti armour – their Soviet-made BMP-2 and amphibious vehicles are much envied by the Marines – deployed in parallel lines across the desert. 'We could go much faster if we wanted,' an American special-forces major said. 'The guys are being very careful.'

But they were not. Beside the road dozens of Iraqi anti-personnel mines were piled high and on several highways the Kuwaitis had ignored the mines, blithely driving over the detonators in their tanks and trucks.

Around the smashed Iraqi lorries lay the unexploded rocket-propelled grenades and boxes of machine-gun ammunition, broken open – the brass cartridge cases sparkling in the thin sun.

Thin it was because of that forbidding cloud. And because of one deeply disturbing phenomenon – the absence of *people*.

Much of the land here is desert, but in any war there would have been refugees, the wounded or civilians who had been cowering in their homes in the coastal towns. In Kuwait yesterday however, we saw not a soul, not a single Kuwaiti, save for the newly arrived soldiers.

The electricity pylons have soldered in on themselves under huge explosions, the roads had been dug up by the Iraqis in preparation for the great battle which they never fought. There were new cars – Mercedes and Chevrolet limousines – turned over on their roofs, their wheels ripped off. It was like a dead land.

There was no doubting the lengths to which the Iraqis had gone to fire their berms. There were swamps of oil hundreds of yards wide, liquid trenches of oil cut into the sand, settling into the desert to leave a black scum along the berms.

Could they not have been set alight? Or were the US jets too fast for the Iraqis? The bomb craters told their own story. Around the roads there were the casings of cluster bombs, long plastic tubes of hygienic white. They were scattered too, beyond the wreckage of a tank transporter, torn in half.

Artillery fire from the south punctuated the air, then a tremendous roar of explosions followed by the keening of jets high above us. Strange things caught our attention – a field gun neatly tossed upside down by an explosion, abandoned bulldozers in the middle of the sand, as if left on a building site, at the end of a busy week, camouflage netting still sheltering trucks which had burned out, mattresses and clothes on the roads.

The Iraqis had looted the customs station on the Kuwaiti border. It had later been hit by shell-fire – but the notice marked 'Kuwaiti Ministry of Immigration' instructing motorists holding Gulf Co-operation Council passports to turn left remained untouched.

Col Haddad said his men had taken 400 Iraqi prisoners. There are supposed to be at least four Iraqi infantry brigades still in front of us, although scarcely a shell was fired in our direction. 'They may be all dead after the B-52 bombing,' a US Marine muttered. 'The only reason we are not moving faster is we want to make them surrender rather than kill them.'

A Kuwaiti special-forces soldier did not share this sensitivity. Ahmed – he said his name was – was brought up in California. He had fled Kuwait on 21 September – six weeks after the Iraqi invasion – and returned to work in the resistance, only to be arrested by the Iraqis, interrogated for three days by military security police and then having to escape again. 'I don't care if they all die,' he said.

LOS ANGELES RIOT, 30 April–1 May 1992
'West Coast Correspondent', Economist

The acquittal of four policemen who beat black motorist Rodney King torched off the most lethal urban riot in American history, leaving 50 dead and over $1 billion worth of damage in the South Central area of Los Angeles.

In front of the smoking electronics store, the small black boy had a problem. He had looted six items, but he could carry only five. For around fifteen minutes he hesitated, shielding them from other, older pillagers, while he tried to arrange them. Then flames spouted from the shop, driving out the remaining looters. A scuffle broke out across the street and the boy loped off down an alley, leaving a radio-alarm clock behind. It was probably his most valuable booty and it would have made a good present for a friend. A bearded (white) hippie, muttering an apology, picked it up instead.

Barely twenty-four hours before, Los Angeles had seemed its usual smoggy, complacent self. The first news of the acquittals in the Rodney King beatings arrived in the late afternoon. When asked for their reaction, two policemen parked opposite *The Economist* office at the *Los Angeles Times* gave a non-committal grunt. At first, the most distraught people seemed to be guilty liberals (some journalists burst into tears). Then a young mob appeared downtown. They smashed the windows and doors of the *Times* building and burnt the local coffee shop. But the television pictures from South Central were much more frightening.

After that first angry night, what followed in most parts of

Los Angeles was more pillage than riot. The fires were started by thugs (supposedly gang members who had pledged to add ten new fires every hour), but the looting was done by petty thieves. The atmosphere was usually like a disorganized rock concert; at its worst, it resembled an angry English soccer crowd – with guns. One Hispanic man scurried away carrying several cartons of tampons. Television coverage, with its maps and pictures of defenceless stores, provided a looter's guide to the best local bargains.

Gradually the fires spread northwards and westwards towards the prosperous 'Westside' that tourists visit. There a different type of riot was taking place. A supermarket on the border of West Hollywood and Beverly Hills was packed with queues 30-deep. Each shopper seemed to be carrying enough provisions to last a month. There was a screaming match at the kosher food counter. Gossip spread that a British billionaire's daughter had said the riots were boring, 'but if they ever heave a brick through Tiffany's window, I might join them.'

She never got her chance: West Los Angeles survived largely untouched. Even in heavily looted areas like Koreatown and Mid-Wilshire, many of the rioters like the small black boy, seemed almost innocently childlike. However, in South Central, the atmosphere changed. The shops – particularly those owned by Asians – were stripped bare. The crowds hanging on street corners seemed to be looking for victims rather than bargains. Women screamed about their neighbourhood being destroyed; onlookers were no more welcome than at a funeral.

The most enduring memory from the riots was the signs in shop windows. In South Central, they pleaded pathetically 'Black owned business'. Some stooped lower, putting 'blak owned business' in an attempt to mollify one gang, the Bloods, who dislike the letter 'c' because it reminds them of their arch-enemies, the Crips. On Rodeo Drive, where there are fewer black-owned businesses, shops at first bravely sported signs saying 'No Justice' to show that their sympathies lay with Mr King. When the riots died down the signs disappeared.

'ETHNIC CLEANSING' IN BOSNIA, YUGOSLAVIA, July 1992

Roy Gutman, Newsweek

Hasnija Pjeva witnessed the execution of her husband Nenad, from the terrace of her house outside Visegrad.

It was 7.30 a.m., June 24, and Nenad was returning from his overnight factory shift when the armed men in Serbian paramilitary uniforms spotted him. Nenad started running to the nearby riverbank, but the irregulars shot him dead on the spot. They dragged the corpse onto the bridge, then threw it into the green water of the Drina.

'I didn't bury him,' Hasnija said of her husband two days later, tears welling in her eyes. 'The river took him away.'

Abdulahu Osmanagulis was at his home in Visegrad, a virtual prisoner since Serb forces seized the predominantly Muslim town three months before. They burned down the two ancient mosques and roamed the streets, firing small arms day and night. Early last week three of his neighbours were shot in their home.

'The bodies were just left lying there in the courtyard,' Osmanagulis said. He knew it was time to get out of his house.

Emina Hodzic's husband was abducted one noon, her son that same evening. Mediha Tira's husband was taken away by men with blackened faces.

The killings all happened last week in the Bosnian town whose Turkish-built 'bridge on the Drina' was immortalized by Yugoslavian novelist Ivo Andric. There are now two bridges, and after last week's events, both will find their place in the literature of war atrocities.

Except for an unknown but apparently small number who escaped, all the able-bodied Muslim men and youths of Visegrad who had not fled the occupiers were shot, according to a dozen survivors.

'Most of the executions were committed on the bridge. Their bodies were thrown into the river,' said Osmanagulis, the unofficial leader of the survivors. It appears that dozens were executed, perhaps hundreds. No one knows exactly.

'If the Drina River could only speak, it would say how many dead were taken away,' said Hasnija Pjeva.

Visegrad (pronounced VEE-shih-grad), with a population of about 30,000, is one of a number of towns where Serb forces carried out 'ethnic cleansing' of Muslims in the past two weeks, according to the Bosnian government.

'There was chaos in Visegrad. Everything was burned, looted and destroyed,' said a Visegrad expellee, 43, who spoke of the terrible events over coffee in the Miratovac cafe but would give neither his name nor his profession. He escaped only because he was an invalid with a gangrenous leg.

The survivors of the massacre are the old, the infirm, the women and the children. They are traumatized by what they witnessed, barely able to speak or to control their emotions. Two of the women had been raped, Osmanagulis said. But the heartbreak was compounded by the humiliation they endured at the hands of the local Serbian Red Cross.

Against their wishes, 280 people were shipped in a convoy of five buses across Serbia, the principal state in the new Yugoslavia, to Macedonia, a breakaway state, a journey of about 275 miles. The Serbian Red Cross gave them food and clothes but insisted they sign papers saying they had been well treated and wanted to go to Macedonia.

'We all wanted to go to Kosovo or Sandzak,' two mainly Muslim areas of southern Serbia, said Osmanagulis, 'but they directed us exclusively to Macedonia. There was no other choice.'

He carried a paper requesting that the Macedonian border authorities provide passports and admit the entire group. But Macedonia, which has more than 30,000 Bosnian refugees but has yet to be recognized by Western countries or to receive any real assistance, has stopped accepting any refugees, particularly Muslims, due to substantial problems with its own Muslim minority, according to Mira Jankovska, a government spokeswoman in Skopje.

And so the Macedonians refused to allow the survivors of the Visegrad massacre to cross the border. It was 4 a.m.

Osmanagulis conferred with the drivers, and they agreed that everyone should disembark and try to enter on foot, but the Macedonian police turned them away. 'I ran back to the buses and everyone followed, but when the drivers saw us, they turned the buses around and left,' he said.

For sixteen hours on June 25 the survivors found themselves stranded in a no-man's-land on an international highway without food, water, shelter or assistance, abandoned by the Red Cross and welcomed nowhere. Fifteen of them were over eighty, and there were at least as many children under the age of two. They stood and sat from 4 a.m. until 8 p.m. through the hot midday sun and a fierce summer rainstorm.

Albanian Muslims in this impoverished farm village in southern Serbia, about a twenty-minute drive from the border crossing, brought bread, water and tomatoes. Then in the evening they arrived with tractors and taxis and took them to a small mosque here. On the advice of a local doctor who feared the spread of disease, the survivors were moved to private homes two days later.

'If the people of the village hadn't helped us, half of us would be dead of starvation or illness,' said Osmanagulis. One woman, ninety-two, died after the ordeal. She was buried on Sunday.

Now the survivors of Visegrad sit in this village at the end of a potholed dirt road, sleeping on the floors and couches of its simple houses, caught between the hostility of Serbia and Macedonia, unattended by any refugee organization, unable even to contact anyone outside, for there is no telephone.

'We have a saying,' said Osmanagulis, summing up their plight: 'The sky is too high, and the ground is too hard.'

THE END OF APARTHEID: NELSON MANDELA VOTES IN THE SOUTH AFRICAN ELECTION, INANDA, 27 April 1994

Karl Maier

'Out of the darkness into the glorious light' reads the inscription on the tombstone of the African National Congress's founding president, John Dube, who was buried at the Ohlange High School where Nelson Mandela fulfilled a life-long ambition yesterday by casting a vote in South Africa's first all-race elections.

Sunlight had just broken over the hills of Natal province when a motorcade escorted by South African Defence Force troops and police brought Mr Mandela to the sight of the tomb.

Mr Mandela, 76, laid a wreath then walked down towards the high school where 300 journalists were cajoling officials of the ANC and the Independent Electoral Commission to set up the ballot box to capture the most famous vote in South Africa's history in the best possible position.

As he moved towards a verandah where the ballot box was poised, Mr Mandela was asked which party he planned to vote for. 'I have been agonizing over that question,' he replied, and went inside to mark his ballot.

Mr Mandela returned beaming. His was probably the most choreographed vote in history. Lifting the ballot paper above the box, Mr Mandela turned to face photographers then deposited the answer to his agonizing question.

'An unforgettable occasion,' he called it. 'We are moving

from an era of resistance, division, oppression, turmoil and conflict and starting a new era of hope, reconciliation and nation-building.

'I sincerely hope that the mere casting of a vote . . . will give hope to all South Africans,' he said. Hope perhaps, but that vote yesterday gave officials at Ohlange a big headache. Hundreds of voters boycotted their local voting station and headed to the school, demanding to cast their ballots where Nelson Mandela did.

SOURCES AND ACKNOWLEDGEMENTS

The editor has made every effort to locate all persons having any rights in the selections appearing in this anthology and to secure permission from the holders of such rights. Any queries regarding the use of material should be addressed to the editor c/o the publishers.

'Nagasaki' is an extract from *Nagasaki 1945* by Tatsuichiro Akizuki. Copyright © 1981 Tatsuichiro Akizuki and Keiichi Nagata; 'Winning the race for the South Pole' is an extract from *The South Pole* by Roald Amundsen, trans. AG Chater, John Murray, 1912; 'Announcing the end of the Second World War' by Maxine Andrews is an extract from *The Good War: An Oral History of World War II* by Studs Terkel. Copyright © 1984 Studs Terkel; 'Lech Walesa leads the strike' by Anon. Gdansk shipyard worker is and extract from *The Book Of Lech Walesa*, Penguin Books, 1982. Copyright © Wydawnicto Morskie 1981; 'The shooting of the students at Tiananmen Square' by Anon. Beijing student is from *New Statesman & Society*, 16 June 1989; 'The Private Life of Adolf Hitler' by Anon. is an extract from *Eyewitness Adolf Hitler*, edited by Allen Churchill, 1979; 'The SAS relieve the siege at Prince's Gate' by Anon. SAS trooper is an extract from *Soldier 'P SAS* by Michael Paul Kennedy, Bloomsbury Publishing Ltd. Copyright © 1989 Michael Paul Kennedy. Reprinted by permission of Bloomsbury Publishing Ltd; 'The Home Front: The Great Man Chase' by Anon. is an extract from *Speak for Yourself* edited by Angus Calder & Dorothy Sheridan. First published 1984 by Jonathan Cape Ltd. Copyright © 1984 the Tom Harrisson Mass-Observation Archive; 'The Berlin Wall' by Mark Arnold-Foster is from the *Observer*, 26 November 1961; 'Troops go into Northern Ireland' by Anon. is an extract from *Northern Ireland: Soldiers Talking* by Max Arthur, Sidgwick & Jackson, 1987; 'The Battle of Britain' by John Beard is an extract from *Their Finest Hour* by Allan A. Machie and Walter Graebner. Copyright © Harcourt, Brace and Co. 1941; 'The Wall Street Crash' by Elliott V. Bell is an extract from *We Saw It Happen* copyright © 1938 Simon & Shuster Inc; 'A Hall at the Paris Opéra' is an extract from *Journals*, Arnold Bennett, ed. Newman Flower, Cassell, 1932; 'The Great Train Robbery' is an extract from *Ronnie Biggs: His Own Story*, Michael Joseph, 1981; 'Medical Experiments at Dachau' by Franz Blaha is an extract from *The Trial of Major German War Criminals: The Proceedings of the International Military Tribunal at Nuremberg*, 1946. Copyright © HMSO; 'A Meeting with Hitler' is an extract from *In the Shelter with Hitler* by Gerhard Boldt, The Citadel Press, London; 'D-Day: The Landings' is from an unpublished memoir by H.T. Bone, the Imperial War Museum, London; 'A Spanish Civil War Diary' is an extract from *Spanish Cockpit* by Franz Borkenau. Copyright © Franz Borkenau 1937. First published in the UK by Faber & Faber. Reprinted by permission of the publishers; 'The Blitz' by Kathleen Box is an extract from *Speak For Yourself* edited by Angus Calder & Dorothy Sheridan. First published in 1984 by Jonathan Cape Ltd. Copyright © 1984 the Tom Harrisson Mass-Observation Archive; 'Victory in Europe Celebration' by James Byrom is an extract from *Unfinished Man* by James Byrom, 1957; 'A Tank Charge' by Bert Chaney is an extract from *People at War*, ed. Michael Moynihan, David & Charles, 1973; 'The Anschluss' is from

Eye-Witness
The 20th Century

Other books edited by Jon E. Lewis and published by Robinson

The Mammoth Book of the Western
The Mammoth Book of True War Stories
The Mammoth Book of Modern War Stories
True Stories of the Elite Forces
Eye-Witness D-Day